FRANCO

FRANCO

THE MAN
AND HIS NATION

BY

GEORGE HILLS

THE MACMILLAN COMPANY

NEW YORK

Library of Congress Catalog Card Number: 68-11428

FIRST AMERICAN EDITION

First published in Great Britain by Robert Hale Limited, London

The Macmillan Company, New York
Collier-Macmillan Canada Ltd., Toronto, Ontario

Printed in the United States of America

CONTENTS

Ε4ΓΕ4

ILLUSTRATIONS

Following Page 256

MAPS

FOREWORD

On 20th July 1936 the London *Times* included a General Francisco Franco in the list of those who had risen two days earlier against the Government of Spain. The most that the paper could find to say of him was that he was the "brother of the well-known flyer", Ramon Franco. Ten weeks later the insurgents appointed General Franco their military and political leader. Thereupon he became the centre of controversy. Men to whom Spain was hardly more than a name had hastened to take sides about the rising within a few hours of its occurrence. Men now argued: Franco's cause is good and therefore he is above criticism; or, his cause is bad and therefore he is an evil man.

In his book on the Spanish Civil War, Hugh Thomas showed how that event was more complex than the foreigner imagined. In preparing it Thomas discovered that Spaniards "mellowed by time (were) willing to speak in the language of history to the dispassionate observer". For the preparation of this present biography, General Franco, notoriously indifferent to what foreigners say or write about him, allowed me to question him and I, understand, gave orders that those under his command should answer with complete sincerity whatever I should ask of them. I had access to all the papers in his Military Household. I conversed at great length with his cousin, General Franco Salgado. His Chief of Operations went through the whole war with me as seen from General Headquarters. Hitherto inaccessible archives which are rich in documents relating to both sides of the war were placed at my disposal. General Franco's close relatives spoke with complete frankness about him from childhood. They knew the purpose of my questioning: and I acknowledge my great debt to them. At the same time they are the least likely to approve of my portrait of Franco. I must therefore apologise for any offence this book may give them, if they should come to read it.

I must apologise also to those hundreds of others who were not aware of my intention to extract the facts which they revealed, sometimes willingly, sometimes unwittingly; and especially to those who must have felt as I talked to them that I was interrogating them as if they had been my prisoners of war, or cross-questioning them as if they were in the witness box and I a counsel for the other side. If I may say so, where interrogator and subject are both natives to a language, it is not difficult to establish the limitations of the subject's powers of observation and memory. It is easier to distinguish between eyewitness and hearsay evidence.

These interrogations—there is no better name for them—were carried out over a period of twenty years, not indeed principally for this biography, but for the wider purpose of finding out what was happening in Spain behind the curtain of censorship, and what had happened over another period of twenty years which were not entirely free from censorship, albeit many men had been able to publish memoirs which were almost invariably apologias for their actions rather than dispassionate statements.

It was not only into military archives that I was allowed to research, but whatever I asked of other ministries was given me either directly or through the Ministry of Information. Nevertheless, wherever possible I have quoted from published documentary evidence of non-Spanish origin on such subjects as foreign relations and economic affairs—for example the German and Italian documents on foreign policy, O.E.C.D. and Bank of London and South America Reports—in preference to Spanish archival material. My reasons will be obvious.

This biography is written to no thesis except that it should provide the necessary facts and circumstances which the reader will require if he wishes to pass judgement. Since no man can be assessed for good or ill in a vacuum, therefore the circumstances have been given almost as much space as the man. Franco declared that he would be judged only by God and History. A biographer must therefore place him in his own historical setting. That setting is here seen principally from a Spanish point of view: Franco—it seems ridiculous to have to stress the obvious —is a Spaniard. Spain is Spain, and not what we from London or any other place would wish it to be or to have been so as to justify our own actions and decisions. The book is being published at the time when perhaps non-Spaniards have also mellowed and can now listen dispassionately to the language of history.

London   G.H.

FRANCO

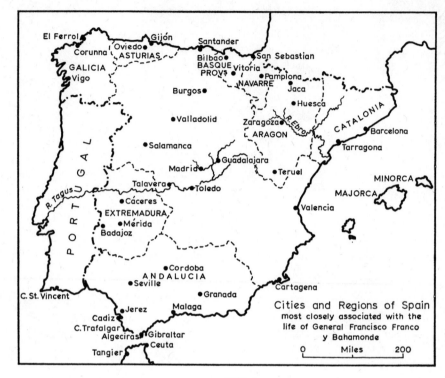

El Ferrol
Corunna
Oviedo
ASTURIAS
Gijón
Santander
Bilbao
BASQUE
PROVS
San Sebastian
Vitoria
Pamplona
NAVARRE
Jaca
GALICIA
Vigo
Burgos
Huesca
Valladolid
Zaragoza
ARAGON
CATALONIA
Barcelona
R. Ebro
Salamanca
Tarragona
PORTUGAL
R. Tagus
Madrid
Guadalajara
Teruel
Talavera
Toledo
MINORCA
MAJORCA
Cáceres
EXTREMADURA
Valencia
Mérida
Badajoz
C. St. Vincent
Cordoba
ANDALUCIA
Seville
Cartagena
Granada
Cadiz
Jerez
Malaga
C. Trafalgar
Algeciras
Gibraltar
Tangier
Ceuta

Cities and Regions of Spain
most closely associated with the
life of General Francisco Franco
y Bahamonde

0   Miles   200

MAP I

1

EL FERROL 1892

Thirty minutes after midnight on the morning of 4th December 1892 Francisco Franco was born.[1] His birthplace was El Ferrol, the Spanish naval base on the north-western corner of the Iberian Peninsula.

Ships making for the port of Corunna twelve nautical miles to the south-west of El Ferrol pass as close as half that distance to the base; no one on the bridge will see it: not even the man in the crow's nest will catch a glimpse of it. The traveller coming inland over the mountains will look down upon a valley with a stretch of water which he might well compare to a loch. He may suffer a high wind on the crests, and yet except upon an occasional day meet scarcely a ripple below. From the heights he will see upon the northern shores of that apparent lake a town of one hundred thousand inhabitants, which stretches away from a promontory with shipyards where tankers are built and men-of-war repaired: he will notice the town's encroachment on agricultural land from an obviously older nucleus of a perfect grid pattern of six long streets and six transverses. He may wonder how those ships escape to sea; there is seemingly no exit. Only if he flies overhead will he realise that the water is not a loch but an inroad of the sea. It runs from the open sea and a deep bay into a narrows, almost a canal, a full nautical mile and a half in length but never wider than two cables lengths; and from the narrows it flows into that apparent lake, which even at low tide is never less than three miles long and one in width.

In 1892 El Ferrol was much smaller. It had at the most twenty thousand inhabitants wholly contained within the promontory by a massive wall erected one hundred and sixty years earlier—soon after 1726 when the Bourbon Philip V of Spain had decreed the establishment at El Ferrol of a new, better and bigger naval base than those which had long existed at Cadiz and Cartagena. For Philip never lost hope that he would recover Gibraltar lost to England early in the

century. To that end, he needed a northern shipyard and base. El Ferrol
offered an ideal point of departure for a fleet whose task would be the
interception of ships hastening from England to the aid of Gibraltar.
Two strong points opposite each other in the narrows were developed
into formidable fortresses, and subsidiary batteries and forts were
mounted further along each bank. They made it impossible for any
eighteenth-century would-be emulator of Drake "to singe the King of
Spain's beard". With its array of defences El Ferrol was made impreg-
nable for as long as warships had no revolving turrets and could fire
broadside only. A British attempt with fifteen thousand men to capture
the base overland in 1800 was unsuccessful. A sea blockade in the early
part of 1805 had to be abandoned.

Spain was less fortunate in the attack. She was in no position to
mount a major offensive on Gibraltar until 1779 when the senior branch
of the Bourbon family in Paris agreed to co-operate with the junior
branch in Madrid, and together they began the famous Great Siege.
El Ferrol had then twelve slipways and a labour force of fifteen
thousand men working incessantly; but it must be remembered that
Spain needed ships not only to blockade Gibraltar, and to attack the
British fleet, but also to protect her convoys to and from her vast and
scattered empire overseas. The convoy work in the Atlantic and
Pacific demanded the best seamanship; the blockade the best marksmanship. Off Cape St. Vincent the British Admiral Rodney had little
difficulty in driving away the scratch force which went out to meet
him. Worse was to come. The forty thousand Spaniards and Frenchmen
in La Linea, and the combined Bourbon fleet, did not take the Rock.
In 1783 the Siege was called off. Yet thirteen years later Spain was again
at war with England, and, more even than before, at the service of
France. During those thirteen years the Spanish navy had been neglected. The twenty-seven ships of the line which then sailed under Admiral
Córdoba against Admiral Jervis in Lisbon were under-manned. Their
gunners were press-ganged at the last moment and untrained. Once
again the navies of Britain and of Spain met off Cape St. Vincent.
Córdoba did well to make Cadiz with no more than four ships lost. The
third and decisive round was about to begin. The French Admiral
Villeneuve was chosen to lead a combined force of eighteen French
men-of-war and fifteen Spanish out of El Ferrol and Cadiz to battle
with Nelson. So at Trafalgar the Spanish navy received what a Spanish
historian[2] calls "a mortal blow". Ten of the best ships of the line based
at El Ferrol were lost. Three officers of admiral rank, thirty-two others,

and 1,268 sailors were killed; a further forty-three officers and 1,428 men were wounded, many dying subsequently. The families of the greater number of these men were from El Ferrol.

Though these events took place long before Franco was born, they were a living memory into the middle of the twentieth century. He grew up with the name before him in one of the streets of El Ferrol of Gravina, the Admiral-in-Chief of the Spanish fleet at Trafalgar, and with an obelisk to the memory of the great Spanish hero of the battle, Churruca.

The development of El Ferrol as a naval base occurred in the life-time of Franco's great-great-great-grandfather, a Manuel Franco, born on 17th August 1717.[3] He arrived in El Ferrol from Madrid on 24th May 1737, but it would seem that Manuel's father and grandfather had been born in Andalucia. In 1738 he married a member of a junior branch of an ancient family, Doña María de Viñas y Andrade.[4] Manuel's son, Juan Franco de Viñas, born the following year, obtained entry into the administrative or clerical branch of the navy. In Juan's days, those of the Bourbon *pactes de famille*, El Ferrol came to have the twelve slipways for ships of the line and the labour force of fifteen thousand men; and he lived on into the days of the battles of Cape St. Vincent. He too married into the Andrades: Doña Josefa Sanchez Freire de Andrade. Juan's son, Nicolás Manuel Teodoro Franco y Sanchez, that is Franco's great-grandfather, was nearing his thirtieth birthday when the news came of the disaster at Trafalgar. Nicolas had followed his father into the administrative branch, after "proving" in 1794 that he was of "pure blood, of Hidalgo family and a man of property".[5] This Nicolas died at a great age, after three wives had borne him fifteen children and he had retired as a *Comisario de Guerra*, a rank equivalent to a lieutenant-colonel in the Army or a commander in the Navy. The tenth of his children, and the first by his third wife, the half-Italian María Josefa Vietti Bernabé, rose to a more distinguished rank and position. His name was Francisco Franco Vietti, born in 1830, who at his death in 1887 was an *intendente* or Director of Administration of El Ferrol with the personal rank of *Ordenador de Marina de Primera Clase*, equivalent to a brigadier-general or commodore. He and his wife, Hermenegilda Salgado Araujo Perez, a daughter of an officer in the Navy Ministry, had as their first child Nicolás José Saturnino Antonio Francisco Franco y Salgado Araujo on 22nd November 1855, and as their second, on 1st December 1856, a girl christened more simply Hermenegilda.

The Franco family therefore did rather better than the Spanish navy over the hundred and fifty years following the arrival in El Ferrol of the Andalusian Manuel Franco. The immigrant was a Master Sailmaker.[6] His son, Juan, is described in the family papers as being "an officer in the administrative corps". His grandson rose to commander or lieutenant-colonel rank, and his great-grandson to brigadier. The Ordenador-Brigadier-Commodore Francisco Franco Vietti had a basic salary of fifteen thousand pesetas a year, a sum with a purchasing power of about five thousand pounds in 1965.[7] He was therefore a man of some wealth. He bought a house in almost the best part of the town, a building of four storeys and an attic in the Calle de María, a block away from the main square;[8] a typical Galician town house, of narrow frontage, with a single door on the ground floor and with glazed-in galleries or balconies to the upper floors; indoors a staircase along the right-hand wall leading to landings giving on to two or three rooms on each floor. Franco Vietti was the first of the family to travel abroad. Soon after the birth of his second child, Hermenegilda, he was posted for a time to Manila in the Philippines.[9]

Hermengilda was to die an eccentric spinster in her eighty-fifth year in October 1940. She distressed her parents in her youth by forming an attachment with a cousin whom she was not allowed to marry. The boy, Nicolás, followed his father Francisco into the administrative branch of the Navy, and in time was to rise to the highest permissible rank in that branch, that of *Intendente-General*, or vice-admiral. He outlived his younger sister by two years and died in his eighty-eighth year, in 1942. Long service (he entered the Navy at nineteen and did not retire until he was sixty-nine) and honesty in his work rather than any other distinction accounted for his rise to the top.

Nicolás, by the standards of his forebears, married late. He was thirty-four and both his parents were dead when on 24th May 1890, "at nine o'clock at night" he married María del Pilar Teresa Baamonde y Pardo de Andrade, the twenty-four year old daughter of Ladislao Baamonde,[10] then *Comisario* (commander or lieutenant-colonel) in charge of naval equipment at the arsenal. Pilar had a reputation for piety and fortitude; her husband, a notoriety as a not so young rake.[11]

Don Nicolás took his bride to his late parents' house in the Calle de María. His pay as *Contador de Navío* (paymaster-lieutenant) was less than a third of that of his father at his death. Not surprisingly therefore the couple let out the ground floor. On the third floor Pilar bore Don Nicolás five children.[12] The first, born at midnight on 1st July 1891, was christened Nicolás after his father. The second was born half an hour after midnight on 4th December 1892, and given the names on baptism thirteen days later Francisco Paulino Hermenegildo Teódulo. The remaining children, Pilar, Ramon and Paz, followed over the next six years to 1898.

Such was Francisco Franco's family, an occupationally in-bred society. For just over a century and a half its members were concerned exclusively with the administration of a particular naval base, within a walled city, on an extreme corner of the Iberian Peninsula. The males married the daughters of administrators. They had little choice. There was a wall between executive officers and the rest; and another between those who went to sea and those who did not. The Administrative Corps was looked upon as an adjunct of the treasury and its officials were suspected usually of corrupt practices. No wife of an executive officer could allow her daughter to "demean herself" by marrying a pay-master. No administrative officer could aspire to the hand of the daughter of an executive officer.[13] There was also another wall between the Navy and the Army, while between the armed services on the one side and civilians on the other there was an impassable moat—the civilians in their turn having their own divisions. Society in El Ferrol resembled the cemeteries of Galicia where the dead are not buried but slipped into niches above ground. Each family according to its descent had its occupation and allotted niche from which it could move neither sideways nor upwards.

Such a caste system existed elsewhere in Europe, but its rigidity would seem to have been greater in El Ferrol than say in Portsmouth, perhaps because El Ferrol shrank after Trafalgar where Portsmouth expanded, perhaps because El Ferrol was isolated from the hinterland in a peculiar way.

The houses in El Ferrol resembled those of Corunna or Vigo or any other Galician city in their glazed-in balconies. Straight narrow streets without side-walks and with carriage ways of large rectangular paving stones were common elsewhere in the region. In those streets however, were to be seen mixtures of facial features alien beyond the city wall. The workers at the arsenal and the dockyards came from Asturias and the Basque provinces; the sailors were from Cadiz and Cartagena, while those from El Ferrol were taken southward. To this day Spanish as spoken by an Andaluz is more likely to be heard than Spanish as spoken by a Galician. The language of the region, the Romance tongue rooted in Latin but as different from Spanish as French from Italian, older than these, and with a lyrical poetry of exquisite refinement written when elsewhere in Europe only crude narrative was possible, is to be heard only among servants, or a few erudite civilians.

The country inland from El Ferrol, south-west for some sixty miles to Cape Finisterre, due south for one hundred and twenty to the Portuguese frontier and east for fifty miles, the land of that language, is Galicia. It was once an independent kingdom. Today a region of Spain, it retains characteristics which few foreigners associate with Iberia. Until the coming of radio, Flamenco was never heard there; the bagpipe remains the instrument for the accompaniment of the peoples' songs, melancholic more commonly than merry, and of dances closer in kinship to the reel or strathspey than to the fandango and bolero. The land is owned in small parcels, so much so that the problem there is of the *minifundia*, holdings too small to be economically viable. Its green lushness and rolling mountains recall the west of Scotland or of Ireland; and even today in the villages there are many young girls of fair skin and dark hair and men with an unmistakeably Celtic cast of face. Their turn of phrase suggests a Celtic approach to life and a Celtic ancestor to their own peculiar Romance language.

Such is the situation now even after a generation of good roads and air transport. At the end of the nineteenth century and well into the twentieth, Galicia was to the rest of Spain almost Ultima Thule. The Galician fisherman would think nothing of going out to fish off the coast of Cornwall, but the Galician would think twice about journeying to Madrid. By road it was unthinkable: by rail it took two days. Ferrol in its turn was isolated from Corunna the railhead. There was a stage-coach when the road was passable. The normal route was by paddle-boat steamer across a choppy sea, a journey longer than from England to France. In El Ferrol the navy kept itself aloof. In the navy the Administrative class kept itself to itself.

Thus it was that Franco's family lived an isolated life: the family in the widest sense, let it be noted, to include cousins and aunts and uncles. The children were of course allowed to play with other children of middle-class parentage. Nevertheless, if there be any truth in the Spanish Saint Ignatius' famous dictum "Let me teach a child during the first seven years of his life, and you can do what you like with him afterwards but you will not change his character", and if there be any factual basis in the modern psychologists' assertion that the impressions of childhood remain ingrained in a man's character until he dies, then the aloofness, the coldness of the adult Franco, noted so often by men who served under him, may have its roots in these family circumstances.

Franco was six when the news reached El Ferrol of the greatest disaster in Spanish history since Trafalgar. It was of such a magnitude that it remained the talking point of upper and middle class Spaniards throughout his childhood, adolescence and early youth. Since it was primarily a naval disaster it was particularly pertinent to his family. It came to figure prominently in his speeches as Generalissimo and in his writings. It has indeed an importance in the life and times of General Franco, so great as to be missed particularly by the foreigner. To consider it in detail will be no digression.

The situation of the Spanish Navy in 1880, that is when Franco's grandfather was the Director of Administration at El Ferrol and his father a paymaster-lieutenant at the same base, was summed up by the American Naval chief engineer J. W. King[14] in these words:

> The ships belonging to the navy of Spain are mostly of obsolete types, the armoured ships being too thinly protected to resist modern projectiles, and the unarmoured ships having neither guns of sufficient power to fight, nor sufficient speed to elude an enemy. There are no modern sea-going armour-clads, and no cruisers of the rapid type. Recent constructions have been confined almost entirely to small vessels of slight power or speed.

A second American investigator went into more accurate detail.[15] Spain had a sizeable fleet of unarmoured little wooden boats of no value except in the interception of smugglers. Her two best ships were the iron-hulled *Numancia* (completed in 1864 in France) and *Victoria* (completed in London in 1868). They are described as "fully armoured, broadside frigate cruisers with a ram-bow, single screw and full sail power". In sheer numbers, Spain had more warships than the United States, but the American ships had anything up to double the thickness of armour; in them sail power had been replaced by steam, and breech-loading guns were mounted in turrets. The Spanish ships still had muzzle-loaders.*

The disparity between the two navies increased as the century neared its end. At the beginning of 1898, the thirty-one year old *Victoria* was still in commission; so was the even older *Numancia*. Spain had six other sail and steam ships described in the First Edition of

---

* Rifled breech-loading guns could be fired with incomparably greater speed and accuracy.

Jane[16] as "of no fighting value". Her strength lay in five cruisers of reasonably recent construction and in a handful of torpedo boats; but although the cruisers were quite new, they compared most unfavourably with those current in the navies of nearly all the other European powers and even of one or two of the new powers of South America. In a hundred years the Spanish Navy had fallen from its position as the third most powerful in the world to insignificance. Not only was it no match for Britain, France or Germany in Europe, but its strength was palpably inferior to that of her ancient colony Argentina. A comparison with the United States was now ludicrous; yet to judge from the speeches and actions of Spanish politicians and servicemen of the time they were either ignorant of the situation or would not admit to it publicly.

As the century neared its end the United States had completed its drive to the west and, in the process, annexed half of Mexico. She was now looking enviously at what remained of the Spanish Empire for further expansion. All that did remain were the islands of Cuba, Puerto Rico and the Philippines. Cuba was particularly tempting. The southern slave owners, having lost the Civil War, saw in the annexation of the island a chance to recoup their losses. The sugar plantations yielded dividends to their Spanish owners which the southerners believed they could better with a more efficient use of the labour available. Spain had never fully exploited the resources of the island. The Spanish slave owner had rarely been as inhuman as the American.

For some seventy years Spain had been battling against rebels in Cuba. Spain still did not realise at the end of the nineteenth century that her continental empire had broken away from her and fifteen new nations had come into existence at its beginning because the leaders of the revolt against the mother country were so Spanish in character. Cuba was ready for independence at the same time as Venezuela or any of the continental nations. However, governments in Madrid, liberal or conservative, now headed by generals, now by civilians, spent freely Spanish capital and lives in an enterprise that was doomed to failure. Merciless repressions of rebels merely created new converts to the cause of Cuban freedom. Paradoxically one of the measures to which Spain agreed after a ten-year battle with the rebels—the abolition of slavery in 1878—gave the independence movement a new field of recruitment. There had been abolitionists on both the Spanish side and that of the insurgents; the anti-abolitionists had all been on the Spanish side. They now felt themselves betrayed by Madrid. The southern U.S.

ex-slave owners did not welcome Spain's move, but even without slaves, Cuba's climate still made it a potentially more profitable zone for sugar growing than the north could ever be; as the century neared its end southern commercial groups in the U.S.A. saw their chance to turn the sympathy with which other North Americans looked upon the struggle for independence led by Martí to their own advantage. At the same time military strategists in Washington, no longer having Confederates to combat, were beginning to think in more global terms. The best place for a naval base to protect the southern coasts of the U.S.A., or from which to launch operations against the countries to the south of the Rio Grande was somewhere on the island of Cuba.

In February 1898 the U.S. battleship *Maine*, not the most modern, moved into Havana harbour "to protect U.S. nationals and interests". On the 15th it exploded. Two hundred and sixty-six American sailors lost their lives. The navy department attributed the explosion to a mine. The influential and popular Hearst press went into action. No American could doubt that this was a deliberate act of war on the part of Spain. American nationalism was stirred, and war hysteria swept the States. The whole of the considerable U.S. Fleet and 125,000 soldiers were mobilised. On 20th April President MacKinley demanded Spain's withdrawal from Cuba by the 23rd. On the 22nd, before the ultimatum had expired, he declared a blockade of the island, and issued a call for a further 125,000 men. If ever a steam-roller was going to be brought into action to crush a nut, this was going to be the occasion. On that same day twenty-eight vessels, including the powerful modern battle-ships *Iowa* and *Indiana* and the cruiser *New York*, sailed from Key West. On the 24th Spain declared war, but on the 25th the U.S. Congress declared that war had existed since the 21st.

From El Ferrol and Cadiz a task force was assembled under Admiral Cervera off the Cape Verde Islands. It left for Cuba on the 29th. The fleet consisted of three 7,000-ton seven- and eight-year-old cruisers, the *Oquendo*, *Vizcaya* and *Maria Teresa*, a corvette, the *Cristobal Colon* (laid down over twenty years previously) and three torpedo boats. The force took twenty days to make Santiago harbour. It could not enter Havana because of the blockade.

The Spaniards had in the meantime been unable to prevent the occu-pation of Guantanamo by U.S. marines and the landing on Cuba of 17,000 American officers and men with field and heavy artillery. Four thousand five hundred of them, led by the then Colonel Theodore Roosevelt, attacked a fort held by 520 Spaniards. The Spaniards resisted for nine hours during which 320 of them were killed or wounded. The Americans were able to capture only one hundred, for the remainder escaped to the hills. Then 11,500 Americans attacked a second fort manned by 700 Spaniards. Half of the Spanish force was dead or wounded before the Americans broke through. American casualties in this attack numbered 1,500.

Admiral Cervera thereafter faced an impossible situation. His ships in the harbour were of little value in the defence of Santiago. With the American land forces now in possession of the main obstacles to the capture of the city, it was only a matter of time before they would be able to bombard his ships from all sides while he would be inhibited against replying by the damage that he would do to the city: yet the fleet could leave the harbour only in line ahead, and each ship would be picked off on its own as it left. There were over one hundred and twenty U.S. warships round the island by 1st July. Cervera of course was in a situation in which he should never have been placed. However, Madrid now ordered him to re-embark such of his men as might be ashore helping the army, and to sail out. At 0931 on 3rd July, the cruiser *Maria Teresa* came out to face four American battleships and two battle cruisers. The *Vizcaya*, the ancient *Colon* and the *Oquendo* followed at eight hundred yard intervals. The *Teresa*, *Oquendo* and *Vizcaya* were quickly on fire. The *Colon* got away in the confusion; but not for long. The battleship *Oregon* had it within range of its 13-inch guns in a very short time and the *Colon* lay a burnt out wreck beached on its side. Five hundred Spanish sailors had been killed or wounded. One solitary shell had landed on an American warship. It had caused the death of one American sailor and wounded ten others; and that was the sum total of the damage inflicted on the American Navy. Santiago fell fourteen days later and Puerto Rico on 21st July.[17]

The United States had defeated a once mighty European power in three months; though it is a wonder that it took 250,000 Americans with excellent ships and military equipment as long as that to overcome an out-of-date navy and 100,000 ill-armed Spaniards. From it all Franco would draw the conclusion that bravery was worth hundreds of tons of superior equipment.

As in October 1805, so now in July 1898, El Ferrol was a harbour of mourning. Of its four thousand households at least two hundred and fifty were bereaved. Franco's immediate family had suffered no loss, but those of its neighbours had. His companions at play included some who were now orphaned. He and they were told: "*El deber es tanto mas hermoso cuantos mas sacrificios entraña"*—"Duty is the more beautiful the greater the sacrifices in its train."[18]

It was Trafalgar all over again; yet worse, for this time there was no foreign allied admiral upon whom the blame could be heaped: but all the blame should not be laid either at the feet of the politicians in Madrid or at those of the armed forces. The politicians in Madrid had refused to grant Cuba self-government when that would have satisfied the colonists; they had agreed to self-government only when full independence alone would satisfy. On the other hand the troops on the island were neither well-armed nor well-disciplined. They behaved at times rather like the Black and Tans in Ireland. When their behaviour had been criticised in a newspaper, led by their officers they had wrecked it. Their commander, General Weyler, knew of only one way to pacify a rebellious people. The responsibility here was therefore equally military and political.

Spanish politico-strategic thinking was also sorely behind reality. By 1890, not one of Spain's neighbours or traditional enemies had any desire to invade her. France, because of the German threat, needed a *grande armée*, while for colonial purposes she had to have a navy and a colonial army. Spain would have been well advised to concentrate her resources on a small but thoroughly up-to-date land force, such as Britain had, and on a small fleet of fast, modern ships. Instead she had a cumbersome army and kept in commission ships which should have been scrapped many years previously. Now the politicians, if not the military as well, should have been aware of American ambitions in the Caribbean. Since Spain by herself could never have warded off a determined American attack, she should have sought alliances with other powers. France and Britain who also had colonies in the Caribbean would not have been unwilling partners. The Spanish politicians sought no such alliances: but again, the military and naval advisers to the government committed yet another and more grievous strategic error. Given that at any time in the 1890s there was no likelihood of a war between Spain and her neighbours, but that Spain intended to keep Cuba and the Philippines, then the places where all the best Spanish warships should have been stationed were Santiago (Cuba) and Manila, not Ferrol and Cadiz. Admiral Cervera's task force arrived in Santiago with its coal bunkers empty. The Key West ships had long been blockading the island. The original twenty-eight were by then being reinforced by many more. Had Cervera *started* from Santiago, the battle would have been between four Spanish cruisers on the one

side and on the other only two battleships and a cruiser, instead of four
battleships, two battle cruisers and a cruiser. But there remained yet
another consideration in the apportioning of blame for the disaster.
Who had issued the Spanish ships mainly with shrapnel shell?[19] In
Manila the U.S.S. *Olympia* had been hit thirteen times without damage
being caused. The gunners obviously had good aim; but who had
supplied the guns and the shells? A comparison of the Spanish navy of
the time with those of other nations puts into high relief two pecu-
liarities: Spanish warship and gun design were out of date, and even if
it is borne in mind that men in uniform performed admiralty tasks
which elsewhere were done by civil servants, the number of administrators was inordinately high.

The navy and the Press of El Ferrol gave prominence to the many
acts of heroism of the men on the ill-fated ships at Manila and Santiago.
The army gave a full account of the battles against impossible odds at
the two forts before Santiago. No explanation, however, was given as
to why the defenders of those two forts had had to face such heavy
odds when there were on the island so many more Spanish troops.
There had been incompetent leadership in the field. Not a word was
said of this. The surrender of the garrison of 13,000 in Manila to
18,000 Americans, with a loss of only twenty killed and 105 wounded,
was on the other hand justifiable as an act of commonsense, either on
the part of the local general if he acted on his own initiative or, if under
orders from Madrid, on the part of the Government. For the general in
command knew or should have known that the situation was hopeless.
His ammunition was limited. There was not the remotest possibility of
fresh supplies or reinforcements. There was nothing to stop the build-up
of more and more American forces. A Christian theologian would judge
that not to have surrendered when he did would have made the general
guilty of the blood of those killed, friend and foe.

That was not how Franco was taught to look upon the episodes: for
it must be remembered that the Spaniard in arms was heir to the pre-
Christian tradition of the heroic but pragmatically utterly useless defence of Saguntum and Numancia, so that the men who defied the
order to surrender were held in higher esteem than those who laid down
their arms. They were the men who in El Ferrol and the garrisons of
Spain were upheld as examples to be followed: "duty is the more
beautiful the greater the sacrifices in its train".

Late in life, Franco was asked to list the chief influences on his life's
thought and action.[20] He enumerated among others "the meditation

and analysis of the events of Spanish history": a meditation and analysis by no means only of its military and naval aspects. After the end of the Second World War, when the United Nations ostracized Spain in an attempt to bring about his downfall from supreme power, he wrote a series of articles under the pseudonym Juan de la Cosa.[21] They were printed in the Spanish press and voiced for him over the National Radio. Later they were collated into a book. The articles were the fruit of that meditation and analysis which began, if the memories of his contemporaries are true, at a very early age: that is, his contemporaries remember that as a schoolboy he delighted in history. They are important as evidence of what Franco believed to be true or wanted to be true. His passage on the Spanish-American war has revealing omissions and points of emphasis. After attributing the debility of Spain to the machinations of unnamed foreign powers and international Free-masonry, he continues:

> The Government rushed into the war without plans or resources and in a defeatist spirit; and, despite the high morale of the fighting men, the plunder was consummated.
>
> When General Blanco received the order to surrender, he answered that the Army wished to fight and believed they had enough strength to do so, and that he did not consider the situation warranted such desperate measures. In spite of this, the Spanish Government relinquished the island of Cuba, being too abject to appreciate what even our enemies acknowledge—the high courage and morale of the Spanish soldiers, so brilliantly displayed at Caney and Santiago.
>
> The Spanish delegates to the peace conference in Paris received no other instructions from that worthless Parliament than to treat for the surrender of the Island of Cuba; but when they got to Paris they exceeded their commission and also handed over the Philippine Archipelago.[22]

Franco is thus anxious to leave his readers in no doubt that the Navy and Army were the victims of international agencies who had long sought the destruction of Spain and of an incompetent system of government, the "impotent democratic regime of the time", as he calls it on another page.[23]

Some years before the Juan de la Cosa articles, in 1940, Franco looked around for a theme to illustrate the virtues of the Spanish race as he saw them. He wrote then, under the pseudonym Jaime de Andrade, the script of a film with the brief title "*Raza*", The Race.[24] The climax of its first part was the war of 1898. Here, as in the later work, the defeat has the threefold explanation: Spain was the victim of foreign powers jealous of Spain's greatness: foreign powers undermined Spain with freemasonry which spread like a malignant disease among the colonials and destroyed their sense of duty to the mother country and of honour: they corrupted politicians who in any case were contemptible nincompoops.

There can be little doubt that though he wrote as Jaime de Andrade when he was in his middle forties and as Juan de la Cosa in his fifties, the basic theme of Spain the victim of an international plot was planted in him in his earliest years, when the inhabitants of El Ferrol and especially the naval administrators at the base had to find a scapegoat or admit their share of responsibility. However Franco must be judged by his acts as well as his words, and in his acts we may see other deductions from his "meditation and analysis" of the Spanish-American war.

The bereavement of so many families in El Ferrol was accompanied by a lack of work at the arsenal and dockyard, and consequently by the misery of unemployment. Within three years the forty-year-old school for naval administrators had been closed. There was to be a run-down of that over-staffed branch of the navy. Unless circumstances changed again, none of the three boys of Nicolas Franco would be able to follow his profession or that of five generations of forebears.

For the moment the Naval Cadet Ship (*Escuela Naval Flotante*) remained open. The problem for the Franco family therefore was whether to set the children on civilian careers or to aspire to the higher branch of the navy hitherto almost totally barred to the sons of admininstrators. The only civilian career which could be considered was the Law. For the Law a boy would enter a university and then continue his studies for a minimum of seven years. The first degree was that of Doctor. University entrance and success depended more on application to work and a retentive memory than on intelligence.

Now the universities of Spain at the time were substantially influenced by men directly or indirectly connected with a free-thinking institution, the Institución Libre de Enseñanza. Middle-class mothers under by no means ill-informed though illiberal clerical influence did not relish the thought of their children entering such an environment and remaining in it for seven years. Pilar Baamonde could have no illusions over her husband who lost interest in her sometime after the birth, in November 1898, of their fifth child Paz, and returned, though discreetly as yet, to his pre-marital habits. Nicolas Franco might be a

bad Catholic but still a Catholic. On the other hand young men who
left El Ferrol to study law came back, if at all, often with ideas which
she knew were condemned by the Church. A civilian career, therefore,
was not to be contemplated for her children. The Army, though inferior to the Navy, was respectable: so the Navy it had to be, if at all
possible, for all three boys and, if not, the Army.[25]

The problem was not absolutely immediate. The age of entry into
the Cadet Ship was fourteen; at the time when the Naval Administration School was closed, the eldest boy Nicolas was ten, and Francisco
was in his ninth year. They were then both attending the local preparatory school for children of middle-class parents—the Escuela del
Sagrado Corazón. It was a small private school in a corner house
overlooking the main square. It had been established a short time
previously by a local priest Marcos Vazquez Leal, from all accounts
an exemplary character. He died soon after Francisco's entry, and his
place was taken by a Manuel Comellas Coimbra who believed in the
clouting of heads as a means of energizing brains.

Nicholas was quick witted but an inattentive student. He did his
homework with the rapidity of the child who has a receptive memory.
Consequently he gave his father the impression that he was lazy and
lackadaisical and was constantly chivvied for not working hard enough
at his books. Francisco was a plodder: "He was meticulous; he was
good at drawing but otherwise quite average, quite ordinary. He was
a nice lad, of a happy disposition, thoughtful; he took his time in
answering questions but he was a playful lad." Ramon was "naughty,
a madcap".[26] The three, together with sister Pilar "who would have
made an excellent Commander-in-Chief had she been a man", lunched
regularly with their Baamonde grandfather Don Ladislao. So did their
first cousins, the Puente Bahamondes, a family of twelve children whose
father was an Executive Branch lieutenant-commander and whose
mother was Doña Pilar Baamonde's sister. In the afternoon, after the
siesta, Nicolas Franco would take all the youngsters for long walks and
for kite flying on the heights above Ferrol. In the Summer the de la
Puentes would move out of Ferrol to a house by the beach at La
Graña, two miles away. The Francos had no summer residence of their
own, but the children would go out at six or seven o'clock in the morning to the de la Puente's, bathe and, at weekends, go fishing. The
lieutenant-commander had a sailing boat, the particular delight of the
boy Francisco Franco.

At the age of twelve Nicolas and Francisco in turn passed into the

Naval Preparatory Academy run by a Lieutenant-Commander Saturnino Suances. From there Nicolas moved to the naval Engineering
School as he wished, and so did Franco's close friend at school and eventual Admiral, Suances. Francisco was anxious to enter the naval cadet
ship. He was at the right age in 1907, but although on 25th January
1907, the Prime Minister Antonio Maura had been returned to power
on a programme which included the restoration of the fleet, entry to
the cadet ship was restricted.* Barred from the Navy, the only career
to be considered was the Army. Accordingly, Franco competed for
entry into the Infantry Academy at Toledo. He was accepted with
381 others.

Franco was now in his fifteenth year and about to leave home. His
younger sister Paz had died four years previously. His younger brother
Ramon was at his old preparatory school. His elder sister was ado-
lescent. His elder brother was at the Naval Engineering School and a
very frequent visitor at the Calle de María in his uniform. His father
was still living at home, but his mother was already being secretly
admired for the fortitude with which she hid her private problems,
and openly loved and respected for her modest and sober, not to say
old-fashioned, mode of dress, her willingness to listen sympathetically
to the troubles of others and to do what she could to alleviate them.
Round the corner from her house she had hired some rooms to run a
night school for workers. Their only hope of a livelihood, with no work
at the arsenal or dockyard, was in emigration, either to other parts of
the peninsula or better still to Argentina and other Spanish ex-colonies.
An emigrant who was literate and had a trade had no cause to fear the
unknown. The political chaos of the new countries did not seem as
serious as the economic decline of their own land. In the New World
cities were growing, land was cheap and workers had a "seller's
market". There a man could break through class barriers if he amassed
sufficient wealth. Therefore, from El Ferrol hundreds, and from
Galacia generally tens of thousands, left for the River Plate in the early
years of the century: and for many it proved to be a river of silver.†

Franco, too, was to leave home. True enough it was only to a city a
mere two days away by sea and rail from which he would return

---

* Maura began the task on 27th November 1907. A Royal Decree of 21st
October 1911 replaced the *Escuela Naval Flotante* with a shore-based *Escuela Naval
Militar*.

† The Gallegos retained throughout life a romantic nostalgia. They spoke
frequently of the day they would go back to the "*madre-patria*", the mother-
motherland. Few did.

regularly during the academic holidays; and again he was not going away entirely on his own but with two other youngsters of El Ferrol. It was not a complete break and yet it was violent enough. Franco's family had been closely-knit under the patriarchal figure of Don Ladislao Baamonde, seventy-one years old in 1907 and with yet nineteen more years to live, who on the death of his wife had moved into the ground floor of the Calle de María house making it the meeting place of the Puente Bahamondes as well as of the cousins on his father's side, the Franco Salgados. However, soon after Franco's departure to the Academy at Toledo, his father Nicolas left wife and home. He was posted to Madrid. On leaving El Ferrol he laid a strict injunction on his wife not to follow him. In Madrid he set up a second establishment to the scandal of the rest of the family. Other members of the family pressed Doña Pilar to disobey her husband and confront him and his mistress in Madrid. It was not her way; and she insisted that the young Franco should pay his respects to his father each time he passed through Madrid on his way to and from the Academy. He did so grudgingly.

Franco himself also was to provide sure evidence of how long the memories of childhood hovered in his adult mind. The adult Franco, as we have said, wrote an extended essay on the history of Spain. He published much on military affairs as a junior officer and as a general. The texts of his speeches were to fill volumes; but his one truly creative literary work was the film script *Raza* to which we have already referred. It is more than a meditation on Spanish history. Over a third of it is set in the Ferrol of his childhood. The opening shots are of its fjord "with its water rippling to a light breeze and silvered . . . upon a brilliant summer's day . . . sea gulls upon its sand . . . vast flat stretches of dark sands furrowed by winding sweet-water streams . . . gullies framed by mounds and hillocks . . . maize fields . . . arrogant eucalyptus trees", and further afield "joyful beaches . . . and fishermen at their nets". The children of El Ferrol in the film play the very game in which Franco took delight: "cops and robbers" or "cowboys and Indians" in the local version, "Loyalists and Rebels", that is Spaniards versus Cubans. The children's terms of opprobium were *insurrecto, masón*, and *mambís*, rebel, mason and mambi, this last from the alleged habit of the Cuban rebels of chewing coca leaves.

The story of the film is a cavalcade of Spanish events from 1898 to 1939, from the disaster of the Cuban war to the end of the Civil War. The Prologue sums up well its argument:

You are going to live scenes in the life of a generation, unpublished episodes of the Spanish Crusade presided over by the nobility and spirituality which are the characteristics of our race. Of a family of hidalgos are the chief characters in this work and they are a faithful image of the Spanish families who stood the brunt of the fiercest attacks of materialism. Sublime sacrifices, heroic deeds, grandiose heroism and acts of the highest nobility will be shown before your eyes. You will find here no invention, no fictions. Every episode will bring to your lips the names of various real persons. Of such is Spain and such is the true nature of the Race.

However, the family of hidalgos which the film first calls to mind is Franco's own. His choice of pseudonym Jaime de Andrade, was like all Franco's acts, deliberate. On his father's side he was a distant relative of the Andrades, a most ancient and noble family with a castle in Pontedeume, a village at the head of the fjord next to El Ferrol. On his mother's side there was a double connection.

Two characters stand out in the not over-distinguished film: one is a patriarchal figure; the other bears the name in the film of Doña Isabel de Andrade. She is the real heroine, left with three sons and a daughter to rear when her husband goes down with his ship off Cuba. Franco's mother was left (less heroically) with Nicolas, Francisco, Ramon and Pilar. She is portrayed, as Franco's mother was in fact, as a gentle and pious lady; she is a *mulier fortis* of biblical stature.

In the film the eldest boy goes into the Navy as Nicolas did; the middle one into the Army as Francisco did; the third becomes an un-principled lawyer. Ramon followed Francisco into the Army: but Doña Isabel's youngest was to prove the prodigal son who returned to his family's spiritual fold only at his death, as it could be said that Ramon did, when renouncing his Anarchist affiliations he took sides with his brother in the Civil War, and was killed on active service. By accident or design, it is the mother who remains the central figure as the history of Spain from 1898 to 1939 is presented episode by episode, and though Franco's declared intention was to praise The Race into which he was born, the major subtheme is contained in his phrase: *"cuánta ha sido la sabiduría de la excelente madre en la formación y cuidado de los niños"*, most accurately translated when rendered freely as "there is no greater wisdom than that of the good mother who looks to the education and care of her children". And in Franco's view the greatest service a mother could do for her child was to instil in him a love for the *patria*.

Franco left El Ferrol already schooled in patriolatry, yet at the same time disappointed. His ambition to be the first of his family to ascend the bridge of a naval vessel had been thwarted. He was away to an academy for infantry officers and he was passionately fond of the sea. The day would come when he would be piped aboard and given all the honours due to the uniform of an Admiral and Commander-in-Chief of the Navy. In this, as in so much else, he would get his own way in the end.

NOTES

1. Registers of Garrison Church of San Francisco, El Ferrol. *Bautismos Lib. 17 Folio 105.* Entry 218. Municipal Registers Vol. 61. Sec. Va. Fol. 50 back, entry 97.

2 José Montero y Aróstegui *Historia y descripción de la ciudad y departamento naval de El Ferrol.* (Madrid, 1859.)

3 This is as far back as the Franco Family Papers go, but Lieut -Colonel Esteban Carvallo de Cora y Gonzalez Fariña (*ABC* 9th October 1965) has discovered a Juan Franco who married a Josefa de la Madrid, and who as a widow lived in La Graña, by El Ferrol. This takes the family back to the beginning of the eighteenth century.

4 The Andrade lineage goes back to pre-1492 days.

5 Municipal Registers and Franco Family Papers. By 1794 this was a mere formality. The applicant had to supply the names of parents and grand and great-grandparents. It was a two-hundred-year-old anti-semitic measure. The surnames Franco, Andrade, La Madrid, Freire and Baamonde, or Bahamonde, are all associated with sephardic descent, but any Spanish family (other than Basque) claiming racial purity would have a herculean task to prove it.

6. *Maestro de Vela.* As a Master Sailmaker he would be a Board of Admiralty employee. It seems unlikely that a boy born and bred in Madrid would be a Sail Master, that is the "petty officer" responsible for the sails on a ship.

7. Tax free. At 25 ptas. to the £, 15,000 ptas. would be £600, and this figure multiplied by eight or nine seems reasonable to equate 1850 with 1965.

8. *The Plaza de Armas.* The house was then numbered 108. The lengthening of the road subsequently led to its renumbering. It is now Calle de Frutos Saavedra 134.

9. His name is among the subscribers "in the Philippines" to Montorio's History of El Ferrol.

10. Municipal Registers. Sec. 2ª, Vol. 20, Folio 85. Entry 47. Here Don Nicolas gave his age correctly. As his cousin Carlos Franco-Salgado, the family

chronicler, noted in the Family Papers, he usually took a year off his age: "Nicolas was born on 22nd November 1855 at 7.30 in the morning. In all official documents he is down as having been born in 1856. That is not so. (*Y no es así.*)

11. Even allowing for popular imagination in retrospect among those aged 80 and over in 1965.

12. Both the Municipal Registers and the Franco Family Papers are meticulous in details.

13. But an officer in the executive grade could marry the daughter of a paymaster. Thus a young Lieutenant de la Puente married María del Pilar's sister.

14. *The Warships and Navies of the World* by Chief Engr. J. W. King, U.S.N., Boston & London, 1880, p. 363.

15. *Navies of the World* by Lieut. E. W. Very, U.S.N. Sampson & Low, 1880.

16. *Jane All the World's Fighting Ships*, giving the position as in November 1897.

17. Firing details from *Jane* 1899. Other sources: F. E. Chadwick, *Spanish-American War* (2 vols., 1911); Gomez Nuñez, *La Guerra Hispano-Americana* Madrid, 1900)

In the Pacific the U.S. Commodore George Dewey steamed towards Manila with four modern cruisers, the *Olympia, Baltimore, Concord* and *Boston* and a number of other fast vessels. The American ships with eight-inch rifled and breech-loading guns were faced by a pitiful seven ships armed with obsolete weapons. The best of them, the *Reina Cristina*, was a twelve-year-old 3,000-ton cruiser; the others: the *Castilla*, a frigate, and two sail-and-steam "ships of no fighting value", the *Don Antonio de Ulloa* and *Don Juan de Austria*, and a 500-ton torpedo boat. The *Castilla* and *Ulloa* were unable to raise steam. The other five attacked the Americans. The torpedo boat fired its improvised torpedoes before it was sunk. They did not hit their mark. The other ships were quickly set on fire and sunk; they landed thirteen shells on the *Olympia* without doing it any injury; but they did manage to hole the *Baltimore* and the *Concord* below the water-line and cause a small fire on the *Boston*. A total of seven U.S. sailors were slightly wounded in the encounter. The Spaniards had 167 killed and 1,214 wounded. Then the Americans set about the silencing of the shore batteries which they did without difficulty. Dewey rather unaccountably waited for the arrival of reinforcements to take the city. They landed in July and, after a token resistance, the Spanish garrison in Manila surrendered.

18. A key-phrase in *Raza*: see below.

19. *Jane* 1899.

20. To Saenz de Heredia in the film *Ese Hombre* to commemorate the twenty-fifth anniversary of the end of the Civil War.

21. *Juan de la Cosa* was the name of Christopher Columbus's navigator whose

maps of the New World made him internationally famous. Not all the articles and talks under that name are General Franco's, but I have been assured that those collected into the book *Spain and the World* (Spanish Themes for the World. Publicaciones Españolas, Madrid) are his as far as Ch. IX. To that point, the Spanish original has the same characteristics of style which are to be found in General Franco's other works.

22. P. 102 in the English version.

23. P. 101.

24. A splendidly bound limited edition of the "book of the film" was published in Madrid, 1942 "on 18th July, a day glorious to the Spanish Race".

25. In *Raza*, the black sheep of the family chooses the Law and Politics.

26. I am particularly grateful to General Franco's older cousins on both sides for their unvarnished reminiscences of their family when they were children and adolescents. El Ferrol being a very small town, few secrets could be kept whether worthy of praise or condemnation.

2

SPAIN IN 1892

The Spain into which Francisco Franco was born was a country with military, artistic and literary glories accomplished in a remote past. It was also a nation-state with a hundred years of turbulence immediately behind it and an unsettled present.

Three days after Francisco Franco was born, there was a change of government. Cánovas del Castillo, the Prime Minister and Head of the Liberal Conservatives, took umbrage at a remark in the *Cortes* or Parliament. A member said in a rather involved sentence that the Party leaders were fallible and weak beings whom back benchers had to tolerate.[1] Cánovas punctiliously resigned the premiership. In accordance with the provisions of the current Constitution, he and his followers automatically went into opposition. Equally automatically the leader of the opposition, and of the Progressive Liberals, Praxedes Mateo Sagasta formed a new government.

In their youth, Cánovas and Sagasta had been on opposite sides of street barricades. In their sixties they were happier with this game of political pat-ball. They had agreed upon it in 1875. The game had another thirty years to run. The ball of power would be passed between Liberals and Conservatives another thirty-seven times into the 1920s, though not always smoothly. To prevent the ball from going out of play, the racket-holders had had in the past privately to adjust election results before their publication. Cánovas had upheld that it was more important that liberty should be seen to be exercised than actually allowed to be exercised. As it was, this would be the last time that he would be free to resign in favour of Sagasta. Sagasta duly passed the ball back to Cánovas, but before Cánovas had reciprocated, an Italian-born anarchist tired of the game and shot Cánovas dead.

That was in August 1897, while Cánovas was taking his summer holiday with his wife in the Basque seaside resort of Santa Agueda.

Not all Spaniards were being born "little Liberals or else Conservatives!" They could be anarchists. The Anarchists had indeed become quite determined to kill Cánovas ever since the very year of Franco's birth.

1892 had been an eventful year. On 5th January the Anarchists had risen in Jerez. Cánovas had seen no reason why the leaders of the revolt should not be executed.

Furthermore not all Spaniards considered themselves Spaniards. On 25th March a group of Catalan nationalists had issued a declaration demanding nothing less than home rule.

Not all Spaniards believed that their lot was unchangeable. On 20th July the Post Office workers had gone on strike for higher wages and better working conditions. For among the more intellectually-minded workers the belief was gaining ground that the only way to a happier future was along that signposted by Marx and Engels.

Finally not all Spaniards were happy about their international status. Cánovas had channelled all his enthusiasm later that year to the celebration in a worthy manner of the fourth centenary of the discovery of America; but with Spain enjoying no more fruits of that discovery than a pair of islands in the Caribbean, and a handful more in the Pacific, the fanfares of the official functions had had a hollow sound. There was more therefore to the fall of the Government in the December than "a punctilio of honour".

Such was the political environment of Spain at the time when Francisco Franco was born. A century was drawing to a close which had begun with the loss of the Spanish Navy at Trafalgar. Napoleon, mistrustful of and dissatisfied with his ally, the King of Spain, had replaced him with his own brother. Before the restoration of the legitimate King, French troops had devastated the country with a barbarism unequalled by any previous invader. Subsequently there had been a republic, a King by election of republican politicians, and a second restoration of the legitimate line. Superficially there were similarities between the Spanish situation and the contemporary scene in France, Italy, Germany, Russia, or even England. The disciples of Bakunin and Marx were active in all those countries. Not all the people of Germany readily accepted Bismarck's imposition of political unity. France, like Spain, had a recent history of contrasting periods of republic and monarchy. The Catalan demand for home rule was an aspiration which Britain could dismiss as Spain's "Irish problem", and believed it understood; the alternation of Cánovas and Sagasta recalled Disraeli and Gladstone.

There was, however, one important difference: most of the countries of Europe were developing whereas Spain was diminishing. Spain had lost an empire greater in territorial extent, in manpower and mineral wealth, than that of Alexander, of the Caesars, or of Napoleon. Her authors, composers and painters of bygone ages delighted readers, audiences and art collectors throughout Europe, but those of the present were little known outside the Peninsula; and where they were, they were dismissed as imitative of other Europeans. Germans held the Spanish seventeenth-century Calderon in higher esteem than Shakespeare. Italians admitted Victoria to a place beside Palestrina. Velasquez was much sought after by British collectors. Don Quixote was popular enough in Paris to warrant several well-bound and printed local editions in Spanish; but where Spanish literature had once influenced Racine, Molière and Corneille, Spanish writers turned now to the French for style, and to the Austrian Krause, for ideas. Krause was a minor follower of Kant and precursor of Hegel.

The writers were, in the majority, *Liberales*. Cánovas himself was a journalist, novelist and popular historian before he became a revolutionary and later a staid politician. They attributed Spain's failure to develop materially at the rate at which they saw Britain and Germany advancing, principally to the Catholic Church, with its insistence on orthodoxy in matters of faith and morals. In the major novels of the prolific and most popular writer of the time, Perez Galdós, the heroes were engineers, *Liberales* in politics and free-thinkers in religion, the villains narrow-minded, bigoted, elderly women in the hands of unpleasant caricatures of priests.[2] Their Catholic opponents who were prominent only outside the Cortes and the literary cafés of Madrid, maintained that it was the flight of so many Spaniards from orthodoxy which had led to Spain's decay.

Monarchists and Republicans, Conservatives and Liberals, freethinkers and Catholics, Socialists and Anarchists, centralists, federalists, and separatists, all sought in the history of Spain matter for their arguments against each other; and when the arguments changed into violence, justification for their resort to arms. There was a general preoccupation with history. Perez Galdós gave the people a Liberal version of what had happened from the beginning of the century. He had a style which pleased both the critic and the general reader; in his *Episodios Nacionales* he shaped to his own fashion the history of Spain from Trafalgar to his own time.[3] All went into several editions. For those with pretensions to a higher intellect and a greater affection for rhetorical outbursts, there was Emilio Castelar, and Cánovas himself. On the opposing Catholic side there was no one to equal Galdos or Castelar, or even Cánovas, as a popular writer. The influence of the prolific Marcelino Menéndez y Pelayo was to be felt more widely and deeply in the twentieth century than in that to which he belonged, although his astonishing erudition was recognised from the first. Menéndez y Pelayo went further back than Galdos had done and forced the Liberals to follow him.

Look at the past, said the Catholic group, and you will know how Spain will recover the unity, greatness and liberty which her peoples once enjoyed. Look at the past, said the Liberals, and you will see from the mistakes of the past how Spain can be brought at long last to unity, greatness and liberty. Look at the past, argued the anarchists, and you will have proof of the contention that man will not be free to pursue good until all Government is swept away; look at the past, the Socialists said, and you will find Marx's historical determinism proved to the hilt, and know then that inexorably the people of Spain will yet be free. The preoccupation with the past was not academic.

To understand the Spain into which Francisco Franco was born and in which he was to acquire and retain absolute power for longer than any other man before him, it is indeed necessary to recall the history not so much of Spain as of the peoples of Spain. The various Celtic and other tribes of Iberia were given political unity by Rome, but even Rome discovered that it was more practicable to administer the Peninsula when divided into more than one province. The Germanic Visigoths destroyed such unity as there was, just as their cousins did in Britain: but in neither case did conversion to Christianity yield anything beyond a unity in religion. Internal political divisions helped the Muslim invader of Spain as they helped the Dane in Britain, but in the Peninsula there was no Alfred the Great who could be called 'Rex Hispanorum". In Britain there were no major physical geographical barriers to unity: in Spain there were. In both the Romans had left a network of roads to facilitate central administration, but their mileage in Spain, when related to the area was far inferior to that of the British system. The Arabs who, when united, had overrun the divided Christian kingdoms, came to absorb far more of the Roman–Germanic culture of their conquered peoples than is generally appreciated; and then themselves dividing into kingdoms and principalities, fell piecemeal to momentarily united Christian princes.

Isabella and Ferdinand did bring the crowns of Castile, Leon, Aragon and Valencia together and by conquest added to themselves the last Arab kingdom in Spain, that of Granada. Ferdinand annexed by conquest the Kingdom of Navarre south of the Pyrenees, while by a mixture of political and military methods their great-grandson, Philip, added that of Portugal momentarily. To make that unity more real, Isabella and Ferdinand sought to encourage unity of language and of law and administration. To such an end they and their Hapsburg successors sought to destroy the local liberties of their subjects established from time immemorial and to curb the powers of their several very democratic Cortes, or Parliaments. The kings succeeded in that by the end of the eighteenth century the Cortes were mere rubber stamps of Royal Accessions; yet the kings failed to unite the peoples of Spain. The Basques, the Navarrese, the Catalans and the Valencians remained linguistically and culturally separate from the Castilians and from each other, and ready at any moment to defend by arms what little remained of their legal autonomy, and even to seek in war the restoration of the independence they had lost.

"Unite to rule" has been the obsession of Spanish monarchs ever since Isabella, and in seeking this unity they created the social, ideological and religious disunity of Spain so evident in Franco's lifetime.[4] Expanding the medieval idea that if a man provided the money for an ecclesiastical foundation he was in a limited sense its "patron", the Spanish Crown claimed first that in reconquering Granada it had "refounded" all its religious institutions, next that all such foundations in the New World were theirs, and lastly that this "Royal Patronage" was applicable to the Church throughout their dominions. The Papacy was forced to agree to each successive step at moments of particular anxiety. The "Royal Patronage" came almost to make meaningless the distinction drawn by Christ between "the things that are Caesar's" and "those that are God's". Charles and Philip obtained administrative control of the Catholic Church throughout their dominions such as even Henry VIII did not have as head of the Church of England. Nowhere was the control more absolute than in the Americas, to which no priest could go without royal licence and where no ecclesiastic could hold any office except under the king's seal. The king defined diocesan and even parish boundaries. No church could be built without royal consent. All tithes went to the king's treasury in the first place for the king to reissue salaries to the bishops. It paid him of course to keep dioceses without a bishop for years on end.[5]

The Spanish Crown should thus have been able to avoid "trouble-some priests" in authority. The wonder is that so many, particularly in the New World, proved as bishops to be fighters for the independence of the Church from the State when before appointment their character warranted the assumption that they would be flexible to the will of the sovereign who had chosen them. Where popular sympathy lay can be seen from the wide cult of Thomas à Becket, the name of whose see was corrupted into the very Spanish-sounding "Cantórberri".

The King was against the Church, but the Church was also against the King, not only in Rome but in Spain itself. The Dominican Las Casas is universally known and quoted for his account of the earliest Spanish methods of colonization. He nevertheless drew attention merely to the immorality of the methods; so did the Papal pronouncements of 1537 and 1568.[6] A whole school of Dominican theologians at Salamanca condemned as immoral the very act of conquest. Francisco de Vitoria, in his *Relectiones de Indiis* left his readers in no doubt that the kings of Spain had committed a serious crime of injustice in sending soldiers to conquer the lands of others in the New World; for all the subtleties of a corps of royal jurists, chief of them Gines de Sepulveda, who twisted the Papal concession to Spain of a monopoly of missionary activity into a warrant for the unprincipled reduction of fellow human beings to a state of slavery. Those *Relectiones*, which by inference judged im-moral also most if not all of the wars of the Emperor Charles in Europe, were in their turn distorted totally; and to this day are quoted out of context as books of rules for "just wars".[7]

In Philip II's time a new school of philosophers, Jesuits this time, renewed the attack upon the Crown—in the defence of the human being. Francisco Suarez judged anew and, like Vitoria, condemned colonial wars and absolutism.[8] A fellow Spanish Jesuit went too far in the opinion of some of his colleagues during the following reign of Philip III. In his *De Rege et Regis Institutione*, he argued that it was the duty of a Christian Head of State to ensure the proper care of the unemployed and unemployable, the sick, the widows, the orphans and the old (thus anticipating modern British social practice by three centuries). He urged the nationalisation of land not being properly exploited; he also put forward the theory that if the king became a tyrant the people could judge him and if guilty execute him. The State could indeed complain against the Church, and it did so often.

And yet, in spite of the financial depredations of the Crown and its interference with the government of the Church, Catholicism did flourish in the Spain of the Hapsburgs.[9] It is to the credit of the Spanish people that they remained true to their Church and that the Church inspired the writers and artists of the Golden Age, in spite of their erastian rulers.

The dynastic break which occurred in 1701 with the death of the demented and childless last Hapsburg, Charles II, provided no change in the religious or political orientation of the Crown. The Bourbons merely carried to their logical conclusion the centralisation of government on themselves in Madrid and the ascendancy of the Crown over the Church.[10] Incidental circumstances helped them.

The European war that the Bourbon Philip's accession occasioned was more than the background to Marlborough's mastery as a general. The armed conflict between the Grand Alliance and the Bourbons *over* Spain was also a civil war *in* Spain, and an opportunity for the eventual victor to effect a revolution under cover of the smoke of war.

Castile had no doubt that Philip the Bourbon's title was unquestionable. Catalonia, on the other hand, and Barcelona in particular, had suffered severely at the hands of the French four years previously. When therefore, the Archduke Charles, Philip's contender, promised that Catalonia would have restored to her all her ancient liberties and parliament, the Catalans sided with the Grand Alliance. Aragon and Valencia followed Catalonia.

The division, however, was not as clear-cut as that. For example after Philip's accession there were Castilians who resented the introduction of Frenchmen into the Royal Councils.

Now the cleavage between the wealthy and the poor in Spain was already deep at the beginning of the eighteenth century. The sixteenth century had been one of neglect of agricultural development, as peasants had flooded to the cities attracted by the wages which the new *indiano* class, the returned successful Spanish-American, was prepared to offer for services. The influx of American gold, in so far as it remained in Spain, had led to a vertiginous rise of prices in the towns. The differences were more marked in Castile and the south than in the north and east. On the other hand, Church and people were still one, though the clergy were by no means as well instructed as they had been a century earlier. The clergy, however, were divided over the accession. Those bishops who had come to put on a par the anointing of kings with the chrism of their own consecration and to whom a king's last will was therefore binding in conscience had no choice. Those on the other hand who did not equate the king's anointing with their own had a more difficult decision to make. They knew that the Church had little for which to thank the Hapsburgs, but the Bourbons had made the Gallican Church even more a tool of the State. In France even the Jesuits seemed to have accepted Gallicanism. Significantly the clergy of Aragon and Catalonia, the zones most in contact with France, sided with the Hapsburg claimant; the further away from France, the more preponderant the party of the Bourbons. To all this there was a counterweight. The Hapsburgs' allies, Britain and Holland, were notoriously Protestant, credited popularly with a long record of atrocities against Catholic missionaries captured on the high seas on their way to South America and the East. France was said to be a Catholic country. Yet again one king of France had been, according to the Spaniards, a heretic, and the behaviour of the reigning sovereign over Jansenism was equivocal; and one of the leading French philosophers, Pierre Bayle, had been allowed to publish a book, the *Dictionnaire Historique et Critique*, in which he had put forward the theory that what was true in philosophy was not necessarily true in theology, and that religion was of its nature incompatible with reason. With the division of the Church it was natural that there should be a division among the people. The war of the Spanish Succession was thus also a civil war.

Even before the war had ended the new dynasty set in motion a process of change in the religious and political structure of Spain which was seriously to exacerbate the social inequalities and sufferings of the peoples of Spain. With the war over the process was accelerated.

In spite of the occasional rifts between France and Spain, Madrid became little more than an annexe of Paris. The Court of Madrid became a mirror of Versailles in ways which were to affect much more the course of Spanish history. The Hapsburgs had been no saints, but the Bourbons took little care to disguise from the people their physical and moral degeneracy. Philip V developed chronic hypochondria; his successor Ferdinand VI melancholia; Ferdinand's brother Charles III was himself free from disease, but his eldest child was mad. Charles IV, the last of the eighteenth century Spanish Bourbons, was physically weak and had an insane obsession with clocks and embroidery. Some at least of their queens behaved in a way which profoundly shocked the Spanish conception of womanhood. That republican ideas should also have percolated from France is therefore not surprising. The Government of Spain was trimmed to the French pattern: the Bourbons completed the creation of the Hapsburgs of an absolute monarchy and a central national government through royal councils; the French ministerial system was introduced. Yet here is the paradox, that these fully absolute kings who claimed that the nature of kingship gave them power of life, exile or death over any subject and a position above the Church and churchmen in their lands, were even more in the hands of favourites than their Hapsburg predecessors; and for their favourites they cast their nets more widely. Lerma, Uceda and Olivares, the favourites of the Hapsburgs, had been noblemen and Spaniards: the Bourbons chose in turn Orry, a French agent of Louis XIV, the castrated Italian singer, Farinelli, a Parmesan full-time politician and part-time priest, Alberoni, and a Neapolitan shopkeeper, Squilace. The Spaniards who shared with them the ear of the monarch were *afrancesados*, Frenchmen in all but birth, like Macanaz in the first half of the century, a paladin of regalism, and in the second half, Aranda, Grand Master of the Spanish Orient and Voltaire's hero of heroes.

Franco as Head of the State was to insist before the Vatican that the Royal Patronage of the Church dating from Isabella was his by virtue of his position as Head of the State, and the Vatican was to resist the claim for as long as it could. Franco, however, eschewed another word which makes its appearance early in the sixteenth century and recurs ever more frequently thereafter in the State's Church legislation. The word was *Regalía*, which in preference to *Real Patronato* became the keyword in the struggle between the Bourbons and the Church. *Real Patronato* retained the connotation that the king had powers over the Church by virtue of a deed of gift from the Pope. For Philip V's favourite, Macanaz, and subsequent writers, where not before, *Regalía*[11] came to mean "those powers of the monarch which are inherent in the quality of a king", that is to say all power over any subject or over any organization of men within his territories. The king could not merely do no wrong; everything he did was right provided it were for the good or the aggrandisement of his kingdom, that is himself. If therefore he needed money for any purpose, he had full authority to acquire it from anyone and by any means. There was money in the Church. Succeeding generations of men who had not led exemplary lives had bequeathed funds and property to religious orders, to dioceses and to parishes in expiation. Kings themselves had done this. A part of this money had gone to university and other scholastic foundations, hospitals, orphanages and homes for the old and incurable, a part on the over-embellishment of churches; a part had remained as land which, by terms of bequeathment, the Church could not sell. Here then was a goldmine to replace the ever-dwindling mines of Mexico and Peru.

To Macanaz, as to the French economist Orry, whom the French King sent to his grandson as an adviser, the austerity of the Escorial was an insult to the majesty of kingship; and they held that a country as rich as Spain was capable of providing the king with an income sufficient not only to conduct wars, but also to build new palaces such as befitted royalty, and to equip them adequately with Officers of the Royal Guard and courtesans. Orry and Macanaz placed before the King a plan to despoil the Church. If the Church replied that though its monies might seem substantial when considered as one single unit, it should not be forgotten that the sum had to provide for several thousand human beings, then the argument should be advanced that there were too many priests. The plan was put before the Council of Castile. Those who in speaking against it showed opposition to Gallicanism were dismissed; however both its sponsors fell from grace for reasons quite alien to it before it could be fully put into effect. It did not matter to this extent: the number of priests whom the monarch would permit to be ordained was subsequently severely limited and the King's encroachment on the spiritual authority of the Pope and the Church's finances reached such proportions that in 1737, the Pope was prepared to negotiate a concordat or peace treaty, one of the first between any modern State and the Vatican.[12] The encroachments none the less continued, and within sixteen years, in 1752, the Spanish Crown forced upon the Papacy a second concordat, giving the Crown of Spain control of the appointment to vacancies in all but a few benefices, and the power to derive from the Church substantial contributions.

Up to mid-eighteenth century, the Regalists were mostly men who accepted all the doctrines of the Catholic Church, substituting only the supremacy of the king for that of the Pope in greater or lesser degree. From that time onwards another type of Regalist becomes more numerous; he is not himself a believer yet he is not opposed to those same doctrines as a means of keeping the masses in their place. The local parish priest, to whom parishoners would look for leadership, would be subject to the bishop, who in turn would be a man whose appointment had been the gift of the State, and who could therefore be expected to be loyal to the State; but, since in the past, particularly under the Hapsburgs, not all the clergy so indebted to the Crown had proved subservient to it in higher office, the Crown would come to use against them the other para-religious weapon of theirs, the Inquisition.[13]

In the second quarter of the eighteenth century yet a third type of Regalist arose. He believed in the necessity of a king in society at that juncture of national development but not in the institution of kingship as immutable.

Pedro Pablo Abarca de Bolea, tenth Count of Aranda, was the first of such men to rise to the position of supreme authority in Spain. His career has some interesting parallels with that of General Franco. Born on 18th December 1718, he was a captain at twenty-two and a lieutenant-general at thirty-seven. At forty-five he was a captain-general of the new Spanish regular army which the Bourbons of Spain created to the model of the French. He was to be the first Spanish general in history to become the Head of Government.[14]

As a young officer Aranda came into contact with Franco-Masonic lodges, the first peninsular one of which had been established in Gibraltar in 1726.[15] He became a member of "La Matritense" in Madrid. Either through the lodge, or in carrying out one or other of the diplomatic missions with which he was entrusted, he established a close friendship with Voltaire, D'Alembert and Raynald, then collaborating on the famous encyclopedia. He shared Voltaire's vague deism and implacable hatred of all religion and of *l'infame*, the infamous beast of Rome in particular. With Voltaire Aranda appreciated that an international Church was too difficult to destroy all at once by frontal attack. In Spain, as in France, the only part of the Church still acting independently of the national monarch was the Jesuit order. In Portugal Voltaire and Aranda had an ally in the powerful Marquis de Pombal and the three decided on the destruction of the Jesuits as the first objective. They would carry it out in their three countries. Such a destruction would have far-reaching results. The Jesuits provided the greater number of schools for middle and upper class boys, and even some for those of the lower classes. They were prominent not only as professors in seminaries for future secular priests but also in the universities where they taught mathematics, physics, chemistry, astronomy and allied sciences as well as philosophy and theology. Without this learned body of several thousand men, who somehow always reconciled the findings of new scientific research with Christianity, the field would be clear for the new French philosophy. Future generations of middle and upper class boys would be freed from the Jesuits' *ratio studiorum*, which somehow gave an agility of mind even to boys of quite average intelligence and enabled them to parry the thrusts of their intellectual superiors such as the editors of the Encyclopedia. Future generations of secular clergy would be even less well instructed. The new intelligentsia would be an elite, limited in numbers. Already for a variety of causes, not least the constant depredations of the State, there had been a falling off from the standards and numbers of the early seventeenth century, when a nation of under five million male persons had had a university membership of at least 25,000.[16]

In 1767 the Jesuits were expelled. The story is a shoddy one of calumny and of brutal suppression by the army, at Aranda's orders, of popular demonstrations in favour of the expelled.

A number of reforms followed the expulsion. The teaching of Duns Scotus, Aquinas and Suarez was forbidden. Calderon's plays were banned. With the money confiscated from the Jesuits homes were built for the orphans and widows of army officers. Voltaire was to say of Aranda: "Half a dozen men like Aranda and Spain would be regenerated".

There are, it is true, a number of learned foundations in Spain which date from the eighteenth century—the Academy of the language and that of history for example. They were for an élite. There were new colleges for the sons of gentlemen, but their number was small compared with that of the closed Jesuit colleges which had been open to any person of ability. There were also agricultural reforms. Campomanes, in his book *Tratado de la Regalía de Amortización*, published two years before the expulsion of the Jesuits, had put forward a plan for the sequestration of entailed property held not merely by religious orders but also by town councils and village corporations. In 1770 the Crown began to take over what in fact were common lands. At the turn of the century the hospitals, hospices, university colleges and other social and educational organisations run by the religious orders were deprived of their income. Lands on which they depended were taken over. The new owners of the lands were less tolerant of the difficulties occasioned by bad harvests on their tenants than their predecessors had been. The gap between the rich and the poor widened yet further.

From the middle of the eighteenth century onwards, therefore, must be dated some of the problems of twentieth-century Spain: an army which could provide the Head of Government; a limited élite which believed itself the intellectual superior of all others; an unlettered mass of the people who could be provoked to violence; and the clergy, which would henceforth look upon "reformers" with almost pathological suspicion and fail to distinguish the good from the bad. The resistance of the Church to reform, even where it was reasonable, would enable its upper class enemies to drive a wedge between the Church and the common people; the unlettered mass would be swayed

by demagogues of different schools; the upper classes would divide into
a traditionally Catholic group, not well instructed in their religion, and
a "liberal" group intent on the fulfilment of Aranda's and Voltaire's
command, *Ecrasez l'infame*; while the army would see no reason why,
having once provided a Head of Government, it should not provide
others, and even a Head of State.

In the early nineteenth century the divisions of Spain became even
more marked.

Napoleon sent Murat with an army into Spain after Spain had lost
her fleet fighting England on his behalf. The French profaned everything that the people held sacred. On 2nd May 1808 two young army
officers distributed arms to the people of Madrid. Led in many places
by parish priests, the people attacked the French. The insurrection was
suppressed so pitilessly that the painter Goya turned from his por-
traiture of the Royal Family and the satirizing of the Church to the
pictures of the horrors of war by which he is perhaps better known.
That rising by the people of Madrid began the War of Independence
against Napoleon. The Mayor of Móstoles, a village near Madrid,
issued a national call to arms. In Seville the Archbishop himself led the
revolt. Priests and local government officials everywhere were the
leaders. A National Junta was formed. On 24th September 1810 a
National Cortes met to draft a new constitution. In that Cortes, after
the first few sessions, the priests and the laymen to whom Voltaire and
Rousseau were anathema came to be outnumbered by those who had
embraced such philosophies; but then, since Napoleon had abolished
all religious houses in Spain, the masses and the clergy were keener to
fight him as *guerrilleros* than to do battle with fellow Spaniards in the
Cortes. The constitution was completed in 1812 in Cadiz. In its final
form it had 384 Articles. It recognised Ferdinand VII as King of Spain,
albeit as a monarch whose absolutism would be restricted to the will
of the Cortes; it gave equal rights to all Spaniards in the peninsula and
overseas; it recognised the Catholic religion as that of the State; it
subordinated the army to the civil power; it guaranteed all sorts of
freedoms. It was also meaningless.

From that moment to 1875 Spain knew no peace. In 1814 General Elío
issued a proclamation in favour of Ferdinand as an absolute monarch
and Ferdinand made his way back to Madrid. Ferdinand then proceeded to persecute brutally all those who had dared to propose at
Cadiz his relegation to the status of a constitutional monarch. In despair

six years later, an Asturian battalion commander, Rafael Riego, issued a proclamation in favour of the Cadiz constitution. Ferdinand swore to it, and then allowed the victors to persecute their enemies without mercy. This in turn led to a civil war, with colourful non-professional soldiers on either side, on the one a monk dubbed El Trapense and on the other a shopkeeper nicknamed El Empecinado—the stubborn one. No quarter was given on either side in this war. Peace was restored by French intervention. In 1833 Ferdinand died leaving an infant daughter, Isabella, but the throne was claimed by her uncle, Don Carlos. A further six years of civil war followed, again with little quarter on either side. This was the first of what are called the Carlist Wars. Half-way through this war, a number of sergeants forced the Queen Regent to swear to the Cadiz constitution. Like her late husband Ferdinand, she allowed it to run for a time. In 1840, however, a General Espartero deposed her. He and two other generals, Narvaez and O' Donnell—*the* O'Donnell on the death of an Irish cousin—then took over all effective government and held it for the next twenty-seven years, while Isabella, after a few early years of virtuous marriage, acquired a reputation which would have set a modern Martial to work on epigrams. Isabella then selected a fourth general, Prim, to take the place of Narvaez and O'Donnell, but he joined yet another general, Serrano, an Admiral Topete, and a civil engineer, Sagasta, in a rebellion against her. The army-navy-civil engineer coalition made up a new constitution; looked around for nearly two years, for a king to fit it and finally prevailed upon the Savoyard Amadeo to accept it. Prim was assassinated, almost certainly the victim of a private feud. Amadeo had enough of Spain in twenty-seven months. He abdicated and the Cortes declared a republic. The Republican government was divided within itself; some wanting a federal constitution; others a unitary State; some a revolutionary programme; some a conservative; and a General Pavía wanted a military dictatorship under republican forms. Old Don Carlos, Isabella's uncle had died, but his son Carlos Luis headed north to join the Basques and the Catalans who had rebelled against Madrid in his favour. Thus there was another Carlist war. Simultaneously in the southern cities of Malaga, Seville, Cadiz, Granada and Cartagena, there were mass movements which looked to new writers, and not to Rousseau, for inspiration, and fought against authority. The Republican government decided it could no longer hope to maintain itself in office. One of its members, Cánovas, sought out Isabella's son Alfonso at Sandhurst in England and obtained from him a promise to return and head a constitutional monarchy at the appropriate moment. First one general in Valencia and then the Captain-General of Madrid, Fernando Primo de Rivera (whose son and grandson were to be even more prominent in politics), declared for Alfonso XII. Cánovas and Sagasta worked on a new constitution which would enable Spain to present herself to the outside world as a peaceful democracy for the rest of that century. This was the constitution discussed in 1875, and approved in 1876, which was to remain in force until 1923 when Primo de Rivera II replaced it by his own military autocracy.

Such is the commonplace history of nineteenth-century Spain: such a review of events misses the essence of the history of the people of Spain in the nineteenth century. Had it been such and no more, it would have had no relevance to the twentieth. It was to be expected that Ferdinand and then his widow, on behalf of their daughter Isabella, should resist by force the surrender of their absolute power to a Cortes and a constitution; and they had many to support them, for the Bourbons, after a century of absolutism, had created a class of men servile to them. It was to be expected, in a country already over-full with legalists, that some would oppose Ferdinand's will and support his brother Carlos. Carlos argued that the Salic impediment to a woman's accession was irremovable by or on behalf of a Bourbon, and that therefore Isabella was a usurper. Again, it was to be expected that the army, having tasted the delights of power, should lord it over the civil authorities even while claiming to support a constitution which placed it in a subordinate position. All these struggles, however, were of their nature between small groups. They do not account for the intervention of the masses throughout the century. Yet in the Civil War of 1821, in the subsequent Carlist wars, and in the risings in the Spanish cities under the First Republic, the greater part of the population of Spain took part. They were fighting for principles less arid than Salic law, and precisely because men held other tenets, or their derivatives, dearly, civil wars in Spain did not end with the nineteenth century.

Non-Spanish and Spanish historians alike have rightly called the Cadiz constitution "liberal"; and in that word is the whole crux of the matter. No Spanish word could be more different from its English dictionary equivalent than that very adjective "liberal". Liberalism in Spain was a philosophy in the first place, a religion in the second, and only incidentally a political doctrine. It had next to no connection with economic theories nor with Liberalism as understood in England. As a philosophy it shared with Catholicism the tenet that every man has a free will. Beyond that it deviated. The Catholic said that free-will was the gift of God to serve God, and in order to serve God better men had to form themselves into societies or States. Accordingly the authority of the State was derived from God through the people—the doctrine Suarez developed so fully. The Liberal said that whether or no there was a God, free-will was of the very nature of man; but while in theory every man was born free to do whatever he liked, and to think as he liked, freedom without limit would make impossible life in society which was seen to be necessary to human beings. Hence there had to be law and authority, even if it cut down individual freedom. But since the only authority was that of the individual, the authority of the State could not be but the sum of the freedoms of the individual. The sum being greater than its parts, logically the State had to be all-powerful, and as there was no law or restriction for the individual except what he decided was good or useful to him, so there could be no law or restriction on the State except as decided by the State. Again, the sum being greater than its parts, any society within the State had either to be an integral part of it or conform to it, or be destroyed.

Such a political philosophy pursued to its logical conclusion would of course make the State totalitarian. Subsequent generations of Spanish intellectuals would in fact find the transition from their forms of Liberalism to Marxism or Falangism easy.

Obviously in denying the existence of any but human law, that is in stating that, whether or no there was a God, there was certainly no divine law, the Liberals were heretics in the eyes of Catholics. The matter however was not left on a purely philosophical plane. Discussions in the Cortes as to whether it was more correct philosophically to talk about the "liberty of man" or the "concrete liberties of the individual" were followed by a direct attack on the Church, through the Cortes and outside it.

Liberal historians and the novelist Galdós were to present the events of 2nd May 1808 and subsequently as the outcome of a resurgence of Spanish national spirit against a foreign invader. So it was; but the sequence of events suggests that patriotism was secondary to something else. There was no immediate popular reaction against the French troops. The movement against the French began *after* they had begun the looting and destruction of churches. It surged as Napoleon ordered the closing down of one out of three monasteries and conventual houses. It became a nation-wide flood as he ordered the scattering of the dwellers in every one of them. The Liberals became "patriots" in any number only as the defeats suffered by Napoleon's armies in Spain coupled with British and Prussian determination to pursue the French made it reasonably certain that Napoleon's days were numbered. The Liberals had then to ensure that the policy initiated by Aranda and continued by Napoleon should be made constitutionally sacrosanct.

Although it would seem that there was general Liberal agreement that the Church should disappear in Spain, there were diverse opinions as to how such an objective should be reached. At Cadiz and for the rest of the century, Liberals fell into two groups: those who sought the destruction of the Church by gradual constitutional means; and those who were for an all-out attack. The two parties, who called themselves by different names from time to time,[17] corresponded thus roughly to the Marxist-Socialists and the Communists of today, both agreed on the final object, the disappearance of the State, but opposed on practical grounds even to the point of fighting one against the other. The periods of maximum civil disorder coincide with the periods of maximum pressure by the extremists. On the eve of the 1821 revolution, the Government ordered the suppression of all religious orders. The outcome of a popular revolution prevented the law from being carried out. From 25th July 1835 to 29th July 1837 a whole series of laws were enacted whereby all Church property in Spain was confiscated piecemeal. It was put up for sale so much at a time in a half-hearted attempt to obtain a reasonable price for it. The Church authorities excommunicated all the buyers, thereby playing straight into the hands of the Liberals, who were able to purchase from the State what they wanted, or could afford, for as little as one-third of the true value of the property. Thus the confiscation of the properties of the Church did not benefit the nation but only a small group within it, a group smaller than that which had been deprived. What little remained unsold by 1844 remained in the hands of the State.

The situation was regularised by a concordat with the Vatican in 1851. The state then undertook the payment of fixed salaries to all bishops and secular clergy after the Vatican had reduced their number. The highest salary—some £1,400 per annum[18]—was allocated to the Primate, the Archbishop of Toledo; a parish priest might have as little as £50. Nominally the Church received irredeemable national debt bonds at a low rate of interest to the value of the property still in the hands of the state; but the interest from these bonds counted towards the state's settlement of the salaries.

The 1851 Concordat should have been a peace treaty. The Vatican had accepted as an accomplished and irreversible fact the spoilation of the first half of the century; but the Government had recognised the Church's right to acquire property in the future. This was a compromise which satisfied neither the Catholic peoples of the north of Spain nor the extreme Liberals. The extremists lost no time in breaking the terms of the Concordat. Relations with the Vatican were strained to breaking point. The army generals who dethroned Isabella II in 1868 embarked upon a veritable religious persecution. In 1869 bishop and priest had to swear unqualified allegiance to the "Atheistic and Masonic" Amadeo of Savoy or forego their "pay". In the following year the peoples of the north of Spain rose in revolt in what is called the Second Carlist War. Peace was not restored until Cánovas in 1876 had promised adherence to the Concordat. His constitution had recognised the church as that of the state. Thereafter for the rest of the century there was relative peace, even though the extremists saw in the Concordat the surrender of the state to the church, and the more devoted Catholics abhorred it as the exact opposite.

There were many other aspects of the struggle between Catholicism and Liberalism than the purely financial one. The extreme Liberals wanted civil marriage only to exist in Spain, and they were, of course advocates of divorce. The less extreme lacked the courage of their convictions, and strangely enough one of the chief sources of trouble for the rest of the century and into the twentieth was the repeated refusal by the Church authorities to bury in consecrated ground those who had not shown any allegiance to the Church in life. Such social aspects increased in importance as the Church came to be identified more and more with the governing upper classes. The first was inevitable following the conversion of the clergy into state pensioners; the second was the outcome of two factors. First, churchmen sought from the upper classes financial means to reopen the schools, colleges, hospices and hospitals which the Church had had in the past. Secondly, until new funds were obtained, only the fee-paying schools could survive. Thus at a time when Church schools "for the deserving poor" were multiplying in Britain in both urban and rural districts, the number of church schools in Spain did not increase. Towards the end of the nineteenth century the great majority of the Spanish clergy were still of very humble origin, but these men of humble origin were very rarely able to compete successfully for the canonries and prebends.

Promotion was by means of *oposiciones*, or examinations in which the man who had been to a fee-paying school had more experience. Appointment was, in any case, subject to state approval. The wealthy Liberal might disapprove of the Church but he would seek to satisfy his pious wife's request for a benefice for her nephew.

More important for the Church than the loss of all her property was the loss of her contact with the masses of the people. It was gradual. Church and people acted as one throughout the country in 1808. Fifteen years later the peoples of Spain all the way to Madrid rallied behind the French army sent to aid Ferdinand VII against the extreme Liberals who had dissolved by force all the religious congregations. Nevertheless at that time the extreme Liberal leader, Colonel del Riego, gathered a city mob to attack church buildings. By 1835 the situation had changed even more. Only the Basque Provinces, Navarre, Aragon, Catalonia and a part of old Castile had rallied to the Carlist cause. In Madrid, the Liberal government had merely to accuse the clergy of responsibility for the first of the two terrible outbreaks of cholera of the nineteenth century for the mob to murder out of hand over one hundred priests. Theophile Gautier who visited Madrid soon afterwards and saw Seville Cathedral empty of people asked whether Spain was Catholic any longer, and although the Catholic philosopher Balmes answered the question optimistically, he too posed the question whether it was true that Spain was still Catholic.

The persecution of the Church in Spain, was no more intense in the south, where the loss of contact first became apparent, than in the north. Nevertheless the re-christianisation of the south and also of the eastern coast of Spain following the reconquest from Arabic rule had been left preponderantly to the religious orders. To this day the ratio of parish churches and secular clergy to inhabitants is far inferior in the dioceses of those areas than it is in Old Castile or the north generally.[19] The church lost contact in the first place where it was numerically weakest in priests. Then, in the second half of the nineteenth century Spain underwent a double economic revolution which was bound to increase that loss of contact. On the one side, as we have said, churchmen came more and more to be identified with the upper classes: on the other the further concentration of land ownership following the confiscation of the church lands made absentee landlordism with all its well-known evils an even more general characteristic of Andalusia than it had been for centuries. The expulsion of the religious orders swelled by tens of thousands the number of peasants not merely landless but workless. They formed a mass of half-starving families understandably too concerned with keeping body and soul together to consider the nature of the soul or the purpose of life. Such unfortunates needed a simple straightforward religion: Catholicism was altogether too complex.

That new religion had in the first place to appeal to their outraged innate sense of justice. It was self-evidently unjust that they should be set upon by the police at the orders of the servants of the landowners when they attempted to cultivate a piece of land to grow food for themselves and their children. If the law of property as decreed by the state forbade it, then the law was wrong. If that law was wrong then all other laws might be so also: indeed the whole legality of legality might be questioned. Now watching their own children, if they survived malnutrition, growing into miscreants, they could with justice argue that the laws of the state had distorted the natural goodness of their *criaturas inocentes*. It was therefore not as churchmen said that "man is prone to evil from his very childhood", but that the Laws of Men deflected Man from natural goodness. But churchmen claimed that they taught what they did by the authority of an omnipotent being and that the laws of men were sanctioned by that God. That God then was evil, which was impossible, or he did not exist. If he did not exist, there was no sanction for either Church or State. To restore man to his natural goodness, both Church and State had therefore to be destroyed.

In the second half of the nineteenth century the Rio Tinto mines in the south-west, others in Oviedo, and industrial developments in Bilbao and in Catalonia provided work for some of the starving southerners. The conditions of work imposed upon them by their British, German or Spanish masters, were at the start no worse than those of their contemporaries elsewhere in Europe, but they remained inhuman where those of Britain improved. The Spanish Liberal came under the influence of English economic liberalism precisely at the time when in England the consequences of Adam Smith's *laissez-faire* were beginning to revolt upper-class English philanthropists. Neither Sagasta nor Cánovas were Lord Shaftesburys. The workless and the working classes of Spain never had in the Spanish Cortes of the time a single true champion, and they could expect no redress from the Government. In their desperation they turned to whosoever promised salvation in this life: one was Marx and the other Bakunin.

The "father" of Spanish socialism was Pablo Iglesias, born in El

Ferrol in 1850. Its early development in Spain was similar to its contemporary growth in other countries, though in Spain its appeal was
limited rather to the semi-skilled worker than either to the skilled or
unskilled. A Socialist Party was founded in May 1879, and after 1888
it had a well-administered weapon in its workers' organisation, the
Union General de Trabajadores. In Catalonia where there were a high
number of skilled workers and even more in the south with its unskilled workers, anarchism was far more successful than socialism.

Anarchism was the religion which satisfied the oppressed masses in
their thirst for justice and in their zeal for vengeance against their
oppressors. Furthermore, there was something very Spanish about
anarchism. Carlism and Liberalism were both manifestations of the
Spaniards' love of liberty in their different ways: so was Anarchism.
Marxist Socialism was a way to liberty in theory, but only through a
purgatory of collectivism and the suppression of liberty. Bakunin
therefore did well to despatch his disciple Fanelli to Spain. He and his
first disciples wisely concentrated on Andalusia. They made converts
by the thousand. The Spanish delegate at the Bakuninist Conference
in Geneva in September 1873 claimed that there were already 300,000
members in the movement. It may be that he exaggerated: the Spanish
Marxist Francisco Mora alleged there were a mere 60,000. Even so
this was an astonishing figure for a body without funds and without
organisation as the world understood it. Andalusia was the area with
greater numbers; but the two hundred and seventy Anarchist groups
included one in Franco's home town of El Ferrol, and one of the
movement's ten newspapers was printed there or in Corunna. Over the
next nine years there were minor incidents involving anarchists. They
took to bomb-throwing in Spain, as elsewhere in Europe, not with
any hope of bringing about their millenium but to "register a protest"
against its non-arrival. Cánovas would not be the last of their victims
of standing.

Such, then, was the Spain into which Franco was born. It was a
country with a wide gulf between the rich and poor, between an
educated minority and an illiterate mass. It was a region with four
mutually irreconcilable religions, Catholicism, Liberalism, Socialism
and Anarchism, and a State which was not a nation but a collection of
peoples called Castilians, Catalans, Basques and others. It was a Spain
in which a man had to be a Spaniard to harbour any hope.

NOTES

1. Francisco Silvela, Cánovas's Deputy: "*Ya es sabido que los políticos tienen que soportar a los jefes de los partidos.*" By the nineteenth century *soportar* was losing its original meaning and acquiring its modern meaning of "to put up with, to suffer".

2. *Passim* but particularly in *Doña Perfecta* (1876) and subsequently in *Gloria, Leon Roch, Nazarín* and *Halma*: all "best sellers".

3. Published at irregular intervals between 1873 and 1912. It is through them rather than history books that the mass of the reading public still glean their knowledge of the Spanish nineteenth century.

4. There is a grave need for a history of Spanish Church and State relations. It is a centuries-long story of discord, and not, as Spaniard and foreigner have been taught to believe, one of harmony. Ferdinand threatened a schism before ever his son-in-law Henry VIII: Isabella expelled priests before ever she laid a hand on Jew or Muslim. Charles V sacked Rome. He and his son Philip II, who also went to war against the Pope, tried at every turn to impede the progress of the Council of Trent. The Hapsburgs repeatedly mulcted the Church of considerable sums of money. The expulsions of Jews, Muslims, Christian Jews and Christians of Moorish descent coincide too well with the periods when the Spanish Crown was in particular need of money, either to replenish an empty treasury or to service the debts it incurred in its European wars, not to put in doubt the official explanation that they were "in the service of religion and the discharge of the Royal Conscience". Hints that the established view is unhistorical were given by R. Trevor Davies in *The Golden Century of Spain* (Macmillan, 1937). For greater detail on Philip II *v.* R.H.S. Transactions, Fifth series, Vol. XI, pp. 23-42, by Professor J. Lynch. For other very important aspects *v.* J. Brodrick's *The Origins of the Jesuits* (Longmans, 1940) and *The Progress of the Jesuits 1556-1579* (Longmans, 1946), both very well documented. For the powers of the Crown I have used the *Recopilacion de las Leyes de los Reynos de las Indias*, especially Bk. I (facsimile edition Consejo de la Hispanidad, 1943), and for the general history the archives of Simancas, Seville, Asuncion and Buenos Aires.

5. There are gaps of up to twenty years in appointments to South American dioceses and of up to seven years in peninsular. Charles V took one-ninth and Philip III two-ninths of all tithes, and the whole of the tithe paid by the manor or largest house in each tithe district. Occasionally there were special levies. The Benedictines had to sell the silver ornaments of their churches and abbeys to provide Philip III with the 12,000 dubloons (or 24,000 ducats) he demanded from them. On the other hand it must be admitted that the Crown would help struggling dioceses and that it did transport missionaries across the

Atlantic: under seventy-five in an average year for the whole continent. (Archivo de Indias Seville for years 1500-99.)

6. The first, *Sublimis Deus sic dilexit* 17th June 1537 condemned the enslavement of "Indians", that is non-whites. The second followed a report by a committee of four cardinals.

7. *De Jure Belli*, the name by which Vitoria's treatises are better known, was only a sub-title.

8. Passim in *De Legibus*; specifically in *De Triplici Virtute Theologica*. Suarez, like Bellarmine in Rome, was preoccupied with the menacing theory of the divine right of kings. His *Defensio Fidei Catholicae* was written more with the Spanish Hapsburg in mind than James I, who had a copy of it ceremonially burnt in London as an act of reparation to his divine person. His ten-volume *De Legibus* re-examined from first principles the whole nature of law and society and came to conclusions more truly democratic than those of Rousseau and less acceptable to absolutists.

9. The Cortes of 1626 gave 9,088 as the figure of conventual houses, including hospitals, orphanages and schools in Spain at that date. There were also about 12,000 town and village parish churches, and the religious population (that is all those claiming protection from the Church for legal reasons, but not religious in the modern sense) may have been as high as 100,000 out of a population of at most 9 millions. These are credible figures. J. P. de Oliveira Martins in *A History of Iberian Civilization* (Oxford, 1930) gives the quite impossible figure of 400,000 monks, 312,000 priests and 200,000 in monastic orders as at 1570. This would mean that for every five laymen, including boys and infants, one was a clergyman and that every conventual house in the country was at least as large as Montserrat is today. "*Convento*" is a generic term covering monastery and hermitage alike.

10. There was, at the moment of accession of the first Bourbon, one attempt to reverse the political process of the previous two centuries. The Marquis of Villena tried to have the Cortes of Castile summoned for more than the formal recognition by them of Philip, the grandson of Louis XIV of France, as King of Spain; Villena wanted the Cortes to extract from the Frenchman an oath to observe the ancient liberties.

11. Usually derived from the neuter plural of *regalis*: the matters that pertain to royalty. Such a derivation seems to me to offend against philological principles. In sixteenth-century documents moreover the word is usually preceded by "*per*" or "*por*", suggesting rather the vulgar Latin *per regale via*—by way or virtue of kingship.

12. The history of concordats seems to be little known even in Spain. A concordat is a peace treaty rather than a treaty of friendship. Concordats have been negotiated by the Papacy only with regimes with which the Vatican has not

seen eye to eye. Thus there is no concordat between the Irish Republic and the Vatican. On the other hand there had to be a concordat with Hitler, Mussolini, the new Poland, and, as we shall see later, with Franco.

13. Para-religious in that the chief judges were appointed from the beginning by the king. For some little known aspects of the Inquisition *v*. the Liberal historian Madariaga's classic works on Spanish America.

14. *Presidente del Consejo de Ministros.*

15. There are numerous books on Freemasonry in Spain. They suffer from uncritical scholarship. The article in the *Espasa Calpe Encyclopaedia* is more restrained. The nature of Aranda's Freemasonry is well documented.

16. In thirty-two universities. V. Fernandez Navarrete: *Conservacion de Monarchias.* B.A.E. No. 25, pp. 539 *ff*. Madrid, 1881. By 1750 the number of university students may have been as low as 7,000.

17. Spanish Liberalism became in the second half of the century something like a river delta. Cánovas's Conservatives and Sagasta's Liberals were the main streams but there were a third and fourth, if not a fifth. The third was composed of men who deviated from Rousseau and turned to the minor philosopher Krause. Krause, or rather his Spanish disciple Sanz del Río, taught a queerly amorphous, almost pantheistic, rationalism. Its political importance lies principally in that Sanz del Rio's pupil Francisco Giner de los Ríos, founded in 1876 an institution for secondary and higher studies, the *Institución Libre de Enseñanza*. It provided the sons of political and religious free-thinkers with as good a secular education as any ever run by the dispossessed religious orders. It was staffed by men of ability who refused at the 1876 restoration to swear allegiance to Church, Crown and dynasty and so were deprived of teaching posts in the state universities. The institute first created a school of remarkable writers: next it was a cradle of men of ability who took to politics.

18. 40,000 ptas. for Toledo, 1,500 ptas. for a parish priest. The Archbishop had to pay all archdiocesan expenses out of his salary. *Cf.* Canterbury £15,000 in 1850.

19. The *Annuario Pontificio* statistics for the various dioceses of Spain shows this clearly.

3

TOLEDO 1907

Franco reported at the Military Academy for Infantry Cadets on 29th August 1907.[1] It was housed in the Emperor Charles V's imposing Alcazar at Toledo. The Spanish Army was still generally accommodated in old fortresses and strongholds where not in equally old monastic buildings appropriated by the State during the nineteenth century.

In Toledo Franco was as far from the sea as he could be in Spain. The Alcazar dominated the city. The city had nearly two thousand years of history to El Ferrol's under two hundred, and ten times the number of inhabitants of Franco's native town. The landscape was harsh and bare, and in its rocks there were none of the soft curves of the Galician hills. The Al-Kazr (a strange combination of the Arabic definite article and a corrupt form of the Latin *castra*) rose high above the height of the dwellings of the civilian population; but it had a rival in the great cathedral where Mass was sung daily according to two distinct rites, the Latin and the Mozarabic, this last developed during the long Moorish occupation when Toledo had had little contact with the western church. Although at the beginning of this century no one could say that "the real masters of Toledo" were "the priests", nor of the Archbishop Primate of all Spain that he was "the richest prelate in Christendom",[2] the militant and artistic glories of the Spanish Church of other days were visible in almost every street. El Greco had yet to be "rediscovered" by the art critics of northern Europe: in the city of his adoption he had never been lost. The pious were moved to prayer by the painting of the "Disrobing" and a score of other pictures; a pupil of the free-thinking *Institución Libre de Enseñanza* admired their draughtsmanship and colouring.[3] Toledo was no longer the "spiritual power-house of Spain", the meeting-place of men of learning, poets, writers, musicians and painters nor even any longer one of the world's centres of silk and woollen cloth manufacture: the last of the "foxes",[4] the sword craftsmen, was long dead. With all this, and however much a young man might be bound by his duties to the walls of the Alcazar, he could not unless totally insensitive remain unaffected by the presence of the past. He might, revulsed, grow to hate it and seek its destruction: more frequently he came to view it myopically. The peculiar distortion that the Alcazar created was that the greatness of Toledo had been made possible only by the prowess of Spanish arms on land and sea. It would be so in Franco.

With Franco, 381 other youngsters, aged between fourteen and fifteen, entered the Academy. They came from all over Spain. They were sons of noblemen and *hijos de algo*, of commissioned officers and the non-commissioned, of captains of industry and commerce and of men even less exalted in social or economic status. The Army did not observe class distinctions as rigidly as the Navy. There were sons of Conservatives and Liberals, of Freemasons and practising Catholics. There were young men whose fathers and grandfathers had fought on opposing sides in the Carlist wars: others whose background was republican; and a few had fathers who had fought in Cuba and the Philippines. Of the intake, some would perish on the battlefields of Morocco over the next twenty years, others on both sides of the Civil War that lay ahead, and yet others in Russia at the side of Germans. On 13th October all took the same oath of allegiance. They swore to God and promised the King "to follow his flags, to defend them to that last drop of their blood, and not to desert those in command over them in the pursuit of war or in preparation thereunto".[5]

At the time, Franco stood out among his academic contemporaries only because of the pallid colouring of his face with its unmistakably semitic features, and his short stature. Already by that October he had learnt that suffrance would be his badge. Pilar Baamonde was petite: Nicolas Franco was squat and somewhat corpulent. Franco at fourteen was very small. In Ferrol his lack of stature had not been remarkable, for the average height was low.[6] In Toledo it was otherwise. At the armoury on arrival he was handed in derision a musket or carbine instead of the standard rifle. The episode cannot have endeared his companions to him. "Franquito"—best rendered as Frankie-boy—he inevitably came to be nicknamed, and equally inescapably, such a small boy, studious and introspective, and unwilling to follow his fellows into sexual or alcoholic experiments in the town, became the object of malicious bullying and 'initiations".[7] His books were hidden by his room-mates under his bed. He was punished for not having them in their proper place. They were hidden again. The Cadet Officer was about to punish him when Franco picked up a candlestick and threw it at his tormentor's head. A riot broke out. Franco was taken before the Commanding Officer. It was said of him that "he behaved in an exemplary way in refusing to disclose the identity of his tormentors", behaviour considered as meritorious at Toledo as in contemporary Sandhurst.[8] He was saved from severe disciplinary measures by companions who had come to admire his courage. It was a courage which would earn him the respect of his enemies throughout his life.

Life at Toledo had its parallels with Sandhurst: but there were also marked divergencies between the Spanish and British systems of training the future officers of the Army. The British cadets began their professional preparation at an average age of nineteen, after a normal upper class education which was considered equally suitable for politics, the administration of the home country or colonial territories, the liberal professions, the arts, or the management of family or public industrial or financial enterprises. Thus Montgomery, who qualified for Sandhurst in the same year as Franco gained admittance to the Alcazar. Franco was segregated from his civilian fellows three or four years earlier, and so were all the military leaders of Spanish Civil War fame. The British cadet at nineteen was more mature than the Spaniard at fifteen, the average age for entry to Toledo. The Spanish cadet was still a boy usually with no more than seven years schooling behind him as against the twelve to fourteen years of the British. True, the Spaniard would have three years at his Academy as against the Briton's eighteen months, but if not expelled or considered totally unsuitable, he would be sent out as a junior officer at an age when the British boy was just entering the architecturally quite undistinguished but functionally more suitable Sandhurst.

Since dexterity in fencing, riding and rifle-shooting was considered as essential to the Spanish as to the British officer, these subjects figured as prominently in the curriculum of Toledo as of Sandhurst. So did arms drill and gym: team sports were favoured in Sandhurst where at Toledo the emphasis was rather on those in which the individual has himself only to consider. The Spanish passion for football had as yet to be aroused. History, and in particular military history, was given a much greater importance in Spain than in Britain. The "military" subjects, topography, tactics, elementary field engineering, figured in both courses of studies, but the approach in Britain was practical whereas that of Spain was theoretic. The Spanish cadet spent more time in the classroom than in the field, in the acquisition of encyclopaedic knowledge beyond the digestion of the ordinary pupil. It was to the prejudice of experience in the practical application of elementary principles. The cadet was more likely to pass out with a smattering of Moltke and the name of Clausewitz on his lips than with the practical knowledge which might make him a competent platoon commander.[9] Memory was developed rather than initiative, a misdirection of education which occurred also in the universities and in the much vaunted *Institución Libre.* The Spanish cadet was called upon to memorise a mass of facts of a hundred battles and never made to analyse a single one in detail. He was encouraged not to question the decisions of the famous or the opinions of his teachers. In this particular the methods of Sandhurst or of Woolwich were incomparably better than those of Toledo or the other Spanish Academies. If competent junior officers emerged, it was in spite of and not because of their academic training. However, the Spanish Army officers were victims of a national attitude as much as contributory culprits.

During the South African War it had been said of the British Army that it was "of lions led by donkeys". The freedom allowed to the Press to condemn generals, as well as to argue for or against the morality of the war against the Boers, led to major changes in the organisation and training of the Army and its officers because not all criticism was destructive. The more influential Press put the more intelligent public opinion behind Army officers who recognised the need for fundamental changes. *The Times* appointed in 1905 a renowned lieutenant-colonel as its first regular military correspondent so as to "stimulate thought concerning the art of war", and in 1909 Oxford established a chair in military history. The links between the Army and the nation were thus reinforced. *The Times* and the *Morning Post* pointed out that apart from the 'asses' in command in South Africa, the Army had also had its brilliant men, and that it was time that their ideas should be put into practice. They were. Some at least of the lessons of the war were incorporated into a series of manuals adopted between 1902 and 1907. They were handbooks for junior officers. The text books in use in Spain in 1907–10, Franco's years at the Academy[10] were of more value to the batallion or brigade commander than to the young subaltern: but even as such they were outdated.

The Infantry Manual took little cognizance of the introduction of the quick-firing rifle, let alone the machine gun. Fortified positions in the way of an advance had to be taken by frontal assault with platoons in strict formations. A large formation, but not a battalion or a company, might seek to outflank an enemy. Though the Spanish troops had suffered heavily from the Cuban rebel's developed individual initiative and the use of ground, the former was discouraged and the last hardly mentioned. The Cubans, like the Boers, had been masters of the use of ground and the skill of sharpshooting. No inference either had been drawn from the Spanish defence of the forts barring the way to Santiago. With the Press concentrating only on the heroism of the few hundred defenders or on the politics of the war, none asked why there had been no mobile divisions to come to their aid; none raised the question as to what the ninety to a hundred thousand men on the island had been doing while the few hundred tried to withstand the onslaught of a concentrated enemy force. In Cuba too "donkeys" had led "an army of lions". The Spanish forces had been scattered in the role of static and isolated armed policemen.*

In 1907 as in 1897 the Spanish Army was in no position to go to war either in the defence of Spain or Clausewitz-like in extension of a foreign policy; yet Spanish politicians were as we shall see, pursuing a foreign policy in Morocco which required for its fulfilment the use of more than a police force. Disaster was forseeable.

No clearer or fairer evidence of the outmoded state of the Spanish Army of 1907 can be adduced than by a comparison of its artillery strength with that of the British Army: fair because Spain and Britain were the two west European powers without compulsory military service: clear from the figures. The Spanish Army was on paper roughly twice as numerous in men as the British. It had eighty-eight batteries of all kinds with a total of 352 pieces: the British one hundred and ninety-eight with 1,380 pieces. The Toledo Academy which was for infantry alone had an annual intake of three hundred and eighty cadets: the Artillery and Engineer Academies were very small. Sandhurst had a twice-yearly intake of 160–70, for cavalry, communications and supply services as well as infantry: Woolwich for Artillery and Engineers was almost as large as Sandhurst.[11] Franco's contemporaries at Toledo were to pay dearly for the lack of serious thinking on army organisation by generals and politicians.

* Earlier in the century, in South America the rebel colonial General Bolivar had defeated Spain more because he was allowed to overcome piecemeal the loyal garrisons in Venezuela, Ecuador and Colombia than because he had an army with an ideal, or a legion of 6,000 British veterans of the Peninsular War to strengthen it. So also General San Martin in the south of the continent.

As the intellectual in Spain looked to German authors for inspiration after 1898 so did the military. The authors of the military textbooks of Franco's Academy had borrowed freely from German books of an earlier generation. Memories of what Spain had suffered at the hands of the French may have predisposed the Spaniard to believe in German military supremacy and almost omniscience after Paris fell to the Prussians. What those authors seemingly did not know was that the Germans had themselves recognised by the turn of the century the freakish nature of their success and that their military thinking was along quite different lines. The German Army of 1907 was already very different from that of 1870. The proportion of infantrymen and officers to those of other arms had been drastically reduced, or rather the numbers of artillerymen, engineers and communications personnel had been very substantially increased. France, too, had begun to appreciate that high explosive and the British contribution of shrapnel from quick-firing rifled guns had introduced new factors into the organisation and composition of efficient armies. In future warfare artillery would play a predominant role. Little of this was said in Spain. The infantry had won wars in the past, and would continue to do so: that was the unchallenged teaching of Toledo.

At the level relevant to the cadet the major faults in the text books and curricula were first that, as Mola was to say, they encouraged the cadet to think that he was competent to move armies across the face of Europe while he had little practical experience in the handling of a platoon (he naturally enough saw himself in the position of his immediate superior, the company commander and knew by heart the regulation: "the Captain will place himself where he considers most opportune: he will dismount when he comes under accurate fire and will have around him the Corporal with standard, a drummer or bugler and two runners"),[12] and second that they encouraged a German-like rigidity of mind. His sections had to be just so. The men in the sections had to be so many paces apart. True enough there were occasional references to the use of ground and "the best firing positions":[13] but there was little guidance to instructor or pupil as to how ground should be used or what were the best firing positions. All this too was to cost the lives of hundreds of officers. Only twenty years later, under the influence of Franco, would the text books for and the training of cadets be changed radically.

Discipline in the Alcazar was strict. As at Sandhurst there were at Toledo senior students who as under-officers had considerable powers to punish juniors. The instructors had greater powers. Cadets were taught by exhortation and by disciplinary measures which included corporal punishment, to obey all commands and regulations to the letter. The system created a mentality best exemplified by the following mild and involved criticism of it printed in the *Cavalry Review* of May 1913. "The terms of reference 'to take no action and do nothing more than what is laid down or ordered' have created a problem now of long standing as to what is correct at and proper to each rung in the ladder of command. Praiseworthy initiative has often been killed by the question, 'Where is your authority for that?' However richly provided with regulations a corpus of doctrine may be, and ours is perhaps too rich, it is impossible to foresee all the circumstances and the rules to overcome all difficulties which may arise."[14]

"The task of the infantry demands great hardships. It is their mission to cross the most deadly zones. . . . The said arm therefore must be livened by an exalted spirit which will impel it till it comes into contact with the enemy which will enable it to surmount the greatest difficulties and obstacles, and to win at all costs. To this end the heart of the soldier must be educated. Patriotism, love of the flag, the king, valour, discipline, honour and the feeling of Duty must be graven into that heart."[15]

This was certainly done at Toledo. Moral training in this sense was hardly surpassable.

Theoretically all the cadets were *católicos*, that is as babies they had been baptised, and as young children they had learnt elementary catechism answers as a preparation for their "first communion". Franco's at ten was rather later than average. For the rest Franco's own experience was typical. While at home, he had attended Mass regularly with his mother, and with her climbed the steep hill above El Ferrol known as *El Chamorro*, "the short cropped", to the shrine of a medieval statue of the Virgin. In his mother's presence Franco would never fail to fulfil any religious duty lest it should displease her. His *pietas* or sense of duty to his mother lasted all his life. Years later when he was in Morocco the editor of the local newspaper used to be on the lookout for telegrams for the Calle de Maria. By their arrival he knew, long before receiving agency tape which had had to pass through censors, that there had been a battle. Franco wired briefly always: "Me safe".[16] *Pietas*, however, was not piety, or as we shall see, devotion religion.

Franco's first school had been founded by a local priest, and the learning by rote of the Catechism was expected of the pupils; but it has been said of even the best colleges run by religious orders in Spain until recently, that they provided "a secular education conducted by teachers who happen to be priests or nuns". At the age of twelve he had passed to the Naval Preparatory Academy where theology was limited to the repetition of Churruca's signal at Trafalgar: "I promise every man that dies today a place in heaven", and dicta such as Franco incorporated into his film script: "there are no bad sailors, for if a sailor commits a fault he expiates it by his punishment. He is purified and at peace. He is a new man": pre-Christian, and many would say non-Christian doctrine. There were chaplains to the Army, and the major ceremonies such as that of the cadet's Oath of Allegiance to the Flag were preceded by an open air mass. The Oath,* which Catholics would judge of doubtful orthodoxy, was followed by a quite remarkable statement from the chaplain: "And I, *in fulfilment of my sacred ministry* ask God that if you do so (that is, defend the flag to the last drop of blood, etc.) He reward you for it, and if not call you to account theretofor"—an extension of the office of a Catholic priest without a single theologian's, let alone conciliar or Pope's authority.

Religion, by which in Spain was meant Roman Catholicism, was at that time at its lowest ebb. The population of Spain was Catholic generally only in the sense that the great majority of babies were taken by their parents to be baptized, that they made their "first communion" to enable their parents to show off their *inocentes criaturas* prettily dressed, that the adults who bothered to marry usually did so in church and that there were also many death-bed repentances. The original medieval legend and first post-Tridentine play of *Don Juan*, which had been a sermon against the sin of presuming that God would always allow a sinner time to repent at the moment of death, had been turned in the nineteenth century into the romantic tale that the loyal love of a woman would save a man from hell. Catholicism was more deeply understood and more devoutly practised in the Basque Provinces and in pockets of Catalonia and Galicia than generally in Spain; but El Ferrol was only marginally Galicia. It was more an outpost of Andalusia and Andalusia was already notoriously de-christianized. In Madrid, the geographical centre, only four per cent of the population fulfilled their Easter duties.[17] The Archdiocese of Toledo included Madrid.

In the Academy for Infantry Cadets there was a chaplain and cadets

* See above, p. 61.

were expected to attend church parades.[18] However, there was no formal study of religion. There was little interest in the theological virtues of Faith, Hope and Charity, nor was the practice encouraged of six of the seven virtues contrary to the seven capital sins. Of humility, generosity, chastity, meekness, temperance, brotherly love and diligence, only diligence was pertinent to the cadet, the diligence not to fail his final examinations. Brotherly love and generosity had to be limited to brother officers or at most officers and men; humility and meekness were unthinkable: worldly prudence had to guide the cadet as to how far he should neglect chastity and temperance. Offences against these virtues were considered serious only if they brought the army officer into public disrepute. Discreet liaisons, visits to brothels, drunkenness in the mess might have led to fatherly advice from an instructor. More formal discouragement was reserved to cases where the matter could become public. Gaming was a favourite leisure occupation, sanctionable only when gaming debts went beyond redemption.

The virtues fostered in the cadet were essentially the Roman-Visigothic. As an officer he would be a guardian at all times of the honour of the motherland, as an extension of the honour of his mother. A writer in 1914[19] struck an appreciative chord in the heart of the soldier and his mother when he wrote: "Do you know the secret force which empowers our Nation always to override adversity? Do you know why it has not perished and will never perish? It is the strength of the patriotism of our women. Spain cannot die so long as her women are like those of Numancia and Zaragoza.* In their dedication to hard work, in their beliefs and their patriotism is the great might of the nation. Our courage in battles is our mothers' more than our own, for they taught us to love Spain and it is they who send us out to fight for Spain. They weep for us dead, but they would disown us if we proved cowards. All our wounds pierce their hearts yet they do not desist from the battle and give more children to the fight. Remember always that your mothers are Spaniards and that Spain is mighty and will be strong because of the virtues and the heroism of woman." He was right enough: the women of Spain were themselves to perform countless deeds of valour and to inspire men to follow their example on both sides of the Civil War. Heroism in itself however is a natural virtue which may derive from any ideal or religion of its exponent: so also is patriotism. Love of one's country as an extension of love of one's

---

* In both the Seige of Numancia by the Romans and that of Zaragoza by the French the women were the more steadfast defenders.

mother, however is clearly an extension also of Roman–Spanish *pietas*, or sense of duty.

A serious sense of *gravitas*, of responsibility, was also impressed upon the cadet. He should tolerate no slight nor insult to the flag or his uniform: even the smallest sneer was too great to overlook. Yet the virtue of *simplicitas* should make the army officer see clearly that the flag and the uniform were symbols of the nation, that the nation therefore was the greater, and that accordingly the honour of the nation was even more ardently to be defended than that of the army or the flag; and consequently also: *Where a government by its actions brought the nation to dishonour in the eyes of the world, either by proving itself unable to maintain order, or by placing it under the control however remote of a foreign power, then it was the bounden duty of the army officer to rise in defence of the country against the government:* for however lawfully instituted, it had ceased to be lawful by its bringing dishonour to the nation. Army officers as guardians of the honour of the motherland were therefore singly or collectively above any constitution. The authors of the frequent military *pronunciamientos* of the nineteenth century, of the revolts and the civil wars, were logically not to be condemned because they had risen against the constituted power, king or republic, but according as they had acted in the defence of the honour or to the dishonour of the motherland.

St. Ferdinand was put before the cadets as the ideal King. By obscuring the sanctity of his life and highlighting his military prowess against the foreign invaders, he could be presented as a paragon of *disciplina*, that is steadiness of character in military success and adversity, of *industria*, hard-work, *constantia*, firmness of purpose, and *virtus*, manliness and energy, all virtues of pre-Christian Rome.

Nevertheless Ruy Diaz, the Cid, was a more satisfactory ideal. His Visigothic ethic of brooking no offence or even shadow of an offence to his honour, of wreaking vengeance on his equals or inferiors who had wronged him or his family, of exercising *clementia* or a willingness to surrender his rights to his natural lord, of retaining towards him unswerving loyalty however iniquitous the injustice with which that natural lord treated him, was all wholly acceptable to the early twentieth-century Spanish military concept of honour and authority. Redress to the last ounce had to be drawn from an inferior who was guilty of a fault. Since by his punishment "he is purified and is a new man" clemency in the Christian sense, that is mercy, could be a fault in his superior. Therefore also, it was heinous for an inferior not to accept even injustice from a superior. He might appeal against the injustice, but he had in the first place to prove his loyalty by his acceptance; as the Cid had done when quite undeservedly his foolish King had banished him.

There was nothing either in the Visigothic or the Roman ethic to encourage forgiveness of enemies. A victor might extend his hand to his defeated foe who had fought well, but this was very far from the Christian commandment that a man should love his neighbour as himself. The Roman *humanitas* renewed itself in the Spanish officer. He held in esteem human personality, but understanding his own to be superior to anyone else's, it became his duty to impose his concept of civilisation on others. The Spaniard, like the Roman, believed he had a divine mission to conquer the barbarian. The loss of an empire strengthened rather than diminished the faith of the officer that such was his duty. Spain had legitimate rights, the cadet was told, to Morocco, Algeria and Indo-China,[20] and the day was bound to come when Spain would rise from the ashes of the present. A "foolish politician" had argued with the loss of Cuba that the sepulchre of the Cid should be sealed with seven locks. On the contrary the Cid's theme "*quant grant es Espana*" should be their ejaculatory prayer; "never lose this faith and this love for Spain" was the counsel that Franco gave youth in his film Raza: "We are the spiritual reserve of the western world. We have a lofty mission" was the considered opinion of his old age that he hoped young Spain would inherit from him.[21] For Franco was the Academy of Toledo's most receptive pupil of his generation.

Shortly before Franco's entry into the Academy Sagasta had followed Cánovas out of this world, but less spectacularly, of natural causes. The pendulum of alternating Liberal and Conservative governments had then stuck. At each swing the escapement of managed election had creaked more loudly. In 1907 the most internationally famous of early twentieth-century Spanish politicians, Antonio Maura, became Prime Minister. He had no one of any ability to the right. To the left of him there was the Count of Romanones and in the ascendant a one-time Minister of Justice and Religion*[22] of Sagasta's, more radical and anti-clerical than he, José Canalejas, yet another demagogue who delighted in tours of the country preaching legislation to reduce the number of religious houses and the size of land holdings. As a good

* Gracia y Justicia.

Liberal he believed also in lightening the tax burden of commercial and industrial enterprises. Canalejas had been born in El Ferrol thirty-eight years ahead of Franco. To the left of Canalejas's Radical Liberals, the Socialists were becoming a power in the land with seats in the Cortes in spite of all the efforts of the Liberal and Conservative bosses to exclude them. To the left again, or rather above left and right since they abhorred all parties, the Anarchists had been organising "acts of protest" increasingly more spectacular than their success at Santa Aguada. Cánovas had been a mere Prime Minister. In 1904 they had tried to assassinate the young King Alfonso and wounded Maura instead. In June 1905 they had made a second attempt. On this occasion the target outside the Opera House was not merely the King of Spain but for good measure the visiting President Loubet of France. On 31st May 1906—the frequency was becoming almost equal to that of the changes of Prime Ministers—they made headlines throughout the world. As the English Princess Victoria Eugenia of Battenberg, a bride of an hour, rode in an open carriage with her husband Alfonso XIII of Spain at her side, a bomb was thrown. Twenty-three bystanders were killed and the bride's dress was spattered with blood. Madrid thereafter became too well policed for them, whereupon they concentrated on Barcelona; and it was to be there that in July 1909 they were to celebrate their Sabbath.

Of Antonio Maura, Franco was to write with some warmth:

At this juncture, a great politician appeared upon the scene. He was Antonio Maura, an intelligent, honest, and patriotic man who endeavoured to achieve what he called "the revolution from above" by getting those in office to reform everything that was rotten or ineffectual. From the time he took Office in 1907, he engaged in important legislative work and addressed himself to the reconstruction of the Navy, the reorganisation of Local Government, and other such tasks. Spaniards began to believe in their country's revival.

Franco did. Had more than a faction of the Spanish political world done so as well, Spain might yet have developed into a democracy: for Maura saw the evils of rigged elections, and tried to introduce reforms which, had they been allowed to be put into practice by Conservatives and Liberals alike might have changed the Cortes into an organisation from which the masses could have hoped for a redress of their grievances; he was too one of the few Madrid politicians who recognised virtue in regionalism. Against all this must be weighed

his inability, a serious deficiency in a politician, to suffer fools gladly, or
at least to appear to do so, and his certainty that any man who did not
see eye to eye with him was a fool.

Antonio Maura was undoubtedly otherwise an able politician. He
had entered Parliament as a Liberal under the aegis of his father-in-law,
also a close associate of Sagasta. In 1892, as Minister for Overseas
Territories, he had drafted the too-long delayed Constitution granting
Cuba self-government. He had broken with Sagasta over the Government's handling of the peace negotiations. He did his best to root out
corruption especially in the Treasury and he did appear to be more
aware than his contemporaries of the practical consequences of his
countrymen's religious and philosophical dissentions. It was an aware-
ness which he passed to his son Gabriel whose summary of the state of
Spain in the last ten years of the nineteenth century held good well into
the twentieth. "In Spain there was neither justice nor education, nor
army nor navy even when the people of Spain paid the heavier sums
demanded by the Treasury for such noble ends. Politicians were ever
mindful of the armed services, but their interest was in the support the
armed services might give them in this or that policy, not in the making
of them the efficient fighting forces which were required. . . . The
cossetting and praise to all who wore military uniform which poured
from governments and opposition were in marked contrast to the neglect and banishment from the mind of the reforms necessary if the
country was to be able to defend herself."[23] Antonio Maura did seek
to increase the educational facilities available, and, as Franco says, to
restore the Navy. However, what really placed him, though a politician and a liberal-conservative, above the reproach of the army and
of Franco, was his dexterity in the negotiation of a secret treaty three
years before he became Prime Minister.

With the loss of Cuba and the Philippines, Spain had been left with
no overseas possessions except some unimportant islands off the West
coast of Africa, a portion of the Sahara desert and the two ancient cities
of Ceuta and Melilla on the coast of Morocco. Two years later France
agreed to the extension of the Spanish holding of desert sands to include
the Rio Muni area. France coveted all Morocco as well as Algeria,
countries to which Spain had better historical claims if the right to the
conquest of Africa by European nations be admitted. To pursue her
aims France had in the first place to ensure Britain's agreement. Britain
had long wanted Egypt. Accordingly in April 1904 France gave Britain
a free hand in Egypt and in exchange Britain promised France a free

hand in Morocco. Spain was in no position militarily to oppose France's territorial ambitions, but France dared not antagonise Spain. Germany too had her eye on Morocco. An irritated Spain might turn to Germany whose army enjoyed great prestige among the Spanish Army and politicians: as we have said, some Liberal intellectuals in their despair at the events of 1898 had renounced their faith in the French philosophers of the eighteenth century and worshipped at the feet of the German latter-day philosophers. Spain, weak though she was, could seriously harass French lines of communication to Morocco. Even if the Spanish Government had not "got wind" of the secret treaty, France would have had to let Spain into her confidence and make a gesture of friendship to safeguard those lines of communication.

The half-truth, half-fiction propounded to justify French intervention in Morocco was that the Sultan was in dire need of protection. He was beset on all sides by rebel tribesmen. France promised aid to the Sultan in the recovery and maintenance of control over all his territories whenever he should be in need of such, and the Sultan would be expected to pay for such a service with concessions to the French which would in fact make Morocco a French possession. Maura, with the full knowledge and approval of the British Foreign Office obtained from the French the right to "protect" the hinterland of Ceuta and Melilla. The agreement was in all but name a partition of Morocco, France keeping for herself the major and potentially less troublesome and more profitable share. It was signed in October 1904.

The agreement was welcomed by Liberals and Conservatives alike. To the Liberal Romanones "Morocco was Spain's last chance to keep her position in the concert of Europe."[24] It was also an opportunity for him and other politicians to invest heavily in the company to which the Spanish government gave mining concessions in the Riff. There was also, it must be added, a body of opinion which held that Spain could not be regenerated unless it had a will to Empire. There were few dissenting voices. Archbishop Nozaleda of Valencia and formerly of Manila who dared to speak aloud his views that Spain's African policy was morally wrong, suffered persecution.

The Sultan of Morocco did not require military protection from the moment that the Hispano French treaty was signed. France, Spain and Britain were agreed that "peaceful penetration" was preferable. European enterprises multipled. These welcomed the establishment in March 1907 of police forces officered by the protecting powers in their respective zones. In August 1907 Spain and France put on a show of

force at Casablanca "to protect European lives and interests". There
was a minor skirmish between Moorish irregulars and Spanish troops
in the following February. By 1909 it had become evident that if
Spanish business interests were to be served Spain had to be ready to
use force. The Spanish Army had large reserves of officers, especially
of senior officers who had never seen a day's active service in their
lives and who were anxious to prove that Spanish arms were as capable
as those of any other European nation. The young men in Africa
could have told them what Mola eventually published: "the other
ranks and the officers did not know each other. The soldiers had just
about learnt how to fire a rifle, but hadn't an idea in the world how to
fight in battle. The majority of the rifles were out of true: the machine
guns jammed as soon as they were fired . . . the pack animals had no
trainers and their scratch drivers were inexperienced."[25]

No one should have known better than Maura that the army was in
no fit condition to embark on a war. In the Spring of 1909 he sought to
introduce conscription. Such advanced countries as France whose
prowess in every field was so much admired by one group of intellectuals and Germany, worshipped by another group, had compulsory
military service, so why should Spain not be numbered among the great
in that particular sphere? The conscription bill was not approved.
What was needed however was not a larger but a more efficiently
equipped and trained army. Events were now to move too fast for him.

Spain had built a railway along the coast from Melilla which served
well the interests of the Spanish Mining Company. On 9th July 1909
a force of Moroccans attacked a military outpost protecting some
workers. Four of these and one sentry were killed. The strength of the
attackers was given as four hundred. Here was the long awaited act of
war. The news delighted chair-borne army circles. At long last the
excuse had been provided for the incursion of armed forces deep into
Morocco in their role as protectors. War fever spread among the upper
and middle classes as jingoistic then in Spain as they had been in England
at the outbreak of the South African War. Few among them dared to
voice dissent. To be labelled unpatriotic was to suffer more than social
ostracism. Spain however had already more Marxist-Socialists than
England. They and the Anarchists denounced the actions of the business
interests in Morocco which they said had provoked the attack. In
seeking to satisfy the militarists and jingoists within and outside the
army, Maura would drive the socialists and anarchists into direct action
within the Peninsula against the war.

On 13th July a body of Moroccans, six thousand strong according to Spanish army estimates, engaged a force of two thousand Spaniards of which eleven were killed and sixty wounded. Alfonso XIII went the rounds of Spanish battalions ordered to stand by in readiness for service overseas, exhorting them to do their duty to their country. Mass anti-war demonstrations were held in Madrid, Barcelona, Valencia and Bilbao on the 18th and again on the 20th. They were not orderly. On 23rd July there was a further engagement in Africa in which the Spanish officer casualties were four killed and thirteen wounded. General Marina, the Commanding Officer, now estimated that the rebels numbered sixteen thousand. To cope with the emergency he asked Madrid for the immediate despatch of forty thousand men. Maura ordered the call-up of reservists. His opponents asked what General Marina was doing with the fifteen thousand men he already had in Melilla. In Barcelona the Socialists called for a general strike unless married reservists were excused recall to the colours. Maura stood firm: all reservists would have to obey: neither he nor the army could have had it otherwise. Their argument was: "Without obedience there can be no discipline, without discipline there can be no army, and without an army there can be neither colonies nor State."[26] On the evening of 26th July Barcelona became a city of barricades.

What happened thereafter was profoundly to affect Franco's thought at all times and action in similar circumstances.

The Socialists had called the strike, but within a few hours the strike had turned into an orgy of destruction over which they had absolutely no control, and for which not they but the anarchists were to bear the blame. "The dregs of the community rose to the top, lorded it over the city, and committed every kind of outrage. They murdered, satisfied personal grudges, and . . . burned churches, killed priests, raped nuns, and danced through the streets with exhumed bodies of dead religious."[27] Such, and worse according to all accounts, were the four days known as the "Tragic Week". Maura ordered the Army to restore order. They fired point blank at the barricades with field-artillery. The rebels who surrendered were summarily tried and condemned to death by courts martial. The untidy clatter of firing squads was heard from Montjuich, the famous mountain on the outskirts of Barcelona. Barcelona was left a city with three score buildings gutted by the incendiarism of the anarchists and numberless others with holes in the walls caused by shelling. The dead were buried by the cartload.

Justice may have been done but was not seen to have been done when the schoolmaster, Jose Ferrer, an internationally famous anarchist, was arrested on the charge of being the instigator-in-chief of the events. He had not been in Barcelona during the vital period. All over Europe meetings were organised to protest against the government in power. Maura refused to consider Ferrer's release on nationalist principles, however expedient it was politically. Ferrer was convicted and shot. The Liberals to the left of Maura now saw to it that Maura should fall. He was vituperated in the Cortes as no man had been for over thirty years, and on 21st October, nine days after Ferrer's execution, Maura resigned. The incoming left-wing Liberal government under a man of otherwise little historical importance called Moret, sent the notorious General Weyler to pacify Barcelona. He showed himself capable of as total a ruthlessness towards his countrymen who were rebels as he had shown in another decade against Cuban insurgents.

As the strike in Barcelona turned into a blood-bath, the Moroccans had pressed to the walls of Melilla. On 27th July over five hundred Spaniards had been killed, including a general, and between one and two thousand wounded. Marina had increased his demands to seventy-five thousand men. Spanish losses during July had been given officially as ninety officers and one thousand other ranks killed. In August, with the arrival of reinforcements, a Spanish army of forty thousand had had the initiative. They had done well. By September the Sultan was complaining that the operations seemed to be something more than a punitive expedition against the Riffs. A General d'Amade of France agreed with him and was promptly dismissed by the French Government. On 12th October the chief of the Riffs had sued for peace. Disease was decimating his troops, the weather was impropitious for further campaigning and the Moroccan tribesmen wanted to get back home in time to do the ploughing. On 9th November Moret accepted a sum equal to £2,400,000* from the Sultan as reparations for the damage done to Spain. The government, having settled Barcelona and Melilla, now turned to the favourite pastime of the Liberals—baiting the Church.

The rapidity with which protests were organised against the very arrest of Ferrer in so many European cities, the pressures from foreign governments exerted upon Maura to release him, the theme recurrent in the editorials of many European newspapers that the persecution of Ferrer proved that in Spain the spirit of the *auto-da-fe* burned brightly was to confirm Franco in his belief that Spain was and had been the

* 65 million pesetas, as part of 190.9 millions repayable over seventy-five years.

victim of an international conspiracy to destroy her as a nation. He had yet to determine the identity of the chief conspirators.[28]

Franco pondered on these matters as his time in Toledo came to its ordained end. He passed out on 13th July 1910. (There had been another political crisis and change of government on 9th February. The undistinguished Moret had been replaced by the flamboyant Ferrol-born Canalejas who bulldozed a bill through the Cortes to tax some religious houses out of existence. Canalejas too was to deserve well of the Army but Franco was not to speak favourably of him for he was too notoriously a Malleus Monachorum). The seventeen-year-old second lieutenant[29] was refused permission to volunteer for service in Morocco. He was told he was too young and that in any case there were senior lieutenants awaiting posting to Africa. He was commissioned into the 8th Regiment of Foot, the Zamora Regiment. It provided the army garrison for the naval base of El Ferrol. So Franco had to go home.

El Ferrol was less economically depressed than when Franco had left three years previously. Maura had discovered that his naval programme was beyond the capabilities of Spanish shipyards without considerable modernisation. That meant revising budget estimates or giving orders to foreign shipyards. He had decided on the latter and weathered the consequent nationalist storm. Nevertheless the programme had brought some small ship work to the dockyard at El Ferrol.

In the Calle de María life was much as it had been for some years. Franco's grandfather, Don Ladislao was living on the first floor, and his mother on the third. They were company for each other. Francisco Franco was able to slip home from barracks on most days.

Garrison life was as onerous as it was exciting. There were for the young second lieutenant parades and drills to attend in the morning, and there was riding in the afternoons. There was not the remotest hope that a foreign enemy would suddenly loom over the hills, and that the alarm trumpets would sound. There were socialists and anarchists among the workers, but they did not have the mettle of their Barcelona comrades. There was no opportunity to put to the test his courage, to show his devotion to duty or to exercise the enthusiasm for the motherland which had been fostered into him for three years. Every so often it was his turn to be orderly officer. His main tasks were then to supervise the men's meals and to ensure that the guard was ready to turn out at the approach of his commanding officer under pain of being confined to the mess for a few days. He was free in the early evening to take part in the town's *paseo* along the *Calle Real*; the stroll of the young men and women up and down the main street, the greeting and brief word with friends, the sexes strictly segregated but young men and girls casting glances of appraisal at each other, with maybe a compliment or a glance being exchanged theoretically unbeknown to the parents. He would then proceed to a very late dinner at home or in the mess. The days slid into weeks. The weeks into months.

Franco, now sporting a moustache, and with the pill-box of his regiment at a jaunty angle on his head, soon began to understand the facts of society. He had neither the naval uniform of his elder brother Nicolas nor the charm and mischievous good looks of his younger brother Ramon. To the matrons of El Ferrol, little "Frankie-boy", the army son of a libidinous administrative officer who had left his wife, was no great match, and no encouragement was given to any young girl to return any look of admiration cast in her direction by the young officer. There was no glorious army or home future for Franco in El Ferrol.

NOTES

1. This and other dates are taken from General Franco's *Hoja de Servicio*, the original of which is kept in the military household of the Head of State in what was the Royal Palace in Madrid. All other *Hojas de Servicio* are kept in the Army Records Office in Segovia. I consulted those of the principal military figures of General Franco's lifetime as well as General Franco's. The *Hoja de Servicio* is a document, until recently manuscript, containing a very full record of an army officer's career from his entry into an Academy until his death. General Franco's was kept very carefully to his elevation to Head of State. The record of an individual officer includes not only promotions, awards, punishments, postings, secondments and the like, but also in considerable detail the part taken by that officer in active operations. The accounts are invariably dryly factual and countersigned by senior officers.

2. A. Navaggero in his fascinating *Viaggio in Ispagna*. Venice, 1563.

3. Manuel B. Cossío whose book on El Greco is still worth reading.

4. "O Signeur Dew, thou diest on point of fox"—*Henry V*, iv. 4.
   "I had a sword . . . a right fox i faith." Porter: *Two Angry Women of Abingdon* (1579).
   The great sword maker was Julian del Rey whose trade mark, a dog, looked like a fox.
   The "Toledo swords" now sold to tourists are unworthy of Toledo's past.

5. *"Seguir constantemente sus banderas, defenderlas hasta vertir la última gota de vuestra sangre, y no abandonar al que os estuviere mandando en función de guerra o en preparación para ella."*

6. Franco's adult height was 5 ft. 5½ in. (1·645 m. in his *Hoja*). The tall, gaunt Spaniard is usually a Castillian or a Catalan.

7. *Novatadas:* horse-play as well as initiation.

8. cf. Hugh Thomas, *The Story of Sandhurst* (Hutchinson, 1961), p. 173.

9. This judgment of the 1907 cadet system may appear harsh to the Spanish reader. It is based on my own research and enquiries; but it is more than backed by General Mola's own views in his *El Pasado, Azaña y el Porvenir. Las tragedias de nuestras instituciones militares,* written in Aug.–Dec. 1933. (Included in Obras Completas, Madrid.)

10. The most important is the *Reglamento Provisional para la instrucción táctica de las tropas de infantería:* 1908.

11. The small number of foreign students in the British academies does not substantially affect the comparison.

12. Reglamento, etc. Sec. 389. Army text books contain traps for translators: a *pelotón* is a section and a *sección* is a platoon. So also a *batería* is usually best translated as a *half*-battery, a *grupo* being usually a battery.

13. ibid., *e.g.* Secs. 314 and 439. Even so the exhortations to make use of the ground were more for formations than individuals.

14. Article on the Lessons of the Riff Campaign, pp. 92 *ff.* I have tried to retain in the translation the awkward style of the original. Articles in the professional reviews show that there were field and junior officers aware of the short-comings of the Army and with ideas as to how they might be corrected.

15. *Reglamento.* Sec. 4.

16. Evidence of Editor of *El Correo Gallego.* The text was: *Yo salvo.*

17. E. Vargas Zúñiga. *El Problema Religioso en España.* Razón y Fé. Vol. 108, p. 302 (1935), quoting from a report by Cardinal Sancha, Archbishop of Toledo, in the first years of the twentieth century. It must however be borne in mind that Catholic clergy in such reports tend to exaggerate the more to impress the faithful: but even if the real figure was 6 or 8 per cent it was still low.

18. A Colonel Labrador was sentenced to six months imprisonment in 1914 for refusing to be present at Mass (Annual Register for 1914).

19. Juán Valdés Rubio, *Acción de España en Marruccos,* Madrid, 1914. Pt. I, p. 38.

20. The claims were developed to the full in *Reinvindicaciones de España, v.* Ch. XIV, n. 20.

21. Interview at the end of the film *Ese Hombre,* 1964.

22. Two ministries were concerned with religious affairs: the Ministry of Foreign Relations in all matters in which the Vatican was involved; that of Justicia y Gracia in all questions from which the Vatican could be excluded.

23. Gabriel Maura: *Historia Crítica del Reinado de Alfonso XIII en su minoridad*, Vol. I, p. 33. General Emilio Mola op. cit. *passim*, said much the same.

24. Romanones: *Notas de Una Vida: 1912-1931*, p. 34.

25. Mola op. cit., p. 936. Mola, five years Franco's senior, was commissioned into the infantry from Toledo on 13th July 1907. He was posted to Melilla in January 1910 (*Hoja de Servicio*).

26. Evidence of elderly Spanish officers. The argument is developed in Mola op. cit.

27. "Juan de la Cosa" op. cit., p. 103. The most useful account is that of J. Brussa, *Revolución de Julio en Barcelona*, 1910. The outburst had more causes than the Moroccan war.

28. There was no "international agency" at work. Romanones and the Liberals were able to make most political profit from the event, but they were in no way responsible for it.

29. Spanish biographers all say "*alferez*" or ensign, but his *Hoja de Servicio* says *segundo teniente*: the name of the first commissioned rank in the Spanish Army was not changed back to *alferez* until later.

4

AFRICA 1912

Franco did not suffer patiently the frustrations of garrison life in El Ferrol. Some time in 1911 he again volunteered for service in Africa. There were two factors against him. In the first place he was only eighteen; in the second the Spanish army respected seniority where there was no influence. There were full lieutenants awaiting posting. By the end of the year, however, the situation had changed. The Commandant of the Toledo Academy of Franco's years, Jose Villalba Riquelme, had been given command of the 68th, or African Regiment. The Colonel pulled the necessary strings and in February 1912 Franco received his movement orders. He was to report forthwith to the regiment's depot in Malaga. So were two mess companions at El Ferrol, Second-Lieutenants Alonso Vega and Franco Salgado-Araujo. The latter was a cousin.[1]

The situation in Africa had not been allowed to stand entirely still since the Sultan had agreed in November 1910 to pay Spain for the damages done by his rebellious subjects round Melilla. The heights above the town, the *Gurugu*, captured by the Spaniards at the end of the 1909 campaign, had been fortified with a line of forts. Beyond them Spain had established a measure of control over a *cordon sanitaire* stretching to the right bank of the River Kert, almost fifteen miles due west of Melilla, and southwards for about twenty miles. In January 1911 Canalejas had taken King Alfonso on a tour of inspection of the forts. The Liberal Prime Minister had written "a new era has begun for our expansion and a new chapter for the history of Spain". The Liberal newspapers which supported Canalejas, no less than the more right wing which traditionally favoured colonial military operations, dug out the references in the Last Will and Testament of Isabella I to Africa as the land of promise for Spain. Morocco was presented to readers as an inexhaustible fountain of milk and honey, as well as one rich in

mineral wealth. Mining shares rose. There was talk of new ports being
built on the north African coast. Then, to the consternation of Spain—
and of Britain—France landed troops at Casablanca and cut inland to
occupy Fez.★ The pretence of Article II of the April 1904 secret treaty
between Britain and France was now blown to shreds. It was difficult
to reconcile the French action with her declared intention not to change
the political status of Morocco, or to judge it as one necessary to "the
tranquillity of Morocco" and pursuant to the French promise that she
would merely "lend her assistance in all the administrative, financial
and military reforms" which Morocco needed. France had also gone
beyond any of the provisions of other international treaties publicly
negotiated later. What infuriated Spain was that Fez was within the
Spanish zone as agreed upon in the October 1904 secret treaty between
France and Spain with Britain concurring. Spain's reply was to land
troops at Larache on the Atlantic coast fifty miles south of Tangier and
occupy Al Ksar-el-Kebir twenty miles inland.

Muley Ahmed Er-Raisuni, who held the western Riff for the Sultan,
accepted the Spanish moves. Not so the tribesmen of the River Kert
where a colourful "holy man" El Mizzian exhorted the tribesmen
never to submit to the Christian leaders. On 24th August 1912 a small
force of Moroccans attacked a Spanish survey party which was being
escorted by two companies. The Spaniards suffered five casualties.
Seven days later a column of five thousand set out from Melilla "to
punish the rebels". The Melilla force was reinforced to a strength of
forty-four thousand men. The River Kert line was re-established, but
the tribesmen proved to be masters of infiltration, and there were
skirmishes uncomfortably near Melilla till the time for ploughing
approached and the tribesmen infiltrated back or, if residents of the
area theoretically under Spanish control, hid their rifles till the campaigning season should come round again.

One general and three colonels were among the ten score Spaniards
who lost their lives in these operations. The wounded and the sick were
repatriated, so that Spain had a new crop of men who could give the
lie to the pro-war articles and speeches. Africa was not a land of plenty.
The minerals might enrich a few exploiters but the earth would not
provide a living for the landless mass of Spain. The sun burned even
more than in southern Spain; there was next to no fresh water;
mosquitoes infested the air. There were reports, too, of the inadequacy

★ For good measure Germany sent a gun boat to Agadir. The Germans had to
withdraw. They were as yet unprepared to go to war with Britain and France.

of the military equipment in the field and of a scarcity of ammunition and rations. The anti-war made the most of such eye-witnesses.

Political affiliations placed the individual in one or other camp. To the anarchists war, being the exercise of an army which was an instrument of government, was as damnable as war by individuals with explosives was praiseworthy. However, following the Barcelona "tragic week" they had suffered months of active persecution and they were too weak to protest too loudly. The Socialists were able more publicly to talk of the sacrifice of human life to the Moloch of Capitalism. Not another man or peseta should be wasted in the interests of the mining companies. Liberals and Conservatives had supporters in both camps. They were divided on the matter as in others. Those with financial interests were for it. Some of those without them were in favour, and others not. The belief that the honour or glory of Spain demanded that she should not surrender colonialism, when not only France, Germany and Britain were adding to their territories but even Italy which had no history of greatness in battle, settled the matter for many. A contrary belief, that it was to a nation's dishonour to deprive other nations of their lands, was not as rare as might at first appear from a reading of the mass of literature and speeches in the Cortes and elsewhere; but on the whole the men with memories of Vitoria or Suarez salved their consciences by insisting that the Moroccans were not a nation at all, let alone a civilised nation. Others, it would seem, genuinely believed that Spain had a divine mission to fulfil; that God had appointed their nation to civilise, that is to Europeanise North Africa.[2] To that end war became a sacred means. It was so to many who were not in the army. The army, in fact, had its doubts at least on the political strategy of the war. It was beginning to realise that there could be no end to hostilities in Africa so long as limits were imposed as to how far a defeated enemy could be pursued. For defence the Kert line was nonsense. Spain had either to withdraw to Melilla or push beyond the Kert. The takeover of Larache and Al-Ksar-el-Kebir was foolhardy unless a land link were established with Ceuta. Ceuta and Melilla, too, should be linked. However, the more influential politicians and writers seem to have been inspired in their utterances for and against the war less by philosophical, religious, humanitarian or military considerations than by purely political calculations. Which aspects of the war could serve to embarrass or better still to bring down the government? Which could serve Canalejas to maintain himself in power? At the beginning of 1912 he had been Prime Minister for a full twenty two months, twice the average for over as long a period of politics as any one could remember. In the flexing of principles to serve political expediency the members of the Cortes were as adroit as those of any other elected body in Europe. Canalejas, standing as he did well to the left of where Maura had stood, was the better placed to prevent those to the left and right of him from combining and bringing about his fall. With his anti-religious legislation he now had his own group of Liberals the more solidly behind him. To widen his support he reintroduced Maura's conscription bill. The financiers (Liberals) for the most part recognised here a declaration of intent to "pacify" all the Riff whose mountains were rich in lead, manganese and iron ore; the nationalists (mainly Conservatives) the glory of the Spanish flag along the mountain tops.

Conscription was also welcome to the army. To the rank and file it promised a less arduous future. Service in Africa had been partly on a volunteer and partly on a lottery basis. All conscripts would be in the draw as well as volunteers to the Colours. In particular the odds against the recall of the reservist in times of crisis were now to be considerably lengthened. To the officers it presented an opportunity of quicker promotion since there would be more units to command. The effect nevertheless would not be immediate; and Franco was in a hurry.

For an officer, service in Africa had one general attraction. He could live on his pay there. As against that Melilla was an unhealthy, unhygienic and neglected shanty town with a bedraggled population living at subsistence level. It did offer a plethora of opportunities for the indulgence of all vice, but always in squalor and in repugnant smells. Ceuta was only slightly less malodorous.

For an ambitious man volunteer service in Africa was the passport to quick promotion in the field, albeit at considerable risk of sickness, wounds or death. For the young man with a sense of mission, with a faith in the myth of a nation chosen by God to bring civilisation to others, to volunteer for service in Africa was compulsory.

Franco had a sense of mission; he was ambitious; he was frustrated in El Ferrol; he was sensitive to the domestic strains of the Calle Maria. He volunteered.

Bad weather had cut the land route from El Ferrol to the Madrid railhead at Betanzos twenty miles away when Franco received the orders that he was to report immediately to his African regiment. The only alternative route was by sea to Corunna; the only ship available was a coaster, the *Paulina*★ The captain, who for some unknown reason, was anxious to venture out of El Ferrol in the teeth of a gale, agreed to take him and his two companions at their own risk. They spent five storm-tossed hours standing as best they could in a gangway.†

Two nights and two days travelling saw them in Malaga; another sea crossing followed, to Melilla. The regiment's field headquarters were by Tifasor, one of the forts outside the town. Franco saluted his old-new commanding officer on 24th February. One of his first tasks was to have his sword scabbard fitted with a leather cover. The glint of metal had already cost several officers their lives at the hands of snipers.

The situation as Franco arrived was promising for a young officer. El Mizzian was stirring up the tribes. During March and April the Spaniards moved in columns down to the river bed and back again, and southwards and north again to Melilla without encountering any organised opposition and never catching El Mizzian who boasted that no bullet could kill him unless it were of gold. El Mizzian was then reported more to the south beyond the mountains, in the Garet Plain, and to have a fair force with him. Three companies of Franco's regiment and three cavalry squadrons were put under the command of a colonel who later was to rise to general, then face a court martial, and later still be asked by the King to form a government. He was Damaso Berenguer.

A year earlier Damaso Berenguer had been instructed to study the French use of local levies. His suggestions for the recruitment and formation of a force which would be known as the Moorish *Regulares*, to be used in the vanguard of attacks on irregulars, had been approved. With some difficulty he had acquired the necessary volunteer officers of the right calibre. The recruits for the *Regulares* were mostly Algerian, tough good fighters when well paid and led by men of courage, but unscrupulous and liable to desert if suffering from a grievance or if a battle began to go against their side. Stories of their unreliability under French officers deterred many a young officer from volunteering to join them in the beginning, and many a seasoned and senior officer had grave doubts about their potential value. However, under Berenguer's leadership they had done well in several combats in the winter of

★ Franco's second christian name was Paulinus.

† Half way between El Ferrol and Corunna, and close by a rock called the Marola, or Seixo Branco the tides and currents meet of three *rías* or fjords. At the best of times the water is so rough that the local verdict is that: Quien pasó la Marola/Navegó la mar Toda.

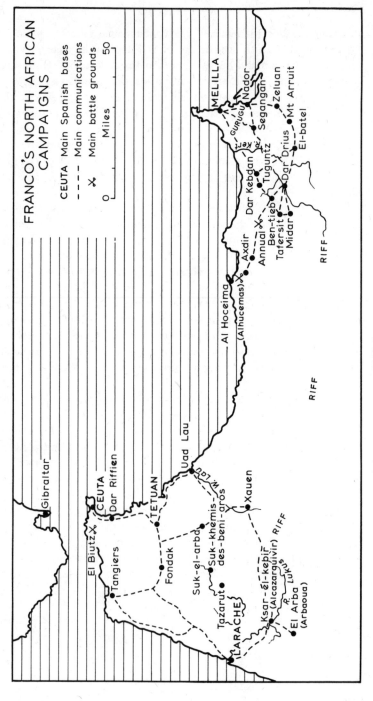

FRANCO'S NORTH AFRICAN CAMPAIGNS

CEUTA Main Spanish bases
- - - - Main communications
✕ Main battle grounds

0   Miles   50

Gibraltar

El Biutz ✕
CEUTA
Dar Riffien
Tangiers
TETUAN
Fondak
Uad Lau
Suk-el-arbd
Tazarut
Suk-khemis des-beni-aros
R. W.
Xauen
LARACHE
Ksar-el-kebir (Alcazarquivir)
El Arba (Arbaoua)
R. Lukus
RIFF

RIFF

Al Hoceima
Axdir
(Alhucemas) ✕
Annual ✕
Tafersit
Midar
Ben-tieb
RIFF

MELILLA
Nador
GURUGU
Segangan
Tuguntz
Dar Kebdan
R. Kert
Zeluan
Mt Arruit
Dar Drius
El-batel

MAP 2

1911-1912. Their fighting worth was now recognised and in May 1912 they were again to be in the vanguard of the column under his command whose objective was the dispersal of El Mizzian's concentration in the Garet and if possible his capture or death. They had their battle honours, but were still not to be trusted. On this occasion they were to be taken two days march from their base. The possibility had therefore to be guarded against that during the overnight stop they might turn on their officers. They were ordered to settle for the night away from the rest of the column. Their officers, as well as those of the Spanish main guard in which Franco figured, spent a sleepless night "with one hand on their pistols".[3]

On 14th May the vanguard made contact with El Mizzian's forces. The main guard was deployed. Franco's platoon was to make a frontal attack on the village of Hadu-Allal-U-Kaddur. He deployed his platoon strictly according to the book, and advanced in perfect formation. At the head went Franco, with his sword in one hand and his *parabellum* pistol in the other. Dámaso Berenguer watching the battle from a hillside, noted the copybook perfection of the manoeuvre and asked for the officer's name. Franco had made his mark with a man who would remember him and who had the ear of the King.

At the height of the battle El Mizzian made a cavalry charge with himself at the head. An ordinary lead rifle bullet fired by a corporal went through his head. The battle was over. El Mizzian's body was left exposed for all his followers to see.

Franco was not the only young man to attract the commander's attention. One of Berenguer's own hand-picked officers of the *Regulares* also carried out his allotted tasks with distinction. He was Emilio Mola, then a full lieutenant, with the *Regulares* since their formation, and already held in honour by the Algerians and Moroccans under his command for his habit of sitting fully exposed on parapets with his arms crossed nonchalantly, and relishing the sound of bullets fired in his direction. In the battle Mola's platoon had been checked momentarily and he had had to make a slight withdrawal. With four others he had then gone to the rescue of two of his men who had been wounded. A bullet pierced his thigh, but he saved the men from being hacked to pieces, Moorish fashion, by the enemy. His behaviour earned him promotion to captain in the field.

Mola was five years Franco's senior. No two men could have been less alike in physical appearance or in ancestry. Mola was over six foot high, gaunt, unquestionably Spanish in facial features. His great-grandfather, a sergeant in the Napoleonic wars, had lived to take part as a lieutenant-colonel in the First Carlist War on the side of the Liberals. His grandfather, an ensign at the astonishingly early age of fourteen and a captain at seventeen had played a prominent part in one of the Liberal army *Pronunciamientos* of 1848, and had also fought with determination against the Carlists; and Mola's father had been among the defenders of Bilbao in the third and last of the Carlist Wars. He had then been posted to Cuba where Emilio Mola had been born. Back in Spain before the 1898 war, he had filled his son with long stories of the great Liberal generals of his own and his father's generation, the makers and destroyers of kings and republic. He encouraged his son to read Galdós as history. A Liberal to the marrow he was a disciplinarian at home, organising his household on military lines with his wife and family as his subordinates. Paradoxically he wanted his son to become a scientist, and so break the family tradition; true to his Liberal principles he allowed Emilio to enter the Toledo Academy where he absorbed the Spanish military doctrines of honour and discipline to such a degree that he came to be known as the "Prussian". Later in life Emilio confessed that he would rather have been a surgeon than what he chose or what his father wished him to be.[4]

From the time of that capture of a village and the death of the Holy Man El Mizzian, a friendship began between the gaunt, quixotesque Mola and the little, but as yet otherwise not sanchoesque Franco. Twenty-four years, two months and four days later they were to be two of the four key figures in the grand climacteric of Spanish twentieth century history. The third was a plumpish round-faced man of medium height, José Sanjurjo y Sacanell; in 1912 a major in the forces operating from Melilla. The fourth was Gonzalo Queipo de Llano y Sierra, a cavalry major risen from the rank of bugler; in 1912 on the eve of leading one of the last spectacular and successful cavalry charges in history, in the region of Al-Ksar-el-Kebir.

With the bearded El Mizzian dead, resistance on the Melilla side of the River Kert came to an end in 1912. The Army commanders were given strict injunctions not to venture across the river, nor with any permanence further south than Mount Arruit twenty-five miles to the south of Melilla. The international situation had changed: and 1912 was not going to come up to expectations as a vintage year for Spanish territorial expansion. France had dangled a slice of French Congo before Germany. Germany had swallowed the sop, and France knew that Germany would not now snap at her if she banquetted on Morocco.

With Germany no longer a potential ally of Spain, France had no cause to consider Spain's sentimental attraction to Africa or claims based on over-simplifications of history. The French had no patience with the arguments advanced over and over again in Spanish newspapers, journals and books of the time that only a geological accident had separated Gibraltar from Ceuta, that North Africa physically was identical with the Iberian Peninsula and a part of it, and even that the inhabitants of North Africa were of the same race as those of Spain and had been since Carthaginian times. The length of time that Spain had been really "present" in Africa was equally irrelevant, except in so far as guns in Ceuta were as well placed to interfere with traffic through the Straits as were those of Gibraltar. Accordingly France came to a new bilateral agreement with the Sultan whereby he would regard France as his sole protector but at the same time, with Britain insisting, she entered into new negotiations with Spain offering her, as it were, a sub-lease of an area smaller than that agreed upon in 1904. The negotiations were still in progress when on 12th November Canalejas was assassinated. Spain accepted the new terms a fortnight later.

At the end of 1912 José Villalba was promoted Brigadier General and left the 68th African Regiment. Franco asked for a transfer to the *Regulares*. It was sanctioned the following April.

Franco was to be much more "at home" in command of Algerians and Moroccans, of *"moros"*—to give them their generic Spanish name—than of *"cristianos"*, that is of Spaniards whether Christian or no; but it is not to be doubted that service with the *Regulares*, always in the vanguard of an attack, gave a young officer opportunities for the display of courage, and that Franco was always anxious to prove to others that no man was braver than he. *Hacer el blanco viviente*—to present themselves as living targets—was a point of honour with officers of the *Regulares*. Mola would summarise their Muslim-like fatalism with the phrase *"Las balas son como las cartas. Cuando escriban el sobre de la mía . . . tendré que recibirla"*:[5] "Bullets are like letters; when someone writes my address on its envelope, I'll be getting it." When in due course, Franco became entitled to lead his men on horseback, he would choose for preference a white horse, halt it while he exhorted his men to push forward with his somewhat high pitched but very penetrating voice, and smile seemingly unperturbed as bullets whistled all around him. It was the way to decorations and quick promotion, wounds or death. Over the next thirty months, thirty-five of the forty-one officers of the *Regulares* of Melilla whom he joined had been killed or wounded.[6]

Not, however, round Melilla. Except for the occasional franc-
tireurs' attacks, all was quiet in the spring of 1913, and for the rest of
the year operations were limited to what was really police work. It
had been decided that the turn had come for expansion, pacification,
protection, call it what you will, in the West. On 18th February
General Alfau, the Commander in Ceuta, marched a column of 2,500
men down to Tetuan, twenty-three miles away, and occupied it without firing a shot. Soon after Franco had joined them, the *Regulares*
were shipped to Tetuan across the one hundred miles of sea separating
it from Melilla. By June the Spanish troops were ready to advance
across the promontory of which Ceuta is the head; but the tribesmen,
offended at the sight of a Spanish flag in Tetuan, were also ready to do
battle with them. On 12th June the forces met six miles from Tetuan
and there were heavy casualties on both sides. In the meantime, however, whether as part of a concerted action or whether because he did
not wish to be outdone by the Ceuta commander Alfau, General
Silvestre in command of the Spanish troops at Larache on the Atlantic
side of the promontory set out with a column from Ksar-el-Kebir on
a punitive expedition. A heliograph station near to Larache had been
attacked. Er Raisuni's reaction to the punishment of his tribesmen was
immediate. He issued a general directive to fight the invader.

Neither side wasted any time.

On 9th May General Alfau informed the government: "Er Raisuni
desires to provoke a war to avenge injuries which he believes he has
received". Within a month the tribesmen from the environs of Tangier
and Ceuta down to the approaches to Larache and Ksar-el-Kebir were
ready to support Er Raisuni. On 13th June the Tetuan forces advanced
six miles from the road to Tangier, and though they carried their
objective, the capture of a village, they did so with heavy losses.
On 13th June Silvestre in the south-west moved southwards from
Ksar-el-Kebir towards the line of demarcation with the French, and at
El Arba (Arbaoua) was similarly brought to a halt. Now it was the turn
of the Moroccans. They ignored the Spanish advance positions. In
July they broke into Ksar-el-Kebir and Silvestre forced them out again
only with difficulty. The coast road from Tetuan to Ceuta came under
constant attack. A Spanish gunboat in support of supply columns ran
aground. It was over-run by the enemy, and the commander and most
of the crew were killed. Tetuan was cut off from Ceuta; it was held but
only just, in a series of actions in which Mola and Franco both distinguished themselves. One enagement was particularly notable out of

the many skirmishes, ambushes, attacks and counter-attacks. On 22nd September, south-west of Tetuan, the *Regulares* attempted to retake a crest from which they had been dislodged. The leading company of *Regulares* was surrounded on three sides and engaged in hand to hand fighting. Its commander was killed. Captain Mola led his company to their rescue and to retrieve the body of the commander of the first company. A third company was brought into action. Franco whose platoon was to the flank, on his own initiative, turned his men towards the pocket and the Moroccans, to avoid being themselves attacked from the rear, broke off the engagement. His initiative was commended because it was successful; but it would have been disastrous for him had it failed, for it was not according to the book.[7]

The *Regulares* took the brunt of the defence as well as the attack. They had to do so. The conscripts from Spain were poorly instructed youths. They included many whose health and morale declined rapidly. Their stomachs could not absorb the uncooked and insalubrious food which they were given. Untoughened by exercises before being sent to Africa, those who came from sedentary occupations in cities crumpled in the long marches under a blazing sun. In any case, they were conscripts, unwilling participants in a war that passed their understanding. The *Regulares* were men who had chosen to make their living at the service of a master who paid them better than any other they knew. They were natives of North Africa. Army rations at their worst were better than they would otherwise have had.

There were other factors behind the constant use of the *Regulares*. Quantity of conscripts was lacking as well as quality. The conscription law allowed many exemptions; it was possible for a parent to "buy out" a son. Furthermore 1913 was a particularly difficult year for the governing classes of Spain. It had begun with the publication in the Conservative newspaper *Epoca* of an open letter in which Maura, now the leader of the Conservative Party, had written that the Liberal Party could no longer be considered monarchist. There were mass resignations from the Cortes, a change of Prime Minister, another anarchist attempt to shoot the King, and, more disturbing than such by no means unprecedented occurrences, Pablo Iglesias, the leader of the Socialist Party called a general strike as much to show the strength of socialism as the socialist disapproval of the Moroccan war and the sham democracy of the 1876 Constitution. The strike as a show of force was a magnificent success. It was broken by the expedient of mobilising all transport workers and putting them under military law. With the

situation bordering on civil war in Spain there were few troops to send
to Africa. The *Regulares*, the volunteers and the small number of conscripts already there had to manage as best they could.

It was as well therefore that Berenguer had chosen well his officers.
Desertions from the *Regulares* during the period were relatively few.
The officers knew how to foment in their men personal loyalty to themselves and their corps. The secret of their success, other than their
unquestionable valour in action, may well be that they were not Catholics à la Français or à l'Espagnol. There was a close affinity between a
Muslim and one imbued with the creed taught at Toledo. The Muslim
respected justice untempered by mercy. He believed that punishment,
particularly severe corporal punishment, expiated faults; but of course
he had to be convinced that what he had done was a fault before he
recognised justice in the punishment. The officers for their part thought
highly of the Arabs' disregard for death. The bravery of a man who
exposed himself to bullets in the way that the *Regulares* did, covered
the fact that as often as not the individual Algerian or Moroccan did
so for no nobler reason than to loot the dead. The officers marvelled
at the Arabs' ability to withstand physical hardship. The Muslim
observance of Ramadan was all that the Christian Lent should be and
was not. Their polygamy, their propensity for rapine, the less savoury
aspects of their behaviour, could be explained away by the officers
with the authority of no less than Napoleon.[8] The religion of Moham-
med was the religion of simple folk, he had said. It would be replaced
by something more adult as they became more Europeanised. Even
more commendable to the Spanish officer was the Arab's care of his
rifle. Though the Arab might himself rarely wash, he never put away
his rifle without cleaning it. He checked every round before he
put it into his bandolier, and again before inserting it into the
clip. The *Regulare* was never caught with a jammed bolt or a bent
firing pin, or a dud round or one that was not of the calibre of his
rifle. In the *Regulares* the irregulars had met their match—and vice
versa.

By the end of 1913 a stalemate had been reached. The Spaniards
held the towns of Ceuta, Tetuan, Larache and Ksar-el-Kebir. The
Moroccans were therefore in a position to operate with all the advantages of having internal lines of communication. They could attack
now towards Ceuta, now switch to Tetuan and, when least expected,
appear off Ksar-el-Kebir. They could concentrate at will. Nevertheless
they could not dislodge the Spaniards from the towns: nor did they

attempt it seriously. They had realised that they could wear away the Spanish army at little cost to themselves.

The Spanish forces in the south-west could communicate with those in the Ceuta Tetuan area only by sea; and between each pair of towns only sporadically by heliograph. The key to the control of the western Riff was Fondak-es-Ain-Yedida astride the north-east–south-west 'road'. It should have been permanently fortified and not merely held momentarily. Its strategic value was not appreciated for years. Instead the effort was dissipated in erecting lines of blockhouses between Ceuta and Tetuan and again between Larache and Ksar-el-Kebir. Theoretically they kept open communications between each pair of towns, but in practice they were exceedingly expensive in men and materials to maintain. They were simple sandbag erections manned by handfuls of men who had to be supplied with water, rations and wood for any cooking which they might do. They had to be relieved at regular intervals. Every time supply or replacement was necessary, a company, a battalion or even a regiment would have to escort the convoy. The Moroccans would first subject them to no more than sniping from the tens of thousands of boulders on the hillsides. Hunting the snipers who had as good rifles as the Army and a plentiful supple of smokeless powder, was a time-wasting operation, and no escort cared to be caught by nightfall away from base. The Moroccans would then permit several convoys to pass totally unmolested thus lulling the Spaniards into the belief that resistance was at an end; and suddenly, when the time and place was propitious, where there was good cover and usually in the afternoon when the troops were returning to base and therefore tired from the march of the morning, the Moroccans would pounce, aiming in preference at the officers; and before the Spaniards had deployed according to the book, they had vanished from the scene. Behind the official communiques' "all quiet in the Protectorate" there were scores of Spanish casualties.

One hundred and eighty-four million pesetas (£7,360,000) had been voted for the war in Morocco in 1913, 8 per cent of the total budget; but directly and indirectly the total cost was somewhere in the region of 300 millions (£12 million). The sums seem insignificant today. Their contemporary enormity may be assessed if it be remembered that £12 million was a sum equal to the income at the time of a quarter of a million families in the south of Spain, or the total income of the million Arabs in the Spanish Protectorate. It would not have been out of character for Er Raisuni and the tribal chiefs to have come to terms with the Spaniards in exchange for pensions which would not have cost as dear. Such an appreciation of the situation may well have been behind an offer publicly made in December 1913 by a German firm of entrepreneurs, Messrs. Mannesmann Brothers. If granted a charter giving them certain exploitation rights they would undertake to bring Er Raisuni to heel and ensure Spanish possession of their nominal protectorate. The firm's offer was bitterly resented in the Peninsula. The Cortes voted for 1914 sums similar to those of the previous year for the pursuit of the war in Morocco.

In Morocco the war in 1914 was much as it had been in the latter part of 1913: the stalemate costly to Spain in men and money continued. For their bravery in the year's operations in which neither side could attain more than very local and temporary ascendancy, Majors Sanjurjo and Queipo were promoted lieutenant-colonels, Emilio Mola a major and, in April 1915, the twenty-two year old Francisco Franco a captain. This last promotion, though first proposed by Berenguer earlier[9] created some resentment among lieutenants of longer standing. There were no captains' vacancies in the *Regulares*. Franco refused to accept the command of a company other than in that force. After some argument, he was carried for a month on its strength as a supernumerary. A vacancy occurred in the May and Captain Franco became a company commander.

For 1915 the war budget was again as for 1914. More Spaniards lost their lives in skirmishes; no major operations were, or could be, undertaken. The high commission was instructed to come to terms with Raisuni. Troops under Silvestre fired on Er Raisuni while he had a safe conduct in his pocket from the High Commissioner. An agent of Raisuni's, Alkalay, was found assassinated in Tangiers. He was a gunrunner but he too had a safe conduct from the High Commissioner. Marina was retired and replaced by a General Gomez Jordana, and Silvestre was recalled to Spain where his face was saved by being given a post as an aide-de-camp to the King. Jordana came to an agreement with Er Raisuni but as neither side trusted the other the pact was not faithfully observed except in one particular; Er Raisuni allowed work to proceed on the railway from Tangier through Ksar-el-Kebir and south to the French zone.

The Spaniards had laid great store by this railway. For all the many assertions that Spain had conquered an Empire to spread Christianity and that she had a divinely ordained mission to Europeanise North Africa whereas the British had been shamefully mercantile in their

expansion of Empire,[10] there were Spaniards who believed firmly that
"trade followed the flag". It would appear that quite a sizeable group
seriously thought that given a railway line from the north to the south
of the continent, goods to and from anywhere in trans-Pyrenean
Europe and Africa would be rail-borne through the Peninsula, on a
train ferry from Algeciras to Tangier, and then right across the Spanish
Protectorate: "It is irrelevant for the enemies of what we are doing in
Morocco to point out that the land is sterile. Were it desert sand . . . its
geographical importance would be the same. It is enough that rails
can be laid upon it, and warehouses constructed for the [inevitable]
international traffic. . . ."[11] The railway was supposed to have another
advantage: "The Moroccans like railways. . . . The prestige of the
French in Algeria is due in great measure to the fact that there are many
railway lines there".[12] The construction of railway lines was judged to
be as important for the pacification of Africa as the establishment of
justice and incorrupt administration.

The year 1915 passed into 1916. The tribes of Anyera and Yebala
between Ceuta and Tangier left the railway but not the military lines
undisturbed. In June the Moroccans were reported to be massing in
the heights above Ceuta, in and around the mountain top of El Biutz,
a crest six miles to the west of Ceuta and at the end of what is today
a much frequented tourist scenic route, with a panoramic view of the
Straits of Gibraltar. From the reverse slopes it commanded the road
from Ceuta to Tetuan. Accordingly in Tetuan a strong column of
Spanish troops was assembled. It set out after breakfast on 28th June,
with the *Regulares* as usual in the vanguard. It proceeded along the coast
road and reached Dar Riffien at dusk, after a twenty mile march. The
Spanish force was now about five miles from the Moroccan. At midnight the column resumed the march across country. At dawn on the
29th they were in a position to assault.

Franco was in command of the leading company of the leading tabor
or battalion. The Moroccans had a line of trenches on the facing slopes
plain for the Spaniards to see. The battalion was ordered to storm them.
This was precisely what the Moroccans hoped that the Spaniards
would do. The entrenched riflemen and machine-gunners would halt
the attack: more Spanish formations would be ordered into the frontal
attack, and in the meantime the main body of Moroccans, behind the
crest, would move to the flanks and trap the column. The Spaniards had
been trapped that way before, but the Spanish field regulations did not
really allow a variation from the rule that defence positions should be

stormed. In all three tabores were thrown at the trenches. The three commanders were killed. Franco in the leading company could see beyond the trenches the enveloping movement. There was no possibility now of withdrawal. The moment he could close in with a bayonet the situation might be retrieved. Men fell all around him. He stooped to pick up a rifle dropped by one of the wounded and loaded it. He called once more to his men to rush the trenches. As he did so a bullet pierced his abdomen. A few steps later he had fallen, but the position had been taken. With the crest in Spanish hands, the Moroccans on the flanks took flight.

Franco remained conscious for quite some time. He had with him the Company's pay—20,000 pesetas (£800). The *Regulares* were due to be paid that night, being a Thursday. They were mercenaries and they required payment whatever the circumstances at the appointed moment. He handed the money over to a lieutenant. Franco might well have believed himself mortally wounded. He, better than anyone, knew that the chance of survival in African war from a wound in the abdomen was rather less than a hundred to one. Two rank and file *Regulares* took him to the First Aid post. The medical officer stopped the profuse bleeding as far as he could, and sent him on to the casualty clearing station on the outskirts of Ceuta, believing that he would not reach it alive. There was no transport available so that he had to be jogged all the way on a two-man stretcher. There it was debated whether it was wise to move him, or indeed whether it was worth moving him at all. Gangrene was imagined to have set in already; but in the end he was moved to the military hospital at Ceuta. His parents were sent for from El Ferrol. He was expected to survive only a few days. An X-ray was taken[13] more out of academic interest than of any hope. To the astonishment of the medical officer the X-ray revealed that the bullet after penetrating the abdomen wall had missed every vital part. Had the bullet entered at the point it did a split second earlier or later, had it penetrated him an inch up or down, or at a fractionally different angle, it would have pierced one or other of his vital organs; and the diagnosis of the medical officers at the First Aid post and the casualty clearing station would have been proved true.

The communique for the battle of El Buitz singled out Captain Francisco Franco Bahamonde of the *Regulares*. "He is mentioned as having highly distinguished himself by his insuperable valour and his gifts of leadership and energy displayed in a tough combat in which he was seriously wounded. His Majesty's Government and Parliament congratulate the forces which took part in this important operation carried out brilliantly."[14] General Gomez Jordana, the High Commissioner, recommended him for promotion to major. Such recommendations had now to be considered by the Cabinet which had at its doorstep a pressure group of Peninsula-based officers objecting to the promotion in the field of juniors according to the seniority list. Instead of promotion Franco was awarded the Cross of Maria Cristina which entitled him to a major's pay though not the rank. He was far from satisfied. While convalescing, he appealed to the King. The High Commissioner endorsed the appeal adding that if promotion was being withheld because Franco was still only twenty-three, then his youth should be considered an added reason for the promotion rather than put in the balance against it. The promotion was reconsidered, approved and ante-dated to 29th June, the day of the El Biutz operation.

Franco had temporarily caught up with Mola, but as he replaced his three small stars for the larger single star of a major, Sanjurjo acquired his full colonelcy. It had taken Sanjurjo, a veteran of Cuba as well as Africa, fifteen years to rise from second lieutenant to major; Franco had done it in six. In six years he had risen as far as most cadets hoped to rise in a lifetime; there would be little doubt that he would eventually become a general. The "eventually" could be shortened if he remained in Africa. However, this time there was no hope that he would be allowed to do so. The vacancies created by the death of the three majors at his side had had to be filled immediately: as a major supernumerary to the establishment he could not be borne beyond 4th March 1917. On that day he was posted to the 3rd Regiment of Foot, the Prince's. That meant garrison duty in Oviedo. After a further period of convalescence, he joined his new regiment on the last day of May 1917.

By no means the least important aspect of these five years which Franco spent in Africa as a junior officer is that they were in one sense of a pattern with his early years in Toledo and El Ferrol. Franco in Africa was away from Spain: Franco in the *Regulares* was a member of a select body of officers having spasmodic contact only with their fellows in the Spanish regiments and little with the Spanish rank and file. They were officers in the Spanish Army but not really of the Spanish Army. A second and perhaps even more important aspect is that Franco was for five years with men who had little cause to respect or be grateful to the politicians in Madrid. True enough they were relatively well paid, but they had been repeatedly the victims of political expediency. Political expediency had demanded orders and counter-orders as to what was or was not to be done in Africa in such profusion that the result was chaos and useless loss of life and money. The weapons with which they had had to attempt territorial gains when these had been commanded, or to defend themselves when the orders were that they were to withdraw were mediocre. Their rifles were mainly but not all Mausers of the 1893 pattern. The ammunition was defective. They had no more machine guns than the enemy. Typical of the few artillery pieces which they had are those described by the then Lieutenant of Artillery Jorge Vigon:[15] "ancient Krupp 90-milli-metre pieces which only by a miracle were not muzzle-loading". The maps available were primitive and small-scale, and there was no possibility of the use of artillery except as close infantry support weapons usually firing over open sights. There were no field kitchens. Each man setting out on a march had to carry a kilo of wood to cook his meals individually at the end of the day. Not surprisingly many men with the heat of the day bearing down on them threw away their kilos of wood, or if they did not, arrived at their night's stop far too tired to think of making their own little individual fire to cook their food. They ate it raw, if the sun had not putrified it already. Dysentery was endemic. Even at a later date Berenguer had cause to complain of the issue clothing. Men froze in their light drill uniforms in the winter. Their rope sandals (*alpargatas*) were no protection in snow or mud: if the men lost them they had to continue barefoot for there were no reserves.[17] Medical supplies were equally scarce. The medical officers were men of adequate knowledge and skill, but they had to work in conditions which were far from asceptic even in the base hospitals of Ceuta and Melilla. The orderlies on whom the medical officers had to rely as nurses were men who were unfit mentally or physically for any other duties.

Franco was now to come face to face with the reality of the Spanish Army in the Peninsula. It was, as Mola was to write in anger[18] "an army which existed on paper rather than in fact". Battalions should have numbered about 600 men but in fact could be down to a third of their strength. Too many of their officers were engaged in desk jobs. N.C.O. promotions were based more on beautiful handwriting on examination papers than on ability to command or teach recruits. The army was "the plaything of politicians . . . a prolongation of the police force . . . and a source of bakers, drivers and postmen in times of strikes".

Spain had realistically opted for neutrality at the outbreak of the 1914–18 war. She could have provided manpower but not an army. There were however political considerations as well behind her neutrality. Though there were pro-British Spanish Army officers and even some pro-French, the sympathies of the greater number were with the Central Powers. They had a case. Britain was not merely Spain's traditional enemy: she had within living memory insisted on the internationalisation of Tangier which would have been a better base than Ceuta or Melilla for the operation in Spanish Morocco. Not satisfied with having despoiled Spain of her American Empire, Franco was to write,[19] not content with the possession of the major part of Africa and of the Indian continent, Britain had in the current century denied Spain even the crumbs of the colonial feast. Germany, it was true, had also had a hand in the internationalisation of Tangier; but then Germany was to be excused. She, too, had been the victim of the "unjust distribution . . . of Colonial possessions . . .". When with the end of the nineteenth century "the lands' end had been reached, it was found that three powers—England, France and Russia—had cornered practically the whole Colonial world. Germany and Italy had obtained a few possessions of small economic and strategic worth. Henceforth in the civilised world, men began to distinguish between the great colonial powers and the so-called have-not states, whose ambitions were frustrated". By 1914, according to Franco, war had become "a necessity" to England because Germany was beginning to draw level with her in naval power and because goods marked Made in Germany were displacing those Made in England on world markets. "A glance at the map is sufficient to make us realise the clever way in which British policy created the situation at the start of the First World War." Thus for Franco, as for many of the officers who served in Africa, Britain was the villain of the 1914–18 war and partly responsible at least for Spain's misfortunes in Africa.

Upper-class civilian Spain had divided roughly equally into pro-German and pro-Allied, or perhaps rather anti-Allied and anti-German. Kant and Hegel battled with Voltaire and Rousseau in the liberal intellectual mind; Henry VIII and Cranmer with Martin Luther and Bismark in the clerical: in the King's, the fact that his wife was British but his mother was Austrian. In folk memory the odds were heavily weighed against Britain, the trickster of Gibraltar and the perfidious despoiler under Canning of the Spanish–American Empire, and against France the destroyer of ancient monuments and thief of priceless treasures. Among the urban masses, Socialists and Anarchists were anti-imperialist, but until 1917 they were unable to make up their minds which side was the more imperialist.

Franco on his return to the peninsula however was not going to become embroiled in the pro-German versus pro-British controversy, but in the complex web of internal troubles. There was a revolutionary ferment in Spain. Catalans were becoming restive again: civil service pay had not risen with the cost of living: neither had army pay, and the officers who had never fought in Africa were not taking kindly to promotions for distinguished active service: and there was a proletariat with greater grievances than Army officers, civil servants, or Catalan "home rulers".

The Catalan "home rulers" had coalesced to form a single party, the Lliga, under a highly respectable member of society Francisco Cambó, a lawyer with a flair for economics. Cambó sought home rule for Catalonia through the Cortes and not by revolution, though he was a revolutionary in a new way. By 1917 he had come to the conclusion that in the Spain of the time there was nothing more reactionary than to be a revolutionary.[20] While home rule for Catalonia was dearest to his heart, he believed that the whole of Spain needed a facelift, a renewal. He became the mainspring behind a movement called *Renovación*—Renovation. It was a movement which was anarchist in the sense that it had no definable organisation, and no more definite an aim than "to renew Spanish life and institutions"; it advocated the replacement of the sham electoral system by true free elections, and of government by rotation of liberals and conservatives with government according to the real views of the people, the cleansing from the monarchy of the lickspittles and courtiers of favour and the keel-hauling of all government administration to rid it from the barnacles of peculation and corruption. It had a newspaper, *El Sol*, printed on better than usual quality paper, owned and run by an engineer turned publisher and journalist Nicolas Maria Urgoiti, a Basque who put into practice in his workshops and relations with employees ideas which even a Rowntree★ would have thought extreme as basic principles of social justice. *El Sol* advocated the establishment throughout the country

★ He was the founder of the *Editorial Calpe* which later amalgamated to become Spain's leading publishing firm, *Espasa-Calpe*.

of Juntas or Action Groups—almost Syndicates by anarchist standards. Renovacion attracted adherents among respectable middle-class and politically middle-of-the-way men in the main cities, including Oviedo.

The first manifestation of action by Juntas came from the least expected quarter—the Spanish Army. On 1st June a Colonel Benito Marquez, Commanding Officer of the Regiment of Vergara in garrison in Barcelona, addressed a petition to the Minister of War through General Alfau, now Captain-General of Catalonia. He did so not on his own behalf but as head of a body calling itself the Juntas de Defensa del Arma de Infantería. More than a protest, it was almost an ultimatum. The Juntas demanded: an end to the favouritism in promotions and appointments shown by the Casa Militar or Military Household of the King, a sense of proportion in awards and a stricter adherence to seniority; the reorganisation of the Medical and Service Corps; better pay for junior officers; and, the exclusion of military forces from civilian political *embrollos* which were separating the army from the people. The Junta stated that it was not seeking power, but that it believed itself to have the right to demand that power should be in good hands.

There was a Junta in Oviedo. Franco was no hothead. This was not the way laid down by the regulations to express a grievance; it was tantamount to mutiny. Were the awards which he had received for service in Africa disproportionate to his personal sacrifices? He did not believe them so. Was his promotion a mark of favouritism? Hardly, since he had had to appeal against an earlier decision not to promote him; but the rewards and the promotion might well have seemed to the officers who had little or no knowledge of service in Africa typical of the practices of the Casa Militar against which they had publicly protested. He had no objection to an increase of pay for officers; he, more than most, had suffered from the inadequacies of the Service Corps, and knew the consequences of the inattention paid to medical services. Publicly he declared himself neither for nor against the Juntas.

The government ordered the dissolution of the Juntas. Colonel Marquez and his officers in Barcelona refused to obey; they were put under arrest and confined to Montjuich Castle. Thereupon Juntas of Valencia and Zaragoza also asked to be put under arrest. The centre-Liberal government of Garcia Prieto resigned and the King offered the Premiership to the conservative Dato. Dato chose as his Minister

of War General Primo de Rivera. Primo de Rivera sent Marina to
replace Alfau. Marina released the officers. The Government promised
military reforms. Politicians to the right and to the left expressed their
strong disapproval. By the end of June unrest was general throughout
the country, and the government suspended the "constitutional
guarantees", in effect thus declaring martial law. Martial law did not
however deter civilian government employees from forming their
own committees of defence and presenting their own demands for
higher pay.

Now it was to be the turn of the Catalanists as such. Under Dato's
Liberal predecessor Garcia Prieto there had been a remote possibility
of the case for home rule being given a hearing in the Cortes, although
the Liberals even at the centre had little understanding of Catalonia's
uniqueness and national aspirations;[21] under the centre-Conservative
Dato there was no possibility without the exertion of public pressure.
On 5th July twenty Senators and forty members of the Lower House
met in Barcelona and demanded a constituent assembly to consider
not merely the demand for home rule, but the "renovation of the
Spanish Constitution, public administration, the armed services, justice
and national economy". Dato refused to consider it. The Catalans then
called on all members of the Cortes who sympathised to meet in
Barcelona. The government threatened that the meeting if held would
be considered subversive, yet seventy-one of the 760 members of the
Cortes did assemble on 19th July. The *Municipios*, or City Governments, of several provincial capitals including Oviedo, sent messages
of encouragement to the men who dared to defy the government. The
defiance was kept within peaceful limits, but links between Cambó
and Colonel Marquez on the one side and Socialists and Anarchists
on the other blurred the distinction between Catalanism, as an ideal on
its own, and Catalanism as a weapon of left-wing revolutionary
activity—and not merely in Franco's mind.

In Catalonia the Anarchists had recovered sufficiently for the heavy
punishment meted out to them immediately after the "Tragic Week"
and sporadically years later to dream again of the establishment of their
Utopia in their own lifetime. Their local workers' organisation, the
Confederacion Regional del Trabajo, had become national; the
Spanish government had given them a martyr in Ferrer, and the
surviving persecuted leaders had established the Confederacion Nacional
del Trabajo, or C.N.T., at Seville in 1910. It was not a trade union
movement in any Northern European sense. It did not organise either

craft unions or company unions, but local groups or syndicates of men. Their subscriptions were infinitesimally small, at most 50 centimos a month, that is, roughly one penny a week. The syndicates were in no way to be concerned in negotiations with employers for juster wages or less intolerable working conditions. Their final objective was to be "the dissolution of government and state in the economic organisation" by a general strike, to which the prelude would be what were called "the daily revindicative tasks", minor industrial sabotage leading to major and to assassination of the bourgeoisie which had to be eliminated. The general strike would bring the final victory, the abolition of the state, and the take-over by the syndicates of all production and distribution. Accordingly, there was no need for the C.N.T. to have talks with employers since they would soon be extinct, to have a strike fund since the general strike would end all strikes, to have social insurance, or to seek in Parliament a voice and redress by legislation since there would soon be neither a Parliament nor national laws. By 1917 the C.N.T. was fighting fit—especially in Barcelona—and with the Army divided over the Juntas and the Lliga causing a stir among the upper classes, the moment seemed propitious for action.

The Socialist Party's Union General de Trabajadores—U.G.T. (General Union of Workers), now under the direction of the already internationally famous Largo Caballero, had a membership not far short of two hundred thousand. It had an even more complete national coverage than the anarchists' C.N.T. Socialists and Anarchists alike had hailed events of the Russian month of March as the dawn of the workers' millenium. And as the industrial middle-classes began to press the Spanish government to declare the country on the side of the allies, the Socialialists and Anarchists decided that to help the allied cause was to aid the hated Czars. They had knowledge, too, of the German Socialists' yearning to emulate in their own country what was happening in Russia. Against the advice of the veteran Pablo Iglesias, his deputy in the Spanish Socialist party, the Professor of Logic Julian Besteiro and Largo Caballero decided that the time had come for the general strike which would be the immediate prelude to the triumph of socialism in Spain. They established contact with the C.N.T., which agreed to co-operate. Both Anarchists and Socialists had converts among N.C.O.s and rank and file of the Army. Among the officers there were also many Republicans.

The 10th August was fixed as the date for a railway strike to begin, and 13th August as a date for the general strike. Revolution was its declared intention. Its aims were the establishment of a republic, the recognition of the working-class syndicates and their power to veto laws passed by the Cortes, a seven-hour, five-day week, higher wages and better working conditions, dissolution of the Army and its substitution by a militia, separation of Church and State, the dispersal of religious and the closure of churches, divorce laws, nationalisation of land and no declaration of war except after a plebiscite and with those who voted for it being the first to be sent into battle. The Anarchists who had more than a streak of puritanism in them also wanted the prohibition of all bullfights and indecent cabarets.

The Government now formally declared martial law. The Army decided to back the government. N.C.O.s and rank and file showed no hesitation in firing on demonstrators when called upon to do so. In Barcelona the strike was over in a week.

In Oviedo Franco set out to "pacify" the miners with an infantry company, a platoon of machine guns and a platoon of the Civil Guard. Only the Civil Guard platoon was up to strength, and the whole force was under 150 strong.

At the very time that Franco arrived in Oviedo, the capital of the most ancient of all the kingdoms of Spain had acquired a new importance. It had long been the centre of the Spanish coal-mining district. With the world at peace three factors had inhibited its development. The railway line to Oviedo went through difficult mountain terrain and narrow passes subject to heavy snowfalls. It was single track. The transport of coal out of the mining valleys was therefore expensive. Secondly, the cost of extraction was high. Thirdly, the quality of the coal was poor. Coal from Britain could be delivered to most areas of Spain more cheaply than coal from Oviedo, and it was of far better quality. However, with the war, Britain could not export as much coal, and it was liable to be sunk in transit. The output of the Oviedo mines was therefore freed from a competitor. The mine owners were grossly and disproportionately the chief beneficiaries, but the miners, having less cause to worry whether there would be any work for them on the morrow began to consider the nature of their oppression and the Socialist General Union of Workers, the U.G.T., gained adherents by the thousand.

The Government intended Franco's column of 150 men to guard the mines against sabotage, and to show by their presence with rifles and machine guns that the Government "meant business". They were not, and could not be, from their numbers,[22] a body to do battle with the several thousand miners on strike; nor were the miners as yet able to give battle. There had, however, been cases of fights or disputes between Civil Guard detachments and individuals before the troops' arrival. Under the terms of martial law which had been declared, Franco had to act as judge in such cases. He did so according to the strict letter of the law, deciding now against the strikers, now against the Civil Guard. Franco had to apply the law and not to judge it. The episode was to remain one of Franco's most vivid memories:

> I came to ask myself what was it that drove people, ordinary decent people, to strike action and acts of violence, and I saw for myself the appalling conditions under which employers were making people work— but as I deepened my enquiries I began to see that no easy solutions were possible. So I began to read books on social questions, on political theories and economics, to search out some solution. Those put forward by socialists and anarchists could lead only to chaos and to an even worse state of affairs than the ills they sought to remedy.[23]

The "show of force" lasted inside of a week: the strike three weeks. Franco thereafter became well-known for his reading of books into the early hours of the morning.

The official figures given in the Cortes for the casualties inflicted by the strikers on the Army were of seven officers, thirty-six N.C.O.s and 180 soldiers dead and wounded. It was said that civilian casualties had been far fewer. Socialist and Anarchist authors differ among themselves as to how many of their men were killed; there may well have been as many as seventy in the whole country: nearly all of them were in Barcelona.

These totals were to be exceeded several times over in the period 1918–23 when in Barcelona alone about 700 persons were assassinated; for after the failure of the 1917 strike, German *agents provocateurs*, working to disrupt Barcelona's supply of textiles to the Allies, reached the climax of their activities. They would provoke an anarchist into action and then betray him to the authorities. The authorities organised their own gunmen to shoot down anarchists. The employers, exasperated by the apparent inefficiency of the government in bringing men to justice also bought gunmen. By the end of 1918 there were at least four and possibly five gangs of assassins. The most coherent group was one which gloried in the name of Jóvenes Bárbaros, under the Radical Alejandro Lerroux who, in 1909 had exhorted the mobs to murder, arson and rape.* These gunmen were prepared to accept commissions for anyone. When the Armistice was signed between the allies and their enemies, gun-law, with its rule of reprisals and counter-reprisals and no overall authority, was too firmly established for an analagous end to violence in Spain.

With the strike over, life for Franco in Oviedo settled down to routine: parades, route marches and exercises with and without troops. In September 1918 he attended a field officers' course in marksmanship at which he met a Major José Millan Astray, a cadaverous man with rather wild eyes, thirteen years Franco's senior.

Millan Astray, whose retort to Unamuno "Death to Intelligence"† was to resound throughout the world in 1936 was a real Gallego, born in Corunna. His father was a lawyer who wrote poetry, newspaper articles and librettos for highly successful Zarzuelas, and who lived out the last years of his long life as a prison governor in Madrid. Millan Astray had a sister, Pilar, who in her day was a popular novelist. He had seen active service in the Philippines in 1898. After a period as an instructor in Spain, he had gone to Africa to organise a native police force in Larache. Silvestre had then had him transferred to the local *Regulares* which he had recruited on the lines similar to those of Berenguer. However, the *Regulares* of Larache had never been near those of Melilla and Ceuta, so that until the encounter at the rifle shooting course, Franco and Millan had never met. Both however had arrived at an important conclusion—that the text books on infantry tactics were sorely in need of revision: above all that Spanish infantry should be taught the use of ground in attack and defence. Soon afterwards Millan was posted to the *Comisión de Táctica* whose task was to be advisory on the re-writing of the text books. Franco returned to Oviedo, but neither officer would forget the other.

In Oviedo Franco tried to enthuse his fellow officers in the use of ground by showing them the practical advantages. In European terms, there was nothing revolutionary in his ideas on the use of cover or on the deployment of rifles and machine guns in mutual support, but they

---

* Before his assassination Prime Minister Dato appointed Martinez Anido, an ex-Africa officer nearing his sixties, to put an end to the political warfare of Anarchists, Socialists, Jóvenes Bárbaros and other groups of gunmen. His methods may be imagined from his confession that "he was but a surgeon and a doctor would have to take charge at a later stage". Martinez Anido was appointed "National surgeon" at a later stage in Spanish history by Generalissimo Franco.

† A mistranslation of *Muera la inteligencia*. It should be "Death to Intellectuals".

were novel enough to his Spanish contemporaries. He now asked to be sent to the Staff College (Escuela de Guerra). He was refused. The Staff College was for captains and lieutenants. Franco replied that it was not his fault that he had been promoted Major at such a young age.

Franco however was not entirely loath to remain in Oviedo. On his arrival he had attracted attention as one unusually short and young to be wearing a major's star. In photographs of the time his waist was not slender, but it must be remembered that he had been wounded in the abdomen and that Spanish officers' uniforms were not tailored to the body as skilfully as those of German or British officers.* The people of Oviedo had dubbed him the "Comandantín"—the mini-Major. He became a familiar figure on horseback and as a visitor to the house of an upper middle-class family with a marriageable daughter, Carmen Polo. Her parents gave their consent to their marriage in the Autumn of 1920. However, in the September, Franco received a telegram from his friend Millan Astray who was now a lieutenant-colonel. It was a definite offer of a new appointment. Franco had been waiting for it for a longer time than for his marriage. His presence away from Oviedo was required as soon as possible. That meant either a quick wedding or none at all: but a quick wedding was out of the question. No Army officer was allowed to marry without the King's consent. The King's consent was unobtainable until after the whole machinery of discreet enquiry had been set in motion. The enquiries had to cover the social and political background of the bride's family, the sociality of the bride, and her strength of character and moral rectitude: it was all intended to avoid as far as possible scandalous behaviour after marriage and to ensure a measure of compatibility with other officers' wives.[24] The wedding had therefore to be postponed.

A few days later Major Francisco Franco was off to Africa, to soldiers who would sing of their new commander (to the tune of the Madelon) verses, the official text of which was the following:

> El Comandante Franco es un gran militar
> que aplazó su boda para ir a luchar.
> (Franco the Major is a military toff:
> To go out and fight he put his bride off.)

In Franco's three years of peace in Spain more Spaniards had met a violent death than in the Africa at war to which he was now returning.

* In later photographs his Sam Browne belt is drawn tighter.

NOTES

1. Francisco Franco Salgado Araujo: a first cousin of Nicolas Franco Salgado Araujo on both sides of the family, and therefore Generalissimo Franco's first cousin once removed: born 16th July 1890, he entered the Academy at Toledo a year later than Franco on 31st August 1908. He was posted to El Ferrol on being commissioned. He was to serve with Franco in Africa, in Asturias, become his cousin's aide-de-camp during the Civil War and Head of his Military Household after it. I am indebted to him for long talks and for placing at my disposal General Franco's personal records and his own manuscript life of Franco. It is adulatory, as could be expected, but it is factually most accurate, and rich in anecdotical detail.

2. Spain was in this respect thoroughly European. cf. Britain's views on her mission in the rest of Africa.

3. The Government's orders were that the *Regulares* were to be used as "shock troops" in the vanguard. The Spanish African Regiments were to be brought into action only when inevitable. Casualties to the Spanish troops it was hoped would thus be kept to a minimum.

4. J. M. Iribarren in *El General Mola*, Madrid, 1945, pp. 181 *ff*.

5. ibid.

6. Officer casualties in Africa were high and out of all proportion to O.R. casualties: a fact not to be ignored when considering the accuracy of the often repeated *simpliciste* statement that "the Army kept the war in Africa going".

7. Engagement details co-ordinated from Franco's and Mola's *Hojas*.

8. Quoted by Juan Valdes Rubio: *Acción de España en Marruecos*, Madrid, 1914, p. 25.

9. Franco was gazetted Captain on 15th April 1915 but his promotion was antedated to 1st February 1914, bearing in mind distinguished conduct in the relief of Izarduy on 12th January 1914.

10. cf. Juan de la Cosa, op. cit. *passim*.

11. Emilio Zurano Muñoz, *Consideraciones comerciales sobre España y Marruecos*, Madrid, 1913, quoted by Valdes op. cit., p. 20.

12. Valdes, p. 25.

13. Still extant in 1966.

14. Recorded in Franco's *Hoja*.

15. Jorge Vigón, *El General Mola*, Barcelona, 1957, p. 25.

16. Juan de la Cosa, op. cit., pp. 72 *ff*.

17. Dámaso Berenguer, *Campañas en el Riff y Yebala 1921–1922*, Madrid, 1923. Letter 4th February 1921 to Minister of War, pp. 232 *ff*.

18. Op. cit., pp. 963 *ff*.

19. Juan de la Cosa, pp. 72 *ff*.

20. Quoted by Burgos y Mazo, p. 109.

21. Cf. Madariaga, *Spain*, ch. XV.

22. Luis Ramirez in his book on Franco, p. 22, quotes an unnamed "senior officer" as saying that Franco and his men went out like "beasts of prey" to hunt down the miners.

23. Conversation with the author, June 1966 (abridged).

24. Queipo de Llano was a month in prison for marrying without the King's authority (*Hoja de Servicio*).

5

AFRICA 1920

New infantry tactics had not been the only subject of conversation between Millan Astray and Franco during their marksmanship course. Millan had a plan for the conduct of the war in Africa more personal and dearer to his heart. As Lenin believed that no revolution could succeed unless led by a body of professional revolutionaries, so Millan Astray was convinced that the war could be won only with a body at the vanguard of which every man from the private to the commanding officer was a professional soldier. Such professionalism could in neither case be expected from men of one single nationality. The patriotism of the Spaniards in the defence of their country had been proved second to none in their defeat of Napoleon's best troops. They had been enthusiastic to a degree marvelled at by Wellington who had nonetheless also expressed the wish that such enthusiasm had been backed by professional knowledge and skill.* In Africa Spanish troops had lacked enthusiasm. Though politicians and army officers drilled it into them that to fight in Africa was *"hacer patria"*,[1] that they were extending the frontiers of the motherland and therefore defending it, such subtlety spurred only the few. Only officers had had the three years of instruction in the fine points of what *honor* implied or meant. The enthusiasts on both sides had been the Moroccans, as *Regulares* or Irregulars, the professional *Regulares* led by professional Spanish officers having the edge on the enthusiastic irregulars.

According to Millan, it was not so much experience in Africa as a

* Franco, as Juan de la Cosa, *op. cit.* p. 92, with his conviction that Britain has ever been Spain's jealous and bitter enemy, misses the point of Wellington's views on the Spanish *guerrilleros*. British historians of the Peninsular War have rarely given them their full due, but so also on the other hand have Spanish historians of what to them were the Wars of Independence underestimated the importance of the British Expeditionary Forces under Sir John Moore and Wellington.

reading of the history of Spanish Civil Wars which led him one step beyond. "When I was a captain, and General Luque, Minister of War,* I was inspired by a study of the (First) Carlist War to think of a foreign legion for Morocco. In that war, an expeditionary force five thousand strong of the French Foreign Legion came to Spain to fight on the Liberal side. The Carlists recruited other foreign troops.† In June 1837, on the field of Barbastro, the two standards faced each other. They fought with ferocity. They were people who did not know of surrender."

This page of the history of the French Foreign Legion[2] led Millan to study its use in Africa, and to ask the sensible question: "If the French can do it, why can't we?" In July 1919 he submitted his ideas for a Spanish Foreign Legion to the Minister of War, General Tovar. Tovar was impressed both with the ideas and the man behind them. He passed them to the General Staff. Millan was sent to Algiers to study the French Foreign Legion's organisation, methods of recruitment and use in the field.[3] On 28th January 1920 a Royal Order in Council (*Real Ordenanza*) was published approving in principle the formation of a unit of foreign volunteers subject to further study by the Minister. General Villalba, Franco's old C.O., was now Minister of War—the tenth in just over three years; for Ministers of War naturally succeeded each other with the same frequency as Prime Ministers.‡ Villalba withheld the implementation of the Order in Council pending "the total reorganisation now being studied of the army in Africa". Villalba went out with the government in May. The new Minister, the Viscount of Eza, heard Millan lecture on the subject in the Circulo Militar.§ The proposed unit had been dubbed by critics within and outside the Army: "the misbegotten child of an unbalanced mind". It was said that it would attract no one but old lags, criminals, ne'er-do-wells, rebels against society and fools. Alternatively, that it would be a body

---

* General Luque was Minister of War between December 1915 and April 1917 under Romanones. He was of Republican sympathies when involved in the 1917 Juntas.

† Including quite a strong British detachment—but they were enthusiasts for the Carlist cause rather than professionals.

‡ The practical consequences to the Army are obvious: no man was ever long enough in office to reform it, or re-equip it properly and economically. What one Minister decided would be countermanded by the next; a matter unresolved at the moment of a change had to be studied from scratch by the new incumbent; the chances were that he would be out of office before he had finished his study of the matter. Each Minister, however, apparently believed that he would be longer in office than his predecessors. (cf. Mola, *op. cit.* pp. 950-63.)

§ Spanish equivalent of the R.U.S.I.

available to all countries wanting a disciplinary force. Millan Astray disabused the Minister who in the end promised the lecturer: "I'll give you your Legion." True to his word, on 31st August the Minister put before the King for his Royal Assent the warrant formally authorising recruitment to commence. Millan Astray, now promoted to lieutenant-colonel, was appointed commander. A second warrant, dated 4th September, laid down the Unit's composition. It would have in the first place three *banderas*, "Colours" or battalions, each battalion with two rifle and one machine-gun company, a platoon of sappers and miners and baggage and ammunition trains. It was a more compact and mobile organisation than the ordinary Spanish infantry battalion which had four and sometimes more rifle companies. Immediately afterwards large posters showing a soldier in the act of running up a flag, his eyes fixed on the sky, were pasted on hoardings and put up in recuiting offices, of which the Spanish army had so many that no less than fifty-four colonels were employed in their administration. The legend on the posters read: "*Alistáos en la Legión de Extranjeros.*—Join the Legion of Foreigners!"*

---

* The original January Order-in-Council and subsequent Warrants all speak of a Tercio de Extranjeros. Millan Astray and the officers sympathetic to his ideas called it La Legión, and would never refer to it as the Tercio. Each word has interesting connotations. The great Spanish infantry before which the armies of Europe had trembled and fled in the sixteenth and even well into the seventeenth century had been composed of units of pikemen, arquebusiers and crossbowmen combined into *tercios*. That long invincible Spanish infantry had admitted foreigners into its ranks. The name therefore was not inapt for the new formation with its combination of rifles and light and heavy machine guns. The Legion's Badge recalled the *tercio*: a crown superimposed a combination of a crossbow, arquebus and pike. However, the word *legión* conjured in the Spanish mind the legions of the Roman Empire (in which so many Celt-Iberians served). It was much more in keeping with the Roman ethic of the Spanish officer. The battle cry which Millan Astray would give his Legion—*Viva la Muerte*—was in the Roman tradition. That is not to say that his Legion was not consciously modelled on the French legion (called by the Spaniards *Legion Extranjera*) whose real and fictitious exploits were the subject of paperback novelettes on sale in Spanish kiosks. Millan Astray was a rare bird: he was Franco-phil. He and all who were to belong to it would refer to it always as La Legion; if an officer asked Millan for news of the Tercio, he would reply—"Do you mean the Legion? I don't know anything about a Tercio". Eventually it would come to be known to the whole nation as La Legión; but notice never La Legión Extranjera, the Foreign Legion, the popular titles of the French prototype; in full it was La Legión de Extranjeros, the Legion of Foreigners. The distinction was subtle, but nationalistically impor-tant. Later, when the Legion was expanded to six and more banderas, the Tercio had two Legions, each legion having three (or more) batallions. but the Tercio was still La Legion—to the confusion of outsiders.

Millan Astray anticipated correctly that there would be no shortage of recuits. With the 1914–18 War only recently over there were mature men of many nationalities with no will to return home, no home to which to return, no office or profession to resume, or with habits of behaviour developed in war and socially unacceptable in times of peace. There were young men whom the armistice had defrauded of the occupation which the propagandists of all the nations at war had placed before them as ideal above all others during their formative years. Thus Germans, Austrians, Frenchmen, Italians and even Englishmen and a North American Negro were among the first to join. There were also Central and South Americans, exiles from revolutions at home, or men to whom Spain was still their true home even after a century and a half of legal independence. Finally, there were Spaniards who had completed their compulsory or enlisted service with the Colours of the Spanish army, the Civil Guard or the Carabiniers, young men with the spirit of adventure, men who, as Franco wrote, "were born to be soldiers and nothing else".[4]

In his mind Millan had already selected his corps of officers long before his Legion had been approved and he had been appointed to command it. "From the day I had the luck to meet Franco, I perceived, as all did, very clearly and in high relief, his extraordinary qualifications and aptitudes . . . appreciating to the full the magnitude of the task, I was right on the target in judging that it would need the help of extraordinary men and in particular of the one who would be my second-in-command. He had to be complementary to me, to fill in all that I lacked to bring the undertaking to full development. I thought of no one else than Franco for the job. I explained briefly to him my ideas and wishes. Equally quickly he answered: 'I'll be your second-in-command'."[5] Thus it was that towards the end of September Millan Astray had wired Franco in Oviedo formally offering him the post, and that Franco had wired back his acceptance, postponed his wedding indefinitely and now on 10th October took the ferry boat at Algeciras for Ceuta and Millan Astray.

Franco kept a diary covering the period October 1920 to May 1922 and he published it that same year in Spain under the title *Diario de Una Bandera*, the Journal of a Battalion. It is a book halfway between the war diary of a British Army formation and the memoirs of an army officer. He wrote nothing more self-revealing. Its uniqueness can be appreciated only when its style and contents are compared with those of his military and civilian contemporaries. Millan Astray also wrote of the Legion and later of Franco himself. No two writers could be more different. Franco is the cold, detached observer who only rarely uses the first person, who prefers the impersonal form of a verb. By Spanish standards he is restrained in his use of epithets and in his praise of other men—or of himself. He would never have written of himself "I perceived . . . I appreciated to the full the magnitude of the task. . . . I was right on the target. . . ." Millan Astray was right. Franco and he were complementary. Millan Astray was an heroic figure, a dashing commander with flashes of inspiration, impetuous in thought, word and deed—some would say half mad. Franco was meticulous, the organiser, a hard worker, staid and rarely perturbed. Notoriously fearless in battle, his was the bravery of the cold-blooded: Millan Astray's that of the exalted, the phrenetic.

The crossing was uneventful. There were on board with Franco a hundred or so recruits for the new Legion. He watched their somewhat rowdy behaviour on deck "with the understanding of those who are about to tread a common path".

As the ferry approached Ceuta, a figure in a launch waved to them. "There's the C.O." writes Franco, momentarily warm, "and the boat brings the raw material for the work." The C.O. and second-in-command embraced. Millan Astray spoke to one of the recruits: "Do you know why you have come? I'll tell you. You're here to die. Yes. To die. This side of the Straits you have no mother, girlfriend, family. From now on the Legion will be your all. You've still got a moment to make up your mind whether you're prepared for the sacrifice. Think about it and tell your Captain of your decision." He addressed the men briefly on the quayside. They were marched to the barracks where on a parade ground, Millan Astray addressed them again, now with his more usual eloquence and at greater length. The Legion, he said, offered oblivion of the past, honour and glory for the future. They would receive the promised pay and allowances promptly; they would be able to earn the stripes of N.C.O.s and even the stars of commissioned officers, but at the price of constant sacrifice, hardship and danger. Many would die, he said, perhaps all of them. They were still free to go.

Franco confesses that he was moved by the address.

Together the batch then swore to die for the Legion; but a medical inspection weeded out twenty as unfit for service, among them a youth who had returned to the world on the eve of taking his vows in a monastery. Later he had asked the Prior for re-admission. According to his story, as retold by Franco, the youth had been told by the Prior to join the Legion and if after four years he still felt he had a vocation, he could return.[5] Appeals against the medical decisions were rejected. Those accepted were given their engagement pay which they spent "in a few days of orgy, in farewell to the pleasures and attractions of town life".

It was goodbye also to the town. The new formation was to camp at Riffien, four miles outside the city. Millan Astray's immediate orders to Franco were to improve what was there. Riffien was to become the depot. Franco ordered drilling for water to begin immediately. Until they found it they were dependent on supplies brought in jars from Ceuta. In a few days they had enough for their immediate needs. Millan next ordered the establishment of a farm to supply fresh meat. Franco planned it, and put his old friend Alonso Vega, whom he had brought with him from Oviedo, on the job. It proved to be a most successful commercial venture.[7] Its piggeries alone brought a net profit of 60,000 pesetas (£2,400) to the Legion in its second year of operation, and there were cattle, rabbits and chickens as well. The Legionaries demanded better food than the Army supplied.* Some years later Franco had a reservoir built for one hundred thousand gallons of water. The water was piped from a mountain spring some distance away. With leather and shoe workshops and weapon and wagon repair shops, stabling and good permanent quarters, the Legion came to have a depot of which it could be proud. It became the envy of other Spanish regiments. We may add, not in a spirit of criticism but of fact, and to give Millan Astray and Franco their full due, that what they provided for their Legion was no more than any British regiment of the time enjoyed. Millan's praise of Franco as "a great engineer— planner . . . above all a town-planner" was hyperbole, but no less so than the criticisms levelled against them by their civilian compatriots as "men who pampered the army and who saw to it that the best was for the army".[8] In the Spanish, no less than the British Army since Sir John Moore, young officers had been instructed that their prime concern was the welfare of their men. Millan, unlike many of his contemporaries in the army as well as in civilian life, realised that a fighting force had to be fed well at all times and that it had to have the opportunities for real rest, when rest was possible, if it was to be efficient.

* Franco-Salgado, who joined the Legion with his cousin, placed a standing order for tea with a London store—for British legionaries. (Conversations with the author.)

By 16th October the first and other batches of recruits had been sorted out into three companies which together formed the first *Bandera* or battalion. Millan appointed Franco as its Commanding Officer. Franco was therefore again in command of non-Spanish troops. He ordered training square and rifle drill to begin immediately. It was as well he did. Within a few days his battalion had its first General's review. The companies, in parade order, were called to attention by the bugler. A Spanish military band struck up "God Save the King". The General passed down the lines to the tune of Tipperary.[9]

Two weeks later Franco's battalion was again on the move.

During Franco's three years in Oviedo the situation in Africa had changed very little. In the east, Spain continued to exercise some control of the zone bounded by the River Kert, the Garet Plain and the Mulaya River. In the west General Gomez Jordana had succeeded under orders and against his judgement in negotiating a pact with the Raisuni, as a result of which Spain was able to occupy and move freely along a coastal strip of up to ten miles from Larache, round the Straits to Tetuan. With that, some 20,000 men had been repatriated to Spain. Each of the six governments in power during the years 1917 and 1918 had ordered Jordana to keep the Raisuni quiet, though he warned each in turn that the Raisuni was not to be trusted; he repeatedly informed them that the Moroccan rebel had been in touch with the Germans—presumably offering to harrass the French if they in turn provided him help against the Spaniards—that he was making impossible demands of arms and money on the excuse that he needed them to keep his tribesmen in peace as Spain wanted, that he treated the High Commissioner with contempt, and that he would break with Spain at the moment he thought it would give him maximum advantage. Under the terms of the pact the Raisuni had agreed to the passage of Spanish troops through Fondak. In fact, as Jordana informed his government in November 1918, the Raisuni did so only when it pleased him. There had been attacks in the outskirts of Larache and Ceuta. Many *Regulares* had deserted to the Raisuni because it had become evident that he could do what he liked against the Spaniards. In brief he was the real master of the Spanish Protectorate in the west, except for the coastal strip. Jordana died urging the Spanish Government to act. They did—as usual half-heartedly. Jordana's successor, Berenguer, was authorised to break with the Raisuni if the Raisuni did not mend his ways; and in October 1919 Berenguer at long last occupied Fondak. With that, however, the Spanish effort had been spent for the year. In this the troops had pushed along the mountain ridges from Fondak. They occupied the holy city of Sheshawen (Xauen) on 20th October, but their hold was precarious as the road to it over the mountains passed dangerously close to the Raisuni's headquarters at Tazarut in the Ben-Aros region of the Riff. So Berenguer now pushed along the coast some thirty miles to the mouth of the Lau Wadi (Uad Lau) from which there was an alternative route to Xauen. However, flanking tribes of the Gomara had not yet formally submitted to Spain, so it was essential to reinforce the position at Uad Lau with whatever troops were available.

Accordingly on 2nd November Franco was ordered to take there his half-trained men. It was a three-day march from Riffien. They passed Tetuan at midday on the second day. That evening the wagon train lost its way along the mountain tracks; and there was no meal for the men that night. Maps were primitive. However both the main body and the wagons met at their destination.

For the moment nothing more was required of Franco's battalion than to hold Uad Lau against possible attack. Franco, therefore, had the opportunity of converting a chance conglomeration of men into a coherent fighting force. The men were of so many different nationalities and of such different backgrounds. Even the Spaniards were a mixed bunch. There were a couple of circus clowns. There was another who was recognised by a young officer returning his salute as his father. Among the foreigners there were veterans of a major war to whom the equipment and weapons with which they were issued must have seemed exceedingly antiquated and inadequate; Mausers of 1893 vintage: the earliest of Hotchkiss machine guns, and ammunition mostly of the right calibre but of very mixed origin. Franco's task therefore was not easy. There was nothing except the future to bind the men together. There was no common patriotism. The very Colour on which they swore allegiance was, as Franco wrote, "not their own as yet". Even their marching song, the Madelon, was borrowed.

The battalion took over the Uad Lau camp from Moorish *Regulares*. It was in an ideal position, just over a mile from the sea, and with the River on one side. Franco had the dirty brown canvas tents of the camp followers struck and taken to its outskirts. The lines were tidied and made habitable. Discipline would make up what was lacking in quality of equipment. Legionaries were expected to wash in the river on rising, and take a swim in the sea during the day. They were allowed to rise late only on Sundays; but Sunday afternoons were for football, and boxing matches. The weekdays were fully taken up with arms drill and tactical exercises. In the evenings, when they were free, they could wander down to the beach, to the wells frequented by the Moorish women from the villages, or towards the Moorish bars and coffee tents. Wine was available only to those provided with a chit signed by a captain. "Too much drunkenness", writes Franco in his account of those early days, "made necessary the limitation of the consumption of liquor." Gaming was totally forbidden to officers and men; but a man could wager to beat another in boxing or marksmanship. The battalion champion shot was a Swiss; the boxer the North American Negro. Quarrels between the men had also to be resolved with gloves. As a special concession Franco allowed intoxicating spirits on Christmas Day.

Early in January security precautions were redoubled at Uad Lau as rumours multiplied of an impending Moroccan attack. Barbed wire fences were constructed. Machine-gun posts were manned by night and outposts were established to watch the fords across the Wadi. A few shots were fired one night at a party taking coffee to the outposts, and the Legion had its first casualty: the coffee orderly was wounded in the leg. Otherwise, either Army intelligence was at fault, or the Moroccans had second thoughts. There was no attack.

In April Berenguer decided that the time had come for an all-out offensive against the Raisuni. The first stage would be receiving the submission of the Gomara tribes, after the use of force if necessary. With the flank guaranteed for an advance up the Lau, a major force would move up to the holy city. With the holy city fortified, a junction would be established across the mountain down to Ksar-el-Kebir and Larache. Thus the Raisuni and the Ben-Aros Mountains would be rounded. The final stage would be a combined attack from Larache, Tetuan and Xauen on Raisuni's stronghold.

Uad Lau then became the assembly point and point of departure of a column under the command of a Colonel Castro Girona. Three battalions of the Legion, one thousand *Regulares*, a body of Moroccan cavalry, light infantry and artillery—say about three thousand men in all—prepared to proceed along the Gomara coast. Franco notes at the eve of departure: "The legionaries slept little . . . an invasion of liquor cellars left a train of drunken men . . . hard liquor had to be strictly prohibited."

The pacification of Gomara took a week. There was no resistance and the column returned intact to its base. The next stage was not quite so peaceful. To the chagrin of Millan Astray and Franco, Castro Girona, the Column Commander put the Legion in the main guard as the Column advanced up the Lau towards Xauen. Franco seemingly learned a lesson here from the veterans of the European war. Sniped at as they advanced, Franco asked an Austrian corporal: "Why don't your fire back?" The Austrian corporal replied: "There's no point in wasting ammunition when you can't see your attacker."

Franco had long dreamt of seeing Xauen with its dozen minarets. His account gives the impression that he was not disappointed with the reality: "It has the peace of Maghreb population centres: steep narrow streets cover the higher part of the town where olive trees glimpse through high-angled red tiled roofs: there is a high crenellated wall round the city giving it a resemblance to our picturesque Andalusian towns. The thick walls of the citadel rise above the centre . . . the lower part of the town is more interesting . . . with its box-like shops offering cloth and hooded cloaks of rich wool made on primitive looms. Sellers of sandals abound . . . with their wares suspended forming as it were columns flanking the niches that are the shops. The mill quarter to the south is one of the city's prettiest. The River jumps over the boulders and moves the mill wheels." What really impressed him was: "The crystal clear water of the city runs through canals between leaf-laden trees. Water is the real treasure of this town. . . ."

The blockhouse system was extended northwards towards Zuk-el-Arba and westwards to establish the link with Ksar-el-Kebir. The Raisuni was now surrounded. The time had come for the final stage of the operation to begin. The net was drawn tighter. To reinforce the troops which had originated from Larache, the second battalion of the Legion was detached. The first and third moved into Zuk-el-Arba. There they came under command of Sanjurjo now a Brigadier. Millan and Franco prevailed upon Sanjurjo to let the Legion lead the attack on at least one occasion. It did so on 29th June in what proved to be a heavy engagement. In his despatch of the day General Berenguer who had had his doubts of their value paid tribute to the *Tercio de Extranjeros*. The Moroccans fell back on Ben-Aros. Franco's battalion entered Zuk-Khemis-des-Beni-Aros, the townlet nearest Tazarut, on 16th July. An ultimatum was sent to the Raisuni. He had till Friday, the 22nd, to surrender or face the final onslaught of fifteen thousand Spaniards. On the night of 21st Franco and his 1st battalion settled down on the slopes overlooking the white houses of their final objective. The 3rd battalion of the Legion was alongside. The two battalions were confident that they would take it on the morrow. So were the newspapers on sale in Madrid that day.

At two o'clock on the morning of the 22nd Franco heard Millan Astray shouting for him. "What's happened? I asked. 'A battalion has got to leave for Fondak as quickly as possible. I don't know what for or where. Toss up for it with the 3rd battalion. It's as likely to be a garrison job in the rear guard as action.' " It fell to Franco to prepare to move northwards to an unknown destination.

That weekend the newspapers of the western world carried news of a reverse. By the Monday, 25th July, the Feast of St. James and Spain's National Day, correspondents in Tangiers and Madrid had pieced together enough details of what had occurred on the previous Thursday to know that Spain had suffered a major defeat. By the Monday Franco also knew, as did every officer in Africa; but as he and the commander of the 3rd battalion tossed for who should have the honour of capturing the Raisuni on the following day, and who should answer the call for what might be "perhaps a rear guard job, perhaps a garrison job," only a "hunch" told Franco that "something was wrong in Melilla". That "something wrong" was to absorb the minds of politicians for half a generation.

Spanish troops in the eastern end of the Riff had not been inactive while Berenguer encircled the Raisuni. General Silvestre, either under orders which everyone subsequently denied having given, or on his own initiative with or without the approval of King Alfonso XIII himself, had decided to open up the way from Melilla to Al-Hoceima. The distance was eighty miles by the shortest and one hundred by the easiest route. Spain had for centuries held the little island fortress in the Bay of Al-Hoceima. The two enclaves would now be linked. In May 1920 Silvestre had crossed the Kert, and over the next seven months had advanced the Spanish front over broken and difficult mountain between ten and twenty miles westward and to a depth of twenty miles from the sea. On 15th January 1921 he had occupied the village with the name that was to haunt Spain for the next fifteen years—An-Nwal. Even more difficult terrain lay ahead. Snow began to fall. Silvestre hibernated. In the Spring he pushed forward of An-Nwal outwards to Abaran, on the very edge of the descent to Al-Hoceima, and Igueriben. Igueriben was only about three miles from An-Nwal, but to reach it the Spaniards had to negotiate an awkward escarpment.

There Silvestre halted the advance. He was now stretched to his utmost. The Spanish troops in the region totalled twenty-five thousand, but his long lines of communications by mule absorbed a large number of them. Furthermore ahead of him, a young Moroccan who had been educated in Spain was rallying the tribes against him. He had a grievance against Spain, His name was to be in every newspaper in the west for years to come—it was Abdel Krim. During the 1914–18 war he had shared pro-Kaiser sympathies with many Spaniards. From Melilla he had helped Abdel Malek to harrass the French. At France's request, he had been imprisoned in Melilla. In an attempt at breaking his confinement he had broken a leg. On his release after the war he had returned to his homestead at Axdir-des-Beni-Urriakel, five miles the Melilla side of Al-Hoceima. Against Silvestre's advance, he now had the tribes around him.

On 1st June Abdel Krim attacked Abaran. He went for a Spanish battery. It was situated on top of a hill, as was Spanish practice, and exposed to any infantry attack. It was bravely defended by a young lieutenant, but the forces deployed against him were overpoweringly strong. Six days later one thousand *Regulares* who were supposed to have gone to his assistance murdered their officers and joined Abdel Krim. These officers were no longer of the calibre of Mola or Franco. Berenguer's volunteer basis had been superseded by a rota system. All army officers now had to do a two-year period of foreign service. The incentives—quicker promotion and monetary awards—for service in Africa had been abolished. Few of these new officers suffered easily the discomforts of service in the field after the ease and luxury of Peninsular garrison duty. They had a minimum of Arabic, whereas older officers had been reasonably proficient in the language of the men under their command. They made little conscious effort to understand the Muslim religion or culture, and had little sympathy for it or for its adherents.

Silvestre wrote to Madrid of "a dark cloud which gives rise to serious doubts". News of the dissertion of the *Regulares* with their arms and ammunition was kept from the general public. The despatch of more troops from the Peninsula was politically inexpedient. There had been yet another change of government. In the March the Prime Minister, Eduardo Dato, had been despatched by three Anarchists, one of whom had sought refuge in Moscow and another in Bonn, leaving the third to pay the price of their joint action. The new government had promised the Radicals and Socialists that the troops in Africa were adequate for the plans in hand.

Abdel Krim now lulled the Spaniards into a false sense of security by doing nothing for week after week. Then suddenly, on 17th July, Igueriben was surrounded. Determined attempts were made to supply the position with water. Spanish officers—other than Franco, one of whose men was to complain to him that he did not know he had joined the Legion to dig wells like a black—were still indifferent to the high cost in lives of not making posts self-sufficient in water. Igueriben had been held for several months. There had been enough time to find water or to reconsider its value in defence. The escarpment had made access to it from An-Nwal awkward enough even without thousands of men attacking supply columns. At the end of forty-eight hours in the blazing July of Morocco, the situation was desperate. A whole company failed to reach the besieged men even under covering fire from the whole of the forces at An-Nwal. From Melilla General Silvestre ordered the men in Igueriben to withdraw. They were beaten back to their isolated positions. He now decided to take over command personally in a desperate attempt to save the men. He gathered what troops he could and hastened to An-Nwal. From An-Nwal on the morning of the 21st, he led his men in the classic nineteenth-century column formation towards the besieged garrison now raving with thirst and drinking urine sweetened with sugar. Silvestre, beaten back to An-Nwal, ordered the garrison of Igueriben to break out if it could. A handful of men succeeded. By the end of the day four thousand Spaniards were dead or missing.

Silvestre's surviving officers held a Council of War that evening and decided to take no more orders from their general. There are several contradictory versions as to what happened next. According to the Spanish military unwritten code, Silvestre should have gone out to the field when his defeat was self-evident, and exposed himself to enemy fire until he was killed.[10] He had not done so. According to the same code, the Council of War was not necessarily an act of mutiny but a trial for incompetence—the sentence being death by suicide. Whether or not Silvestre carried out this sentence, totally contrary to his nominal religion, has been argued ever since. Suicide was the "correct thing", and his fellow officers long gave him the benefit of the doubt.

Without Silvestre the remnants of the An-Nwal garrison scurried to the next post ten miles back. They were short of ammunition. Abdel Krim came after them in hot pursuit. The morale of the Spaniards was broken; they panicked. The withdrawal became a rout. There were deeds of heroism as individual officers tried to rally their men. The troops however were now terrified. Abel Krim was taking no prisoners. Those who surrendered were "passed under the knife". By the Saturday night close on seventy fortified positions had fallen. Silvestre's second-in-command, General Navarro, held out in Mount Arruit twenty-two miles from Melilla, but the enemy by-passed the position and took to the mountains, the Gurugu of Franco's earliest days in Africa, and appeared on the crests overlooking Melilla.

By the Saturday night Franco was aboard the old ferry boat *Ciudad de Cadiz* with his battalion. The second battalion which had not had so difficult a journey from Suk-el-Arba—and which had not lost its way —was also aboard; so in another ship were two *tabores* (battalions) of *Regulares* and three mountain batteries. The commander of the rapidly gathered force was Sanjurjo, with Millan Astray as his second-in-command as well as Commander of the Legion. Their plan to capture the Raisuni had been abandoned. Berenguer, the High Commissioner, who had taken the fastest boat he could find to Melilla that morning, now radioed Sanjurjo from the city he had just reached: "Make full speed". A telegram was followed a few hours later by a second: "Make full speed. Presence of troops urgently necessary". It was Sunday morning. Franco adds succinctly: "A day of obligation. They tell us there's a Mass on: we go, but our thoughts are with the [Navarro] column in retreat".

The old boat even with its boilers at bursting point did not reach Melilla until two o'clock in the afternoon. There was a mass of people on the dockside, and on the balconies of the houses by the waterside. One of the High Commissioner's aides-de-camp rushed aboard: "Army HQ in Melilla has been laid flat: Army has been defeated: The city is wide open: the town has gone mad, panic-stricken: no news of the Navarro column: your job is to raise the morale of the inhabitants: restore its confidence: anything you can think of will be less than sufficient".[11]

Spanish *colons* were the destroyers of the Army headquarters—enraged at both the inefficacy of an army which had allowed itself to be defeated and at the Spanish Government which "had let them down". It had been the arrival of terrified dishevelled men women and children from the hinterland which had caused the panic, rather than the imminence of the Abel Krim troops; for the enemy had in fact turned away from their military targets to the looting of the dead and the slaughter and castration of the wounded. In the final reckoning the number of the Spanish dead and missing from 17th to the surrender of

Navarro who held out in Mount Arruit until 29th was to reach the total
of fourteen thousand, seven hundred and seventy-two men. 29,504
rifles, 392 machine guns and 129 field guns had been captured by the
enemy. Abdel Krim had deprived Spain in a few days of all that she
had gained in twelve years of fighting and of negotiations with
Moroccan tribesmen.

The propensity of the Moroccan to turn away from battle in order
to loot the dead and dying and the fidelity to Spain of one Arab chief-
tain, Abdel Kader, with lands immediately to the south of the city,
saved Melilla from capture in the early hours of the Sunday. Now in the
afternoon, it was up to the Legion to save the people from themselves—
the Legion alone, for the people feared that the *Regulares* who had
arrived with them—might be no more loyal than those who were now
with the enemy. The legionaries were given orders, which they
obeyed, to laugh and sing and shout Long Live Spain; and the crowd
took up the cries and applauded the Legion as it marched in full dress
order through the streets of the city, Franco at the head of the 1st
battalion with its black standard, and behind the 2nd battalion of
Franco's friend Fontanes with his red standard. This was the Legion's
finest hour—or rather it was that of Millan Astray. In his sharp and
penetrating voice he had addressed the people at the quayside: "people
of Melilla: the Legion which comes to save you salutes you. We are
prepared to die for you. We are under the orders of the heroic General
Sanjurjo and we shall triumph! Away with fear! The breasts of the
Legion stand between you and the enemy. Long live Spain. Long live
Melilla. Long live the Legion."

In a very real sense the Legion, two battalions strong, had captured
a city without firing a shot. Months of hard fighting lay ahead. Sanjurjo
sent the battalions out post-haste to man the defences on the southern
approaches to the city, the most vulnerable: the *Regulares* were dispatched to the western approaches, the Gurugu positions. The Legion
moved southwards. It met survivors "naked, or with no more than a
shirt, half-conscious, half out of their minds. They tell of being hunted
down and of Moroccan women cutting off the privy parts of those
caught on the run." On the Tuesday Franco looked down from the
slopes of Sidi Hamed, on Nador, a township ten miles south of Melilla.
Let Franco here take up the story: "We could see Nador clearly. There
were groups moving round the church. The town was on fire. Big
columns of smoke rose from the railway station and the tobacco
factory. Other houses were already gutted. On the plain we could see

mules laden with booty. From a house rather higher than most, and closer to the sea, we saw the flash of a heliograph. We advanced to the very limit of the slope. Orders forbad us to go further. Since we were so near, we asked permission to go to their relief. The order to advance not even one step more was repeated. We must bide our time until the fortifications are completed. We speak to the General. Our lieutenant-colonel is with him. We again ask permission to go to the aid of those holding out. The General expresses sympathy. He, too, would like to go to Nador but our job is to save Melilla and to defend it, and we are alone." There occurs then in Franco's diary a phrase in which the answer may lie to one of Franco's more inexplicable military decisions in the Spanish Civil War. From the context it would appear that he is quoting Sanjurjo: *"En la guerra hay que sacrificar el corazón"*— *"In war the heart must be sacrificed"*.[12]

Franco did not give up immediately: if not a battalion, a company: if not a company, a platoon. At which Sanjurjo agreed "provided you can find Moroccans to go with you". None would. Over the next week Franco watched the garrison of Nador die a slow death.

Nothing beyond a holding operation could be undertaken until a new army had been built up with reinforcements from Ceuta and Spain. During the next seven weeks the Legion was employed on three tasks. It was used piecemeal to stiffen inexperienced or untrustworthy formations—a platoon here, another there, and a company in the third place. It manned the more dangerous strong points and blockhouses, and it established new ones. It took the vanguard of columns covering the transport of supplies of water, food and ammunition to outposts. The Legion was here, there and everywhere. Casualties were frequent and on occasions heavy, as when in the supplying of the 120-strong advance position of Casabona, ninety out of a total of three hundred legionaries in the operation were killed or wounded as well as one hundred of a *tabor* of the *Regulares* who were with them. Nevertheless the relief of Casabona was the turning point. The Moroccans were entrenched waiting for the supply column to pass. Franco led the vanguard away to attack the Moroccans before they should attack him. Making full use of available cover his troops remained unobserved until they were almost on top of the Moroccan trenches. The Moroccans were forced out at bayonet point. Next, and again contrary to normal Spanish practice, Franco made his men stand their ground for the inevitable counter-attack. Moroccan losses were far heavier than Spanish. Abdel

Krim had suffered his first serious reverse. On the column's return to base, Sanjurjo embraced Franco, and the Legion received a special mention in Berenguer's despatches—the first of many.

By mid-September Berenguer had between fifty and sixty thousand men in Melilla. They were, he wrote: "a hotchpotch of units, deficient in armament, instruction and fitness, with battalions of as few as four hundred and fifty".[13] Their value in an offensive was extremely doubtful. However he decided to do what he could, using the Legion and the *Regulares*, now under command of Lieutenant-Colonel Emilio Mola, as the spearhead. The first objective was to be Nador. A column was assembled under the command of General Sanjurjo. Franco's battalion was to lead the advance, with Emilio Mola's *Regulares* on his right. The column was ready to move at 0700 hours when floating batteries began shelling the Moroccan positions at Nador from the sea. Millan Astray, who had been absent for most of August on a recruiting mission in Spain, moved up to Franco's forward sections to point out to Franco his objectives in the assault. As he stood beside Franco a bullet went through his chest. As he was carried away Sanjurjo ordered the advance. Franco took over command of the whole legion, the spearhead of the attack.

In the diary Franco is at his best in his description of the battle. It is almost a film shooting script.

The legionaries advance with determination running along the edge of the wadi. They leave behind the fallen whom indefatigable stretcher bearers carry to cover. Some stretcher bearers are carrying a wounded soldier. The enemy lead downs one of them. The other pushes the stretcher into a ditch. Another soldier dying wants a word with us. We stop for a few seconds. He dies making the efforts to speak. Another with a bullet in his chest runs to our side. He continues to fight. . . . The advance retains its momentum. The first slope is crowned. . . . Long Live the Legion! The enemy turns to flight. . . . It's a pity that having to leave detachments on the way: we are left without reserves to pursue the enemy.

Colonel Castro Girona comes up to our side.

. . . Shall we push on to Monte Arbos?

—Straightaway.

Without one waiting for the others we advance rapidly before the enemy can reform. On the way we pass dead Moors. There is a young and pretty Moroccan girl on the field. Her white clothes have over her heart an enormous red stain: her forehead is still warm. Poor little dead child, a victim of war.[14]

The day's casualties in Franco's battalion were light: eight dead and twenty-five wounded.

Franco entered Nador on the following day. The town had an unbearable smell. The Spanish dead of several weeks were still unburied. The Rebels had killed also all the Spanish civilian inhabitants and sacked the town.

Franco's battalion rested six days there, burying the dead and clearing up the chaos of the town.

The offensive thereafter had the River Kert as its objective along the two roads to it from Nador. The Legion, and in particular Franco's battalion, was switched from one to the other repeatedly. Franco therefore took part in all the major engagements—the storming of the Gurugu which he knew so well, and of height after height on the northern route to Segangan, the recapture of Mount Arruit and of Dar Drius on the southern, townlets where the Spaniards found scenes of horror as repugnant as those in Nador. The Legion suffered heavy losses at some points and Franco complained that the replacements he was being sent were under-trained. Even so the Legion remained the spearhead of a whole army. There were days of triumph and others of anxiety. There was a moment in the Gurugu operation of which Franco wrote cryptically: "The moral co-efficient of the troops is being overtaken and the left flank wavers at a number of points. They are moments of great emotion. We pour men and spirit into the threatened sector. The Legion's wagon line runs to help and attack the enemy: the muleteers of our machine gun sections and combat train leave their animals and go in counter attack. The Moroccan attack is beaten back all along the line. On the heights the legionaries outdo each other in enthusiasm . . . some regain a machine gun from another unit which with its crew dead is in danger of falling into the hands of the enemy. . . ." Franco now insisted on his officers and men making full use of natural cover in the approach, but he still believed in leading the final assault in person and in the value to the morale of his troops of exposing himself to enemy fire. He was a fervent disciple of the bayonet school. No weapon in his opinion could break the enemy's morale more quickly.

Franco was now a by-word, almost a legend, among his men as a commander who did not waste lives unnecessarily; among the *Regulares* who were usually to one or other flank of him, he was regarded as the beloved of Allah whom no bullet could touch even when "a sitting target on horseback": among army officers generally as a remarkable innovator in the tactics of advance and withdrawal—they were new to the Spanish Army. Newspaper readers in Spain were repeatedly reading of his exploits.

Dar Drius was recaptured in January 1922. February and March were spent in consolidating the ground gained. Political crises at home and constant opposition to the continuance of the war any further now that national honour and prestige lost at An-Nwal had been retrieved led to the withdrawal of twenty thousand men from Melilla. While it was being argued whether the advance should be continued up to Al-Hoceima and until Abdul Krim had been punished for his rebellion, Franco took a few days leave to visit his mother at El Ferrol. He returned just in time to see the first use of tanks in Africa. Their sight disconcerted the enemy. However, they ran out of petrol and were abandoned—to the delight of conservative officers but not of Franco who saw in them their possibilities. "Tanks are no good for Morocco," became a favourite cry among army officers.[15] On the contrary, said Franco, they were the answer; but they would have to be like those in use in foreign armies, that is with two machine guns and not one which broke down. The Hotchkiss was not bad in its way, but it had to have good ammunition "not the mixture we use". The enemy had nothing to stop tanks; but their crews would have to be trained to perfection. Tactics to ensure the mutual support of one tank by another had to be worked out. "Men, not materials, are the dearest commodity in war."

Franco, too, had shown his colleagues the use of aircraft in a way which they had not considered. His brother Ramon, who had transferred from the *Regulares* to the infant Spanish Air Force, had arrived in Melilla in 1921. Thereafter Franco had used his brother's seaplane to reconnoitre enemy positions. On one occasion his brother ditched him in the sea.[16]

That is not in the *Diary*; but what is is Franco's own assessment of Spanish Army shortcomings. Franco recommended an increase in automatic weapons and a consequent reduction in rifles. He notes sourly that there were neither hand nor rifle grenades available in this campaign, vital though they were in blockhouse defence. His men had to improvise them out of nails, food tins and gunpowder.[17] His main criticism, however, was of men rather than materials: "In the *quality* and not the quantity of troops lies the answer to the problem. . . . Recruiting officers must have volunteers, and the volunteers must have incentives. . . . Rest and good living standards . . . but the volunteer depends like all soldiers on good officers . . . enthusiastic and brave, to instill in them ideals which need more than a handful of pesetas . . . there must be incentives for an officer to become a specialist in war and to know the enemy and not to be dreaming of the day he will return home to Spain. . . . Well-trained officers, not those of which the native troops say 'Lieutenant X not know how', men tied to text-books . . . in this campaign we have frequently seen cases in which because of 'not know how' the number of casualties has been high." Of An-Nwal he writes: "Let us examine our conscience: let us look at our dormant virtues and we shall find there the crisis of ideals which turned into a rout what should have been no more than a slight set-back. . . ." He ends his *Diary* with a panegyric for the men who stood their ground—*Regulares* and Spaniards alike.

Franco's treatment of death seems at first reading truly Spanish. It is stoical, Senecan. He can on occasion permit himself a moment of human grief or pity: "At that moment my faithful adjutant fell with his head pierced . . . from the forward positions two soldiers take his lifeless body. With sorrow I see going from my side for ever my faithful and loved Baron de Misena." The Baron had long been his adjutant. At second reading it is less Spanish, that is, it is not the treatment normal in a Spaniard of Catholic upbringing even when he is no longer a believer. There is nowhere a "God have Mercy".

Franco mentions religion five times only.[18] The first time he does so is in giving an account of Christmas Day 1920: "Christmas Eve was celebrated by the legionaries with a splendid supper; wine was plentiful and in brotherhood they spent the feast singing happily. The Germans asked permission to gather together. A Christmas tree with many lights marks out their place of feasting. The officers had hung bottles of German beer on the branches and they repaid the compliment by singing for us the songs of their country. As they sang their war hymn, there was sadness on their brows, and the eyes of an old man full of tears. The feast lasted till dawn when there was quiet in the camp. Wine flowed and yet there was not one incident." The second occasion was on board ship to Melilla when he confesses that he attended Mass but that his thoughts were not on the Mass. There is a reference to a Father Antonio Vidal, a Scolapian, attached as a volunteer to the Legion "dying gloriously" on the same day as Fontanes, the Commander of the second battalion. On another occasion he notes "at the foot of a cutting to the left and under cover from enemy fire the Chaplain of some formation aids the wounded. The stretchers are halted for a

moment as they pass and there is a hold-up as the blood-covered warriors receive absolution. The Legion's stretcher bearers bare their heads
and stand to attention as they watch the moving spectacle." There is
one reference to Mass in the field, and Franco mentions the Christian
Brothers burying the dead in Zeluan and Mount Arruit.

By the end of 1922 nearly all the territory lost after An-Nwal was
back in Spanish hands. The Legion took up a semi-permanent position
at Dar Drius. It was here that according to Franco it would have been
possible to have stopped Abdel Krim after An-Nwal.

Franco's *Diary* is written in praise of his men. For his own part in the
decisive engagements it is to his Army Record of Service, in the writing
of which he had no part, that we must turn. In June 1922 General
Sanjurjo recommended him for immediate promotion to lieutenant-
colonel for his part in the capture of Nador.[19] Berenguer, the G.O.C.,
recommended him for the Military Medal as well as promotion. Franco
did not get his promotion. The excuse was that there could be no further
promotions for distinguished conduct in battle while the question of
responsibility for the An-Nwal disaster was under review. In a welter of
recriminations and counter-recriminations the King had called upon
Maura to form a government, and Maura had appointed a General
Picasso to investigate the facts. Nevertheless Sanjurjo went up to
major-general and Millan Astray to full colonel. With the latter's
promotion the command of the Legion became vacant. If Franco
expected to be named Millan's immediate successor, he was disappointed. A Lieutenant-Colonel Valenzuela, with a distinguished
record in the *Regulares*, took over the Legion.

On 12th January 1923 the Military Medal was pinned on Major
Franco at Dar Drius. Franco now sought a posting back to Spain. He
was given back his post in the Prince's Regiment in Oviedo. He went
back by way of El Ferrol where his mother took him on a pilgrimage of
thanksgiving to the rock shrine of El Chamorro above the town. His
brother Ramon, also awarded the Military Medal, followed him out
of Africa at about the same time.

Ramon was now becoming as serious a family problem as his father.
In the words of his cousin Carlos Franco-Salgado, the family chronicler,
Ramon "lacking religious convictions, allowed himself to be carried
away by the unbridled licentiousness of life in Africa . . . he turned up
one day with a woman Carmen Diaz who was well known in the
cabarets of Melilla".[20] Carlos Franco implies that Ramon was not

married to her, or that if he was, there was no more binding a contract than that of civil marriage which few Spaniards considered valid. However, at home he presented her as his wife, "and persuaded his pious mother that it was so". Ramon had forgotten about Carmen Diaz within two years.

Francisco Franco arrived in Oviedo on 21st March. He was welcomed by his fiancée Carmen Polo. After the inevitable *Festejos*, banquets, dinners and other social gatherings in honour of Franco—his distinguished record was known locally in minute detail—it was time for arrangements to begin again for what the Polo family wanted to be a socially memorable wedding. The King had named Franco a Gentleman of the Bedchamber in the January, but he had not as yet issued his assent to the marriage.

The King's throne was tottering: a *simpliciste* explanation for An-Nwal was gaining popular credence: Silvestre had stretched his lines of communication to breaking point under orders from the King and against the advice of the Government and the Army: therefore the King alone was to blame for the deaths of so many thousand Spaniards.

There had been three governments in 1922. Maura had resigned when the allegedly disbanded *Juntas de Defensa* had tried to force his hand over the Picasso report on An-Nwal. The report had unearthed serious misappropriations of funds all the way from the Ministry of War to the African bases of the troops in the field. His successor as Prime Minister, Sanchez Guerra, had appointed an inter-Party parliamentary committee to study it. The Committee had heard more witnesses, and out of it three reports had emerged: one by the Conservatives stating that the disaster was due to causes beyond human control even if some persons had been guilty of irregularities; one by the Liberals affirming that the government of the time deserved a vote of censure; and a third by the Socialists who named definite persons against whom criminal proceedings should be instituted. Following a debate on the matter, that government had resigned, and a new one had taken office in December. It also had realised quickly that the Picasso report was too hot to handle and settled on the diversion of opinion away from it by entering into more anti-clerical legislation.

This was the major talking point when Franco arrived back in Spain. The Government proposed to appropriate all Church funds and treasures amassed since the State had last done so. The Archbishop of Zaragoza, Cardinal Soldevila, protested loudly, pointing out that the move was impossible without breaking the terms of the Concordat. On 4th June he was assassinated.*

Life in Spain was "normal" therefore as Franco waited for the King's permission to his marriage with Carmen Polo. In Africa during April Abdel Krim had allowed the Spaniards to keep their forward posts without hindrance. Then on 28th May he cut off one of the positions. It fell to the Legion as always to re-establish communications. The morning papers of 7th June carried banner headlines: Colonel Valenzuela had been killed in action. On the following day there arrived in Oviedo a copy of a telegraphed general order despatched by King Alfonso XIII himself as Commander-in-Chief of all the armed forces of Spain. It read: "One of my best soldiers has fallen in battle. Respect always his glorious memory. I confer the command of those *Banderas* to Lieutenant-Colonel Franco".

> Colonel Franco is a military toff,
> To come out and fight he put his bride off.

Franco's return put new life into the Legion. As a harbinger of "good luck" he was proverbial. Legionaries noticed that the only reverses they had ever suffered were those when he had been on leave. Whatever was being said at home, in Africa both in the Legion and outside it, there was nothing but praise for Franco's promotion. His value to morale was proved almost immediately. On 2nd July a message was flashed to another forward position which had been cut off, that Franco was back in Africa. It was enough to put new heart into the last survivors, an engineer ensign and a few men. On that very day the official gazette carried the notice that His Majesty had graciously consented to the marriage of Lieutenant-Colonel Francisco Franco y Bahamonde to Doña María del Carmen Polo Martinez Valdes.

The first attempts to relieve the outpost were unsuccessful. The Moroccans deployed an unusual number of men both to capture the position and prevent its relief. Franco finally threw the text books over. After aerial reconnaissance on 23rd August, he used one *bandera* to launch a feint frontal attack while he took a second a long way round to attack from the rear. Moroccan casualties were heavy.

Before Franco could return to the Peninsula at train of events which was to have considerable bearing on his thought and life took

---

* The assassins were Anarchists, but they appear to have believed an anonymous note to the effect that the Cardinal had ordered the assassination of a prominent C.N.T. leader, Salvador Seguí.

place in Spain. Oscar Perez Solís, an ex-Artillery captain just appointed Secretary-General of the nascent and still much divided Communist party of Spain, tried in Bilbao to have the Socialist leader Indalecio Prieto blown up. Prieto had refused to call out the Socialist workers of Bilbao on a strike to coincide with the departure from Malaga of a battalion for Africa. The strike in Bilbao was a failure, though a handful of Communists anxious "to die in honour" fought the Civil Guard from the *Casa del Pueblo*, the Socialist Party centre which they had seized from their owners. In Malaga between fifty and seventy members of the battalion refused to embark. They were quickly overpowered, though not before an engineer N.C.O. had been killed by a Corporal Sanchez Barroso. Barroso was tried rapidly by court martial and sentenced to death. On 28th August the Cabinet issued a statement. The King had exercised his Royal Prerogative of Pardon at the request of the government which had acted in accordance with an appeal signed among others by the Primate of Spain. The Army reacted furiously: "If there is no discipline, there can be no army. If there is no army there can be no State."

On 13th September the Captain General of Catalonia, General Miguel Primo de Rivera, rose against the Government. The Captain General of Zaragoza was on his side. So was Martinez Anido, now Commander-in-Chief in Africa but at that moment at San Sebastian. Sanjurjo, Martinez Anido's immediate underling in Africa, declared for the insurgents. The garrison at Valencia expressed its loyalty to the Government and that of Madrid awaited the King's orders. The King ordered acceptance of Primo de Rivera as the new ruler of Spain.

With the situation quiet on all fronts in Africa, Franco was given forty days leave to get married. He had first to "kiss hands of the King".[21]

The King received me most cordially but was very depressed about the situation in Africa. He asked me to give him a full report. I did so.

"I think that we'll have to pull out of Africa. I don't see how we can hold on to what we've got, let alone overcome our present difficulties there."

"I beg leave to differ." I said to the King that the defeat of the rebels was well within our capabilities. After all, the whole of the Protectorate was no bigger than one of his Spanish Provinces—no bigger than the Province of Badajoz. The King said: "But how, how? Everyone else tells me that everything that can be done has been done." I said: "Well, there is a way."

We went into the next room where there was a large map of Africa. "All we've done so far is to attempt to take crest after crest piecemeal and drive the enemy back without destroying him. That's a useless waste of men and materials. We know from experience we can get nowhere that way. What we've got to do is to make straight for the Beni Urriaquel region and Abdel Krim's headquarters at Axdir by the shortest route. The shortest route is by sea. We can hold the enemy where we are at the moment in the East. We can organise a large force in Ceuta and Melilla, embark it and make for the beaches at Alhucemas (Al Hoceima).* We take the war right into the heart of the enemy territory and we capture his capital. This operation should not be beyond our capabilities." The King thought for a moment, asked a few more questions, and then said to me: "You must tell Primo de Rivera this."

"If I were to do that, Your Majesty, wouldn't he throw me out saying—Who's this whipper-snapper telling me what to do? Besides, isn't he rather busy cajoling municipal governments? [*Granjeándose Ayuntamientos*]"

"He can take time off." The King moved over to a telephone and, as he did so, he said: "You'll be dining with Primo de Rivera tonight."

It wasn't until late that Primo de Rivera said to me: "What's this plan of yours all about?" I told him what I had told the King, but it was about 2 o'clock in the morning and he was in pretty high spirits (*muy eufórico*) so I reckoned that he wouldn't remember much about the conversation. "What are you doing now?"

* Alhucemas was the name given both to the offshore island fortress held by Spain through the centuries and the mainland opposite. A small-scale landing from the island to the mainland had been considered in support of Silvestre's advance along the coast which had ended with the An-Nwal debacle. References to this appear in various accounts of the Riff war. Franco's *Diario*—published almost simultaneously with Berenguer's first memoirs (*Campañas en el Riff y Yebala 1921-22*, Madrid, 1923)—emphasised the need to land in Alhucemas and make straight for the rebel headquarters in a passage so worded as to be clear to the Spanish military reader that Franco had in mind something different from what had hitherto been proposed without telling him exactly what it was. Its curiously cryptic phrasing led me to ask several Spanish senior officers whether they knew who was the originator of the idea not of a landing ahead of and in support of a crawling slow operation along the coast, but of a concentration of force at the point nearest Abdel Krim's headquarters, with a push along the coast only when the headquarters had fallen. The answer in every case was: "It must have been Primo de Rivera's". "Couldn't it have been Franco's?" "I don't think so: remember, he was only a lieutenant-colonel. You can't have a lieutenant-colonel telling a General what he should do". Accordingly, I asked General Franco point blank: "Was it *your* idea?" He sidestepped characteristically—"It was in the air". He then went on to tell the story given in the main text.

"I'm off to get married."

"When do you come back?"

"In about twenty days."

"Fine, come and see me when you do."

The twice postponed wedding took place on 16th October in Oviedo. The rather dull church of Saint John was crowded to the doors. His "padrino"—the equivalent of best man—was the King by proxy. There was quite a gathering outside the church to watch the couple pass: Franco booted and spurred with his bride in white on his right, taller than he in her very high heels.

On his way back to Africa he called on Primo de Rivera. Primo told Franco to put his Alhucemas scheme down on paper; he would himself take a trip to Africa as soon as he could spare the time to see the general situation for himself; and there, for the moment, was the end of the matter.

Between November 1923 and March 1924 climatic conditions reduced military activity. Abdel Krim was now much more than a rebel tribesman. He had turned the enormous quantity of war material he had captured to good use. The Russians had sent him a colonel of Artillery, Serge Kugushchev, to train his men in the use of the 75 and 105 mm. Schneiders in his hands. Tribe after tribe had accepted his leadership and paid him tribute as he began to call himself the Emir of the Riff, and Head of the Riff State. His gold, whether come by way of tribute or of ransom for prisoners, was good enough for the private arms manufacturers of Britain, France and Czechoslovakia. He now had an army as good as that of the Spaniards. With this army he sought to march onwards, and expand eastwards and westwards. By mid-1924 he was master of all Spanish Morocco except the quadrangle in the east reconquered by the Spaniards after An-Nwal, and the towns of Larache, Xauen, Tetuan and Ceuta.

Primo de Rivera at long last fulfilled his promise to visit Africa. He saw the absurdity of the Spanish situation in the west. To hang on to Xauen and maintain a link between it and Tetuan, a large force was pinned down in about four hundred outposts with between ten and fifty men in each. In the east the general defensive line was good though the salient pointing at Axdir had no purpose unless an offensive was contemplated. However, Primo de Rivera had come to agree with the Army in Africa that the real point at issue was not whether this line or that line should be held, but whether Spain should make an all-out effort to conquer the Protectorate or else get out. Given the choice "all or nothing" Primo had come to the conclusion that it would have to be nothing since all was not possible: that is in his opinion all was not possible. In that of the African Army, it was.

Over the winter, Franco had become a founder and the head of the Editorial Board[22] of a new publication, the *Revista de Tropas Coloniales* whose avowed object was "the encouragement of African Studies". He had contributed an essay on leadership[23] to its first number which was published in January 1924. "In this land of life and mystery," he had written in a more florid style than in his *Diario*, "we must not walk in darkness. We must lift the veil and identify ourselves with the Moroccan way of thinking." Leadership required a comprehension of the mentality of the men led. The essay had then developed (or digressed deliberately) into a consideration of leadership in politics and army: "There cannot for ever be a divorce between political and military leaders", words into which perhaps too much might be read with hindsight. More likely he intended them as a declaration of support for Primo de Rivera, General and Head of Government, in view of the fact that the review would pursue the anti-Primo policy, "we must not give up Africa". The cover of this and subsequent numbers had a drawing of Alhucemas. Primo was sent a complimentary copy.

Franco met Primo in Melilla on 13th July and on the 19th took him to Dar Drius and then to Ben Tieb in the salient. At dinner Franco made an impassioned speech. Accounts vary[24] as to how forthright he was in telling the Primo that a withdrawal from Africa would be over the dead bodies of the Legion: in other words that Franco would not obey.

> I brought up again the plan for Alhucemas. To have given up what we had would have been a grave mistake. Primo de Rivera promised to study the matter further."[25]

The story is credible that as the General subsequently inspected the Legion lines he read the so-called "Creed"[26] of the legionaries—one whose twelve articles read: "The spirit of the Legion is of blind and fierce combative spirit before the enemy". Primo is said to have suggested that it should read: "The spirit of the Legion must be of blind obedience to orders etc. . . ."

Hardly had Primo gone when the Riffs attacked in strength on both fronts. The Tangiers–Tetuan road was cut and Tetuan itself was threatened. The Legion was hurriedly switched from the East and stopped the enemy at the gates of Tetuan. Primo de Rivera ordered the rescue of the Spaniards now cut off in Xauen. Franco and his Legion, now five *banderas* strong, were formed in the vanguard of a relief column set out from Tetuan on 23rd September. The *banderas* battled their way to Xauen. They arrived decimated on 2nd October. They had been given no quarter and given none. The outposts beyond Xauen were now evacuated. A visitor to the area round about this time[27] noted that the posts had "no reserve trenches, no barbed wire and no precautions against sudden attack". Equally at least to the point they were so isolated one from another that units of the Legion had to sally out from Xauen to cover their individual withdrawal. Primo, returning from the Peninsula, ordered the evacuation from Xauen of all Spaniards. On 17th November Franco ordered all civilians, Spanish, Jewish or Moroccan, who wished to leave, to pile into lorries prepared for them. Franco suggested to Castro Girona, the commander of the column, that as far as possible movement back to Tetuan should be by night. He agreed, though it was a novel idea. Progress with so many civilians would be of necessity slow. The road was barely fit for vehicles. Night would afford some protection from attack.

Franco and his Legion now formed the rear guard, the most vulnerable part of a column in retreat. It took them four weeks to pull back the forty miles to Tetuan, but they arrived there on 14th December with ten thousand men from Xauen and the little outposts scattered along the route safe and sound. Franco wrote for his *Revista* a highly-coloured article on the sadness of withdrawing from the "Holy City". He had obeyed Primo de Rivera, but obviously did not approve of the surrender of so much hard-won territory. Primo de Rivera rewarded both his skill in the withdrawal and his obedience to orders by approving his promotion to full colonel, a rank to which he had long been entitled since he was in permanent command of a force five battalions strong. The promotion was announced in the following February, but it was ante-dated twelve months.*

Primo de Rivera promised the Army that Xauen would one day be recaptured. He had changed his mind about surrendering Morocco and had come to the conclusion that the defeat of Abdel Krim and the reduction of Spanish Morocco were within the capabilities of Spain. He had told Franco after the withdrawal that he had accepted the Alhoceima plan in principle. It was now up to Franco to work it out in greater detail. He would be given all the necessary facilities.

* 7th February 1925 to 31st January 1924.

Primo de Rivera asked me who should be in command. I said I supposed it would have to be the senior commander in Africa—that was Sanjurjo, with the G.o.C. Mellila as his second in command—"Quite right—that's as it should be".

Franco now had to find out for himself what a sea landing would involve. The only precedent he knew about was the not very happy Gallipoli operation. He decided on a "pilot scheme". In January 1925 he put two *banderas* in landing craft and set out from Ceuta for Ksar-es-Sethir, halfway along the coast to Tangier. Bad weather led to the cancellation of the operation, but a second attempt in March was successful.[28]

With Xauen in his hands Abdel Krim was now triumphant. He began 1925 by capturing Er Raisuni who had made his peace with the Spaniards fearing his fellow Arab more than the Christian. Spain's old enemy in the west died a prisoner that May. Then Abdel Krim, who had had no hand in the partition of Morocco, turned south with Fez as his objective. The French deployed eighteen battalions of infantry, six squadrons of cavalry and twelve batteries to stop him. France and Spain buried their hatchets temporarily and agreed on joint action against Abdel Krim. Pétain, then Commander-in-Chief of the French Army, rushed to Fez and stabilised the front; then in August met Primo de Rivera off Algeciras and agreed with him on a combined offensive. A French army of 160,000 men, mainly Colonial, would attack from the south over a wide front while Spain would bring into action 75,000 men, mainly European. The Spaniards were to land at Al-Hoceima and push from the Melilla rectangle. Franco's plan was at long last to be put to the test.

The landing force was organised into two brigade groups, each of 5–6,000 men, at Ceuta and Melilla. Sanjurjo was appointed the overall Commander. The Ceuta brigade would land first. In the first wave, after a preliminary bombardment by a Spanish fleet of two battleships, one cruiser, one old cruiser and various gun boats, and one French battleship, Franco would lead off landing craft, ten light tanks, two battalions of the Legion, three battalions of *Regulares*, one mountain battery and two sapper companies. He was to have a free hand in establishing a bridgehead.

The Ceuta brigade group sailed on 6th September. They hugged the coast—and in one case too closely. There was no attempt at surprise. The soldiers sang uproariously most of the night. The fleet sailed with all lights blazing. On 7th September they arrived off the sandy beach later called La Cebadilla. They were ready to go in when Franco received the order to hold off for another twenty-four hours while a feint landing was made twenty miles to the east. This was a last minute change in which he had no part and which could have had serious consequences. In the afternoon the sea grew choppy. They were hove to and the soldiers were naturally disconcerted. Let Franco here take up the story:

8 September. Day dawned with our craft scattered and the convoy disorganised. The current has taken us westward: as there are so many boats getting them back in position takes longer than calculated. The morning wears on. It's after 10 before the column is ready. At long last, boats farthest away appear over the horizon. The lines of landing craft which are to ground on the beach are drawn up. The tugs and the gun boats tow them in, a pair each. The first line has the Legion, the Moroccans and light tanks . . . the bombardment begins . . . a thousand metres from the shore the tugs and gunboats cast off the landing craft and the craft continue under their own power. The enemy fires cannon and machine guns at us. . . . We come within rifle range. . . . We run aground. Down come the ramps. We are still fifty metres from the shore . . . the tanks cannot be unloaded . . . the moment is critical . . . a bugle sounds the attack. . . .[29]

Exciting—but it is difficult to keep in mind that the date is 8th September 1925. One battalion of the Legion captured one of the enemy batteries protecting the beach and the other the second. Seemingly the naval bombardment had not knocked them out—but they had had better luck with others. The feint landing had drawn no Moors away from the Alhucemas area. The enemy waited in force beyond the first range of crests. There were anxious moments on the right flank where the *Regulares* were, but by nightfall the bridgehead was established. Franco' diary of the event has the sinister phrase "those who resisted too much were put to the knife"—the very phrase which in his earlier diary he had used with reference to the massacre of the Spaniards by the Moroccans after An-Nwal. On the following days the rest of the troops disembarked—and once again the weakness of the Spanish Army organisation revealed itself. They were far too weak in artillery once beyond the range of the ships' guns, and shore-to-ship communications were poor anyway. Next, ammunition and food began to run short: they had wasted time off-shore and to crown their difficulties there was a storm at sea. Fifteen days passed before the order was given to advance beyond the bridgehead, and when it was, Abdel Krim's mortars (so much more effective in mountain country than Schneider 75s) began to take heavy toll of the Spanish troops. Once again Franco distinguished himself with his sheer grit and determination. On 30th September the Riffs fell back setting fire to their capital Axdir.

Al-Hoceima had been a success. Conducted as it was without the advantage of the element of surprise, without adequate reconnaissance —the landing craft should not have grounded so far out as to make the tanks unemployable—without due care being given to the maintenance of adequate food and ammunition supplies after the initial bridgehead had been established, it could well have proved a costly failure. These were matters to which the Commander-in-Chief should have attended. The composition of Franco's landing force was unbalanced. There should have been much more artillery. Again, this was a matter for the General Staff and not for Franco alone. It can be argued that the French attack in the south was vital to the success of Al-Hoceima, drawing away a part of Abdel Krim's forces. With all this, Franco was way ahead of his superior officers, in the first place in his strategic thinking and in the second after the landing in his tactical handling of adverse circumstances.

Franco would learn from Al-Hoceima many lessons. As Supreme Commander-in-Chief he would insist over and over again to his Corps and Divisional Commanders: "Reconnoitre; make sure you know where the enemy is; know what you're doing; ensure everyone else knows what he is supposed to do; find out what the weather is going to do. . . . Surprise, surprise . . . time is gold: you can lose a battle by dilly-dallying . . . once you have broken through, exploit your success: don't delay."[30] As Generalissimo he would be in a position to tell others what to do. In Africa he was merely a colonel under orders of a major-general who recognised a clever and courage-young officer in Franco but who had a happy-go-lucky attitude to the planning and conduct of operations.

With the French pressing hard from the south, the end of Abdel Krim was merely a matter of time. French and Spanish cavalry met. On 2nd November Sanjurjo, now a lieutenant-general, took over from Primo de Rivera. Bad weather then set in. In the Spring there was a slow restart to the operations. Sanjurjo seemed to be in no hurry. The driven and defeated Emir of the Riff surrendered to the French in May but it was not till 10th July 1927 that Sanjurjo declared the war ended.

Morocco had cost Spain tens of thousands of lives from 1909 to 1927. Its monetary cost is difficult to assess except in relative terms: in the year 1923 for example, 500 million pesetas were spent on the Army, 127 million on the Navy and there was a supplementary estimate of over 320 million for Moroccan affairs. The budget for education was 160 million pesetas; and it must be remembered that the State relied on the devotion of men and women in religious orders to attend to the education of many children at grossly uneconomic rates.

Franco was not in at "the kill' in Africa. Indeed, he had left Africa, of which he had had enough,[31] during the winter lull.

On 3rd February 1926[32] Francisco Franco Bahamonde aged 33 had been promoted brigadier-general—the youngest man of that rank in the Spanish Army for several generations. He had been given command of the most important brigade in Spain—the First Brigade of the First Division with headquarters in Madrid.*

* Millan Astray took back the Legion from Franco. It was then eight *Banderas* strong and had a nominal total of about 5,000 officers and men. Millan Astray was himself promoted brigadier on 18th June 1927. In his speech of farewell he gave the following figures of casualties to the formation between its foundation on 4th September 1920 and the day of his promotion: 116 officers killed and 319 wounded, 1,871 other ranks killed and 5,775 wounded. The Legion had lived up to its famous battle cry: "*Viva la Muerte*"—Long live death. Millan had been wounded four times, losing an eye and an arm; Franco-Salgado had been wounded twice; Francisco Franco never in the Legion.

NOTES

1. Franco's phrase in an article refused publication in the *Memorial de Infantería* but included by him in his *Diario de Una Bandera* (see below, Ch. VI, p. 151).

2. For an account of this battle to the death *v*. Edgar O'Ballance, *The Story of the French Foreign Legion*, Faber, 1961, pp. 34 *ff*.

3. Millan Astray's stay with the Foreign Legion was of twenty days duration: 7th to 27th October 1919 (*Hoja de Servicio*).

4. This and other quotations are all from the *Diario* unless otherwise stated.

5. Prologue to *Diario* by Millan Astray.

6. To call this recruit "a monk" as Arraras, Valdesoto, Ramirez, etc., do is tantamount to calling a would-be medical student a doctor of medicine. The lad obviously took a superior's facetious remark too literally, proving he was no man for a monastery.

7. For such general background to the Legion I have relied extensively on Franco-Salgado's very vivid memories, as well as on ex-legionaries of that

time and on Millan Astray's own memoirs. Franco-Salgado was for a while in charge of the farm.

8. Mola, *El Pasado*, etc. (pp. 936-78), rejects thoroughly the idea that the Army was always pampered and gives the evidence against the popular verdict. At the same time the Army did eat better than the southern Spaniard in his misery.

9. Unfortunately his name has been forgotten.

10. Another feature of the Spanish Military Code difficult, not to say impossible, to reconcile with Catholic dogma.

11. Berenguer in his *Campañas 1921-1922* (p. 91) confirms the story and is eloquent in his praise of the way the Legion carried his orders out.

12. *Diario*, p. 97. See below, Chapter IX, pp. 35-6.

13. Nominal strength with muleteers 800.

14. *Diario*, pp. 191 *ff*.

15. Franco and Berenguer (op. cit., p. 189) were almost the only two Spanish officers who believed in tanks in Africa. The tanks used in this campaign were a dozen 6·5-ton Renaults, armed with a single 7-mm Hotchkiss, bought in January 1922. (Article in *Ejercito*, January 1966, on the history of tanks in the Spanish Army.)

16. Family papers. Cf. Valdesoto, p. 29.

17. Franco has praise for the supporting artillery although on a number of occasions Spanish shells fell among his men. This is hardly surprising. The contemporary artillery manuals ignored the effect on shells of variations in barometric pressure, temperatures and wind speeds and directions: nor was there any service in the field to provide the information to the gunners. On quality of ammunition see Berenguer op. cit., p. 233.

18. *Diario*, pp. 57, 91, 133, 171, 181.

19. When an officer was recommended for promotion in the field, a court had to be convened under a member of the Judge Advocate's department (Cuerpo Juridico). It held a *juicio contradictorio* at which evidence was taken for and against the promotion from the nominee's superiors, equals and juniors. Among those who spoke in favour of Franco's subsequent promotion from Lieutenant-Colonel to full Colonel were the then Lieutenant-Colonels Miaja and Pozas who would be prominent on the Popular Front side in the Civil War (*Hoja de Servicio*).

20. Family papers.

21. Conversation with the author.

22. *Jefe del Consejo de Redacción*.

23. *Los Mandos* (in all he was to write forty-six articles for this review).

24. Cf. Galinsoga, pp 89-91, Arraras, pp. 100-1, etc. It is my considered opinion that Franco was very outspoken on this occasion, as on a subject about which he felt deeply.

25. Conversation with the author.

26. Luis Bolin (*Spain, The Vital Years*, Cassell, 1967, p. 77) adds this detail: "When Primo arrived at Ben Tieb ... he found a repetitive menu with a hidden meaning not used in polite society." The Legion's "Creed", of which Franco and Millan Astray were the authors, was the following:

The Spirit of the Legionary: unique and second to none: blindly and fiercely combative: seeking always to close in on the enemy with the bayonet.

The Spirit of Companionship: a sacred oath never to abandon a man till all have perished in the attempt to save him.

The Spirit of Friendship: sworn between one man and another.

The Spirit of Union and Help: on hearing anywhere and at any time the cry '*A mi la Legion*' all will hearken to the appeal, and rightly or wrongly they will defend the legionary who has asked for help.

The Spirit of the March: a legionary will never say he is tired till he drops exhausted: the corps will be the fastest and most enduring.

The Spirit of Resistance and Toughness: the legionary will never complain of fatigue, pain, hunger, thirst or lack of sleep. He will do all tasks: digging, manhandling of guns, vehicles, outpost duties, supply column work. He will do whatever is ordered.

The Spirit of Seeking out the Battle: the Legion, one man or the whole body, will race to wherever firing is heard, by day, by night, always, always, even if under no orders to do so.

The Spirit of Discipline: he will do his duty: he will obey till death.

The Combat Spirit: The legion will always, always ask to take part in combats, out of turn, without counting the days, months or years.

The Death Spirit: Death in battle is the highest honour. One dies once only. Death comes without pain. To die is not as terrible as it seems. The most horrible thing is to live a coward.

The Legion's Standard: will be the most glorious for it will be stained by the blood of the legionaries.

All Legionaries: are men: brave: every nation is said to be brave: here each nation must prove which is the bravest. Long live Spain. Long Live the Legion.

27. Brennan, *Spanish Labyrinth*, p. 60.

28. *Hoja de Servicio*. Bolin (pp. 79-82) speaks of the use of K-craft in the rescue of the Uad-Lau garrison in November 1924. It was undertaken by a force of 250 *Regulares* under the command of the then Major Muñoz Grandes with an old warship in support. In point of time, therefore, this must be considered Spain's first essay in combined operations.

29. Account published in the *Revista de Tropas Coloniales*.

30 *El Reglamento para el empleo táctico de las Grandes Unidades* with commentary by Generalissimo Franco. Printed version of August 1938.

31. "If the truth be told, Franco agreed to Millan Astray's offer of second-in-command of the Legion in the belief that he would be free to return home once the Legion was organised; but there it was, the Legion had to go into action straightaway, before its training was completed; then he had to return again at the King's command; and then Primo de Rivera wanted him there" (Franco-Salgado to the author).

32. Antedated to 26th January 1926—two years to the day after his promotion (as antedated) to colonel, the legal minimum.

6

THE FIRST DICTATORSHIP

On the very day that Franco's promotion was announced, the newspapers were full of the success of a most spectacular adventure. Franco's brother Ramon had piloted a Dornier flying-boat, the Plus Ultra, across the South Atlantic. It was a pioneer achievement comparable to that of Alcock and Brown across the North. Francisco was eclipsed. The event almost crowded out another item of news: Marshal Pétain had arrived in Madrid to receive the Spanish Military Medal. That night the Marshal dined with the King. Amongst the guests was the new General Franco—but the nation was talking about the Major Franco who had heroically shown what Spanish aviators could do. Nothing could have suited Primo de Rivera and General Franco better than such a coincidence.

Ramon and his crew of three would all be heard of again over the next ten years. Juan Manuel Duran, a naval lieutenant, the navigator, who had to be dropped at Dakar to lighten the load, was killed shortly afterwards piloting a Savoia. Ruiz de Alda, a captain in the Air Force, Major Ramon's co-pilot, lived to become one of the founders of the Falange and to be shot for it in Madrid's "model prison" by order of the Republican government of 1936. Rada, the mechanic, was to be the chief provider of the petrol with which churches and priests' houses were set alight in 1931. After the Civil War, he lived out his long life quietly in Mexico. Ramon was to have a more ebullient career.

The Plus Ultra flight added international lustre to the régime of Don Miguel Primo de Rivera, second Marquis of Estella, who nationally and internationally had taken all credit for the success of the Al-Hoceima landing.[1] He was now at the very apex of his popularity. He had risen in September 1923 against the Government certainly not "with the nation's unanimous applause" as Franco wrote[2] but undoubtedly with the approval of the King, and with the foreknowledge that a sufficiently large proportion of the Army would support him immediately for the remainder to declare for him without too long a delay. Nevertheless it is true that many Spaniards reading the manifesto of his revolt had been disposed to give him a chance as a ruler. "The Army, as interpreter of public opinion has decided", Primo declared in his manifesto, "to put an end to the political oligarchies which have long shared out power between themselves." The second part of the sentence was an incontrovertible fact. The Liberal and Conservative parties were oligarchies which had violated, each in its way, the interests of the masses over many years. The manifesto's summary of the history of that half century and of the immediate past was likewise no gross caricature of the truth. Prelates, ex-Governors, agents of authority, employers, foremen and workers had been assassinated. Assaults had gone by unpunished. Justice had been twisted to political ends. The value of the peseta had fallen: agriculture and industrial production was decreasing; millions had been spent for purposes unknown to the public; Ministers had been corrupt; the Moroccan war had been used to cover political intrigue; the war had to be decided one way or another, whichever it was to be, but quickly. In Primo de Rivera, therefore, the Church, the Army, the industrialists, the middle and lower classes all saw promise of a happier future. The only sections of society who were opposed to the manifesto were the Anarchists, some of the professional politicians and, for a short while, the Socialists.

The Anarchist opposition was logical. Dictatorship whether of one man, of an oligarchy or of the proletariat was a negation of the very principle of anarchism. The politicians were those who feared in the final sweeping away of the Cánovas–Sagasta alternation by arrangement the end of their careers: not that a military dictatorship would condemn them all to earn their living by some other way than politics, for even a dictator would not want all his Cabinet Ministers to be fellow-generals. Besides the Anarchists only a handful of intellectuals opposed a dictatorship in principle; for there were good Aristotelean reasons why an intellectual could judge a dictatorship theoretically permissible in the circumstances; and there were examples in ancient history of beneficial dictators. It must be remembered that these were the days of Ataturk, and of Mussolini who was "making the trains run on time in Italy". Not that Primo de Rivera was in any way a Fascist. He was not a thinker. To him all things were either jet black or pure white. He had no Party and no political ideology beyond the simplest: for him the time had come to save the nation from its enemies, and no one could do it better than he.

The Socialists, solidly against him at first, reconsidered their opposition. A military dictatorship might be a paroxysm of a dying bourgeois capitalism, and yet a definite advance towards the establishment of the dictatorship of the proletariat, and therefore a form of government with which they could co-operate. The elderly Pablo Iglesias was too shrewd a man to identify Primo de Rivera's move with Fascist reaction. He left it to the wags of the Liberal and Conservative clubs to repeat *ad nauseam* the originally clever quip "Primo de Rivera *ma secondo di Mussolini*". Primo was no upstart corporal but a general and the nephew of a captain-general of Liberal traditions: a revolutionary general in the tradition of the O'Donnell, Prim and other makers of *pronunciamientos*. Don Miguel was a Marquis, though admittedly only the second of his line. He was the owner of large tracts of land in Andalusia, the descendant of a family which had not been deterred by the churchmen's anathemas against the acquisition at knock-down prices of monastic lands. Nevertheless he was not a harsh landlord. Like others of his class he kept women, wine cellars and a plentiful larder, but he was contemptuous of that class, and he would pour out gifts for the poor and scorn fine garments for himself. Though he made no particular secret of them, his private habits of gluttony, of drunkenness and lust—from time to time he would retire with a supply of women to one of his country palaces—were not common knowledge when he rebelled, else he might have aroused the suspicion of the church-going public and of Socialists; for although as Madariaga says[3] "Spanish people do not feel that incurable horror of sin in others which afflicts some races", nonetheless the Spanish middle and lower classes (other than the Liberal and Republican) did believe that a dissolute private life so undermined a man as to make him unfit to govern. Not a few Catholics had turned Republican because of the, to them, immoral private behaviour of so many Bourbons, while there were Carlists who had been strengthened in their peculiar faith by the fact that the original Don Carlos had been a paragon of virtue compared with the errant Queen Isabella II.

When Franco arrived back in Spain in the third year of Primo de Rivera's rule, he had every cause to compare the order of Madrid and Oviedo with the chaos he had seen at any previous time in his life. The first impressions were to remain with him, and thereafter he would look upon dictatorship as the ideal form of government for Spain. At

that moment Primo de Rivera had the confidence and the support of
the majority of the population. He had destroyed the political bosses,
the *caciques*, and cleaned up local government. He had in the process
found jobs for under-employed army officers. He had set up compulsory arbitration boards to the disgust of the industrialists, but industries
were doing well; there was industrial peace, for Largo Caballero had
accepted on behalf of the Socialist U.G.T. Primo de Rivera's invitation
to co-operate with him. There was far less unemployment than at any
time before in the twentieth century. Primo de Rivera had embarked
on a programme of public works which created work for tens of
thousands. He had acquired the services of a clever young economist,
Calvo Sotelo, who allowed his Chief credit for his successes and was
eventually to shoulder the blame for Primo de Rivera's intuitive but
arbitrary and stupid economic decisions. Ancient monuments were
being restored. Spain was being made a haven for tourists.

   Primo de Rivera's manifesto had contained a threat to another group
of Spanish society besides the Anarchist and the professional politician.
He had spoken in it of "the unashamed separatist propaganda" undermining the State. It was a term so vague that the most law-abiding and
truly nationalist Catalans thought that Primo de Rivera would lend a
sympathetic ear to their advocacy of home rule within a Spanish State.
Primo de Rivera had no such ear to lend. He hated Catalanism. He was
to confess that the primary motive force behind his revolt had been his
belief in the need to maintain the unity of the nation at all costs, that is
to supress all regionalist aspirations. He began to implement his promise
in mid-1925. He dissolved the Catalan *Mancomunidad*, the very limited
form of local government which had been granted to Catalonia in
1912. He went on to forbid the teaching of the language,* the speaking
of it in public assembly, the flying of the white and red flag of Catalonia
and even the dancing of the *Sardana*. Doing so he discredited the
moderates who had been seen to co-operate with him in the beginning.
Denied even these safety valves, the Catalanists would turn towards
the Republicans and even the revolutionaries who posed as Catalanists.

   In 1926 Primo de Rivera began to screw down other safety valves.
He appointed Martinez Anido his Home Secretary. Press censorship—no
new thing in Spanish life, for Liberal governments had made use of it

   * Enemies of Catalan separatism have said repeatedly that Catalan is not a
language but a dialect. Madariaga's arguments (*Spain*, pp. 146-8) could be used
with equal validity to identify Welsh with Irish, or for that matter English with
German. Be that as it may, Madariaga's old university, Oxford, now recognises
Catalan studies as a separate discipline in its own right.

no less than Conservative—became oppressive. Private letters were opened and telephone conversations tapped. Unamuno, the philosopher, was deprived of his Chair of Greek at Salamanca University after he had written a letter criticising the régime to a personal friend in Buenos Aires. The Ateneo, the meeting place of the famous in arts and sciences, was closed. Even men of moderate opinions came to be hounded for speculating when it would be that Primo de Rivera would fulfil his manifesto's assurance that his régime was only provisional and that the army would give the people the chance freely to choose a real government in place of the sham which had existed for so long. As month succeeded month there appeared to be fewer and fewer signs of any intention on Primo de Rivera's part to surrender power.

The first signs of trouble came from the Army itself. They had various reasons to be discontented with Primo de Rivera. In the first place he was held to have been too complacent over the international settlement of the government of Tangiers. It was so justifiably a Spanish town. In the second he was considered to have mishandled Spain's claim to a permanent seat in the Council of the League of Nations so that even Germany and Brazil appeared to be better placed to obtain such a seat. Thirdly at home the Army had not had it all its own way. In November 1924 a handful of men had been brought by the Civil Guard before a military court martial and accused of causing the death of two civil guards. The military court had found the prisoners not guilty. The members of the court had then been arrested.[4] That was merely a beginning. The real trial of strength was to come in 1926 over the long-standing difference of views within the Army—a matter directly affecting General Franco's promotion, the announcement of which so happily coincided with Marshal Pétain's visit to Madrid and Ramon Franco's arrival in Brazil.

In the Spanish Army, as in others, there was rivalry between the members of one branch and another. The cavalry believed itself socially and militarily superior to the infantry and the artillerymen and sappers could prove their intellectual superiority over horse-riders and "foot sloggers". In the case of the Spanish Army, each branch had its own Officers' Academy—the infantry's in the Alcazar in Toledo, the artillery's in a sequestrated monastery in Segovia, the cavalry's in Valladolid, the engineers in Guadalajara and so on. The infantry and cavalry courses were of three years duration: the engineer and gunner of five. To compensate, the infantry officer was commissioned as a second lieutenant rising to lieutenant after two years whereas the sapper and gunner were commissioned straightaway as full lieutenants. Thereafter promotion had long been theoretically subject to identical conditions: by strict seniority (subject to the passing of examinations and recommendation) or by outstanding action on active service. However, spectacular action was more readily possible for infantry or cavalry men than for gunners and engineers. Dissatisfaction with the heavy weighting of promotions in favour of the infantry had led the artillerymen all to swear an oath on commissioning that they would not accept promotion except when due according to strict seniority rules, and oppose, as far as they could, the promotion for active service of all others. The law recognised their oath, and an artilleryman recommended for promotion could opt out of it by accepting a medal or some other similar award. Now the Spanish Army, both in Africa and in the Peninsula was essentially an infantryman's army. In 1923 there had been in the peninsular forces at most a ratio of four guns to every thousand rifles as against ten guns minimum to every thousand rifles in the other armies of Western Europe.* There had been 1,777 artillery officers as against 5,900 infantry, that is roughly four infantry officers to every gunner. There were twice as many cavalrymen as engineers. By 1926 the figures of artillery officers had expanded to 1,811, but the infantry had also swelled according to the old proportion.[5]

Primo de Rivera, every inch an infantryman (like Sanjurjo and Francisco Franco), began to mention in public speeches that he proposed a reorganisation of the Army. No one was told exactly what he intended. Rumours that he had in mind a whole batch of promotions of infantrymen to reward good service in Africa were rife in mid-January, and there was considerable unrest in all the artillery units. Primo de Rivera very assuredly outmanouevred the opposition by announcing the promotions at the very moment when, if the artillery had acted, they would have turned on themselves the full anger of the people as well as the rest of the Army. Nothing could be done which might dishonour Spain in the eyes of a Marshal of France, and the masses would not have stood for a show of force at the very moment that a Spanish aviator—ex-infantry major Ramon Franco—had conquered the South Atlantic skies: but Primo had to guard against delayed reaction.

---

* On paper there were 16 field and 16 medium regiments, but in fact there were only 14 field and 8 medium in existence. They were up to strength neither in pieces nor in men.

Franco deserved his promotion if anyone did, but Primo de Rivera was a shrewd man. To appreciate how shrewd we must consider briefly the territorial distribution of the Spanish Army. Spain was divided into eight military regions, each under a Captain General. Each region had on paper two divisions and each division two brigades. In fact there was so much "buying oneself out of" compulsory military service that only the senior brigade of the senior division in each region really mattered. If this brigade stood firmly on one political side, the rest could be trusted to follow suit. The key men in each region were therefore the Captain General, the commander of the senior division, and the commander of the senior brigade. The key regions were those with headquarters in Barcelona, Zaragoza and Madrid. Against a rising on the part of the artillery, whose headquarters were for conspiratorial purposes their Academy at Segovia (a short distance away from Madrid), the first brigade of the first division in Madrid was the one to have in the hands of someone absolutely trustworthy. Primo de Rivera had done what Franco had told him to do at Ben Tieb. He had changed his mind about surrendering Morocco, and he had made a direct attack on Abdel Krim via Al-Hoceima. Franco, promoted out of turn from lieutenant to captain and subsequently every single step to brigadier-general, had stated in article and book what he thought of the infantry and promotion in the field. With pride in the record of his branch of the army and great warmth he had argued the case for special awards and promotions for the infantry in an article refused publication in the *Memorial de Infantería* but put by him into his *Diario de una Bandera*.

[The infantry] are the creators of the motherland. The Moroccan military problem is for the most part the work of infantrymen: they are the main nucleus of this army, and with cavalry, but in a lesser number, fill the ranks of the front-line troops. Infantrymen are they who in the frosts and storms of night watch over the sleep of camps, climb under fire the highest crests, fight and die, without their voluntary sacrifice receiving the just reward of heroism. . . . The painful casualties of recent operations speak with greater eloquence than can these written lines. . . .

Franco, therefore, was the man to command the first brigade of the first division of the most important military region in Spain at that critical moment.

Primo de Rivera could not let well alone, for he was a simple man, obsessed with the virtue of unity. Spain had to be united: regionalism could therefore not be tolerated, nor could political parties which divide nations, nor could a parliament which of essence implies a dychotomy at least of government and opposition. On a speech-making tour in April he made it clear that he would tolerate none of these offences to the unity of Spain, whereupon in their clubs, in cafés, in Spain and beyond her frontiers, Monarchists joined with Republicans and Conservatives with Liberals to plot the downfall of the dictator who was beginning to lord it over Spain like some Eastern potentate. Neither the plotting nor Primo stopped there. If Spain had to be united, *a priori*, the Army had to be united. There could not be two sets of rules, one for the infantry and one for the artillery. If he chose to pick out infantry officers for accelerated promotion, he must be free also to reward artillerymen whether they liked it or not, and if they had sworn an oath, he would have them forswear it. On 9th June 1926 he issued an Edict on the matter through the King. All artillerymen who had opted for the commutation of promotions out of turn for decorations or other awards at any time since 1920, were to consider themselves promoted as from the date of the awards, and move up in the seniority list accordingly. Eight days later Primo de Rivera confessed to the Press that there had been some trouble with the artillery, but he assured them that all was now settled.

So it was, for the moment; the mutinous artillery and Primo had had word of one of the strangest plots in the long history of military conspiracies in Spain.

On 24th June 1926, the Feast of Saint John the Baptist, which in Spain is a day for fireworks, masked balls and atavistic junketings, a *Monarchy* was declared. The signatories were the 87-year-old General Weyler and the 68-year-old General Aguilera who once had been Minister of War. The conspirators included the King's physician, Dr. Gregorio Marañón, a pair of young cavalry officers and a handful of artillery sergeants. It was a pitifully ill-organised plan with no idea of security. Most of the conspirators were under lock and key long before 24th June and the plot came to be known as the *Sanjuanada*, the clowning of Saint John's Day. At the subsequent courts martial, Weyler was found Not Guilty though he is remembered to have pleaded that he was, Aguilera was condemned to prison for a mere six months and a day. He was also fined 200,000 pesetas, a sum which everyone knew would never be paid.

On 27th July Primo de Rivera issued new and somewhat compli-cated rules for promotion. As from the forthcoming 1st October, there would be no more promotions on active service, but there would be a percentage of accelerated promotions at all levels. The artillery could not accept the compromise. It was a matter of honour. The temperature of revolt rose during the heat of August. On 5th September, without the authority of the Ministry of War or any other governmental department, all artillerymen, officers and other ranks, returned to barracks of their own volition and closed their gates. Primo de Rivera had the King declare a "State of War". Anyone disobeying orders would be court martialled. The whole of the artillery was suspended and declared under arrest. The infantry was ordered to take over all artillery establishments, and they did so without a shot being fired on either side except in Pamplona where one artillery officer, one sergeant and one gunner were killed. The Spanish Royal Regiment of Artillery had ceased to exist. Obviously 1,811 officers could not be court martialled. Primo de Rivera decided to proceed only against Colonel Jose Marchesi Sagarra, the Commander of the Academy at Segovia. He was condemned to death. Popular reaction to the sentence deterred Primo de Rivera from having it carried out. Towards the end of the year the Dictator gave the others the choice of re-employment on condition they accepted his promotion rules or of voluntary early retirement. Most officers returned since there was little hope for them of civilian employment. Charitable employers would not have been popular for harbouring enemies of the régime.

Primo de Rivera had in the meantime decided that the root of the trouble was the fact that there were separate Academies for each branch of the Service. Here, therefore, was yet another simple problem requiring a simple solution. He summoned Franco. He would replace the existing Academies with a single General Military Academy. Franco agreed that the idea was good. He suggested that Millan Astray was the man to carry it out: Millan had been working on the re-writing of the antiquated Service manuals: he would know what changes were needed in the training of cadets. Primo dispatched Franco to study the École Militaire de St. Cyr then under the direction of the friendly Marshal Pétain. Franco returned full of ideas how a similar but Spanish institution could be established in Spain. Alfonso XIII approved the general plan on 20th February 1927.

In the following month Franco was appointed a member of the commission which would examine all aspects of the new foundation, and he was told that he would be its commander. Franco wanted it at the Escorial. Primo de Rivera insisted that it should be in Zaragoza. Primo would later regret his decision. Three and four years later Franco would not be able to come to the help of the Dictator or the King across 225 miles.

The summer holidays then intervened. Franco spent a few days in Oviedo and on the beaches of Asturias with his wife, and they then went to pass their "usual fortnight"[6] at El Ferrol with his mother.

The previous year Franco had had in El Ferrol his first taste of what mass popular applause could mean. The whole of his native town had turned out to acclaim him, his brother Ramon and their mother. After a Te Deum in a neighbouring church for the prowess of the Franco brothers, the Mayor had unveiled a plaque on the wall of the home where they had been born. The Mayor, who had a deep love and respect for Doña Pilar, handled the absence of Don Nicolas, the errant father, with extreme tact.[7] To the surprise of some of the townsfolk, the plaque showed Francisco more prominently than his brother, and the Mayor sang the praises of the elder just perceptively more loudly than those of the younger. There were private reasons for the Mayor's distinction. He had gone to Huelva with the King to greet the returning trans-Atlantic airman. Ramon had affronted the King. Immediately after arrival he had disappeared to spend his day more pleasurably than in lunching with the Sovereign.

The King did not allow the flagrant discourtesy of the brother to affect his personal affection for Francisco: and Franco retained a respect for the person of Alfonso XIII, if not always for kingship.

In the Calle de María house there is today a large glass case with some of Franco's personal treasures, such as his pistol of the Moroccan campaign, the dress sword presented to him by the officers of his class in the Toledo Academy when he became a General, the binoculars he used during the Civil War. In a frame within the case there is an autograph letter from King Alfonso. It is dated 1st May 1925:

Dear Franco,

On visiting the Shrine of Our Lady of the Pillar in Zaragoza and hearing a brief memorial service* before the grave of the Commander of the Tercio Rafael de Valenzuela, killed so gloriously leading his Standards, my prayers and my regards were for you all.

The beautiful pages of history that you are writing with your lives and blood is a living example of what men can do who stake everything in the fulfilment of duty.

* *Un Responsorio.*

The King now changes from the plural with which he had been addressing the Legion, to the singular for Franco alone:

> I am sending you a medal (of the Virgin). I ask you to wear it always for she, every inch a warrior and a Spaniard* will assuredly protect you. My congratulations and thanks for all you have done. You know how much you are loved and appreciated by your very affectionate friend who embraces you—Alfonso.

After the 1927 Summer holidays, Franco accompanied the King and Queen on an official visit to Africa. The highlights were the giving of new Colours to the Legion at Dar Riffien, and the redress of Franco's old commander General Damaso Berenguer. He had been found guilty by court martial of neglect of duty as Commander-in-Chief in Africa at the time of An-Nwal. Dismissed the service he had been subsequently amnestied but left on the retired list. Alfonso now created him Count of Xauen.

While Franco went ahead with his plans for the new Academy—Primo de Rivera was giving him a free hand—the Dictator undertook a measure of reorganisation of the army. He brought reality and paper strength closer together. He reduced the number of infantry regiments to sixty-four and the artillery was to consist of sixteen field, eight medium and three mountain regiments. Franco now moved to Zaragoza. Work was begun on the site for the new Academy. Brigadier General Franco chose his teaching staff—five lieutenant-colonels, sixteen majors including his inseparable friends Alonso Vega and Franco-Salgado, twenty-one captains and eleven lieutenants—a formidable body of fifty-three officers of whom twenty-five were infantry, four general staff corps (ex-infantry) seven cavalry and eight artillery. He told them that entrance examinations would be held that June and that the Academy would be opened that 5th October. The staff were kept hard at work preparing the curricula.

On the appointed day the 215 boys chosen out of 785 applicants reported at Zaragoza. Primo de Rivera was present. In his opening speech Franco naturally did not mention St. Cyr nor the German military schools at Dresden and Berlin which he had also visited. He recalled the precursors of a single Academy, the first of which, he pointed out, had been founded by an artilleryman. He exhorted the students to love country and King—in that order of priority—and to

---

* *Tan militar y Española.* The Spanish monarchs ever managed to pour nationalism into their Catholicism.

expect glory in the Army only through a life of hard work and heroism. He introduced them to his *Decálogo*—the technical word in Spanish for the tablets of the Mosaic Law.

Franco had had prepared new text books with new ideas on tactics and he was to give at his academy a prominence to practical work which was quite revolutionary in any branch of Spanish education and not merely the military; but the most personal of all his contributions were his Ten Commandments:

> I—Love your motherland dearly: be loyal to the King. Show this love in every single act of your life.
>
> II—Show always a great military spirit; be totally dedicated to your vocation and to discipline.
>
> III—Be ever zealous of your reputation as a gentleman purified as it were in a crucible.
>
> IV—Fulfil your duties faithfully and fully.
>
> V—Grouse not and tolerate no grousing.
>
> VI—Make yourself loved by your inferiors and desired of your superiors.
>
> VII—Volunteer for every sacrifice. Ask for and desire to be called upon on occasions of greatest danger and fatigue.
>
> VIII—Feel a noble companionship. Sacrifice yourself for your comrade. Rejoice in his successes, prizes and progress.
>
> IX—Love responsibility and the taking of decisions.
>
> X—Be valiant and self-sacrificing in all things.

Of all these clauses the two on which Franco laid the greatest stress were: "Love your Motherland. Love sacrifice."

Of men who knew him personally, even those who came to look upon Franco as a fiend retained a respect for him, as a man utterly devoted to what was his duty or to what he believed to be his duty. It was so in Zaragoza. He would work if necessary twelve hours a day for weeks on end. He was a young enough director of the Academy for himself to take part in all its practical exercises. The favourite zone was round Canfranc in the High Pyrenees, splendid for the purpose and no region for the physically unfit. He took a very personal interest in the education of the boys who were to become army officers. He suppressed rigorously the *novatadas*, the bullying and initiations from which he had suffered himself as an undersized boy of fourteen. In his speech at the opening of the second course, in 1929, he issued the order: "The evil and ugly custom of the *novatadas* common in such centres as this in Spain and abroad must be banished for ever". At the same time he allotted every cadet to a tutor with strict injunctions to the tutor that he was to devote himself to the character formation of the boy as well as the supervision of his military studies.

Franco had become a family man, and though his child was still a baby and a girl, it changed his outlook.* Up to now his deeply ingrained sense of responsibility had led him to seek "glory even in the cannon's mouth", to instill in men fearlessness in battle by his own example. Henceforth he saw it as his responsibility that he should prepare young men for the battle he already begun to see ahead. For the Franco who was remembered, as a youth in his native El Ferrol for ever reading books even in public cafés while other ensigns ogled at the girls, as a young man in Oviedo courting his future wife but yet again at his books, and in Africa as a field officer whose tent light shone late into the night long after the Last Post had sounded, now as a General began to take an ever greater interest in politics, economics and social problems.[8]

It was while I was director of the Zaragoza Military Academy that I began to recieve regularly a Review of Comintern Affairs from Geneva.[9] Later I discovered that Primo de Rivera had taken out several subscriptions and thought I might be interested in it. I was. It gave me an insight into international communism—into its ends, its stragety and its tactics. I could see communism at work in Spain, undermining the country's morale, as in France.

Communist propaganda circulating in the Spanish Army was then largely a straight translation of matter addressed to the French Army. It was therefore not as effective as it would have been if adapted to its other rank recipients. Franco however credited the men whom he began then to see as his country's chief enemies with sufficient sense to know this for themselves. His worry was what might be going on under the surface, particularly among officers and N.C.O.s, not the leaflets and pamphlets confiscated from time to time in barracks. The Communist party of Spain was small, divided and seemingly so effete as not to worry Primo de Rivera unduly. Franco was already becoming aware that there were other groups of individuals to whom a later age would give the names of crypto-Communist and fellow-travellers. It was the flank attack and not the frontal feint that he considered dangerous: "the enemy massing beyond the immediately visible crest".[10]

* His one child Carmen was born in 1928.

In this early assessment of Communism as the enemy of Spain religion must have been a factor (the Spanish equation Spain is the Faith and the Faith is Spain) but it would be unwarrantable to suppose it to have been a major factor.

In Africa the barrack rooms of his Legion had borne such exhortations as *"Ni misas ni mujeres"* and *"Ni copas ni curas ni mujeres"*—"No wine, women nor priests"—counsels of perfection which could be explained as a product of a puritanical streak in his nature, but equally as sheer logic from a man inebriated with "the military spirit". For wine and women, it could be argued, debilitated a man physically and rendered him less fit than he might otherwise be for battle; religion made thinkers out of men on subjects inimical to war and could therefore be psychologically dangerous—unless the religion were that of the Prophet.[11] They were 'counsels of perfection", let it be noted, and not orders, but woe betide the legionary unfit for service through drink or venereal disease. This was to be so for the cadets at Zaragoza. Nevertheless there was nothing essentially Catholic or Christian in Franco's Ten Commandments—and it could be argued much that was anti-Christian. In his known addresses to the cadets the nearest to a reference to religion was his warning at the opening speech of the 1929 course against the "positivism of our times"; but then the old militarism arose: "Winds of pacifism will blow across your path, Utopian illusions which contradict the History of the World, and the laws which nature obeys. Those winds always rise just when the loud voice of force dictates treaties, forms nations or shares out worlds. Chimeric illusion that of the leading nations to stop the clock of history when the moment is favourable to their [continued] dominion [of the others]."

Franco was referring to Britain and France and to the contemporary proceedings at the League of Nations; nevertheless it is perhaps not unwarrantable to consider the passage as evidence of his Catholicity at that time. For a well-informed Catholic in Spain would have known of Pope Pius XI's many allocutions of the period on Peace and references to militarism in connection with his battle against Mussolini's establishment of the *Ballila* and suppression of the Boy Scouts. Franco would himself one day come to ban all boy scouts and imprison their Catholic scout masters in favour of an organisation not unlike the *Ballila* in organisation and ideals—but that was years ahead. Primo de Rivera's half-hearted attempt at a very quasi-Fascist party to support his dictatorship, the Union Patriotica, was proving a dismal failure.

Primo de Rivera was beginning to fail. He had had one rebuff after another. He had envisaged a National Assembly by limited suffrage. The Socialists would have no part in it, and neither would any other respectable organisation. The Socialists could justly have been described as one of his four props. The second was the Church; that is to say in a country where religion had been persecuted for over a hundred years anyone who did not persecute it was considered to be a friend of the Church. Primo de Rivera then went further. He insisted on his officials showing in public respect to churchmen and to being seen attending services. To the fury of the Liberals he began to allow an increase in the number of Catholic schools and he had textbooks offensive to Catholics withdrawn. An aspiration dear to the Church at the time was that two colleges for clerical higher studies, one Jesuit and one Augustinian, should be recognised as faculties of theology with a right to grant university degrees. Primo agreed to let the Church have its wish. The moment he did so, he had major and bloody riots in all the university cities. Students and professors defended jealously and with the violence of conviction the century-old monopoly under the State.* The Dictator won. But nevertheless the Church thereafter sought to separate itself in peoples' minds from the régime, and it ceased to be its second prop. The third was the Army. The artillery corps which he had reformed was proving as intransigent as its precursor. The regiment in Ciudad Real had risen at the end of January as part of a national plan to overthrow the Dictator. The infantry had smothered the revolt rapidly, and the corps had been dissolved a second time, but Primo de Rivera was left with a major problem. The *political* leader of the rebels, the Conservative ex-Prime Minister Sanchez Guerra, had deliberately surrendered himself when he could have escaped. In the October he was brought before a court martial. He revealed all his seditious activities but the court martial found him *Not Guilty* against all the evidence which the accused himself had furnished. All the members of the court were brigadiers.

For the Dictator the inference was obvious.

Burdened now with diseases of the flesh he became ever more arbitrary. His collaborators began to desert him. Foreign financial organisations began to wonder how long he could continue. Capital began to leave the country. The peseta fell to a record depth. The King

---

* One of the consequences of French and Liberal influence was the destruction in the eighteenth and nineteenth centuries of the autonomy of the medieval universities such as Salamanca whose government was originally not unlike that of Oxford or Cambridge. They were placed under direct State control. The new universities were State foundations.

was now his one and only prop. On 28th January 1930 Alfonso XIII summoned the Second Marquis of Estella, his Head of Government, to explain how it was that two days previously he had sent a telegram to all the Captain Generals of the eight military regions without the authority or even the knowledge of the Commander-in-Chief of the Spanish Army. In the telegram Primo had asked the Captain Generals point blank whether he still had their support. He now knew he no longer had the King's. He asked to be relieved of his duties. The King graciously accepted Primo's resignation and ordered the Chief of his Military Household, General Berenguer, Count of Xauen, to assume the government of the country.

In Zaragoza Franco bowed quietly to the change; a very old friend of his now was the Government.

Berenguer was a kindly man. His rule came to be known as the *Dicta-blanda*, the soft dictatorship, as opposed to his predecessor's *Dicta-dura*, the harsh dictatorship. It was too soft to last and the man he appointed Director General of Security, Franco's old comrade General Mola, was no Martinez Anido.

In the October Franco saw to the opening of the new academic year. He introduced yet another innovation. Professors and students of Zaragoza University were invited to meet his staff and pupils in the mess. Then, at Mola's request, he hurried to Madrid. Mola had incontrovertible proof that Ramon was conspiring with men of the extreme left. As an act of friendship he told Francisco that if Ramon continued, he would have no choice but to order his arrest. Franco duly warned his brother. Ramon however was by now bitterly anti-King and anti-establishment. An attempt at a flight to New York had ended with his rescue by the British aircraft carrier *Eagle* after he had been seven days in the water. A court martial had found him guilty of negligence and put him on the "unemployed" list. Ramon believed himself in no way responsible for what had happened. After the warning he continued as before, going from garrison and airfield to airfield exhorting the troops to rebel. Mola ordered his arrest; but Ramon, remembered by his airforce and other companions in their more sedate days as a *pirata, pillo, botarote*, pirate, playboy and madcap, eluded his captors.

Ramon was no lone wolf. He was an agent of a revolutionary committee which had been formed on 17th August in San Sebastian and now planned to declare Spain a Republic on Monday 15th December.

Spaniards of almost every political view were now agreed that Spain could not go back to the "controlled democracy" under a king of the Cánovas–Sagasta convention. The choice was now between a new Constitutional Monarchy and a Republic. Berenguer was pursuing a self-contradictory policy. He was seeking a means of saving the monarchy, but at the same time he was allowing the Republicans a very free rein in their propaganda—or perhaps it would be truer to say that he had neither the means nor the ability to prevent the avalanche of leaflets, pamphlets and books advocating a Republic. He certainly did not have the stomach to put into force rigorously the repressive measures which would have been necessary at that juncture to stop the all-out attack against the Monarchy. There were three columns in the offensive. One was of Catholics inspired in greater or lesser measure by the Papal Encyclicals and allocutions on Social Justice. It had at its head Niceto Alcala-Zamora and Gabriel Maura, the son of the now very monarchist Antonio Maura. The second column was of free-thinking intellectuals headed by Unamuno and Ortega y Gasset. The third was of the Socialists, the largest and best organised of all. Within the second there were men of the old Liberal stamp, Freemasons to a man, sworn to destroy Catholicism but otherwise divided among themselves into a plethora of groups ranging from backwood capitalism to not-so-mild socialism. They included the very able physically deformed Manuel Azaña, a man of the most unsavoury personal reputation[12] and Fernando de los Ríos, the son of the free-thinking founder of the Institucion Libre de Enseñanza; Fernando had flirted with communism, written a book in praise of communist Russia but had been unable to let himself go in his Muscovite love affair.

The plan for 15th December was straightforward. The politicians would declare the Republic established. General Queipo de Llano would take command of all the armed forces in Madrid on behalf of the new government. Republican army officers (of whom by now there was a substantial number in the infantry as well as the artillery and who ranged in rank from general to lieutenant) would take over the Army units in the Provinces. Ramon Franco and his fellow airmen would take off from the airfield at Cuatro Vientos and shower leaflets over nearby Madrid. The Army would be confined to barracks so as not to prejudice the action of the workers who would come out on strike. The revolution would be bloodless as far as possible, but if the King did not surrender immediately, then Ramon Franco and his squadron would threaten to bomb the King's palace. Mola knew all about the plot but events were to surprise him no less than the plotters.

In the October Maginot had pinned on Franco in Zaragoza the Insignia of a Commander of the Legion of Honour and invited him to Versailles to attend a course for brigadiers and colonels. Franco was back in Zaragoza by 4th December, just in time to be almost in the centre of the unexpected.

In the early days of December some light vans were observed heading north through Zaragoza. They carried young men with skis. The occurrence was not considered unusual although skiers usually took the train. Their stay in Jaca, ninety miles further north, was more surprising, for there was fog and sleet but no snow. However, they appeared to have friends among the military officers in the small garrison, and their overheard conversations and telephone calls to Madrid about the number of trees in the neighbouring forests seemed innocent enough. Then on the morning of Friday, 12th December, a telephonist got a message through to the Military Governor of Huesca, a town halfway between Jaca and Zaragoza, before the lines were cut. She reported that something appeared to be wrong. Later that day it had become public knowledge at home and abroad that Jaca was a centre of yet another military revolt in Spain. The Military Governor of Huesca went north to reason with the rebels. He was greeted by the leader, a Captain Fermín Galán, with joy, until the Military Governor demanded his surrender. "But aren't you one of us?" asked Galán. There was a brief tussle during which the Military Governor was shot in the arm.* Fermín Galán with a handful of fellow junior officers and about six hundred men prepared to push towards Huesca. Some civilians of republican sympathies joined him. By the evening, however, they suspected that all was not as they had expected it to be. They had been told by Galán that a republic had been declared throughout the length and breadth of the country, yet radio stations mentioned only the events of Jaca, continued normal programmes, and on closing down for the day played as usual the Monarchist National Anthem. In the meantime the Captain General of the region, from his headquarters in Zaragoza, had got together three regiments with supporting cavalry and artillery, at least six thousand men in all, and dispatched them by train to Huesca. In case they did not reach it before the rebels, and these pushed towards Zaragoza, he ordered Franco to place his cadets astride the Huesca–Zaragoza road. There was no need. The column reached Huesca in the early hours of the morning of the Saturday, detrained, formed and began their march up the Jaca road. Contact was established two miles

* He died fourteen days later, but almost certainly not directly of the wound.

outside the town. Three rebel officers sought parley with the column's commander on behalf of Galán. They were promptly arrested. A brief engagement followed in which several dozen rebels were wounded before they were all routed. Galán, his right-hand man, a fellow infantry captain García Hernandez and some companions, surrendered that very evening to the Civil Guard at the village of Ayerbe. They were taken to the Army headquarters in Huesca. The cavalry swept into Jaca and tore down the republican red, gold and purple flag which had been flying for two days.

On the Sunday morning a court martial assembled at 0930 hours to try Galán, García Hernandez and four other officers. The others had escaped into the mountains or into France. All those before the court pleaded guilty to a charge of making war on the King. At 1015 hours all the evidence had been heard, and the Prisoners' Friend had argued the extenuating circumstances in their defence. After the briefest of retirements, the court announced sentence: death by shooting for Galán and García Hernandez, life imprisonment for the others. Galán and García were taken to a field outside Huesca where in 1848 other revolutionaries had been shot. The sentence was carried out at 1510. Galán gave the orders for his own execution. Both died bravely.

Franco knew both the dead men well. They had been subalterns of his in the Legion and both had been decorated.

On the Sunday morning Mola ordered the arrest of all the National Revolutionary Committee, civilians and generals alike. Queipo de Llano escaped. Alcalá-Zamora kept the police waiting till he had heard Mass. He and all the others denied any connection with the events in Jaca. On the Monday, as if nothing had happened, Ramon Franco took off with his fellow pilots and dropped the leaflets over Madrid. He then flew on to Portugal. In exile he and Queipo put all the blame for their failure on Galán; Queipo adding: "Galán wanted something more than the Republic, and to take over control of the Revolution he acted three days before the agreed date." Galán's rising was certainly out of the ordinary, for he called on civilians to arm themselves and join him, and several dozen did.[13]

The case against the National Revolutionary Committee was heard by the Supreme Military Tribunal in March. The Prisoners' Friend argued that if the accused were guilty of violating the Constitution, so was the King in accepting Primo de Rivera's dictatorship. The President and several fellow generals were for the acquittal of all the accused: others for sentences not exceeding six months. As they had already been in prison for three months and all had behaved in an exemplary fashion in prison, either way the court was for their immediate release. Obviously there were other senior officers besides those who were known to be implicated in the defeated plot who no longer considered themselves in honour or duty bound by their oath of allegiance to the King: but Franco was seemingly not one of them.

On 28th March in Jaca Franco presided over the court martial of four officers, a sergeant and others. After a five day hearing the court sentenced one of the officers to death and the others to imprisonment.[14] It was all in strict accordance with military law. The sentences would not be carried out; but that was no concern of Franco's.

The question now was not whether there would be a Republic but when and how bloodlessly it would be established. Berenguer resigned as Head of Government and took office in its successor as Minister of War. That the King had lost the confidence of a large proportion of his people was obvious to all but the King.

Berenguer had restored the machinery for municipal elections. The Government agreed on their use as a barometer. Candidates would be able to present themselves under any Party ticket. There would be freedom of the Press and assembly to facilitate their campaign.

Voting took place on 12th April. The electors knew everywhere that the choice was the single one—Monarchy or Republic.

On the day following the election, all the Captain Generals in the country received a telegram from Berenguer. Franco was also among its personal recipients. It read:

> The scrutiny of yesterday's vote suggests that the monarchist candidates have been defeated in the principal cities: Madrid, Barcelona, Valencia, Seville, etc. The elections have been lost. This presents the Government with a most delicate situation which it must consider as soon as it has the necessary facts. At such an important moment your Excellency will not be unaware of how absolutely necessary it is for everyone to act with calm, with our hearts on the sacred interest of the motherland of which the Army is the guarantee at all times. Keep contact with all the garrisons in your regions. Commend them all to place their absolute trust in the maintenance of discipline so as to help public order. If they do this, they will guarantee that the destiny of the motherland will follow the logical course set to it by the supreme national will without disasters which could seriously harm it.

In simpler words Berenguer had issued orders to all the Army to accept without demur an impending change from Monarchy to Republic.

The Army did so. On the following day it was public knowledge that in all the major cities the Republicans had outnumbered the Monarchists. When the results from rural towns were also known the balance was against the Republic. In absolute terms 41,224 Monarchists had been elected as against 39,248 Republicans (including Socialists and sixty-seven Communists). Since that date to this the exact meaning of the result has been debated by writers in Spain and abroad.* This much however is certain: that the cities had voted for a Republic. There were enough Republicans, whether they were only 48·7 per cent or as many as 60 per cent, prepared to fight for the imposition of their system of government on the rest if the King did not surrender. On the other hand, even if the 51·3 or mere 40 per cent which were Monarchist had been prepared to a man to rise in defence of their King, they would have been defeated in double quick time since their strength was not in the cities. The army was divided. General Sanjurjo, then in command of the para-military Civil Guard, thereupon informed the King that he could not answer for the loyalty of his men, a statement that may have meant that Sanjurjo himself had become a Republican or, less likely, a confession out of character that where he might lead, others under him would not follow.† The choice now before the King was to cause bloodshed without any hope of victory, or by resigning to give a chance to another form of government and men who were firmly convinced that they had the solution to the many and complex problems which had eluded absolute Monarchy and Republic, controlled democracy and dictatorship. The King, advised by his physician, Dr. Marañon, by his Secretary of State, Romanones, and his Minister of War, Berenguer, left the country after Romanones and Marañon had negotiated with Alcala-Zamora a peaceful transition, and Berenguer had virtually ordered the Army to accept a Republic as the destiny of the nation.

The King in his farewell message confessed that he might have erred.

---

* It is generally agreed that the elections were free and exemplary in the cities but that there was some rigging in the rural districts. In the absence of sufficient trustworthy evidence it is impossible to say how much "fixing" here was balanced by "adjustments" there.

† The Civil Guard, a para-military organisation founded in the nineteenth century to suppress brigandage consequent on international and civil wars has had its panegyrists and its denigrators as a police force. It was much more of the people in officers and men than the Army.

He appealed against any use of force on his behalf. Alfonso may not have known how to reign, but he knew how to abdicate. The legal fiction that he was renouncing none of his rights might hearten the die-hard Monarchists, but they had been given a strict injunction to do nothing violent. Speed was now essential. Without waiting on events in Madrid, the Republic was already being declared in one provincial city after another. Even in Madrid before the King had finally made up his mind, the Civil Guard had stood motionless as the centuries-old red and gold flag of Royal Spain was replaced in public buildings by the Republican purple, gold and red. Sanjurjo had already put his para-policial army at the disposal of the Republic. There was no harm in letting a jubilant crowd chant "Death to the King and Death to Berenguer".

The danger point at that moment was the Fourth Military Region with headquarters in Zaragoza. The Captain General, Fernandez Heredia, was renowned as a Royalist, and he was surrounded by Royalist officers. The Jaca rising had revealed who were the Repub-licans in his region. Franco, the Gentleman of the King's Bedchamber, was already being looked upon by Monarchists and Republicans alike as the young man who could command the loyalty of a large section of the Army and who therefore had to be watched. Franco kept in close touch with the Captain General. Both had personally received their orders from Berenguer, yet the red and gold flag was not lowered at the Captain General's headquarters until midnight on the 14th, by which time the King was well on his way to exile.

On the morning of the 15th Franco addressed a parade of the whole Academy. He read out a brief impersonal General Order:

A Republic having been declared in Spain, and the supreme national power being now vested in a provisional government, it is the duty of all, in discipline and in exercise of solid virtues, to work together that peace may reign and the nation be orientated by the normal process of law.

The discipline and exact fulfilment of orders which has always prevailed in this centre are more necessary at this moment than ever before. The Army, calm and united, must sacrifice all personal thought and all ideology for the good of the nation and the tranquility of the motherland.

It was a warning for any hothead who might take Franco's Ten Commandments too literally—or not literally enough. For Franco had placed the motherland before the King. The royal flag continued flying at the masthead for a few days longer. Elsewhere in Spain crowds were wrecking statues and monuments of the kings and queens of Spain and royal arms wherever they were and however old they might be. Street names with royalist connections were being changed. Local enthusiasts were opening prisons and releasing everyone irrespective of whether the prisoner were a political detainee or a dangerous convict.

On the 18th, the principal and widely distributed monarchist newspaper, the A.B.C., carried a picture of General Franco on its front page. The caption described him as "the new Spanish High Commissioner in Morocco". Franco immediately wrote indignantly to the paper:

> Neither the provisional government which now directs the nation can possibly have thought [of such an appointment for me], nor would I accept any post which I am not in duty bound to accept lest anyone should interpret such an acceptance as proof either of my approval of the recently instituted government before it came into power, or of having been in some way lukewarm or half-hearted in the fulfillment of my duties or in the loyalty which I owed and kept to those who till yesterday were the representatives of the Monarchy. On the other hand it is my firm purpose fully to respect, as I have done till now, the sovereignty of the nation and my desire that that sovereignty be expressed through the proper channels of law.[15]

What was behind the publication of Franco's photograph at that moment? It could not have been a hint to the Monarchists that he was a man whom they could trust, for the caption had him as being among the first Generals to accept a large size plum from the new régime. It was now established that the High Commissioner in Morocco had a higher authority than any army General in Africa although he might in the army be junior in rank. Was it merely wishful thinking, that if Franco had been appointed High Commissioner, he might rally the Army in Africa to the Monarchist cause? Or was the photograph and caption slipped in by some sympathiser with the Republic within the editorial staff of the A.B.C. to goad him into a definite declaration one way or the other? He was the only General with an outstanding record who was as yet not committed. Berenguer and Mola had supported the King in his bid to rule as well as reign, and would be dealt with accordingly over the next few days. Sanjurjo had jumped on the Republican wagon in the nick of time. Franco's prompt rejoinder was perfectly balanced. He had argued in effect that his primary loyalty was to Spain. Because he had been so faithful to the established order in the past, therefore he would be loyal to the established order in the future. It was a matter of honour and of duty.

A month later Alfonso declared in London to the Marquis Luca de Tena, the editor of *A.B.C.*, that he would put no difficulties in the way of the new Republic adding: "I do not want Monarchists to incite anyone in my name to military rebellion". It was doubly now for Franco a matter of honour and duty not to conspire against the Republic. Lerroux, the ex-Emperor of the Paralelo, was now a minister in the Government. He took it upon himself to tempt Franco[16] and cleared him of conspiratorial intentions; but the Republican Government would still look upon Franco with suspicion.

It was a matter of honour and duty for the members of the new régime that they should fulfil their promises—among them arrange elections for a constituent Assembly, examine what reforms were necessary in the civil and armed services, respect the religious beliefs of the individual, guarantee the individual's rights and respect private property, yet at the same time ensure that land was properly utilised. The reform of the Army was to hit Franco personally in two ways.

NOTES

1. Madariaga in his *Spain* gives the best brief account of Primo's dictatorship.

2. Juan de la Cosa, op. cit., p. 104.

3. *Spain*, p. 254 (1942).

4. The *Vera* incident. Madariaga is one of the few writers of the period who has given it its due importance (pp. 263-4). For a severe criticism of Primo de Rivera's dealings with the Army, cf. Mola, *El Pasado*, etc., pp. 1024: 'In his dealings with the Army, as in everything else, Primo de Rivera was right in some things and wrong in others." Mola's major criticism was the following: "Primo de Rivera did nothing to raise the cultural level of the other ranks for all his pandering to their vanity".

5. Spanish Army *Anuarios* and other records.

6. Franco-Salgado's phrase.

7. Evidence of the then Mayor; the local Press did its best not to draw attention to the absence of the father.

8. Franco-Salgado and others.

9. Conversation with the author.

10. One of the leaders of the Ciudad Real revolt (see p. 159) was a Colonel Antonio Cordon Garcia who came out into the open as a communist in 1936.

He was expelled from the Communist Party in his old age, on 18th May 1965 (Radio Independent Spain). The question whether or no Ramon Franco was ever a full member of a Communist party is immaterial. He was unquestionably "a fellow traveller"—and that is all that the Party would have required of a man with his reputation and family background.

11. In Africa it was the Mizzian, the Raisuni and Abdel Krim who could legitimately preach a "Holy War", not the Spaniard and certainly not any Spanish Catholic. The Spanish Government insisted before the Vatican that only Catholic missionaries who were Spaniards should be allowed to enter the Protectorate, but while the Vatican would have preferred them to have been missionaries first and Spaniards only incidentally, the Spanish Government preferred Spaniards in missionary habits. In practice the Catholic missionaries in Spanish Morocco had been and were to be to the end of the Protectorate restricted in their activities.

12. For a ridiculously hostile view of Azaña v. Arraras's introduction to his edition of Azaña's *Memorias*. Thomas accepted it in part in the first edition of his book on the Civil War (pp. 23-5) but not for the paperback edition. He had the reputation to which I allude—how far it was based on truth is another matter.

13. Madariaga, op. cit., pp. 291 *ff*. (1942) called Galán and García Herñandez "Communists". They may not have been, but what is important is that even such a balanced observer as Madariaga thought they were. Galán persisted courteously in his atheism to the last. García Herñandez died a Catholic.

14. *Hoja de Servicio.*

15. *A.B.C.*, 21st April 1931.

16. Lerroux, *La Pequeña Historia* (B.A. 1945), p. 568.

7

THE SECOND REPUBLIC

The history of the second Spanish Republic falls naturally into three parts. The first extends from its inception on 14th April 1931 to December 1933. It is a period which, insofar as Radicals and Socialists dominated the political scene, can be described as of the Left. The second extends from that December to February 1936: it is a term of uneasy coalition of parties of the Centre and the Right. The third and last ends with the victory in Civil War of General Franco and his supporters.

The same period of eight years in Franco's life divides more naturally into four parts; the first ends with the defeat of a rising headed by General Sanjurjo in August 1932. The second finishes with the suppression of what is inadequately known as the Revolt of the Asturian Miners in October 1934. The third ends with the election of General Franco as Commander-in-Chief of the so-called Nationalist forces on 1st October 1936, in the third month of the Civil War. The fourth comprises the remainder of the Civil War.

In this chapter we shall consider the period April 1931 to October 1934.

The actions of the first and provisional government of the Spanish Republic which had a direct and immediate bearing on Franco's life were those instigated by the Minister of War, Manuel Azaña. For years this civil servant-turned-politician had been engaged on a study of the Spanish Army. He had come to the conclusion that Spain had an army too big for its foreseeable needs, and that its ratio of officers to men was too high. He offered the 21,000 officers on the active list the chance to retire on full pay. It was a generous proposal, and many accepted with alacrity. There would be 7,600 in his new model Peninsular Army of 105,000 men, and 1,700 officers for a Moroccan force of 42,000 men; that is one officer to fifteen men in Spain but one to twenty-five in

Africa—a curious reversal of what might have been expected.[*][1] In Africa he cut the Legion by two *banderas* from eight to six, but otherwise made few changes beyond the fundamental that in future the African contingents would be officially a colonial army on its own divorced from the Peninsular. In Spain he reduced the number of infantry divisions from sixteen to eight, one for each of the eight regions instead of two. There would therefore no longer be Captain-Generalcies (the post was abolished) so that the normal senior army post would be that of a General of a Division (or Major-General). He reduced compulsory military service to one year.[2]

Army officers subjectively described the cuts as cruel and vicious: so they were in numbers; but objectively the Spanish Army did require for its own good and the needs of the national economy a reduction at least as severe as the one that Azaña carried out. Nevertheless it was a reform only in so far as what is chopped in half is of a different shape from the original. The eight divisions which survived were left with the same infantry-heavy structure of old: each had eight clumsy battalions short of automatic weapons, and inadequately supported by artillery, tanks or cavalry, engineers, signals and supply services.[†] Azaña might have earned the gratitude, if not of the conservatively-minded majority of the older generals, at least of those who knew of the complete rethinking that Liddell Hart and Fuller of England had started off in Germany, Russia, the United States and France, had he really studied the requirements of modern forces. His claim that this army was of a quality which might enable it "to compete with those abroad in an international war" was nonsense.[3] Nor did Azaña's cuts substantially help the national economy.[4] Over 100,000 men went into a glutted labour market eventually to be recruited as militias by the Socialists, Anarchists, Carlists and the soon-to-be-born quasi-fascist *Falange*.

On 14th July the Minister of War's changes hit Franco personally. Azaña ordered the closure of the General Military Academy. There was a surplus of subalterns as well as of Generals. The day appointed for the closing was 14th July.

In a long farewell speech, Franco made no secret of his feelings. He

* The British Army was reduced from December 1921 onwards. In round figures there were then 282,500 Other Ranks for 14,600 officers. In 1935 there were 10,000 Officers for 186,000 men. The ratio of officers was therefore increased from 1 to 19 to 1 to 18.

† The one Cavalry division he retained was organised as if the internal combustion engine had still to be invented.

began by regretting the fact that they had no flag to grace that year's Passing-out Ceremony—(with the perfect logic of an atheistic government, cadets could no longer swear anything to God, so that the Oath had been abolished). He referred to his three years as their teacher, to the praise that the Academy had merited from foreign visitors, the new systems and text books he had introduced, his banishment of the *novatada*, the absence among the cadets of venereal disease "through vigilance and adequate prophylaxis", and to his Ten Commandments. "The machine is being dismantled," he continued, "but its product remains; you, the seven hundred and twenty officers who tomorrow will be in contact with soldiers of whom you will take care, and whom you will lead; you will be the great nucleus of the professional army; and I know that you will be paladins of loyalty, chivalry and discipline, in the fulfilment of duty and in your spirit of sacrifice for the Motherland." He laid special emphasis on discipline, and on love of Motherland and Army: that is of Army as opposed to regimental *esprit de corps*. He ended with the cry "Viva España"—Long Live Spain, and not with the recently ordained "Long Live the Republic".

As yet the cry "Viva España" had to acquire the anti-Republican overtones which could cost a man his liberty, but the speech was nonetheless forthright. Franco had called for discipline, that is, obedience to orders, but in sentences such as this:

> Discipline, which acquires its full value when thought counsels the opposite to what we are ordered to do; when the heart swells in inward rebellion against what is ordered: when one knows Authority is wrong and acting out of hand.

Franco published the speech as his Order of the Day. Azaña duly received a copy of it. On 22nd July the Minister of War and Prime Minister ordered the General commanding the Vth Division in Zaragoza to administer Franco a severe reprimand for daring

> to utter in effect words of criticism albeit in a veiled fashion and under cover of emotional motives against certain measures taken by the Government, thereby displaying disrespect to discipline;" the General reprimanding Franco was also "to order him thereinafter to abstain from such manifestations, and to temper his conduct to the elementary principles of discipline.[5]

Azaña allowed Franco five weeks of peace to hand over the buildings of the empty Academy. Franco swore "to serve well the Republic, obey its laws and defend it with arms".

Franco was then sent home to Oviedo "pending posting". He asked in September to be allowed to defend General Berenguer who had to face a new court martial over the An-Nwal business and his collaboration with Primo de Rivera. The Republican Government wanted no doubt to remain that Alfonso rather than his politicians or generals had been responsible for that long-past disaster. Franco was ruled out of court on the grounds that he was resident outside the military command in which the trial was taking place.

Eventually on 13th February 1932 he was posted to Corunna, as Commander of the XVth Infantry Brigade. It was a post which carried with it also the military governorship of the city. It was not that Franco was forgiven, but that Azaña did not wish to break so quickly his own rules for appointments and promotions. Franco was the next on the list for any vacancy in brigadier's appointments. Azaña went to see him in Corunna in the Summer, and insisted[6] on photographs being taken of him with Franco.

Disastrous as these army changes were to Franco personally and to the Army, by themselves they would not have been historically important to Spain had the first Republican government not dedicated by far the greatest part of its effort to the destruction of religion. It has been said that in seeking to cremate the Church it buried the Republic. Spanish writers of nearly all political and religious views date the beginnings of the Civil War from the provisional government's inaction over events which occurred on 11th May 1931, that is four weeks after its peaceful takeover from Alfonso. The inaction however was only a logical consequence of what they had already done and promised to do positively in the immediate future. On that day a gang of youths led by Ramon Franco's mechanic Rada poured petrol all round the main Jesuit church and house in Madrid. They were cheered by a crowd of some hundreds. Police and Civil Guards impassively watched them complete their preparatory work, and set a match to the petrol. Firemen did nothing to save life or property. The inmates escaped by jumping on to the roofs of neighbouring houses which were partly damaged as the firemen did not bring their hoses to bear on them until the religious buildings were well ablaze. Next the fire raisers turned to a convent which they sacked first. From there they were moved to set ablaze a non-fee paying school for five hundred boys run by the

Brothers of Christian Doctrine, then a non-fee paying convent for three
hundred girls: another church, and next an orphanage, and finally
Madrid's best equipped technological and skilled crafts college. It was
one run by the Jesuits.* A Colonel of Hussars round the corner from
the college gave orders for his regiment to turn out to save the building,
but he foolishly telephoned the G.O.C. of the Madrid region to tell him
what he proposed to do. General Queipo de Llano was the G.O.C.
He strictly forbad the Colonel to move, warning him that the Government had "a long dossier" against him.

The Government had known for at least forty-eight hours what was
going to happen. Gabriel Maura, as deputy Prime Minister, had
appealed to the Cabinet to order the Civil Guard to protect the buildings: but the Government was overwhelmingly anti-church. Azaña
put the majority view in the famous words: "A single Republican life
is worth more than all the convents of Spain." During the next forty-
eight hours over a hundred religious houses were attacked, mainly in
the south of Spain. What augured ill for the future of Spain was the fact
that the Government of Republican Spain had countenanced civil
disorder—whatever the justification.

The Church, or rather the Archbishop of Toledo and Primate of
Spain, Cardinal Segura, had officially accepted the Republic in a
Pastoral issued ten days previously and made public on the 7th; but he
had done so in lukewarm terms. He had instructed the faithful to render
the *de facto* government "respect and obedience in the maintenance of
order for the common good"; but the Cardinal, who owed his appointment to Alfonso XIII, had thanked the King for the favours that he
and his ancestors had shown the Church. He had warned the faithful
that "difficult days lay ahead for the church", a forecast which had
already been made in Catholic newspapers and which any intelligent
Catholic of the time could expect from past experience of such men as
now held most of the portfolios of government; he had asked the people
to pray. In the forthcoming elections he told his Archdiocese, they were
to unite "so as to elect candidates who offer full guarantees that they will
defend the rights of the church and of social justice".

Like all carefully phrased and balanced pronouncements, it could be,
and was, quoted out of context. It was even used by those so minded
as proof that the Church was planning a counter-revolution. The more

---

* These burnings were fully covered by film and newsreel. The cameramen
were very well placed—proof of their skill and speed in getting to the right place
or of their foreknowledge.

thoughtful wondered how this could be so, since so many of the senior Spanish Army officers were members of Masonic Lodges, had sworn an Oath contrary to Catholicism, and were *ipso facto* excommunicated.[7] The provisional government had in fact not waited for a mandate from the people to declare "complete religious liberty"—that is to ban the teaching of religion and the placing of the crucifix in schools. It had already prohibited government officials, civil servants and members of the armed services from being present at religious functions. It had made illegal open air religious services. It had, it must also be added, given non-Catholic religious bodies the same "liberty" as the Catholics. It now promised that in a new Constitution there would be a legal separation of Church and State, to which many a Catholic might have agreed since in history the Church in Spain had suffered as much as it had benefited from the State's "protection", had the new State had in mind the religious liberty allowed the Church in the U.S.A. for example, and not, as it became evident from the very first decrees, the suppression of Catholicism.

On 18th May, the State expelled the first Catholic Bishop, Mateo Mújica of Vitoria in the Basque country. On 14th June Cardinal Segura was seen off the country by the Civil Guard.*

These measures against the Church were carried with objections only from Alcala-Zamora and Maura, and they were principally the work of the agnostic Fernando de los Ríos, then Minister of Justice, and Marcelino Domingo, the self-confessed atheist head of a Party which called itself Radical Socialist, a quasi-Jacobin society, of which Ramon Franco was a member.†

The provisional government's anti-religious policy was duly made sacrosant by the vote of the Constituent Assembly. It was elected on 28th June. It was representative of the country to this extent: that there were men and women deputies, laymen and men in clerical orders, rich and poor, intellectuals and men who made the intellectuals writhe with their uncouth grammar, men from every Province and every city. They totalled 454. A few owed their election to their personal reputations: most to the Party labels which they wore. There was a multitude of such labels, Separatist, Centralist, Federalist, and of the European Left, Centre and Right. However, the only Parties to count were the Socialists with 117, Lerroux' Anti-Socialist Radicals

---

* It is an interesting point that these two prelates were also to be active opponents of General Franco in the years ahead.

† He was to leave it for more extreme associations.

with 93, Fernando del Río's Radical Socialists with 59* and Azaña's personal following of 27.

That these Parties should have dominated the results was only to be expected. The Socialists were the only party with an efficient, almost nation-wide organisation through their *Casas del Pueblo*, and the U.G.T. Radicals and Radical-Socialists, and Azaña's Acción Republicana had the use of the Masonic Lodges in existence in all the larger towns. Common to these four groups was a hatred of religion, though in individuals it ranged from the passionate to the lukewarm. Any anti-religious measure was therefore assured an over-whelming majority; but Socialist measures were not. There were Left-wing Catalans and others prepared to vote Socialist, but the Anti-Socialist Radicals could call upon the Centre and Right where religion was not an issue.

The Constitution which this Assembly discussed and approved over the following six months to the end of the year had 121 Articles. It was original with borrowings from Mexico, Russia and Weimar. It defined Spain as "a democratic Republic of workers and all classes in liberty and justice". It established the office of a President and Prime Minister over a single Chamber. It agreed to universal suffrage, in spite of an impassioned anti-feminist speech from a woman member. There were clauses on the usual liberties of the individual, but only "subject to the security of the State", and also on the right to property "if not contrary to the national interest". It separated Church and State.

Had the Assembly then turned to legislation to improve the miserable lot of the urban masses of Spain and to make Spanish agriculture especially in the South more productive† the Republic might have lived; but its directors were obsessed with the Catholic Church. Azaña in particular wanted to make true his dogma "Spain is no longer Catholic". Therefore in the Constitution and in supplementary legislation the Assembly, urged mostly by Azaña, went out of its way to offend Catholic sentiment, by insisting on the burial of non-Christians in consecrated ground, by introducing divorce by consent—a law which enabled Ramon Franco to arrive in El Ferrol with a new wife and small daughter, and to leave them when he tired of them. It was per-

---

* Including Ramon Franco who, elected for both Barcelona and Seville, chose to be a member for Barcelona.

† The Socialists ignorant of its failure in Russia proposed collective farming: eventually they and their opponents agreed to a distribution of the large estates in the South but at a rate which would have taken a century to accomplish.

haps true that only 20 per cent of the nation* went regularly to Mass on Sundays but the great majority did take their children to be baptised, were married in church and many of the most rabid atheists would plead for a priest to come to their deathbed. The law did leave the private individual free to go to Mass. However his clergy were to be denied even the small pittance of 60 million pesetas a year which the State had been dividing among some 30,000 priests—ever since that figure had been agreed as just compensation for the property of which they had been deprived earlier in the nineteenth century. Religious houses with their 45,000 inmates (not all religious) were relieved of "all such property as is not directly necessary to their functions". They were forbidden to engage in commerce, industry, purchase of shares in enterprises or teaching. Azaña would have driven them from medical and social work; not that there were the teachers, nurses or social workers to take their place. By the closure of schools run by religious, nearly 45,000 children were deprived of schooling in Madrid alone bringing the total there without teachers to 59,000 out of 136,000. Alcala-Zamora pleaded in vain that even if Catholics comprised only a minority, it was still the duty of the State to protect minorities. From January 1932 Spain was left without the men to teach in ten centres of higher studies. They were Jesuit foundations. The Jesuits were expelled from Spain with no more than they could carry on foot. There had been the wildest stories that they had hundreds of millions of pesetas. All their goods were confiscated; and when valued the sum was disappointing. The explanation was then circulated that the trouble was that their "vast investments" were in the names of private individuals.[8]

The passing of the anti-religious clauses of the Constitution in October had several far-reaching consequences. Alcala-Zamora resigned from the government leaving Azaña in power. He returned as President at the end of the year with Azaña as Prime Minister. There were always Spaniards who believed that they could change a régime from within as well as those who were prepared to take to arms. As a Basque priest and Member of the Cortes put it, for the Catholic the choice thereafter was between passive resistance, resistance within the established order or resistance by open rebellion.[9] The last possibility could not be entertained at that jucture. The Spanish Army was not the organisation in

---

* There had been some return to the Church since the early days of the century. The 20 per cent is a rounded estimate for the nation. It was as high as 80 per cent in the Basque Provinces and Navarre and as low as 3 per cent in Malaga and district.

which to look for militant Catholics in any number. The Basque and Navarrese delegates withdrew from the Cortes. Thereafter they would evolve tragically in opposite directions. After a long struggle with the central government and in particular the Socialists and the intellectuals, the Basques would acquire a measure of autonomy which enabled them to continue practising their religion and prove that monarchy and catholicism were not synonymous; the Navarrese on the other hand would revive the Carlist spirit of God and King and begin to train militias, just like the Socialists and Anarchists.

However, it was not from the Catholics, Republican or Monarchist, nor yet from the Monarchists that the Republican Government of Madrid had to face its first armed challenge, but from an *ad hoc* and uneasy combination of left-wing extremists which included Communists and Anarchists. The Anarchists now had a fascinating underground organisation, the Iberian Anarchist Federation (F.A.I.) as well as the more visible workers' C.N.T. The Communist Party was gradually sorting out its internal difficulties but as yet it was in no position to embark on any ambitious plan on its own initiative. It agreed therefore to collaborate with the Anarchists. More as a reminder of their existence than with any real hopes of success, this extreme left agglomeration prepared to take over Seville on 22nd July 1931. Ramon Franco was with them. Sanjurjo was sent post haste to scotch the plot. He dealt successfully and rapidly with the military adherents of the revolt, and the Communists beat a hasty retreat. The Anarchists fought tenaciously from a public bar which they had fortified. Resistance did not end till the building had received twenty-two direct hits with H.E. shell. There were thirty dead and two hundred wounded in the affray. Ramon Franco escaped punishment. As a member of the Cortes he was "immune".

The government now created a new armed police force, the *Guardias de Asalto*, with orders to shoot on sight anyone committing an act of sabotage. It was a gift of an organisation for the trigger-happy to join, and the Communists to infiltrate. It would play a vital part in the events immediately preceding the Civil War.

From then onwards there were outbreaks of violence in various parts of the country. In the October Azaña rapidly took through the Cortes a law for the Defence of the Republic capable of as arbitrary an interpretation as any act of the late dictatorship. It authorised the government to fine anyone considered to have incited anyone else to political, social or religious strife up to 10,000 pesetas or to deport him anywhere.

With it Azaña was able to suspend newspapers, fine and expel Catholics, and imprison Catholics and Anarchists at will. The Anarchists in their turn declared war on the central Republic, and since one of their strongholds was Catalonia, against the autonomous government of Catalonia which had come into *de facto* existence at the beginning of the Republican period. In January 1932 they established a Libertarian Communist régime in the valley of the Llobregat, which put up a three-day defence against a strong combined Army and Civil Guard force. Azaña deported 104 of its Anarchist and Communist members.

Socialists, though not as a body for their official leader, Indalecio Prieto, counselled moderation and backed Azaña, were perturbed by the prodigious advances being made by the Anarchists, whose C.N.T. in a recruiting drive was asked for and gave membership cards to 1,200,000 between April 1931 and June 1932. Perhaps originally no more than in an effort to prove that they were not pusillanimous (the red flag was to be seen much less frequently than the black and red of the Anarchists) the more extreme socialists began to take a hand in the violence of the time. They chose as a target the Civil Guard. A fire-eater of a socialist revolutionary, Margarita Nelken, a woman of German–French parentage, incited the people of the region of Badajoz into an attack on the Civil Guard. At a village of mud houses called Castilblanco, the detachment of a corporal and four men were stoned to death. It was a signal for similar attacks throughout the south and south-east. The guards began to defend themselves and there were deaths on both sides. Azaña tried to justify the Civil Guard in the Cortes but Nelken, who was also a deputy, demanded the expulsion of Sanjurjo from his position of command. Azaña gave way. On 5th February he designated Sanjurjo head of the Carabiniers or Customs Guards.

It was demotion. Sanjurjo saw Lerroux,[10] who was having second thoughts about the Republic's progress and his alliance with the Socialists among whom the revolutionary element was gaining the upper hand. The one-time mobster wanted to move his party to the Right, a Right which would approve of the anti-religious legislation but not of active religious persecution, of agrarian reform but not in one lifetime. The General saw in Lerroux a kindred spirit and told him that in his opinion the Republic was being too soft with lawbreakers.* Lerroux counselled Sanjurjo to bide his time.

* The Liberal novelist Pio Baroja[11] on the very day of Sanjurjo's demotion calculated that in the ten months of the Republic more people had been killed on the streets of Spain than in the preceding forty years of Monarchy. It is impossible to arrive at any reliable total.

There were strikes and acts of violence throughout the Summer of 1932. Prieto and other moderate Socialists in the Cortes began to worry about the effect that so much stoppage of work was having on the economy of the working classes, but the Socialist with real power was Largo Caballero who was leading the strikes as head of the U.G.T. It was a matter of life and death in the struggle, bloodiest in the south and Catalonia, between the C.N.T. and the U.G.T. The U.G.T. could not afford to appear less revolutionary than the C.N.T. if the workers were to be solidly behind the next step in "the revolutionary movement which started with the fall of the Monarchy" as Largo Caballero called it. Socialist militias began to make their appearance. In the face of these developments left-wing intellectuals were already reiterating Unamuno's famous cry that this was not the Republic of their dreams "*No es esto! No es esto!*" (Not this, Not this!) Other political bodies could not allow the Socialists alone to have militias. In the North the Carlists, and elsewhere members of what were called Juntas de Ofensiva Nacional Sindicalista—National Syndicalist Action Groups—a movement more important in the years to come, began to clash with the socialist militias.

In the newspapers (when Azaña allowed them to circulate) the main news however was of the troubled progress through the Cortes of a statute to give *de jure* status to the limited autonomy already being exercised in Catalonia, and of another similar statute on behalf of the Basque Provinces—which Fernando de los Ríos christened "the Vatican Gibraltar" and opposed.

Lerroux, who had now broken with the Socialists, was again approached by Sanjurjo. Sanjurjo asked him "to save the unity of Spain". The Spanish Army officers (so few of whom were Catalans) felt very strongly what they called "the dismemberment of Spain". As they saw it, the government was destroying the Motherland. It had to be stopped by any available means. Sanjurjo again asked Lerroux to consider the lawlessness of the country and the activities of Largo Caballero, whom he was convinced now had in mind the overthrow of the Republic which Sanjurjo had helped to establish. Lerroux still did not see any imminent danger.

Turned down by the Radicals, Sanjurjo turned towards the Monarchists. They encouraged and were encouraged by Sanjurjo's discontent with the Republic. He sounded out fellow officers, and obtained a sufficient number of promises of support to come to the conclusion that if he raised the troops in Seville, other Generals would do the same in other cities. Faced with rebellion everywhere he reckoned Madrid would capitulate.

Early in August Franco paid a visit to Madrid "to choose a horse".[12] He was asked repeatedly if he were in on the conspiracy about which everyone, including the Government, seemed to know everything. He answered wilily that while he did not himself believe that the time had come as yet for a rising, he respected those who thought otherwise. He planned to be on holiday for the 10th August, the date that everyone knew had been fixed for the revolt by Sanjurjo. In the event he had to cancel his trip as his immediate superior in Galicia fell ill; but on 10th August he did not move.

The rebellion began according to plan at 0400 hours. It was all over by the same time the following morning. The main army figures implicated had had second thoughts and the support of a mere handful of Monarchists divided among themselves into Carlists and Alfonsists was not enough with which to go ahead. Sanjurjo fled but was captured. The only real fighting was between the supporters of Sanjurjo and government troops together against Anarchists in Seville who could not let such an opportunity pass for a show of force.

Of the many plots against the Republic this was one of the least costly in men or property and one of the shortest lived. Nevertheless Sanjurjo was condemned to death and over a hundred Monarchists were deported to an island off the coast of Africa. However, after reflection, the Cabinet took a vote on Sanjurjo's condemnation and a narrow majority decided that the sentence should be commuted to life imprisonment.

Azaña and his government got down once again to their all-absorbing occupation. On 17th May the Law of Religious Congregations was approved and at least one third of a million children were left without education.[13] This was too much for a large body of parents dependent on these schools, for though the Government promised thousands of new schools, they could not suddenly come into existence. People began to rally to a new Catholic party, Accion Popular,★ whose leader, a Professor of Law, Gil Robles, formed a coalition with parties to the right of him into the C.E.D.A., the Confederacion Española de Derechas Autonomas, coherent only in that they agreed that the persecution of the Church had to stop. But it was not the C.E.D.A. but his own left-wing which was to bring Azaña down.

In the January the Government had sent a detachment of storm

★ A precursor of the Christian Democratic parties of post-war Europe.

troopers to cope with Anarchists who had killed some Civil Guards in a village called Casas Viejas. The troopers were brutal. Brought to account for their actions, their Captain claimed that the Minister of the Interior, Casares Quiroga, had given him orders "to take no prisoners and to shoot in the belly". A government enquiry duly exonerated the Government—but the Socialists could not be seen to support ruthlessness against the very men whom they were trying to win. Towards the end of the year, therefore, they withdrew their support from Azaña. Without them he could not rule. Lerroux took over briefly and then Martinez Barrio, a member of Lerroux's Radicals, but well trusted by the Left as the Grand Master of Spanish Freemasonry. Martinez Barrios supervised elections for a new Cortes.

In the new parliament the main parties were the C.E.D.A. with 115, the Radicals with 102, and the Socialists with 60 seats. The remaining 200 went in dribs and drabs to nineteen other Parties and 18 Independents. Azaña's *Acción Republicana* gained 5 seats against the 27 they had had, del Rios' Radical-Socialists totalled 4 against 60. With the Basques and others, the Catholic vote could about balance the antireligious. The Socialists could count on the support of about another 30 to 40 deputies, that is a total of about a quarter of the House. Rapid legal progress towards socialism was therefore out of the question. Indeed, nothing very startling could be expected from an Assembly in the largest single body was itself a coalition, and the second largest led by an opportunist.

The total vote for all candidates who could be called of the Left was 2·82 millions: for the others it was 5·19 million. Within the left-wing vote, Indalecio Prieto, the Socialist who counselled the Party to keep the law, headed the list, whereas Largo Caballero, ever more clearly a revolutionary in deed and speech was a long way down. The country had rebelled against the Left and in particular against the Marxists.[14]

President Alcala-Zamora called on Lerroux to form a government. He upheld the view that the Radicals were the majority party, since the C.E.D.A. was a coalition: furthermore, he asked, was Gil Robles a Republican or not? Gil Robles, for his part, had maintained that the question of Monarchy versus Republic was immaterial. He was a parliamentarian, and if that was not enough for the President, then Gil Robles would form no government.

Over the next six months Lerroux tried various Cabinet combinations, always with Radicals, but for survival he had to rely on the C.E.D.A. vote, so he allowed the lower clergy two thirds of their old salaries,[15] and he did not enforce the law against the religious congregations so that their schools were quietly allowed to re-open. Martinez Barrio left the Radicals in protest and formed his own Party. The weakened Lerroux needed now the right-wing vote as well as the C.E.D.A.s; the pursuit of agrarian reform, to which the Centre was committed as much as the Left, stopped; and under right-wing pressure he next sanctioned the reduction of the wages of workers. Such actions could only infuriate the Socialists and weaken the position of the moderates among them. As a sop to the Army and the Monarchists he proposed an amnesty for all those imprisoned over the 1932 Rising. Here his own Cabinet and the President differed with Lerroux. The amnesty went through as a package deal: some Anarchists were released[16] and Sanjurjo was taken from prison and exiled to Portugal; and Lerroux had to surrender his premiership. The next Prime Minister was one of his subordinates, Ricardo Samper. Thus, once again Alcala-Zamora ignored the claims to power of the largest single group in the Cortes, and given the premiership to the Radicals. With the passage of the months it was only natural that the C.E.D.A. should begin to insist that if their vote was necessary to keep the Radicals in power they should have at least some share in government, if not government itself. Lerroux was now beginning to realise that Sanjurjo's warnings of Socialist intentions were not wholly unfounded and began to consider a coalition with the C.E.D.A.

Salvador de Madriaga, who briefly in the Spring of 1934 held office under Lerroux, gave it as his considered opinion that by that time "the whole country was rapidly moving towards Civil War". By then indeed only a minority represented in the Cortes by some of Gil Robles Accion Popular and of Lerroux's Radicals, a few independents and some of the Basques and Catalans, believed in parliamentary democracy. The majority did not. There were men who wanted an absolute monarch, others a dictatorship, here of one man, there of an oligarchy under the name Dictatorship of Proletariat, and yet others who yearned for the Libertarian Communism, the anarchy which they sincerely believed could alone bring happiness to mankind. Before there could be a civil war, however, there had to be at least one sizeable united side to fight the rest.

It was in the spring of 1934 that Largo Caballero determined on an effort to unite behind him as many as stood to the left of the Radicals in office. The elections had proved to him that any further advance towards Marxist-Socialism through constitutional means was not desired by the majority of the inhabitants. The Government which had been in power since the elections had moved the country away from Socialism in as much as they had done anything. If now Gil Robles's Accion Popular were to be given a chance to carry out the social reforms of their programme, the less tepid adherents of the Socialist Party might also change their allegiance. For the future of Socialism it was essential therefore that the C.E.D.A. should be kept out of power: but it was even more desirable that the "Democratic Spanish Republic" should be replaced once and for all by the dictatorship of the proletariat. The first obstacle, however, was the disunity at the top of the Socialist Party itself. There was the intellectual group led by Professor Besteiro. In Largo Caballero's (not incorrect) assessment, Besteiro did not accept Marx blindly. Secondly there was Pablo Iglesias' heir Indalecio Prieto who lacked revolutionary fire.

Largo Caballero sought and obtained control of the Socialist Youth Organisation. With the U.G.T. and the Youth behind him, he was in a position to dictate to the more faint-hearted Prieto and Besteiro. The point must here be stressed that the main body of the Spanish Socialist Party, that is all except the Besteiro group, did not differ one whit in ideals and principles from the Communist Party of the Soviet Union except that the Spanish Socialists refused dictation by the Comintern. The Spanish Socialist Party was not, as foreign visitors too readily assumed, Social-Democratic in the Central or West European sense or Socialist in the British way. But if foreign Social Democrats thought of Spanish Socialists as their co-religionists, so did Spanish Socialists judge what they heard from abroad in a Spanish context. Largo Caballero was able to convince Prieto that Gil Robles was the Spanish Dollfuss. Gil Robles' refusal to declare himself a republican or a monarchist was adduced as testimony that he was a crypto-fascist.

By the summer of 1934 Largo Caballero had convinced the mass of the Party that the time had come as prophesied by Marx and Engels for a Socialist revolution in Spain. Arms and ammunition were obtained by stealth and purchase and the Casas del Pueblo and other Socialist buildings were fortified. The Youth was organised into militia units and their conscript service training was refreshed and supplemented. Socialist newspapers carried inflammatory articles and promises that the signal for revolution would be given soon.

Largo Caballero sought also an alliance with the Spanish Communist Party and the Anarchists. The Communist Party was small, but its few thousand members were enthusiasts and in the training of their militia, the Communists had the services of the brother of the ill-fated leader of the Jaca rebellion, Francisco Galán, an able infantry officer. The Socialists, too, had professionals giving their services. Largo Caballero worked hard throughout the country to establish a single workers organisation, the Alianza Obrera, and he called for a Frente Unico of the extreme left. His success varied from area to area. Part of the trouble was that the official Moscow line was then action through "the bourgeois parliamentary democracies", and not revolution; the Spanish Communists had some difficulty in persuading their foreign masters that they could not allow the Socialist Party to appear to be the more revolutionary section of Marxism in Spain and only belatedly were the Communists given authority to support Largo Caballero in a tactical alliance. In the case of the Anarchists anything more than local tactical alliances was out of the question from the very nature of the anarchist movement. Largo's main problem areas, however, were the Basque Provinces where the Socialists had a weak hold (other than in Bilbao), and in Catalonia where the workers were overwhelmingly by preference C.N.T. members. The Basques could not see the Radicals helping them to autonomy. Gil Robles seemed unwilling or unable to make up his mind whether to support them or their no-less Catholic opponents, the Carlists, who wanted a monarchy where the Basques had had enough of kings. The Basques believed that they could handle their own left wing. To them the immediate and important matter was greater autonomy. The central government at that crucial moment helped Largo's call to unity by trying to interfere with the autonomous Basque fiscal system which had survived over fifty years of monarchy and dictatorship. In Catalonia a left winger, Luis Companys, had taken over from the revered figure who had headed the semi-autonomous government from the time of the inception of the Republic. Companys was a demagogue who attracted part of the working class (immigrants from the south of Spain in large measure it will be remembered) to the cause of Catalan nationalism. Here again, the Radical Government chose this moment to intervene on behalf of the owners of vineyards against a new law favouring the leaseholders. The Government thus gave Largo the allies he required. In the rest of the country Gil Robles now played splendidly into the hands of Largo by holding two mass rallies to tell his own hotheads that it was impolitic and inexpedient to press for a share in the government, but that the time would come. The left wing Press likened the rallies to those of Dollfuss and Hitler. The Communists now stopped calling the Socialists the Fascists of

Spain and joined the Socialists in giving that title to Gil Robles. The fact that there were already in the country groups of blue shirted young men engaging in pistol fights with the green shirted Socialist militias, and that those blue shirts had a twenty-seven point programme much of which was at least superficially similar to that of Fascist Parties elsewhere, added further evidence of a pending Fascist *Putsch*. It was not for the Socialists to point out that the Blue Shirts were spiritually far closer to socialism than to Catholicism and that they had more in common with Largo Caballero than with Gil Robles.

In September the extreme left Press more than hinted that the coming month would be their October of revolution. Readers were instructed to look out for the signal. The moment that Gil Robles were to demand power they would attack. All workers would be called out on a national general strike to paralyse "the forces of reaction".

On 3rd October Gil Robles announced that C.E.D.A. could no longer give its support to the government headed by the insignificant Radical Samper. The President called not on Gil Robles, but again on Lerroux to form a new government. Lerroux gave three places in his new government to C.E.D.A. members. The orders for a general strike were issued. Armed men began to attack government buildings in Madrid.

The revolution to destroy the Republic and to establish the dictatorship of the proletariat had begun. The Radical Minister of War, Diego Hidalgo, mistrustful of his own Army generals, called on two men to save the Republic. One of them was Franco.

Franco had had no finger in the Sanjurjo plot. Azaña, however, could not reasonably trust him. Here was a general who was known to spend his free time, when not riding, fishing or shooting, in the reading of history and book after book on politics and economics, and to have done so for many years.[18] It was inconceivable in Spain that such a man should have no political views. The very fact that he had reached general rank at an early age pre-disposed him to turn to a new career, and traditionally for a general there was only one career, that of politics. To the businessmen of Spain the inclusion on boards of directors and letter-heads of men with military titles did not have the same commercial value that it had in England. What was known of Franco's political views was far from a guarantee that he might not prove troublesome to the Republic. He had neither welcomed nor condemned it at its inception. He was not bound to it through Freemasonry in the way that even self-confessed monarchist generals were. The fact that those sent to watch him could not discover what he had in mind made him the more dangerous. In Corunna he was as far away from Madrid (in terms of lines of communication) as anyone could be in continental Spain, but it was still too near. To send him to Africa was unthinkable for he was known to have respect and trust in both the Moroccan forces and the Legion: indeed, more than when he had been in command of either; for as time passed, so the memory became blurred of how strict, not to say cruel[19] a disciplinarian he had been, of how he appeared always to be wanting to prove his power over men physically far more imposing than he, of how he punished, with justice, admittedly, but without mercy. Moroccans and legionaries recalled rather his fearlessness in battle and his handling of battle situations in attack and withdrawal. To have sent him to Africa would have been to have provided him with an army loyal to him. Azaña's problems had been solved when in March 1933 the military command of Majorca became vacant.

Now Franco's wife's sister had married a young lawyer called Serrano Suñer. Serrano, like many a Spanish lawyer, was determined on a political rather than a legal career. He joined the Party which seemed to him the up-and-coming, and which did not offend his religion, Gil Robles' Acción Popular, and his enthusiasm led him to the position of head of its youth organisation. Possibly at Serrano's suggestion or merely because Acción Popular, like other Spanish political parties, liked to have names on their list which could attract votes,* Franco was approached by the Party in the Autumn. He declined an offer to stand for the equivalent under the list system of a 'safe seat'. He remained aloof and untouchable by Right, Left or Centre.

The following February, Doña Pilar, Franco's mother, decided to go on a pilgrimage to Rome. Franco went dutifully to Madrid to escort her to the coast. She fell a victim of the capital's sharp changes in temperature, developed pneumonia and died. During his stay her son came into contact for the first time with Lerroux's Minister of War, Diego Hidalgo, on whom he made a very favourable impression. Later Diego Hidalgo went on a tour of inspection of Majorca and returned even more convinced of Franco as an Army General. Franco had made a special study of the 1914–18 War and seemed to know more about "modern warfare" than other high-ranking officers of the Spanish Army. Hidalgo promoted Franco to major-general in March, and

* For Madariaga's account of how he was elected *v.* his *Spain*, pp. 375–6.

invited him to attend army manoeuvres in the Province of Leon in September as his personal adviser.

On their return to Madrid the Minister of War asked the General to remain in the capital.[20]

The news of the entry of the three C.E.D.A. members into the Cabinet was given out on the evening of 4th October. Middle-class Madrid woke up the following morning to a totally paralysed city. Firing could be heard from all directions. The socialist militias were discharging their weapons into the air to give the impression that more was afoot than there really was. The Civil Guard and the storm troopers, however, stood by the Government, and shops began to reopen. On the evening of the 6th the Government declared martial law. It was hardly necessary by then in the capital, but the news coming in from Catalonia and Asturias made the Government realise that they were facing a real revolution and not merely a strike.

In Barcelona Companys had declared Catalonia "a state of the Federal Spanish Republic", a curious pulling of the punch for full independence. He could count on a nationalist militia organised by a curious fellow called Dencás who may later have become an agent of Mussolini. The Commander of the storm troopers, Lieutenant-Colonel Riquart, was with him, and it was thought that the rank and file would follow their leader. Companys seem also to have believed that the local army division might prove friendly. The Commanding Officer, General Batet, was a Catalan. In the event Companys was deserted by the Socialists and the Anarchists: the storm troopers did not follow the Commander and General Batet followed orders from the Ministry of War to move against the insurgents. In brief engagements the Army suffered 26 casualties: the rebels 47 killed and 117 wounded.

By then the Minister of War, Diego Hidalgo, had two specialist departments in full operation in the Ministry: one under General Goded Llopis and the other under Franco, to direct operations in Catalonia and Asturias respectively. The two had suggested to the Minister the use of troops from Africa against the rebels. However, by the time that a battalion of the Legion and a light infantry battalion of Spaniards landed in Barcelona from Africa, the Catalan rebellion was already well under control. In Asturias, however, the situation was still quite different. There a real civil war was in progress.

Prior to October, Largo Caballero had concentrated his weapons in

Asturias—with good generalship. The U.G.T. was particularly strong and militant in the region. The C.N.T. was weak. The workers were not the starvelings of other areas but sufficiently well fed to withstand the rigours of campaigning if it became necessary. Among them there were several hundred miners highly skilled in the use of explosives: they knew far more about them and had much more experience in handling them than army sappers generally. The broken-up nature of the terrain made it possible to train men in the use of machine guns, as well as rifles, without much interference from the police. The local army garrisons did not total more than 2,000 men. Asturias was difficult to reach except by a narrow pass leading from Leon. If the revolution failed in the rest of Spain, Asturias could fairly easily be turned into a stronghold tenable indefinitely, and thus keeping up the spirit of the revolution in the rest of Spain until such a time as conditions became favourable again for a new national effort. The weapons imported were adequate for the first stages of the rising: thereafter it was hoped the rebels would be in possession of the small arms, artillery and munition factories of Asturias whose workers were instructed not to go on strike.

There was a good historical precedent for the choice of Asturias. There alone had the Spaniards held the Moors in the seventh century. From there Christians had sallied on the reconquest of Spain.

At the start everything went according to plan. The rallying cry "U.H.P. (Union, or Unídos Hermanos Proletarios)—Union of or Unite—a command—proletarian brothers" brought Communists, Trotskyists, peasants and Anarchists together with the Socialists. Their headquarters was in Mieres, a mining town ten miles from Oviedo, the Asturian capital.

On 4th October "at about 8.30 in the morning", writes the Socialist Manuel Grossi, "I declared the Socialist Republic".[21] The orders to begin the revolution had been received at 2300 hours the previous evening and the several revolutionary committees in Asturias had gone into action. According to the strength in them of Communist Party members, some declared with Grossi a Socialist Republic and others a Soviet Republic. The militias, at least ten thousand men[22] attacked Civil Guard posts, churches, schools and other religious institutions, municipal buildings and the houses of middle and upper class citizens. In Mieres they liquidated members of a Catholic Trade Union. A column marched on Oviedo and by the third day it was in possession of half the city. By then they had twenty-nine pieces of artillery from the

factory and other sources, 200 heavy machine guns and 208 light machine guns, and more rifles than men to fire them. The attack, however,
lacked cohesion, and units would detach themselves to form firing
squads to shoot civilians, in some cases with brutality; but the defence
was at first equally chaotic. In the main barracks of Oviedo, there were
two colonels, two lieutenant-colonels, nineteen majors and over nine
hundred other ranks. They merely barricaded themselves.

On his return to Madrid from the army manoeuvres in Leon,
Franco had asked Hidalgo for a few days' leave in Oviedo. He had not
yet departed when the general strike began. However, it was not until
the evening of the 6th, that he walked into the Ministry of War.
Hidalgo had had search parties out for him all day.[23] He explained to
Franco the position. Franco, who as Hidalgo would explain later, "had
been resident for long periods in Asturias, had relations there and knew
well not only the capital and the mining valleys but also the coast and
the lines of communication of the region",[24] recommended the dispatch of forces from Leon in the south, from Galicia in the west and
from the Basque provinces in the east. He set up an office in the
Ministry with his cousin, Franco-Salgado, and two naval officers. He
had in mind the landing of troops in the two Asturian ports of Gijon
and Avilés. He ordered the cruiser *Libertad* and all available gunboats in
El Ferrol to embark troops and marines and the cruiser *Cervantes* and
battleship *Jaime I* to embark three *banderas* of the Legion,* a tabor of
Moors, two light infantry battalions and a mountain battery at Ceuta,
and made for Asturias as fast as they could. He tried to contact the
Air Force headquarters and air base in Leon. He wanted the very
Republican General Lopez Ochoa to go there, take command of the
troops in the Province and with them advance through the passes to
the north. However, the commanders of both the Air Force headquarters and the air base were for the rebels. He ordered their arrest.
The commander at the air base was his own first cousin Ricardo de la
Puente Bahamonde. Still unsure of the situation in Leon and whether
the passes into Asturias were in enemy hands or no, he sent Lopez
Ochoa to Lugo in Galicia. There Ochoa was able to raise sufficient
transport for the whole of the depleted battalion, about four hundred
men. With these he reached on the 11th the barracks at Oviedo and took
command of the self-encloistered one thousand men. The cruiser
Libertad and the gunboats had arrived three days earlier at Gijon. The

* Azaña had reduced the Legion's strength to six *banderas*.

troops and marines from El Ferrol had been disembarked and taken up defensive positions. The column from the east had been halted. However, Franco had re-established contact with the air base, and its aircraft, of 1918 vintage, were pounding the rebels with their heaviest bombs: eleven pounders. There was also a telegraph link between Oviedo, Gijon and Madrid. Franco decided on the daring scheme of using the ship's guns in support of the land forces, using his office some 270 miles away from the scene of the fighting, as the necessary land-ship link. There was no other way of transmitting forward observers' directions to the gunners at sea.

The African troops arrived on the 10th. Franco sent his trustworthy friend, Colonel Yague, to command them.[25] Yague landed on the beach of Gijon by autogiro. The troops from Africa had been slightly delayed. *Cervantes* had had to put in at Corunna on Franco's orders after he had received a report that the commander of a light infantry battalion had made it known that he intended to order his troops not to fire on their fellow countrymen.

The rebels in Oviedo fell back before the combined pressure from Lopez Ochoa and Yague. The revolutionaries blew up the university with its excellent library, and withdrew to the mining centres of Mieres and Sama. Two days later, on 15th October, the main body of the revolutionaries sued for peace. Their main condition was that the Moors and the legionaries should not form the vanguard of the advance in the mining areas. Lopez Ochoa put them in the rear, to the fury of Yague. Yague was to confess that he was on the point of shooting Lopez Ochoa.

The Legion and the Moors had acquired a reputation for barbarous behaviour in and after battle. Only a properly constituted independent court could have sifted the truth from the false accusations of conduct contrary to the contemporary rules of war. Relatives of victims would satisfy an interrogator thirty years later that there had been *prima facie* cases against legionaries as also against Socialists. Some Socialists were tried, but no legionaries. Left- and right-wing newspapers vied with each other in reporters' stories of atrocities, They exacerbated hatred at the very time when Spaniards needed to be calmed. A left-wing editor was shot dead in Oviedo by a Legion officer called Ivanov. Of the editor's allegations, one at least was certainly true. The Legion shot men who surrendered to them. There is no other way of accounting for the casualty figures.

By the middle of October Lopez Ochoa had under his command

some fifteen thousand men. Army casualties totalled about one thousand of which some 200 were killed. There were over 1,000, perhaps as many as 3,000, dead on the rebel side.[26]

Franco arrived in Oviedo with the Minister of War on 24th October. He was hailed by the majority of the middle and upper classes of Oviedo as their saviour—even as the saviour of the Republic.

NOTES

1. The exact figures are: in the Peninsula—Officers 7,661, O.Rs. 105,367; in Africa—Officers 1,756, O.Rs. 41,774 including 9,080 Moors (Anuario, 1932).

2. Curiously exaggerated figures have been given of the number of generals before Azaña's reforms. In the last days of the monarchy there were 18 lieutenant-generals, 34 major-generals and 96 brigadiers on the active list (Anuario, 1931); total 148. Azaña reduced this to 20 major-generals and 64 brigadiers: total 84.

3. Azaña in the Cortes on 23rd May 1931 and 30th July 1931. Weapons and equipment were not changed. The structure two battalions per regiment, two regiments per brigade, two brigades per division, looked pretty on paper: and that is about all that can be said in its favour.

4. The only saving was in pay. As a private got 1 peseta a day, the overall saving was under £2 million a year.

5. The reprimand is recorded "as ordered" in Franco's *Hoja de Servicio*. If Arraras's edition of Azaña's *Memorias* are to be trusted (pp. 307-8) the Minister made sure that it was recorded.

6. Witnesses of Azaña's visit in Corunna. Local papers published the photographs.

7. It may be that this pastoral has so often been misquoted by foreign authors (as opposed to Spaniards who have quoted from it out of context) because it is not easy to come by a full text. Cardinal Segura had one copy in Seville in 1950. It was popular belief that many—some say most—of the senior Army officers were Masons. All the Masonic records fell into Nationalist hands during the course of the war, and there is a museum of them in Salamanca: but I have been informed by a trustworthy source that they were severely "expurgated" and that the names of many supporters of the Nationalists were expunged. The records were also "added to".

8. The Spanish Jesuit provinces had 3,630 members, of whom 650 were missionaries in India, the Far East and South America. In Spain they ran 21 secondary and 163 primary and vocational schools, the Spanish leper colony

and the 10 centres of higher studies (science as well as theology). Fees (where charged) were at best uneconomic and in most cases nominal. The Jesuits did have considerable investments, mainly in public utility companies, and of course in their school and other buildings. Collectively the investments and nominal value of the buildings may have run into the 200 million pesetas which their bitterest enemies claimed for them—55,000 pesetas, or £1,800 per head—not much for men of renowned learning with fifteen years minimum of higher studies behind them. It is, of course, as foolish to think of the Society as wealthy as it would be to consider the Dean and Chapter of Westminster Abbey as multi-millionaires because the buildings they occupy are on lands worth millions of pounds in theory. The Jesuits lived frugally. They allowed themselves for personal expenditure a few pesetas a week. Today they refer to their large house in the Calle Serrano as the Serrano-Hilton. As the headquarters of considerable missionary activity as well as local it looks imposing enough from the outside, but the bed and board provided might be euphemistically called "good bed and plain cooking".

9. The then Canon Antonio Pildain and Zapiain, Basque nationalist member. Canon Pildain was appointed Bishop of the Canaries on 18th May 1936. He was not consecrated until 14th February 1937 because of the Civil War.

10. Lerroux, *Pequeña Historia*.

11. Speech in Villena 5th February quoted by Arraras in *Historia de la Segunda República Española* in 1 vol. (Madrid, 1965), p. 104. The Arraras of this abridged *Historia* is hardly recognisable as the Arraras of the Azaña *Memorias*, of the first biography of Franco, or even of the earlier two-volume version.

12. Franco-Salgado. I see no reason to doubt it.

13. The educational record of Azaña's Government has received praise from foreigners owing to a misunderstanding. In Ministerial publications "*una escuela*" was not a school but a classroom. This was not changed until the 1960s when Spain took part in the O.E.C.D. Mediterranean Regional Project.

14. However, in considering these figures it must be borne in mind that some Anarchists had voted for the Left but that others had abstained. The Anarchists had their own way of showing how strong they were. In four days of sabotage and fighting with dynamite and petrol bombs (the "Molotov cocktails" of another war) eighty-nine persons were killed and 164 were hurt.

15. As Madariaga says (p. 325), strictly speaking this was an unconstitutional act.

16. Under Azaña, 9,000 had been imprisoned.

17. Op. cit., p. 327.

18. He took out a personal subscription to the bulletins on Soviet affairs from Geneva when, with the advent of the Republic, the subscription would no longer be borne by the Government (conversation with author).

19. A relative term. Punishments in the Spanish Army did not undergo the same

changes as those in the British Army after 1918. Those who have complained to me of Franco's "cruelty" admitted that he always kept within the bounds of the Law, and that he did not demand of others what he did not demand of himself.

20. *Hoja de Servicio.*

21. Grossi: *La insurreeción de Asturias* (Valencia, 1935), p. 25. Grossi, however, was only a local leader. The Generalissimo was Gonzalez Peña.

22. The Asturian left wing newspaper *Avance* (months of September and October) gives the impression that there were more. There may well have been.

23. Franco–Salgado.

24. Diego Hidalgo wrote a long defence of himself and his actions during the October Revolution and after: *Porqué fuí lanzado del Ministerio de Guerra,* Espasa Calpe, 1934. His praise of Franco was unstinting; and it is of particular interest since it was written before there was any possibility that Franco might rise to power.

> "I met this general in Madrid in February [1934]. I got to know him during my [ministerial] tour of the Balearics, and in those four days I became convinced that his reputation was justified. Totally dedicated to his profession, he possesses to a high degree all the military virtues. He is a hard worker; his clarity of thought, understanding and general education are all at the service of arms. Of his virtues the highest is his capacity to weigh, examine, analize, penetrate and develop problems. He is meticulous in carrying out his duties, to the point of criticism, hard in giving necessary orders, exigent and yet understanding, unruffled, determined... he never meanders [*no divaga jamas*]... his knowledge of modern military science has the solid foundation of a study of all that the great captains accomplished in history... he has a thorough knowledge of the Great War and its lessons."

For these reasons, Hidalgo says, he invited Franco to accompany him in the manoeuvres.

> "Why shouldn't a minister have the best adviser?... Everyone has praise for Franco, but not a word of praise for the Minister who chose him. I have the right to tell people that *I* was that minister."

Hidalgo then goes on to parry objections:

> "Franco was made a brigadier-general with due regard to all regulations: but he should have been one anyway. Then on 28th January 1933... he was 'frozen' in that rank. *I* raised Franco to major-general when the one vacancy occurred in my time [as minister]. I'm proud to have promoted him."

25. Yague's *Hoja de Servicio.* Juan Yague Blanco joined the Toledo Academy and was commissioned on the same dates as Franco. Their paths met again in Africa during the Riff War when Yague was with the *Regulares.* He had been

promoted lieutenant-colonel and posted to one of the independent mountain infantry battalions in Spain in 1932. He was given his first permanent command of Legionaries in January 1936, as O.C. the 2nd Legion (that is one-half of the Tercio) and was still a lieutenant-colonel at the outbreak of the Civil War.

26. Casualties: the official army figures were: killed—22 officers, 25 N.C.O.s and 173 other ranks; wounded—(all ranks) 743; and missing 46. Once again it is worth noting the inordinately heavy officer deaths. Estimates of civilians killed vary from the official 855 to 14,000. The last figure is an absurd exaggeration (Brennan gives 3,000); but even a four defenders killed in action to one attacker ratio is greater than could be expected in an action of this nature. A reference to the 1916 Easter Rising and a comparison is not unfair. The Sherwood Foresters alone suffered 250 casualties when attacking at one point no more than a dozen Irishmen. In Dublin, it is now admitted, individual British officers and men killed "rebels" who had surrendered or been captured: but the Army still had the greater casualties. The Asturian miners were not fools. They had done military service. The attackers should have had the greater casualties.

8

THE RELUCTANT REBEL

It is not only of the Legion in Oviedo that it can be said that "they behaved with the same primitive instinct as the masses whom they feared".[1] Insofar as it excuses them for what they did in action, it must be added that they were fighting against forces which far outnumbered them and that in such circumstances the military of most times and most nations have rid themselves of the encumbrance of prisoners. Fear, however, cannot account for the actions of the military and the police after the majority of the rebels had surrendered.

There was a sizeable discrepancy between numbers of the weapons captured and those known to have been taken from the factories alone. Several of the leaders were at liberty. The task now was to discover the hideouts of leaders and material. A Major Doval, expert in obtaining information by torture, was drafted to Oviedo.[2] Doval was a master of his craft, and although over a hundred wanted men escaped to Moscow, by the end of the year he had closed the net on Gonzalez Peña and a Sergeant Vazquez whom the Army was even keener to apprehend as a notorious deserter to the enemy on the field of battle.

While the Asturian revolt was still being suppressed, courts martial had been busy in Barcelona. The fact was that Companys had taken arms against the constitution of the Spanish Republic. Some of his followers had acted out of the fear that they might be about to lose the limited autonomy approved under the Constitution. Their participation had thus been paradoxical. They had attacked the Republic to uphold the constitution of the Republic. That, however, was not the position of Companys. His goal had been the complete independence of Catalonia. Nor was it the position of the military officers, Riquart of the assault guards, Perez Farras of the militia, and others. They had more than rebelled against the Republic: they had violated their oath of allegiance to the Army Command.

In all, the courts sentenced twenty-one Catalans to death. Cardinal Vidal, the Archbishop of Tarragona, was among the many thousands who signed a plea for mercy. In Madrid however all government was brought to a standstill by arguments and intrigues for and against the executions. The basic point was that whatever was decided about the Catalans would be a precedent for a decision on the fate of the Asturians.

For the legalists there was no problem: Catalans and Asturians had alike rebelled against the Constitution and no distinction could be made. For the growing number of ultra-nationalists, the Catalans were guilty of a greater crime than the Asturians. The former had sought the division of their idol, Spain, as constituted over the previous 450 years. Calvo Sotelo, who had returned from exile at once a rabid monarchist and nationalist, was to utter in the Cortes before the end of the year "Better a Red Spain than a shattered Spain". Many an army officer agreed with him. To them the socialist Gonzalez Peña was almost blameless compared with the separatist Lieutenant-Colonel Riquart. For the socialist, too, there was no problem. The fate of the Catalans, other than the socialistic Companys, was of no concern to them. That of Gonzalez Peña was; for he had proved himself both an able leader in revolutions and a match for communists anxious to take over the Socialist Party and control the rate of progress towards the goal ordained by Marx. The fate of the master-mind behind the October Revolution, Largo Caballero, was also still open. Lest he be condemned to death, it was expedient that the Catalans should not be executed.

For the leaders of the two Parties in office the problem was insoluble. Neither could afford to alienate the Army, and they were aware that the cancer of nationalism had spread into their parties. At the same time both parties had supporters of limited Catalan autonomy. And again Gil Robles had to consider the conviction of many of his followers that unless the socialist leaders were executed, there would be a second rising during which the Socialists would murder tens of thousands of people. Gil Robles himself appears to have been convinced that unless a coup de grâce were given wounded Socialism it would revive to attack again with even greater ferocity. Eventually the Cabinet decided on confirming the sentences: the President intervened with doubtful legality and overruled them. Companys, Riquart, Perez Farras and others survived to fight again.

It has often been said that during the period December 1933 to February 1936 Spain was under a Right-wing government. There were nine different governments, and apart from Lerroux there were three other Prime Ministers. After Asturias Lerroux and Gil Robles did come to realise that unless they kept together, the country would be handed over to the left-wing, and in that sense it was a period of right-wing rule; but both were constantly harrassed from within their Parties as well as by their opponents. It is therefore truer to say that the country was not governed during this period, and in the last analysis, Spain was set on the course that led to the Civil War more by the omissions of government than by acts of government.

What Spain needed was a more equitable distribution of such wealth as there was, and more wealth for distribution. At a time when the rest of the world was emerging from the economic morass of the "slump", Spain was sinking lower. At the beginning of 1935 six hundred thousand workers out of a total labour force of under seven millions were registered unemployed and six months later there were one million: figures which do not take into account the situation in the more remote rural areas. No country in Western Europe had a higher percentage of illiterates or a lower percentage of skilled workers in agriculture or industry; there was a dearth of technicians, trained managers and professional men—other than lawyers. No Western European country had proportionately as many civil servants, and yet in none did an administrative problem take as long in resolution.

In the fifteen months that followed the suppression of the October Revolution there was only one serious attempt to remedy the ills from which the country and not merely the Republic was dying. It was a three-part agrarian reform introduced by Gimenez Fernandez, the Professor of Canon Law at Seville University who for a brief time was Minister of Agriculture. The combined opposition of landowners— monarchist and republican alike, Radicals and C.E.D.A. (the Professor's own Party)—brought it to nothing. Gimenez Fernandez was vituperated as a "white Bolshevik", and when he tried to win support for it on the grounds that it was based on the principles of social justice laid down by Leo XIII in his *Rerum Novarum*, the cry arose "If you take away our land with your encyclicals, I shall declare myself a Protestant". The men of wealth were not prepared to listen to reason.

No one was prepared to follow close argument. In the Cortes and out of them politicians talked incessantly. Rhetoric had long covered a lack of logic in the Cortes; now progressively demagogy began to drive out rhetoric. Deputies were prepared to let their opponents talk only to pick out debating points, and to accuse each other of duplicity, contradiction and insincerity. The dialogue of government and oppo-

sition turned into pandemonium. The Cortes became a Tower of
Babel where everyone spoke one language yet no one understood his
neighbour.

Perusal of the speeches of the period, especially as truncated in the
Press, has led subsequent writers to the most divergent opinions as to
what the principal figures and especially Lerroux and Gil Robles meant
or intended. They puzzled their contemporaries and compatriots. The
Socialists, allowed to return to the Cortes, made no secret of their
ideals. Nor did the Monarchists with Calvo Sotelo at their head. He
and Jose Antonio Primo de Rivera, the young lawyer son of the
dictator, ranted and thundered against the Republic and the Republican
Constitution as ardently as any Socialist or Catalanist who had risen
in arms. Neither Robles nor Lerroux could take such a clear line.
There were religious clauses in the Constitution which Gil Robles had
in conscience to do his utmost to change; but Gil Robles had ever to
keep his eye not merely on the right-wing of his C.E.D.A. (a coalition,
let it be remembered, of which his own Catholic Accion Popular was
its only progressively-minded component), but on the men behind
that right-wing, men of wealth whose Catholicism was pre- and even,
it could be demonstrated, anti-Tridentine, let alone anti-Leonine.

Salvador de Madariaga said of the 1930 Jaca Rising and subsequent
events that "the extreme left betrayed the left. It is the law of Spanish
progressive politics".[3] If the Government of this period was a government of the Right, then it must be said with equal truth that "the extreme Right betrayed the Right". The conclusion of the French
philosopher Jacques Maritain in 1937 is applicable to the men in power
in 1934 and 1935: "In the defence of order and intelligence, they did
not use order and intelligence."[4]

Franco remained in Madrid until the month of February 1935 when
he was appointed General Officer Commanding-in-Chief of the
military forces in Morocco. Three months later he was on his way back
to Spain.

The Government with Diego Hidalgo as Minister of War had fallen
in April, when the three C.E.D.A. Ministers refused to be signatories
to the commutation of the death sentences which courts martial had
passed on Gonzalez Peña and others guilty of common law crimes in
Asturias. The new government, exclusively Radical, discovered that
it could not manage without C.E.D.A. support. It lasted under a month.
Lerroux was then again asked to form a new one, his sixth. He regained

C.E.D.A. support by giving them five portfolios, still a minority in a Cabinet of thirteen men, including the Prime Minister.[5] In this government Gil Robles held the Ministry of War. From the start he showed a capacity for getting things done which must give cause to speculate on what he might have accomplished in Spain as Prime Minister, had the President, Alcala-Zamora not had a pathological distrust of the man, and so, steadfastly refused him a chance to form a government.[6]

Gil Robles' first act was to summon to Madrid all the Divisional and other senior commanders. He asked them for a detailed report on the state of their commands. They reported that they had ammunition sufficient only to maintain a battle for twenty-four hours: that there was a shortage of uniforms: that in Asturias men's wounds had become gangrenous because there had been no field dressings available.

On 17th May Gil appointed General Fanjul his Under-Secretary. Fanjul would be loyal in the Minister's absence and do his best to carry out ministerial policy. Gil Robles then chose General Goded, Hidalgo's aide of October, as Commandant of the Air Force. Goded's known antipathy towards the Republic since he had been Azaña's Inspector General of the Army, made the left look awry at the choice. However, the appointment which really caused a stir among the men of the Left was that of Franco as Army Chief of Staff. Changes in divisional commands could be expected and they were announced with surprising speed. Among the first to be replaced were Miaja and Riquelme, both men with African war backgrounds. Miaja was an officer of no particular distinction. Riquelme had a political past: he had plotted against Primo de Rivera. In all eighty officers were put on the unemployed list. Some were grossly incompetent like Hernandez Sarabia, still a colonel at fifty-eight. Others were men disliked or mistrusted by either Franco or Goded, like a Colonel Mangada whom Goded had once put under arrest. Others again were officers of extreme Left sympathies and even of secret affiliations with extreme Left parties. The vacancies so created were filled with officers whom Azaña had dismissed. Mola was recalled and instructed to study and modernize mobilisation plans; but he had hardly begun when he was re-posted to command in Africa.

Franco dedicated himself to his new task with a fervour of which even his enemies speak as characteristic of the man. He was in his office by not later than a quarter to nine. He took his lunch break at about 3.30. Back at 5 o'clock he would stay there until 11—a twelve-hour day six days a week. On Sundays and holidays he called at the Ministry for a few hours.

Most of the work was routine. Delegation was not a feature of Spanish bureaucracy. The simplest requisition required the rubber stamp of the highest civil servant or Army officer, when not of the Minister: a disposition which made it easy for the perpetration of the frauds which it sought to prevent; for the senior official, inundated with papers to sign, could not read them all, nor could he remember subsequently which he had signed and which not.

Gil Robles, as Minister of War, was prepared to delegate to an unusual degree. He instructed Franco to effect such reforms in the Army calculated to improve its efficiency as did not involve extra-budgetary expense. There was plenty of scope. In view of the international tension over Mussolini's African adventures, Franco was instructed also to overhaul the defences of the Balearics and Cartagena. He did so, and he put on call an independent brigade in the Gibraltar region and another which, while stationed on the Portuguese frontier, could be quickly switched to any of the Spanish southern Mediterranean ports: dispositions which backed Spain's declared preparedness to act in consort with Britain and other members of the League of Nations against Mussolini.[7] On paper he gave the eight infantry divisions more fire power: their lack, by contemporary standards, of machine guns and mortars was to be diminished. He ordered anti-aircraft guns and steel helmets. He sought to interest the civilian population in defence against air attack. He began negotiations for the necessary licences from foreign patentees to construct aircraft of more modern design than 1919 in a factory in Guadalajara. He worked out for his Minister a three-year plan for the re-equipment of the armed services at an estimate of 1,100 million pesetas.

Political changes were to baulk Franco of a rich harvest for his labours. Gil Robles, who survived one change of government in October, lost his post in December. Franco himself would be out of the Ministry two months later. Nothing came of the plan for the Army's re-equipment. Indeed, Franco's rearmament remained largely on paper. Though he had the workers in arsenals and armed factories placed under military law, they could not suddenly go from virtual standstill into top gear, and in any case their directors could not forgo their traditional two months summer holidays whatever the Chief of Staff might demand. The Madrid Division received its steel helmets, mortars and machine guns but other divisions did not.

In spite of the cold fact that Franco was Chief of Staff for too short a period to reform the army, his reputation as a go-ahead general was enhanced. He further attracted to himself the loyalty of those army officers who believed, as he did, that scandals and criminal acts involving army officers should be kept from public knowledge and punished severely but secretly, when he restored the Courts of Honour which Azaña had suppressed. The code under which they operated was different from the civilian and from that exercised in public courts martial, harsher here, and more lenient there, but in them the accused was judged by his peers, from whom he could expect a fair trial. By the end of 1935 an intelligent appreciation of the situation would have concluded that the greater part of the officers and N.C.O.s of the Army would follow Franco for good or ill. They trusted his judgement. If he decided that it was his duty to support the establishment, they would do so: if he were to call for a revolt against it, they would answer it. The greater part but not all.

The political changes which brought to nothing Franco's rearmament plan were triggered off by two major scandals which destroyed whatever prestige the Radicals still had. Back in 1933 a Jew of Mexican nationality, David Strauss, and another of Dutch birth, Perl, had demonstrated to Companys in Sitges an electrically-operated roulette wheel which from the surnames of their inventors was called the *Straperlo*. It was a clever device which gave gamblers the impression that their success depended on their personal skill, their quickness of sight, memory and mental arithmetic, and on their remaining cool. It was a complete fraud giving the operators far greater dividends than the standard hand-worked model. Companys refused its promoters a licence for Catalonia. They moved to Madrid where Lerroux' adopted son Aurelio and a number of men with influence, or powers of persuasion, over the Secretary to the Radical Minister of the Interior who would have to issue the licences, and over the Radical Director-General of State Security who could prohibit the machines, formed an exploiting company with Strauss and Perl. The Minister was not consulted, and the Director of Security was almost certainly duped. The roulette began operating in the high-class casino at San Sebastian and an equally high-class hotel in Majorca. It had hardly been in action three hours in the Spanish summer capital when the police moved in on orders from the Ministry of the Interior. The matter might have ended there, but that Strauss, who had dispensed eighty thousand Dutch florins and two very expensive gold watches, wanted his bribes back or a return of some kind for the money he had "invested". He came across the Socialist leader Indalecio Prieto and Azaña in Belgium. They agreed to take up the matter on his behalf but in their own time. Strauss, dissatisfied, now wrote straight to Lerroux demanding of him the return of the money under threat of exposure of his adopted son. Lerroux refused to be blackmailed. A government commission was appointed. Lerroux was absolved of any responsibility: but not so other Radicals. A month later a second scandal came to light. A General Nombela proved to the satisfaction of the Cortes that through one of Lerroux' Under-Secretaries a shipowner had been allowed to receive over 3,000,000 pesetas for losses in Africa originally assessed at 600,000. The extreme Right and the extreme Left joined in an all-out propaganda offensive against the Radicals as corrupt to the core and against the C.E.D.A. for having been their partners in office. Lerroux resigned. Alcala-Zamora, unable now to call on any Radical to replace him, would still not turn to the leader of the largest group in the Cortes. The only course open was the dissolution of the Cortes and new elections. A nonentity in poor health, Portela, agreed to form a caretaker government until the elections could be held.

Portela took office in December. He did not retain Gil Robles as Minister of War.

On hearing the news, Franco organised a small farewell party for the out-going Minister. He made a brief speech in praise of Gil Robles who had "never once urged the claim to promotion of any friend of his" and who had restored "honour and discipline and all the basic concepts of the Army" in his seven months of office. In reply Gil Robles thanked those who had worked with him for doing their duty, and left the Ministry.[8]

So much for the Gil Robles in whom the Socialists had seen a Spanish Dollfuss; and not only the Socialists. The Monarchists had looked on the Franco–Gil Robles combination with hope—and despair. The Madrid stage had had a play[9] whose protagonists were two characters which the dullest member of the audience identified as Franco and the Minister. The moral of the story was that it was the duty of such a pair to seize power once and for all. Whether this was an attempt by the Right to discredit Gil Robles or whether the Monarchists hoped thereby to shame Gil Robles and Franco into action, both Minister and General ignored it. Gil Robles, however did give way to the pressure, which elements of his own C.E.D.A. coalition placed upon him, to this extent: he summoned Franco, Goded and Fanjul. As the lawyer that he was he put to the Generals these questions: "Given that the President has made Prime Minister a man who has no political following in the Cortes, and that that man has formed a Government representing no body of opinion, has the constitution been violated? If it has, would the Army be prepared to rise in its defence?" Franco, Fanjul and Goded asked for time to consult their army colleagues. They reported that the Army was not of one mind.

It did not become public knowledge until March 1937 that Gil Robles had discussed with Franco the theoretic possibility of a rising in 1935. Two contradictory versions then became current: the first that Franco had urged Gil Robles to rebel, the other that it had been vice versa. Franco then wrote Gil Robles a letter. As often when angry, he expressed himself in an involved style; but his meaning was clear enough: neither had urged the other. "The fulfilment of the duty of obedience to authority, the situation in Spain which though in a difficult trance was not in imminent danger, and the correctness of your behaviour throughout your term of office as Minister, gave me no authority and made it impossible for me to suggest what at that moment would have been unjustifiable and impossible of fulfilment." It was "unjustifiable" because the Motherland was not in "imminent danger".[10]

Franco's attitude was as incomprehensible to the Right as to the Left. The Left could not believe that he was not a conspirator: the Right could not understand why he was not.

The professional plotter-in-chief among the Monarchists, the airman Ansaldo, recalled in his famous Memoirs—¿Para Que?—(What was it all For?) the Franco of the days when Sanjurjo was preparing his un-succesful coup: "In all our efforts to recruit sympathisers and supporters there was a curious phenomenon. Everywhere, and very specially among wealthy civilians, we were asked "Is General Franco with you"; we could not answer Yes or No. Franco was a fellow who said one thing and then contradicted it, who came close to one and then went away again, who swerved and wheeled out: always vague, never clear nor forthright. He was seen to be the most monarchist of all the young Spanish generals. Before the King he had always shown himself as such and the King had believed his behaviour. He had been his Gentleman of the Bedchamber when it was a very special grace and a sign of un-qualified loyalty. And yet, although we had all long taken it for granted that he would support the coup, shortly before 10th August, he openly declared that he would have no part in it, and counselled several officers to follow his example."[11]

Once again during the October rising in Asturias Ansaldo had approached Franco. The Monarchists were prepared to carry out a coup with Sanjurjo as the figurehead in the midst of the general confusion. Ansaldo was to fly Sanjurjo out of Portugal to Oviedo where they could count on the allegiance of Yague, and the Foreign Legion. Everything was ready. Then according to Ansaldo, "a journalist came from the Ministry of War. Things have changed, he said. General Franco does not believe this is the moment to act".

He was right, whether he was in sympathy with the plotters or no. Yague was not the whole army, even in Asturias. The strength of the enemy was far superior to the combined Lopez Ochoa–Yague force. In the event of a monarchist rising Lopez Ochoa's troops might have sided with the enemy against the African force on the grounds that a Spanish enemy of the Republic was preferable to one using foreign mercenaries.

The remark was also cleverly worded. Franco judged the plot not merely untimely but definitely immoral. Again, let us look at the situation through Franco's eyes. Because even the combined Lopez Ochoa–Yague force was inferior in numbers to the enemy, it was essential that it should be kept together. An outright declaration that Franco was not with Yague and Sanjurjo might have alienated the one commander of the one force whom he could trust against the rebels. No intelligent general, therefore, could have been more specific.

Where in fact did Franco stand? If he was a Monarchist why did he not join Sanjurjo in 1932 or 1934? If he was a Republican why did he take no part in the pre-1931 plots? If he was a man of the Left, why did he proceed so firmly against the Asturians? If he was a man of the Right, why did he not rise in December 1935? Why, finally, did he rise seven months later in July 1936, under Sanjurjo but at the side of a very Republican Queipo de Llano?

There is one way in which Franco's actions can be seen as consistent, and into which all the known facts fit: that he acted always from principles firmly engraved into him in his early years.

As we have seen, at home and as a cadet, it was drilled into Franco that "there is nothing more sacred than the *Patria*". What did this mean?

(1) *Patria* in the mind of the Spaniard into whom the concept was drilled was presented as a mother-father figure: a figure to be adored as sacred. It is no mere accident that the word is feminine from a Latin masculine root.

(2) If the *Patria* can be thought of as the mother-father, then the Chief

of State becomes the High Priest to provide, care for and protect the *Patria*. The High Priest might be a King, President or Dictator—it does not matter which. He might have as assistant ministers a Council, a Prime Minister and Cabinet, or even a House of Representatives, but this too is ritualistic detail.

(3) The Temple of the *Patria* is the National Territory. The National Territory as Franco understood it was all of the Iberian Peninsula (less that part defined as Portugal), and certain islands and African territories. The African territories were, as it were, annexes to the temple; but the provinces of Spain were its pillars: the removal of any of them, therefore, endangered the whole.

(4) Though an analogy must never be pressed too far, the inhabitants may be seen as at once the children of the *Patria* and its worshippers.

(5) The *Patria* and the Temple had its guard—the Army—guardians of the congregation, of the Assistant and High Priests, but above all of the mother-father figure and her honour. Therefore, if the High Priest dishonoured the *Patria* by worshipping foreign Gods, or if he was so incompetent as to endanger the fabric of the temple, or if the congregation became so unruly as to imperil the temple, it became the duty of the guard to save the *Patria*. However the danger had to be real and imminent for the army to rush in and save her; for in doing so, it might well do more damage than it was seeking to prevent.

Bearing all this in mind Franco's conduct up to the end of 1935 can be seen as consistent. He had to protest vehemently against Primo de Rivera's proposal to give up the annexes. A King could serve the Patria as well as a Republic: he could therefore not plot against the King; but a Republic could also serve the *Patria* as well as a King: he could therefore not support his friend Sanjurjo in his plots. In 1934 however he had had to serve the Republic with arms, against those who sought to remove the pillars and those whom he believed were creating conditions in which the temple might have been ruined. But in 1935 the question facing him was Gil Robles or Portela. Neither constituted a danger to the temple.

"Remember that our duty is not to this or that form of government, but to the motherland, and that the men and arms entrusted to us by the nation may be used only in its defence."[12] Mola had written these words to the ill-fated Captain Galan hoping to dissuade him from his action in Jaca. Franco shared this view. At the same time every Army officer knew by heart the Second Article of the Army Act:

The Army's first and most important mission is to uphold the independence of the motherland and defend it from external and internal enemies.

"Developments in Spain towards the end of 1935 were disturbing. There was growing violence and disorder. What worried me however was not so much what was happening *within* Spain as outside and the relations between people in Spain and Moscow. I had had a full report of the proceedings of the VIIth Congress of the Commitern. I had however to be certain that what had been decided upon in Moscow was in fact going to be carried out in Spain."[13]

Year in year out the Spanish Communists had reported at Comintern and C.P.S.U. Congresses increased membership—3,000 in 1931, 20,000 in 1933 and in 1935 30,000.[14] The Congresses had listened to long reports bespattered with statistics of work accomplished—numbers of strikes organised, protests, deaths and imprisonments at the hands of "Fascists". They claimed that in the December 1933 elections Communist candidates had received "more than 400,000 votes" as against 60,000 in 1931. Moscow had been far from impressed. They asked: Where had the Communist Party been in the Jaca rising? Why had the Communists not been the leaders in the October Revolution; if, after October 1934, the Socialist Party was bankrupt, as the Spanish delegates said, why were they still the vanguard of revolutionary activity? In 1932, Jesus Hernandez, the Spanish delegate, had spoken of "the butcher government of Azaña and Largo Caballero"; at the XVIIth Congress of the C.P.S.U., in January 1934, the flamboyant Dolores Ibarruri had compared Largo's Law for the Defence of the Republic to Hitler's. Yet nine months later Largo was at the head of an armed rising to establish the dictatorship of the proletariat and not Ibarruri or any of her male companions. Largo, and no member of the Spanish Communist Party, was being hailed in Spain as "the Spanish Lenin".[15] Insofar as there had been a united front in the October Revolution, it had been the outcome of Largo Caballero's initiative.

Matters had come to a head at the VIIth Congress of the Comintern held in July 1935. The Spanish delegates confessed their faults. One of them, Ventura, admitted that they had failed to convince the working class. Then came the extraordinary volte-face: "Behind Largo Caballero stands everything that is healthy and revolutionary in the Socialist Party. He is ready to co-operate in a united front." The Comintern however now advocated a much wider union. Communist parties were to seek agreement with petit bourgeois organisations and form "popular fronts". The tactic was to be the seizure of power through democratic means, that is to say the petit bourgeois parties would be helped to win elections by the communists so that subsequently the communists would take over from within. Dimitrov, the Comintern Director called it the tactic of the Trojan Horse. In the final declarations of the VIIth Comintern Congress, Largo's name was linked with that of Thaelmann and Rakosi as the three men for whose release from gaol communists were to agitate throughout the world. Moscow accepted Largo as "the Spanish Lenin".

Largo Caballero had been released from gaol in November; he had declared that he now had a clearer understanding of Marxism than before his imprisonment.[16] He had been accepted as the link between the Communist Party and the Socialist; but he was also to be the link between the revolutionary Marxist left and the *petits bourgeois*. He had considerable personal influence over Azaña who, even as early as 1933 had said; "I consider myself in and out of government united for always to the Socialists."[17] Azaña, who after being cleared of complicity in the Catalan rising had successfully fused a number of petit bourgeois organisations into a party of his own under the title *Izquierda Republicana* was to be in turn the link with his fellow Mason Martinez Barrio, who under the title *Union Republicana* had rallied under him elements of the discredited Radical Party. The *Izquierda* and the *Union* were already close to each other and looking for allies when the left approached them.

Martinez Barrio, it will be remembered, had seceded from Lerroux's Radicals in protest against the relaxation of the anti-religious laws. He was Grand Master of the Spanish Orient and his chief political aspiration was to see Voltaire's command *"Ecrasez l'infame"* fulfilled at long last. His following was middle-class, and in other matters Poujadist. Azaña had two bêtes-noires—the Church and the Army. He believed in principle that some social reform was necessary, but the important step was "to educate the people"; not that the proletariat could ever aspire to the intellectual heights of his own élite. Three groups were discernible in the Socialist Party—one headed by Professor Besteiro, a Spanish Laski with no great numerical following, a second headed by Indalecio Prieto who counselled moderation in revolution but still believed in revolution as a necessary stage in human development, and thirdly the followers of the Spanish Lenin, Largo Caballero. The goal of the Spanish Socialist Party was the establishment of a national communist state.[18] Largo had the masses behind him, and officially control over the U.G.T. and the Socialist youth. He believed that he could control the Communists who in the matter of tactics were to the *right* of him and not revolutionary enough: and because he was more revolutionary than the Communists he was able to attract the Trotskyist party, the *Partido Obrero de Unificacion Marxista*, and some Anarchists.

Negotiations for a coalition between these six groups—Union, Izquierda, Socialist, Communist, Trotskyist and individual Anarchists— under the Comintern title of Popular Front were almost complete when in the second week of January Alcala-Zamora signed for Portela the order for the dissolution of the Cortes and the holding of elections.* They agreed to fight the elections as a single unit, Azaña being given its nominal leadership. They prepared a single programme for the elections.

The Popular Front programme put before the electorate was calculated to appeal to the *petits bourgeois* and the peasants uncommitted to any particular ideology. There was in the country, as Mendizabal wrote,[19] a general feeling of sympathy for the imprisoned. There were still several thousand persons in gaol for their part in the October Revolution;[20] the Popular Front promised to free them all as its very first step in government, and to redress the gross injustice in law whereby workmen had been dismissed from employment because of their political views. (Since the jobs had been filled few realised that in righting one injustice another would be committed). It pledged itself to seek out corruption—the Straperlo and Nombula affairs were in everyone's mind. It promised to restore the Catalan Statute—that was worth a million votes to any party. For the rest it proposed mild social and economic land reforms and better educational opportunities for people of ability. It was in no way a socialist manifesto.† The only ominous phrases were those which referred to the restoration and enforcement of the 1931 Constitution: that meant the renewal of religious persecution, but anti-religious legislation was never in Spain, as we have seen, the monopoly of socialist or even left-wing Parties.

---

* In Catalonia an analogous Popular Front was formed with the Esquerra Catala under Companys as the principal non-Marxist unit.

† The differences between the socialist and left-liberal parties were "noted" in the document, but not stressed; or rather put in such a way as to allay non-Marxist fears. Thus, for example, on land reform "(the Republicans) do not accept the principle of State ownership of the land . . . requested by the Socialist Party . . . or) control (of the means of production) by the workers."

The decisions of the Comintern had been implemented in Spain this far when an event abroad took Franco away from Spain. As Chief-of-Staff, and because he had once been an officer in the 8th Regiment of Foot of which the King of England was Honorary Colonel, Franco was ordered to attend the funeral of King George V. He arrived in London on 26th January and stayed at the since-demolished Carlton Hotel in the Haymarket. On the following day he was received by King Edward VIII at Buckingham Palace. On the 29th he attended the Service in Westminster Abbey, and marched behind the coffin with the representatives of other foreign States. On subsequent days he was taken over Sandhurst and Camberley—and the Caledonian Market.

Franco was then very concerned about developments in Spain. He had asked the Spanish Military Attaché in Paris, the then Major Barroso to accompany him to London as his aide-de-camp:

> General Franco seemed very worried about the situation, but we never had an opportunity to talk properly until we were on our way back. There was a storm in the Channel. Franco said, "Let's go up on deck". He's a good sailor, and luckily I was just about able to stand it. The deck was deserted. He took me behind the smokestack where there's some shelter from the wind. "Now we can talk", he said, and he told me all about the Comintern meeting, and how like him there were other officers who were worried—Mola and Goded, and so on—and Sanjurjo was being kept informed. He said that of course the Popular Front hadn't yet won the elections, but that he believed they would. Again, it all depended on what the Popular Front did *if* they won. But the Army had to be prepared. If the worst came to the worst, then it would be our duty to intervene. If the Popular Front won, of course, he would not be kept on as Chief-of-Staff. I said I was at his disposal. He said I was to remain in Paris—"If you hear of me going to Africa, you'll know we have decided there's no other way but a rising. When that happens, your lot will be to explain to people in Paris, to people likely to be well disposed, what it is all about".[21]

At the Spanish Embassy in Paris Franco convinced Dr. Marañon that though he feared a communist takeover at or after the elections, he did not intend to pre-judge the issue by taking part in any coup.[22] He arrived back in Madrid on 5th February, eleven days to polling day.

The people of Spain had had two years of so-called governments of the Centre and Right which, as we have seen, had accomplished nothing to alter the economic condition of the country or reduce the social misery of the majority. The right wing, and especially the Monarchist faction led by Calvo Sotelo, was preaching war against the Republic, and promising that in victory it would restore the Monarchy, from which the populace had no cause to expect better treatment in the future than in the past. The C.E.D.A. had proved itself a coalition which could keep together only when idle. The Radicals were discredited. There were in all twenty-five distinct political parties outside the left-wing Alliance. The people were faced, therefore, by a solid left-wing front with a simple programme, and a chaos of contradictions. The wonder of the results is that the Popular Front did not have a walk-over.

Thirteen and a half million Spaniards were entitled to vote on 16th February. One in three did not vote, although all Parties had stressed that the elections were to be the most important in Spanish history. How many did not do so because they were intimidated or prevented, or because with thirty Parties to choose from they could not make up their minds, because even with thirty Parties none represented what they wanted, it is now impossible to say. Preliminary results gave 4,206, 000 votes to the Popular Front and 4,464,000 to the others. In circumstances which we shall describe later, the Popular Front then took over the government. Under the provisions of the highly complex electoral law, elections were held again in nine provinces, and it was then reckoned that the Popular Front had gained 4,540,000 and the rest only 4,200,000.[23] There were further subsequent revisions to cut down the Centre and Right, and in particular Gil Robles's C.E.D.A. The final official figures were 4,700,000 for the Popular Front and 4,446,000 for the remainder. The C.E.D.A.'s claim to 120 seats was whittled down to 96 and finally to 88. In the end all Parties not in the Popular Front had to be content with 195 seats while the Front shared out 278 according to pre-election arrangements: 87 Socialists, 81 Republican Left, 35 Republican Union, 15 Communist and the rest for the Catalan Popular Front and minor allies.[24]

Franco spent election day in the Ministry of War, close to the Cibeles Fountain and the G.P.O., one of the focal points of Madrid, though in those days not as important as the Puerta del Sol.

16th February was a Sunday. The booths closed at 4 o'clock, that is during the lunch hour.* A mere three hours later the streets of Madrid

* 1530 to 1630 or 1700 was the popular pre-Civil War lunchtime.

began to fill not only with the usual evening promenaders but also with bands of men and a few women chanting Popular Front slogans, giving the clenched fist salute and shouting *Viva Rusia*! They implied that they had won the elections. With memories of what had occurred on the declaration of the Republic five years earlier Franco telephoned General Pozas, the Director of the Civil Guard, giving it as his opinion that the crowds might get out of hand. Pozas, who would one day join the Communist Party, assured Franco that there was nothing more than high spirits. Franco then telephoned General Molero who had succeeded Gil Robles as Minister of War. He suggested that the Declaration of *Estado de Guerra** was necessary to prevent disorder. Molero replied that he could issue the order only with the Prime Minister's authority.

The left-wing attribution of victory to itself continued overnight into the next day. Portela's secretary announced over the radio that the Popular Front had indeed won in Barcelona, though how the result in a city so far away in a country notoriously poor in communications could be known so quickly has never been satisfactorily explained. Franco sought out an old friend, a Liberal ex-Minister of monarchist days who was a close acquaintance of Portela to arrange an interview with the Prime Minister. Such was Spanish protocol that the Chief-of-Staff had no direct access to the Head of the Government. Portela had by then proclaimed an *Estado de Alarma*, and Franco now pressed him to make it an *Estado de Guerra*. Franco–Salgado's memory of the conversation is credible in its general outline.[25] Portela put to Franco the question: Why didn't the Army act on its own initiative? Franco replied that without a governmental order it would split: furthermore the Prime Minister had authority over the Civil Guard whose co-operation was essential. Portela dismissed Franco with the phrase: "Let me sleep on it". He slept on it after lunch. While he did so, Goded, Fanjul and a third General, Rodriguez del Barrio, Inspector-General of the Army, urged Franco to give the signal for a military rising since the government would not act. Franco asked them to inquire of the garrison commanders whether, if it were given, they would obey it. The majority answered "No".

At 2000 hours on 18th February, Portela was visited by Martinez

---

* The Law of Public Order provided for the suspension of civil liberties in three degrees: the first was *Estado de Alarma*—mainly affecting the freedom of the Press, and the last was *Estado de Guerra* when the Army's help could be sought in support of the civil power.

Barrios. Pozas and Nyñez del Prado, the Commander of the Storm Troopers, entered to announce that Goded and Franco were preparing a military coup and that the leaders of the right-wing parties were all assembled together. They pledged the Civil Guard and Storm Troopers to the Popular Front. Portela insisted before Martinez Barrios that the Popular Front should take over government immediately. The situation was getting out of hand. Martinez Barrios tried to persuade Portela to remain in office for another week. With that he left. On the following morning *El Socialista* carried the rumour that Franco and Goded were planning a military revolt. Portela went to the President and handed in his resignation, to the chagrin of Alcala-Zamora who also felt that it was premature. He then summoned Franco and gave him the news of his resignation. Franco accused Portela of having deceived him. Portela excused himself as being too old and too sick to carry the burden. He told Franco of the profession of allegiance to the Popular Front of Pozas and Nuñez. The rumour was then current that Goded and Franco were under arrest. In announcing his resignation, Portela denied it.

The President, notwithstanding the fact that election results were incomplete and the Popular Front victory debatable, now called on Azaña to form a new government. He did so, in accordance with his pre-election pact with the Socialists and Communists giving them not a single portfolio in the Cabinet.

Two days later a number of army officers received new postings: Mola, out of Africa to unimportant Pamplona; Goded to the Balearics, and Franco to the Canaries, that is as far away from Spain as was possible.

The overall history of the five days following the elections is even more complicated than the part of it which directly concerns Franco. This much however seems quite clear: that in February 1936 Franco was not prepared to take part in any army intervention in the political affairs of Spain except on the authority of the civilian government or some part of it. Whether his inaction was based on moral grounds or on practical considerations the fact is that he stood by the Government. And yet Azaña's exclusion of Socialists from the Cabinet confirmed Franco's belief that the Popular Front was a smoke-screen. Expressed as a military operation it could be put this way. The Popular Front was not going to seize Spain by an attack in width but in depth. Thus not

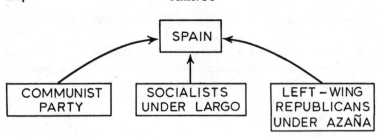

Communists, Socialists and left-wing Republicans side by side, but:

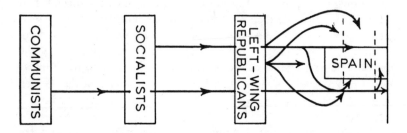

That is, in the first phase the Republican Left only would attack and bear the brunt of capturing the first objectives—the amputation of Catalonia and the Basque Provinces from the body of Spain, the release of the several thousand Socialists in prison for their part in the Asturian revolution, the restoration and reinforcement of the anti-religious laws: and a measure of land distribution to seduce the Anarchists into the socialist camp. Commanders in this first phase would be Azaña and Martinez Barrio. Once the *petits bourgeois* objectives had been reached, then the Socialists would be brought in through them, under Largo Caballero. In the final phase the Communists would come in, perhaps under Caballero if he really were the Spanish Lenin, perhaps under someone as yet to make himself known.

Not all army officers were being as slow in making up their minds that the Popular Front would have to be overthrown by force. Mola, Goded and Fanjul were now certain, and to the exiled Sanjurjo the Popular Front was only just another facet of the type of régime he had grown to hate within a year of its inception. They brought under their wing the members of an inchoate body of discontented men called the Union Militar Española, an organisation which Franco as Chief-of-Staff had distrusted since it remined him of the *juntas* of

1917. He knew about them as also about a Communist-front rival, the Union Militar Republicana which later changed its name to Antifacista. However, even a military rising had to have some civilian support. The conspirators could count on the Alfonsist Monarchists and the men of the extreme right generally, but they would hardly be enough.

The 1898 disaster had led to much heart-searching among writers as to how Spain could be regenerated. It had set in ferment the ideas which seethed in the minds of the founders of the Republic in 1931; but already in that year a new generation of young intellectuals had concluded that their immediate elders had failed: Spain had still to be regenerated.

One of these young "intellectuals" was Ramiro Ledesma Ramos, the son of a schoolmaster in Zamora. He had studied philosophy under Ortega y Gasset who encouraged him while still in his early twenties to contribute essays on German philosophers to his exclusive *Revista de Occidente*. Ledesma had then branched out on his own. He founded and edited a politico-philosophic review with the provocative title *La Conquista del Estado* (The Conquest of the State). Like the Anarchists, he was exasperated with the Establishment, of the left and right alike. He advocated the nationalisation of the means of production: but not in State ownership; rather he subscribed to the theory that workers in syndicates, if self-disciplined, could regenerate the land. At the same time he exalted the State, or rather the nation above the individual. He hated religion and Catholicism in particular; thus there were points in common between his philosophy and both Fascism and Nazism on the one hand and Marxism and Anarchism on the other. There was every reason why it should be so. All were derivatives from the same German School of Philosophy. Ledesma had a particularly deep admiration for the Anarchists' determination and attitudes on death and violence. He attracted some fellow university men but few others.

A second young intellectual was Onésimo Redondo Ortega, born like Ramos in 1905. He was an outstanding law student at Salamanca. The University of Mannheim employed him for a year as an Assistant in its Spanish department. During that time he read German philosophy and came to admire the discipline of the Nazis, but not their ideals. He returned to Spain with a zealous desire to give Spain "a new life" based on "the spiritual and human values" which he believed had made Spain, or rather Castille, great in the past—an iron will to overcome adversity, hard work and honesty and respect for the family. He professed love for the working classes and the peasants and a hatred of all things bourgeois. He accepted Catholicism as a factor in "Spanishness". He was anti-clerical, but religious, and even it is said pious. He believed that his new Spain could be born only through bloodshed and violence.

Redondo and Ledesma joined together in October 1931 to found National-Syndicalist action groups which they called Juntas de Ofensiva Nacional Sindicalista (J.O.N.S.). They adopted the yoked arrows motif of Isabella's and Ferdinand's coat-of-arms in admiration of the Spanish past, and a black shirt with a red tie and a red-black-red flag to show their spiritual connection with anarchism. They issued a sixteen-point programme which was a curious mixture of anarchist and nationalist ideas.[26] Their most important decision was the adoption of the battle cry "*España, Una. Grande, Libre*"; for a whole philosophy would evolve out of each of these four words, "Spain, One, Great, Free". A few hundred university students and some *pistoleros* (gunmen) with whom the anarchists were displeased joined the juntas.

In 1931 also the ex-Dictator Primo de Rivera died. His son Jose Antonio was then twenty-eight years old. He had acquired a law degree at Madrid University, but by preference he was a dilettante. An avid reader of Spengler, Marx, Lenin, Ortega, Hitler, Rosenberg and Trotsky, he took to politics, he said, to vindicate the memory of his father. He stood for the Cortes as a right-wing candidate where he impressed men of all political colours with his consummate charm and his gift of words in verse and in public speeches. After a brief flirtation with a monarchist group he branched out on his own with a following of university lecturers and poets. With Ortega he believed in government by an élite. After wavering left, right and centre, early in 1933 he tried with Ledesma to launch a new weekly with the inflamatory name, *El Fascio*. Jose Antonio understood fascism to be "the idea of unity . . . a faith in the nation". A fascist state was one run by workers in syndicates agreed on the principle of order. Violence might be used as a means to its creation, but the violence was the means and not the end.[27] The Socialists who were then being called by the Communists "Social-Fascist" were indignant. Azaña's government vetoed the sale of the first issue and any further editions. Ledesma who had welcomed the joint action with Jose Antonio in the hopes that the Dictator's son might give new life to the moribund J.O.N.S. now discovered that there was a gulf between his amorphous National-Syndicalism and

Jose Antonio's vague Fascism. They parted. Ledesma however lost to Jose Antonio Ramon Franco's co-flyer of the South Atlantic Ruiz de Alda. Ruiz was an organiser, which Jose Antonio was not. Together Jose Antonio and Ruiz de Alda went on to found their own movement. At the end of October 1933 they obtained the use of the Madrid Comedy Theatre to launch it. Ruiz de Alda named it the *Falange Española*—a nationalist title with military overtones, and one whose initials F.E. made the Spanish word for "faith". The faith of the Falange was in Spain, that is in the total synthesis of all individuals and classes, which thus synthesised into a new individual, had a divine destiny. Within this synthesis, there could not be political parties: religion would be tolerated so long as it did not interfere in undefined affairs not of its competence: there could be no drones nor parasites in the new society: all men would have the right but also the duty to work for the community: to achieve the new society, violence might be necessary, but it was not an end in itself. In brief, it was a hotch-potch of Hegel and Nietzche with a sprinkling of Marx.

The movement was given funds by several right-wing elements who hoped it might develop into a rival to the Socialist Youth. However in the first place it attracted the weapons of the Socialist Militia rather than its members. The Socialists stabbed to death their first Falangist on 2nd November 1933.[28] In December, when Jose Antonio had been elected to the Cortes in his own right and not as the Number One Falangist, the Socialists shot two more youths who were selling their periodical *Fé*. Five more Falangists fell in January. Nevertheless, within limits the movement prospered in the universities, and Falangist students took to carrying pistols with them on their way to lectures. Ruiz de Alda then persuaded his fellow-pilot Ansaldo to join the Falange in order to organise a squad of gunmen to even the score which was weekly getting more unbalanced. From March till October Falange and Socialists obeyed the Old Testament law of retribution in their dealings one with another. However, when Ansaldo discovered for himself that Jose Antonio was no monarchist, he left, or was expelled, from the movement. In the meantime, however, Ledesma and Jose Antonio had been reconciled, and they had fused their two organisations into a single one ruled by the triumvirate Primo, Ruiz de Alda and Ledesma. Ansaldo compared its full name Falange Española de las Juntas de Ofensiva Nacional Sindicalista to that of the Compagnie Internationale des Wagons-Lits et Grands Express Européens.[29] According to Ansaldo the total membership at the end of 1933 was not much more than one thousand youths—almost all of them university students.

With the end of the university year the frequency of street battles diminished. Then came the October Revolution. Jose Antonio offered the Government his *"centurias"* of which he had eight, that is a total of eight hundred youths, to fight the Asturian miners. The Government rejected the offer. In spite of the revolution in progress, the Falange held its first congress during the first week of October. Jose Antonio emerged from it as the Falange's sole leader although he had written earlier[30] "To be a leader one must be something of a Prophet. Faith, good health, enthusiasm, anger, are essential ingredients: they do not mix with good breeding. I would be the last person to be any good as a fascist leader". He issued a twenty-seven point manifesto—the work of an angry young man rather than of a philosopher or party theorist. At the end of 1934 he offered Gil Robles his support in any bid for power but Gil Robles would have none of it: not so Serrano Suñer, Franco's wife's sister's husband (and by Spanish custom referred to as his *cuñado*—brother-in-law). Serrano Suñer thereafter sought to direct the Accion Popular's youth movement towards the Falange. The Falange's membership increased during 1935. In June of that year Jose Antonio sought an alliance with the U.M.E. The U.M.E. as a body rejected his overtures, though individuals sympathised.[31]

Jose Antonio, Redondo and Ruiz de Alda and other Falangists stood for election in February 1936. They received in all 40,000 votes. As a political force, therefore, the Falange was even weaker than the Communist Party, but they did have by then between 6,000 and 8,000 youths behind them, a force worth taking into consideration by anyone looking for semi-skilled fighters: and in Yague they had a convert who would not belittle their numbers or fighting qualities. Yague had joined the U.M.E as well.

After the elections more young men hastened to join the Falange. Jose Antonio now had a daily, *Arriba*, to spread his doctrine. In that daily he flayed right-wing politicians and praised Prieto. He then even offered to make his Falange more Socialist in outlook if Prieto would take it over from him.[32] Prieto who was not unaware that his position as a leader of the Socialist Party was now purely nominal, admired Jose Antonio personally but rejected the offer.

Soon afterwards Largo Caballero handed over the Socialist Youth to the Communist Party. The united Socialist and Communist Youth now turned on the Falangists in earnest, and the old game of murder and reprisal began again. The Government outlawed the Falange and placed all its leaders in Madrid's model prison, and some thousands of its members in gaols throughout the country. The U.M.E. which had once rejected Jose Antonio's advances now began to consider the Falange an ally. It found ways of keeping in touch with the imprisoned leaders.

There was in the north of Spain another force more attractive to the Military Union than the Falange. It was the body of Carlist activists who, under retired and suspended military officers, not all of similar sympathies, had been secretly drilling and training for guerilla war. Their spokesman was a tough ultra-simplifier of moral problems called Fal Conde. Fal Conde reckoned in the Spring of 1936 that he could put in the field 8,400.[33]

Mola's posting to Pamplona, the very heart of Navarre and Carlist conspiracy, would have filled the conspirators' cup of happiness to overflowing had Franco not been under orders to proceed to the Canaries. Most of its members were still anxious to have the reluctant Franco on their side. In between packing his belongings, he accepted an invitation to go to the house of a civilian at which Fanjul, Goded and Mola were among the many present. In five hours of discussion they came to no agreement among themselves as to what form of government should replace the Popular Front, some wanting to install the Carlist Pretender, others to restore Alfonso and others to reconstitute a non-socialist Republic. The meeting however did produce a concensus of opinion that all those present should proselytise the cause of revolt against the Popular Front since they all believed imminent a Communist takeover of Spain. Mola was to be the organiser-in-chief of a simultaneous declaration by army units throughout Spain that they considered the Popular Front no longer the legitimate Spanish government. He was to ensure that no garrison acted prematurely: the rising was to be a co-ordinated and rapid move. It would depend on rapidity for success. Therefore no action was to be taken until nationwide support was certain, and all the committed understood that this discipline was expected of them—unless the Popular Front embarked on any of these contingencies: the dissolution of the Civil Guard, the disbandment of the Army, the dismissal of its officers, or a definite takeover of government by Largo Caballero or the Communists.

Both the revolutionary and counter-revolutionary forces now began to move rapidly towards an armed conflict. The history of the five months 16th February to 18th July has been examined many times. It is our purpose to review it once again only insofar as it is relevant to Franco's change of heart. On 16th February, as we have seen, he refused to join any armed rising against the Government. On 18th July he was issuing a general call to arms.

For Mola in Pamplona, Goded in the Balearics, Sanjurjo in Portugal and several hundred other army officers the die was cast if not by 16th February, certainly by 8th March, when a whole party of them went to see Franco off on his way to Tenerife. He still refused to commit himself. They promised to keep him informed of developments.

On the train with him were his wife, his daughter and his inseparable cousin Franco-Salgado. As they neared Cadiz the following morning they saw a pall of smoke from churches set on fire the previous evening. Franco refused to shake the hand of the military governor of the city sent to escort him to the packetboat for the Canaries, because he had taken no action even when the fire raisers had struck next door to the barracks. Again, as they neared their destination, they saw a crowd on the quayside. It had been organised against him as "the butcher of Asturias". To Franco it was an insult to his uniform.[34] The two events he witnessed shifted him towards the rebels—still he would not give the word. Franco-Salgado remembered him often saying from this time onwards: "People are quite mistaken who think this business will be a brief affair. Far from it. It's going to be difficult, bloody and it'll last a long time—yet there seems to be no other way, if we're going to be one step ahead of the Communists".[35]

In Tenerife, the newspapers subject to ever-increasing censorship told him little enough about events in Spain, but he was kept informed by both military and civilian friends: of the political murders, of attacks on harmless individuals such as Sunday-school teachers whom rumour had distributing poisoned sweets to workers' children, of the hundreds of acts of arson and wanton destruction, strikes and the establishment of Soviets in the factories and the countryside, of the attribution of blame for all deeds of violence to "fascists", of the imprisonment of twelve thousand such by mid-May, and of the refusal of the Government to act against perpetrators of such acts who were members of the Socialist or Communist Parties, or Anarchists.[*]

Cuenca and Granada were among the nine provinces where elections had had to be held again. The results of the first re-take were challenged

---

[*] The figures which Gil Robles gave the Cortes on 16th June were 269 dead and 1,285 wounded (*Diariode Sesiones*).

by the non-Popular Front parties. A second re-take was arranged. In Granada quite barefacedly the Popular Front made a mockery of them.[36] The C.E.D.A. then withdrew from recontesting Cuenca, but four right-wing candidates' names were put forward. One was that of Jose Antonio then in prison, and the other that of General Franco. The right-wing were certain that the two would be elected. The Government would then have had to release Jose Antonio, and Franco would have been free to return to Madrid which was where the Union would have preferred him to be when the moment came for revolt. Franco's candidature was challenged on the grounds that these elections were to be a re-take and that only the original candidates could be allowed to stand. Walls of buildings carried the legend "Death to Franco". Franco himself withdrew his candidature. The greatest praise for his action came from the lips of Indalecio Prieto, at a May the First rally which was also an electioneering speech in Cuenca. Indeed, Prieto uttered a veritable panegyric in the General's defence: "I will not say even half a word to reduce the stature of that military figure. I saw him fight in Africa, and for me General Franco represents the purest formula of courage. I must do homage to the truth. We cannot deny, whatever our political creed, that among the military, in considerable numbers and over wide areas there is a subversive ferment, an urge to rise against the Republican régime, not so much surely because of what it now is, but *because of what the Popular Front which dominates national policy implies in terms of a near future.* General Franco, being young, gifted, having a network of friends in the Army, is the man who at a given moment has it in him to lead such a movement with maximum probable success because of the prestige he enjoys. I do not dare to attribute to General Franco any such designs. I accept wholeheartedly his declaration that he stands aloof from politics . . . but I cannot deny that there were people who, with or without his authority, tried to put him up as a candidate for Cuenca, so that vested with parliamentary immunity, he might come to interpret the desires of his proposers and become the leader of a military revolt."[37] Prieto was then trying his utmost to thwart Largo Caballero. Largo, who had handed over the Socialist Youth to the Communists, was now preparing the fusion of the parent body with the Communist Party. In his newspaper *Claridad* and in speeches he was justifying his title of "the Spanish Lenin" to a degree which did not suit the Comintern at all, for he had in mind a IVth International of independent Communist States. Prieto at that juncture did not know where to turn. In the hopes of ingratiating himself with the bourgeois parties of the

Front, he had led an attack on the President, Alcala-Zamora, on a technical constitutional point as to whether Alcala-Zamora had dissolved the Cortes once too often in the constitutionally allotted span of a Presidency. The President had been dismissed ignominiously and Azaña had taken his place. Azaña had offered Prieto the Premiership, but the Socialists at Largo Caballero's instigation had vetoed his acceptance of the post. Azaña and his friends, Casares Quiroga, Martinez Barrios and Marcelino Domingo, might continue for a while theoretically in government, closing Catholic schools, attempting to keep factories open, putting the blame on non-Marxists for Marxist and Anarchist violence, and even in the end seeking ineffectually to protect private lives and properties; but they could govern only in so far as Largo Caballero (and the Anarchists) would allow. To these, Prieto had spoken in Cuenca "in the language of the privileged classes". In their view it was unbefitting a Socialist to talk of Spain as presenting "a more tragic panorama than ever in history, a madness and disorder which would lead not to democracy, nor socialism, nor communism, but to the anarchy of total despair".[38]

On his arrival in the Canaries, as we saw, Franco had been met by an organised hostile crowd. Physical attacks against members of the armed forces—by no means always officers—increased in frequency with the passing of the months. But perhaps nothing frightened the conspirators into speeding up their preparations for a rising and turning from conspiracy to action, or swayed those who still doubted whether Spain was on the brink of being turned into a Communist State, than the march-past in several cities on 1st May of thousands upon thousands of excellently disciplined militias.[39] When Largo Caballero referred to them as nuclei of a new army to be used against workers who refused to accept the new order no less than against capitalists and the old army[40] any military observer could judge for himself that Largo was not uttering vain boasts. Those militias, ex-conscripts with supplementary training, were likely to be a more formidable force than the half-trained conscripts wearing army uniform. Franco, as Chief-of-Staff, had carried out an enquiry into how many conscripts already belonged to extremist organisations on call-up. The findings had surprised him: one in four of the 1935 class had been members of the C.P., F.A.I., C.N.T. or Socialist Youth. So the "enemy" was not only before the Army in the militias but within it. And now in mid-1936 anti-army literature circulated freely, and a mutinous attitude was encouraged by the left-wing publication *El Ejercito Rojo* distributed in the barracks.

In Pamplona Mola continued his task of organising the rising. The Carlists would not join until he promised them that they would not be prevented from flying the old red and gold Monarchist flag. The Falange which preferred the Republican colours, demanded action immediately. Jose Antonio from his prison wrote a circular to all army officers to do their duty. Incarceration had changed his opinion that it was useless to count on generals on the payroll—"Old hens and the biggest old hen of all Franco". From Portugal Sanjurjo wrote to Mola: "With little Frankie-boy or without little Frankie-boy we shall go ahead and save Spain."[41] The Republican Queipo de Llano had joined the Union when his relation by marriage Alcala-Zamora had been ousted from the Presidency. At the beginning of June the Prime Minister, Casares Quiroga, began to dismiss officers from their commands and replaced them with those who had been favourable to the October Revolution or the Catalan separatists. On 23rd June Franco wrote Casares a letter warning him that the changes were causing grave unrest. Franco waited in vain for an answer.

At the beginning of July Franco informed Mola that the time had come to strike.[42] Prieto's appreciation of Franco was about to be proved correct.

NOTES

1. Maritain's phrase in his introduction to Mendizabal's *Aux Origines d'une Tragedie*, Paris, 1937 (on p. 7 of English translation: *The Martyrdom of Spain*, Bles, 1938).

2. Doval acquired his unsavoury reputation during the left-wing first period of the Republic. *v.* Arraras, *Historia*, p. 108.

3. Op. cit. (1961), p. 378, cf., p. 455: "What made the Spanish Civil War inevitable was the civil war within the Party."

4. Op. cit., p. 7.

5. Thomas, p. 128, oversimplifies calling it a right-wing and Catholic government, but he is right in saying that it wasted its opportunities.

6. Alcala-Zamora's *apologias* do not provide a complete explanation of his attitude.

7. *Servicio Histórico* on Franco's reorganisation. On Spain and Mussolini *v.* Madariaga (1961), pp. 471-3.

8. Franco-Salgado who was present.

9. *Quien Soy Yo?* (Who am I?) by Ignacio Luca de Tena.

10. The sentence quoted was compounded with the following: "for the army, which may rise in arms when a cause so holy as that of the Motherland is in imminent danger, must not play referee in a political struggle." Franco's answers to Gil Robles were therefore in effect: "It is not the Army's role to judge a constitutional point." Madariaga, no ideological nor political ally of the C.E.D.A., had no shadow of doubt that Gil Robles was a true parliamentarian. (*Spain passim* references to Gil Robles). As such Robles proved to be one of the eventual rebel and victorious Franco's most awkward opponents. He had already stated disapproval of Franco's New Spain by March 1937. Gil Robles is unique among the men prominent during the Republican record in not writing an *apologia* of what he did or failed to do.

11. Op. cit., p. 92.

12. Mola, *Obras*, p. 474.

13. Franco. Conversation with the author.

14. *The Communist International 1919-43*, Selected Documents, Vol. III, O.U.P., 1965, pp. 180-7, 244-6, 328-31, 345, 349, 386 *ff*. These figures have been challenged as exaggerated, but it is difficult to see how their many "front" activities would have been possible with smaller numbers. A scholarly independent history of the Spanish Communist Party is still needed. There is some excellent material in Bolloten's *The Grand Camouflage* (Hollis and Carter, 1961), and in David T. Cattell's *Communism and the Spanish Civil War* (Berkeley, 1955), and in the memoirs and histories written by Dolores Ibarruri and other Spanish Communists. Colmin Colomer includes in his massive History profuse documentation, but he spoils his book by its obvious propagandistic purposes and his obsession that Masonry is intertwined with Communism.

15. The first time was at the 1933 Socialist Summer School in Torrelodones, after a major revolutionary policy speech (*El Socialista*, 13th August 1933).

16. Largo Caballero's own *Mis memorias* (Mexico, 1954) reveal him as a better pupil of Marx than some of his Communist contemporaries.

17. At a meeting in Azaña's honour.

18. Spanish socialist literature of the time makes this quite clear. So do the speeches of Socialists as reported in *El Socialista* and *Claridad*. For a selection that the Socialists were out to establish in Spain "*lo mismo que en la Union Soviética*". *v.* Arraras, pp. 373-5. The quotations have been checked against originals.

19. Op. cit.

20. For electoral purposes the figure chosen was 30,000. It was a good number: "*treinta*" is easier to say than "*cuarenta*" (40) and it has a more emotional sound than "*veinte*" (20). Two facts suggest that the real figure was considerably lower. The returns for the prison population on 15th February 1936 were

34,526; it is unbelievable that there were only 4,526 common criminals, as opposed to political prisoners, in a country of over 20 million inhabitants. The other is a rambling speech by the Anarcho-syndicalist deputy Benito Pabón in the Cortes on 2nd July 1936. Pabón declared his disapproval of the use of a number "which was not the true one . . . there were not 30,000". *Diario de Sesiones.*

21. General Barroso to the author.

22. The late Dr. Marañon to the author. Cf. Thomas, p. 135.

23. *El Sol,* 3rd March. Gil Robles' *El Debate* gave 3,912,086 for the Popular Front and 4,654,000 for the others. Any distinctions between "Centre" and "Right" cannot be other than arbitrary. For what is still the best analysis of these figures, *v.* Madariaga, pp. 340-3. His important point is that even if the Popular Front did win the election the people of Spain did not give it a mandate beyond what it had stated in its manifesto, that it was a vote for the Left-centre, but not Left.

24. These final figures are those given in Mendizabal, p. 245.

25. MS. Also in Centinela, p. 180, Arraras, *Franco,* pp. 229-31. Portela's statement of 1st October 1937 (as quoted by Brennan, p. 300) that Gil Robles and Franco urged Franco "to carry out a coup" is suspect if only because Portela was a sick man and he and Gil Robles were not on speaking terms.

26. A tautologic programme which can be reduced to eight points: (i) the Political Unity of Spain intolerant of separatism; (ii) respect for the erastian-catholic tradition of Spain; (iii) the return of Gibraltar and acquisition of all Morocco and Algeria; (iv) "controlled democracy" with a non-Party Cortes; (v) compulsory membership of workers' syndicates, the workers being given a place in the machinery of government; (vi) a one-class society; (vii) extirpation of all Marxist parties; (viii) government by young men.

27. Jose Antonio, *Obras* (Madrid, 1954), pp. 43 *ff.* S. G. Payne's *Falange* (Stanford 1962) is a well-documented book on the subject albeit tilted in Jose Antonio's favour.

28. *El Sol,* 3rd November 1933. As the Press was subject to censorship during most of the Republican period, not all deaths were reported.

29. Ansaldo is quite cynically frank about his activities in the Falange. *v. Para Que?,* pp. 63 *ff.* He retained a liking for Jose Antonio.

30. Jose Antonio to the *A.B.C.* in protest against monarchist disparagement of *El Fascio,* 16th March 1933.

31. The Spanish Army's attitude to the Falange was in many ways similar to the German Army's to the Nazi Party.

32. Cf. Jose Antonio, *Obras,* p. 1103. Zugazagoitia, *Historia de la Guerra de España* (B.A., 1940), pp. 7-8. Bravo, *Historia de la Falange,* etc. (Madrid, 1940), pp. 218-58. Buckley, *Life and Death of the Spanish Republic* (London, 1940), p. 128.

Jose Antonio was taken by Surrano Suñer to see Franco in March 1936. Franco asked questions, and said little more than "keep in touch with Yague" (Franco-Salgado).

33. Lizarza, *Memorias de la Conspiración*, etc. (Pamplona, 1953), p. 90.

34. Franco's Spanish biographers play down this episode and go on to talk of a counter demonstration. Centinela (based on the Franco-Salgado MS.) is more outspoken than most.

35. Franco-Salgado MS.

36. *V.* Arraras, *Historia*, pp. 420-1.

37. *El Socialista*, 2nd May 1936.

38. A picture of Spain very similar to Prieto's would be painted by Franco a few weeks later.

39. Such newsreel film as there is shows the militia as a well-disciplined force.

40. *Claridad*, frequently from April onwards.

41. Ansaldo, pp. 121 and 125.

42. Martin, *Franco*, pp. 155-7, takes the view that the letter was to allay Casares Quiroga's suspicions.

9

FROM GENERAL TO GENERALISSIMO

17th July 1936 was a hot summer's day in Madrid. It was a Friday. Casares Quiroga had had a difficult week as Prime Minister, but now everything seemed set for a quiet weekend.

The talk of the town centred on the accounts available that day of speeches at a meeting the previous Wednesday of the Standing Committee of the Cortes.[1] The Government had suspended the Cortes proper without realising that the *Estado de alarma* which had given it the powers to arrest without trial, censor the Press and break up political meetings since the February, was due for renewal; but the Standing Committee's approval would be constitutionally enough. The Government had known that it would have to listen to plain speaking from the opposition; but the real point at issue had been whether the Socialists were still prepared to support Casares Quiroga as Prime Minister. All had gone well. Gil Robles had read the latest list of major disorders: during the period 16th June to 13th July sixty-one persons had been assassinated and 224 wounded: there had been 132 bomb explosions: nineteen private buildings and ten churches had been set on fire. What use, he asked, had the Government made of the powers already given them to suppress disorder? Since the beginning of June construction workers, public works employees and lift operators in Madrid had been on a strike whose motivation was political. Largo Caballero and his U.G.T. were engaged in an open struggle with the C.N.T. for the control of the workers. The C.N.T.'s orders to workers to obey the principles of "libertarian Communism" and "not to pay in cash for food and groceries" had got them many converts. Largo Caballero had at first spoken of the strike as "mighty ram-blows at the gates of power". Immediately he had realised that the continuance of the strike was favouring his enemies, back-pedalling he had then argued that strikes were not in the best interests of the proletariat. The Minister of

Labour had offered higher wages, a 40-hour week and paid holidays;
but the workers had remained on strike. Gil Robles' figures for killed
and wounded included those in gunfights between the U.G.T. and
C.N.T.—a feature of Spanish working class "solidarity" which Largo
Caballero did not mention to his Socialist "brothers" when he paid a
visit to London in the first week of July. Gil Robles had then gone on
to talk about the latest and most remarkable assassination, that of the
Monarchist opposition leader Calvo Sotelo. In the early hours of the
Monday a posse of Government storm troopers under the command of
a Captain Condés, the paramour of the Socialist firebrand member of
the Cortes Margarita Nelken, had enticed him out of his house into a
Black Maria. They had shot him at point blank range, and with macabre
humour had dropped the body at a cemetery as that of "an unknown
stiff". Gil Robles did not know it at the time, but another police car
with two captains and three lieutenants of the Storm Troopers had
gone in search of him. They had failed to find him because he was
away for the weekend. At Calvo Sotelo's funeral, the police had fired
at the mourners, killing four of them. Gil Robles recalled the threats
against Calvo Sotelo uttered in the Cortes by Government speakers
including Casares Quiroga himself. Popular Front spokesmen justified
the storm troopers on the ground that "Fascists had killed a Lieutenant
Castillo on Sunday afternoon".* The Government claimed that it was
doing all that was necessary. It had the driver of the Black Maria under
arrest and it had appointed the *juge d'instruction* to question the officers.
Indalecio Prieto had then argued that what had happened was no worse
than what had followed the suppression of the October 1934 Rebellion.
In the voting which had followed the debate, the Socialists had voted all
with the Government. Indalecio Prieto appeared to have re-established
his supremacy over the more revolutionary Largo Caballero. Casares
Quiroga had weathered the storm.

During the Thursday and Friday morning forty police cars with
motorised Socialist militia escorts had toured Madrid searching houses
and detaining whom they willed without opposition. However they
had not interfered with the exodus of middle-class women and children
off to the northern seaside resorts, or with the departure of Gil Robles,
Alcalá Zamora, Lerroux and other non-Popular Front politicians to

---

* So they had. Castillo, prominent as a Training Officer of the Socialist Youth
Militia, had killed in the April Andrés Saenz de Heredia, a first cousin of José
Antonio, when attending the funeral of a Civil Guard killed by Storm Troopers
in the belief that he was pointing a pistol at President Azaña.

France and Portugal. Throughout the country Army units were depleted with men and officers on leave: the date on which a military rising had last been expected was a week past. The Prime Minister's personal bodyguard and the Presidential Guard★ were hand picked and fully to be trusted. Casares Quiroga had every reason to expect a quiet weekend.[2]

On 17th July 1936 General Franco, G.O.C. the Canary Islands, knew that he had a long journey ahead of him that weekend. He was in Las Palmas. He had travelled overnight from his headquarters in Tenerife with his wife and daughter and his cousin Franco-Salgado. He had been authorised by the Ministry of War to attend the funeral of General Balmes, the Military Governor of the Grand Canary, who had shot himself accidentally on the previous day. What Casares Quiroga, Minister of War as well as Prime Minister, did not know was that there was a de Havilland Dragon Rapide on charter from the Olley Airways Company of Croydon waiting on the apron at Las Palmas to take Franco further way from and not back to Tenerife on the day after the funeral. It had been there since the Wednesday, having left London on the previous Saturday.

Late in the afternoon of 17th July Casares Quiroga received in Madrid a tiresome report of an untoward event in Melilla. A Lieutenant-Colonel Seguí had been holding a meeting with other army officers and civilians at which he had handed out instructions for a rebellion. Casares Quiroga tried to contact General Romerales, G.O.C. Eastern Region of Spanish Morocco, to obtain more accurate information and to order the arrest of the officers concerned. A voice at the other end replied to his telephone call *Viva España*. Romerales in fact was already the prisoner of the insurgents. After more telephoning the Prime Minister located the G.O.C. African Army, General Gomez Morato, in the Casino at Larache. The General, unable to answer the Prime Minister's question "What's up at Melilla?" was ordered to fly there and find out. He walked out of the aircraft straight into a hostile reception committee. He refused to side with them and joined Romerales and over a score of other officers in prison.[3] The gaol also held the survivors of a brief battle between the Socialist militia and the Legion at the *Casa del Pueblo*. Later the insurgents would start bringing in known Freemasons as well as the local leaders of the Socialist, Anarchist,

★ A body dubbed by Madrileños the "Pretorian" or "The Queen's".

Communist and other left-wing organisations. In the meantime Casares Quiroga had telephoned the High Commissioner in Tetuan urging him to resist. Tetuan town fell to the Legion more quietly than Melilla; the only fighting of any consequence was at the airfield outside the town where Franco's cousin, Major de la Puente Baha-monde,[4] commanding the local air squadron, held out for a while and then disabled his aircraft before surrendering.* At 2300 hrs. Yague took over Ceuta without firing a round.

By 11 o'clock all Madrid knew that something untoward was happening in Morocco: indeed the Socialist Party had known sooner than the Government, for the original information on the Melilla army officers' meeting had come from a spy in the service of the Melilla *Casa del Pueblo*. The U.G.T. were clamouring round the President's palace and the Prime Minister's office for arms. Special editions of Largo Caballero's *Claridad* and Prieto's *El Socialista* took up the demand with banner headlines: *Armas, Armas, Armas*. They considered the eight thousand militia armed with rifles and automatic weapons and the thousand-strong storm troopers with armoured cars an insufficient force for battle against those whom they called Fascist. Casares was in a dilemma. He could trust the Commander of the Madrid Infantry and Cavalry divisions, but Romerales and Gomez Morato had also been his men. He might trust Prieto, but not Largo Caballero nor the U.G.T. rank and file who had been urged for so long and repeatedly to seize power. He preferred to await developments, and so did most of the provincial governors, some perhaps influenced by Casares' threat to have anyone shot who handed out weapons to the populace. He telephoned garrisons all over Spain. Everything seemed normal.

In Las Palmas Franco went to bed unaware of the events in Africa. His cousin Franco-Salgado awoke him with the news at 3 o'clock in the morning. The Army in Africa had moved some hours earlier than planned:[5] it was no matter. Everything was ready in the Canaries. He dressed in mufti and went from his hotel to the local military head-quarters where he changed into uniform. From there he issued orders to all the garrisons under his command to take over public buildings and headquarters of left-wing parties. He telegraphed Africa: "All Glory to the heroic Africa Army. Spain Above All. Receive enthusiastic Salute these Garrisons who unite themselves to you and other companions in Peninsula in these historic moments. Blind Faith in

---

* All the officers who did not side immediately with the rebels were later shot, Puente included.

Triumph. Long Live Spain with Honour". He sent copies to all naval and military commands in the Peninsula.

Franco then issued his first manifesto, for broadcast by Radio Tenerife at 0700 hrs.: "Spaniards! All those of you who feel the holy love of Spain, those who in the ranks of the Army and the Navy have made an act of profession in the service of the Motherland, those who have sworn to defend her against her enemies till death, the nation calls you to her defence." "The internal situation of Spain," he went on, "grows more critical from day to day: anarchy prevails in most of its fields and towns; authorities appointed by the Government preside over where they do not actually foment upheavals. Differences between gangs of citizens are resolved by shots from pistols and machine guns. In treason and counter-treason they assassinate each other and the public authorities do nothing to impose peace and justice. All manner of revolutionary strikes paralyse the life of the nation, ruining and destroying its foundations of wealth and creating a situation of hunger which will drive to desperation the workers. Monuments and artistic treasures are the object of the most determined attacks by revolutionary hordes obeying orders and commissions received from abroad . . . the most serious crimes are committed in cities and fields while the forces of public order are kept confined to barracks, eaten away by the desperation provoked by a blind obedience to Governors who seek to dishonour them. The Army, the Fleet and other armed forces are made the targets of the dirtiest calumnies precisely by those who should watch over their good name . . . the Constitution suspended and wounded by all suffers a total eclipse. There is no equality before the law and liberty is shackled by tyranny: neither is there any fraternity where hatred and crime have taken the place of mutual respect." "Unity of the Motherland," Franco continued, was being destroyed by regionalism and separatism, by listening to foreign broadcasts preaching destruction, by Soviet agents. "Can we tolerate one day longer the shameful example we are giving the world!" Franco offered "justice and equality before the law, peace and love among Spaniards . . . liberty and fraternity without libertinage and tyranny . . . work for all. Social justice . . . a progressively fairer distribution of wealth without endangering Spanish economy". He promised "war without quarter to the deceivers of the honest workman, the foreigners and the foreignisers who openly or by subterfuge" intended to destroy Spain. "We shall preserve what is just: fraternity, liberty and equality. Long Live Spain. Long Live the Spanish people in honour."

Here was a manifesto worthy of any nineteenth-century Spanish
Liberal General or indeed almost of an eighteenth-century French
revolutionary. Only years later would commentators notice the fact
that Franco had nowhere mentioned the left-wing war on religion.
He had spoken of the destruction of "monuments and artistic treasures"
but not of churches as such. Only the love of Spain had been called
holy by him.[6]

Captain Bebb, the English pilot of the Dragon Rapide, was ordered
to stand by. Franco asked a friend of his in the Judge Advocate's department, a Lieutenant-Colonel Martinez Fuset, to say goodbye for him
to his wife and daughter and to put them aboard a German liner which
was due to sail the following day for Cherbourg and Hamburg. He
handed over command of the Canaries to the arch enemy of the
Republic, General Orgaz.[7] Units of the Army were still battling with
Socialist militias and the Civil Guard as Franco made his way to the
airfield with his cousin and two other companions. Bebb took off at
1400 hours and then amazed watched his principal passenger put on
Arab dress and throw his uniform overboard. The others changed into
more ordinary mufti. The aircraft refuelled at Agadir and flew on to
Casablanca. Night had fallen and there were no landing lights, but
Bebb put down his aircraft safely. Franco showed the French police a
passport which had his photograph but described the holder as a man
several inches taller than he was. It was all the same to them. They did
not even question the fact that Franco-Salgado had no passport at all.
It was a Saturday night. Luis Bolin, the London correspondent of the
Monarchist paper *A.B.C.*, who had chartered the Dragon Rapide had
booked rooms for them in a small out-of-the-way hotel. He would
accompany the General to Africa.

Bebb took off from Casablanca with his passengers at break of day
on the Sunday. As he approached Tetuan Franco told him to fly low
as he did not know in whose hands Tetuan might be. Some of the naval
units despatched from the Peninsula were in the area. As Bebb flew
low, Franco recognised the face of one of those waiting. It was that of a
friend. Bebb brought his aircraft down. Saenz de Buruaga, the leader
of the revolt in Tetuan, saluted and reported "All quiet in Morocco,
sir" (*Sin novedad, mi general*).

It was quiet in Morocco, but it had not been so earlier. The previous
day a government aircraft had dropped eight bombs. One had landed
on a mosque and three on the Moorish quarter killing fifteen
Moroccans. The immediate Moroccan reaction had been to threaten

all Spaniards, but the 66-year-old grand visier Sidi Ahmed el Gamnia had ridden among them turning their anger exclusively against the Madrid government. The Jalif, Muley Hassan, had already sent Franco the message "Paternally at the side of the glorious army of Morocco, I send greetings to General Franco and pray God for the triumph of the Spain being reborn". Colonels raising the standard of revolt had done so in the name of Franco. Franco was beloved of the Moroccans. One of the officers embracing him at the airfield was Major El Mizzian, nephew of Franco's very first military opponent.

The colonels and lieutenant-colonels who now greeted Franco had not been idle while awaiting his arrival. Aboard the destroyer *Churruca* and a cross-Channel steamer, they had sent part of a *tabor* of *Regulares* to establish a bridgehead on the mainland. These had helped local troops to capture Algeciras and were now fanning out towards La Linea, Jerez and Cadiz. The destroyer, however, had not returned to base. It had in fact been seized by its crew and was being sailed to Malaga where its officers would be shot. Three destroyers had appeared off Melilla. They had not bombarded the town as ordered from Madrid, but on the other hand they had sailed away. Franco would learn later the details of what had happened aboard. They had sailed from Cartagena as ordered by Madrid. Their commanders had heard the broadcast of his manifesto from Tenerife and called upon their crews to join them in rebellion. The crews had elected to side with Madrid, imprison the officers and sail back to Cartagena. These officers, too, were shot.

It was all quiet in Morocco but the African Army was needed urgently in the Peninsula. In Seville the bon viveur and late riser Queipo de Llano had heard of the rising in Morocco in the late morning of the Saturday. He had rushed to the barracks where he found that of a whole regiment nominally garrisoned in the town there were only 180 men. With these he had taken Seville, shouting defiance at Madrid with the cry "Long Live the Republic".* Such an easy take over had not been expected by the insurgents, but on the other hand Franco had thought that the Navy would by now be rallying to their cause. From intercepted wireless telegraphy messages signed by Jose Giral, the Navy Minister, Franco had an inkling of what was happening. Giral was ordering the crews to take over from their officers. The crews

* He too had not mentioned religion, and in his case it would have been wholly out of character.

in many cases interpreted this as permission to kill them.* Among the bodies they threw overboard was that of the one member of the Franco family who had made the executive grade, his inseparable cousin's brother, Hermenegildo Franco-Salgado, Captain of the heavy cruiser *Libertad* which had put out from El Ferrol on the Friday night. The ships which had remained in base at his home town would become available to his side in days to come, but for the moment he was in command of an army of 24,000 men† and no means of getting them across the Straits other than two cross-channel steamers, one gunboat, one coastguard vessel and one torpedo boat. On the gunboat he sent another *tabor* of *Regulares* to the mainland, and on small boats two companies of the Legion making the total who had got across about one thousand. The bridgehead was being widened, but there was a sizeable gap between it and Seville.

Queipo de Llano was broadcasting that he was Master of Seville and claiming that he had received massive reinforcements from the Army of Africa. Franco packed a handful of men into a Breguet bomber to give colour to the lie. He did not know it at the time but Queipo was in fact already doing that. Queipo had ordered his force of 180 men to blacken their faces and ride round and round the town giving the Socialist militia and storm troopers the impression that the insurgents numbered many more than they did. It was to be hoped that the troops landed in Algeciras would reach Seville before the deception was discovered. The situation was not heartening on the morning of the 19th. Twenty-four hours later it was worse.

The plan of the Rising which Franco had joined was a simple one.

The Spanish Army in the Peninsula consisted of eight infantry divisions and one cavalry division. The cavalry and one infantry division had their headquarters in Madrid. The headquarters of the others were in Seville, Valencia, Barcelona, Zaragoza, Burgos, Valladolid, and Corunna. The divisional commanders were all Masons, all trusted by the Popular Front and all, with the exception of Cabanellas in Zaragoza, worthy of their trust. Each infantry division had two brigades. In each of the divisional H.Q. cities there was also a brigade headquarters; the others were in smaller towns, such as Pamplona, where Mola was in command. Each brigade had two regiments. The divisional H.Q. cities had a regiment quartered in them apiece: the

---

* Gln. Rojo (Republican) to author: "75 per cent of all officers". That is about correct according to Navy Records.

† See below, p. 240.

MAP 3

three other regiments of each division were scattered in small parcels, sometimes as insignificant as a platoon.

The plan of action was the following:

On D-Day Cabanellas would declare for the Rising: the other divisions would be taken over by generals or colonels in the plot. At lower level the same pattern would be followed: that is to say if the brigade, regiment or battalion commander was in the plot, he would lead the rising on behalf of his command: if he was not, some junior officer was designated to take over from his senior. The plotters did not overlook two facts: that the officers in the plot were a small minority of the total: that the rising was not only against the Popular Front government but also against most of the senior officers put in command by that government.* The D-day first objective, therefore, was the

---

* Of the twenty major-generals on the active list, only seven were in the plot, including Franco. Of the remainder at least eight remained voluntarily with the Popular Front after the rising—one of them, Lopez Ochoa paid dearly for his loyalty. He was shot by the Popular Front for his part in the October Revolution.

overpowering of the Popular Front army officers. The second objective varied from region to region. The populace was expected to be hostile to the rising in the regions of the Ist Division (Madrid), IInd (Seville for Andalucia), IVth (Barcelona and Catalonia) and VIIIth (Corunna for the Galician ports and Asturias). These divisions would therefore remain in their scattered garrison state. In the others where the populace was expected to be friendly, the divisions were to be concentrated. On D plus 1, or as quickly as possible thereafter, the three divisions assembled in Valencia, Zaragoza, and Burgos and Valladolid would begin a converging advance in columns towards Madrid.

The African Army fitted in to the general plan in this way: the Army in Africa was to rise on D minus 1 in the name of General Franco who would arrive on D-day. It was anticipated that the Government's immediate reactions to the news of the rising in Morocco would be to order out warships from Cartagena and El Ferrol. These would be the ships which, if all went well, would take and escort the Army in Africa to the Peninsula to form a further column to tackle Madrid from the south.

On D-day the Monarchist flyer Ansaldo was to take his dilapidated Puss Moth from Pamplona to Lisbon. On the following day Ansaldo would fly in General Sanjurjo either to Burgos or Pamplona. Sanjurjo would then be declared Commander-in-Chief.[8]

Little went according to plan. Friday, 17th July, the date of the rising in Morocco, was not the D minus 1 day which most of the plotters had been expecting. In the preparatory stages the plotting had been weakened in its lines of communications. Counter-orders would arrive at their destination before the original orders, to the extreme annoyance of Yague in particular.[9] In the immediate pre-D-day period the date for D-day had been changed more than once because of disagreements between the insurgent Army officers and the civilian groupings on whose support they wanted to rely. The Falange was prepared to co-operate with the Army but not under its command. The Carlists would follow no flag other than the old monarchist standard. On the other hand several of the insurgent officers were republican. Then the murder of Calvo Sotelo united the dissenting factions. If there was to be a rising, it had to be as soon as possible. On the Wednesday Mola had despatched the prearranged telegram: "On the 15th last at 4 o'clock in the morning Helen gave birth to a beautiful child":[10] that is the insurrection is to take place on 19 (15 + 4), on the mainland, and 15 + 4 − 1 in Africa.[11]

The news of the rising in Morocco on the 17th disconcerted the plotters on the Peninsula. Were they to obey the telegram, or were they to follow the earlier instruction that if one garrison were forced by circumstances to rise prematurely all others would follow immediately? Queipo in Seville followed the earlier orders. So did Saliquet in Valladolid; but all the others waited till the 19th. In the early stages of the plotting, Mola had himself stressed that "the rising must be rapid in the extreme, to defeat the enemy which is strong and well organised".[12] The delay made no difference in most of Old Castile, Aragon and (eventually) in Galicia; but Mola himself took over a VIth Division depleted by prompt action on the part of the Basque Government of garrisons in two out of the three Basque provinces, while the miners in Asturias neutralised the VIIth Division's detachments over a wide area. The cost of the delay in the east and to the south was wellnigh disastrous.

In the late evening of the 18th, that is 24 hours after the news of the rising in Morocco had become general knowledge, the left-wing General Llano de la Encomienda[13] commanding the Barcelona Division reported to President Companys of Catalonia that there was no sign of revolt among the troops. While the troops remained in barracks, the C.N.T. assaulted arms depots and by the end of the day had 12,000 men under arms. By 2 o'clock in the morning they were in position along the main avenues—the Ramblas—with the storm troopers and Civil Guard on their side. Numerically they outnumbered the divisional troops actually in the city by at least four to one. Far too late, at 0400 hours, the troops began to move out of their barracks. Though they fought well on the whole, the issue was never in doubt. General Goded arrived from the Balearics to take over the revolt in Barcelona halfway through the morning. By that time the battle had been decided. By early evening Goded was a prisoner and the Division lost to the insurgents. Barcelona had been lost, and with a failure at Barcelona the revolt collapsed also in Valencia, where the plotters dithered.

The situation on the Monday morning was therefore this: the insurgents had lost the IIIrd Division in Valencia, the IVth in Barcelona and all that isolated units of the IInd in Andalucia. They were sure only of the whole of the VIIth in Valladolid, most of the Vth in Zaragoza and three-quarters of the VIth centred in Burgos. A part of the VIIIth in Galicia was being saved, but not the detachments in Asturias; and it was evident by that Monday morning that the loss of the Ist

Infantry and the Cavalry Divisions in Madrid was only a matter of time.

In Madrid on the 19th Casares Quiroga had resigned rather than succumb to the Socialist clamour for handing weapons to the masses. An army officer was in fact already distributing five thousand rifles to the Communist–Socialist militia nearly doubling their armament. Martinez Barrios, momentarily Prime Minister, had offered Mola the post of Minister of War as a peace offering. Mola had refused. Barrios had then stepped down for Giral. Giral had then authorised the distribution of arms already begun. The First Brigade commander, Miaja, stood by his side.[14]

Franco's advice to General Fanjul, the insurgents' man in Madrid, had been that he should act immediately and lead the troops out of their barracks northwards to join Mola's column which would be advancing southwards. Fanjul ignored the advice. He made no move till the evening of the 19th when he assembled the officers in the Montaña barracks and persuaded them to give battle. By then the few hundred men within the barracks were being surrounded by several thousand militia and loyal troops supported by storm troopers and artillery. On the 20th they were subjected to a five-hour not very accurate bombardment from the air and a pounding at point blank range from artillery. On surrendering most of the officers were slaughtered. The militia and loyal troops then reduced the other garrisons in Madrid and region in turn. The cities and towns of New Castile were lost to the insurgents. Only in one place were the militia checked. That was in the Alcazar in Toledo where General Moscardó, the elderly Commander of the Physical Training School, barricaded himself in with 100 other Officers, five cadets and 190 other ranks, 800 members of the Civil Guard and about 200 civilian combatants. His action was to have far-reaching consequences to the conduct of the war.

On 20th July another event occurred, the long-term consequences of which were perhaps even more far-reaching. On the previous day Ansaldo had duly coaxed his elderly Puss Moth to Lisbon—or rather to an airfield 70 kilometres away. The Portuguese authorities were already friendly to the insurgents, but not wishing to attract too much attention to the departure of Sanjurjo, they refused permission for the aircraft to take off with the General anywhere but from a field near Cascaes, used as a horse-race track. The ground was hard but lumpy. The wind direction was from a line of tall trees. Ansaldo protested but confessed that he had taken off from smaller fields in worse conditions. Seconds after take-off the aircraft was a wreck in flames, and Sanjurjo was dead.*

The insurgent movement was now without a Generalissimo. Franco was Commander-in-Chief of the Army in Africa: Mola was Commander-in-Chief of the Army of the north; Queipo was Commander-in-Chief of the non-existent Army of the south.

* Ansaldo survived with severe injuries, being pulled away from the burning aircraft by a shepherd. Iturralde op. cit. Vol. II, pp. 46-50 suggests that in some mysterious way Franco arranged this accident. There is not a shred of evidence to support the suggestion. Ansaldo who later became one of Franco's bitterest enemies wrote a perfectly credible explanation of the accident. (*Para Que?*, pp. 139 ff.): "The General got into the aircraft and an enormous and very heavy case went in behind him. I demurred at the overloading. I had in mind the weight of the petrol I was carrying in view of the long and devious flight ahead (an extra 80 litres). 'They are the General's uniforms,' someone said, 'he can't arrive in Burgos with nothing to wear on the eve of his triumphal entry into Madrid'. I didn't dare discuss the matter, and I trusted in my many successful take-offs in complicated circumstances. I went carefully to the end of the field and turned the aircraft towards the trees at the other end. I asked the General to stand up, so as to get my tail up quickly. I put the engine on full throttle with the brake still on. Then, with the joy-stick up against the dashboard, I let go. The trees came up at a terrific speed: but keeping the aircraft on the ground and with my eyes on the wind-speed indicator I watched till the needle marked 15 k.p.h. above flying speed, so as to take-off abruptly with this margin of safety. (This was my habit when taking off in awkward conditions.) A fraction of a second later I heard a sharp bang and felt the aircraft shudder. Used to blow outs in similar circumstances, I pulled the stick and rose . . . I am not trying to excuse what I did. I've paid hard enough for the consequences. But there are many people who say I took off with insufficient speed. That is not so. I cleared the trees, and the accident occurred more than one kilometre away from take-off.

". . . as I passed over the trees still climbing I had the awful sensation that my airspeed was . . . falling off, and that the shuddering was increasing to the extent that I felt the aircraft might break up in the air. 'My air-screw is broken', I thought to myself. Almost at stalling speed I put the nose downwards towards a ploughed strip . . . and cut out the engine . . . There was a metre-high stone wall between us and the field I had chosen. I had to clear it but the heat of the day and the weight of the overloaded aircraft made it impossible: and I crashed into it, failing to clear it by a few centimetres . . . " Ansaldo reckoned that in his anxiety to lift his tail, he had put the nose down too far and had broken the air-screw on one of the bumps on the ground. That is possible. So is the explanation suggested by Wing-Commander Asher Lee from my description of the field, the surrounding country and the winds common in that area (near the notorious Boca do Inferno, or Mouth of Hell) on a hot summer's day: that once clear of the trees, Ansaldo ran into air currents with which an overloaded Puss Moth with a well-worn engine could not cope.

To say, as Thomas does (*The Spanish Civil War*, p. 162) that Sanjurjo was a victim of his sartorial vanity is to do this general a gross injustice: he was rather a victim of the convention of all European armies before World War II to be "properly dressed" according to occasion.

Let us examine now the military situation outside Africa.[15] Though the paper strength of the Army in Spain was 121,000 men, all ranks,* in fact its ration strength on 17th July was 60,230.† If we consider the geographical distribution of the garrisons we arrive at the following: Army personnel in the insurgent zone 23,595; and in the Popular Front zones 36,685. Not all those in the insurgent zone were insurgents or vice versa: hence the severe casualties during the weekend 17–20th. After that weekend 23,000 remained with the insurgents and 33,000‡ with the Popular Front. Even the officer distribution gave no definite advantage to one camp or the other. Of the 8,500 officers in the Peninsular Army the insurgents were left with 3,000: the Popular Front killed or imprisoned 3,500 but 2,000§ chose to fight for them.

The relative strengths meant a stalemate. Each side had the remnants of an army, but no army. We must however consider also the paramilitary Civil Guard, *Asaltos* and *Carabineros*. The Civil Guard had a paper strength of 24,300.‖ Its exact strength at the outbreak of hostilities is unknown. In view of the "State of Alarm" few should have been on leave. The total in the insurgent zone including those who managed to cross over in the first days was 14,200.¶ The total in the Popular Front's zones was therefore 20,100. There it was disbanded but practically all its members were incorporated into a new force, the *Guardia Republicana*. Exact figures for the *Asaltos* are also not available** but we may estimate 500 with the insurgents and 3,500 with the Popular Front. The *Carabineros* numbered 14,750 of whom 6,000 were in the insurgent zone and 8,750 in the Popular Front.†† This frontiers and ports

---

* 8,851 officers, 112,228 O.R.s.

† Ration returns last week before the Civil War (Servicio Historico Militar). There were 40,000 on leave.

‡ Exact figures are not available, but may be calculated from the mass of accounts of the early days of the fighting, desertions, etc.

§ The figure 2,000 was given me by the late General Vicente Rojo shortly before his death in June 1966. Alvarez del Vayo's often quoted 15,000 with the Insurgents and 500 with the Republicans was absurd on both counts. The officers who remained loyal in Madrid alone came close to 500.

‖ 1,516 officers; 22,869 O.R.s.

¶ Servicio Historico Militar.

** The Republic, like other Spanish régimes, had a large Secret Police force. In returns it was grouped together with the *Asaltos* proper. The Servicio Historico Militar estimates the combined force under the Popular Front at 31,200, rather a high figure to my mind. Of these they say "about 9,200 were to be found in the Insurgent zone". How many were *Asaltos* and how many were Secret Police? I can find no evidence that more than 500 *Asaltos* were trusted by the Insurgents: 3,500 is the lowest figure with Madrid. It may well have been much higher.

†† Paper strength: 678 officers; 14,112 O.R.s.

force however was not particularly mobile. While those on the Portuguese frontier would fight against the insurgents when the war moved into that area, and others with the insurgents elsewhere, their military importance was nugatory compared with that of the Civil Guard or *Asaltos*. The mobile para-military forces were therefore: Insurgents— 14,200 Civil Guards and 500 Asaltos; and Popular Front 3,500 Asaltos and—immediately available—about 10,000 Civil Guards out of their haul of 20,000.*

Again, these relative strengths meant a stalemate.

So much then for one-half at least of the generally accepted story that the armed forces rose as a body against a determined but unarmed people. Nothing, as we have seen, could be further from the truth. The rising had been engineered by a small body of officers, some of them generals but mostly of more junior rank. The greater number of army officers had followed them, but in terms of all ranks the Popular Front had retained well over half the land armed forces. What of the people? At the outbreak of the war, the *trained* militia in hand were:

Insurgents
  Requetes (Carlist and associates)   8,400†
  Falange   4,000‡
                                            ——————   12,400
                                                          ——————

Popular Front
  Socialists and Communists   12,000§
  Trotskyist and Anarchist   15,000‖
                                            ——————   27,000
                                                          ——————

* The Socialists by and large did not share the Anarchist's or southern peasant's hatred of the Civil Guard uniform. The same men as Guardia Republicana were generally acceptable to all. The figures for Security Police, Civil Guard and *Asaltos* incidentally do not confirm the myth that the Popular Front was left without the means to prevent the wholesale murder of priests, nuns and other civilians which took place over the first weekend and for some months after.

† Lizarza.
‡ Crusada IX 511
§ Vicente Rojo.
‖ By the end of July when the Requetes reached a total of 16,000 and the Falangists 20,000, the left-wing militias had swollen to 100,000, or if Peirats (*La CNT en la Revolución Española*) is to be believed, 150,000. Accordingly the ratio was then at best one to four. At the end of the war the Falangist units totalled 35,000: the Requetes, once 40,000, had after heavy casualties been reduced to 23,000.

The militia balance was overwhelmingly favourable to Madrid and Barcelona, but only in a one to two ratio: not enough for attackers to dislodge determined defenders—as the Government quickly found out when they deployed 7,000 militia (trained and untrained), strengthened by Army units, against the Alcazar in Toledo defended by 1,300 Civil Guards, soldiers and militia; and 5,000 militia and soldiers against 200 insurgent militias in the mountains to the north of Madrid.

Once again, therefore, both sides knew they were facing a stalemate.

The people (if we exclude the militia) were unarmed at the very beginning; but they were not defenceless. The fact has been almost totally ignored that the "people of Madrid" or other cities to whom arms were issued over the weekend were not like those of London or Glasgow, New York or Toronto. Every since 1912 there had been compulsory military service in Spain, so that in theory every man under 42 in 1936 knew how to handle small arms at least. In fact, a far greater number of workmen had handled them than clerks and a far greater number of the less prosperous than of the wealthy. Conscription had been universally hated, but it had been relatively easy for upper middle and upper class parents—that is for those whose sympathies now tended to be with the insurgents—to have their boys excused military service.

In this fact that the Popular Front had retained control over the major population centres (Madrid, Barcelona, Bilbao and Valencia in particular), and therefore the greater number of men already partially processed for war during their compulsory military service, there was reason to expect—as the German Ambassador in Madrid did[16] a Popular Front victory in the long run.

The Popular Front, moreover, was in possession of the arms, ammunition, motor vehicles and aircraft assembly plants, of the textile mills, and indeed of all the means of producing the weapons and supplies of war. The insurgents had a small artillery factory in Seville and minor railway repair shops. They had one naval base, at El Ferrol, as against their opponents' two, at Cadiz and Cartagena. Their opponents, too, had the shipyards of the north. Prieto could with reason broadcast to the insurgents "I don't understand what the rebels are after. They have gone off their heads. How can they hope to be saved? We have in our power the major cities, the industrial centres, all the gold and silver of the Bank of Spain, limitless reserves of men, the fleet. . . ."[17]

The Government had the gold reserves of Spain. The insurgents had only such wealth as persons who sympathised with them had in foreign holdings.*

In the long run a Popular Front victory—but how long a run? If on the one side men were flocking to join the Socialist, Communist, and Anarchist militias, so on the other men of all ages were rushing to Requeté and Falange recruiting offices. Like for like there might be little to choose between the Falange militiaman and the Anarchist (Prieto was never more right than when he referred to the FAI-lange†) but the Requetés had a century-old tradition of fighting against enormous odds till death. In the nineteenth century Carlist guerillas had held out for years in the mountains of Navarre against overwhelming odds. Mola's plan in the event of a failure of a general rising had been a withdrawal of all insurgents to the mountains of Navarre, where every peasant and bourgeois was on their side.

The situation must have looked hopeless enough alike to Mola in Pamplona, Franco in Tetuan or to Giral in Madrid. However there were two factors in the situation which might yet save the insurgents on the Peninsula.[18] The first was the solidarity under Franco of the Army in Africa: the second the reputation for military ability and for ruthlessness of that Army and of Franco.

Including the units already across the water Franco had six *banderas* of the Foreign Legion,‡ ten *tabores* of *Regulares*, seven Spanish infantry battalions, six Spanish cavalry squadrons and six field artillery batteries, supporting services and garrison units—a total on paper of 32,800 men and in fact 24,000.[19] The Jalif had also placed at Franco's disposal his Mehalla or Moroccan equivalent of the Civil Guard—a further 6,000 men. Of these 30,000 Franco could afford to take 17,000 men and still leave Spanish Morocco well policed.

These 17,000 men, added to the 23,000 on the Peninsula, would give the insurgents a slight numerical superiority over their opponents: but more than that, they were for the most part professional soldiers. Nine years had passed since the official end of the Moroccan campaign but they had been kept well trained and well disciplined in arms. The "Moors" and the Legion had a reputation in the popular mind for

---

* Fortunately for them one of the sympathisers was the reputed millionaire Juan March; but even his wealth was insignificant compared with that on hand in Madrid.

† The FAI, being the Anarchist "inner cirle".

‡ Since his days as its commander the Legion had progressively become less foreign. As *The Times* correspondent said (23rd July 1936), 95 per cent of its members were Spaniards at the outbreak of the war.

extreme military ability, endurance and mercilessness. Before them the morale of inexperienced, indifferently-led men, even if superior in number, might well crumble. The sooner this army could be got across to the Peninsula the greater its potential value: if it could strike at the enemy camp while its inmates were fighting each other, it might yet win the day. Contrariwise, if Giral could prevent it from getting across, he might give Madrid time to settle its internal affairs and produce a new model army.

To get his army across the Straits Franco needed transport; ships or aircraft. He had immediately available a few old aircraft and two channel steamers: and to protect them one gunboat, one coastguard vessel and a dozen obsolescent fighters and bombers.[20]

To prevent him from getting it across, the Popular Front had in the area one battleship, three cruisers, fourteen destroyers, six submarines and six torpedo boats.[21] Out of its force of 111, it should have been able to concentrate fifty-nine bombers and fighters. However, the fleet with 75 per cent of its officers killed and thrown overboard was of doubtful fighting value, and Giral judged his airforce insufficient, if not inefficient.

There was only one course open to both Giral and Franco, and both took it. Giral appealed to the French Popular Front Government for modern bombers and bombs heavier than he had. On 26th July thirteen Potez 54 bombers, the best the French had to offer, were shipped at Marseilles and must have arrived in Spain a day or two later. Within a few days[22] a further seventeen bombers, fifteen fighters and ten other aircraft were flown to Popular Front airfields by well-paid French pilots. On 2nd August Giral approached Berlin for fighters, bombers and bombs. Franco's men had got there first.

Franco had held a council of war on 20th July. The agenda was the consideration of how the African Army might be transported across the Straits.

Immediately after his arrival, Franco had realised that his most pressing need was aircraft, to replace those damaged by his cousin in Africa, and to bomb the airfields from which Tetuan had been bombed. Accordingly he had dispatched Luis Bolin in the Dragon Rapide with a hurriedly written note which read: "I authorise Don Luis Antonio Bolin to negotiate urgently in England, Germany or Italy the purchase of aircraft and supplies for the Spanish non-Marxist Army." In pencil he had added: "Twelve bombers, three fighters, bombs. . . ."[23] Colonel Alfredo Kindelan, the senior Spanish airforce officer with Franco, a

Monarchist first and foremost, now undertook to contact British friends in Gibraltar and Britain. Eventually he obtained three Fokkers. In connection with the Sanjurjo rising in 1932, the Monarchist airman Ansaldo had flown to see the Italian Air Marshal Balbo. Balbo had prevailed on Mussolini to promise small arms which never left Italy. In 1934 a joint Carlist–Alfonsist delegation had obtained a donation of a million and a half pesetas (£50,000) to their cause, and the promise of small arms if there were to be a rising: and subsequently four hundred young Requetés had gone to Italy for training. The Carlists were allies of the insurgents, so Mussolini might now agree to a request for aircraft. Accordingly Franco now diverted Bolin who had reached Biarritz on his way back to England. With Luca de Tena, the Editor of the *A.B.C.*, he was to go to Rome. Through them Franco told Mussolini,[24] that with a mere one dozen aircraft he would be able to win the war in a few days. This was merely a ruse on Franco's part to get what he wanted immediately. If Mussolini was incapable of working things out for himself or chose to believe him, the more fool he. Mussolini's immediate reaction was to refuse to help but changing his mind on the Friday, he ordered the dispatch of twelve Savoia Marchetti 81s—three-engined bomber/transport aircraft, of which nine reached Nador on 30th July.[25]*

Franco appreciated that Germany would be a more difficult trout to land than Italy. He had with him in Africa a Lieutenant-Colonel Beigbeder, once Military Attaché in the Spanish Embassy in Berlin, and Yague was a friend of the local Nazi Party leader and German businessmen. Beigbeder, in the name of Franco, asked the German Military Attaché in Paris to obtain for them "ten troop transport planes with maximum seating capacity through private German firms".[26]

The German Ministry of Foreign Affairs passed the message to the War Ministry with the observation that compliance with the Spanish request was out of the question.

Franco's other line of approach was to prove the more productive. On 23rd July he ordered a Lufthansa JU 52 to be seized in Las Palmas. In this General Orgaz travelled to Tetuan. There were immediate German protests. The German acting Vice-Consul in Tangier rushed to see Franco in Tetuan. Franco informed him that the rising had been

---

* One crashed into the sea and two others landed short of fuel on French territory. Bolin, who flew back to Africa in one of the Italian machines, confesses that the nine survivors all landed with hardly any fuel left.

necessary to forestall a Soviet dictatorship: and explained that he needed
the JU 52 to despatch the Nazi party's man Langenheim and the busi-
nessman Bernhardt with personal letters to Hitler and Goering. Hitler
saw the emissaries on the 26th in Bayreuth after a performance of
Die Walkyre. There were sound reasons why he should acceed to
Franco's request. The choice was no longer between democracy and
military dictatorship in Spain but between a dictatorship of the proletariat and the military dictatorship: that is in Hitlerian terms between
a Spain which might be an ally of what Germany then called the
Franco–Russian bloc[27] and a Spain which might give Germany
concessions in the raw materials of rearmament. Goering was anxious
to give his Luftwaffe battle experience and therefore all for help
to Franco over and above the transport aircraft which had been
requested.

Twenty JU 52s[30] and six Heinkel bi-plane fighters were quickly sent
to Africa via Seville. They were operational by the beginning of the
second week of August.

Franco however had not waited for them to begin his airlift. Using all
available aircraft from the 20th onwards, and the Italian Savoyas from
the 29th, he had got 800 men across by 1st August. At a rate of a little
more than 100 men a day, Franco would have needed almost six months
to complete the operation. He decided, therefore, albeit against the
advice of all his colleagues, on a sea crossing of as large a force as the
ships at his disposal could carry. Their chief danger was the strong
enemy naval force in Tangiers. Since the day of his arrival in Africa
Franco had spent a great deal of effort trying to get the International
Commission to deny this fleet harbour. He had still not succeeded. He
could wait no longer. He loaded cross-channel steamers and some small
boats with 3,000 men, their beasts of burden, some guns and fifty tons
of ammunition. Early on 5th August aerial reconnaisance showed that
the Straits were reasonably clear. He ordered the troop carriers,
escorted by his one gunboat and six of the Savoyas as bombers (with
Italian crews) and eleven Spanish fighters, to race across. Only one
enemy destroyer attempted interception. It was driven off by the gunboat and the bombers.

What had been done once could have been done again more easily
after 9th August when the International Commission had ordered the
fleet to sail to far away Malaga and Cartagena—but there was no
need.

With the arrival of the JU 52s the airlift gradually built up, and by the end of September 12,800 men had been ferried with about 400 tons of equipment.*

To return, however, to 1st August. On that day Franco ordered a Lieutenant-Colonel Carlos Asensio Cabanillas to leave Tetuan for Seville by air and take over a "column". His orders were to proceed north to Merida so as to establish contact with General Mola and deliver him seven million rounds of small arms ammunition. Mola was desperately short.[29] The "column" would consist, he was told, of the Fourth *bandera* of the Legion, the best part of a *tabor*—troops which had been taken across by sea and air in the first few days—half a battery and supporting services: little more than 1,500 men in all. Queipo de Llano was to provide transport—a few old requisitioned lorries.

The "column" set out from Seville on 3rd August.[30] During the first two days it advanced eighty miles with nothing to hold it up more than a broken bridge and occasional small arms fire. At that rate it could be in Madrid in another week after establishing contact north of Mérida with Mola; but on the third day it faced soldiers, carabiniers, assault guards and militia men from Badajoz. There was a seven-hour engagement before the enemy withdrew. Casualties were heavy on both sides. On the following day another battle. On the 6th the column suffered even heavier casualites when it was attacked from the air for the first time. It was then by Almedralejo, 100 miles from its point of departure: in the previous four days it had advanced twenty miles: at that rate it would take nearly two months to reach Madrid. Almedralejo fell only after another stiff engagement. The enemy fell back still intact

---

* These facts do not substantiate two myths. The first is that without the Italian and German aircraft Franco would never have transported the army out of Africa. More accurately without those aircraft it would have taken him longer, but he would have done it. The second is that Franco won a great victory with this convoy. It is officially called the *convoy de la victoria*. He was right in his assessment that the enemy fleet would not intervene, its nearly officerless crews demoralised by the few bombs which had been dropped on them by the old machines in Franco's possession in the first days of the war. This however does not explain the inaction of the Popular Front's air force. Madrid had the aircraft to bomb Franco's convoy out of the sea and shoot down his bombers and fighters. The Heinkel 51 was to prove Germany's grave disappointment. It was no match for the French fighters, let alone the Russian machines which appeared later. Indeed, as Ansaldo records, their major successes were against insurgent de Havilland light aircraft which the Heinkels' German pilots mis-identified. The Popular Front's failure to use the aircraft at their disposal where it mattered must therefore be judged the decisive factor, together with the failure of their fleet to sail out from Tangiers to battle. The Popular Front "atomised" their air force in useless little raids in ones and twos on the Alcazar in Toledo and other points and cities in the hands of the insurgents.

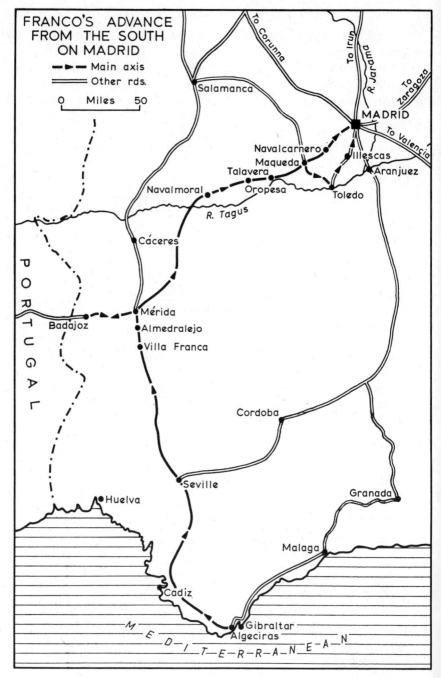

MAP 4

on Mérida. Queipo ordered Asensio to wait for reinforcements. The arrival in Seville of the sea-ferried troops had made possible the formation of two more columns under the Lieutenant-Colonels Castejón and Tella. Castejón's was raced to back Asensio's. On the 10th Asensio, Castejón and their three thousand tired men faced a fresh force despatched from Madrid. Franco ordered the colonels to combine and assault Mérida. It fell the following day.

With Mérida in the hands of the insurgents tenuous contact was established between the northern and southern zones. Mola got his ammunition and a *bandera* of the Legion. Badajoz, a name that was to figure prominently in foreign newspapers, was cut off from Madrid, but not defenceless. A force five-thousand strong stood in the way of the insurgents if they should decide to attempt its capture, or ready to pounce on them from the rear if the insurgents now turned eastwards towards Madrid.

On 1st August Mola's need for ammunition had been the overriding factor behind Franco's decision to send Asensio due north. On the 7th he had established his headquarters in Seville. On the 10th, with Mérida almost in his hands, he could consider the next step. Though anything approaching the original insurgent plan of several columns making for Madrid was out of the question (with Mola pinned down to the north of the capital and threatened from Barcelona), the capture of Madrid was still the objective. He had a choice of two routes—via Mérida or via Cordoba. The Cordoba was the easier route; on the other hand the enemy would be expecting him that way. Furthermore, to go via Cordoba he would have to recall his columns back from Mérida. That looked like a withdrawal. And any move that could be interpreted as a withdrawal could not be considered. Accordingly, the way to Madrid had to be via Mérida.[31] The columns were now to become one with Yague in command. Yague took over as Mérida fell. But now, before the newly combined column could set out from Madrid, the enemy in Badajoz had to be destroyed. Badajoz was, moreover, the gateway from Portugal. Prime Minister Salazar had declared himself for the insurgents from the beginning. He would allow the passage of the weapons which Franco had in mind to purchase from Germany if his drive to Madrid was halted.

Yague was instructed to destroy the enemy in Badajoz. The 5,000 soldiers, armed police and militiamen fought bravely but proved no match for the 3,000 from Africa. Yague then decimated in cold blood the prisoners he captured.[32] His excuse was that he had to deal with the enemy

in an exemplary fashion to safeguard the rear. The insurgents shared with
their enemies the view that the Geneva Convention did not apply in
civil war. Franco intervened only to prohibit the castration of dead bodies
by the Moors.[33] Several days were spent in "cleaning up" operations.
The main guard did not move out of Mérida until 20th August.

The advance on Madrid had begun at long last. The column covered
the 150 miles to Talavera in fifteen days—not a fast speed even bearing
in mind the fact that it was not motorised and that it was subject to
air attacks. Ground opposition was sporadic until the column reached
the outskirts of Talavera. There Yague did have to face a determined
and well-equipped enemy force which counter-attacked at an awkward
moment. The column gained the day killing 500 of the enemy and
making several thousand prisoners, capturing forty-two guns but themselves suffering "over one thousand casualties".[34] The column then
halted for twelve days. Reinforced by local volunteers who joined the
Legion, and by fresh units air-ferried from Africa, it moved again
7 to 8,000 strong, and again halted for three days. On the 19th it took
Santa Eulalla, sixteen miles beyond Talavera which had fallen on the
3rd: sixteen miles in sixteen days; Franco was chivvying Yague.
Yague "collapsed through exhaustion"[35] on the 20th. On the 21st
Asensio, temporarily in command, took Maqueda, and Franco now
had an important decision to make.

Two roads lay ahead: one to Madrid, the other to Toledo: to Madrid
45 miles, to Toledo 24.

In Toledo the 1,300 men in the Alcazar were still holding out. Their
resistance against incredible odds had become a symbol to the insurgents of heroism, tenacity, discipline and duty—Franco's highest
ideals. A month earlier he had promised the defenders to hasten to their
help. It had taken him longer than he anticipated to be in a position to
do so. Was he still bound by his promise? The news from Madrid was
that the Communists' so-called Fifth Regiment[36] was about to re-
organise the rump of the Army which had not joined the insurgents,
and the militias into a new model army. The longer Franco took
making Madrid the less chance that his seven to eight thousand men
might capture it. Kindelan[37] warned him that saving the Alcazar might
cost him Madrid. Friends abroad were warning him that though the
rumours that Russia and France would send troops to Spain might be
false, there were plans for the formation of an international force, men
whom he had no reason to suppose would be inferior in any way to the
excellent foreigners whom he had commanded in Africa in the early

days of the Legion. In spite of all this, Franco decided to relieve the Alcazar.

It is legitimate to wonder whether at the back, if not at the front, of his mind there was the memory of the men of Nador* to whose rescue he had been forbidden by the now-dead Sanjurjo to go when he was little more than a youth.

For the Alcazar operation Franco needed a man with a flair for rapidity of movement and the calculated risk. He chose a proven man, Jose Varela Iglesias. Varela had risen from a boy bugler at eighteen to a Brigadier at forty-four winning Spain's highest award for bravery twice. When Queipo had been worried about the force reported to be advancing from Madrid to Seville via Cordoba, Franco had sent Varela to do what he could to strengthen Cordoba. With no more than a battalion to begin with, he had frightened off the force descending from Madrid, saved Cordoba, and gone on to gain definitely Granada and Ronda for the insurgents. On the 23rd, Franco gave Varela six days to take Toledo. He took over command of the column on the 24th. By the 28th he had scattered the forces sent to stop him— and Madrid had made all-out effort to do so—and his men were embracing the defenders of the Alcazar. On the following day, 29th September, Franco arrived in Toledo in triumph.

While Franco's column had pushed all the way from Seville, Mola's troops had not been inactive. Mola had gone to see Franco in Seville on 13th August. The two generals had agreed that while Mola had neither the men nor the weapons to drive towards Madrid from his precariously advanced positions in the Guadarramas twenty-five miles to the north of the capital, he might attempt to deny the Basques their frontier with France. French materials and volunteers were reported entering Spain through Hendaye and Irun. A strike force would be formed. Franco would provide a battalion of the Legion and the ammunition once Merida was taken, to reinforce a column of 450 Carlist militiamen, as many Civil Guards and perhaps 400 Falangists supported by insurgent artillery. According to plan, this column had taken Irun on 5th September after fighting in which the Carlists on the one side and the Anarchists on the other distinguished themselves for their utter disregard for personal safety. But this column had not destroyed the enemy. One group, mainly of French Communists and Spanish Anarchists had withdrawn across the International Bridge

* See above, Ch. V, p. 125.

after setting fire to the town which had already suffered considerably from bombardment by Italian aircraft. The bulk of the defence force, Basques with some Communists and Anarchists, had fallen back on San Sebastian which the Basques had surrendered eight days later to prevent the Anarchists from setting fire to it.[38]

Elsewhere in the north during August and September success and failure had balanced out. Gijon defended by 180 insurgents, fell to a determined attack from several thousand Asturians, but the insurgents in Oviedo held out. With 30,000 men Mola had established also a 600-kilometre line of defence (rather than a front) with the key towns of Jaca, Huesca, Zaragoza, Belchite and Teruel. Against it Anarchist militia under the legendary Durruti, together with Catalan Communist–Socialist militia, reinforced with several hundred Germans, Italians and Central Europeans (men who were at the Workers' Olympiad in Barcelona when the rising had occurred), French, Belgian and even a few British Communists, and Trotskyist militia, had not prevailed.

Towards the end of September it was becoming possible to talk of "fronts" and to define with some accuracy which parts of Spain were in the hands of whom. Behind those fronts there were some points of similarity and some differences. On the non-insurgent side, Largo Caballero was now Prime Minister of a mainly Socialist government. He exercised such authority in military matters as he was permitted by the men running the Communist "Fifth Regiment" headed by the Italian Vidali (Carlos Contreras). In civil affairs too, Largo Caballero was attentive to Communist insistence that Socialist revolutionary exuberance had to be checked if "Republican Spain" was to retain the sympathy of Western Europe: that it was essential that the revolution which had taken place in Spain should be camouflaged by retaining in the government representatives of the less revolutionary elements of the Popular Front. There had to be an end to the slaughter of priests and nuns: it was necessary to retain some semblance of moderation. A limit had to be imposed on the confiscation and collectivisation of property in wartime if the national economy were not to break down completely.* Above all no war could be won without discipline and

---

* Another of the popular myths about the Civil War to account for the shortage of food in Madrid, etc. is that the insurgents held the food-growing areas. They had some of the best wheatlands but not all. To quote merely one example Cuidad Real was the centre of good wheat and fine cattle. The most agriculturally productive areas then as now were the northern strip (half of which was held by the insurgents and half by their enemies), and Catalonia and the Levante (eastern

unity. Russia might be prepared to provide arms, but not to a rabble which one day chose to fight with insuperable bravery and the next to throw away rifles and ammunition. Such discipline and unity would be possible only if it existed in government. Thus, order of a kind was being brought to Madrid but neither the visible government of Madrid, nor the Communists had any power in Andalusia, or in Valencia, or in Catalonia. Catalonia was theoretically under Companys, and Valencia under a junta headed by Martinez Barrio as agent of the Madrid government, but in practice in both areas, as in Andalusia, the Anarchists had triumphed (though in Catalonia temporarily in alliance with the Communists–Socialists and the Trotskyists). To complete the picture, local revolutionary and defence committees ran military and civil affairs in the north; in Asturias, Santander and the unconquered Basque provinces. These last were given autonomy on 1st October. In them only were the democratic freedoms exercised which the British and other liberal foreigners imagined were characteristic of all Republican Spain.

Behind the lines the other way, there was superficially more law and order. Men and women could practise their religion—if it was the Catholic: they could dress as they wished.* They could go about their businesses in normal fashion—provided that they had not been prominent Masons or conspicuous in the parties which had formed the Popular Front, the U.G.T. or C.N.T. Even then, if they put on the Falange blue shirt they were safe. Tens of thousands did, though thousands did not and, accused of having committed some atrocity, could consider death before a firing squad almost inevitable. For the military courts assumed guilt and took too short a time to allow innocence to be established. The one hope for a man so accused was that his case might be referred to Franco for confirmation. Franco spent several hours a day going minutely through cases, and a stickler for the law then as before, he would draw the attention of his Judge Advocate, Colonel Martinez Fuset, to inconsistencies, hiatus, unreliability of witnesses, and to the application of penalties on the basis of precedence. The more educated the accused, the higher his rank, the less chance of

region centred on Valencia). The truth of the matter is that collectivism did not work in town or country even if Borkenau[39] discovered one or two satisfactory examples; and secondly that Madrid could exercise no authority over Valencia or Barcelona.

* The wearing of a tie in Barcelona or Madrid could cost a man his life.

mercy.* But Franco was not as yet Commander-in-Chief, let alone
Head of State.

The side in the hands of the insurgents was in military matters
divided into the northern zone under Mola and the southern zone
under Franco. In civil affairs it was all theoretically subject to a junta,
established on 24th July with the 64-year-old General Miguel Cabanellas
at its head and Generals Saliquet, Ponte, Davila and Mola as members.
On 3rd August Franco and Queipo de Llano had been co-opted on to
it. In fact by mid-September the Junta had no authority in two areas.
One was the island of Majorca, where after helping in defence of the
island against an attack launched from Barcelona, an Italian fascist
aviator "Count Rossi" had assumed the powers and practices of a
medieval Bad Baron, acknowledging Mussolini rather than any
Spaniard as his "natural overlord":[40] the second was Andalusia where
Queipo de Llano, ignoring the existence of the Junta of which he was
a member, lived and ruled like a legendary Sultan. Franco, while in
Seville, had intervened only to the extent of insisting on 15th August
that the official flag of insurgent Spain should be the old red and gold of
Monarchist days, and Queipo, who had shouted "Long Live the
Republic" on rising, had stood by his side as Franco had ceremonially
unfurled it on the balcony of the Town Hall, saying to a crowd
assembled (they did not quite know why): "Here you have it. It is the

---

* Franco-Salgado insists strongly that this was so. His evidence is corroborated
by all other members of Franco's General Staff including those to whom Franco
was not a flawless hero. It would seem to contradict Thomas op. cit., p. 222.
I, too, have heard the story many times that Franco gave orders that no appeal
should reach him until after the execution of a sentence, but my informants were
not in a position to have seen or heard the orders themselves. What does appear
to be true is that Franco would not consider relevant to a case the social status of
a person making a plea for clemency on behalf of the condemned.

His attitude throughout his life may be said to have been this: Is the man
guilty? Is the sentence in accordance with the law? In possible extenuation, to
what extent can the man be said not to have appreciated the turpitude of his
crime? What is his background and education? From this it followed that an
illiterate peasant had a greater chance of survival than a judge, a soldier than a
general, or a Liberal (as the less intelligent) than a Communist. Thus in December
also sixteen Basque priests would have no chance once proved militant nationalists.

That 10,000 people should sign a petition, that the signatories should include
those of Church prelates, national or foreign intellectuals: that the condemned
man was a blood relative of his: all this was irrelevant in Franco's view. His
attitude of mind is further exemplified by a remark he made in the course of
several after-dinner conversations: "If I am captured alive I shall of course have to
stand trial for rebellion. Make no mistake about it. I shall not have a defending
officer. I shall tell the court: Gentlemen, you know your duty. Do it and be
done". (Evidence of his staff.)

one which belongs to you . . . which they tried to rob from you . . . this is our flag, the one on which we all swore, for which our fathers died . . . the flag a hundred times covered with glory." A crowd of cheers had greeted him from the many Monarchists present, and a show of outstretched arm salutes from the (non-Monarchist) Falangists. On the following day he had gone to Burgos, the Junta's headquarters. He had been enthusiastically welcomed as the redeemer of Badajoz. The advance of Franco's army from the extreme south looked impressive on any map. Mola, as befitting a brigadier in the presence of a major-general, had taken second place. On 26th August Franco had moved his headquarters to Caceres leaving Queipo to lord it over his "subjects" and taunt the enemy from Seville Radio in words which served only to make the less religious of his followers laugh, and to strengthen the determination of his enemies to resist the new "Moorish invasion" of Spain.

All this time the need for the appointment of a Commander-in-Chief was becoming more evident. There were substantial differences on strategy, and the allocation of aircraft coming in from Italy and Germany was causing trouble. Yague had complained to Franco that his air cover was inadequate. The Germans and Italians were also quite bemused by requests for help coming from more than one source and unrelated.

Kindelan, as Commander of Franco's air force, was particularly anxious that there should be a Supremo, and that the Generalissimo should be Franco.[41] He sounded out Franco who gave non-committal answers. Satisfied, he persuaded Orgaz, Millan Astray (who had hastened back to Spain from Argentina on hearing of the rising), and Yague to back him. He drafted notices convening all the generals in the field and the Junta for 1100 hours on 21st September at the airfield in Salamanca. Franco kept the notices a week before signing them.

That when the Junta should get round to naming a C.-in-C. in succession to Sanjurjo Franco would be chosen was never in question. What was needed was a man whom all those under arms on the insurgent side would support. The insurgent army was comprised of a part of the old Peninsular Army, of a part of the Civil Guard who were ex-Army, of the African army of legionaries, Spanish units and Moors and of Monarchist (Carlist and Alfonsist), and non-monarchical Falange militia. The possibilities were Cabanellas, Queipo and Franco among the major-generals, and Mola among the brigadiers. Cabanellas at sixty-four was no longer in his prime. As a Republican he was unacceptable to the Alfonsists and as a Mason doubly unacceptable to the Carlists. Queipo had risen from bugler, but at sixty-one he was too much of a sybarite to lead half the nation. Mola, aged forty-nine, had organised the rising, but he had left many ends untied; he had a very good African army record, but on this score Varela far outstripped him; he had shown some skill in his dealings with the Falangists on the one side and the Carlists on the other, but still he was only a brigadier, junior even to Orgaz. Franco still appeared to the Monarchists to be secretly a Monarchist. At the same time he was backed by Yague and therefore by the Falangists. Still the youngest general, aged only forty-three, still a byword among the Moors and Legionaries for skill and courage, revered although or perhaps because he had been a martinet by the junior officers who had been his cadets, Franco had a personal following which Mola could not match. To add to his past glories, Franco's army was on the point of relieving Toledo. He was at the gates of Madrid.

The question therefore was not who would be Commander-in-Chief but when. Nevertheless correct procedure had to be observed. Kindelan duly proposed the nomination of a C.-in-C. Mola seconded him. Cabanellas dug his heels in: "A war can be conducted as successfully by a committee as by a Generalissimo." Mola issued in effect an ultimatum: "Either there is a C.-in-C. within eight days, or I quit—and that's that." The appointment of a C.-in-C. was put to the vote. All but Cabanellas voted in favour. Franco was next proposed. All but Cabanellas voted in favour.

Days passed. Cabanellas did not issue the decree as President of the Junta. Kindelan, Nicolas Franco who had become head of Franco's political administration of "reconquered territories", Millan Astray and Yague—on their own initiative but with Franco's passive consent—now plotted to make Franco more than a Generalissimo. Each for his own reasons wanted Franco to be Head of State. Kindelan, like many Monarchists, believed that the war would be of short duration and that when it was over Franco would restore the monarchy; Millan Astray believed in military dictatorship: Yague in dictatorship of a Fascist type: Nicolas's reasons may be guessed. Kindelan prepared a draft decree.

A new meeting of the generals was convened. Nicolas obtained one hundred Falange and a like number of *Requetés* as "a guard of honour" on the airfield. Kindelan then presented his draft. There was an uproar as he read the Article appointing the Commander-in-Chief Head of

1. Francisco Franco

2. Franco as a child with his sister Pilar and elder brother Nicolás

3. Doña María del Pilar Teresa Baamonde y Pardo de Andrade de Franco
(Franco's mother)

4. Franco, aged 18, as a Second-Lieutenant in the 8th Regiment of Foot

5. Major Franco, aged 28, immediately after the capture of one of the heights in the Melilla battle zone, 1921, with officers and men of the forward company of his battalion of Foreign Legionnaires

6. Franco with General Sanjurjo in Africa, November 1921

7. Lieut.-Colonel Franco and his bride, Doña María del Carmen Polo Martinez
Valdes, 16th October 1923

8. Brigadier-General Franco and Nicolás with their younger brother Ramon
on the latter's return to Spain after his pioneer South Atlantic flight

9. Franco in a forward area, winter 1938

10. Franco's brother-in-law, Ramón Serrano Suñer, at Franco's Field Headquarters, spring 1931; Franco in the background

11. The Saluting Base for the first Victory Parade, 1939, with the panoply of a military dictator

2. The much simpler Saluting Base for the twenty-fifth Anniversary March-Past. Prince Juan Carlos, the 'heir apparent' to the vacant throne of Spain, stands extreme left.

13. Franco and Hitler before beginning their discussions in Hitler's railway coach at Hendaye, 23rd October 1940

14. Franco and Serrano Suñer with Mussolini at Bordighera, 12th February 1941

15. The scene from the balcony of the Royal Palace in Madrid on 9th December 1946 as the U.N. voted to ostracize Spain

16. Franco meets with President Eisenhower, Madrid, 1959

17. Franco and Sir Alec Douglas-Home

18. Official reception of Franco, and the Sra. de Franco, in a cathedral church, Franco exercising the right claimed by the Spanish kings to 'honours' un-paralleled elsewhere

19. Franco, his son-in-law, Dr. Cristóbal Martinez Ortega Bordiú y Bascarán, his wife Doña Carmen, his only child Carmencita, and her children

Government as well. Mola opposed it on the practical grounds that a Commander-in-Chief would have enough to do in the field without having to consider political questions. Cabanellas was livid. Kindelan won the assembly over one by one. Cabanellas bowed. He sent the decree to the printers the day the Alcazar fell. As published on the following day, 29th September, it gave Franco all powers in the new State of Spain.

On 1st October in Burgos Cabanellas formally handed over the supreme command of the insurgent armies and the headship of the new State of Spain to Francisco Franco Bahamonde. From that moment he ceased to be *"un caudillo de España"*, a Commander of Spain, an ancient honorific title which an Oviedo newspaper had given him at his wedding, one which had been given also to Sanjurjo, Valera, Millan Astray and most of the distinguished military leaders; and Franco became *El Caudillo*.*

* It is an over-simplification to say that "caudillo" was "a bad translation of *fuehrer* or *duce*". The Falange would later use it as such, but in September-October 1936 the Falange was not as yet the dominant political grouping on the insurgent side.

NOTES

1. A full and accurate account is given by Arraras in his *Historia*, pp. 514 ff.

2. That is, in Madrid, where Casares could still exercise governmental authority. Elsewhere it had already broken down. Since the murder of Calvo Sotelo the whole country had been on tenterhooks and was expecting either an Army rising or a Socialist revolution. In Bilbao, for example, the Socialists were ready for both. They began rounding up the opposition on 16th July. Doña Paulina Puente de Bahamonde, Franco's first cousin, and her mother, were warned by a newspaper seller not to return home. With other relatives they took refuge in the house of British friends called Simpson who kept them hidden for many weeks.

3. Agustin Gomez Morato (b. 11th December 1879) was seventh in seniority on the list of major-generals. He was a personal friend of Azaña and Casares Quiroga.

4. A major in the Air Force, but a lieutenant in his original regiment, the Engineers (Anuario, 1936).

5. See (11) below.

6. Franco's description of the State of Spain was in essence no different from that given on 1st May by Indalecio Prieto (reported in *El Socialista*—see Ch. 8).

Too much has been made of the fact that Franco made no mention of San-jurjo and that Sanjurjo's nominal leadership is played down by all Franco's Spanish biographers. The latter was only to be expected: the former fact must be placed in juxtaposition with the manifestoes issued by Mola, Goded, Fanjul, etc., not one of which mentions Sanjurjo (or for that matter Franco). *The Times* (20th July) talked significantly of an exiled general as coming from abroad to lead the rising: and that could refer only to Sanjurjo.

7. Brigadier General Luis Orgaz—senior on the active list to Mola, but *"dispon-ible"*—that is, unemployed. For the fullest account of the chartering of the Dragon Rapide by Luis Bolin, with the help of the English man of letters Douglas Jerrold, and of its flight from Croydon to the Canaries and thence to Africa, *v.* Bolin, pp. 9-54. As Sir Arthur Bryant writes in the introduction to Bolin's Memoirs, it is "as exciting as a John Buchan story".

8. All the conspirators recognised Sanjurjo's claim to be their leader. He was still a lieutenant-general to them. At 64 he was still active. He had a distin-guished African war service record. Though a Monarchist in 1932, he had been a Republican in 1931.

9. Since 5th June there had been eight changes of date for D-day.

10. Why Elena, Helen, no one seems to know.

11. Franco-Salgado MS.: "On 13th July, at about 1430 hours, we received a signal to put back the rising 24 hours: that is to say it was to begin on the 18th (in Africa) at 1800 hours."

12. Mola's orders in June.

13. b. 17th September 1879; a brigadier, though in command of a division. He had been promoted brigadier-general by Azaña (on 13th November 1931) at the very time when Azaña was cutting down on officers and "freezing" those who in his opinion had been promoted out of turn.

14. The 1st Division's commander was Virgillo Cabanellas, a younger brother of Miguel Cabanellas of Zaragoza. The family connection did not help him when the rising took place, though there was no evidence that he was other than loyal to the Government. Miaja was another Azaña promotion to brigadier-general (30th May 1932).

15. I am greatly indebted to Lieutenant-Colonels Martinez Bande and Gárate Cordoba of the Servicio Historico Militar for making available to me the fruits of their own research, and to the Ministry of War for allowing me to consult the archives. Some of these statistics were published in the *Revista Historica Militar* (Año VIII Num. 17). That they should have been kept secret till 1964 can easily be explained: the extreme left wing could never have admitted that a substantial proportion of a body that they called an agent of capitalism, etc., should have stayed on their side while their non-Marxist allies had to pretend that they were without an army or armaments so as to

retain the sympathy of the Western World; the insurgents in the first place had to hide the grimness of the situation, while later they had to pretend that the army had been "untainted" by "foreign intellectual perversions".

16. *Documents on German Foreign Policy*, Series D, Vol. III (hereafter referred to as D.G.F.P. followed by the number), No. 11. I am not suggesting that the conscripts and ex-conscripts could be considered a first-class fighting force: German observers had the lowest opinion of the whole Spanish Army. My point is that between the men in the Army doing their military service and those who had gone through it, there was little to choose. Major MacNeil Moss's appreciation (*The Epic of the Alcazar*, Rich and Cowan, 1937, p. 29) is a very sound one:

> The regular army was a conscript one. The officers and higher N.C.O.s formed the permanent cadre, but the other ranks consisted of boys of seventeen or eighteen who were undergoing their one year of not too strenuous military service. It was on an average but a bare six months since they had left their villages. Much of their time in the army had been spent in the necessary fatigue duties and not infrequently in learning to distinguish their right foot from their left. I hope to give no offence when I say that while their officers had a higher standard of theoretical and military education than officers in corresponding British regiments, the short-service conscript army of Spain was not in the summer of 1936 a very efficient military force. The quality of its higher command and its general tone had lately and deliberately been weakened by a government promoting to key position only such officers as it believed held its own political views.

17. Quoted in Franco-Salgado's MS.

18. In retrospect Franco added a third factor in his favour: in giving out weapons to the masses, the Popular Front destroyed itself. General Vicente Rojo, Chief of Staff on the Republican side (see below, Ch. 10, p. 264) and General Barroso, Franco's Chief of Operations, also gave me this as their considered opinions. It is interesting to note that the military men on both sides expressed the same view and one so opposed to that generally accepted.

19. Army records.

20. Operational orders for 5th August listed six Breguets and two Nieuports, but there are discrepancies in the records of what aircraft were available for Franco in Africa, as opposed to the insurgents as a whole.

21. Cf. *Revista de Historia Militar*, No. 5, 1962.

22. There are discrepancies as to when they were shipped. Cf. *Les événements survenus*, Vol. III (Paris, 1946), Malraux's and Pierre Cot's reminiscences and G.F.P.D. Nos. 17, 24, 25. My information is that the aircraft were already being loaded on 25th July when the then Major Barroso as Military Attaché in Paris refused to sign a cheque for them. Aircraft identification was not a

strong point of any of the combatants in Spain. Potez aircraft took part in air attacks on 27th July. Whether they were old Potez or new or whether they were Dewoitines would require considerable investigation. Of this, however, there can be little doubt: that at the beginning of August, Giral was in a position to stop Franco from getting his army across.

23. Bolin, p. 53 and photograph of Franco's commission countersigned by General Sanjurjo.

24. ibid., pp. 165-70 and private information.

25. Roberto Cantalupo, *Fu la Spagna*, Milan, 1948, pp. 61-2. Bolin, pp. 171-2.

26. D.G.F.P. 2.

27. *International Military Tribunal Nuhremberg*, Vol. IX, pp. 280-1. Goering: "I urged the Fuhrer to give help, first to stop the spread of Communism, and secondly to test my young Luftwaffe." He sent "transports and experimental units". For the part possibly played by Admiral Canaris, an old friend of Franco's, in persuading Hitler to help *v*. Ian Colvin, *Chief of Intelligence* (Gollancz, 1951), pp. 31-2.

28. The official statistics for the airlift with all types of aircraft is as follows:

July	837 men in 102 flights			
August	6,543	,,	,,	353	,,
September	5,455	,,	,,	324	,,
October	1,117	,,	,,	89	,,
	13,952			868	

   plus 44 guns, 92 machine guns and 500 tons of equipment.
   This tallies with the capabilities of twenty JU52s: if there were thirty as the D.G.F.P. state, they were underemployed. The other ten may of course have gone to Mola.

29. At one time he was down to 26,000 rounds.

30. I have based this account on Asensio Cabanillas' own report in *La Guerra de Liberación nacional* (University of Zaragoza, 1961), pp. 149 *ff*., and on the *Hojas de Servicio* of Yague and other officers. They all dovetail excellently, and do not substantiate (let us not say that they contradict) Aznar's *Cruzada*, the original "official history of the war".

31. I do not believe that Franco could have judged decisive for his choice the presence on the Cordoba route of a strong force under Miaja. At the rate he knew his columns could move, even when unopposed, there was no possibility of a surprise advance on Madrid.

32. Not merely in the bullring, though perhaps not by any means as many all told as the *Chicago Tribune*'s reporter Jay Allen's "2,000" for the bullring alone. Army commanders of other nationalities have used Yague's argument as well.

33. He gave strict orders, which are unlikely always to have been obeyed: the Moors are unlikely suddenly to have given up the habits of a lifetime. Rape by a Moor or Legionary was made punishable by death—that is a Spanish officer was empowered to kill any man caught in *flagrante delicto*: the officer was not encouraged to bring a man who had disobeyed this or other orders before a court martial. Cf. Kemp, *Mine Were of Trouble* (Cassell, 1957), pp. 115-18 and 169 *ff.*, for aspects of morality which will surprise only those who have an idealised concept of men at war.

34. Yague's *Hoja de Servicio*.

35. ibid. Assensio who had been in the vanguard since 3rd August kept in excellent health.

36. The four regiments of the virtually intact Madrid division were numbered 1-4. The 5th was not a fighting regiment but a training school. It was officially commanded first by the Spanish communist Enrique Castro Delgado (who wrote colourful memoirs) but its real commander was its Commisar, the Italian communist Vittorio Vidali. One of its officers for a time was Jose Martin Blasquez—the vividly imaginative writer of *I helped to build an Army* (Secker and Warburg, 1939). The "Red" army was worthy of a better historian.

37. Kindelan, *Mis Cuadernos de Guerra* (Madrid, 1942), p. 54.

38. The Basques were caught in this war between the insurgents on the one side and the Marxists of the Popular Front on the other. Theirs, in miniature, was the case of Poland between Russia and Prussia. For a ready-to-hand account of their tragedy see G. L. Steer, *The Tree of Guernica* (London, 1938).

39. *The Spanish Cockpit*, 1937—one of the more perceptive propaganda books by foreign observers written during the Civil War.

40. Cf. Bernanos, *Les grands cimitières sur la lune* (Paris, 1938); allowances must be made for Bernanos's wrath and indignation getting the better of him at times. He was in Majorca at the relevant times. His evidence cannot be classed with Antonio Bahamonde's *Memoirs of a Spanish Nationalist* (London, 1939) and Ruiz Vilaplana's (*Burgos Justice*, London, 1939) which are largely hearsay.

41. Kindelan's is the fullest printed account of how General Franco became Generalissimo. It appeared in *Mis cuadernos* (pp. 50-6). Mola also claimed that he suggested Franco for C-in-C. Irib., p. 210.

10

GENERALISSIMO

On being invested as Head of the new State of Spain, and the Supreme Commander of the National Armed Forces, Franco said with poetic licence: "General [Cabanellas] and fellow Generals. You can be justly proud. You took over a broken Spain. You hand over to me a Spain united in a single great ideal. Victory is on our side. . . . I shall not fail. I shall take the Motherland to her summit, or die in the attempt. . . ."[1] In fact he had not been handed over the political control of Spain but only of those two-fifths of its territory over which the insurgents had established their authority by force of arms. The ten and a half million inhabitants of that zone were by no means "united in a single great ideal". The behaviour of the insurgents in victory had not converted to the "national cause", as Franco's was now called, the thirty or so per cent who had voted in the Popular Front. The thirty per cent who had voted against it were determined never again to suffer the lawlessness of left-wing government and doubtless they had been joined in their determination by some of those who had not voted at all but had suffered all the same: these were prepared to pray, work and fight at the side of but not necessarily for Franco. Franco was the man whom they might believe the most likely to defeat the enemy, but no Falangist could acknowledge as his leader anyone other than the imprisoned Jose Antonio; no Monarchist could recognise Franco as more than a *locum tenens* for Alfonso XIII or the Carlist Pretender; no Republican (and it must not be forgotten that there was many a Republican on the insurgent side) could accept him as more than a stopgap "for the duration".

Franco, of course, had friends and sympathisers among the thirteen and a half millions in the remaining three-fifths of Spain. The crimes committed by Anarchists and Socialists had converted possibly more to the national than to their own cause. Nevertheless, before such could declare their sympathy they had to be rescued from their present masters. Franco's top priority task therefore was to destroy the will and ability to fight of those masters. Two courses were open. One was to destroy their armies; the other to capture Madrid. For there was a particular mystique about Madrid among all Spaniards not Catalans or Basques. If Franco should capture it, his enemies would psychologically consider their cause lost. But Madrid had also a practical military value. The Spaniard as the heir of Rome had made his capital even more the hub of all communications. The master of Madrid could send out troops quickly in any direction—towards Bilbao or Barcelona, or any other recalcitrant city. But did Franco have the means?

Franco's title of Supreme Commander had almost as hollow a ring as that of Head of State. He had by now about 150,000 men under arms, but they were a motley collection of men with obsolescent weapons, and all but 20,000 were pinned down holding what had been gained against numerically superior forces. Of those 22,000, 2,000 were engaged in an operation to rescue Oviedo where the remnants of a thousand men were holding out against Asturian militiamen no less tenaciously than the defenders of the Alcazar had done. These 2,000 were too far committed to be withdrawn and in any case the bravery of the men in Oviedo was of the sort that Franco believed merited the reward of relief at all costs.

Franco now summoned Varela. "*Siempre tienes suerte*"—"You are always lucky. Have a go at taking Madrid. We might yet do it, if we go about it quickly." There would not be time for his forces to work round to the north of Madrid, the classic easy way, easy in that the attackers would be advancing from higher to lower ground. Varela would have to approach Madrid from the south and west—literally an uphill fight; in Franco's estimation Madrid would be defended by between 40 and 60,000 men but Franco clung to his deep-rooted belief in discipline and morale as irresistible forces in battle. He knew his men.[2] He underestimated the enemy.

Franco reinforced Varela's original "Madrid column" which had relieved Toledo to a total of just over 10,000 men, and had it re-divided into four "columns". They would have in support, as throughout their advance from Merida, cavalry squadrons in command of a Lieutenant-Colonel Monasterio. This thrust force would move up astride the Mérida–Madrid and Toledo–Madrid roads. At the same time a subsidiary group—some five thousand—under a General Valdés Cabanillas would move through a gap between the Guadarrama and Gredos Sierras due west of Madrid.

Franco, having outlined the plan, appointed Mola over Varela and Valdés to co-ordinate their efforts. A job was found for Yague as Valera's second in command.[3]

The offensive began on 6th October. The point of departure varied between 60 and 80 kilometres from the outskirts of Madrid. Ten days later Franco's troops were 35 kilometres away at their nearest point, Valmojado, on the Merida road. The going everywhere had been tough against an enemy more numerous and more determined, and better disciplined, than expected. The enemy command had been confused at the top, but it had some first class professional officers in the field, the equals in training background and ability of those under Franco: indeed one of them, the then Major Vicente Rojo, would come to be recognised as the best military brain on either side.[*] Brought more or less to a halt astride the Mérida road, the thrust was switched to the main road from Toledo. Monasterio's cavalry swept up to Illescas, thirty kilometres from the southern approaches to Madrid.

And now, the war was about to change from a colonial-type struggle of the turn of the century, which it had been since 18th July, into a postscript to the 1914–18 European War or an introduction to that of 1939–45. There was a new push on the Mérida road to Navalcarnero, much the same distance from Madrid as Illescas. In this new thrust Fiat-Ansaldo 3·5 ton tankettes preceded the infantry as if they had been lumbering Mark I tanks of 1916 instead of the fast, ridiculously thinly armoured machine gun carriers which was all that they really were.

---

* Vicente Rojo, two years Franco's junior, rose in the Republican Army to the rank of lieutenant-general. On weekend leave in Madrid on 18th July from his post as Instructor in Tactics at the Toledo Academy, Rojo believed it his duty to stand by the Government every scruple as much as the insurgents considered it theirs to rise against it. After the Civil War Rojo lived for a while in exile in Mexico. Subsequently he asked to be allowed back into Spain. He was not only allowed to do so in 1957, but Franco granted him the retired pay of a lieutenant-general. He lived out the last nine years of his life to 15th June 1966 quietly in a flat opposite the New Ministries. Though his ability was generally recognised by his enemies, they could hardly have expected to make public their views (although at his death, the Falangist newspaper *Arriba* published a glowing tribute to his integrity), while those for whom he fought also had their reasons for not singing his praises. A reassessment of the history of the war, based on military documents and a study of the ground or the maps, rather than on what men on either side wrote to justify themselves, might well confirm the view of some of the staff officers on the winning side that had Rojo's advice rather than that of Russian generals been followed at various critical moments in the war, its course might have been different.

But their use in this way was justified in that it gave Franco's infantry with months of fighting and many leagues of marching behind them fresh courage. These tankettes were not the makeshift private vehicle conversions which they had called 'armour' till then. But three days later, on 24th October, Franco's troops on the extreme right flank heard a new sound from enemy lines, the rumble of tracked vehicles accompanied by the pum-pum of guns, and on the 26th, the Fiats came face to face with nine-tonners carrying a three-pounder (45 mm) high-velocity gun in a revolving turret. They were Russian tanks based on the famous Vickers model. They made short work of the Fiats. One single Russian tank knocked out eleven of the Italians.* The insurgent advance was renewed yet again, but very slowly; and every day that passed more Russian equipment came into action. On 29th October Monasterio's cavalry ran into the Vickers tanks commanded by the Russian General Pavlov.[4] There followed an encounter as gallant and as unequal as when the Polish cavalry met German and Russian tanks three years later.

Franco had known of the arrival of several shiploads of Russian arms on 13th October and subsequent days. However, he was placing his trust in the pending deliveries of weapons—and of men—from Germany.

At his headquarters in Salamanca, on the evening of the day on which the Madrid offensive had begun, Franco had wined and dined Dumoulins, the Counsellor at the German Embassy in Lisbon. Franco had sent telegrams round the world informing governments of his appointment as Head of the Spanish State. Dumoulins had been instructed to express verbally Hitler's congratulations. Franco now went on to say all the right things to Dumoulins for transmission to the man from whom he hoped to get the weapons he needed to capture Madrid. Franco wanted more aircraft because what the Germans and Italians had sent him that far had not given him air supremacy over Madrid. He wanted anti-aircraft guns to protect his own cities, and field and anti-tank artillery, machine guns and tanks. Franco had seen in Britain and France more formidable vehicles than the toys which Italy had sent him, and thought that Germany might have something comparable. He did not ask for anything, however, through Dumoulins. Instead he merely expressed his optimism with regard to the military situation and his belief that he would take Madrid in the near future. Dumoulins—that is, Hitler—was

---

* This is an episode which was hushed up by all interested parties for obvious reasons.

to have no fears that the former privileges of the nobility and the Church would be restored. He left Dumoulins with no doubt of his sincere veneration for the Führer and sympathy for Germany. The Führer had raised the banner of civilization.[5]

Now the Germans did not have the same high opinion of Franco's army as Franco himself had, nor indeed of the nationalist leadership.[6] Franco had repeatedly told German military observers that the Marxist enemy was an ill-disciplined, demoralised rabble. Why then had Franco taken so long to get to Madrid? The answer was of course that the degree of motorisation of Franco's forces was infinitesimally small, that his assault force was far smaller than he pretended, and that the enemy had fought his troops with courage—on the whole, even if on occasion they had run away. But whatever the past, the immediate future was none too rosy. The Russian equipment arriving in Spain was sufficient in quantity and quality to turn the scales, unless Germany sent immediately the aircraft, guns and tanks which Franco had requested.

Germany agreed to let Franco have the equipment, under conditions which must have offended Franco's national pride. On 30th October Admiral Canaris was instructed to tell Franco that Germany did not consider that the combat tactics which the "white side" had hitherto employed in ground fighting or in aerial combat could lead to success "in view of possible increased Russian help for Red Spain". In particular Franco's use of aircraft in ones and twos would lead him nowhere. Germany and Italy would recognise the "white government" (that is Franco) only when Madrid was taken. Only then would Germany be in a position to send Franco help on a large scale. In the meantime Franco could have a German force consisting of a bomber group of forty-eight aircraft, one of a similar number of fighters, a squadron and a flight of reconnaissance aircraft, three anti-aircraft batteries, some searchlight platoons, and the necessary signals and operating units—all under a German commander; provided that all German aircraft and airforce personnel already in Spain were placed under that commander, who would be responsible only to Franco, and who would advise Franco on how the German air forces were to be used; provided also that Franco undertook to pursue a "more systematic and active conduct of the war", and to deny the enemy the harbours through which the Russians were landing supplies.[7]

Franco accepted the conditions. Thus it was that by 6th November the formation which came to be known as the Condor Legion was ready for action. So also was a further batch of German tanks and, what Franco wanted most, anti-tank guns, with German personnel to train Spaniards in their use.*

In spite of German views on Franco's conduct in the war, the "white troops" were within assault distance of Madrid by 6th November. Russian tanks had slowed down the advance, but they had not stopped it. In general lines the pattern over the last days of October had been: attack by the insurgents: gain of a few hundred yards: counter-attack: loss of a few hundred yards: immediate counter-attack—substantial gain: pause and recommencement of cycle. The world at large, even the Germans,[14] believed the fall of Madrid imminent, knowing nothing of the numerical weakness of the assault force. It imagined a great Army whereas in reality the assault force did not now number above 8,000†

* General Sperrle, the Commander "responsible only to General Franco" gave 6,500 as the number of Germans in Spain at the end of 1936.[8] The Condor Legion's fighting strength was subsequently considerably increased to a total of 288 aircraft as against the original 111.[9] But the number of Germans was *reduced* to 6,000 as Spaniards took over from Germans the ground defence of airfields and the training of Spaniards in the use of modern weapons. 14 to 16,000 Germans may have fought, or rather made Spain the European Aldershot[10] but they came and went in relays. Von Thoma, who was in charge of the tanks and anti-tank weapons says that there were never more than 600 German *Army* men in Spain. This figure tallies with Spanish Army records. How often Germans went into battle with their tanks or guns may be judged from German casualties. In all Luftwaffe and Wehrmacht lost 300 men.[11] They must have been almost entirely Luftwaffe. The German tanks were Panzers Mks. I and II, as ineffective as the Fiats against the Vickers tanks.

As Thomas says (Appendix 3, p. 793) "the total amount of foreign aid to the two sides in the war is difficult to calculate exactly". The qualitative aspect is at least as important as the quantitative, and this has not been given the attention it deserves. As Vicente Rojo said[12] "the Russians sent us some first class material superior to anything on the other side; at the same time they also sent us junk". The same could be said of the German and Italian equipment. The Russian Vickers tanks did meet their match in this way: they were lured into townships where Moorish *Regulares* and Legionaries waited for them on the balconies of houses: "we told them to stock up with Molotov cocktails. Our 'cocktail' was pure petrol in a wine bottle with a hand grenade tied round it. A really good shot destroyed the rubber mountings of the caterpillar tracks—that was their weakest part; but a drop on the front part of the tank was a terrifying sight. There was a loud explosion and a sheet of fire and out would come the crew. The Moors would then jump off the balconies on to the crew, take the tank over, repair it as necessary, and we would use it ourselves."[13] Von Thoma stated that out of 180 tanks which he had under his command in 1938, 30 were captured Russian tanks. According to Spanish Army records, however, some more of these were taken off intercepted ships. A few Panzer Mark IIIs which were a match for the Russians reached Spain only just before the end of the war.

† And it was at times as low as 6,000. Strengths fluctuated considerably day by day with the heavy casualties being suffered. The records are confused and confusing.

exhausted after a full month of constant battle. It had been convinced
by colour writers and propaganda that there was no one to stop the fall
of the capital but "ill-armed civilians fighting for democracy"; whereas
in fact not only was there the infantry and artillery which had remained
loyal to the Popular Front, but a new if small Army which had been
created by the Communist Party through its so-called "Fifth Regiment":
several hundred professional Spanish Army officers as well as Russian
and other foreign generals and less exalted commanders: and a woman
orator, Dolores Ibarruri, who had the powers of persuasion of Hitler
and Lenin combined. There were in Madrid at least 40,000 men at arms,
and possibly as many as 100,000. Some had no more than shot guns, but
others had the latest automatic weapons from U.S. factories (supplied
through Mexico) and from Russia, France and Czechoslovakia.

Such was the situation as Varela ordered the assault to begin at dawn
on 7th November. It would have been a miracle if it had succeeded.
He had before him a river to cross—even if only an "apprentice of a
river". He had heights to scale. Every one of his men would have at
least six of the enemy with which to contend.

Varela's men advanced, and then had partially to withdraw. The
pattern of previous days was repeating itself. They were not dis-

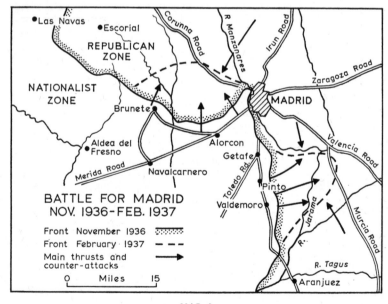

BATTLE FOR MADRID
NOV. 1936-FEB. 1937

Front November 1936
Front February 1937
Main thrusts and counter-attacks

0   Miles   15

MAP 5

heartened. The morrow or the day after a substantial gain would come. That is to say on the next day or the following, they would be in the heart of Madrid. Correspondents within Madrid itself, certain that the attackers were more numerous than they were, believed the city's fall inevitable. Largo Caballero, the Spanish Lenin, had given the city up for lost on 6th November and fled. Vicente Rojo rallied his men, and Dolores Ibarurri hers. But that was not all. On Sunday, 8th November a force of between two and three thousand men marched in perfect formation through the streets of Madrid. The people called them *Rusos*, Russians, though in fact they were Central and West Europeans— Germans and Italians for the most part—the first of the communist-organised International Brigades. Over the next nine days Varela's men crossed the river, mounted the University City and even had tanks rattling down Madrid's Calle de la Princesa. That was the limit of the advance. The university buildings were reduced to ruins, and they became a battlefield in which neither side could or did win.*

The question has long been debated whether the "people of Madrid" or the International Brigades saved the city. The "people" had checked Varela on the 7th: but they had done so on several previous occasions, and on each the check had been followed by a further advance. This check was in fact so followed. The strength of the first International Brigade,[15] however inadequate it might seem in European terms, must be weighed against that of the assault force which was also surprisingly small. The crucial dates were certainly 7th to 9th November. Whether the credit be given to the "people" or to the Brigades, there is another question which must be asked. Supposing that, at that moment, Franco had thrown into the battle a reserve force of fresh troops, what would have been the outcome? Should he not have had such reserves, even if it meant weakening other fronts at some risk? Later in the war Franco would warn his Commanders: "You must have reserves. You must not expect too much from exhausted men".[16] Publicly Franco would maintain to the end of his life that but for the International Brigades *and* the mass of war material poured by Russia into Spain during the month of October, he would have taken Madrid in November.

Within twelve days of the petering out of the attempt to take Madrid by force, Franco had made good Varela's losses, and increased the over-all strength of his troops. He then ordered Varela to thrust north and

---

* This should have taught the Germans a lesson. In miniature it was a foretaste of Stalingrad. But then the Allies of World War II learnt nothing either from Toledo, else they would not have bombed Monte Cassino.

cut the Corunna road, that is the lines of communication between
Madrid and some of the enemy's Guadarrama positions. The first
attempt, as usual, was only partially successful. He let Varela have
12,000 men now, supported by 100 guns (the proportion of artillery to
infantry was beginning to assume the 1914–18 proportions) and 40
tankettes. The attack this time was foiled by Pavlov and his tanks and
the International Brigades. Varela was wounded on Christmas Day.[17]
Orgaz took over and released a third attack in appalling weather.
Orgaz succeeded, but the enemy, throwing everything into a delaying
action, saved their troops in the Guadarramas. Franco now ordered a
similar attempt to be made to cut the Madrid–Valencia road. Varela
was back. Franco let him have 20,000 men. The enemy brought into
action fifteen brigades, national and international. Between the
"whites" and their objectives ran the River Jarama. Half the attacking
and defending forces were killed on its banks over the next four weeks
to mid-February, when both sides, exhausted, agreed to let the river
keep them apart. The Valencia road remained uncut. What the Germans[18] had believed the right strategy for the capture of Madrid, its
encirclement, had been proved beyond the capability of the troops
that Franco had at his disposal.

By mid-December, when Franco began the attempt to encircle the
city, his allies had in fact other ideas on what the strategy of the war
should be. Behind the façade of solidarity and mutual back-slapping,
Franco was at loggerheads with Germans and Italians. At that moment
also the Rome–Berlin axis was not perfectly aligned.

Germany initially had recognised Franco as Head of State rather un-
expectedly on 18th November. The German Government, which had
earlier resisted Italian pressure to do so before Madrid had fallen,[19]
had taken the initiative vis-à-vis Italy when the "red government"
threatened to stop German ships trading with "white" ports.[20] Germany had then gone on to seek from Franco economic concessions.
Italy had gone much farther. Mussolini, whose immediate reply to
Franco's first request for help had been No, had come with his son-in-
law Ciano to the conclusion that Italy's interests were seriously at stake
in the Spanish Civil War. The concept of the Mediterranean as Italy's
mare nostrum and of the new Roman Empire like to the old implied the
conversion of Spain into a province, as Albania was to become, or at
least made desirable the presence there in power of an ally so indebted
as to be malleable. A Spain bound not to subscribe to economic sanctions nor to allow the passage of French troops through her territories,

would make Mussolini's project of extending his African Empire at the cost of France easier to realise. Italian naval and air forces based on the Balearics would be better able than in Pantellaria to intercept French communications with Africa. Such considerations had existed since July. But since November Spain had become the scene of an Italian civil war in a very real sense. How far the Italian Dictator can have hated Communism as an ideology is open to the surmise of debate, but he certainly saw in it a rival to his own (philosophically not diametrically opposed) Fascism, and Italian Communists as personal rivals. In purely Italian terms, the defeat of Franco would have been a victory for Toggliati, Longo and de Vittorio, with consequent serious repercussions on his own dictatorship over the people of Italy. The many Italian Communists already in Spain were sincerely fighting against Fascism in the true sense, that is the peculiar Italian aberration and not merely the amorphous bogey of Communist propaganda. For such self-interested reasons, therefore, when Franco asked Italy to replenish his depleted stocks of arms and ammunition, Mussolini sanctioned the request but on condition that Franco promised to align his Mediterranean policy to Italy. Franco, in an agreement which in no way offended Spanish sovereignty, promised to do so. For good measure he conceded that he would look favourably on Italy as a buyer and seller of merchandise—a feature of the agreement which angered the Germans[21] till they saw that what Franco had agreed to did not prejudice their, or any other trading nations', interests.* There was on the other hand one point on which Germany and Italy were in agreement: that the Spaniards did not know how to fight or win a war. Hitler had appointed as his first Ambassador to Franco a retired General Faupel. Though Hitler's instructions had been that the conduct of the war was not within his Ambassador's province,[23] Faupel could not help expressing his views on military affairs. In a telegram sent on 5th December[24] he declared that Franco's best troops were committed in an unfavourable position in Madrid and implied that Franco was being foolish in not withdrawing them. In order to prevent Bolshevism from taking hold of all Spain, "then one strong German and one strong Italian division would be required". In a second longer dispatch five days later he described General Franco as a man "whose military training and

---

* The agreement, details of which were not published, bothered other nations which believed firmly that Franco had promised Italy bases in the Balearics.[22] In retrospect it can be seen as Franco's first major victory in international affairs. He appeared to give much whereas it pledged him to remarkably little.

experience do not fit him for the direction of operations on their present scale".[25] In the meantime, in Rome Mussolini had said to the German Ambassador in less diplomatic language[26] that there were "evidently very few real men in Spain" and had proceeded to prepare a whole division of Black Shirts – presumably to show Spain what real warriors were. In December, while other nations of Europe had sought to put an end to the conflict in Spain by appealing to both sides to accept a mediator or at least to limit the war by preventing non-Spaniards from going to fight in Spain, thousands more passed through France to join the International Brigades, and Mussolini began to send "real men", his Black Shirts, with a plan to win the war. From bases in and around Cadiz the Black Shirts would strike at Malaga, then race up the coast to Valencia. With a wide encircling movement they would then cut inland to Guadalajara. Finally, Italian and Spanish troops together would encircle Madrid. Madrid would fall: the bulk of the enemy forces would be "in the bag".[27] As commander of this victorious modern army, Mussolini appointed his trusty and well-beloved 50-year-old General Mario Roatta (Mancini)—(one time head of his Military Intelligence and already in Spain).[28]

The Internationals went into action immediately. Franco gave the Italians until the end of February to organise themselves.

As the Italians arrived, Franco had already decided to allow the Spanish forces under Queipo de Llano a chance to gain battle experience. His intelligence informed him that the enemy in the Malaga region, though 40-50,000 strong, was quite the most undisciplined and ill-armed of any. On 14th January Queipo's field commanders, the Duke of Seville, a regular Army colonel and a Prince of Bourbon, and a Colonel Gonzalez Espinosa, began a pincer movement from the West and from Granada. It brought the front all round Malaga to a distance of roughly thirty miles. Nine Italian battalions were selected and reinforced by Falangist *banderas* and Requeté *tercios*** to form three brigades. Franco went down to Seville from Salamanca to see all was well and left Queipo and Roatta to go ahead.

The assault began on 5th February. Spanish insurgent warships shelled the coast which thirty-five years later was to be the delight of English tourists. The Duke of Seville set off from Marbella. The Italian and mixed brigades descended from the north. It was a walk-over. Malaga fell on the morning of the 8th, and a Spanish column closed the gap to the east at Motril. Over 2,000 square miles of Spain had changed

* In this case both equivalent to battalions.

hands. The Republic was also 40,000 men the poorer. The "clean-up" took as many weeks as the assault. Roatta, to his credit, worried over the execution of so many of the defeated. He consulted Cantalupo who had just taken office as Italian Ambassador to Franco. Cantalupo confronted Franco with the evidence. Franco recognised the excesses of his troops, and realistically added that he was in no position to control the local courts. Queipo indeed recognised Franco's authority only in so far as it pleased him, and did nothing to restrain either the Falangists out for blood nor the Moors in their barbaric practices.*[29]

Mussolini hailed Malaga as a great Italian triumph. He promoted Roatta major-general[30] yet the original plan to proceed up to Valencia was abandoned. Franco was rather anxious over the pressures on his troops at the banks of the Jarama. With the build up of the Italian troops to 35,000 men he had an assault force at his disposal (though at his orders only through Roatta) the like of which he could have done with three months earlier. 31,500 of these Italians were organised into four divisions.[31] With the rapidity that their complete motorisation was expected to give them, they were to descend from the direction of Soria, north-east of Madrid, towards Guadalajara. It was expected that they would draw off the forces facing Franco's troops on the Jarama. These troops would then assault the river and make for Aranda on the Valencia road. (See Map 6.)

The attack began on 8th March. The Italian advance was pusillanimous. The two forward divisions took three days down the main road to reach the objectives appointed for the first day, 25 kilometres from their point of departure. Spanish troops, acting in support on their right flank, did almost as well cross country on foot and moving their supplies by mule. The three days' delay enabled the enemy to organise a counter force. Its vanguard alone brought the Italians to a halt. Then there was a sudden change in the weather. The rain put out of action the airfields on the Italian side, but not the more southerly from which their opponents were operating. Snow and sleet fell on the Italians;

---

* There are several accounts of the behaviour of the insurgents after the fall of Malaga. Although what Foltz, Bahamonde and others wrote would not stand up to judicial examination in detail, the members of the court set up to judge those thousands of Malagueños accused of the atrocities which had undoubtedly been committed during the anarchy characteristic of the area since July, were either credulous to the point of stupidity or else guilty of criminal revenge. Franco's rider to Cantalupo that only the clergy could moderate vengeful passions was out of touch with the reality that Malaga's clergy had been slaughtered and that the chaplains with his troops had next to no influence with his men. The repression did create a hatred for the victors which would last a generation.

and they lost whatever heart they had. The two forward divisions were replaced by the two in reserve with orders to dig in. Roatta rushed away to appeal to Franco to launch the Jarama attack there and then. On 18th March seventy Vickers tanks advanced with International and Republican Brigades in strength against the two Italian divisions. Their 250 tankettes were useless. The Italians panicked and ran in headlong

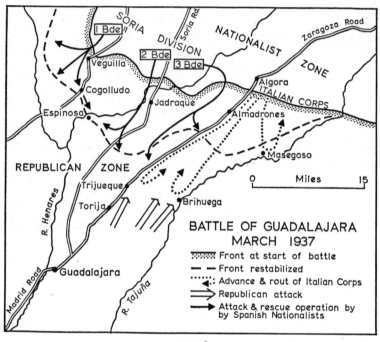

MAP 6

flight towards their points of departure. Franco's Spanish troops not only stood firm but plugged the gap left by the Italians. So much for Mussolini's "real men".[32]

In Franco's headquarters town, Salamanca, Spanish cavalry officers drank toasts when they heard the news of the defeat of the Italians before Guadalajara.[33] Franco's own reaction is reported to have been: "Splendid. We can now begin the strategically important northern operation."[34]

The background to the remark was this: Franco had long been fully aware of the economic, political and military disadvantages of being dependent on German and Italian supplies of war material. The Germans repeatedly made it clear enough that they expected payment sometime in cash and in economic concessions; Franco had argued his way out of any written promise except for a "protocol" signed a few days after Guadalajara which committed him among other vague generalities "to intensify economic relations (with Germany) ... as much as possible";[35] but he could not expect the Germans for ever to be so patient. The main political disadvantage was that Franco had no quarrel with any country except Russia, but no country knew Franco for the crafty politician he was proving;* and they believed or were prepared to believe that Franco was already in the pocket of Hitler and Mussolini. The military disadvantages were two-fold. In the first place non-intervention could become a reality: that is to say the naval patrols proposed by Anthony Eden[36] round the Iberian Peninsula threatened to cut off his supplies.† But not those of his enemies. He could trust the British, German and Italian Navies but not the French Government— and there was a long land frontier between France and his enemies. In the second place Franco had had to accept conditions not entirely in accordance with his dignity as Generalissimo as a *sine qua non* of military supplies.

There was one way to minimise all these disadvantages. The north-west industrial belt had the raw materials and the factories for a substantial war industry. Franco had tried and failed to win the war with a small body of professional soldiers. He would now have to attempt to do so with a citizen army. This large army would require more weapons than he could afford to buy from his allies. In spite of all Faupel's despatches to the contrary, Franco had methodically set about creating this new citizen army. He had not issued a general mobilisation order as the Republicans had done (a call-up so poorly obeyed that it was soon replaced by a more realistic substitute), but with cautious circumspection had added 140,000 to his forces by the end of 1936, and to officer them he already had sixteen training schools by March 1937 when he took Orgaz away from the Madrid front and made him Director of Army Training.‡ He planned to double his army by the end of 1937.§

* And which only a study of the archives of the German Foreign Office and other such documents revealed years later.

†When instituted in April they were carried out by the British, French, Italian and German navies. Russia was invited to participate but put forward proposals which were unacceptable to Italy and Germany and criticised by Britain.

‡ Orgaz was also put in charge of the recovery and rehabilitation of captured equipment. This varied from used and damaged guns captured on the battlefield to such major "prizes" as the *Mar Cantabrico* with U.S. $2·75 million of aero engines and other equipment.

§ He would in fact have over 650,000, and 879,000 by the end of 1938 in spite

The capture of the northern industrial belt was therefore an economic, political and military priority task: but before Bilbao's factories could be geared to produce more for him, he needed a two-fold guarantee: one that the Italians would leave him alone and the other that the Italian factories should continue to supply him with guns and ammunition in the meantime. Franco wrote to Mussolini. Thereafter Roatta had the ear of Faupel rather than Franco, and Mussolini assured Franco that he would not withdraw his volunteers until they had avenged Guadalajara—his way of saying that he would continue with supplies. Franco agreed to include Italians in the northern operation.

The operation would have three phases: in the first Bilbao would be taken, in the second Santander and in the third and last Asturias. The campaign was to prove more costly in men and time than Franco anticipated. Each phase was tough—but none tougher or more tragic than the first, the conquest of the Basque Province of Vizcaya and its capital Bilbao.

For the first phase of the operation Franco chose four brigades made up of army and *Requeté* units. The Italian formations with which he chose to satisfy Mussolini's injured pride were a brigade group called after a date sacred to Fascism—23rd March—and the Black Arrows brigade. This last was in fact only half Italian. The other half was *Requeté*.* Overall, Mola, whom Franco asked to command in the field, had about 25,000 men for the task. Franco's estimate of the opposing forces was 76,000, but he did not believe them to be well-disciplined or high in morale. There were in fact at most 50,000.[37] Some were Anarchist and some Socialist militia, but 30,000 were Basques, and these were fighting for a more powerful ideal than Marxism or Bakuninism. To the last man they shared the determination and courage of men defending their nation and motherland, a fact which Franco—in common with the overwhelming majority of Spaniards whatever their political tenets—would not appreciate. Though heavily bombed by the Condor Legion and hard-pressed by men better armed than they, they yielded their motherland grudgingly. It took Mola's

---

of losses through heavy casualties. In all 608,476 men answered the Insurgents' calls for mobilisation to the end of 1938. 23,991 officers came out of the training units (*Academias*) instituted by Franco as well as 5,132 from the *Escuelas* they replaced. Service in the ranks at the front was a condition of entry to the *Academias*. There were German officers among the instructors at these, but their number was limited since there were not so many Germans who knew Spanish.

* From this the popular saying arose: *Avanti, avanti con el requeté adelante.*

forces twenty-six days to push forward ten miles on a 30-mile front. Franco would now explain to Cantalupo[38] that though progress was slow, it was according to plan. "Franco"—the Spanish Generalissimo told the Italian Ambassador—"is not making war on Spain, but liberating her. I must not destroy the enemy, nor the cities, fields, industries or means of production. That is why I must not be in a hurry. If I hurried, I would be a bad Spaniard; if I hurried I would not be a patriot, I would be behaving like a foreigner." Franco, who had now given strict instructions to his commanders and his troops not to make Vizcaya another Malaga, was about to discover that he had allies other than Queipo de Llano with their own ideas on how to conduct the war.

The Condor Legion's Heinkel 111s and Junkers 52s had bombed tactical targets as required by Mola. As many missiles had gone wild as had found their mark. The German bomb sights of the time were primitive and the bomber crews were learners. In these circumstances, the Germans, without consulting any Spaniard, chose the ancient town of Guernica for the world's first experiment in saturation bombing.* Fifty aircraft in relays dropped high explosive and incendiary bombs. The raid lasted three hours. Only a few buildings remained undamaged. Of Guernica's 7,000 inhabitants, 1,650 were dead or dying, and over 850 wounded.

This was not known at Franco's G.H.Q. "The first news we had of it was from abroad. At first we didn't believe the news and thought it another piece of Red propaganda." The Germans denied it, confusing the issue by telling Franco that none of their aircraft had taken off on the 27th, the date on which Franco's General Staff first thought the destruction of Guernica had taken place. When better informed Franco ordered Colonel Funck to report to him. "Pale with anger, he said to Funck: 'I will not have war made on my own people'." Kindelan was told to make sure that it didn't happen again—if necessary by disabling the German aircraft. "For all that was said publicly, at G.H.Q. relations between us and the Germans were at breaking point for a long time." The Condor Legion's Commander was eventually recalled.[39]

Guernica was occupied by Mola's troops two days later. Some of the Germans were themselves horrified at their handiwork. So was the outside world. Berlin pressed Franco categorically to deny German

---

* Not in *dive* bombing as has often been said. The types used were not Stukas.

responsibility. Franco refused, but he did not order an amendment to his Press Office statement of 29th April—apparently issued without Franco's authority—that Guernica had been destroyed by the retreating Basques.[40]

Guernica hardened Basque resistance. They had eye-witness evidence that the *Franquistas* were as barbarous as the Anarchists from whom they had also had to protect their cities and their churches. The Basques had attempted an offensive in the November to relieve the pressure on Madrid. Now Madrid (or Valencia as it had become) would find excuses not to come to the aid of the "Vatican Gibraltar". Indeed it can be said that they added insult to injury. At that time Valencia concentrated 20,000 men against a little isolated outpost of 250 Civil Guard insurgents in the Sierra Morena—an outpost of no value to either side. The Republicans then set about each other. For five days there was open warfare in the streets of Barcelona between Anarchists and P.O.U.M. (Trotskyists) on the one side and Communists and Socialists on the other. After the death of between 400 and 900 of them Valencia sent 4,000 storm troopers to keep them apart. But in Valencia there was trouble as well. The Communists had grown tired of Largo Caballero and wanted the P.O.U.M. liquidated. They had chosen a Doctor Negrín, a man reputed to have all the grossest vices of ancient Rome, to succeed the Spanish Lenin. With nothing to fear during the month of May on any other front, Franco was able to double Mola's forces to about 50,000. There were no Italians among the extra troops, though the divisions scattered at Guadalajara had been reformed. However, even with 50,000 men at his command, it took him four weeks to advance five miles from Guernica. Between him and Bilbao there then stood an "Iron Ring", a circle of casements and trenches constructed while he had advanced so slowly. Mola knew all about it because its details had been betrayed to him by the engineer officer in charge of their construction. Franco took one look at the plans and expressed horror at an elementary error which would allow him to break through easily. He had expected better from General Llano de la Encomienda in command of the Basques.[41]

Franco now prepared to send Mola his heaviest artillery, guns of up to 305 mm. On 3rd June, however, Mola took off by air to consult Franco. He never reached his destination. The machine hit the mountainside in low cloud. Kindelan took the news to Franco. "A great loss," said Kindelan. "Yes indeed, a great loss. In war we can replace him; but we shall miss him when peace comes"[42]—a not unjust assessment of the man who had planned the half successful rising but who in his writing had revealed the makings of a good politician.*

Mola's death delayed the commencement of the final assault. This was preceded by a bombardment from ground and air of a type developed in World War II. Bilbao fell on 19th February. Its defence had cost the Basques alone 15,000 deaths on the field of battle. Not immediately but only later that year would there be executions and sentences of imprisonment.†

The Republicans, who but for two very small probing attempts, had been inactive while the Basques fought in the north, now prepared a surprise for Franco. Franco was busy planning the details of stage two of the northern campaign, the capture of Santander, when news began to filter from the opposing side of the preparations for an offensive of hitherto impossible proportions. Franco's brigades were developing into divisions, and his divisions into corps: but so were those of his opponents who had had an initial numerical advantage. The question for Franco's G.H.Q. was the usual—where would the enemy strike? Concentrations were reported at various points. Feint attacks were started from Aragon to Andalucia. It was not till dawn on 6th July, when a concentration of armoured vehicles and tanks to a strength never seen before and followed by one of the International Brigades crashed through six battalions six field and thirteen anti-tank guns at a point fifteen miles west of Madrid, that the secret was out. The *Schwerpunkt* could not have been better chosen. It was Franco's weakest point.

The operation as conceived by Vicente Rojo (now Chief of Staff to Prieto who had become Minister of Defence in Negrin's government) was intended to envelop in an area of about 100 square miles Franco's force before Madrid. Rojo envisaged six divisions as pouring through the gap made by his assault force. When well on their way to their objective, Móstoles, through Brunete, Rojo would launch two divi-

---

* Franco has also been credited with having engineered Mola's death. The only shred of evidence to support the allegation is Faupel's comment a month later[43] that Franco seemed relieved at Mola's death and that Franco had told him that Mola had become very touchy, meeting all Franco's observations with the phrase: "Have you lost your confidence in me?" Franco, however, was always impassive at the news of death (see Chapter 5, also below, p. 406). There was also a belief that the Germans had engineered the death, but if anyone was to be killed for protesting against the German bombing of civilians it should have been Franco rather than Mola.

† Proportionately the class to suffer most severely was that of priests and religious. Sixteen priests were shot and 403 sentenced for their separatist views and activities.

sions westward from a point south of Madrid to head also for Móstoles. In all 80,000 men, supported by 200 guns, 130 tanks, 40 armoured vehicles and 200 aircraft, would be brought into play. As the fight in the university city would have its parallel in the streets of Stalingrad, so this operation can be said in planning to have anticipated the Russians' envelopment of Von Paulus. But Rojo was only the planner. Miaja

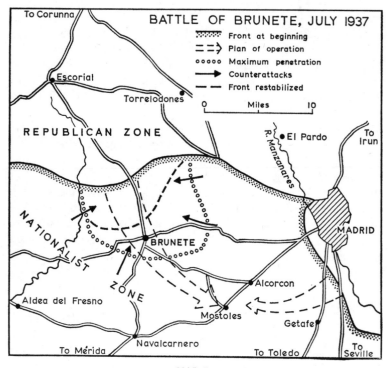

MAP 7

was the field commander; and below Miaja there were the captains and lieutenants of the new popular army who owed their ranks more to their devotion to Marxism than to their military ability. Furthermore, at all levels the chain of command was confused by the presence of Red Army-type political commissars. The line was penetrated, with a rapidity never before seen in this war, through Brunete and beyond: then utter confusion developed. The Popular Army battalions got in each others' way. In their confusion Franco got the time and opportunity to plug the gap and to have troops to blunt the other point of the pincers. He switched troops, anti-tank and heavy artillery and the Condor Legion from the northern front. On 18th July he was counter-attacking with 60,000 men. Eight days later the Popular Army was back, not to its line of departure, but to a line which put them, rather than Franco's army, at a disadvantage as a permanent front. Franco's side had suffered 12,000 casualties: his enemy 24,000.[44]

General Franco, who had come to agree with his Chief of Operations[45] that though Madrid might be taken, holding it would absorb 100,000 men if the enemy still had forces to continue the war, and who in any case was always a man not to be distracted from his main purpose, switched back his forces to the north. He now at long last agreed to give the Italians a chance to avenge Guadalajara. Accordingly for the capture of Santander he lined up eight Spanish brigades, the now 80 per cent Spanish Black Arrows Brigade, and six entirely Italian.[46]

In two weeks to 1st September the phase was over. The Italians did not distinguish themselves but neither did they disgrace themselves. This time Franco did cut off the enemy's retreat and over 50,000 prisoners were taken. However, by 24th August the Popular Army had

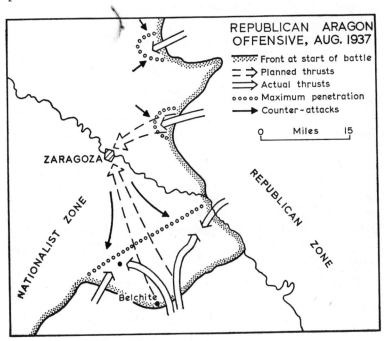

MAP 8

recovered sufficiently to attempt a diversionary offensive directed this time at Zaragoza. It was Brunete all over again. Rojo conceived the plan: the International Brigades fought magnificently, and so did the Spanish brigades of the Popular Army; but once again political and military considerations got in the way of the exploitation of the initial breakthroughs.[47] Furthermore, since Brunete, Franco had been able to build up a strategic reserve: thus, stemming the Aragon front offensive did not hold him up in Santander or in proceeding to the third and last phase of the northern operation, the capture of Asturias. Progress through the battlefields of the October Revolution of 1934 was slow at first, but suddenly in mid-October resistance collapsed.

Though guerillas would harass Franco's forces till the following March,[48] the war in the north was over. He had the factories in which to produce armaments for his ever more numerous army.* The training of everyone from private to corps commander would proceed apace. Von Thoma would say of Franco after World War II, "a general of the old school"—when it came to tanks.[49] Franco could never be pigeon-holed so neatly even as a general. He would not concentrate the German or Italian tanks because they were so lightly armoured and so vulnerable. Only the captured Vickers were capable of facing the Russian anti-tank guns. Furthermore, Franco never had more than 200 tanks, as against the 2,400 with which the Germans would conquer France.[50] He did not have the transport to motorise his infantry. And though he knew his Fuller as well as Von Thoma or Vicente Rojo and would stress to his corps and divisional commanders the need to maintain the momentum of an attack and "to follow through", he, also like Rojo, had to adapt theory to practicability.† To Von Thoma Franco was conservative: to his own corps and divisional commanders he was dangerously revolutionary. In the early days he had despatched his Chief of Operations, Barroso, to Varela lest Varela should wage "una guerra moruña—a war a la Morocco". How much his subordinates rather than Franco had to learn can be seen from a commentary he wrote about this time to the standard work on the tactical use of large formations.[51] He made them study all arms including air power, and rid themselves of the Moroccan war's concept of infantry columns. He stressed the

* Copies of German, Italian and Russian models. Rather significantly, the anti-tank gun chosen for manufacture was the Russian 45 mm which in its turn had been based on the Vickers 3-pounder.

† "Of course you should know what is the right thing to do in theory; but you should also know whether it can be done in practice . . . you must remember Spain was hardly a nation on wheels at that time". (Rojo to author: June 1966.)

importance of concentrated effort and tactical surprise in the attack, and of security and depth in the defence. He advanced the thinking of his subordinates from 1918 (where not 1908), to 1928 (if not 1938); and it must also be said to his credit that there was no man alive in Spain who had ever commanded more than the equivalent of a brigade in the field.

Franco now considered the next step. In his opinion ideally it should be a drive from the Aragon front down to the sea so as to split into two the third of Spain not in his hands. However, bad weather could be expected and the drive to the sea across the mountains would be dangerous before the Spring. After Brunete, he had stopped Varela from pursuing the enemy uphill towards the Escorial so to pinch out their salient to the north-west of Madrid. Franco decided to thrust at Alcala through Guadalajara which would have the same effect and should be easier as it would be downhill. He gave the necessary orders for the preparation of this new offensive and turned his attention to international affairs which had reached a point of crisis.

Hitler had replaced the interfering Faupel and wife[52] with the more obese Von Stohrer. On 31st October Sperrle who had become a *persona non grata* since Guernica would also be replaced. But Sperrle's superior in the Luftwaffe, Colonel-General Herman Goering, still wanted his pound of flesh: payment in good measure for services and goods rendered. In the March Franco had signed an agreement constantly to consult Germany on measures "against the dangers of Communism" and on questions of international policy "of mutual interest", not to join in treaties against and not to attack Germany and to intensify Spanish/German relations.[53] So as to put into effect the last clause there had been a further protocol in July. With the iron ore mines in Franco's hands at long last, Goering expected Franco not merely to export raw materials to him, but to give Germany rights over a number of important mines.[54] Franco's reaction was to sign a decree declaring illegal and null and void all transfers of mining titles effected since 18th July 1936. Next Goering heard of Franco seeking an economic and commercial *modus vivendi* with Britain. The very ores and pyrites which Goering wanted were those required by the British steel industry whose investments were protected by that decree. Germany's pre-war imports from Spain had been mainly of crates of oranges. A fierce diplomatic battle developed. Franco's understanding of the protocols was proved different from Germany's. Franco maintained that the new law did not discriminate against Germany. Germany was in the same position as other foreign powers. No international agreement could be contrary to national laws. He would sanction the export of Spanish products, but when it came to handing over controlling interests in Spain's natural resources, this he could not do.

The discussions were to drag on for many months. Franco employed every diplomatic subterfuge known. Goering sent a personal representative "to hold a pistol at Franco's breast". In the end Germany had to be satisfied with less than she considered her due. Franco, at the height of these negotiations, may have been unaware of the details of the famous Hossbach Conference, but his experience of the Germans in Spain had left him with no illusions as to why Germany was helping him.* Franco exchanged agents with Britain on 16th November.

Franco was prepared to think the Italians less disinterested than the Germans. The Italians pressed their claims to payment from time to time, but their chief complaint against Franco was his refusal to be dictated to by Italian commanders and his use of the Italian troops.[56] They had been re-grouped into two pure Italian and one mixed Italian-Spanish divisions. Franco was keeping them in the rear. Eventually, however, he did agree to let them take part in the limited operation aimed at Guadalajara, but only in support of Spanish troops. Their commander, Bastico, the ex-Abyssinia general who had replaced Roatta as their G.O.C., protested vehemently in a stormy meeting at which Viola, Cantalupo's successor as Ambassador, was present. Franco demanded the recall of Bastico.[57] He would gladly have seen the last of the Italians but to have got rid of them might have meant the departure of the Condor Legion at a time when he still had dire need of them and of the German officers in the cadet schools who, though few in numbers, were doing an excellent job as instructors. These were the men whom Franco prized—for their military value. In standing out at this time against British moves towards the withdrawal of volunteers from both sides, he had these last in mind. He believed also genuinely that the proposals would favour his enemies who would be able to hide the foreign origins of the men in the International Brigades. As fighters Franco had the highest opinion of them. In the event his enemies proved as unwilling to let their volunteers go as he was.

---

* On 5th November at the Hossbach Conference Hitler said that he expected the war in Spain to last a further three years. He did not consider desirable a 100 per cent victory for Franco. He wanted tension to be kept up in the Mediterranean. With Franco in undisputed possession of the Mediterranean, the Italians would have to leave the Balearic Islands. If they did not France and Britain might go to war, and in that war "a white Spain might be on the side of Italy's enemies".[55]

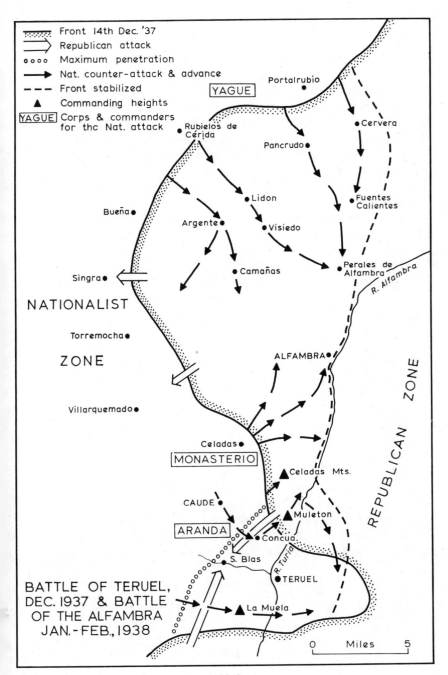

Front 14th Dec. '37
Republican attack
Maximum penetration
Nat. counter-attack & advance
Front stabilized
Commanding heights
YAGUE Corps & commanders
for the Nat. attack

Portalrubio

YAGUE

Cervera

Rubielos de
Cérida

Pancrudo

Fuentes
Calientes

Bueña

Lidon

Argente

Visiedo

Singra

Camañas

Perales de
Alfambra

R. Alfambra

NATIONALIST

Torremocha

ZONE

ALFAMBRA

REPUBLICAN ZONE

Villarquemado

Celadas

MONASTERIO

Celadas Mts.

CAUDE

Muleton

ARANDA

Concua

S. Blas

R. Turia

TERUEL

BATTLE OF TERUEL,
DEC. 1937 & BATTLE
OF THE ALFAMBRA
JAN.-FEB.,1938

La Muela

0   Miles   5

MAP 9

The preparations for the Guadalajara-Alcala offensive took longer than Franco anticipated. He was unable to fix a date earlier than 18th December. But on the 15th, Franco received a rude and unexpected shock. The enemy had begun an offensive north and east of the point where he had concentrated his forces. It was directed at Teruel.

The city of Teruel was in a salient. In two days it was cut off and surrounded by a force of 60,000. To the chagrin of the Italians[58] Franco cancelled the Guadalajara offensive and switched the two army corps under Varela and Aranda which he had destined for it to plug the gap and relieve Teruel. Fortunately for him his enemy had turned to reduce the city instead of pressing inwards through the huge gap which they had created. The streets of Teruel swallowed up the majority of this army, for the "white" defenders of the city resisted as the "red" defenders of Madrid had done. Franco, against the outspoken advice of the German Colonel Funck[59] who urged the sacrifice of Teruel, ordered Varela to relieve the besieged at all costs. Half the inhabitants were his friends even if the other half were not. As Toledo, so now Teruel with Nador possibly in the background. A battle in which no quarter was given developed as Varela counter-attacked. A heavy snowfall followed by extreme low temperatures made further advance impossible for the relieving army. But within Teruel the street fighting continued. Soldiers and civilians held out as long as they could—to 8th January.* Franco was now faced with a choice either of withdrawing a substantial distance back, or pushing the enemy up to 30 kilometres forward, to the River Alfambra, with a bridgehead across it, retaking Teruel in the process. He decided on the latter. Varela and Aranda's corps went over to the attack on 15th January. Franco sent in Yague, now commanding the African army corps to help them. After heavy fighting the Alfambra was reached, Teruel fell on 20th February and Franco had a new and better defence line than before.

Not one Italian had taken part in any of these operations. Ciano, on his own authority, had sent in Italian aircraft to bomb Valencia and Barcelona. Any question of allowing the Italians to avenge Guadalajara

---

* Prieto agreed to an International Red Cross request that the besieged women and children and old people should be evacuated during a truce. He agreed. However, the allegations of the "whites" that the "reds" broke their pledges and that they used the truce to prepare the final assault may have some basis of truth. It is debatable how many civilians were killed, but even the lowest estimates give proof that the "Republican" forces in the field were every whit as ruthless as their opponents. On the other hand, the Colonel who defended Teruel, Rey d'Harcourt, and the bishop who were taken prisoner were not shot till later.

was now out. Still suspicious, however, of the effect that an international agreement on the withdrawal of volunteers from both sides would have, and attributing to the British initiative no more than enlightened self-interest (that is, that all Britain was concerned about was that the Italians should leave the Balearics) he continued his diplomatic game on this matter, now appearing to agree, now finding some objection, while he prepared his next military move.

By ordering his troops to advance up to the Alfambra, Franco had turned loss into substantial gain: and not merely in the field of military operation. He had confounded the new German Ambassador Stohrer's foreboding that Germany would have to send more materials and technical men[60] and Ciano's panic[61] that the whole nationalist front would be pushed back. Mussolini's orders to Italian submarines to attack neutral shipping had been quite unnecessary and equally so the Italian terror raids on Valencia and Barcelona.[62] The offensive aimed at Guadalajara which Teruel had interrupted had been intended by Franco only as a stop gap to give his troops—and the Italians—something to do over the winter. It had been his intention then to drive to the sea in the Spring. It was Spring now, and drive to the sea he would whatever the Italians or the Germans recommended. He now had twenty-five infantry and one cavalry divisions, about 250,000 men, with which to manoeuvre. He grouped most of them into six corps.* He now proposed to bring all these forces into play in a three-stage operation. In the first, using the River Ebro to cover his left flank and pivoting round his new gain above Teruel, there would be an advance along a sixty-mile front from Fuentes de Ebro, twenty miles south-east of Zaragoza, up to the River Guadalupe, Six depleted divisions manned this front for Valencia. Franco proposed to use fourteen plus the cavalry. Yague's Marroqui corps would be the spearhead: the Italian corps would be given the task of advancing in parallel on Yague's right hand but protected by a Navarrese division and the cavalry: the Galicia corps would advance to the right of the Italians.

The attack began after intensive artillery and tactical air bombardment

---

* *Castilla* (four divisions under Varela); *Galicia* (five under Aranda—the hero of Oviedo); *Aragon* (four under Moscardo of the Alcazar); *Navarra* (four under Solchaga); *Marroqui* (three of Moors and Legion under Yague); *CTV* (two Italian and one Italo-Spanish) under Berti who had succeeded Bastico after the row with Franco, and who on arrival had told Franco that Mussolini expected him to conduct the war more vigorously and listen to the advice of the Italian military.[63] The remaining two Spanish divisions were the embryo of a 7th corps, formed later in the year.

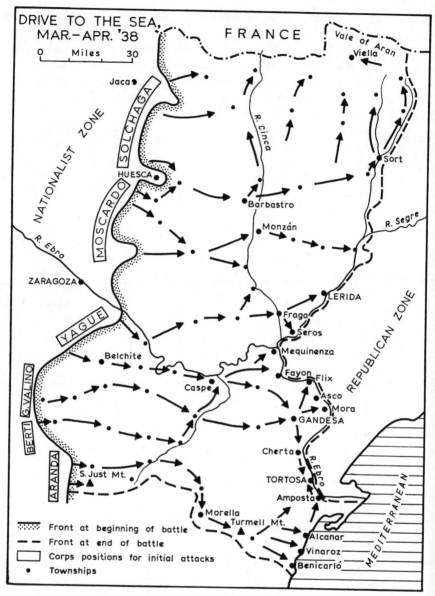

DRIVE TO THE SEA, MAR.–APR. '38

0   Miles   30

FRANCE

Vale of Aran

Viella

Jaca

SOLCHAGA

MOSCARDO

HUESCA

NATIONALIST ZONE

R. Ebro

ZARAGOZA

YAGUE

G. VALINO

BERTI

ARANDA

S. Just Mt.

Belchite

Caspe

R. Cinca

Barbastro

Monzán

Fraga

Seros

Mequinenza

Fayon   Flix

Asco

Mora

GANDESA

Cherta

TORTOSA

Amposta

Morella

Turmell Mt.

Alcanar

Vinaroz

Benicarló

LERIDA

Sort

R. Segre

REPUBLICAN ZONE

R. Ebro

MEDITERRANEAN

Front at beginning of battle
Front at end of battle
Corps positions for initial attacks
Townships

MAP 10

of the enemy lines on 9th March. All objectives were reached by the 17th. The Moors, Legion and Navarrese had as usual the lion's share of the fighting.*

Franco now had a road along the south bank of the Ebro; but the enemy also had one along the north bank, the main road leading to Zaragoza from Lerida and Barcelona. The enemy was exposed on the flank, but so was he. Accordingly, he concentrated Moscardo's Aragon corps and Solchaga's Navarra between Fuentes and Huesca. On 22nd March he ordered them to advance and Yague to cross the Ebro. All three corps were to make the River Cinca the minimum objective. All reached it by the 28th. Franco then told his commanders to push ahead into Catalonia: the enemy resistance was crumbling. Lerida fell to Yague on 3rd April, Balaguer to Moscardo on the 6th and Pobla de Segur, fifty miles north of Lerida, to Solchaga on the 7th. Franco was now only eighty miles from Barcelona, but he was not going to head for Barcelona. Franco considered that Barcelona would be as untenable as Madrid unless he first destroyed the armies in the field. Furthermore, much though, or rather because he hated Catalan separatists so deeply, he looked on Barcelona as a Spanish city, and therefore not one to be destroyed by street fighting or Italian bombardment. Besides, on 2nd April his spare infantry division and the cavalry division which, under Garcia Valiño had been protecting the Italian flanks, had crossed the Guadalupe, and reinforced by yet another spare division, had reached Gandesa twenty miles from the Mediterranean; while Aranda's Galicia corps, which had also crossed the River Guadalupe, had reached points a mere thirty miles from the sea. The road from Gandesa to Tortosa and the sea was easy. That ahead of the Galicia corps was across the craggy mountain peaks of the Maestrazgo. Franco ordered the Italians to take over from Garcia Valiño the easy road, and sent Garcia to help Aranda. The Italians were stopped by the enemy before Tortosa. Aranda and Garcia drove back the enemy from peak to peak. On Good Friday, 15th April, Aranda's forward division—one commanded by

* Ciano[64] exaggerates to absurdity the part played by the Italians in this campaign. A detailed examination of the operational orders and of the ground assigned to them proves how small their role really was. It may be that Franco was not totally averse to the false value given the Italians by themselves and by the Communists alike. His enemies came thereby to deceive themselves. Thus in this first stage of the operation, Rojo rightly considered the town of Caspe at the confluence of the Ebro and Guadalope as the vital point, and prepared to defend it with the pick of the International Brigades against Yague; but the Communists, who had the last say, over-ruled him and squandered valuable time and material on the Italian sector.

Franco's boyhood companion Alonso Vega—took the Mediterranean fishing village of Vinaroz. In the meantime, however, the Italians' situation at Tortosa had become precarious. Garcia Valiño was ordered to save the Italians. He arrived in the nick of time and Tortosa fell to the combined force on the 19th.*

In six weeks Franco had added to his Spain a mountain area roughly the size of the Netherlands or of Wales and Northern Ireland combined. This was no mean feat with an army that still went on foot and whose transport and supplies were almost entirely horse-drawn.

Franco had proved himself a Supremo who knew how to handle twenty-five divisions. He had used them throughout in the right place and at the right time. He had exercised correctly economy of force and concentration of force, mobility and surprise and security. Equally important in a senior general he had learnt when to leave the initiative to his commanders and when to intervene. As once he had acquired fame for intrepidity under fire when personally leading his men to battle, so now his name became a by-word among his staff and commanders for coolness and imperturbability. He received the news of serious reverses at Brunete, Belchite and Teruel with a calm which dumbfounded those present: but his reaction was equally imperceptible when Teruel was turned into a victory and when his troops cut to the sea. Franco now really was in character as in ability, in fact as in title a Generalissimo; and anyone surveying the situation, with the enemy split in two, with Franco in possession of a strike force of a quarter of a million men with battle experience, and another half a million to hold fronts steady, might well have said that the end of the war was in sight. Many did: there were even rumours (which were true) of his enemies suing for peace. Almost immediately after this victory, however, a number of factors compounded to prolong the war another year.

* I consider the suggestions made to me that Franco deliberately here exposed the Italians to near defeat in revenge for the air raids to be unlikely, though not impossible. If "near" had become real defeat, its consequences might have been serious. Nevertheless the Italians were again seen by the Spaniards as lacking in the morale and determination which wins battles. "The Italians were good fellows but you must remember that this was not their cause: this was not their country: that they were not acclimatised: that they were not volunteers and that their officers were bad" (Franco-Salgado to author).

NOTES

1. Full text in Iribarren, *Mola*, p. 223.

2. The accounts of events within General Franco's G.H.Q. are all based on the evidence of eye-witnesses.

3. The *military* part played by Yague in the Civil War, especially in these early stages, seems to me in the light of his own *Hoja de Servicios* and other army records to have been grossly exaggerated by Aznar and all who followed him.

4. Cf. Thomas, pp. 389 and 401. The disparity between the Vickers tank and its opponents (see below, p. 267), and the lack of troop carriers for the infantry made it quite impossible for either side to use tanks tactically according to Liddell-Hart's (not Guderian's or Tukhachevky's) principles.

5. D.G.F.P., 94 and 96.

6. Cf. D.G.F.P., 50, 87 and 90 in particular.

7. D.G.F.P. 113.

8. In *Die Wehrmacht*, special number May 1939. *Wir Kämpften in Spanien.* Sperrle is not likely to have diminished the figures.

9. Cf. Thomas, pp. 652-3 and note.

10. Liddell-Hart, *The Other side of the Hill* (Cassell, 1948), pp. 97-9.

11. Aznar, p. 862, writing in praise of the Germans.

12. Conversations with author May-June 1966. Some of the "junk" is on show in the Military Museum in Madrid—"siege of Sebastopol stuff" (Spanish Army Colonel).

13. Evidence of now senior Spanish officers. Von Thoma claimed in a letter to Liddell-Hart (quoted in *Theory and Practice of War*, p. 161) that German crews manned these in battle. The evidence of Spanish tank officers contradicts this quite flat. They all acknowledged that they were trained by Von Thoma and his assistants but not one could recall any occasion when Germans took these or their own Mks. I and II into *battle*. One would have expected German casualties to have been higher if they did as Von Thoma alleged.

14. D.G.F.P. 109. The Germans went as far as to prepare a note for their Ambassador on the other side to hand over to the Government. It began: 'Since General Franco has captured the city of Madrid . . .' (D.G.F.P. 114).

15. The lowest estimate is 1,900; the highest credible figure is 3,500. The composition of these units whose organisation looked forward to the independent brigades of post World War II lead me to suppose that their full complement was 2,500 for some, and 3,500 for others. Since they had a very high casualty rate they are unlikely ever to have been up to strength. Of the 40,000 who

served in them 8,000 were killed. There were another 5,000 other foreigners on the Republican side in Spanish units (cf. Thomas, pp. 796-7). Varela's assault force on 8th November did not exceed 7,000 men (Spanish Army records). They therefore had the quite inadequate superiority in up-hill attack of at best 7 : 2 alone against the XIth Brigade, as this first brigade was called: Franco's argument is therefore tenable, though it belongs to the "ifs and ands" of history.

16. Advice incorporated into his commentary to the standard *Reglamento para el empleo táctico de las grandes unidades*—issued printed in 1938.

17. *Hoja de Servicio:* by a Vickers tank shell, during a reconnaissance.

18. Cf. D.G.F.P. 87, p. 96.

19. D.G.F.P. 95, 110, 111. Ciano, *L'Europa verso la catastrofe* (Milan, 1948), pp. 87-9. Cantalupo, p. 130.

20. D.G.F.P. 119, 121-4.

21. D.G.F.P. 135 for the text; 139, 142 for immediate reaction. Cf. also 157 and 180.

22. Cf. D.G.F.P. 143.

23. D.G.F.P. 125.

24. D.G.F.P. 144.

25. D.G.F.P. 148, p. 159.

26. D.G.F.P. 129-30.

27. Cantalupo, pp. 65 and 109-12.

28. Professor G. Jackson in *The Spanish Republic and the Civil War* (N.J., 1965) makes two generals out of this one several times, and especially on p. 349.

29. Cantalupo, pp. 131-7.

30. D.G.F.P. 220.

31. These "divisions" were of an experimental pattern which was soon dropped. The remaining Italians were placed with Falange and *Requeté* units into two formations known as the Black Arrows and Blue Arrows (Brigades).

32. Roatta blamed his Chief of Staff killed in the battle for allowing an order to withdraw to become a rout. See footnote, p. 290 and note 6 above. Ciano, *Diary 1937-8* (Methuen, 1952), p. 91, called Guadalajara his "worst day".

33. Cantalupo, p. 207.

34. Franco-Salgado MS. and *Centinela*, p. 288.

35. D.G.F.P. 234. 20th March 1937.

36. Franco would always maintain that non-intervention helped his enemies, as vehemently as they upheld the contrary.

37. It is, of course, wiser for a general to over-estimate the enemy rather than the opposite.

38. Op. cit., pp. 230-4.

39. This summarised account of the bombing of Guernica is based on my cross-questioning of Basque and other eye-witnesses in the 1950s and on information willingly supplied by eye-witnesses of the scenes at General Franco's G.H.Q. Steer's report to *The Times* is proved accurate but not Galland's who attempts to explain it away as "all a mistake". (in *Die Ersten und die Letzten*, Ch. III); Galland, of course, arrived in Spain *after* the event and a Spanish general to whom I showed it dismissed it as "utterly absurd: there was no question of a mistake: Funck admitted that it was done as ordered by Keitel and that it was a try-out". Sperrle and Faupel subsequently quarrelled. D.G.F.P. 386 (which talks of "General Sander") would have the reader believe that Sperrle was meddling in economic affairs (as Faupel was in military). The odd feature is that Kindelan, Franco's Air Chief, should send his senior staff officer with gossip to Faupel. Remembering that Goering was Sperrle's Luftwaffe superior, it is legitimate to speculate whether the despatch was as straightforward as it seems. Either way, Kindelan can be seen fanning the dissention between Sperrle and Faupel to the point when Spain would be rid of both (cf. p. 424 and note on p. 434). My enquiries solicited no further evidence than that (i) Franco did not order the bombardment ("how could he? We had plenty of friends, even in Basque towns"); (ii) Sperrle's recall was "maybe connected with Guernica, among other things: but it took time to be rid of him". The subject was not pursued at Nuremberg (Keitel's trial).

40. For German pressure on Franco on this point see D.G.F.P. 249, 250, 251. For an oblique reference to the power of Germany over the Press see ibid. 598. The Press did not in fact come under full government control (as against its control by the Falange) till 1944.

41. Llano was replaced later by the Basque Gamir Ulibarri who wrote the useful *De mis Memorias* (Paris, 1939). Gamir's conduct of the Basque war was restricted by the Russian Colonel Gorev (see Thomas, p. 568).

42. Franco-Salgado. Also in *Centinela*, p. 293.

43. D.G.F.P. 390, p. 410.

44. Summary based on my conversations with Generals Rojo and Barroso (June, 1966) and on pp. 169-74 of *Revista Historica Militar*, No. 17, in preference to earlier "official" and other accounts. In going through this and other battles with the generals I found no important discrepancies between them, or between them and Lieutenant-Colonel Martinez Conde's extensive article in that review. On this particular battle the only variations were on casualties. The nationalist may have been 14,000.

45. *i.e.* the then Colonel Barroso.

46. These mixed brigades were reckoned by writers inimical to Franco as wholly Italian. Later writers (and the D.G.F.P., *e.g.* No. 390) talk of them as "officered by Italians". Bastico, the new Italian C.-in-C. was a party to this deception

of both Hitler and Mussolini. They were "officered by Italians" from the rank of lieutenant-colonel upwards entirely, partly from the rank of major and hardly at all below that rank.

47. For more details of this offensive *v*. Thomas, pp. 600-4.

48. In D.G.F.P. 390, pp. 410–11, Faupel stated that Franco had hoped to round up the northern campaign "in July or August". For guerilla activity *v*. Stohrer's despatch no. 541, p. 614.

49. Liddell-Hart, op. cit., pp. 98-9.

50. Ibid., p. 100.

51. *Reglamento para el empleo táctico de las grandes unidades.*

52. Serrano Suñer in his memoirs gives maliciously amusing pen pictures of the two ambassadors.

53. D.G.F.P. 234.

54. D.G.F.P. 392 for the July protocol. For the mining concession or "Montana Project" story *v*. 440, 455, pp. 483-4, 463 and 464 and *passim* pp. 508-619. The "pistol" references are on pp. 509 and 523; no. 529 gives a lengthy "state of play" as in February 1938. A key passage "in return for the great sacrifices we have made for the Spanish National movement we have thus far received only meagre equivalents and few assurances for the future", occurs on p. 593. The next German offensive to get the concessions took place in June 1938 *v*. pp. 674-81.

55. D.G.F.P. Series D, Vol. I, Doc. 19, pp. 36-7. Also Nuremberg trials, Vol. XXV, pp. 413-14.

56. D.G.F.P. 489 (Ciano's figure of 40,000 includes Army and Airforce personnel), 494, 495, 497-8, 500 *et aliter*. See also Ciano, *Diary 1937-38*, p. 37, for an instalment on the debt: "10,000 tons of steel".

57. D.G.F.P. 434, 477. Cf. also 363, p. 376. Ciano op. cit., p. 17 (2nd October 1937), cf. p. 22 (17th October): "Franco can hardly wait for (the Italian forces) to clear out . . . He is jealous of our successes and those that are still to come".

58. Ciano, *Diary*, p. 46.

59. Information from eye-witnesses.

60. D.G.F.P. 501, p. 553, and 503: but for a more penetrating analysis made in Berlin *v*. 502.

61. Op. cit., p. 65.

62. Italian bombing of Spanish cities: between Franco's H.Q. and the Italian bomber squadrons at Palma, Majorca, which were supposed to be helping Franco, there was no direct communication. If Franco wanted to enlist their aid he had to ask the Italian Liaison Officer to contact the Italian Air Ministry in Rome which then relayed the request to Palma. That Franco was not only

not responsible for these air raids but did not know about them till he heard the news from other sources is clear from the following jottings by Ciano in his Diary:

26th August 1937 (p. 5) I have given orders for the aircraft at Palma to bomb Valencia tonight. This is the moment to terrorize the enemy.

2nd February 1938 (p. 68) The Duce has intensified the air raids on the coast.

8th February (p. 72) The Duce intends to resume air raids on the coastal cities in order to break Red resistance. I have received and passed to the Duce an eye-witness account of the recent bombing at Barcelona. I have never read a document so realistically horrifying. And yet there were only nine S.79s. . . .

6th April (p. 98) The Duce has telegraphed the Air Force in the Balearic Islands for an attack in force on the back areas of the Spanish troops. *Franco doesn't want air raids on cities*, but in this cases the game is worth the candle.

For a German report on the bombing *v*. D.G.F.P. 550. For a confirmation of Franco's anger *v*. 551, cf. 553, cf. note 34, Chapter 11, below.

63. D.G.F.P. 527.

64. Pp. 87 *ff*., cf. D.G.F.P. 527.

11

HEAD OF STATE AND CAUDILLO

As Franco himself said: *"La guerra era lo mío; de eso estaba yo seguro"*: "War was my job; I was sure of that".[1] Fighting battles and winning them was indeed his metier. Being in command of three-quarters of a million men required basically the same ability as being in charge of a platoon. Forming, training and officering such an army was an amplification of his experience with the Legion. Preparing an offensive with twenty-five divisions and disposing of others to hold the enemy elsewhere was an extension of his staff work before Alhucemas.

The foreign policy of Franco, Head of State, can also be seen as an extension of his war. In him Clausewitz's dictum may be said to have been reversed. By April 1938 Franco knew from experience that as Head of State he had to protect his country not only from the foreign power which he believed was its most dangerous and active enemy, Russia; nor yet only from those which his reading of Spanish history gave him to understand were its traditional foes, Britain and France; but also from those which publicly proclaimed their friendship—the Axis powers. He was, by the spring of 1938, stronger than the enemy entrenched before him; but in the battlefield of foreign policy he still had, and for many years to come would have, no strength but his own personal cunning. Therefore he would have to conduct a diplomatic war in which his only hope was to attract the antagonist into traps by withdrawal, and "waiting upon providences" as Cromwell would have put it; in expectation particularly that the countries which would not leave Spain alone might fall out among themselves. His army training and active service in Africa had prepared him for such diplomatic manoeuvring no less than for his other task as Generalissimo, to win a shooting war. As Head of State and Head of Government, however, he had to have a home policy as well. Of the profession of government he had no knowledge, and in the conduct of civilian affairs, no experience.

In his manifesto of 18th July, Franco had offered[2] justice and equality before law, peace and love among Spaniards, liberty and fraternity without libertinage and tyranny, work for all, social justice and a fairer distribution of wealth without endangering the national economy. Fine words, and fine ideals; but could they be put into practice? If so, how? Spanish army generals and professional politicians had been proclaiming much the same promises for a century and a half. Almost the only visible result of the many and varied attempts to realise these had been the conversion of Spain into the stamping ground of the apocalyptic war, hunger, pestilence and death.

By 1st October, when his fellow-insurgents had chosen and appointed him Head of the new State of Spain, which they hoped would be built above the ruins of the current and materially most destructive of the long sequence of civil wars, it had become clear who among the people was with them and who was against them. Those with them were they who had also come to the conclusion that nothing was to be expected of the Popular Front but violence against the person and property, conducive either to total chaos and anarchy, or the dictatorship of the proletariat, Communism and subservience to a foreign power.

This was the single common factor among all the men and women on Franco's side. To reduce the civil war in Spain to one of army against civilians is, as we have seen, to ignore the facts. Equally, however, to simplify it as a struggle of the privileged classes against those without privilege, of "haves" against "have-nots", of Monarchists against Republicans, of advocates of dictatorship against democrats, of patriots against traitors, of Catholics against the enemies of religion, or Fascists against anti-Fascists, is to distort the truth.

The quasi-fascist Falange was on the same side as Franco, on 1st October as on 18th July; in the February they had been the most insignificant of the thirty and more parties which had opposed the Popular Front; on 18th July they had fielded 5,000 young enthusiasts: by 1st October they had accepted perhaps 200,000 neophytes into the Party.[3] Many were true converts to the dynamism of the imprisoned Jose Antonio whose doctrines were in all essentials identical with those of Spanish Socialism except in two particulars: that he would have the dictatorship of an élite of a party, or of one man, instead of that of an amorphous proletariat: and that the dictatorship would be an end in itself and not a prelude to "the disappearance of the State". Some nevertheless were men who had hurriedly destroyed their C.N.T. or

U.G.T. membership cards before surrender to the advancing insurgents, and who without changing their views had wisely taken Queipo de Llano's advice that Falange membership was a lifeline. Thus, while there were no Fascists on the opposing side, there were on Franco's many who had paid at least lip service to Marxism or Bakuninism.

The Falangists almost to a man were anti-Monarchist; yet all Monarchists were on Franco's side, whether they looked on the exiled Alfonso XIII or on the Carlist Pretender as king; and though the Carlists like the Falangists were upholders of authoritarianism, the Alfonsists differed among themselves as to whether under the hereditary king Spain should have once more the controlled democracy of the days of Cánovas and Sagasta or move towards its development into a full-scale parliamentary democracy such as that for which they admired Britain. But there were yet others to whom the choice between a king and a president as Head of State was of minor importance compared with the choice between a true parliament and a false one. Some genuinely believed that the February elections had been falsified: others that even if they had not been, the elected Popular Front had proceeded to a series of actions for which there had been no warrant in the ballot boxes and which were contrary to the will of the majority of Spaniards. Such believers in democracy however were, it must be admitted, as few in number on Franco's as on the other side; for it must not be forgotten neither of the mass political groupings on the so-called Republican side believed in parliamentary democracy.

Not all the "haves", or the privileged were with Franco, nor was he without many "have-nots" and under-privileged. Azaña, Casares Quiroga and their followers were men of property. On the other hand the upper and middle classes of Spain in the 1930s were far too small to have provided Franco with the vast army he collected. That army was indeed as much of the people as the Popular Army which it fought.

Here indeed was the true tragedy of Spain at war: that it was not divided horizontally according to its class structure but that it divided families. In consequence brothers literally fought against each other and killed each other. There were Bahamondes on both sides. In this particular Franco's film script family, the Andrades,[4] was true to life. Ramon, Air Attaché of the Popular Front in Washington on 18th July, did finally decide to throw his lot in with his brother Francisco, but his extremist earlier history could equally easily have taken him to the other side.

Franco's rallying cry on 18th July was: *"Viva España—Long Live*

Spain." Uttering that cry could cost a man his life at the hands of his fellows on the other side who favoured "*Viva Rusia*" or *U.H.P.*; but equally there were men on the other side who saw the insurgents as no less un-Spanish, supported as they were by Germans and Italians and by a political party which appeared to have its roots in foreign Fascism and National Socialism. Nationalism—or patriotism—was a powerful inspiration at the outbreak of the war; but it did not necessarily lead to Franco's side. Furthermore, Basque and Catalan nationalism was as equally legitimate as Spanish nationalism, and it led tens of thousands of men who had no brief for the Popular Front to stand by its side because the conspirators were intransigently Unionists while the Popular Front had the political foresight to give Catalonia and to promise the Basque Euzkadi a measure of autonomy. The battle cry "*Viva España*" confirmed in opposition men with whose support Franco could have shortened the war by at least a year.*

Finally, in the beginning and until Franco liquidated the northern front, the war was not simply either one between Catholics and the enemies of religion. For the Basques fought against Franco, and they with their fellow-Basques, the Navarrese, who were Franco's bravest troops, were together the most Catholic of the peoples of Spain.†

The propaganda of the time on both sides befogged the real position of the Church in the Civil War. Cardinal Gomá, Archbishop of Toledo

* The history of tragic misunderstandings and enmity between the conspirators of 1936 and the Basque nationalists goes back to 1931 when General Orgaz tried to persuade Jose Antonio Aguirre, the leader of the Basque nationalists, to join in a Monarchist plot.[5]

† Meaningful statistics are hard to come by on the practice of Catholicism in Spain in the period immediately preceding the Civil War. However, on the basis of discussions with anti-clericals as well as with bishops, the parish priests, religious and laity (including the late Cardinal Segura and the now Bishop Benavent of Malaga) during the years 1950-8, in virtually all parts of Spain, I am confident that the Church was stronger in 1936 than at any time since the beginning of the century. This was partly because of the work, inspired by the Papal Encyclicals on social justice, done by priests (especially the Jesuits in the north) and laity, and because of the attacks upon the Church amounting at times to persecution from 1931 onwards. If by a Catholic we understand someone baptised, instructed rudimentarily in his religion and anxious to die confessed and with a priest at his side, then a good 70 per cent of the inhabitants of Spain were Catholics. The 30 per cent who rejected Catholicism were fairly evenly distributed among all social classes but not regionally. If however by a Catholic we understand a person who does not willingly miss Mass on Sundays etc. then the percentage varied considerably, with a virtual 100 per cent in the villages of the Basque provinces and Navarre, to 3 per cent in the city of Malaga; but the qualification "willingly" is important, for the people of the northern countryside did not generally have to travel so far to church as those of Castile, nor there as far as the people of the south.

and Primate of Spain, declared his adherence to Franco's cause on
23rd November 1936, when he said then that "a patriotic feeling (was)
the mainspring for the mobilisation of the mass of combatants".[6] It
was not until 1st July 1937 that the majority of the bishops of Spain
jointly followed suit; and when they did they stressed the following
point: "the Church has neither wished for this war nor provoked it. . . .
True enough, thousands of her sons have risen in arms in order to safeguard the principles of religion and christian justice . . . but they have
done so obeying the promptings of their conscience and of their
patriotism on their own responsibility."[7] Though there were priests
who, with the young men of their flocks, raced to join the *Requetés* in
Navarre following a nineteenth-century tradition, and there are stories
of blood-thirsty priests[8] among them, it was not till after the holocaust
of the priests and nuns and churches of the first weekend in the rest of
Spain that the war began to be seen as one of religion; but not in
Euzkadi—the Basque Provinces—where prompt action on the part of
the Basque authorities prevented the Socialists and Anarchists among
them from emulating their political co-religionists in the rest of Spain;
and all over Spain there were many priests so schooled in the Petrine
doctrine that men must be subject to their masters *etiam dyscolis*[9] as to
be severely censured by their theologically less inhibited pro-insurgent
parishioners for their "blindness in not seeing immediately which side
was undoubtedly in the right".[10] Had the atrocities of that first weekend not been committed, and had the Popular Front government not
proceeded to prohibit the Mass in their zone, the Catholic hierarchy
would never as a body have declared themselves as they eventually did
on the side of Franco.

    To return to the beginning: as we have seen, Franco's first manifesto
was that of a nineteenth-century Liberal rather than a Catholic: but he
evolved, not to say changed. In speaking to the Legionaries and Moors
in Africa on 24th July he referred to his audience as *cruzados*, crusaders
for "Holy Spain", and on the following day he referred to his cause
as a *cruzada*, a crusade: again clearly only figuratively, for he labelled
Spanish barracks as "sanctuaries of the Motherland", though he did
also say that the choice for Spaniards was between Communism and
Moscow on the one hand and Spain and its Christian civilization on the
other. Then the semi-pagan people of Seville took a hand: they be-
decked the Moors with Catholic religious emblems to the scandal of
the Basques and of Catholics abroad; but to the satisfaction of Spanish
Catholics, Franco allowed chaplains back into the army units from

which the Republic had banished them. Propagandists on his side made the most of the atrocities of which they heard from priests who had escaped with their lives from cities where the revolt had failed, or read in foreign newspapers, and of which troops saw evidence as they advanced. Propagandists took up the word *cruzada* and used it literally, and Franco began to do likewise. He went to Mass and was photographed at Mass. When on 15th August Franco unfurled solemnly the old Monarchist red and gold flag, the aged Navarrese-born Archbishop of Seville, Cardinal Ilundaín, was at his side. Books contrary to the Christian faith and morals were expunged from schools: the crucifix was restored to classroom walls—and a place was also found for Franco's photograph.

Churchmen in Spain had two grand obsessions in the 1930s: Communism and Freemasonry. A plethora of pamphlets by a Father Tusquets[11] on Freemasonry convinced its hundreds of thousands of readers that Masons in Spain were renewing their century-old offensive on the Christian religion. Franco was rounding up Masons as un-Spanish and as underminers of military discipline. Details of the intense and horrifying persecution of priests and laymen in Mexico under President Calles had been as widely reported in the Spanish Press as ignored by the British.[12] Though Calles was not a Communist, Moscow's inspiration was (not entirely mistakenly) emphasised. Liberalism to the Spanish churchman meant the century-old attack by the pupils of Voltaire and Rousseau against the Church; what they understood by Liberal Democracy was therefore fundamentally different from what American, English or even German prelates understood. In the remote background, also, was the whole history of regalism and of identification of religion with nationalism. Churchmen were therefore receptive to Franco's description of Spain as threatened by Communism and perverted by Freemasonry and other un-Spanish philosophies. However, there were far fewer Masons in the north than in the south and fewer men with a hatred of religion inspired by Voltaire or Marx: and Cabanellas was or had been a Mason. The Archbishop of Burgos, a Castilian, did not hesitate to put himself on the side of the insurgents; but looking around them, the Basque-Navarrese Bishops of Pamplona and Vitoria did not see the issue unequivocally as one between atheistic Communism and Catholicism. They saw rather impious Spanish Army officers making war with the help of anti-clerical Falangists, albeit also with that of ultra-Catholic *Requetés* on their fellow Catholic Basques. Mola exerted pressures on the two Bishops, in particular on Mateo Mújica of Vitoria who had been expelled by the Republic to call upon the Basques to lay down their arms. With the help of Cardinal Gomá, who by chance had been in Pamplona consecrating the Navarrese priest who was to be his auxiliary in Toledo on the outbreak of war, they were prevailed upon to write a pastoral letter in which, up to a point, they did as the generals and Falangists commanded. It had no effect on the Basques who suspected its authenticity. It would be repudiated later by Bishop Mújica when, after his expulsion by Franco in October, he took refuge in Rome. The letter did not inhibit the Bishop of Pamplona from protesting on 15th August against the executions carried out by the insurgents. He said from the pulpit—*No mas sangre*—Enough blood has been shed.

Publicly nonetheless, Cardinal Gomá took neither side till his Archdiocesan seat was about to be reached. Only then did he decide categorically for Franco in a broadcast permeated with nationalistic sentiment. He had, it seems, just met the General: Franco had made a good impression on him as an honest man, self-disciplined, and a Catholic, and thereupon the Cardinal had accepted at its face value all that insurgent propaganda said. In his broadcast he plaited the cause of Spain with that of Catholicism, and the two with that of Franco. He rated Russians, Jews and Masons as the corruptors of "the national soul". The broadcast, like an open letter *El Caso de España* which followed it, was that of a Spanish ultra-nationalist—although the Cardinal was himself a Catalan and had once been criticised for his Catalanist sympathies—rather than that of a prince of the Universal Church. He would have his readers believe that Franco was fighting for that Church.

From that time onwards Franco had in Cardinal Gomá an ally of prestige. Franco's propaganda organisation gave the letter the widest possible publicity, and it won over to the insurgents the sympathy of many Catholics throughout Europe and America who wrongly assumed that Gomá was speaking for the Spanish hierarchy. The Vatican remained unmoved, but then the Vatican had housed two exiles, Cardinal Segura the victim of the 1931 Republic, and Cardinal Gomá's fellow-Catalan Cardinal Vidal.* Cardinal Segura would never utter a word of praise for Franco: Cardinal Vidal never publicly condemned (or supported) either side.

Before Franco became Head of the State, the only words from the

* Cardinal Vidal Barraguer was so beloved even by Anarchists that the Cata an Generalitat was able to deport him to Rome. His auxiliary was one of the twelve bishops assassinated by Socialists or Anarchists.

Vatican had been politically non-committal. On 14th September Pius XI received in audience 500 refugees from "Red Spain". He had sympathised with their sufferings—and the experiences of some of the refugees had been harrowing—but his words were in no way a pronouncement on who was right in the war. If war was always fearful and inhuman, what, he asked, could be said of civil war; and if the shedding of the blood of one man by his brother was one too many for all the world and all time, how then to describe massacres between brothers? He had then given his blessing to all those who defended "the rights and the honour of God and religion", that is to say, he continued, the rights and dignity of conscience, with a warning that there was a limit to what could be justified as legitimate in the defence of religion.

Thus, the Church-State situation when Franco became Head of State was the following: the insurgents had the support of Cardinals Gomá and the ageing Ilundain, but not of Vidal or Segura; the degree of support from other bishops and from priests varied: the Basques were not with him; the Vatican had spoken in terms which implied a censure of his own methods of warfare no less than those of his enemies: the Vatican retained its Nuncio in Madrid.

The Vatican's attitude was unwelcome to Franco for military as well as political reasons. The northern front against the Basques absorbed men required on the Madrid operation. The Basques being well-instructed Catholics could not accept Cardinal Gomá's "open letter" as infallible. However, if the Basques were as "Vaticanist" as their allies by force of circumstance—the Popular Front—alleged them to be, then a word from the Pope would leave them in a more difficult crisis of conscience. Franco accordingly despatched Gomá to Rome on 11th December. Gomá failed in his mission: that is to say the Pope agreed that Catholics should not help Bolshevism but "complained sharply about the execution of Basque Catholic priests by 'white' troops".[15] It does not appear to have occurred to Franco, or his emissary, that the Vatican, then experiencing severe difficulties with Hitler and Mussolini, would not be as receptive as Spaniards to the doctrine: Franco's Spain is the Church and the Church is Spain. The Pope, however, did offer to act as a mediator in peace negotiations which were begun in January and continued into April 1937 when the Italians and Britain also took a hand. All these came to nothing—and could come to nothing.[16] President Aguirre of Euzcadi, the name given the Basque provinces when the Valencia authorities recognised their autonomy that October, was as intense a patriot (or nationalist) as General Franco. The same concept of honour inhibited both Aguirre and Franco. In Francos' idea of Spain there was no possibility of a region with local autonomy: Aguirre could not surrender his nation to a 'foreign' army. Francos' expulsion of Mújica and his subsequent treatment of the defeated Basques did not endear him to Rome.[17]

Franco had no power over the Church of Rome, but he was in a position to exert progressively greater pressure on the Church in Spain. Forty-one of the fifty-five Spanish bishops were in his zone. They were cut off from the outside world for ten months. They were left free to read only what Franco's Press and Propaganda Department permitted. There was mail censorship as well, and seemingly only Cardinal Gomá heard of Pius XI's outspoken condemnation of Nazism *Mit brennender Sorge* issued in the March. Franco laid a strict injunction on the Cardinal to prevent its publication.[18] Inevitably the bishops' ability to judge issues was left impaired. Ten months after the outbreak of the war, Gomá, at Franco's request drafted a letter. Its purpose was to convince the Catholic world that the Church was on Franco's side.

The letter was without precedent in that it was addressed to the Bishops of the Whole World. It made use of the documents pointing to an impending Soviet *coup d'etat* whose authenticity was to be accepted even by Hugh Thomas in 1961.* Uncritically it took as facts figures which were guesses. Indeed, the Spanish clergy proved themselves as susceptible to propaganda as any group of individuals in any modern war.† In general terms however the account the letter gave of Church–State relations under the Republic was accurate and that of events leading to the Civil War a not unfair one. Gomá circulated the draft to the bishops in Spain asking for their views and suggestions. As amended it was sent in galley proof to the Spanish bishops abroad.

Bishop Mújica in Rome excused himself to Cardinal Gomá, and explained to the Pope the reasons behind his refusal to sign: the letter stated that the Church was free under Franco—in his view it was

---

* P. 108: Eyre and Spottiswoode edition, though not in 1965 when his book was reprinted as a paperback. I have reason to believe that these documents were fabricated in the Propaganda Department. The question whether Franco did or did not forestall a Communist Spain can be argued, and in my view, answered, without reference to them.

† To quote only one example: it was not till the commemoration of the fiftieth anniversary of the Easter Rising that the people of Britain were given facts on which they could make a fair judgement of the event.

enslaved: it said that in Franco's Spain justice was well administered: Bishop Mújica had "long lists of fervent Christians and exemplary priests murdered without trial". Cardinals Vidal and Segura did not sign either—but the forty-one bishops in Franco's Spain did. It was dated 1st July 1937.

Not all the signatories were enthusiastic about it: it was the omissions which worried some rather than what was said: but it would seem they took refuge in the doctrine of the lesser evil. Socialists, Communists and Anarchists and even Liberals could not be expected to allow the Church to survive. Franco might seem to enslave the Church, but he was still "a son of the Church", and the Church in Spain had survived the tyranny of a dozen kings who did not know where to draw the line between the things that are Caesar's and those that are God's.

There is certainly no published evidence that Franco seriously contemplated a break with Rome during the Civil War; yet he appears to have listened patiently to Faupel's reminder that those very Spanish rulers "under whom the country experienced its greatest prosperity, such as Charles V and Philip II, had forbidden any encroachment by the Popes and, on the contrary, had imposed their will on them; while in the periods of Spain's greatest weakness, interference by the Vatican had been the strongest"; and Franco is said to have replied "that this applied also to the present".[19] Again, in his broadcast on 1st October after his appointment as Head of State, Franco had said that though the State as such would have no official religion (*sin ser confesional*) "recognising the tradition of the nation and the religious sentiment of the over-whelming majority of Spaniards", it would seek a concordat with the Catholic Church "which would not infringe the liberty of the State to carry out its specific functions".[20] These words, in the light of the thinking of some Falangists and other nationalists, sounded ominous to some churchmen. For although Jose Antonio had advocated a separa-tion of Church and State such as the Popular Front had brought about, some of his followers, realising the strength of Catholic tradition and sentiment in the Spanish people had seen the logic of a State Church in a nationalist state. There were churchmen not unaware of this develop-ment; and at least one bishop signed Gomá's letter because he believed that the Church would be able to guide Franco by private admonish-ment while public opposition would turn him away from the Church —or towards the "national church" which would have pleased his German allies.

Franco, by 1st July 1937, had won his first major political victory, and this too had a bearing on the bishops' desire to be heard speaking with one voice. He was by then Head of a one-Party or more accurately of a no-Party State.

Franco could conceive of only one Spain: a united one. A united Spain had led to greatness: greatness had given her liberty. Or turning the matter the other way about: Spain had to be free: that is to say it had to be a Spain which would be able to to stand up to attempts at dictation from any other nation, and not at the beck and call of Moscow or Berlin, Rome, London or Paris—Washington barely counted in those days. So to be free, however, it had to be great: great in the sense that other nations were then measured as great—by the territorial expansion of their colonial empires, by their industrial and commercial power and by their visible military might. So to be great it had to be united.

When no power had told Spain what to do, when Spain had ruled half the world, there had been a unity of religion, language and political organisation: this therefore was the unity to be restored. It followed that non-Catholics would not be tolerated beyond what good relations with foreign powers (Germany at that time) demanded; that there would have to be one language and therefore no Basque or Catalan: and that political life would have to be *organica*—that is organised, well-ordered, regimented. Parties implied division.[21]

Among the millions who by choice, geographical accident or surrender, lived in the zone captured by the insurgents, there were only three political groupings recognisable as such by October 1936. The Popular Front parties were proscribed: the Catholic Party, *Accion Popular*, and all its fellows in Gil Robles' *C.E.D.A.* had ceased to exist within a few weeks of the rising. The survivors were the *Renovación Española*, the Alfonsist Monarchist party to which the murdered Calvo Sotelo had belonged—numerically very small; the Carlists who had increased in number but only slightly since the rising had commenced; and the Falangists who were rapidly becoming a mass party. Franco, rejecting his brother Nicolas' suggestion of a Franquista Party on the lines of Primo de Rivera's short-lived experiment, long considered how to make them one. In spite of German pressure to act with speed, he allowed all three to go their ways for the rest of 1936 and into 1937, now appearing to favour the Falange, now the others.[22] His one move in 1936 was on 20th December when, hearing that the Carlist leader, Fal Conde, had set up a Royal Military Academy, he ordered him to leave the country within 48 hours. Later he told the German Ambassador that he had indeed contemplated having Fal Conde executed[23] but restrained himself lest the act should have affected the morale of the *Requetés* among his forces.

The expulsion of Fal Conde left the Carlists without the dynamic leader who somehow had obfuscated the fact that there was now no direct line Carlist pretender. The aged Alfonso Carlos, whose claim to the throne as a descendant of the Prince whom the Carlists called Charles V of Spain was unquestionable, had died childless in Vienna on 28th September. His nephews could succeed only if the Salic Law which the Carlists maintained applied in Spain were broken, as it had been broken when Isabel II had ascended the throne. He had chosen one of them, Jaime of Bourbon-Este as Prince Regent: but this Jaime was almost as remote as Prince Rupert of Bavaria to the latter-day Stuart supporters.

With Fal Conde's expulsion the leadership of the Carlists in Spain devolved on the comparatively docile Count of Rodezno. With the knowledge and approval of Franco, Rodezno began negotiations with Falangists to establish the bases for a fusion of their respective parties.

The Falangists too were without a leader, and divided among themselves. Officially they all still believed that Jose Antonio was alive (he had been shot on 20th November in Alicante). The Falange provincial leaders had formed a Junta among themselves after the war had started, giving its Secretary-Generalship to a Santander mechanic, Manuel Hedilla. By the beginning of 1937, however, several of the Junta members had come to the conclusion that Jose Antonio was dead, and that Hedilla lacked the qualities of a national leader. It was with these members that Rodezno talked. Several weeks of conversations and correspondence produced nothing of lasting value.

At the end of February 1937 Franco welcomed to Salamanca Ramon Serrano Suñer, accompanied by his wife Zita (Franco's wife's sister) and their two children. His own wife and daughter had also joined him there recently. They had not been placed on the liner which would have taken them to France or Germany but had remained in the Canaries. Zita and Carmen Polo, not having seen each other for a year, had much to talk about; and so had Franco and his brother-in-law. Serrano had escaped from Madrid's Model Prison. He had witnessed the execution of Fernando Primo de Rivera, Ruiz de Alda and his own two brothers.[24] These executions had confirmed him in his hatred of 'democracy'; and as he believed that his brothers had been caught because they had been refused asylum by the French Embassy, France had become his implacable enemy as well.

What Serrano Suñer had to report confirmed the suspicion that Jose Antonio Primo de Rivera was also in fact dead.

Franco gave his brother-in-law the task of investigating the political situation and of reporting back to him. Serrano saw the Cardinal, the Count of Rodezno and General Mola. He had interviews with Falangists. Reporting back he delivered Franco a long lecture in the garden of the Bishop's Palace in Salamanca which was then his headquarters. The import of his discourse was that none of the existing parties was suitable for the new Spain, and what was required was a synthesis. Franco listened patiently. When Serrano had finished he produced his own annotated copy of the Falange basic points and of various speeches by Falangist and Carlist leaders. Franco pointed out the obvious similarities; neither party had any use for parliamentary rule; both advocated authoritarianism; both wanted social reforms. This far Franco was with both.

The matter might have rested there for months—Franco was never in a hurry—but for two circumstances. There were clashes between Carlist and Falangist militias in the back areas, and in the forward (although all were now subject to military authority) not enough co-operation between them when on each other's flanks. The second circumstance was the inordinate interest then being paid by Germans to Falangist affairs, and the very close friendship of some Falangist leaders with members of the Nazi Party. In this inter-relationship Franco's very position as Head of State and Supremo was threatened.

Franco was not a general according to German standards. Weighed in the balance of Nazi ideals he was wanting as a Head of State. He was not of the people, as Hitler was. He was too friendly with the clergy and the Monarchists. The Nazis had no use for either. "Franco's chief opponents were the German political and military agents at his side, from the Ambassador-General Faupel downwards. The truth, which I noticed immediately, was that the German support was not for Franco but the Falange." Thus the Italian Ambassador Cantalupo:[25] "I came to the conclusion that the Germans—the very Ambassador himself—were prepared to organise a coup against Franco. Of the despatches I wrote at the time I choose two. On 8th March I sent Ciano the following: '... the German attitude of reserve not merely about Spain's international policy but about Franco himself appears more marked ...' and the second is a sheet of notes of a conversation with the German

Ambassador before I left Spain: 'Germany is making further help to Franco conditional on his handing over all political power to the Falange before he enters Madrid.' "

The Germans who had ample means of knowing of Jose Antonio's execution—a Nazi Party member had tried to rescue him from Alicante earlier—saw from December onwards on the one hand a general who would not do as he was told either in the conduct of the war or in the matter of economic concessions, and on the other a mass party with ideals like to the Nazis but without a Führer. Nazi Party propaganda was distributed among likely proselytes. Their most valuable convert to full Nazism was a journalist, Victor de la Serna, but he was more suitable for the role of a Goebbels than a Hitler. They chose to back Hedilla. Hedilla, either on his own account, or encouraged by de la Serna, now chose to make a bid for full power over the Falange. This immediately antagonised other members of the Junta. They would have none of Hedilla as their leader, and unable to agree among themselves as to whom to have instead argued for the appointment of a Triumvirate in accordance with their Party's statutes. They appealed to Franco. Franco cryptically told them to refrain from violence.

On 11th April, a Sunday, Faupel was summoned to Franco's presence. He reminded Faupel of the insignificance of the Falange at the time of the rising. "Only after the beginning of the nationalist movemend led by Franco had the Falange, with considerable assistance from nationalist-minded officers obtained a great number of adherents and thereby its present importance." Hedilla, Franco told Faupel, was not a leader. He was surrounded by a whole crowd of ambitious young men who influenced him instead of being influenced and led by him. Faupel then heard from Franco's own lips how he had dealt with Fal Conde at the first sign of insubordination. Franco having now consulted Queipo de Llano in Seville, intended to "fuse [the Falange and Monarchist Parties] into one Party, the leadership of which he would himself assume".

Faupel did not inform Berlin of this Sunday conversation for three days—a circumstance which strengthens the suspicion that Franco did not merely inform him of what he proposed to do but intimated that he would stand no further intrigue from the Germans. If it was so, Faupel took the hint. On the Tuesday he saw the Nazi Party representative at the Embassy and the Italian Danzi, and they agreed that "in spite of all [their] inclinations towards the Falange", in a clash between Franco and the Falange they would support Franco.[26]

On the night of the Wednesday a supporter of Hedilla went with a bodyguard to the hotel in which Hedilla's chief rival Sancho Dávila was staying with friends. Shooting broke out. The friend and one opponent of Hedilla's was killed.

Now was Franco's moment to act. With charges of affray and homicide hanging over all the prominent Falangists, he allowed them to meet among themselves, squabble and even on 18th April to elect Hedilla as their national leader. On the very day, however, Franco broadcast a speech.

> In the sacred name of Spain and in the name of all who have died through the centuries for a Great, United, Free and world-wide Spain, I address myself to our people to tell it:
> We are in the midst of a war which takes on with every new day evermore the character of a crusade, of a historically important event, and of a struggle vital to peoples and civilisations. . . . With a clear understanding and firm conviction in my mission in Spain at this moment, and in accordance with the will of all Spanish combatants, I ask of you one thing: unity—[*unificación*]. Be one to end the war quickly: to embark on the great task of peace, to crystalize in the new State the thought and nature of our national revolution. . . .[27]

After referring to himself as the man to whom God had entrusted the life of Spain, he interpreted the history of his country as a constant movement towards the better—in spite of occasional retrogressions: a movement towards the integration which it was now his destiny to effect. He praised in turn Primo de Rivera, the JONS, Jose Antonio and the Falange whose dead he said were "martyrs"; and then, significantly not the Carlists, or the *Comunión Tradicionalista* as they called themselves collectively, but Navarre with "its universalist Spanish and imperial tradition . . . its unbreakable faith in God and great love for our Motherland". And so he continued at some length, at times apparently subscribing to Falangist doctrines, at others to such Carlist ideals as independent universities, and Catholicity: here attacking Liberalism and democracy, there Bolshevism. In future nothing would divide Spain.

> When the prestige of our nation makes her worthy of the respect of other nations: when our ships, powerful and majestic, once again fly the flag of our motherland on the high seas; when our aircraft cross the firmaments and make evident the resurgence of Spain; when Spaniards, all of you, shall uplift your arms and raise your hearts in homage to the motherland; when no Spanish hearth shall be in want of fire and bread and the joy of

life—then shall we say to our fallen and our martyrs: your blood has borne fruit. . . .

What this speech of 2,000 words was to mean in the short term was made clear in a rather shorter decree published the following day. All parties were abolished. (The Alfonsists' *Renovación* had wisely entered into voluntary liquidation a few days previously.) The Falange and *Requetés* were fused "into a single national political entity" which *for the moment* was to be called the *Falange Española Tradicionalista y de las Juntas de Ofensiva Nacional-Síndicalistas*. This organisation would be the intermediary between society and the State. Its principal purpose would be to inform the State of the opinions of the people, and to disseminate among the people the thought of the State. The organisation would be structurised. At the top there would be a National Council, topped by a Secretariat, and at the very summit the Head of the State. With this amalgamation of the old Parties there would be no separate militias but one single National Militia subject to military command. Its Commander-in-Chief would be the Head of State.

Hedilla was present at Franco's side as the decree was read. Subsequently a telegram was intercepted, to the provincial leaders of the old Falange, ordering them to accept no orders except from "superior authority". It was allegedly sent by Hedilla, and interpreted as meaning that Hedilla had ordered them to accept no orders from Franco unless channelled through him. If so, it was a direct defiance of Franco's own telegram through the Civil Governors that they were to follow only Franco.[28]

Whether the telegram was genuine or no, or whether the interpretation was correct, Hedilla was arrested with twenty other Falangists. He was tried and condemned to death. The others received various terms of imprisonment. Faupel pleaded with Franco to reprieve Hedilla and even asked Berlin to back him. Berlin refused, but Franco did in fact commute the sentence to one of life imprisonment.* Thereafter, with only minor whimpers, Carlists put on the blue shirt of the Falange and the Falangists donned the red beret of the Carlists, as decreed by the union of their militias. They exchanged their old Falange and Carlists membership cards for those of the new *F.E.T. y de las JONS*. No man not a member of the new organisation could hope for political advancement, so Civil Servants and others who had hitherto steered clear of either party joined the new group. Franco gave it an *idearium* under

* Hedilla was released in 1946.

twenty-six points superficially resembling Primo de Rivera's twenty-seven. The latter, however, had been the work of a political thinker—even if a woolly thinker. Franco's twenty-six were the work of a general who believed in "the supreme reality of Spain", in the right of Spain to be the equal of any European nation in wealth and military power and in a society organised as fully as an army, with all its branches working in conjunction and in support of each other. The nation being an army, it had to be disciplined and capable of hardship, but for that reason also one which should be well fed, well housed, well clothed, well equipped and with no enormous gap between the wealth of the private and the General.*

With Franco's creation of an army of his own, with the Church's declaration in his favour and with his fashioning of the Falange into a body to his own image, it became customary to say that Franco's rule rested on three pillars: the Army, the Falange and the Church. Neither in this beginning nor at any time during the rest of Franco's long rule was the situation ever as simple as that. In the Spring of 1938, and to his horror, the Nazi Von Stohrer[29] saw priests familiarly frequenting the household of the Head of the State. There were also others then writing ingenious books to confirm the already convinced that Franco's cause was unquestionably morally righteous: among them even two Jesuits, grateful that their order was being allowed to return. Cardinal Gomá worked indefatigably at home and abroad to build up the figure of Franco as that of a Christian Gentleman. Behind that façade nevertheless there were always "troublesome priests" at work: and they would not always limit their actions to "behind the scenes".

As for the *Falange Española Tradicionalista*, between the concept and the reality there would also always be a hiatus. The unity which Franco imposed remained as superficial as that of Isabella and Ferdinand. As the one crown covered the disunity of Aragon and Castille, so within the *Movimiento* there would always be a fissure between the Falangists and the Carlists. Again, as the crown of Castille in itself hid the real divisions between Asturias, Leon and Castille, so there were to be for a generation to come three types of Falangists: first those who had been in the party before the rising, who had worn the Falangist blue shirt of old (they were known as the *Camisas Viejas*) and who continued to subscribe to the "pure doctrine" of Jose Antonio: secondly those who had adopted the shirt between the rising and 19th April 1937 "to save their skins":

---

* A Spanish private received as much as a British private at that time, but a Spanish General only about a quarter of a British General's salary.

and thirdly those forced into it thereafter, the Alfonsist Monarchists and the one-time members of centre and right-wing parties. It was not merely as Faupel said[30] that while one can make a brigade out of two regiments by an order, the merging of two parties takes time, but also that Franco's military conception of Spain and Spaniards enfolded only a small part of the Spanish heritage and tradition. Spain could never be made totalitarian in the strict sense without violence to the Catholic concept of the human person; but even in the loose sense in which Franco used the word, as a synonym for "well ordered, like a human body, its members being in harmony one with another, informing the brain and being motivated by the brain", it was alien to Spanish individualism. Franco, of course, knew this, and realised that it would be his task never to allow any group to become too discontented, or too sure of itself. Though in public he recognised thereafter no division and no party but his all-embracing *Movimiento*, in practice he would always be conscious of its internal divisions, especially in the composition of his Cabinets. It was in February 1938 that he replaced his technical Junta with what was recognisably a government—his first. Its composition was to satisfy everyone and no one. Franco became his own Prime Minister. He appointed the sixty-two-year-old Count Jordana, a retired general, one-time High Commissioner in Morocco and ex-member of Primo de Rivera's government, as his Vice-Premier and Foreign Minister. Jordana was a man of liberal views, a Monarchist, and to the extreme chagrin of the Germans, Anglophile. As his Minister of Home Affairs Franco picked the seventy-six-year-old General Martinez Anido who in the few remaining months of life left to him after his appointment proved that his earlier rigour in the pursuit and suppression of violence with violence remained unimpaired in his advanced age. Indeed, even the German Ambassador spoke of Police Minister Martinez Anido's "terror" as "unbearable".[31]

The Ministers of Finance, Public Works, and Industry and Commerce were specialists—the last was Franco's old school friend, Suances, who had made a name for himself in business after leaving the Navy. Franco gave the Ministries of Education, Labour and Agriculture to old-style Falangists, but that of Justice to the Carlist Count of Rodezno. The portfolio of *Gobernación*, with a role almost that of a Deputy Prime Minister, went to his brother-in-law and neo-Falangist Serrano—the Cuñadisimo.★

★ *Cuñado* means brother-in-law. The satirical implications of the superlative are obvious.

Franco left his brother-in-law to work out the implementation of the Decree of Unity, and thus it was that Spain took on the outward trappings of Fascism. Serrano had a genuine admiration for Mussolini's Italy, and for a long time he saw in Germany under Hitler a model to be envied though not necessarily copied. Franco allowed Serrano to do as he wished and the German Ambassadors to organise visits to Germany from which youths came back impressed with the ultra-efficiency of Hitler's Germany. Nevertheless, there were few true converts to Nazism. As Serrano said, "it would have been very useful to our ends if these youthful and ardent organisers had taken the trouble of translating their experiences into Spanish terms".[32] Nevertheless, the first major act of legislation, the Labour Charter issued in March 1938,[33] was Franco's in conception and ideology, and Serrano's only in so far as he as a lawyer edited it. It was a Law worthy of any enlightened British Labour leader. It introduced security of tenure for tenant farmers, fixed minimum wages, and maximum hours of work for all workers, social insurance and family allowances and holidays with pay. Alas for the intention, careless or incompetent editing left many a loophole: and for many years Spanish wages would be the second lowest in Western Europe; but then again production per man would be equally low. For the real economic problem of Spain was not so much that wealth was badly distributed (this was true) but that even if it had been properly distributed, there would not have been enough of it to go round: and the war in progress was further reducing that national wealth. Three-quarters of a million able-bodied men were engaged in a destructive occupation in Franco's Spain and close on half a million on the other side: and the peak had not yet been reached.

The Army, that is the officers, were at all times far more solidly behind Franco than the Church or the Falange. Yet there were dissidents even in the armed services. The next attack on Franco's concept of unity came, in fact, from an army general.

Yague, whose Corps had suffered heavy casualties taking Lerida on 3rd April,* ordered his troops to take up defensive positions along the banks of the River Segre down to its junction with the Ebro, and hastened to Burgos. He had been invited to attend the celebrations of "a year of unity". There he made a speech in which he spoke with feeling of the fighting qualities of his own troops and of the enemy, and he described the Germans and Italians as "beasts of prey". Had he stopped there, Franco might have welcomed such plain speaking. He

---

* See Chapter 10, p. 289.

was still angry over Mussolini's air raids. He was also putting out feelers to have the Condor Legion withdrawn provided that they left their aircraft and equipment behind.[34] The Germans, for their part, were pressing Franco for more than "very reassuring statements" that the new mining law which after months of discussion was still in draft form would not be interpreted in any way prejudicial to their interests. Yague went on to speak also of the social reforms needed—here he was over-stepping the mark, but as a Falangist he could be excused; but when he went on to attack the imprisonment of Hedilla and other Falangists as a miscarriage of justice, his speech became a very challenge to Franco's authority and an act of rank insubordination. Yague was confined to Burgos and kept there by Franco for some weeks wondering whether he would be court-martialled.[35]

Franco had need, however, of every available senior officer at that moment.

With the division of the enemy into two, the Generalissimo had the choice of liquidating quickly either the northern half or the southern half.

The conquest of the northern half would deny his enemy easy access to further help from abroad. It would place Barcelona and the industrially rich area of Catalonia in his hands. It would shorten his front by over two hundred miles. However, it would not all be gain. As Stohrer reported repeatedly to Berlin[36] 40 per cent of the people in the conquered territory were "politically unreliable". The proportion in Catalonia was likely to be substantially higher. Mussolini's terror raids had not helped Franco (nor had Franco's decree prohibiting the speaking of Catalan). Troops, therefore, would be required in quantity to keep the area quiet. Again, an advance from the line of the Ebro and Segre would mean either using all the corps which had been in action for a considerable length of time, and some of which (like the Marroqui and Italian) were exhausted, or bringing up fresh troops with inadequate battle experience.

The conquest of the southern half would shorten the front by a full five hundred miles. It was not unreasonable to hope that if Valencia, a mere sixty miles south of the breakthrough to the coast, were taken, it would be unnecessary to fight for every inch of the remaining territory. The Castilla and Galicia Corps with eleven divisions between them would be enough for this operation. The other Corps along the Ebro could remain unmoved. With the natural valley of the river to protect them, half their divisions could be put at rest. But as against all this the drive to Valencia would be over the formidable Sierra of the Maestrazgo.

Whether he turned north or south Franco expected the enemy to be demoralised and short of supplies after their defeat. Several of his senior commanders urged him to go north. He chose to go south. In retrospect it is easy to see that this was a mistake. Franco, however, must not be credited with all the blame.

A breach was quickly made, but then torrential rain began to fall. When the rain cleared, the enemy were discovered to have strong fighter and anti-aircraft gun protection. They had plenty of ammunition.

This was by no means what Franco had expected. He back-pedalled on the withdrawal of the Condor Legion. The Germans, however, had allowed the Legion to "run down": and at the end of May its front line strength was down to 150 aircraft and the gun linings of its powerful 88 mm guns were worn out.[37] Franco had known that Daladier of France had been allowing since early April Russian and other ships to use the French canals so as to defeat his blockade of the Straits of Gibraltar and avoid the Italian submarines operating on his behalf in the Mediterranean: but the extent of the war material which poured in through France was a surprise to him. The enemy was reinforced by at least 300 fighters and bombers and other equipment totalling 25,000 tons[38] and some of this came from Germany.[39] Thus, at a vital moment when Franco might have brought the war to a rapid conclusion, his ally denied him the help he required and even helped his opponents. This was, of course, in accordance with the decisions of the Hossbach Conference.* More than that, Munich was only four months away.

The Russian aircraft operated from northern airfields in support of the southern sector. The transport by ship of ammunition from Barcelona to Valencia or Alicante proved easy by night. Though Franco asked the Italians and Germans to bomb the ports, the bombers were more successful in hitting British cargo ships taking on citrus fruit than in sinking the ammunition coasters.

The German diplomatic moves in the period May–July 1938 are particularly fascinating. At the beginning of May, as Franco becomes aware of the extent of the new supplies reaching his enemy, his troops have been brought to a halt and he begins to back-pedal on the withdrawal of the Condor Legion[40] and Stohrer broaches the subject of an Hispano-Germanic Treaty of Friendship. Franco encourages Stohrer

* See Chapter 10, p. 284 and note.

into the belief that he is ready to give the subject favourable consideration. Berlin instructs Stohrer "to commence negotiations now" and presents a draft which had been approved by Hitler a month earlier but which was not to be put forward until a suitable opportunity occurred. Jordana assures Stohrer that the draft is to Franco's liking, but raises time-consuming minor objections.[41] The situation brightens. Ribbentrop orders Stohrer not to press the Treaty since the Spaniards seem to be in no hurry about it. Hitler after all is more anxious to have commercial advantages. Stohrer, having heard that Franco is about to sign the long-pending new law on mining concessions, wants a copy of the draft—which is not given him—and to discuss the matter with Franco personally. The military situation however is still improving. Stohrer is not allowed to see Franco. The law is published. Foreign companies are not to be allowed more than a 40 per cent holding in Spanish mines. Germany is not satisfied. Jordana points out the clause which mentions the possibility of greater foreign holdings in special circumstances and if expedient: he speaks vaguely of the fact that foreign participation higher than 40 per cent could mean 90 or even 100 per cent. The matter is left in abeyance.

In the meantime, however, Volkmann had become worried about his Condor Legion. Berlin had to make up its mind. It had either to be withdrawn or put back into a fighting condition. By mid-June Volkmann reported that it had only sixteen serviceable fighters left and that they were being outnumbered three and four to one. Against such odds he was not prepared to send out bombers in support of ground troops. Kindelan told him that Spanish pilots were prepared to fly them. Volkmann asked for and received permission from Berlin to let the Spaniards do so. Berlin did finally decide to send out new supplies: to have withdrawn the Legion because it had suffered heavy casualties would have looked like a defeat for the Luftwaffe and this could not be countenanced; but the decision came too late to influence the military operations before August. Stohrer was instructed to impress upon Franco how heavy were the sacrifices which Germany was making on his behalf.

At the end of the third month of fighting on the east coast, Franco's troops were at long last over the Maestrazgo. He had sent in the Garcia-Valiño divisions in the June to back those of the Castilla and Galicia corps, and at the beginning of July he sent in the two Italian and the mixed Italian-Spanish divisions after them. Together they broke through what was called the iron ring protecting Valencia between

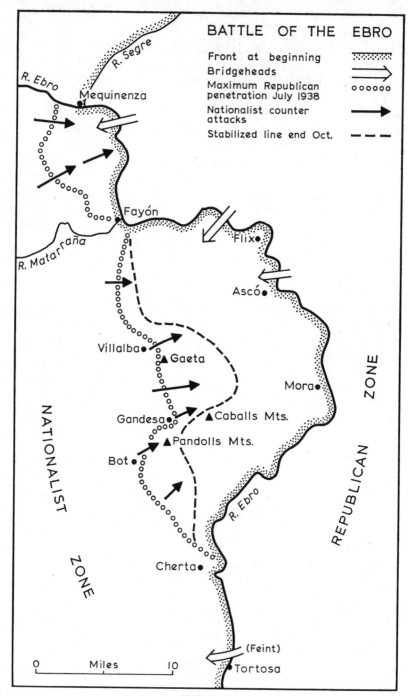

BATTLE OF THE EBRO

Front at beginning
Bridgeheads
Maximum Republican penetration July 1938
Nationalist counter attacks
Stabilized line end Oct.

R. Segre

R. Ebro

Mequinenza

Fayón

R. Matarraña

Flix●

Ascó●

Villalba●

▲Gaeta

Mora●

Gandesa●

▲Caballs Mts.

▲Pandolls Mts.

Bot●

R. Ebro

NATIONALIST

ZONE

REPUBLICAN ZONE

Cherta●

0   Miles   10

(Feint)

Tortosa●

MAP II

18th and 23rd July. Valencia was still twenty miles away, but there was no further major obstacle and it was downhill all the way. Its capture seemed inevitable.

Franco's divisional commanders reported that all was quiet on the Ebro front. They were wrong. The enemy had been far from inactive all this time in the northern sector. A strike force of between 100,000 and 120,000 men had been assembled with about 250 field guns and a number of pieces of heavier calibre. They had acquired from France inflatable rubber boats and pontoons for bridge building.*

At a quarter past midnight on the morning of 25th July, the Feast of St. James, this army freshly equipped moved into action at numerous points across the Ebro, from its junction with the Segre at Mequinenza down to Amposta forty-five miles down river. Franco, in preparing for the final assault on Valencia and a subsidiary operation east of Merida, had denuded Ebro of defenders, confident in the river as a barrier. The whole of this sector was manned by Yague's Marroqui Corps, two divisions up and one in reserve. Equally to the point, the division in the north was very badly deployed, all its positions being under observation by the enemy, and Yague appeared to have had no idea of what was happening directly across the river from him. The enemy established three bridgeheads (see sketch map). From the southernmost, near the mouth of the river at Amposta, they were quickly ousted. At the northern end they broke through to a depth of about five miles in the ten-mile stretch between Mequinenza and Fayon. The middle bridgehead, immediately south of Fayon, was a major breakthrough. A third of Yague's northern division was captured there. More important still, the commanding heights of the Caballs and Pandolls mountains fell to the enemy. Yague's reserve division held the enemy before Gandesa. Franco rushed seven divisions which he had in reserve nearby to close the gap. By 2nd August the breakthrough had been contained: but the advantage of the ground was with the enemy.

Franco now ordered the liquidation of the northern bridgehead. The task was given to Yague, who had been called severely to task for his

* General Barroso, a popular figure in French army circles during his time in Paris as Military Attaché, is certain that the enemy had French officers to supervise their use. Though General Vincente Rojo planned the battle that followed, a detailed examination of its course is so much in the style of the French theory and practice of a "lutte pour les observatoires" that the question must arise as to how far it was conducted under French army professional advice. Unfortunately General Rojo died a few days before I hoped to discuss this battle with him in detail beyond what he had written in his book España Heroica (BA, 1942): he had already given me to understand that there was much that he had left unsaid.

errors. He redeemed himself on 6th and 7th August. The enemy lost 900 dead, 3,000 prisoners and had possibly 2,000 wounded.

For the next stage Franco's original plan may be explained in this way. He looked upon the enemy in the major bridgehead as contained by his own men on the north-south line between Fayon and Cherta, and by the great arc of the River Ebro between those two towns. If the Ebro were kept under constant aerial and artillery bombardment, the 80 to 100,000 men in the area would be trapped as in a bag. To draw the strings tight, he wanted his troops to proceed on the two flanks. On hearing of the breakthrough on 25th July he had merely moved over to a map and said: "I am inclined to let the enemy penetrate as deeply as possible, keeping firm the two ends of the breach, then draw tight the bag and give battle withn it so as to wear out the Red Army and to finish it off once and for all."[42] He now proposed to do this. He knew of the enemy's determination to keep the high ground they had gained. He realised that wresting those heights from a determined enemy would be an expensive operation. The plan however was too revolutionary for Yague and his own Chief-of-Staff Vigon. They appear to have influenced some at least of the divisional commanders. Franco agreed to compromise. The Italian and German airforces were to keep the bridges under constant attack. After minor adjustments to improve his points of observation, he gave Yague four divisions and Garcia-Valiño three to deny the enemy the road linking Fayon and Cherta.* No attempt, however, was to be made by the infantry to advance without considerable artillery and air bombardment. Franco gave the two corps 47 field batteries, 20 medium and 2 heavy batteries, a concentration of fire power never before attempted in Spain.

Franco's conception was in a sense beyond the technical possibilities of the forces at his disposal. The German and Italian bomb aimers had many more misses than hits on the bridges.† As a prerequisite to the economic use of such numbers of artillery, the "white" forces would had have to have had instrumentation such as was employed at Alamein. Nevertheless, the first attack begun on 3rd September was successful. The enemy was shattered. The seven divisions reached their objectives for that attack. They renewed the offensive thirteen days later, and again forged ahead. Rojo had organised a first-class defence system in

---

* The Corps were given the names *Marroqui* and *Maestrazgo*, but only one of the divisions of the former had Moroccan troops while one division under Garcia-Valiño was under the command of the now Colonel Mizzian.

† The ratio is said to have been 500 to 1.

depth, but the artillery was destroying it inexorably. There was then a long pause. On 16th October, however, Franco gave the general order for seven enveloping movements to exterminate the enemy in what remained of the bridgehead. On 30th October the seven divisions concerned began the attack, preceded by the fire of eighty-seven batteries —over 500 guns. Sixteen days later there was not one Red Army fighting man left on the west of the Ebro. Franco's forces had lost 41,000 men; the enemy at least 70,000.[43]

Franco had vindicated his methods. The International Brigades, the cream of the Red Army, had suffered appalling casualties. Franco had in fact destroyed an army, for the 30,000 men who had got away were men broken in spirit by the weeks of heavy shelling, and the enemy had lost its newest and best equipment.

Now Franco fought this battle in the face of extreme difficulties. In Rome, Mussolini unable to understand why Franco was proceeding so slowly, said to Ciano: "Put on record in your book, that today, 29th August, I prophesy the defeat of Franco. Either the man doesn't know how to make war or he doesn't want to. The Reds are fighters— Franco is not."[44] Franco's difficulties were threefold. First, several of Franco's Generals, Yague the chief among them, did not share Franco's new views on the value of artillery nor did they respect the lives of their men to a similar extent. "They don't understand, they don't understand," Franco had told his friends, "I've got the pick of the Red Army in the bag." There was no need for frontal attacks with heavy casualties. There was no point in recovering a few square miles of territory for its own sake.[45] Disagreements at G.H.Q. were so violent that even the Italian and German Attachés heard of them.[46] Franco's second difficulty was a shortage of ammunition.[47] It was this shortage which prevented him from bringing into action more divisions than those he did and which held up the operations repeatedly during August and September once he had acceded to his generals' demand for action. He was not short of men. Indeed his army had grown too fast for his factories. But during September he received no ammunition for his heavier calibre guns from Germany—because of the third reason.

The third reason for the hold-up was the Munich crisis. It was most inconsiderate of Germany not to bear in mind Spanish interests in choosing that moment to take Europe to the brink of war.[48] As Franco saw the situation, if the Maginot and Siegfried Lines were what they were alleged to be (actually since his experience with the Bilbao "iron ring" he had come to the conclusion that defence in depth and not a

"line" was the way to defeat an attack in modern warfare, and he could
see the value of such defence before him in the Ebro battle so that he
had his doubts about the French fortification) neither France nor
Germany would attack each other directly. Either Germany would go
through Belgium again, or France would seek to turn Spain into the

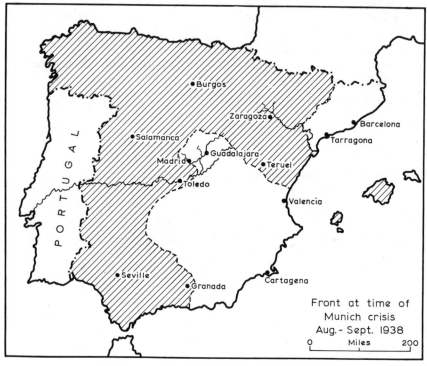

Front at time of
Munich crisis
Aug.- Sept. 1938

0   Miles   200

MAP 12

European battlefield. Alternatively, his enemy might declare war on
Germany, thus becoming the ally of France and Britain, and again
Spain would become the battlefield of the great powers. He would have
none of it. Immediately he was approached by France[49] as to what his
attitude might be, he said that Spain would remain neutral. Subsequently he informed Germany that he was about to declare his
neutrality to Britain and France and Jordana supplied specious arguments which momentarily smoothed over German resentment.

    With the Munich crisis over, Germany came to the conclusion that a
total victory for Franco was in its best interests. Franco had already

turned a deaf ear to several appeals for a negotiated peace which Britain favoured. A strong Spain, the Germans reckoned, would have more in common with them than with Great Britain or France. However, any further war supplies, and Franco was asking for these, would be made conditional on an end to the shilly-shallying over the acquisition of controlling interests in mining companies and a Treaty of Friendship, if not also on the adherence of Spain to the Anti-Comintern Pact.[50] Franco quickly agreed in principle to acknowledge the debts. However, permission for a 75 per cent participation in three mining companies and 60 per cent in one other was not granted until 19th December.[51] Jordana and Stohrer signed a cultural treaty on 24th January 1939 which was never ratified.[52]* After a final rearguard diplomatic battle Spain joined the Anti-Comintern Pact, and at the end of March acceded to a Treaty of Friendship—almost a year after Hitler had approved it.

With the arrival of fresh ammunition supplied at the end of November, Franco could consider the next step. Under international agreements, the International Brigades and the part of the Italian so-called volunteer force had been withdrawn. Franco aligned along the Ebro and Segre sixteen Spanish infantry divisions, the one completely Italian still in existence and three others which were 20 per cent Italian and 80 per cent Spanish: with others in reserve a force of approximately 250,000 men supported by 565 guns. He calculated that his enemy still numbered 220,000 and that they had 250 guns and 120 armoured vehicles.

The offensive was due to start on 10th December, but bad weather led to its delay. The Papal Nuncio in the name of the Pope appealed for a truce over Christmas, but Franco gave the order for the battle to commence on 23rd December. To begin with, the fighting was tough. There was a diversionary offensive on 5th January in Extremadura which caused Franco a few anxious moments, but Barroso gathered for him enough reserves to hold the enemy without affecting the advance on the Catalan front. On 14th January Yague (now obedient to Franco's orders) captured Catalonia's second city Tarragona. After that the battle for Catalonia became a walkover in which Franco had to instruct the Italians not to waste shells against resistance which did not exist and push on.[53] Barcelona fell on 26th January 1939. There was some

---

* The clergy in Spain, now better informed on the Papacy's views on Nazism, saw dangers in the agreement. They at home, and the Vatican abroad, exerted the necessary pressures to prevent its ratification.

wanton destruction by the retreating Anarchists among the Republican troops. The roads to France were blocked by refugees. Colonel von Funck told Barroso that since these columns contained also an army in retreat, they were a military target and that in fact he had had orders from Keitel to instruct the Condor Legion to bomb and machine-gun them. There was a violent scene at Franco's headquarters—the name of Guernica was mentioned. Kindelan was told to see to it that the German aircraft did not take off. He was in fact already aware of what was afoot.* Franco allowed the refugees to escape, and with them 200,000 men. His troops captured only 60,000.

By mid-February the fighting in the north-east was over—except against isolated guerilla units who continued for months and even years to harass the conquerors. Negrin sued for peace. The Communists urged continued resistance. Franco would have nothing short of un-conditional surrender. He met offers of peace with promises of trials and punishment of "war criminals". With that he strengthened the power of the Communists. They talked of huge Russian supplies awaiting shipment at Marseilles, but, as the man who now rose to prominence in Madrid, the regular Colonel Casado pointed out, how could they be got across? Casado, seeing the people of Madrid starving all around him, his troops without shoes or overcoats and Franco massing 600,000 men for the final assault, urged surrender. Further resistance was absurd. What followed was confusion worse confounded with Communists fighting Republicans, and both resisting Franco's forces in isolated groups.†

Franco's troops entered Madrid on 28th March. His supporters within the city rose to help them in the last stages. With the news of this, Franco's civilian supporters took over the remaining large cities.

On 1 April 1939 Franco issued his last war communique:

On today's date, the Red Army having been captured and disarmed, the national troops have reached their last military objective.

The war had ended.

---

* If any German aircraft did manage to carry out Berlin's orders, there were only a few. I have had contradictory reports from refugees on this matter.

† This last "Civil War within the Civil War" is admirably summarised in Thomas, Section 75.

NOTES

1. Franco-Salgado MS. and *Centinela*, p. 312.

2. See Ch. 9, p. 231.

3. The Party claimed at the end of 1936 that it had 50,000 militiamen at the front and 30,000 in rear areas (*Arriba España*, 6th January 1937). Army records and dispositions do not substantiate the former figure. The Falange spoke also of "a million members": my figure of 200,000 for October is based on enquiries of Falangists in various cities of Spain—but even this could be an overestimate.

4. *Raza*, see Ch. I.

5. Cf. Aguirre, *De Guernica a Nueva York pasando por Berlin* (B.A., 1942), and Lizarra (Andrés María de Irujo), *Los Vascos y la Republicá Española* (B.A., 1944)

6. Cardinal Gomá's Letter, *El Caso de España*, 23rd November 1936.

7. Joint pastoral letter, 1st July 1937.

8. Iturralde in *El Catolicismo y la Cruzada de Franco*, 3 vols. (Toulouse, 1955, 1960 and 1965) proves no more, even in Vol. I, pp. 322-476, than that Churchmen were divided among themselves on the Monarchy, the Republic, Catholic parties and the nationalisms of Basques and Catalans. Iturralde in his anxiety to prove that the only real Catholic priests were Basque makes the most of these stories.

9. I Peter 2, 18.

10. As late as 1958 I came across Spaniards who still resented the tepidity for the Nationalist cause shown by members of the clergy in the first stages of the Civil War. As was to be expected Nationalist propaganda gave publicity only to the statements of those who sided with them: the other side had little use for priests or their views. A priest could be anti-Franquist without being pro-Popular Front.

11. J. Tusquets, a prolific writer of pamphlets with an astonishingly popular appeal. He was a rabid anti-Semite as well; though it is doubtful if he ever met a Jew in his life.

12. Anti-religious legislation in Mexico dated back to 1859, but the active and violent persecution which resulted in the death of several thousand laymen as well as some priests began on the eve of the accession to power of General Calles in 1924 and was intensified by him. In England the Catholic Press did keep its readers informed as far as it could of the events of which Graham Greene gave a partial picture in *The Lawless Roads* and in his novel *The Power and the Glory*. Not so the national Press—except for one front-page "story" in the *Daily Express*, published after considerable argument as to whether the persecution of Catholicism was "news". Such was the ignorance of the British

public over the Mexican persecution that the Ministry of Information provided Mr. Bernard Newman with the photographs of the execution of the
Jesuit Father Miguel Pro to illustrate his World War II lectures on spying.
He accepted them in good faith as photographs of "a German spy in Paris in
1870" until I pointed out the error. In Mr. Newman's defence I must add that
there was a superficial similarity in the uniforms of the Mexican soldiers of
the 1920s with those of the French of 1870.

13. Iturralde op. cit. II, p. 299, for the Bishop of Pamplona's protest; pp. 278-368
for a version, albeit confused and not above suspicion of bias, of the treatment
of Bishop Mújica.

14. Texts of Spanish prelates in *Ha hablado la Iglesia*. Burgos, 1937. Quoted in
part with other texts in *The Church and the Spanish War* (Spanish Information
Service 1965). Both books are partisan. The Pope's speech as reported in the
Osservatore Romano is not the pro-insurgent declaration it can be made out to
have been by careful quotation out of context. A heavily edited version of
Cardinal Gomá's *Pastorales de la Guerra de España* was published in Madrid
in 1955.

15. D.G.F.P. 168 of 27th December 1936. Cf. no. 242 of 9th April 1937 for a
reference to German and Italian pressures on the Pope. See also nos. 406
and 565.

16. D.G.F.P. 198. Iturralde III, pp. 203-9, which admits that the evidence on the
course of the negotiations is contradictory and observes that no one will be
able to know all "until the Vatican archives be opened". Other details ibid.,
pp. 217-23, D.G.F.P. 247, p. 276, Cantalupo, p. 185, Aguirre, p. 31.

17. Cf. Inaki de Aberrigoyen, *Sept mois et sept jours dans l'Espagne de Franco*
passim.

18. D.G.F.P. 264, pp. 294-5.

19. As 18, cf. D.G.F.P. 80, p. 87, 455, p. 482, and 586, p. 660. Stohrer, however,
is wrong in saying that "the *original* Falange" wanted a State Church. Jose
Antonio advocated the separation of Church and State as effected by the
Socialists. But he was right if by "original" he meant Jose Antonio's direct
heirs.

20. *Dos Discursos Historicos*. Ed. Fermat, Cadiz, 1937.

21. The above is based on Franco's numerous speeches printed in *Palabras* (Burgos,
1938). For the first complaint against the disabilities of Protestants *v.* D.G.F.P.
134.

22. Cf. D.G.F.P. 207 and 128.

23. D.G.F.P. 243, p. 268.

24. Ramon Serrano Suñer, *Entre Hendaya y Gibraltar* (Madrid, 1947), opening
chapters.

25. Op. cit., pp. 130-1. D.G.F.P. 243, p. 269.

26. Alicante rescue attemp,, D.G.F.P. 102, 104, 108. The command issued on 24th October 1926 (D.G.F.P. 108) that no Nazi was to work towards a National-Socialist revolution in Spain had long been forgotten. *Inter alia* in the German view a return to a multi-party state would lead to political instability but they required a stable Spain to reap their expected economic harvest (cf. nos. 248 and 254).

27. *Dos Discursos Historicos.*

28. D.G.F.P. 248, 252, 254, 286, 296. The main published sources are Serrano Suñer, op. cit. 47-50, and *Cartas entre cruzadas entre el Sr. D. Manuel Hedilla Larrez y el Sr. D. Ramon Serrano Suñer*, Madrid, 1947. Cantalupo, pp. 213 *ff*. For an account based on Falangist sources *v*. Payne, *Falange* (O.U.P., 1962), pp. 166 *ff*. Cf. Thomas, pp. 415-16.

29. D.G.F.P. 586, p. 661.

30. D.G.F.P. 248, p. 277.

31. D.G.F.P., p. 711.

32. Op. cit., p. 50. An often misquoted, and mistranslated, sentence.

33. A fuller summary is available in Allison Peers' *Spain in Eclipse 1937-1943* (Methuen, 1943), pp. 119-21.

34. D.G.F.P. 557, 564, 567, cf. note 62, Chapter 10. The Italian air raids appear to have infuriated Franco even more than the German on Guernica, for he believed Italy more genuinely his ally than Germany, and he was therefore all the more disillusioned. Berti had asked Franco to withdraw the two Italian divisions completely from their holding positions on the Ebro after their battering at Tortosa (D.G.F.P. 579, p. 652). Franco refused to do so before the end of May when they were taken to far away Logroño. Their amalgamation into one division was considered, but Franco had in mind their complete dismissal (private information confirmed by D.G.F.P. 576). Instead Mussolini sent reinforcements (D.G.F.P. 599, p. 683) and the number of Italian army and airforce personnel in Spain and the Balearics rose to between 37,000 and the 40,000 mentioned by Stohrer in D.G.F.P. 648 as their strength on 1st July: Stohrer was wrong in adding 8,000 reinforcements to the figure for 1st August. These reinforcements, not however 8,000, were balanced out by an equal number sent home. Ciano, *Diary 1937-38*, gives quite a different version from the German or the Spanish. Cf. pp. 126, 127, 145, 146, 149, 152, 154 for the situation up to 11th September.

35. On mining law, D.G.F.P. 561, note on p. 637, 566. Stohrer's account in D.G.F.P., pp. 658-9, of Yague's speech leaves out his comments on the Italians and Germans. In deciding what was objectionable to Franco I have followed the opinions of officers present rather than of Stohrer who was not there. Though Stohrer put quite the wrong emphasis in his report to Berlin, nonetheless it was a good dispatch insofar as it warned Berlin that the affairs

of Spain were not to be over-simplified and that the Nazis should not see a kindred spirit in Franco.

36. e.g. D.G.F.P., p. 657.

37. D.G.F.P. 575, 604.

38. D.G.F.P. 580.

39. Franco's protest through his Ambassador in Berlin is mentioned in *The International Brigades*, a booklet issued by the Spanish Government in 1953. I have been unable to establish with any certainty how much was sent, but the quantity may have been substantial. Cf. also Ciano, *Diary*, p. 162.

40. Colonel Janicke's report to Ribbentrop on 3rd June 1938 (pp. 672-4) is quite the best intelligence report in the whole of D.G.F.P., Vol. III. On withdrawal *v*. 581. On bombing of ships and ports, cf. 597-602, 605, 617-23. Not all the raids were as directed by Franco. The Germans and Italians naturally played the innocent.

41. Treaty of Friendship, D.G.F.P. 558, pp. 632-3, 559, 560, 581, 582, 583, 787. On mining: 588-91, 595, 596 (which makes one feel rather sorry for Stohrer) 603, 632, 634, 647; on Airforce: Spanish sources and D.G.F.P. 604, 606, 609, 610, 613, 624, 627, 632.

42. Franco-Salgado MS.

43. D.G.F.P. 660 comments on the lack of co-ordination between the artillery and infantry. Cf. Thomas, p. 561, for estimate of "red" casualties. The "white" total compiled from Army records is 41,414. Lightly wounded men and especially officers, however, were not usually counted as "casualties".

44. Ciano, *Diary 1937-38*, p. 148, cf. 146.

45. *Comentario*, etc.

46. Cf. D.G.F.P., 660, p. 743.

47. D.G.F.P. 685, 686; cf. 651 and 675.

48. The D.G.F.P. relevant to this are Vol. II, 597, 622, 624, 638, 641, 659; Vol. III, 656-9, 664-6, 669, 670-3.

49. General Weygand contacted General Ungria at G.H.Q. before any diplomatic moves were made (F.S.).

50. D.G.F.P., pp. 758-71, 775-92, 795-6.

51. D.G.F.P. 703.

52. D.G.F.P. 716. The clergy now better informed about the persecution of the church by the Nazis in Germany were against its ratification. There was also a Vatican protest (cf. D.G.F.P. 739). Treaty of Friendship text, 773, pp. 884-6, cf. 632-3. Comintern pact, 768.

53. Information about the Italians from General Staff officers at G.H.Q.

12

CAUDILLO *VERSUS* FÜHRER

Franco issued his last war communique from his bed. He had influenza. The illness delayed his triumphal entry into Madrid until 18th May. On the following day he presided over a sixteen-mile long march-past of 120,000 troops and a flyover of 500 aircraft. General Varela, the man risen from the ranks who twice in his lifetime had been awarded in the field Spain's equivalent of the V.C., a Grand Cross with Laurels of St. Ferdinand, pinned that coveted decoration on Franco's tunic.*

The parade filled foreign observers with misgivings. The trappings of Fascism were inescapable: the extended Roman salute—and another Roman touch, the monogram out of the word Victor; the columns flanking the saluting base blazoned each with the name Franco three times; the goose step.

Members of the all-embracing Movimiento, the *FET y de las JONS*, reacted deliriously with joy or disgust according to their particular brand of Falangism, "Spanish-ism", or traditionalism.

On 19th May Cardinal Gomá received the Victor into the Army Church of St. Barbara. Before the altar Franco recited a prayer which might have come from the lips of Cromwell with minor verbal differences:

Lord, graciously accept the effort of this people which always was Thine and which with me and in Thy name has with heroism defeated the enemy of truth of this age.

Lord God, in whose hands is all righteousness and power, lend me Thy help to lead this people to the full liberty of Dominion, for Thy Glory and that of Thy Church.

Lord, that all men may know that Jesus is the Christ, the Son of the Living God.[1]

* Franco, it must be remembered, had been recommended for it during the African campaign.

There was no unanimous Catholic reaction to this prayer. Some approved of it: some considered it heretical: some that it bordered on blasphemy. The Pope had at long last spoken—on 19th April.[2] Addressing his "very dear children of Catholic Spain with immense joy" he had congratulated them on the peace and victory "with which God has deigned to crown the Christian heroism of your faith and charity tested in so many sufferings so generously borne". He had referred to the "most noble and Christian sentiments" of the Head of State, and he had included him in his blessing. Two-thirds of the address, however, had been an exhortation to receive back into the fold with goodwill and love, patience and meekness, those who had been deceived, and for prayers for all the dead. Very few were aware that at long last the Cardinal Primate had come face to face with the reality that there was a wide gap between Franco's and his interpretation of Catholic doctrine. Shortly before the Pope's speech, the Cardinal's Advent Pastoral on the social duties of Catholics and on the Christian forgiveness of enemies had been refused publication by the *cuñadísimo*, and an appeal to the Generalissimo had been in vain.[3]

Serrano Suñer, Minister for Home Affairs, controlled the Press and police. Prisoner of war camps held about a quarter of a million men. They were the prerogative of the Army. However, there were already in existence decrees which empowered Serrano and his police to round up tens of thousands of other persons and hold them indefinitely in custody. The most comprehensive and harshest of the laws was that decreed in the February on Political Responsibilities. Under its provisions anyone over the age of fourteen who at any time from 1st October 1934 was held to have "helped to undermine public order or after 18th July 1936 to have impeded the national Movimiento ... by definite acts or by being *grievously passive*", all who had at any time belonged to any of the Popular Front bodies or to the Basque, Galician or Catalan nationalist organisations or to the Liberals, and anyone who had been a Mason (unless his membership had lapsed on 18th July 1936*) was liable to have all his goods confiscated, to be exiled to Africa, to be deprived of his nationality and to be sentenced for up to fifteen years imprisonment. In certain cases the prosecutor could demand the death penalty. Voluntary service in Franco's forces, a wound in battle while fighting on the nationalist side, the loss of a son or father on that side, and being less than eighteen years old, could be adduced as extenuating circumstances; no more.

* This let out a number of army officers.

The civil courts could not cope, so there were *ad hoc* tribunals whose members were military men or Falangists. Ciano in the July would speak with relish[4] of 200,000 "Reds" imprisoned, of 200 to 250 executions per day in Madrid, 180 in Barcelona, 80 in Seville and 10,000 awaiting execution. These figures must be treated with all the reserve that the poor fantasy-ridden Count Ciano merits. Nevertheless Serrano was out to revenge the death of his brothers, and the Falange the slaughter of the 60 per cent of their pre-war membership at the front and in the prisons of the Popular Front; while the Army wished to wipe out "the ignominy" of fellow-officers who had sided against them.[5] The desire for vengeance did not end there: it was widespread among the people.

How many were executed in the months after the end of the Civil War and into 1940 when Franco transferred his meticulous lawyer and brother-in-law, the "fanatic in bad health" as Samuel Hoare called him[6] from the Ministry of Home to that of Foreign Affairs, cannot now be established with certainty, but they may well have numbered ten thousand.[7]

Franco had handed over to the *Cuñadísimo* the conduct of internal affairs, but he was still responsible overall, as an Army commander, for the conduct of subordinates and "divisional officers". It would no longer have been in character for him to interfere in the "tactical approach" of his Minister to the problem; at the same time it was in character that he should allow the guilty, as he saw it, to be punished for their crimes. "By accepting his punishment, a guilty man becomes a new man."[8] He was attracted therefore to the work of a pre-Civil War Jesuit penologist[9] whose theories on the rehabilitation of prisoners came to be simplified into the slogan "Redemption through Work".

In outline the Jesuit had argued that the imprisonment in crowded and insanitary conditions of a person who had committed a grave crime —murder, rape and the like—was anti-social as well as anti-Christian. In his experience the men convicted of such acts had a diminished sense of responsibility. He wanted them taught a trade and given an opportunity of earning a living for their dependants, of developing their social senses while repaying the debt which society decreed they owed it.

The scores of thousands of war and political prisoners, only a small proportion of whom could be considered criminals, were now to be given a chance to "redeem themselves", and to provide a pittance for their families. They could volunteer for reconstruction work as unskilled labourers. This was not what the penologist had had in mind.

Thousands however did volunteer rather than linger at near starvation level and in abominable conditions in the gaols: and in work for which they were physically unsuitable hundreds would die. Priests among them did what they could to alleviate their sufferings and reconcile them to their religion, but there was no attempt on the part of the State to take pity on the vanquished or to seek to reunite them with the victors. Rather "the cult of the dead" was fostered. For the next twenty years every night at 10 o'clock all radio stations would broadcast a salute "to the fallen for God and Spain". From the first Jose Antonio was singled out for special worship. The Falangists painted a cross and their dead leader's name on the façade or on the side of every large church—except Seville Cathedral to which the Pope appointed Cardinal Segura on the death of Cardinal Ilundain. Cardinal Segura, at the Vatican during the long battle with Hitler and Mussolini, abhorred the Falange as a pagan abomination more dangerous to religion than Communism.[*] In the November Jose Antonio's body was transferred with ceremonies the like in grandeur the modern world had never seen,[10] from its grave in Alicante to a new place of honour in the Basilica of the Escorial, as if greater than any of the Kings of Spain. Franco presided. The Monarchists thought it sacrilege. On the anniversary of the end of the war, however, these were given hope of redress. Franco had decided to build his own Temple of the Dead where Jose Antonio would rest finally. It would be hewn out of the granite of the Guadarramas in a valley to be known as that of the Fallen. In its construction scores of those unfortunate political prisoners would die.[11]

It was not enough however to make a God of a dead hero. Serrano directed his Press to the unbridled adulation of the Caudillo. Statues were erected in his honour. His picture was placed in every public room. However, a people with cults to all the saints of the Church tended to laugh in private at this man-made god.

The material damage of the war quantitatively was not to be compared with the devastation brought about either by artillery in World War I or by shelling and aerial bombardment in World War II. The Barcelona docks were shattered. There were 183 towns, villages and hamlets to be rebuilt: in all about a quarter of a million houses had been totally destroyed. They were valued at 4,250 million pesetas (£140

---

[*] His argument ran as follows: Communism would have a man empty his mind and heart of religion, but sooner or later the victim noticed the vacuum. Falangists, Fascists and Nazis sought to fill a man's mind with a false religion, so a man would never be aware of its falsehood (conversation with author).

million). The railways had lost almost two out of every three passenger coaches, one out of five of their goods wagons and one out of every four locomotives.[12] These figures would compare extremely favourably with the "abomination of desolation" of Europe in the years to come. Both sides together were responsible for these losses to the national economy. However, the Anarchist propensity to destroy before surrender must not be forgotten. In the circumstances, therefore, the figures are a testimony to the fulfilment by Franco of his pledge to Cantalupo that he would seek to minimise the destruction of war. Farmlands suffered relatively little, but the country's life was reduced by about a third, mainly by slaughter to provide food in the Republican zone.

The material damage nonetheless was serious enough for Spain. It can be assessed as equal to a year's national income. The rebuilding would present no insurmountable difficulty, particularly once the prisoners came to be used on it. But this was not all. Nearly two million men had served at some time or other in the armed services, a serious loss to the productive manpower of the nation over the three years of war. A third of a million had been killed in battle and at the end a quarter of a million had crossed into France. This quarter of a million contained a very high proportion of the skilled workers of Spain: and Spain in 1936 had already been desperately short of skilled workers. Thus Franco's problem was three-fold: he had damage to repair; he had a three-year leeway of reduced production to make up; he had been left without the most productive of Spanish workers.

He also had two creditors—Italy and Germany—dunning him. His vanquished opponents had sent 510 tons of gold to Russia and another 30 tons to France while some at least of the exiled leaders had left Spain with millions of pesetas.[13] Franco would get the gold back from France and with it lorry loads of art treasures, but he would never recover for Spain the Russian gold. Indeed, Russia would insist that so far from owing Spain anything, 120 million dollars worth of war material had been left unpaid. The exiled leaders would live well and use their millions of pesetas on propaganda and other activities.

Among the defeated half of Spain there were many men prepared to risk imprisonment and death for sabotaging the new Spain which Franco hoped to create. Many saw nothing final in their defeat. It was merely a reverse. The convinced Marxist was as certain as ever that the dictatorship of the proletariat was as inevitable for humanity as death for the individual man. If by action against Franco a man were to hasten the advent of that millenium, what did it matter if he hastened his death?

Events in Spain were to give the anti-Franco propagandists raw material in plenty. The fair 1938 harvests of the nationalists' zone were almost, but not quite, sufficient to provide food for the whole of Spain during the Summer and Autumn of 1939. Local shortages however were inevitable. Spain's internal lines of communication had been such that a Valencia orange could be sent by sea to Covent Garden at a lower cost than overland to Valladolid; and the war, as we have seen, had deprived Spain of a large proportion of its rolling stock. Franco toured the whole of Spain urging people to produce more.

The efforts of those who obeyed in the countryside were to be vitiated. Spain entered into a long cycle of years of drought which would have brought the country into severe difficulties at any time. The 1939 harvest was poor: that of 1940 was disastrous: that of 1941 no better. Occurring at a time when the whole of Europe was at war, they left the people on the brink of starvation. All food was rationed, poor people being allowed more bread than the rich; it was considered that the rich would be able to supplement their rations anyway. Franco ordered really punitive measures against speculators and black-marketeers, with fines ranging up to £12,500 and sentences of imprisonment of up to twelve months hard labour. In Barcelona fines totalling a quarter of a million pounds were collected within a month. The word *estraperlo* returned to common use with a new meaning—black marketeering. However, too high a percentage of the public were prepared to deal in it for the police to cope—even if all policemen had been prepared to ensure the enforcement of the measures.

Here indeed was yet another of the major problems with which Franco was faced for the next twenty-five years of his rule. His police, and all his civil servants, were paid miserably low wages—as were workmen. To make ends meet, like the workers they would have had to undertake two jobs. Their irregular hours of duty, however, made it difficult where not impossible to do so. In the circumstances the temptation to accept bribes was acute: resistance to it often required heroic virtue—and in no nation has heroic virtue been widespread. The solution might have been to double the wages; but the economy of the country was far too weak to stand the cost. The number of police and civil servants might have been reduced, but they were men untrained for other occupations. Franco's problem here was not shortage of manpower but of skills. There could be no quick solution to it. Demobilisation of a third of his army and the amnesties which released several tens of thousands of prisoners from 1940 onwards had therefore only a slight effect on the economy.

The lack of the required skills went all the way up to the top. Franco's choice of his lawyer brother-in-law was in fact indicative of this shortage. Serrano could draft splendid socially revolutionary laws. Those laws, however, presupposed administrators to put them into practice, and Spain had few. For generations the universities had been turning out a plethora of lawyers, excellent doctors who could win Nobel Prizes, littérateurs and academic men; but few practical men. Practical men would have pointed out the weaknesses of those laws in their draft form, and so perhaps ensured the practicability of their enforcement. Fifteen years would pass before Franco found the pragmatic and incorruptible economists and administrators who might have made the early years of his régime very different from what they were.

Action against Franco was not the monopoly of his old enemies. One of Franco's earliest acts after the end of the war was to rid Seville of its "bad baron", Queipo de Llano. Queipo for all his arbitrariness, let it be said, had interested himself in the welfare of the smallholders: he had embarked on a building programme of houses for workers and sought to bring industry south. However, he grew ever more unpredictable, like the dictator Primo de Rivera, and his verbal indiscretions became more daring. He criticised the centralisation of power on Madrid. Thereupon, in the first months of his victory, Franco offered him honourable exile as Ambassador in Argentina. Later Mussolini agreed to his going to Rome instead. There, Serrano Suñer would publicly insult him.[14]

Four months after the end of the Civil War Franco reformed his Cabinet. General Jordana was replaced as Foreign Minister by Franco's faithful friend Colonel Beigbeder. Beigbeder was forty-nine: Jordana sixty-three. They had the same military and social background. Beigbeder, like Jordana, was a Monarchist. He was likewise pro-British. In the rest of the Cabinet also younger men replaced older, as the Falangists wanted; but Franco carefully balanced Falangist with non-Falangist, pro-British with pro-German and civilians with military men. He divided the Ministry of Defence into three. He gave General Varela, pro-British, the Ministry of War; Yague, Falangist and pro-German, the Air Ministry; and the pro-British Admiral Moreno of El Ferrol, the Navy. He put the mildly pro-German Muñoz Grandes into the job of Secretary General of the Falange. On the other hand, Jordana's office of Vice-President of the Cabinet was abolished. This gave Serrano Suñer, the one survivor from the old Cabinet into the new, still Minister of Home Affairs, even more power than before. Serrano grasped it with both hands. Gossip, never absent from Spanish politics and all the more prevalent under Press censorship, had it that the two Polo sisters[15] had fallen out, and that Franco was giving Serrano enough rope with which to hang himself. It would be years before he did.

Serrano Suñer then was the freer to carry out his intention: to design and construct a permanent régime which would carry out "an orderly and stable revolution".[16] He had long held that "the formula— single commander, single Party and a mass organisation directed by a convinced minority [*minoria creyente*]" was the only practical one for Spain. Now however he would do his best to convert Spain into a Fascist Party-State analagous to the Italian of Mussolini whom he had come to admire even more after a visit to Rome the previous June. Others would try to succeed later where Serrano would fail; but in the end, as he himself was to write[17] "the Falange never came to be the single ruling party, the exclusive base for power: far from it. There was always a counterweight of opposition—and I mean within the national side, even *right at the source of government*.* In the last analysis, the centre of gravity, the real prop of the régime—for all the outward appearances which we put up—was and would be the army. The National Army, politically undefinable, would constitute the substitute for a State that never arrived, that never finally took constitutional shape, that never truly became an organism."

Franco, for his part, would stress in speeches for almost the rest of his life his faith in Jose Antonio's principles. He would reserve his most adulatory phrases for the Falange; but in retrospect it may well be asked if he ever believed in any of them, except in so far as they coincided with his own belief in a "united, great and free Spain". Foreigners would take his words at their face value: the old Falangists never did.

Three weeks after the reform of the Cabinet, Serrano and Franco

---

* *Incluso dentro del poder*—the most telling phrase in this paragraph. It could mean merely "within the Cabinet", but it must be remembered that Serrano's book, published in 1947, had to be approved by Press censors over whom he no longer had control. (He was then a private individual even if still the Head of State's brother-in-law.) His object in writing and publishing the book was to clear his name: but there was a limit as to how far he could reveal Cabinet or family secrets.

had something more important to occupy them than internal developments. Europe was at war.

On Sunday, 3rd September 1939, Franco broadcast an appeal to the nations "whose hands could unchain a catastrophe unparalleled in history". "With the authority of one who has borne the weight of a war to free our country," he called on them "to spare other people the sufferings and tragedies that befell Spaniards." He asked them "to localise the war". He had earlier appealed to Britain and France to negotiate with Germany.

On Monday, 4th September, Franco decreed that all Spanish subjects should observe the strictest neutrality.

On 12th June 1940, two days after Mussolini had entered the war, Franco moved from neutrality to "non-belligerency", the jargon word which implied that Franco, while not at war on the side of Germany and Italy, looked favourably upon their cause.

On 23rd October 1940, Hitler met Franco at Hendaye. Hitler wanted to deny Britain the Mediterranean. He had plans for the capture of Gibraltar overland. He required Franco to come into the war on his side. Hitler was observed going away from the meeting discomforted: Franco smiling. Hitler is reported to have said: "I would rather have three or four teeth out than meet that man again."[18] His troops never went through Spain.

On 22nd June 1941, Hitler invaded Soviet Russia. Three weeks later a force of Spaniards wearing a blue-shirted uniform which was not of the Spanish Army, crossed the Pyrenees on its way to the Russian Front. The Corps was called the Blue Division.

On 17th July 1941, Franco said to the National Council of the F.E.T.: "The destruction of Communism, the terrible nightmare of our generation is now absolutely inevitable. The Allies made a mistake when they declared war, and they have lost it."

On 14th February 1942, Franco addressed a meeting of army officers. He made a fierce attack on Russia and praised Germany as "the defender of European civilisation". He then went on: "If ever the road to Berlin were open, then not merely one division of Spanish volunteers, but a million Spaniards would go there to bar the way".[19]

In 1942, as transports were seen to gather round Gibraltar, Franco mobilised his troops in Morocco. American and British troops invaded French Africa. Franco's troops did not move.

In 1943, Franco moved back to the position of neutrality. These were for Spain the key events and pronouncements of the World War II years.

Franco was inclined on balance to look with greater favour on Germany and Italy than on France and Britain for three reasons. First, as we have seen, in his Spanish interpretation of history, he saw France and Britain as the enemies of Spain through the centuries. Only once had Britain helped Spain: and that was against Napoleon. Secondly, Britain had not merely deprived Spain of numerous islands in the Caribbean, excluded her from Africa and been instrumental in the loss of the Spanish–American Empire, but by treachery she had clung on to a part of Spain—Gibraltar.[20] There was more than a grain of truth in the extreme Spanish view that Britain and France had reduced Spain to a third class power, almost a satellite, a market for finished goods and a source of cheap raw materials. Thirdly, while the British Government had remained neutral in the Civil War, Britain had allowed several thousands of her subjects to fight against him at a crucial moment. Clement Attlee, with a clenched fist, had identified himself with them. The British Press had been hostile. Several thousand French had also fought against him. Of all foreigners they had been the first to enter the Civil War. France had not only supplied his enemies at the beginning, but at a second crucial moment, after the Ebro battle when she had opened her frontiers to a flood of war material. Franco would argue that non-intervention had worked to the advantage of the defeated Republic with no less ardour and conviction than his enemies upheld the contrary. "Britain, in an offensive abuse of her might ruling that the maritime blockade in the Spanish war could be exercised only inside . . . a limit of less than three miles from the coast",[21] had made it perilous for nationalist warships to intercept supplies to the north-west front at the beginning of the war and to Barcelona or Valencia later.

Neither Italy nor Germany had a history of wars upon wars against Spanish interests. Yet Franco's gratitude to Hitler and Mussolini was tempered by his fuller knowledge of the history of that help than the outside world would know for many years. German aircraft had bombed Guernica and the Italians Barcelona without his authority. Italy had hoped for bases in the Balearics, though in the end she had honourably withdrawn her troops. Germany had fought him tooth and nail for economic concessions. Germans and Italians had given him gratuitous advice on how to run his country. The Nazis had encouraged Hedilla to presume above his station.[22]

In the Winter of 1938–9 there had been a dreary diplomatic interchange on whether Franco had acted in accordance with the Secret Protocol of Friendship when during the Munich crisis he had assured

Britain and France of his neutrality if a war should break out.*[23] He had informed but not consulted Germany over his declaration. Nevertheless, Germans and Italians had been killed fighting for him and at the side of his men. In honour he owed Germany and Italy something: though not necessarily Hitler or Mussolini.

Such was the situation in August '39 when he made Beigbeder his Foreign Minister. As Germany began to demand Danzig and the Polish corridor, Franco made it known tactfully to the Germans through Beigbeder that he saw no provocation forthcoming either from Poland or Chamberlain. Stohrer was instructed to correct the Spaniards' "false conception of the situation in Poland".[25] On 1st September he saw both Beigbeder and Serrano to inform them that Germany had begun the war. Beigbeder, for Franco, told the German that Spain would go neutral. Serrano, who had committed himself to the axis cause about June 1939,[26] gave it as his opinion that "should the outcome of the war be victory for France and Great Britain, then all the sacrifices made by Spain in the Civil War would be in vain" and promised to influence the Press in favour of Germany.†[27]

Serrano believed the Axis to be invincible and that an axis victory would be the best for Spain.[29] Franco had his grave doublts. He understood that it would not be in the best interests of his country or himself to be on the losing side: but which was going to be the losing side? In the Summer of 1939 he held in very high regard French Army officers (Pétain of Verdun, then French Ambassador in Madrid, was the hero of his studies of World War I). He had met some brilliant men during his stay

---

* There were minor pinpricks as well in the immediate post-Civil-War period. For example, Goering angled for an invitation to Spain and then expected a Head of the Spanish State to go and meet him on the high seas. Franco, after some hesitation, accepted invitations for a State Visit to Germany and Italy for September-October 1939, but the war came first.[24]

† In fact, all that was required of him was that he should not hinder the gathering of the harvest sown by German Embassy and Nazi Party officials during the Civil War. They had been lavish in their attentions to and entertainment of journalists. The Germans worked on the minds of the ablest and most influential writers, even those originally not particularly well disposed towards them. British information officers started in 1940 with a severe handicap. The Germans came virtually to control one of Madrid's evening papers, *Informaciones*. Serrano, however, was not Franco.

Franco used to tell the story of how, during the Civil War, he wrote an article under a pseudonym in praise of Sir John Moore and in honour of a visit by "an English lady" (?Lady Chamberlain). It was censored (by Serrano).[28] I have the impression that Franco did no more than glance at the Press, either because he lacked the time or the inclination. Even in 1965 it was not "appetising" in format, layout or style—quite apart from the subject matter.

in Versailles. He did not want to believe the pro-allied General Barroso's warning that though there were many first-class men, the morale of the French Army had been sapped. Secondly, Franco, the thwarted naval officer, had the very highest opinion of the Royal Navy. It was unthinkable that Britain could lose the mastery of the seas: he pooh-poohed Goering's theory that airpower could blast it out of existence or that aerial bombardment would cow the civilian population of Britain. The Maginot Line might or might not hold: the French Army might or might not crack—but Britain would remain unconquered and undaunted. The British would never give in, Germany would wear herself out on land. Indeed, all Western Europe would be worn out—and then the Russian bear would pounce.[30]

Franco, however much a dictator, had also to consider the views of the people—or at least of his generals. Serrano and his Falangists might be pro-Axis. So were Generals Yague and Vigon. Kindelan, a descendant of the Irish "wild geese" was anti-English, but inclined to be pro-British because he was a Monarchist, and Britain had a king; but Aranda, a far abler General than Yague, the heroic Varela, Moscardo of the Alcazar and Solchaga who had commanded the ubiquitous Navarra corps, were uncompromisingly pro-British. Franco could not enter a war in which his generals would be sympathisers with the enemy whichever way he sided.

The balance in Franco's mind between the contenders oscillated from pro-German to pro-Allied over the next nine months. With the Russo-German pact it went heavily anti-German. The inaction of the French behind the Maginot Line when Poland was fighting for her life, appalled him. He considered it one of the most dishonourable acts in all history.[31] Through Stohrer he congratulated Hitler on his *brilliant* victory.*[32] Stohrer tried to persuade him that his views on Stalin were out of date: that there had been great changes in Russia. Russian Communism nonetheless remained Franco's obsessive hatred. Churchill's words in defence of Finland therefore met with his complete approval: he would always admire Churchill for his voice of authority and his possession of the human qualities which Franco revered in all men, patriotism, courage and a determination to fight till death. Franco continued exporting raw materials to Britain, in spite of German protests.[33]

Britain's retreat to the Channel and the evacuation of Dunkirk reminded Franco of Corunna: he had in his childhood walked upon the

* The irony was lost on Stohrer.

ramparts where Sir John Moore is buried. Nevertheless, the French Army had been defeated. Hitler's army was approaching Hendaye. Marshal Pétain went to take his leave of Franco: he had been summoned to the wreck of France. Franco revealed later:[34] "I said to him 'Don't go, Marshal. Make your age your excuse. Let those who lost the war sign the peace. You, thank God, were here and in no way responsible. You are the hero of Verdun. Don't let your name be mingled with the others who have been defeated.' Pétain replied—'I know, General, but my country calls me, and I am hers. It may be the last service I can do for her'." Petain, visibly distressed, embraced Franco—and went away, according to Franco, "to be sacrificed".

The war had come to Franco's doorstep.* Italy declared war. Franco's immediate reaction was to declare Spain non-belligerent. On 14th June 1940, with the full consent of Britain and France, Spanish troops entered Tangier "to guarantee the neutrality of the zone": a move legally justifiable since three of the four guarantors of the international city were now at war with each other.[36]

Franco had already surveyed the scene, and realising that Hitler's expansionist policy could lead only through Spain to Africa had decided on a bloodless war to save Spain from defeat.

If the French Army, with all its size and modern equipment, had been swept to one side so spectacularly, what hope for a Spanish Army? The tanks which the Germans had used were not the flimsy Mks. I and II of the Civil War but formidable Mks. III and IV which could knock out Franco's captured Russian Vickers as easily as these had destroyed the Fiat Ansaldos. If Hitler's Panzer divisions had scattered the French motorised divisions, what hope for Franco's infantry and its horse-drawn transport? If Franco were, at that moment, to "exhaust Hitler's patience", Spain would suffer the same fate as Czechoslovakia, Denmark, Norway, Belgium and Holland. Hitler had already looked askance at the Anglo–Spanish Trade Pact signed the previous March,

---

* And over it. When the Germans reached Hendaye in mid-June, the garrison commander at San Sebastian invited them to hold a parade in his city. Franco had him dismissed from his command. The recently appointed British Ambassador to Spain, Sir Samuel Hoare, was fully justified in bringing the matter of the parade to Beigbeder's notice, but there was no need for him to "have a row with the Government"[35] or address the Foreign Minister "with a directness unusual perhaps in diplomatic procedure". Colonel Beigbeder, as Hoare discovered soon afterwards, was pro-British—and so was the Minister of War General Varela. Quite apart from his sympathies, it would have been General Varela's duty to curb such un-Spanish enthusiasm as that of the garrison commander's in any circumstances. For further action within the Army by General Varela, see below.

and the continuing export from Spain of iron ores to his remaining enemy.[37]

Serrano Suñer urged his brother-in-law to go in to the limit on the side of the Axis. France was beaten, and Britain's turn was only a matter of time. The "Spanish high military officer who had prophesied that the French and allied armies would beat the Germans or at least hold them indefinitely"[38] had been proved wrong. Serrano allowed the Press full liberty to praise Germany, and he had it hail the entry of the Spanish troops into Tangier as a great Spanish victory. The long-felt under-current of vague imperialism now became a torrent of demands for Gibraltar, Morocco and beyond.[39] Franco himself joined in the campaign to the extent of saying that it was Spain's "duty and mission" to fulfil Isabella I's injunction to her heirs that they should conquer Africa and recover Gibraltar.[40] The recovery of the Rock was and always would be dear to Franco's heart—but whether he ever believed in the creation of a new Spanish empire is open to discussion. Like all Spaniards who had fought in Africa, he had a sentimental attachment to Spanish Morocco, but he also knew how much Spanish blood had been shed for a few square miles, and with his understanding and sympathy of the Moroccans, he had long previously appreciated the strength of their already renascent nationalism.[41] His attitude might be put this way: if there was to be a new "carve up" of Africa, he would do his best that Spain got more than the crumbs that the Anglo–French imperialists had given her in the nineteenth century. Spanish claims in Africa, moreover, could be a valuable bargaining counter in the struggle which Franco could see coming. He would turn Serrano's and the Falange's imperialism to his own ends. The British Ambassador might be annoyed, but Britain was in no position to come to the aid of Spain if attacked: Franco trusted Hitler no more than Hitler trusted him.

France was beaten: "but those people who urge me to go in with Germany are all wrong, quite wrong", Franco told his generals. "I tell you that the English [los ingleses] will never give in. They'll fight and go on fighting: and if they are driven out of Britain, they'll carry on the fight from Canada: they'll get the Americans to come in with them. Germany has not won the war." Almost all the generals agreed with Franco.*

---

* Vigon and Yague were the only notable exceptions. The airforce was pro-German. At the beginning of May Yague as Air Minister, had sent General Barron to discuss with Goering the provision of spare parts for the old German aircraft in

What of the so-called third prop of the régime? Franco was already at loggerheads with the Vatican on the age-old question of the *Patronato*.† There were nineteen vacant bishoprics out of fifty-seven and the Pope was refusing to allow Franco as Head of the Spanish State to fill them with his nominees. Cardinal Gomá was dying. In May 1940 he had written a pastoral in which he had stated that more and more Spaniards were beginning to realise that Britain and France were fighting to uphold the Christian spirit of morality invoked by Pius XII. The Pastoral had been refused publication in the Press but its contents were known, and Franco knew that the Cardinal's views were shared by many churchmen.

The situation then was as balanced as before: the Falange more vocally pro-Axis, Army no change, Church inclined towards the Allies. These considerations apart, it was now even more imperative than before that Franco should stay out of the war. He was face to face with the ruined economy of the country and the failure of the 1939 harvest. His people were nearing starvation level. In these circumstances Franco could not dream of entering the war: but would Hitler allow him to stay out?

Franco was advised, or from his study of Hitler came to the conclusion, that if he wanted to keep Spain out of the war then he should at all costs avoid giving Hitler a definite "No" for an answer. A point blank refusal would be the way to invasion: rather Franco should appear to go all the way with Hitler, yet always find some difficulty, some point that needed clarification, an *i* to be dotted or a *t* to be crossed:[43] and Franco, who as a general "waited on providences", was the European Head of State best able to say "Yes, but . . ." and mount delay upon delay. It was thus that Franco embarked upon a policy which would infuriate the British Ambassador, Sir Samuel Hoare, on the one hand, and the Germans on the other. Certainly Franco wrote letters and said words which compromised him to the limit as pro-

---

Spain and help in building up the Spanish aircraft industry. Goering at a long meeting had said outright to Barron that he was disillusioned and indignant over the attitude of Spain. The impression they gave was that they did not believe in a German victory. Barron defended Yague pointing out that he had allowed German weather reconnaissance aircraft to operate with Spanish markings and the Luftwaffe to use the Corunna beam transmitters. That, Goering had rejoined, did not answer his question: On whose side was Franco?[42] For the way in which Britain—in particular R.A.F. Coastal Command—turned the beam transmitters to their own use *v.* Churchill *The Second World War*, Vol. IV, p. 255.

† See Chapter 2.

Axis and which would later be used as evidence against him: but his actions did not correspond with his words. *Las palabras y las plumas el veinto las llevan**—was after all so well known a Spanish proverb that even Ciano would use it in his diary.[44]

As France crumbled, Franco sent Vigon to Hitler with a personal letter. He expressed in it his unbounded admiration and enthusiasm for Hitler: but of course, Spain was worn out, and the Allies might occupy the Canaries if Franco were to declare war.† Franco made it known that he would come into the war if Germany gave him a firm undertaking that Spain would be allowed to take Gibraltar for herself, and that she would receive as booty all of French Morocco, Oran and substantial portions of French Equatorial Africa. It was a foregone conclusion that Hitler would not grant these demands, for in the first place he had to keep fallen France faithful to him while wooing Spain, and in the second Germany wanted North Africa for herself: but Franco's extravagant praise of Hitler as a general was ambrosia to the Führer. So also the news Vigon told him of Franco's difficulties with the Roman Catholic Church. Indeed, said Hitler, it was time that the Vatican realised that it was only because National Socialism, Fascism and the Falange existed that the Roman Church survived in Germany, Italy and Spain—so if the leaders of these three acted together, the Vatican would have to change its policy.[45] On 2nd August Ribbentrop wrote to Stohrer that Spain's early entry into the war was now desirable and to that end the High Command prepared an appreciation of Spain's armed strength—on the whole substantially favourable to Spain. At the same time the inadequacy of Spain's roads and railways was noted. Next, in September, Franco allowed Serrano Suñer to accept an invitation to go to Germany (Serrano had been seeking the invitation since early July).[46]

Not too fancifully Franco could be seen in this to be applying to international politics his old military beliefs: that as the best way to defeat the Moors had been to use Moors against them, so now the best way to confound the Axis was to operate through pro-Axis subordinates. True to form Serrano took offence at Ribbentrop's lack of comprehension of Spain's economic difficulties, and his waving aside Spain's territorial ambitions as quite unrealistic: Serrano was further annoyed when Ribbentrop demanded bases in the Canaries and made thinly

---

* Words and quills the wind will waft away.

† Franco was not entirely wrong. For allied plans to take the Canaries if Hitler invaded Spain *v.* Churchill op. cit., Vol. III, pp 123, 388–9, 771.

veiled threats that Hitler might have to occupy the Peninsula in Germany's own protection. Serrano then had a long and less excited conversation with Hitler: they talked vaguely round a number of points, the attitude of the Church, "U.S. imperialism", and the need of heavy artillery to capture Gibraltar if that were to be attempted—and Hitler mentioned that he would like to meet Franco himself at Hendaye.*

It was so agreed. Franco and Hitler would meet on the railway station at Hendaye at 1400 hrs. on 23rd October. By then Hitler had definitely abandoned Sea Lion and decided on Felix. Operation Felix envisaged an attack by twenty divisions through Spain directed at Gibraltar so as to deny Britain the Mediterranean and North Africa. The safety of his long lines of communication depended on the co-operation of Franco. He would need airfields in Spain. Franco would therefore have to come into the war. With Spain in possession of Tangier, Ceuta and Melilla, the Straits would be sealed, but the seal would not be complete unless Morocco and Algeria were kept neutralised. The French, therefore, had to be assured that Hitler did not intend to cross into Morocco and Algeria, lest the French troops there, with or without Pétain's connivance, should side with de Gaulle. But Franco had made it well known that his co-operation would be conditional on his acquisition of French African territories. Hitler's problem therefore was how to satisfy Spanish irredentist aspirations without rousing the French.

Just prior to 23rd October, Franco replaced Colonel Beigbeder with Serrano as Foreign Minister. The change infuriated Sir Samuel Hoare and satisfied the ambitious *cuñadisimo*.[48] The Germans considered it augured well for the future. What neither knew at the time was that at this moment Franco would keep Serrano Suñer strictly to the lines which he, and only he, laid down.

Franco arrived at Hendaye an hour late. He had deliberately delayed the train: "This is the most important meeting of my life," he said to one of the senior army officers with him, "I'll have to use every trick I can—and this is one of them. If I make Hitler wait, he will be at a psychological disadvantage from the start."[49] Actually Hitler and Ribbentrop took little notice: it was a pleasant day in which to walk

---

* Serrano had a second meeting with Ribbentrop before leaving. He saw a map which had marked on it Germany's interests in Africa and it seemed to Serrano that there was little left for anyone else. He was then given a conducted tour of Dunkirk and the Channel ports where he saw the landing craft for Operation Sea Lion against Britain, and off he went to Rome where he told Ciano that he did not like Ribbentrop.[47]

up and down the Hendaye platform. After the embrace, the national anthems, the protocol of a meeting of Heads of State, Franco delivered a set speech in which he laid layer on layer of praise upon Hitler. In the present war Spain, he said, would gladly fight at Germany's side. Hitler in his turn made an exposé of the war situation. England was beaten, but she was not prepared to admit it. The next stage was the capture of Gibraltar. He explained Operation Felix. He then called on Franco to conclude a treaty there and then under which Franco would bind himself to declare war on Britain in January 1941. Panzer divisions would be ready to cross the Pyrenees. So would all the parachute units which had captured the Liege Eben Emael fort. Franco knew from General Barroso, whom he had sent to France as Military Attaché, that every detail of how Gibraltar might be taken was being studied with a large-scale model of the fortress, and that the parachute units were undergoing special training and exercises in conditions simulating those of Gibraltar. Gibraltar, Hitler said, would fall on 10th January. Hitler would then give it to Franco, and maybe Franco would get parts of Africa as well.

When Hitler had finished, Franco remained silent for a while. "From his impenetrable expression", Paul Schmidt, Hitler's interpreter, was to recall, "I could not make out whether he was taken aback by the proposal or whether he was just quietly thinking out his reply." Spain was in desperate need of food. The Allies were allowing Spain to import a certain amount, not enough and subject to the navicerts which Spain found an intolerable restriction on her sovereignty. Could Germany deliver the food and oil that Spain needed? Of course, it was not consistent with Spanish national pride to accept Gibraltar as a present. The fortress would have to be taken by Spaniards alone. That meant providing the Spanish Army with modern armaments and heavy artillery, and time to train Spanish units for the assault. He would also have to protect his long coastline against attacks by the British Navy. Hitler had said that the Panzer units would drive the British out of Africa. "To the edge of the great desert very possibly," said Franco, "but Central Africa would be protected against major attacks by the desert belt, in the same way that an island is by the open sea. As an old African campaigner I am quite certain about that." Britain's defeat was not a foregone conclusion. Even if England were conquered, Franco told Hitler, the British Government and fleet would continue the war from Canada, and America would come in on her side.

"As Franco made these remarks," Paul Schmidt recalls, "in a quiet gentle voice, its monotonous singsong reminiscent of the Muezzin calling the faithful to prayer, Hitler became more and more restless. The conversation was obviously getting on his nerves. Once he even got up saying that there was no point in continuing the discussion, but he immediately sat down again and renewed his attempt to win Franco over." Hitler recalled the help that he had given Franco during the Civil War. It still had to be paid for. Franco's reaction to this made Hitler feel—in Hitler's own words—"like a Jew". However, Franco finally said that he was ready to conclude a treaty provided that Germany could supply the food and armaments Spain required and left Spain to decide when would be the right moment. After dinner in Hitler's banqueting car, there was a further unscheduled meeting between the Caudillo and the Führer.[50] Franco argued that the eastern gate to the Mediterranean should be closed before the western. Hitler disagreed. Franco stood firm. Hitler became more insistent, not to say violent. Franco, impassive, imperturbable, repeated his insistence on 10 million quintals of wheat (1 million tons) without which he could not guarantee that history would not repeat itself. He alluded to the rising against Napoleon. All Spain was not pro-Axis. Far from it. Was Hitler right in his calculations as to how fast Panzer divisions could move through Spain—range after range of mountains with tricky passes, the roads—the one main road—in an appalling state, the weather in January the worst in Europe, snow and ice on the heights and heavy rain in the valleys in which even tracked vehicles would be bogged down. The railways—single line for large stretches and of a wider gauge than the French or German—were short of rolling stock. At the end of two hours, as Schmidt says, they were no nearer to understanding. "Indeed the feelings of both had completely changed." Hitler and Franco parted. Ribbentrop and Serrano were left to work out an agreement. A draft was prepared, but Franco had left and there was no possibility of its immediate signature. "Spluttering with rage, Ribbentrop drove off with me," Schmidt continues, "to Bordeaux. . . . All the way Ribbentrop cursed the "Jesuit" Suñer and the "ungrateful coward Franco who owes us everything and now won't join in with us".

Out of the Hendaye meeting a secret protocol was eventually evolved[51] which left everything as vague as before: Germany declared herself ready to send supplies to Spain: Spain declared that she would enter the war—sometime: Germany promised Spain unspecified territories in Africa. It bound neither side. There was however one sudden act: as it were to remind to the Germans that he was capable of lightning action without reference to anyone, Franco declared the Statute of Internationalisation of Tangiers dissolved on 3rd November. He had acquired the city which Spain had coveted for thirty years. Britain issued a strong protest.★ Germany interpreted as unfriendly the fact that Franco had acted without warning.[52]

Later in November Serrano was invited to Berchtesgaden. Franco's immediate reaction was to ask: What for? He summoned Varela, Moreno, and Vigon. "Someone," according to Serrano Suñer,[53] said, "wouldn't it be better not to go? I answered if we don't go to Berlin we might have to meet him in Vitoria." Franco heard the views of his three Service Ministers, then said to Serrano Suñer, "Spain cannot and must not take part in the war".[54]

Serrano met Hitler at Berchtesgaden on 18th November. On the 4th Hitler had told Jodl and Raeder that he was determined to occupy Gibraltar as soon as possible, but ten days later the German Naval High Command had advised Hitler first that the occupation of Gibraltar and the control of the Western Mediterranean was not enough, that is that the eastern end would have to be closed as well—the point Franco had made at Hendaye—and second that *before* Spain entered the war, the Canaries would have to be reinforced by German troops disguised as Spaniards.† Hitler began his conversations with Serrano expressing disgust with the Italians: they had committed a grave and unpardonable error in attacking Greece. Now more than before it was essential to close the Mediterranean. The Germans would indeed attack towards Suez, but it was Spain's duty to close the West. Hitler and Serrano then went over the same ground covered at Hendaye: Spain's need for food and therefore neutrality: the priority that should be given to the Suez operation before Felix. The only two new points were these: of Germany's 230 divisions, Hitler said, 186 were not in action and could be deployed in any direction. "I have decided to attack Gibraltar. The operation is planned to the last detail. All that is required is the signal to begin, and a beginning must be made." After four hours of discussion during which Serrano, on Franco's behalf, repeated that the Spaniards might resist invasion as in Napoleon's days, but that Spain would continue getting ready to enter the war, Serrano took his leave of Hitler.

On 5th December Hitler sent Canaris post-haste to Madrid to

★ The Khalifa, the Sultan's representative in Spanish Morocco, approved. Tangiers became a whirlpool of intrigue and espionage.

† "In the same manner as the Condor Legion". Fuehrer Conferences 1940. (Board of Admiralty, 1947), p. 123.

inform Franco that he was expected to come into the war on 10th January. Franco received the German Admiral on the 7th. Vigon was present. Franco expressed the view that the Royal Navy was still the master at sea. His war preparations were not complete. He was still one million tons of wheat short. His transport was inadequate to move supplies. While everything possible was being done to complete the necessary preparations, he could give no date for his entry into the war. He invited Canaris to see for himself that there was hunger everywhere. Canaris must have known from his agents how true this was, but also that the only recent troop movements had been in the Irun and not the Gibraltar region.[55]

Hitler postponed Felix the moment Canaris reported Franco's reaction. However, on 27th December the Naval High Command told Hitler that British actions in Greece, Albania, Libya and East Africa had greatly enhanced Britain's prestige. It was now the Navy's view that Gibraltar should be taken as quickly as possible: to relieve the pressure on Italy in Greece and Cyrenaica: to make possible German penetration into Africa through Spanish Morocco: to close the sea route to Malta and Alexandria. Hitler agreed but added that Franco was not ready to co-operate: Britain had promised him food. However, he would try once more. On 31st December he wrote to Mussolini that although Spain had refused "to co-operate with the Axis Powers", he still had hopes that Franco would realise "the catastrophic consequences of his conduct". Halfway through January 1941 he renewed the offensive. There was a barrage of "most urgent" and "secret" notes from Ribbentrop through Stohrer practically demanding of Franco his immediate entry into the war. Franco side-stepped them all. When Hitler promised Franco food as soon as he committed himself to a definite date, Franco replied that January was no month to start a campaign in Spain.[56]

Hitler now wrote Franco a long plaintive letter recapitulating their relations since the Hendaye meeting. Franco's first excuse had been Spain's shortage of grain. Hitler had then promised to let him have 100,000 tons* provided he named the day, however secretly. Hitler had then asked Franco to allow Germany to begin concentrating troops for an assault on Gibraltar in the January:

* There were 100,000 tons of grain in Lisbon awaiting transport to Switzerland. Hitler proposed to let Switzerland have an equivalent amount from German stocks. The Lisbon stock would then become German and Franco would have it on the day he did as Hitler wished.

... only then, for the first time, were our negotiators told plainly that such an early date was entirely out of the question; again, the reasons given were economic. Thereupon I had it pointed out once more that Germany was willing to begin deliveries of grain immediately. Admiral Canaris was thereupon told that these grain shipments were not the decisive issue at all. . . . We had in the meanwhile allocated batteries for the defence of the Canary Islands and intended to use dive bombers for additional protection. We were then told that this was not decisive either. . . .

In these circumstances I fail to understand, to be sure, why one should at first have wanted to declare an operation impossible on economic grounds which is now supposedly impossible simply for climatic reasons. . . .

Caudillo, the climatic conditions of Spain are indeed not unfamiliar to us.

I must deeply regret your views and your attitude, Caudillo! . . . The attack on Gibraltar and the closing of the Straits would at one stroke have changed the entire Mediterranean situation. . . . It is obvious that if our advance units had been allowed to cross the Spanish frontier on January 10, Gibraltar would be in our hands by now. This means that two months have been lost which otherwise might have helped decide world history. . . .

Hitler then pledged himself never to forsake Franco if he came into the war.

We three men, the Duce, you and I, are linked together by the most implacable force of history, and we should therefore in this historic conflict obey the supreme commandment to realize that in grave times such as these nations can be saved by stout hearts rather than by seemingly prudent caution. . . .

Hitler concluded with a veiled threat:

... the world's most tremendous military machine (stands ready) . . . and the future will show how good and reliable that instrument is.[57]

Stohrer handed Franco Hitler's letter on 8th February. He had just the day before sent Berlin yet another set of reasons why Spain could not enter the war, or rather the details of Spain's economic and military needs which would have to be satisfied before Spain could begin to prepare for war: large quantities of rubber, cotton, jute, fertilisers, rolling stock (16,000 wagons and 180 locomotives), thousands of vehicles, 400 anti-aircraft guns and 90 four-gun batteries—demands which Berlin in due course ruled "so obviously unrealisable that they can only be evaluated as an expression of the effort to avoid entering the war under this pretext".[58]

Franco told Stohrer that he agreed with everything Hitler said: he would reply as soon as he was back from Bordighera where he had promised to meet Mussolini on 12th February. Hitler had also written to Mussolini. "To us," Ciano noted in his diary, "is assigned the task of bringing back home the Spanish prodigal son."[59] The prodigal duly met Mussolini.

"I was the more delighted to meet him because our meeting should have taken place sooner. . . . He was still convinced that Germany would win the war . . . he had just suffered severe setbacks in Greece. . . . Genoa had been bombed on the eve of my arrival . . . so, while still asserting that the Nazis were bound to win in the end, he was none too happy. . . . Yes, he was honest with me . . . he was very human, natural. Besides, I think I can say he felt friendly towards me. . . . We spoke absolutely freely about events. He scarcely tried to persuade me to enter the war: he realised Spain should think only of curing her own wounds. I put to him a question. 'Duce,' I said, 'if you could get out of the war, would you?' He burst out laughing and, throwing his arms into the air, cried out: 'You bet your life I would.' "[60] Mussolini wrote to Hitler that Spain was in no condition to enter into war.

Franco saw Pétain at Montpellier on his way back from Bordighera, and asked him to help Spain in preventing Hitler from going through Spain. They agreed not to irritate Hitler. Franco returned to Spain. Several days later, on 26th February, he wrote to Hitler. He called it a "prompt reply" to his letter of the 6th. Praise, protestations of faith and love poured from him—but no action. Hitler fumed. He "expressed himself in very forthright terms", talking of Franco's ingratitude, "cowardly defection" and "underhand game".[61]

Franco had won. Seventeen years later a French correspondent asked Franco outright: "Did you at any moment think of aligning yourself with the Axis?" Franco replied "Never."[62] Perhaps for a brief moment he did so, in the following July: by that time however Hitler was engaged at the other end of Europe.

Franco had left for Bordighera at a time when Stohrer expected a *coup d'état* or a revolution at any moment. The German Ambassador had reported that there was no bread anywhere and hunger everywhere, and that even the Army was under-fed and ill-clad. All that was true. He had also given Berlin a picture of the Army arraying itself against

Serrano Suñer, which was partly true, yet at the same time of a very pro-German Serrano and very pro-German Spanish Army. There was indeed grave dissatisfaction with the *cuñadisimo* and the Generalissimo. In the family partnership no one knew for certain who was the rider and who was being ridden. Some saw Serrano as an arch-Falangist: others as the man helping the Caudillo to betray Jose Antonio's dreams of a nationalist syndicalist Spain. Some thought Serrano Hitler's agent: others the person holding Franco back from joining Hitler. The Monarchists clamoured for the restoration of the monarchy. (On 21st February Alfonso XIII died: Franco attended a Requiem for him, but refused to call Don Juan by any other name than "the Count of Barcelona".) Everyone prayed for the food that Franco did not have to give. Berlin warned Stohrer against supporting any of the dissidents.[63] He was not the only representative in Spain of Hitler's Germany.

Towards the end of 1939 a Lieutenant-Colonel Emilio Tarduchy had organised a clandestine *Junta Política* in Madrid. Tarduchy had been an early convert to Falangism and for a while prominent in the U.M.E. During the war he had risen from captain but his record was otherwise undistinguished. His chief henchman was a Patricio Canales, a fervent admirer of Germany's and as such placed by Serrano Suñer in a position to influence the Press and direct official propaganda. Early in 1940 Tarduchy established relations with the German Nazi chief in Spain, Thomson. He asked the Nazis to help the Junta to overthrow Franco: in exchange he promised the Germans that the Junta, having a Nazi political programme, would bring Spain into the war on their side. The Junta then began to seek supporters. An approach to Yague was obvious, and in the young Jose Antonio Giron then at work on the organisation of workers into unions, Canales hoped to find fervour for the Nazi cause. Giron was a self-publicist who had made the most of his exploits as a militiaman. Neither Yague nor Giron, appear to have discouraged the plotters. Early in 1941 one of Yague's aides-de-camp denounced his general. Franco saw Yague privately. There were witnesses only to Yague's tears as he came out of the audience chamber. The Junta met for the last time and, realising every move they made was known, disbanded. Franco took no action against anyone implicated.[*] Varela was instructed quietly to post away from any strategic point any officer whose adherence to Falangism was likely to influence his loyalty to Franco's amorphous *Movimiento*.[64]

[*] One of them, Jose Perez de Cabo, was later executed on well-founded charges of black-marketeering.

In the Thomson-Tarduchy association may lie the reason for Berlin's orders to Stohrer not to interfere. On 22nd April the Ambassador reported that the food situation was worse, that the Army was about to strike against Serrano, and that a coup against Franco was still possible. The hunger of the people was indeed more acute. On 7th April Britain had agreed to a relaxation of her economic blockade which in all truth was not directed against Spain but against Germany.* Serrano had done his best to frustrate any agreement with Britain, but he had not been a free agent as there had been other negotiators. Spain was to be allowed to import wheat, but weeks would have to pass before the necessary shipping was available, and the permitted quantities could be foreseen as inferior to Spain's real needs.[65]

In Berlin Hitler summoned Espinosa de los Monteros and showed him cuttings from British newspapers which talked of German troops training in Spain and of airfields being built for the Luftwaffe. Espinosa said it was pure propaganda. Not so, said Hitler. It was preparatory to a British operation against Spain or Spanish Morocco. England intended to overthrow Franco. Not so, said Espinosa. Franco was informed of the meeting. His immediate reaction was to send Serrano to Stohrer and express the hope that Germany would not walk into Spain except at Spain's request. Stohrer reported in May that the food crisis was now acute. Then in June he was told to get the Spaniards to repair the bridge at Hendaye. Hitler, however, had by now other plans.[66]

The news of Hitler's attack on Soviet Russia was communicated by Stohrer to Serrano who was out in the country. Serrano was delighted to hear the news and promptly offered Falangist militia to fight on the side of the Germans. Franco modified Serrano's offer. No Army General would want a Falangist militia with possible battle honours independent of the Army. It would be, as far as possible, a volunteer force from Army Regulars as well as Falange.† Stohrer suggested that Spain should

* The requirements of Navicerts did hurt Spanish pride deeply as a slight to national sovereignty. It was a tragedy that at that moment Britain did not have in Madrid a fully Spanish-speaking Ambassador, with a thorough understanding of Spanish mentality and *simpático* to Spaniards, to "sell" the Spaniards the navicert system. There were some excellent men in the British Embassy, but they were not in a position to influence the Spaniards "at the top". In March 1940 Britain had lent Spain £2m. to get trade going and in October 1940 £600,000 to buy food.

† I have come across no person who served in this force who has not eventually confessed that he volunteered in the first place. As with all volunteers, the reasons behind their act of will were manifold: the pay was good, there was a hope that the food might be more plentiful on the Russian front than in Spain; there was a choice of death or glory; some were pro-German and most were passionately

declare war on Russia. Franco would not. Serrano, regretting that "strong opponents [to Germany], above all among the military" had a strong influence over Franco, headed the recruiting drive. On 24th June he harangued a meeting. A number of youths went from it not to the recruiting offices but to the British Embassy shouting "Gibraltar, Gibraltar", attacked the building and did substantial damage. German cameramen filmed the event.[67]

Serrano appears to have been his usual insolent self and Franco conciliatory when Hoare protested. The *cuñadisimo*, bewailing the disunity of Spain over the war, had previously said to Stohrer that a provocation of the English was necessary to bring about Spanish unity, and if necessary such provocation should be provoked.[68] For months, with Stohrer, he had been plotting the downfall of Varela, Minister of War, as the leader of the pro-British party. Varela was now on his honeymoon after marrying into a pro-British Basque family. Here then was Serrano's chance. *Arriba* had a rash of violently anti-British articles.

Now Britain herself had cut away one of the pillars on which Franco had based his policy of keeping out of the war. The imports of grain were proving quite inadequate to Spain's dire needs. On 17th July he delivered his most violent anti-British speech. It was now, perhaps, that he came nearest to entering the war. Britain, he said, was making war on Spain depriving her of the food the people needed. However, that over, Franco went off to hunt ibex.[69]

Serrano remained in Madrid to continue to intrigue and report on his pro-German policy to Stohrer: but Varela also returned, to post away dangerous Falangists in the Army. The Blue Division, the volunteer force for the Russian front, was an admirable destination for many of them.[70] If it came to a "show-down" Franco would have reliable lieutenants at home.

Franco's Intelligence Service now provided him with disquieting

---

anti-Communist. I have even met ex-members of the Blue Division who were as intensely pro-British as they were anti-Soviet. Spaniards were not the only ones to hold that Churchill's verbal identification of the cause of Britain and Russia against Nazi Germany was justifiable only on purely practical grounds. Some of the volunteers repented of their decision; some were disillusioned and others, having come to wonder how they had ever thought of volunteering, would have themselves and the superficial questioner believe that they never did. The Division when at full strength had 641 officers, 2,272 N.C.O.s and 15,780 O.R.s. It suffered heavy casualties, and repaid "Spain's blood debt to Germany" nearly twenty times over.

news. First there was an article in a newspaper edited by Spanish Republicans in New York,[71] suggesting that Britain and the United States were about to attack the Canaries and Azores. There were reports of U.S. intelligence agents contacting the Republican Generals Miaja and Asensio and of the suggested formation of a Division with ex-Republican Army men. The U.S. Department of State naturally denied knowledge of any such plans. The capture of the Canaries, however, was also reported to have been discussed by Churchill and Roosevelt on 10th August. The visit to Hoare in Spain of the U.S. Intelligence Colonel Donovan the previous February seemed to fit into the picture. 15th September was supposed to be the date for the attack. September passed without incident. A note from the Duke of Alba that Churchill had said at a luncheon at the Embassy that England might exert pressure on the French after the war to meet "Spain's just claims in North Africa" was reassuring but not conclusive.[72]

In December 1941, Franco's prophesy to Hitler that he would have to fight the Americans became true. Serrano let the Press rant against the Americans as well as the British. Nevertheless, in private Franco began to maintain that there were two and then three wars. First, he said, there was the war between the nations of Western Europe—a war of commercial and imperial interests in which he would have no part, except it helped Spain's own commercial and imperial interests. Secondly there was the war between Germany and Russia: this was a war of ideas, of western civilisation against "the Asiatic hordes" and "Communism". Here he was wholeheartedly on the side of the Germans. Thirdly there was the war between the United States and Japan. When Japan attacked the Philippines the United States became a defender of the Spanish civilisation of the Philippines against another Asiatic barbarian. This three-war theory became a favourite theme in conversations with American visitors.

Franco now thought out a move which he hoped would be interpreted as a statement of neutrality in the war in the west. He invited Salazar to meet him on 13th February 1942. Salazar was reputedly pro-British: Franco pro-German. Therefore an alliance between the two, Franco hoped, would be proof to either side that he was determined to keep out of the war. Not so, according to Serrano: the Germans would interpret it as an unfriendly act. At the meeting Franco spoke to Salazar in Galaico-Portuguese which Serrano could ill understand. The *cuñadisimo* complained to his friends that he felt "absolutely on my own". But Franco went ahead to prepare the ground for the alliance which matured under the name Iberian Bloc in December. However, Franco was most anxious to make it known that while he was neutral in the west, he was far from it in the east. Such were the circumstances of his speech (the day following the Salazar meeting) to the garrison of Seville, in which he spoke of a million Spaniards barring the way to Berlin if it were to be threatened by "the barbarous hordes of Communism".[73]

The internal situation, rather than international affairs, occupied Franco over the rest of 1942. In the Spring and Summer of that year there was what the recently appointed American Ambassador Carlton Hayes called "a veritable epidemic of students' riots, brawls, and street fighting, so that Spanish jails began to bulge not alone with 'reds' but quarrelsome 'patriots'."[74] To be sure in his 17th July 1942 speech Franco praised yet again "totalitarianism" and poured scorn on democracy. He was sure that the Axis powers were bound to destroy Communism. But all this was secondary to his references in this and other speeches of the time giving dark hints and warnings about the "fraudulent and disloyal conduct of a few Spaniards". All the old divisions of the *F.E.T. y de las JONS* were now intriguing against each other—Carlists and Alfonsists, Conservatives and Progressives, anti-Falange and Falange, though quite what *Falangists* meant no one was quite sure, except that a Jose Luis Arrese who had made himself well known for his *plans* for extensive workers' housing in Malaga and was now the *Movimiento* Secretary-General had ordered a purge of ex-Socialists and Anarchists from the lists of the Falange. Arrese turned to emphasise the Catholicism of Jose Antonio's thought.

On 14th August, General Varela, a Carlist by conviction, attended a Requiem Mass in Bilbao. As he came out of the church a bomb exploded. It missed Varela, but seventy-two bystanders were killed and wounded. The culprits were proved to be Serrano's Falangists associated with the Nazi Party.[75] Just over two weeks later, Franco announced the replacement of Serrano Suñer by the pro-allied General Count Jordana as Foreign Minister, and that of the pro-allied General Varela by the half pro-Axis General Asensio as Minister of War. Stohrer[76] did his best to save Serrano. He failed. Hoare and Hayes were happy. They no longer had "to face a gauntlet of Falange youth" whenever they went to the Foreign Ministry.[77] Ciano in Rome was not surprised. The last time he and Serrano had met, he wrote in his

diary, "Serrano talked of Franco as one speaks of a moronic servant".[*][78]
Serrano thereafter took no further part in politics.

The era of the *cuñadisimo* was over.

The danger from Hitler would continue to exist for a while longer.
Churchill would write even on 18th April 1943 to Lord Ismay: "[We
cannot] exclude the possibility of a German incursion into the Spanish
peninsula, and plans should be brought up to date for an Anglo-
American intervention"—but by then Churchill could continue con-
fidently—"on the assumption, now almost certain that the Spanish and
Portuguese will resist the Germans".[80] Six allied divisions were then
earmarked to help Spain to repel Hitler if necessary.

In the period immediately ahead, however, Franco might have seen
a greater danger of allied than of German intervention in Spain. A new
situation required a new Foreign Minister—a pro-Allied man: but if
the Falange was to be kept quiet, the loss of their champion Serrano
Suñer had to be recompensed. Furthermore, if the Allies were to invade
he should have a pro-Axis Minister of War. Hence the changes. To the
superficial observer they seemed typical of a dictator. In fact, they were
typical of Franco the General.

At the end of May 1940, Lord Halifax sent Chamberlain's ex-Lord
Privy Seal and ex-Secretary of State, Sir Samuel Hoare, as British
Ambassador to Spain. The Germans had taken Poland, Denmark and
Norway. They were in full advance across France. Two years later, in
May 1942, when the tide had not yet turned, President Roosevelt sent
a Professor of History at Columbia University, Carlton J. H. Hayes, as
U.S. Ambassador. Sir Samuel Hoare remained in Spain until the end of
1944: Professor Hayes until 1945. Sir Samuel knew no Spanish and his
knowledge of Spain and Spanish history was no more than could be
expected of a non-specialist English ex-public schoolboy:[81] his acquaintance with Spaniards was limited to a friendship with the Duke of Alba
and Berwick and a few refugees. Professor Hayes could not speak
Spanish either, although he could read it: but he had studied Spanish
history. The Spaniards had a long tradition of appointing men of
learning to ambassadorial posts. Carlton Hayes did not correspond to
the Spaniards' concept of an American: he was more urbane, cultured

---

* The shock of seeing his two brothers executed for no particular reason by the
Popular Front must be taken into consideration, if his conduct is to be judged. In
his *apologia*[79] Serrano promised to let the world have more details of this "chapter
of his life", and further reflexions on Spain's international and internal policies.
He has as yet not fulfilled his promise.

and gentlemanly. Sir Samuel was also a gentleman, cultured and urbane; but he lacked the quality for which Spaniards admire Britons above all the other virtues popularly attributed to them: *flema*— imperturbability.[82] Carlton Hayes was respected even by anti-allied Spaniards, like Serrano Suñer. Each Ambassador published an account of his experiences. In 1946, Sir Samuel, now Viscount Templewood, came to the following conclusion: Franco was never neutral; he believed firmly and hoped for an Axis victory; he helped the Axis to the limit of his ability; he was unfit to collaborate in the United Nations.[83] In 1945 Professor Hayes distinguished: "So long as Axis victory seemed inevitable [to Franco], so long as almost the whole continent of Europe was at the mercy of Germany with German armies massed near the Pyrenees and German submarines infesting the seas adjacent to Spain, he let Hitler, and indeed the whole world, believe he was pro-Axis. Nevertheless . . . at least from the date of his dismissal of Serrano Suñer from the Foreign Ministry and the leader-ship of the Falange in September 1942, General Franco guided or backed the responsible officials of his government in approximating Spain's official position to the pro-allied position of the large majority of the Spanish people."[84]

Sir Samuel Hoare was convinced that Franco had had every intention of coming into the war on the side of the Axis, and that he personally had stopped him.* Hayes,[87] on the other hand, would write: "From what I later learned, I came to doubt that there ever had been any real justification for supposing, on the part of the British Government, or of Sir Samuel himself, that Spain would voluntarily join the Axis."

There was, however, a more important and better informed English-man who was also not deceived by Franco's public protestations of love and friendship for the Axis. That was Churchill, who on 24 May 1944 would say in Parliament:

* The selected fifteen documents of German Foreign Policy published by the U.S. in 1946 to prove Franco pro-Axis ratified his opinion. The very documents taken in their full context with the several hundred others prove Hayes to have been the more perceptive. Sir Robert Hodgson, Britain's first diplomatic repre-sentative in Franco's Spain took the same fifteen documents in his *Spain Resurgent* (Hutchinson 1953) and interpreted them in a way much more favourable to Franco. Serrano Suñer, who disliked Hoare as ardently as did Sir Samuel the *cuñadisimo*, argued that Molotov's visit to Berlin alone kept Spain from entering into the war in 1940 more than "all Hoare's intrigues".[85] Juan de la Cosa's summary of Sir Samuel's Embassy would be: "It was fortunate for Great Britain that the Spaniards looked on her Ambassador as a joke: for the British may be sure that if Spain did not join in the war against them, it was in spite of Sir Samuel and not because of him".[86]

There is no doubt that if Spain had yielded to German blandishments and presence at that juncture (1940-41), our burden would have been much heavier. The Straits of Gibraltar would have been closed, and all access to Malta would have been cut off from the West. All the Spanish coast would have become the nesting place of U-boats. I certainly did not feel at that time that I should like to see any of these things happen, and none of them did happen.[88]

But then Churchill knew the history of Spain's War of Independence, that is her struggle against Napoleon (he referred to it in the same speech): and in Cuba he had been awarded a Spanish Military Medal.*

* The capture of Gibraltar as such would not have been necessary: only its neutralisation, which could have been done by guns over a ten-mile and bombers within a 500-mile radius. At the time Britain was on her own. She could have done nothing effective to help the Spaniards against the Germans. Why did Hitler not invade when Franco refused him passage? Napoleon's fate in Russia did not deter him later. The answer must remain speculative: but a military historian could argue that in Russia Napoleon was defeated by the distances involved and the extreme cold, adverse factors which mechanisation and a better knowledge of geography could offset. In Spain, on the other hand, it was the *guerrilleros* who cut to pieces a whole army of Napoleon's. They could have done the same to a German Army in 1940.

NOTES

1. Franco-Salgado MS.

2. Full text in Iturralde, Vol. III, pp. 551-3.

3. Ibid., pp. 530-1. Cf. Allison Peers, *Spain in Eclipse* (Methuen, 1943), p. 152.

4. Ciano, *L'Europa.* The detail that spoils his figures of executions is "eighty in Seville". Three years had passed since its capture by Queipo. At that rate Seville should have been pretty empty.

5. Payne (*Falange,* O.U.P., 1962), p. 212, says: "It has been estimated that sixty per-cent of the original members of the Party were killed during the conflict." I have often heard the figure quoted by Falangists; I have not found anyone to state on what basis the estimate was made, but it is not an incredible figure. It must be remembered that the Popular Front had rounded up known Falangists months before the rising. Among the Generals executed for not joining the rising were Aranguren and Martinez Cabrera.

6. Sir Samuel Hoare (Viscount Templewood), *Ambassador on Special Mission* (Collins, 1946), p. 57.

7. Cf. Thomas, Appendix II, how the estimates of war deaths have been reduced through the years. Similarly my cross-questioning through the years, of

Liberals, Communists, Socialists and Anarchists and of people in the working-class districts of Bilbao, Barcelona, Malaga and Madrid, as well as of lawyers and others connected with the courts, have led me to the conclusion that there cannot have been more than 10,000 executions, and that the real figure may even be considerably smaller. I understand from Ministry of Justice officials that it would be theoretically possible to establish how many persons were condemned to death after the war, after due process of criminal or martial court—or even by the Special Tribunals. I cannot follow at all Professor G. Jackson's reasoning (*The Spanish Republic and the Civil War*, Princeton, 1965) behind his guess at "200,000 war-time National *paseos* and political reprisals" and a further 200,000 post-war executions: but then few persons with experience of warfare could admit his mere 100,000 deaths for three years of bitter fighting. Perhaps post Vietnam he would revise his figures to include the day-to-day casualties of patrols and skirmishes. Thomas's estimates of war-time 60,000 rear area executions in the "Red" zone and 40,000 in the "White" zone tally with my own calculations. His estimates of 300,000 deaths in action seems to tally overall with Army Records, though I would be inclined to favour 350,000. The popularly accepted "one million dead" can be wholly discounted.

8. *Raza* film script. See Ch. I.

9. Julian Pereda.

10. Described fully in Peers op. cit., pp. 153-4. The cult had been begun officially by a Government decree of 16th November 1938. B.O.E., 17th November 1938.

11. It was completed in 1959. Franco had difficulty in finding a community for the adjoining monastery. Its current abbot, Fray Justo de Urbel, is renowned for his extreme admiration of the Caudillo. In that, he is exceptional. Franco was constrained to make the Basilica a monument of Reconciliation, and it houses the remains of dead from both sides. In the minds of the conquered, however, it has remained one to the victors only, and many of the surviving victors concur.

12. Figures from the reports of the *Dirección General de Regiones Devastadas*.

13. On his death in 1956, Dr. Negrin passed the Russian receipts of the Spanish gold to Franco. Photostats have now been published: *v.* Bolin, pp. 375-82; cf. Thomas, p. 395 and Notes 2 and 3, and p. 396. For a fuller and more recent confession by General Orlov, *v.* article in *Readers Digest*, December 1966. The photostats give a full account of the Russian weighing of the gold between 6th and 10th November 1936, and acknowledge receipt of 510,079,592 grammes. At January 1967 prices, the value therefore was £225 millions. The loss of these gold reserves, between 70 and 80 per cent of the total, had to be kept secret by Franco for as long as possible else the post-war economic difficulties of Spain would have been even worse than they were. The sur-

render of this gold to Russia in October 1936 by the Popular Front Government is a fact which must be taken into consideration whenever the question is discussed as to how far that Government was consciously putting Spain under Soviet domination or as to how naïve it was.

14. Ciano's *Diary 1939-43* (Heinemann, 1947), pp. 117, 119, 294.

15. Ibid., p. 106. Entry for 23rd June 1939.

16. Serrano, p. 67.

17. Ibid., p. 127.

18. Ciano, *L'Europa*, pp. 603-4.

19. Franco quotations from B.S.S., Vol. XVIII, pp. 210-17, and Vol. XIX, p. 130.

20. For the Gibraltar issue see Chs. 14 and 15.

21. Juan de la Cosa, p. 118; Serrano, p. 142. There is no short answer to the question which side profited most from non-intervention.

22. See Chs. 9-11.

23. D.G.F.P., Vol. II, 622, 624, 638, 641, 659; Vol. III, 666, 669, 670, 672, 704, 705, 711, 714, 736. Cf. Vol. VII, pp. 590-3, for an English version of the German translation of a letter written by Franco to Hitler as an act of reconciliation. Franco did not make an apology. He merely told Hitler why he had declared his neutrality, and softened him with an account of British and French pinpricks.

24. D.G.F.P., Vol. III, pp. 902 *ff*; Vol. VI, 605, 634.

25. D.G.F.P., Vol. VII, 96, 136.

26. Cf. Ciano, *Diary*, pp. 99-102; D.G.F.P., Vol. VI, 507; cf. 522.

27. D.G.F.P., Vol. VII, 524.

28. Valdesoto, p. 309, confirmed by General Franco-Salgado.

29. Serrano, p. 139 and *passim* D.G.F.P., Vols. VII-XIII.

30. For Franco's great admiration of Marshal Pétain *v.* "Interview" for *Arriba*, 25th February, 1951; *Discursos 1951-54*, pp. 38-42; and for *Le Figaro*, 13th June 1938; *Discursos 1955-59*, pp. 487-8. Generals Franco-Salgado and Barroso independently recalled conversations with General Franco at the outbreak of the war in which he put forward this appreciation of its eventual outcome. Both agreed that the speed of the French collapse astonished Franco, but that even Dunkirk did not shake his conviction that Germany would not win outright against Britain. Mussolini's letter, D.G.F.P., Vol. VI, p. 902, urging Franco not to place his hopes on Britain and France is significant. Cf. Juan de la Cosa, pp. 128, 131, 133-4, and Ciano, *Diary*, p. 102, "(Franco) is somewhat prejudiced against the Axis", albeit in *L'Europa*, p. 440, "Spain would maintain a neutrality even more friendly to Italy".

31. Juan de la Cosa, p. 131 *ff*.

32. D.G.F.P., Vol. VIII, 173.

33. D.G.F.P., Vol. VIII, 284, 575, 679.

34. *Discursos 1951-54*, p. 41. Variant reading, *Discursos 1955-59*, p. 488: this last appears to be a translation back from the French of *Le Figaro* of what Franco said in Spanish.

35. Hoare, pp. 43 and 53.

36. But of course Serrano had no right to have his Press declare it "a Spanish victory". See below.

37. *V.* note 33.

38. Varela? Franco himself? Serrano, p. 160.

39. Cf. Peers, pp. 155-62, and Hoare, pp. 26-55. The articles in *Arriba* and *Informáciones* of the period are nauseating in a world no longer imperialist but only marginally more so than those in the British jingoist Press of Boer War days. The "will to Empire" had been stressed by Falangist writers since 1931 and by Franco in his (Civil) War speeches. *V. Palabras del Caudillo* (Barcelona, 1939), *eg.* pp. 299-300, 310-314.

40. Speech, 18th July 1940: a demand let it be remembered constant since the beginning of the century.

41. Franco's understanding of Moroccan aspirations is inherent in his articles for the *Revista de Tropas Coloniales*: that is not to say that at the time he believed Morocco capable of full independence in his lifetime, or that he did not consider that the whole of Morocco should by rights have been all a Spanish Protectorate. Ansaldo, pp. 246-7, says that Franco used to laugh Serrano's blatant imperialism to scorn.

42. D.G.F.P., Vol. IX, 330.

43. Admiral Canaris certainly kept in touch with General Franco, and it can be assumed that as friends and as servicemen, they discussed Hitler's psychology. One version I have heard of the advice given runs: "Look at Norway. She said no, and where is she? Look on the other hand at Sweden giving way on points that don't really matter." Cf. Colvin, pp. 124-33. Vigon however was not the channel of communications.

44. P. 339.

45. D.G.F.P., Vol. IX, 378, pp. 509-10. Franco to Führer on 3rd June: 456, pp. 585 *ff.* Hitler and Vigon; 488 for territorial claims; cf. X, 374.

46. D.G.F.P., Vol. X, 87, 250, 274, 313, 326; Serrano, pp. 165-92.

47. *Diary*, p. 295; cf. *L'Europa*, pp. 589, 595, 597.

48. The change was not unexpected. Cf. D.G.F.P., Vol. X, 250; J. M. Doussinague, *España tenía razón* (Madrid, 1950), p. 41. Nevertheless it was brusque. Cf. Hoare, 71-4 and 169.

49. This account of the Hendaye meeting is based on published material and on information provided by officers on General Franco's entourage on the way to and from the meeting. In June 1966 I pressed General Franco to give me his own version of the meeting. "What has been published is accurate enough," he said. What has been published, however, must be a heavily muted version of what took place, else Hitler's "I would rather have three or four teeth out than have to face that man again" (*L'Europa*, pp. 603-4), and Hitler's other remarks about Franco seem rather unwarranted. If Serrano, pp. 165-92, and *L'Europa*, pp. 589 *ff.*, are to be believed, very little that Franco told Hitler at Hendaye should have been news to him; but I have been left wondering whether Serrano, who hardly mentions Hendaye, has not confused the dates on which various arguments against Spain's entry were brought up (see note 53). On the temper of the meeting the remark has been made to me: "Well, you know, Hitler was a violent fellow and not a gentleman." Franco's only public reference to the meeting were published in *Le Figaro* on 13th June 1958 and are to be found in *Discursos*, etc., 1955-9, pp. 479-81. "My train was late and the Führer was ill-at-ease with waiting. . . ." On all other points his brief account confirms Paul Schmitt's in *Statist auf diplomatischer Bühne* (Bonn, 1949), pp. 502 *ff.* English version: *Hitler's Interpreter* (Heinemann, 1951), pp. 194-7. Other sources: D.G.F.P., Vol. XI, 220 and 221; *L'Europa*, pp. 647 *ff.* Serrano has *nothing* on Hendaye. D.G.F.P., Vol. IX, 323, pp. 528-530, has substantial detail on Operation Felix. There were also minor references to it at the Nuremberg trials (*International Military Tribunal*, Vols. V, p. 2, XV, 542, etc.).

50. Schmitt was not present at this further meeting. Franco used his own interpreter, General Espinosa de los Monteros, a man of very long lineage (*i.e.* pre-1492) who spoke German perfectly "with a Viennese accent", according to Schmitt. Franco had sent him as Ambassador to Berlin. Serrano said of him to Stohrer the following July that he had "well-grounded doubts in regard to the honesty of (his) German sympathies"; D.G.F.P., Vol. XIII, 229. Franco thought Hitler "an affected man, with nothing sincere about him . . . an actor on a stage, and one could see the mechanics of his acting!" (*Figaro*)

51. D.G.F.P., Vol. XI, 294, and pp. 466-7.

52. D.G.F.P., Vol. XI, 286. Britain too: Cf. R. A. Butler, House of Commons, 13th November 1940.

53. Serrano, pp. 233-59; D.G.F.P., Vol. XI, 352 and 357.

54. And he sent "someone to make sure that he stuck to his brief". Cf. Carlton Hayes, *Ambassador on Special Mission* (Macmillan, 1945), p. 65.

55. D.G.F.P., Vol. XI, 473 and note p. 812; 476, 479, 497, 500. Serrano, pp. 258 *ff.* *The Führer Conferences on Naval Affairs* (Admiralty, 1947), Vol. for 1940, pp. 113-14, 122-3, 127-8. For troop movements—conversations with Spanish Army generals involved, cf. Colvin, p. 132.

56. D.G.F.P., Vol. XI, 682, 692, 695, 702, 707, 718, 725, 728; *L'Europa*, p. 628; Juan de la Cosa, p. 136; cf. *Führer Conferences*, 1940, pp. 136-7; 1941, p. 2.

57. D.G.F.P., Vol. XII, 22.

58. Ibid., 28, 46.

59. Ibid., 32; *Diary*, p. 330. Hitler's letter to Mussolini was intercepted by Britain, cf. *Churchill*, Vol. III, p. 11.

60. Statement to *Le Figaro*, 13th June 1958; *Discursos 1955-1959*, pp. 482-3. Matching accounts of Bordighera: D.G.F.P., Vol. XII, 49, Serrano, pp. 261-5; *L'Europa*, pp. 637 *ff.*

61. D.G.F.P., Vol. XII, 95; *Führer Conferences*, 1941, pp. 26, 76, 94; *L'Europa*, pp. 650, 672-3. For Pétain meeting H. de Moulin de Labarthète, *Les Temps des illusions*, etc. (Geneva, 1946); Serrano, pp. 265-7.

62. *Figaro*, loc. cit.; *Discursos*, p. 485.

63. D.G.F.P., Vol. XII, 21, 73.

64. In Payne's account of the Tarduchy plot (*Falange*, pp. 213-5), based principally on the word of Canales, the conspirators sought the assassination of Serrano as well as Franco. Berlin certainly did not share Stohrer's complete conviction that Serrano was pro-German. Army personnel I cross-questioned on the plot were certain that Franco's death was envisaged, but expressed doubts about Serrano Suñer's—perhaps because of subsequent events. Stohrer was right in saying that the Army hated Serrano, but wrong in thinking only Varela was anti-German (D.G.F.P., ibid., p. 615).

65. D.G.F.P., Vol. XII, 386—a long despatch on the situation in Spain as seen by Serrano. The chief of the other negotiators was Demetrio Carceller to whom Payne, p. 295, note 31, relying overmuch on Falangist and especially *camisa vieja* sources, does less than justice. On the economic blockade *v.* Professor W. N. Medlicott, *Survey of International Affairs: The War and the Neutrals* (O.U.P., 1956), and *The Economic Blockade*, Vol. I (H.M.S.O., 1952). In assessing quantities Britain would seem, like the Germans, to have under-estimated the ravages of the drought and the natural increase in population.

66. D.G.F.P., Vol. XII, 422, 453, 509, 574, 619.

67. Ibid., 633, 663, Vol. XIII, 12, 34, 70; Ansaldo, p. 262; Hoare, pp. 114-16; Serrano, p. 294, denies he stirred up the crowd against Britain. J. M. Doussinague, a Foreign Office official and eye-witness, pp. 53-4, insists that Serrano attacked Russia even if the youths did go to the Embassy. However, the violently anti-British articles in *Arriba* of 26th and 27th June must cast doubts on Serrano's innocence in the affair, as well of course as his remark to Stohrer that an incident against Britain should be provoked.

68. D.G.F.P., Vol. XIII, 34.

69. Ibid., Vol. XI, 479, Vol. XII, 157; *Arriba* from 26th June onwards.

70. Varela's postings and retirements were by no means all political. There were a number of superannuated officers as the German High Command had reported a year earlier: cf. D.G.F.P., Vol. X, 326. Serrano sought the repatriation of the more rabid Falangists in the following November. Ibid., Vol. XIII, 523. For the continuation of his intrigues, cf. ibid., 273, 392, Serrano went to Berlin in November. Hitler was still resentful of Spain's refusal to enter the war. Serrano excused Franco on the grounds that Spain was disunited. Only the Falange, he said, was pro-German: ibid., 522, 523. Stohrer was again warned not to intervene. Cf. ibid., 467.

71. *España Libre*, 25th July 1941; *Arriba*, 31st July.

72. Cosa, p. 141; Hoare, pp. 107-9; for Donovan's visit, cf. pp. 74-5. On British plans for a landing on Cadiz *at the invitation of Spain*, *v.* Churchill, Vol. II, pp. 551-2; for a landing on the Canaries *if* Germany invaded Spain, ibid., pp. 460, 552-63, 625, 639. However, the Germans also had plans to invade Spain and Portugal *if* Britain landed on the peninsula. This was Operation *Isabella*. Six to eight divisions were earmarked for use if the need arose. *V.* D.G.F.P., Vol. XIII, 469, 7th May 1941. The use by the Germans of the Canaries for refuelling submarines with the connivance of the Spanish Navy could have been held to justify British action to neutralise this activity. For a very well-documented summary of this, see *The War and the Neutrals* (article by Katherine Duff), pp. 266-8. My impression is that General Vigon and Admiral Moreno, with the help of Serrano, kept most, if not all, of the facts from Franco. (They were, it seems, totally unknown even to the Spanish Army High Command.) On board the *Prince of Wales*, 10th August 1941 (*v.* Vol. III, pp. 388-9), Churchill did say to Roosevelt that Britain *might* be forced to act before Hitler invaded the Peninsula. Sumner Welles, before the U.S. Congress hearings on the Pearl Harbour Attack (U.S.G.P.O., 1946, pt. 4, pp. 1785-6) has Roosevelt *dissuading* Churchill from an act which would have appeared to the Latin American world as much an act of aggression as any of Hitler's. In view of Roosevelt's and Churchill's subsequent attitudes towards Spain (see Ch. 13) either Sumner Welles put the wrong emphasis on Churchill's words, or Churchill and Roosevelt switched points of view. See also footnote, Ch. 13, p. 371.

73. As in Seville Franco spoke in Galaico-Portuguese, to the discomfiture of the *cuñadisimo*, Serrano's own account (pp. 267-70) and Stohrer's version of what Serrano told him about the meeting (*Documents secrets du Ministère des Affaires Etrangères d'Allemagne*—trans. Eristov; Paris, 1947 and 1955), 8th May 1942, p. 96, are therefore suspect. The Spanish-Portuguese meetings had greater propaganda than real value. Doussinague gives a full account of them, pp. 115-26. Serrano chose this moment to issue a denial of the use of the Canaries by German submarines. As the Germans knew this was false, perhaps Serrano intended it as a reminder to the Germans that whatever Franco might say he at least was helping Germany surreptitiously. For Franco's two- and then

three-war theory, as later in 1942 and 1943, cf. Hayes, pp. 71-2, 98, 161-2; Hoare, pp. 112-13; Eristov, pp. 133-6. Generals Franco-Salgado and Barroso, however, assured me that it was fully developed by the beginning of 1942.

74. P. 56. For Monarchist plots: cf. Ansaldo, ¿*Para Que?*, pp. 276 ff; cf. also Eristov, pp. 96, 105-110.

75. Doussinague, p. 130; Hoare, pp. 165-6; Hayes, p. 57; Payne, pp. 234-5, gives a Falangist version of the affair as an anti-Carlist. He ignores the international background to the affair.

76. Hoare, p. 166.

77. Ibid., 166-71; Hayes, 58.

78. *Diary*, 4th September 1942.

79. Doussinague, pp. 127-38, has a fascinating account of a Nazi plot to assassinate Franco and replace him by a person wholly subservient to Berlin. The Germans certainly carried on a war of nerves against Spain till February 1943.

80. Churchill, Vol. IV, p. 848.

81. Hoare, pp. 18, 224, 294-5.

82. Ibid., p. 274.

83. Ibid., p. 288.

84. Hayes, p. 298.

85. Hoare, pp. 308-15; Serrano, pp. 302-3.

86. P. 140.

87. P. 35; cf. pp. 303-9.

88. Hansard, 24th May, 1944.

13

THE UNITED NATIONS
VERSUS FRANCO

The era of the *cuñadisimo* was over.

During the next twenty-two months from September 1942 until his death from a heart attack on 3rd August 1944, Jordana, the new Foreign Minister, while pro-British personally, was first and foremost Franco's General Staff Officer (Foreign Affairs) rather than Minister. He put all the facts before the Generalissimo in meticulous detail, discussed with him the courses open, and then to the minutest point carried out the orders given him.[1] He was, according to Hoare, "the most conscientious of all Spanish ministers" with an eleven-and-a-half-hour working day.[2]

Once again rumours multiplied and persisted that the Allies planned an attack on the Canaries if not in the Iberian peninsula itself.* There was a fresh spate of anti-Franco articles in the American Press advocating a rupture of diplomatic relations. On or soon after 16th September[3] Spanish intelligence reports reached Franco that there was inordinate activity on the neutral ground between Gibraltar and La Linea. German intelligence officers, of whose presence Hoare would often complain, were not the only observers of what went on and around the Rock.

Franco ordered his forces to observe but in no way to interfere with the allied aircraft which Churchill would later reveal[4] came to number "600 aeroplanes . . . in full range and in full view of the Spanish batteries", or with the ships massing in Algeciras Bay, within what Spain considered Spanish territorial waters. These were the preparations for

* Operations in the Iberian peninsula were again studied by the Allies in June 1942. *v.* Churchill, op. cit., Vol. IV, p. 345.
Cf. also General Sir Frederick Morgan: *Overture to Overlord* (Hodder and Stoughton 1950), p. 195: cf. note 62 to Chapter 12 above.

Operation Torch, the North Africa landings. Churchill had persuaded a seemingly sceptical President Roosevelt that Spain would not go to war over Torch, and assured him that if the Germans tried to force their way through Spain, it would take them at least two months.[5] Here indeed was the strange paradox. The British Ambassador was certain beyond all doubt that Franco was a belligerent on the side of the Axis in all but name: Hayes was sure that it was not so; yet it was Churchill who maintained in effect that all Franco's protestations of loyalty to the Axis were empty of any non-neutral intention, and Roosevelt who feared that Franco would act against the Allies.* Churchill would say later: "Before [Torch] was begun, Spain's power to injure us was at its highest".[6] Spain at that moment had the guns and the ammunition to have done the assembled forces very grievous harm.[7]

Jordana was worried over the preparations which could be seen so clearly from Algeciras. Though assured by the Duke of Alba that the preparations were for a landing on *French* North Africa, and the Americans had promised Spain at the end of October that they considered Spanish neutrality necessary to the allied cause,[8] at the weekly Cabinet meeting of 4th November, he gave it as his considered opinion that of all likely objectives for the concentrations off Gibraltar, Spanish Morocco seemed to him most probable. Obviously the ships would be moving off any moment. Franco had a shoot arranged for the weekend. He did not cancel it.

At 0100 hours on Sunday 8th November Hayes telephoned Jordana asking for an immediate audience.

> He greeted us in pyjamas and bathrobe and with obvious anxiety. This was not lessened when I requested him to make an immediate appointment for me with General Franco so that I might present to the Caudillo, without delay, an urgent communication from President Roosevelt. The Foreign Minister tried to elicit from me the contents or at least the subject of the communication. I regretted, I said, that I could not divulge it except to the Caudillo. Count Jordana then tried calling the Palace of the Pardo† from his telephone in an adjoining hallway. After half an hour, punctuated by his pacing the floor in and out of our room in ever deepening anxiety, he finally aroused the Pardo, only to learn that the Caudillo was out on a hunting party and wouldn't be back till early morning, at which time he would set an hour for receiving me.

* Theodore Roosevelt led his Roughriders against the Spaniards in Cuba: Churchill, as we have said, was with the Spaniards—as a correspondent.
† Franco's residence on the outskirts of Madrid.

It was then a little after two. . . . Count Jordana looked so inexpressibly distressed that I decided to take him into our confidence forthwith. So, "as a trusted friend", I then and there let him see the President's letter. . . . I have never seen a man's face change expression so quickly and so completely as Jordana's. From one of intense anxiety, it was now one of intense relief. "Ah!" he said, "so Spain is not involved."[9]

The letter contained formal notification of the allied landing in French North Africa, and this assurance:

These moves are in no shape, manner or form directed against the Government or people of Spain or Spanish Morocco or Spanish territories—metropolitan or overseas.

Roosevelt ended with this promise:

Spain has nothing to fear from the United Nations.

Franco accepted Roosevelt's word. In October, when rumours had been strongest that the Allies would attack the Canaries, he had sent reinforcements there. When now Germany occupied the whole of France he ordered a partial mobilisation, for the potential threat from Germany extended now along the whole of the Pyrenees and not just a section of them. He had Jordana tell the Ambassadors of the belligerent powers that Spain would resist any invasion. That done, he seems, as it were, to have opted out of the war about him. Therefore he did not bestir himself unduly over protests by Samuel Hoare against Spanish ports being used on occasion by German and Italian submarine depot ships, and against the existence of German intelligence networks in Spain. He knew that there were allied agents at work as well; and if the Germans used Falangists to their own ends, so did Hoare himself encourage Monarchists, and O.S.S. men meddle with Republicans.[10] He acceded easily to Hayes' request that American airmen who mistook Spain for Africa should be looked upon like shipwrecked sailors and therefore not interned. He knew all about "the escape route" through Spain through which 1,100 American airmen and some British made their way from France back to their units. He gave free passage to 25,000 able-bodied men, most of them on their way to join the Free French forces in Africa.[11]

That the countries of Western Europe should be destroying themselves was to Franco utter foolishness. Europe's common enemy was Soviet Russia and Communism. On 6th January at a dinner he took Hoare aside. He had heard that Stalin was insisting that in the post-war

Europe Russia's sphere of influence should have the Rhine as its limit. That, he said, meant the end of a Free Europe. When Moltke, the "tough" ex-Warsaw German Ambassador whom Ribbentrop sent to replace Stohrer, presented his credentials, Franco urged Germany to come to terms with the West.[12] Ten days later he sent Hoare a long memorandum as though written by Jordana "for transmission to the British Government". The person Franco was most anxious to convince was Churchill.

Two passages at least of this memorandum of February 1943 would be re-echoed by statesmen of the countries of the future NATO in years to come.

> Which is the greater danger not only for the continent but for England herself, a Germany . . . with sufficient strength to serve as a rampart against Communism . . . or a sovietised Germany which would certainly furnish Russia with the added strength of her war industries, her engineers, her specialised workmen and technicians, which would enable Russia to extend herself with an empire without precedent from the Atlantic to the Pacific? . . .
>
> If Germany did not exist Europeans would have to invent her. It would be ridiculous to think that her place could be taken by a confederation of Lithuanians, Poles, Czechs and Rumanians which would rapidly be converted into so many more states of the Soviet confederation.

Hoare replied to the memorandum six days later. Spain's fears were unfounded. Britain, he prophesied, would come out of the war Europe's most powerful military, naval and air power, and her influence would be greater than at any time since Napoleon. Europe would be in no danger from Russia: but in any case he did not believe that Russia could possibly embark on any anti-European adventure having been Britain's ally in war.[13]

Franco next tried to enlist the aid of the neutrals in his scheme for a negotiated peace. Notwithstanding his lack of success, on 16th April, through Jordana, he formally called on the Western Powers to make peace. That very day Cordell Hull reiterated the Allied policy of "unconditional surrender". On the following day Berlin denied knowledge of any Spanish offer of mediation: Germany would fight "until the peril threatening Europe from East and West should be crushed". Hitler now called on Franco to declare war on Russia. After all, Franco in his New Year greetings had wished him well in his war against Communism.

At a Cabinet meeting Franco now instructed his Minister of War to withdraw the Blue Division as soon as it could be conveniently arranged. It could not be immediately since, in the Spanish view, there was still a danger of a German invasion of Spain. Since the January there had been a concentration of considerable forces in the Toulouse-Perpignan area.[14] The Spaniards were not mistaken. The Germans had a plan for the occupation of the north coast of Spain—Operation Gisela—ready by April. In May Doenitz pressed Hitler to occupy Spain rather than defend Sicily and Sardinia. Hitler replied that Germany could not undertake the operation without first-class divisions. "They are the only tough Latins and they would carry on guerrilla warfare in our rear."[15] In his public utterances Franco persisted in his calls for a negotiated peace. Newspaper correspondents in the West interpreted them as an Axis-inspired attempt to split Russia from the West. In fact, Hitler's latest Ambassador Dieckhoff urged Franco to stop.[16]

That was on 15th June. By then a fresh anti-Franco propaganda campaign in the U.S.A. had reached such an intensity that Jordana in all seriousness wondered whether the Germans were behind it (as they were in Spain behind the anti-Allied tenor of the Spanish Press). The U.S. Government was now being counselled to *invade* Spain.* Franco showed publicly that he could still be unfriendly to the Allies. This was

---

* Not only among Spaniards but among Spanish-Americans, irrespective of political opinion, I have always found polite incredulity over the claims of Britain and the U.S. that their Press and radio are not strictly directed and controlled in peacetime, let alone in wartime. Therefore the Press campaign was seen as a government-inspired move to prepare public opinion for what would have been an act of aggression. There were some highly imaginative stories of Spanish oil tankers supplying submarines and Spain sending Germany food and arms, and of building warships for her. Contrariwise, Britons and Americans, assuming that Franco's Spain was as Hitler's Germany or Mussolini's Italy, logically concluded that the Spanish Press too had been used to prepare public opinion for the entry of Spain into the war on behalf of the Axis. But, as we have seen, Franco could not control the Falange fully, and it was the Falange which controlled the Press. However, there were four important differences in the value of Press propaganda in Spain as compared with its power in Britain and the U.S. First Press readership in Spain was proportionately very small. Second, fifty years almost of uninterrupted Press censorship had made Spaniards rather more sceptical of what they read in the Press than their contemporary Europeans or Americans. Again, there were few able propagandists in Spain: the best of them, the writers in the *Socialista* and *Claridad* were in exile. Finally, propaganda or publicity is never as efficient or effective where there is no competition as where there is. The proof, agreed upon by Hayes and Hoare, is that the overwhelming mass of the people of Spain were and remained pro-Allied, or rather almost as anti-Nazi as they were anti-Communist.

in his annual speech of 17th July 1943. That done, however, he received Hayes in audience. Hayes, knowing better than to complain directly of the speech, spoke of the Falange Press censor Arias Salgado's discrimination against the Allies. "Franco appeared to be greatly surprised" at the non-obedience of orders which he had already given to the Falange's Secretary-General.

The Caudillo promised prompt action (and fulfilled his promise). Hayes on his part was surprised when Franco took calmly his next piece of advice: that the Blue Division should be withdrawn.[18] He was not to know that Franco had in fact already ordered it.[19] However, on 20th August, Hoare had an interview with Franco. It was almost a replica of the Franco-Hayes'. Franco talked of his detestation of the Japanese as violators of the Philippines, and of his fears for Europe with Germany in Russian hands.[20] Hoare complained of the Press, of antiallied activities, of breaches of neutrality and of the presence of the Blue Division in Russia. Hoare then went home to England on leave, very satisfied with his work.

There now followed a remarkable sequence of events. When the Spanish Embassy in Washington issued a statement that the Franco-Hoare talks had been friendly and satisfactory and implied that relations were excellent between Spain and Great Britain[21] Hoare issued his own version. This was, in the words of Hayes,[22] substantially similar to what Hoare had told Hayes in Madrid "with one glaring exception. The publicity had it that the British Ambassador had *demanded* the withdrawal of the Blue Division, etc." The effect on Franco—or any other Spaniard—could have been foreseen by anyone with the slightest knowledge of Spain. Franco could not let it be said that he had been *forced* to withdraw the division. A move which might have been rapid took till 12th October, and Franco left in Russia a part of it, which was renamed the Blue Legion, a good while longer. The withdrawal was done quietly. Franco was no longer afraid of the Germans. As they had not invaded Spain when the Allies had acquired bases in the Azores, Franco assumed that they would now never do so. Calmly he had publicly reaffirmed his neutrality on 1st October and the meaningless term "non-belligerency" would never be used again. Germany protested and Franco ignored the protests. What Franco really feared was a violent reaction from the Nazi element in the Falange. By not publicising the withdrawal he kept the disorders to a minimum.[23]

It was the Allies who made life more difficult for themselves than it need have been from 1943 onwards by not always acting in consort either in Madrid (Hoare and Hayes) or in Washington and London.[24] This was particularly true over what came to be known as the Wolfram Crisis.

Right from the beginning of the war Spain had maintained a strict neutrality in trade. Franco was prepared to do business with any country—except Soviet Russia. It was up to the purchaser to bid for what he wanted and outwit his rivals on purely commercial lines. Here, though the Germans should have had the advantage with their agencies established during the Civil War and their hard-won mining concessions, the British and Americans soon established a fair balance. The Spaniards sold to the highest bidder: wolfram "worthless dust in 1939" was selling at £7,500 a ton in 1943. Now the Spaniards insisted on payment. The Allies could provide the food and fuel which Spain needed whereas Germany could not. Thus, for Germany to get anything at all she had to send Spain machine tools, vehicles, chemicals and medicines which she could ill spare: and weapons for the Spanish Army—to be used in the defence of Spain: which could have meant against the Germans just as easily as against the Americans or the British.* The arrangement therefore suited the Allies well: and it kept Spain from economic bankruptcy. Washington, however, grew tired of having to pay 'through the nose' for that precious material, wolfram. The Allies were in fact buying more than they needed, to keep it from being sold to the Germans. Washington now decided to force Spain to prohibit its export to Germany at any price, so that she would not have to buy any herself. Spain saw the move for what it was, and how, if she acceded to the American demand, she would be depriving herself of the income not merely of the few hundred tons Germany was buying, but of the thousands which the Allies were purchasing.† An extraneous episode now gave the U.S. a splendid weapon. The Filipino Jose Laurel informed the Spanish Government that he had declared the Philippines (till then a U.S. colony) independent, under Japanese protection. The Spanish Government sent a reply assuring the Filipinos that their blood ties with Spain were a guarantee that Hispano-Philippine relations would always be cordial. It was not, as the American Press made it, a recognition by Franco of Jose Laurel or of Philippine independence.

---

* Franco ordered weapons from Germany in February and received them in June. In the March, Allied HQ in Algiers received from the Spanish General Staff a copy of its plans for meeting a German invasion from the Pyrenees and asked for fighter aircraft, anti-aircraft guns and mines. It got none.[25]

† During the first eleven months of 1943 Spain allowed the export of 2,313 tons of the material to the Allies against a mere 690 tons to Germany.

Jordana explained, but the U.S. State Department, against the advice of its Ambassador, proceeded to make a mountain out of a molehill— perhaps under pressure from the exiled Republican lobby which gave full vent to a new anti-Franco campaign in the American Press.* Once again in the New Year there were rumours and "documents" that the Allies were going to invade Spain. They were supposed to be planning to out-flank the German Atlantic wall by landings in North-east Spain or Portugal. Franco, as a general, cannot for a moment have believed them. He would know that the choice for a second front was between the French Atlantic, the Mediterranean and the English Channel coasts, and no other; but the rumours were symptomatic of another possibility. The *Maquis* in the south of France had recruited substantial numbers of Spaniards whose principal interest in collecting the arms parachuted to them was not to drive the Germans from France, but to cross the Pyrenees.[26]

To return however to the wolfram business. The Spaniards saw in the affair a parallel between what the Allies were doing and what the Germans had done over mining concessions during the Civil War. So long as the Allies played the game with more subtlety, Franco was prepared to give way gracefully and therefore not too quickly, not only over the wolfram embargo but over other allied demands—the release of interned Italian ships (now that Italy was an ally), the expulsion of German Secret Service agents and the closure of the German consulate in Tangiers. Britain had only a minor interest in the wolfram embargo, and indeed pointed out the economic losses which Spain would suffer. London reminded Washington that the Germans were getting more of the ore from Portugal than from Spain. Washington, however, had made up its mind, and at the end of 1943 it decided that the only way to make Franco hurry was to threaten to cut off his oil supplies. The Foreign Office impressed on the U.S. State Department that in view of what Hoare called "the idiosyncracies of the Spanish character", "direct threats, and particularly direct public threats, were at all costs to be avoided".[27] Spain was to be told that there would be no February shipment of oil; and when asked for a reason, the Allies were to say "the increasing need of the allied armies";

* This is the background to the equivocal answers given by Franco to German Ambassador Dieckhoff on 15th December 1943 (*v.* Hoare, p. 314). Dieckhoff read Franco almost as long a list of "unfriendly acts" as Hoare had done. Franco assured Dieckhoff that his heart was in a German victory: and did nothing about the complaints.

in no circumstances was it to be said openly that the oil embargo was connected with the wolfram business.

This would have been the correct way to deal with Spain. Hoare and Hayes are agreed basically on what happened next. Here is Hoare's version:

> All would, I believe, have worked well on these lines if there had not been a premature leakage of the plan to an American Press agency. Worse still, the agency, no doubt like any other Press agency in the circumstances, dramatised the news into a public and immediate ultimatum. All oil supplies were to be cut off from Spain as long as a single ton of wolfram left Spain for Germany. The B.B.C. took up the agency tale with zest.* The result was that at the very moment when we believed that our organised pressure was likely to succeed, the public announcement of an embargo stirred to their very depths the latent forces of Spanish obstinacy and immediately increased the difficulties of reaching a swift and satisfactory settlement. On the American side the unfortunate publicity made a complete embargo almost a matter of national prestige, while on the Spanish side acceptance of the allied demand meant surrender to an ultimatum.

This allied action put the whole of Spain, even Franco's enemies, behind the Caudillo. The oil embargo did create considerable hardship in Spain. Food could not be distributed to the full extent. Churchill[28] badgered Roosevelt to stop his foolishness; only after he had warned him that if the U.S.A. did not relent, Britain would come to a separate agreement with Spain, and furnish the oil she needed, did Roosevelt give way. At the end of April Franco agreed to release the Italian ships, expel the German agents and close down the German Consulate in Tangiers; but the U.S.A. had to be satisfied with a reduction and not a total embargo on the exports of wolfram.

In May 1944 Churchill referred in the Commons to the fact that Franco's denial of Spain to the Germans in 1940 had been very helpful to the allied cause, and so also his inaction at the time of the North African landings. Of the latter Churchill said in the face of interjections from other Members of Parliament: "I shall always consider a service was rendered at this time by Spain, not only to the United Kingdom, and to the British Empire and Commonwealth, but to the cause of the United Nations": and he had then gone on to express the

---

* According to Hayes: "The B.B.C. began and continued for two weeks a series of broadcasts attacking the Spanish regime of General Franco". The references are to the B.B.C.'s broadcasts in Spanish.

hope that Spain would be a strong influence for the peace of the Mediterranean after the war. This prompted Franco to write Churchill a letter the following October,[29] not directly, but as protocol demanded, through the Spanish Ambassador in London, the Duke of Alba. Franco recalled the Press and radio campaigns against the régime. He implied in numerous ways criticism of Sir Samuel Hoare's Embassy. He alluded to the subversive activities of British agents. The letter throughout lacked a knowledge of the British scene with such phrases as "the Press, including that of the government". Ubiquitously in detail it was not happily worded. Nevertheless it was a letter written from the heart by a man who believed that Europe was about to face her most dangerous enemy of all time—Communist Russia, and that his country was with Britain the best prepared to do battle with that enemy.[*]

In 1954 or 1964 it might have had a sympathetic hearing: in 1944, Churchill had no choice but to remind Franco of his breaches of neutrality in favour of the Axis, and to stress the Anglo-Russian Alliance. Churchill agreed with Franco that Anglo-Spanish friendship and co-operation was to be desired; however, in all honesty he gave Franco this blunt warning: "It is out of the question for His Majesty's Government to support Spanish aspirations to participate in the future peace settlements. Neither do I think it likely that Spain will be invited to join the future world organisations."

That was a friendly warning of what Franco might expect. Churchill's, after all, was a minority view in the Triumvirate whose other members were Stalin and Roosevelt.[†]

[*] What Franco said to Hayes in an audience on 6th July 1944 must be taken in conjunction with what he wrote to Churchill (Hayes, pp. 243-4). The allied landings in Normandy were then just one month behind: there was still plenty of fight left in the Germans. Indeed in July the success of the Second Front looked far from certain. Nevertheless Franco told Hayes that in his opinion the German defeat was assured and would occur within a year. The German rocket bombs would not demoralise the population of Britain. The German General Staff would seek to stop the war before the civilians or the fanatical Nazis. Franco called on the Allies (that is the British and Americans) to be prepared not only to feed, clothe and rehouse the peoples of the liberated nations but to prevent civil wars. He was worried over the impending fate of Finland, Poland and Rumania. He went on to warn Hayes that there was a sizeable section of the Nazi Party fundamentally sympathetic to Communism and that they would rather surrender to Russia than to the Western Allies. Russia would recover her old Empire in Europe, then turn on Japan. The only point on which he was proved wrong was in giving the Japanese till mid-1946 before final defeat: but then he did not know about the atom bomb.

[†] Churchill signed the letter. How far did he agree with what it said? The following memorandum from the Prime Minister to the Foreign Minister dated

Franco had kept Spain out of World War II. As the fears of Britain and France that Franco had mortgaged during the Civil War the Balearics to Italy had been proved groundless, so also had the contention of all Franco's enemies abroad been false that his signature of a treaty of friendship with Germany and of the anti-Comintern Pact would inevitably lead him into active participation in the greater war. Britain and the United States could make long lists of 'un-neutral acts", but so could Germany. Franco had allowed German agents to operate in Spain: but so had British and American agents operated with his knowledge. German submarines had on occasion taken refuge and refuelled in Spanish ports: but so had, also on occasion, allied aircraft; and Franco had not interned the crews of those making forced landings. Franco, for his part, could have complained that the combatant nations had not respected his neutrality. Hitler had planned to make use of Spain to capture Gibraltar: Churchill and Roosevelt had considered landing on the Canary Islands which to the Spaniards were as the Hawaiis to the United States or the Orkneys and Shetlands to Britain. When in the opinion of the Germans or Italians Franco had shown too much friendliness to the Allies they had torpedoed his ships. When in the opinion of the Allies he was straying too far from even non-belligerency, they had cut off his oil and other supplies. Indeed, it had been the Allies rather than the Germans who had harassed him most. Though Britain in the early part of the war had loaned him several million pounds, the quantities of wheat, cotton and oil which they and the Americans permitted at the best of times to enter Spain had been inferior to Spain's requirements in normal times; and they were not normal times but years in which Spain had to make good the ravages of civil war and deficiences caused by drought.

Franco's record as a neutral did not in truth compare unfavourably with that of other European neutrals. As Serrano Suñer would point out,[30] Portugal had been no less friendly to Germany than Spain in

11th December (*Second World War*, Vol. 6, p. 616) is relevant to the answer: "I do not think the balance of help and hindrance given us by Spain in the war is fairly stated. The supreme services of not intervening in 1940 or interfering with the use of the airfield and Algeciras Bay in the months before 'Torch' in 1942 outweigh the minor irritations which are so meticulously set forth".

That Roosevelt and Churchill did not agree on Spain can be seen from the following memorandum of Churchill's to Roosevelt dated 4th June 1944 (Vol. 5, pp. 553-4): "I do not care about Franco, but I do not wish to have the Iberian peninsula hostile to the British after the war. . . . I do not know whether there is more freedom in Stalinist Russia than in Franco's Spain. I have no intention to seek a quarrel with either."

1940, and had supplied her with raw materials as Spain had. Switzerland, at first pro-allied, had later imposed a strict censorship not to
offend Berlin. From 1942 the Swiss machine tool and chemical industries had worked almost exclusively for Germany, and Swiss workers
had gone there. Sweden in 1941 had allowed the passage of a complete
division of the Wermacht on its way from Norway to Finland, and at
all times the transit of German soldiers on leave from Norway and
Finland to Germany. There had been Swedish volunteers on the Russian
front. Until the second front landings Sweden had supplied Germany
with ball-bearings and machine tools. Turkey, under treaty obligations, should have gone to the aid of Greece. Instead in 1941 she had
signed pacts of non-aggression and friendship with Germany. She
would have helped the Allies if she had closed the Dardanelles, but she
did not do so until 15th June 1944 and after the Allies had supplied her
with £20 million of arms.

Such an analysis would have required an unemotional approach to
the facts which was beyond the United Nations, that is the U.S.S.R.,
the U.S.A., Britain and France in the period 1944-6.

The U.S.A., Britain and France had many nationals who genuinely
believed in the *simpliciste* theory that Franco owed his victory to Hitler
and Mussolini, that he in his turn had helped them and that the overthrow of Franco would unquestionably lead to the "restoration of
democracy in Spain". They had also given asylum to tens of thousands
of Spanish refugees. These enemies of Franco found in the nationals
a sympathetic ear. The most fantastic stories of Franco helping the
Germans were readily believed: for example that Franco was manufacturing the V1 and V2 projectiles for Germany, though he had the
means to make nothing more complicated than old 75 mm shell and
flying club aircraft; simultaneously they alleged that all Spain's technicians had been forcibly transported to Germany.[*] The smallest
incident was blown up into a major "news story".[†]

* 20,000 workers, unskilled by German standards, did in fact go, attracted by
pay seven times as high as they could get in Spain.
† In January 1944 one bomb exploded in a British ship carrying Spanish oranges.
One unexploded bomb was found in another ship, in the London Docks. It was
readily assumed that they had been put there by Franco's agents or by Germans
with Franco's connivance. Even *The Times* (20th Jan. 1944) assumed the latter and
chastised Franco editorially. In the absence of other evidence, it may well be
asked: *Cui bono?* Hardly that of Franco then doing his best to establish good
relations with the Allies. In a speech on 27th January Franco reaffirmed yet again
his neutrality and referred to "attempts to draw Spain or force Spain into one
side or another". A second unexploded bomb was found in a crate of onions a
week later. Franco expelled Germans living in Valencia.

Conservative political circles in Britain would have liked Franco to have abdicated in favour of a king—Negrin in Britain did not inspire much confidence in the Conservatives or even among many of the Labour men who came to know him: in the United States the consensus of political opinion was for a Republic, under some middle-of-the-road man like Prieto, or yet better Martinez Barrio, both then in Mexico running a Committee of National Liberation.

The U.S.S.R. could not be other than anti-Franco. In Spain, the Comintern—if not the U.S.S.R. itself—had suffered a grievous defeat.* The Russian Generals Grigorovich, Koniev, Malinovsky and Nedelin, and the Russo-Polish Rokossovski, had all been on the losing side. So had the Comintern magnates Josef Broz (Tito) of Yugoslavia, Togliatti of Italy, Gero of Hungary, Stepanov of Bulgaria and Thorez of France, to mention but a few of the Spanish war veterans already destined by Stalin to create his post-war empire. That post-war empire would be all the wider if at the same time as the Red Army over-ran East and Central Europe, Spain and the Mediterranean were to fall into his hands.†

If Franco faced a completely hostile world, he had himself more than partly to blame. Even people who realised that Spain had never been a democracy, and who had supported Franco and his companions when they had risen against the Government which had permitted, if not created, the anarchy of Spain of July 1936, had come to ask themselves by the end of 1944 whether Franco's record gave him any greater moral right to remain in power. There had been no governmental attempt to reconcile the conquered and the victors. There had indeed been amnesties so that the director of prisons could say in the late Summer of 1943 that there were only 49,000 political prisoners and in the Spring of 1944, when twenty-three prisons were closed down, that the total had been reduced to 25,000. But even if just that number, why still

* The Russian army had also drawn many a wrong conclusion on the civil war: for example, that Russian tanks would always be better than the German, so that whereas the Germans went on to build their Marks III and IV, poor General Pavlov had to lead against these the same Vickers models which he had commanded in Spain. Stalin had him shot in 1941, by which time he had already had executed the Russian General Borov who had also been in Spain.

† The annexation of Baltic countries and parts of Poland, Rumania and Hungary might be explained as a desire of Russia to have more readily defensible frontiers: the establishment against the popular will of Communist governments in these three countries and Czechoslovakia and Bulgaria might also be half-explained away as self-protection; but these were the arguments of Hitler in his expansionist period; and no such explanation is possible for Stalin's attempt to make Communist states of Greece and Turkey.

25,000? The nightly ritual *Caídos por Dios y por España, Presentes*, the victors' cry broadcast nightly and audible throughout Europe and South America belied all the assertions that Franco had at heart the defence of Christianity. The special tribunals to cope with the Law on Political Responsibilities had also been abolished, but in 1943 there had been a new law extending the definition of military rebellion to include strikes, sabotage, conspiracy, illegal possession of fire-arms, the propagation of false and tendentious news, and any word or action calculated to upset the internal order or to lower the prestige of the State, Army or Authorities. Only Communist Russia had a comparable law. Franco's régime looked like a replica of Hitler's and Mussolini's, and Stalin's—with a secret police, and a single party having special privileges before the law,* a large budget allocation and its own militia. The party control of the workers and the party control of the printed and broadcast word, the existence of a secret police in whose training the Germans had helped and which Hitler himself had reviewed, the denial of freedom of speech, movement, assembly or association were all facets then associated in the popular mind of the foreigner with Nazism, as later they would be with the very evil from which Franco was supposed to have saved Spain, Communism. As foreign correspondents had no freedom to gather news within the country, and as their despatches were censored, only close observers could see the differences in degree and those in kind between Franco's system and those of countries properly totalitarian.†

It required the perspicacity of a Carlton Hayes to see how wide was the gap between Franco and the Party. The *FET y de las JONS* was

---

* Since 1941.

† Franco used then to call his régime *totalitario*. However it was only to churchmen like Cardinal Segura who had lived outside Spain that the word had the international meaning of "a state which subordinates the rights proper to the individual to those of the state" and arrogates them to itself—a heresy to the Catholic mind. To Spaniards the word *totalitario* (as eventually accepted by the Royal Academy of the Language) meant "that which is the sum of all its parts without exception": that is to say an "*estado totalitario*" was one which was "all-embracing" in the sense that it could concern itself with all the activities of the individual and pertaining to the individual: it considered it within its rights therefore to take over, if need be, industry and commerce (an activity denied it by Liberals), the land (a claim denied it by Conservatives), education (even to an extent challenged by the Church) etc. Harold Laski's philosophy of government would rightly be called in Spanish "*totalitaria*", and even Attlee's post-war government could also be termed in Spanish *un régimen totalitario*. Nevertheless an examination of the contexts in which Franco used the word in speeches and documents leaves considerable room for doubt whether to him it meant anything other than a synonym for *orgánico*, that is organised.

as far from becoming the new substance *Movimiento* at the end of 1947 as it had been in April 1937 when Franco had forcibly brought together the divisions Alfonsist, Carlist and Falangist. In 1942 Franco had toured the country preaching unity under himself in his *movimiento*, but its elements had remained immiscible. Within his Cabinet, as we have seen, he kept representatives of all groups. Within each ministry he carefully apportioned posts to Falangists, Carlists and Alfonsists. Whoever was at the top could not have his political ally as his immediate subordinate.

Franco, however, did give the Falange uncounterweighted power in two activities of his "all-embracing" State: the organisation of the workers and Press and propaganda.

In his Labour Charter Franco had promised the workers new Trade Unions. It must be remembered that his experience of the matter was limited to the C.N.T. whose avowed purpose had been the destruction of all authority and the very idea of the State, and the U.G.T. whose chief purpose had been the Marxist one of fomenting class hatred and a socialist revolutionary spirit among the masses. Anything approaching the British or American idea of Trade Unions as organisations to better working conditions by bargaining with individual employers had been unknown in Spain except in the few places where the so-called Catholic Trade Unions had existed. The new organisations were to be modelled along the lines, first proposed in Belgium, of vertical syndicates. Theoretically there was much to commend them. They were envisaged as autonomous professional associations bringing together employers and employees as equals. Within them the "two sides of industry" would learn that in co-operation both sides could benefit more than from constant struggle. The idea attracted Franco in all particulars but that of "autonomy", as a means to bring about gradually the social reform which he had long recognised as necessary. He entrusted their organisation to the more radical Falangists. His reasoning appears to have been this: given something positive to do, their revolutionary zeal would have an outlet: being beholden to him, they would accept direction by him. He chose well. However, from being autonomous organisations at the service of all individuals engaged in a particular trade or profession, the *sindicatos* became an adjunct of a party, as inextricably linked in the popular mind with a particular political ideology as the U.G.T. or C.N.T. They therefore failed to attract the loyalty of any person to whom for one reason or another Falangism was distasteful: and since Franco chose to exercise his surveillance indirectly through his Minister of Labour (a Falangist firebrand with *sindicato* connections) what the world saw in the system was a means whereby governmental policy on labour would be carried out at all levels. Self-evidently they were not free trade unions, and as such anathema to the British and American. The holding of elections in the October of 1944 for offices in *sindicatos* did not satisfy the objection that though the workers had been free to choose their officers, the choice had been limited within previously selected lists, and that those officers would have to carry out orders emanating from the top.

Franco was far less successful, as we have seen, in keeping the Falange under control in the field of Press and propaganda. Carlton Hayes' complaints eventually led to the creation of a separate Ministry of Information and the denial to the Falange of its power over the printed and broadcast word. Yet in point of fact the American Ambassador had not been the first to bring the excesses of the Falange to the notice of the Caudillo. Before Serrano Suñer's fall in 1942, he had already been told by the new Archbishop of Toledo Pla y Deniel and the Bishop of Madrid that under Serrano and his henchman José Luna, Nazi influences had reached the point in which Racialism was being preached. There had always been in the utterances of the victors occasional references to Jews (that is the members of the Jewish religion) in the same breath as Liberals, Masons and Communists:* Franco himself had fallen occasionally into the practice; but now true anti-semitism was being fostered, irrelevant though it was to the Spanish scene. Thereafter the Falange had sought to build up the image of Hitler as a great Catholic—to the Spanish hierachy's even greater annoyance.† Franco did not take much notice. The Church seemed perpetually to be complaining.

Franco had allowed the restoration of religious teaching in state schools and the reopening of Church schools: he had repealed all the anti-religious legislation of the Republican period and the easy marriage and divorce laws: he had restored to the clergy the 1851 pensions: he was rebuilding destroyed church property. The Church was enjoying greater liberty than at any time for a century and a half: contrary to the tenets of the strict Falangists he had declared Catholicism the religion of the new state. Yet the Vatican had steadfastly refused

---

* Tusquets, the anti-Mason pamphleteer had also been anti-Jewish in a non-racialist sense.

† The Bishop of Calahorra got hold of a copy of *Mit brenender Sòrge*, published its contents in his diocese, and was punished for his breach of the censorship.

him the prerogative of the Spanish Head of State: the power of "presenting" the candidate of his choice to fill vacant bishoprics and certain other benefices. Only on 7th June 1941, after two years of negotiations and then still begrudgingly, had the Papacy agreed to a system of "presenting" which did grant Franco the final word, but yet allowed the Vatican far more say than before.* By the end of 1944, three and a half years had passed since Serrano Suñer, on his behalf, and Cardinal Cicognani on Pius XII's had signed that agreement, but the Concordat envisaged in one of its clauses as "to be concluded as soon as possible" was no nearer accomplishment.

To the Catholic with any historical knowledge a Concordat was always proof of the existence of discord between Church and State: it was a Peace Treaty presupposing a previous war. It was not difficult, however, to hold it before the less instructed as a Treaty of Friendship, "a Papal guarantee of the Catholicity of the Ruler", almost a chrism. Thus, a Concordat would have been a welcome prop to Franco: contrariwise the obvious reluctance of the Papacy to expedite it weakened him: but to no great extent.

One of the undoubtable results of the Civil War had been a marked return of Spaniards to their religion. The churches were full, not merely

---

* The system of filling vacant Sees agreed upon in 1941 was the following:

(1) The Nuncio in consultation with the Government sends the Holy See a list of at least six priests:

(2) From these the Pope selects three, and returns the 'short list' via the Nuncio to the Head of State:

(3) The Head of State chooses one person and 'presents' him to the Pope who thereupon is supposed to name him the Bishop (or Archbishop) elect.

At stage two the Pope may add supplementary names of his own choosing to the three he selects from the original list. If at stage two none or only one or two of the names on the list are acceptable to the Pope, the Pope may make his own list of three. In that case at stage three the Head of State is bound to declare, within thirty days, any objection he may have on *political* grounds to any one or all of those on the Pope's list. If he does, the process begins all over again. At the Vatican Council this Governmental control over the choice of bishops was implicitly condemned, but the situation remained unchanged even as late as 1967.

That the Papacy and the Head of State often have not agreed over an appointment is a more than reasonable surmise from the inordinate length of time, running on occasion into years, that it has taken to fill many a vacancy. By 31st December 1943 only three had been filled of the thirteen Sees left vacant by the execution of the bishops in 1936.

Cardinal Vidal of Tarragona did not return to his See in 1939. Did he voluntarily remain in exile? It is in the tradition of Cardinals who are titular archbishops not to leave their Sees unless expelled (cf. Cardinals Wyszinki, Mindzenty, Beran etc.): and to return at the earliest opportunity.

on Sundays but even on weekdays. There were, doubtless, a number of men with Popular Front, Masonic and other proscribed antecedents who made a show of conversion as a means of allaying the suspicions of the authorities. They would go to Mass because they were afraid not to do so, as in Communist countries there were Catholics who feared to be seen in church: everything else being equal or nearly equal an applicant to a job armed with a recommendation from a priest had a greater chance of success than one not so provided. However, the conversion of hundreds of thousands in the "Red" zones was beyond question, sincere, especially of those who, out of a sense of justice, had adopted Communism and Anarchism as a religion: what they had seen of Communism or Anarchism in practice had revolted them, and they had come back into the church of their baptism with a deeper understanding of Christianity than when they had left it. The church of laymen as well as priests was stronger than ever in the century. Franco was not the perfect Christian ruler but he allowed the religion of the masses a greater freedom than it had had under the Bourbons or under either republic.

In this negative sense then Franco had the support of this Catholic mass of people at the end of 1944. His main strength, however, lay on three other facts. First, though his Army officers were divided in their political sympathies—Alfonsist, Carlist, Falangist, Conservative and even Liberal and Christian Democrat—their primary loyalty was to their country, Most had seen as clearly as Franco that Spain could not have afforded to enter into World War II on either side; and an even greater number realised, now that the war was ending, that another Civil War would heap further and perhaps this time irremediable ruin upon their country. In Franco they saw the one man who could hold Spain together and thus prevent another civil war. Secondly in their anxiety not to have Spain plunged into another civil war, the Army was at one with the mass of the people. The combatants and the people were the ones who had suffered the hardships and perils of the war and who had no wish to undergo again the experience in their lifetime, neither on behalf of the Falangist or Monarchist leaders who cursed Franco for having betrayed the cause of Jose Antonio or of one or other Pretender, nor on behalf of the exiled Negrin, Prieto, Martinez Barrio, Largo Caballero or Dolores Ibarruri: and least of all on behalf of Roosevelt or Stalin. Franco's régime was oppressive, with its secret police, its trials by courts martial, its censorship of the printed word, its privileged classes, and other denials of the rights and freedoms of the individual; but all these had been characteristic also of monarchist days and more so of the Republican period.

That the people however heavily oppressed by Franco yet preferred him to any exiled politician was a fair deduction from the 'invasions' of Spain which took place in the Autumn of 1944. As the Germans withdrew from the south of France the Maquisards took over, and ruled the area without reference to de Gaulle in Paris. There were with the Maquisards several thousand Spanish and Catalan exiles.[31] They opted out of the pursuit of the retreating Germans. With the approval of the local Communist "governors" they attacked and captured the Spanish Consulates in Bordeaux, Pau, Toulouse, Perpignan and Marseilles. Toulouse radio began to broadcast the wildest of "news" about serious disturbances in Spanish cities. There were supposed to be mass risings in Asturias and Andalusia. A major battle was said to have been fought in Barcelona and 1,500 were said to be lying dead in the streets. Fifty thousand Spanish warriors were stated to have crossed the Pyrenees at numerous points, and, reinforced by tens of thousands of jubilant sympathisers, they were stated to be sweeping down on a cringing Franco in Madrid.

In all this fantasy there was a grain of truth. At the beginning of October five hundred well-armed guerrillas entered the Valley of the Roncal through various passes including Roland's Roncesvalles. A similar number spread out into the Vale of Aran through Bagnères de Luchon; and bands not above platoon strength went through Andorra and points east into Catalonia. In all, and at most, the invaders numbered fifteen hundred. Yague was given five infantry battalions (2,500 men) and under a thousand civil guards to dispose of them in Navarre and Aragon, and Moscardo* moved against them in Catalonia with a smaller force. Within five weeks there was nothing left of the invaders except remnants who took to brigandage and, as brigands, were pursued by the Civil Guard and the French gendarmes with equal zest.†

* The great majority of the invaders escaped back to France. Of the nineteen prisoners Yague took, nine were foreigners. As far as I have been able to correlate the figures, it would seem that the total number of invaders killed did not far exceed 100. In all about 500 were captured.

† De Gaulle sent 100 gendarmes into Andorra in pursuit of the French Communists who had been the Lords of Toulouse. Thereupon Franco sent 107 Civil Guards under Moscardo. The Hispano-French condominium over the Republic of Andorra was thus preserved. Some of the invaders, as also handfuls of men who were mis-guided by Radio Toulouse and took to the hills in Asturias and round Malaga, held out for some time but they were a police rather than a political problem.

There would seem to be no other occasion in modern history in which fifteen hundred well-armed and presumably reasonably well-trained and determined guerrillas have been defeated so easily. The force deployed against them had a mere 3 to 1 superiority where elsewhere even a 10 to 1 superiority has proved inadequate against guerrillas. It was not equipped with helicopters or bombers.[32] The determining factor was that these guerrillas received no help whatever from the local inhabitants except a very few whom they terrorised.* On the contrary the local inhabitants, not merely of Navarre and Aragon but even of Catalonia gave the Army and the police positive help in making known the positions and movements of marauding bands. Thereafter neither the Communist-dominated *Junta Nacional* of exiles established in Toulouse to conduct the invasion, nor the *Junta de Liberacion* in Mexico could have any grounds for the hope they had long cherished that the third of Spain which had voted them into power in 1936, if not the near half which had fought for them in the Civil War, was prepared to fight again given encouragement from abroad. The unpalatable truth was that while few Spaniards had a good word for Franco, fewer still were prepared to see the return of the exiled politicians. It was not a case of "better the devil you know", but of "better the devil we have than the seven devils we might have".

Such then was the internal situation at the time when Franco was being warned by Churchill that Spain could expect to be excluded from the forthcoming world international organisation.

On 4th November 1944 declared to a U.P. correspondent that Spain was "an organised democracy" with the ideals God, Motherland and Justice, with a deep-rooted Catholicism. From then on he sought to change the Spanish image to this mould. As usual he proceeded with caution. There were further releases of political prisoners. The police were restrained in their activities. In May, censorship of foreign correspondents' despatches ceased. The culminating act was Franco's announcement of his *Fuero de los Españoles* or Declaration of Freedoms of Spaniards† in June 1945. Within a month it became law. By this *Fuero* the State pledged itself to ensure that all Spaniards received at least primary education, a living wage, the medical care and medi-

---

* After their defeat, there were cases also of private citizens taking pity on isolated fugitives.

† The Spanish title could be tranlated as Declaration of Rights, but the word *Fuero* has the medieval connotations of the English word Freedoms.

cines they might require and financial help in times of sickness and un-employment. All Spaniards were to be free to reside where they wished, to acquire and hold property. All Spaniards would have a say in their government "through the family, the town council and the *sindicatos*". There would be no censorship of letters. No man would be detained for longer than seventy-two hours without judicial authority and the due process of law. Every man would be free to express his opinions. Men would be free to gather and form associations. Spaniards would be free to hold and practise any religion. There were, however, limits to these last liberties: only the Catholic religion would be allowed to manifest itself in public; freedom of assembly and associa-tion would be restricted to "lawful ends as established by law"; free-dom of speech was to be circumscribed by the clause "provided that the ideas expressed do not constitute an attack on the fundamental principles of the State"; and clause 2 gave the State the power to suspend at will the liberties of the individual granted by the *Fuero*.[33]

To Spaniards who had lived for nine years under Franco this Declara-tion promised an astonishing advance. It was on close analysis a com-promise between the ideals of the Carlists with their insistence that it was the State's duty to serve the individual and to defend the rights of the individual, and the quasi-totalitarian concept of Jose Antonio that while the individual might have some rights, they were to be sub-ordinate to order in the State. The cynical would recall that the Re-public too had promised as many freedoms as Franco now did and then promptly denied them in practice. Commentators abroad fastened on the limitations which were the major concessions to Falangist thought.

The *Fuero* could not undo in June the damage which the Nazi-Falangists had done Franco a month previously. On 1st May *In-formaciones* still had Hitler winning decisive victories over the Russians. On the following day it carried the news of Hitler's death under a five-column banner headline, a part of which read: FACE TO THE ENEMY IN HIS POST OF HONOUR ADOLF HITLER DIES. Beneath it there was a curious farrago of Germanic paganism and Christianity. Hitler, "a son of the Catholic Church", had died "de-fending Christianity", but "like a Nibelung embracing his sword" . . . "for the liberty of Europe"; . . . "God is with his paladins . . . on High there is a major feast . . . and on earth men of goodwill envy the manner of his death."[34]

True enough *Informaciones* was only one newspaper. The non-Falangist *A.B.C.* and *Vanguardia* had stopped carrying pro-German

propaganda ever since Franco had ordered the Falange Press controllers
to be more neutral; even *Arriba* had been horrified over the revelations
of Buchenwald and Belsen and it had come to condemn the persecution
of the Jews. Nevertheless, the pro-Nazis broadcast on 4th May, through
the State Radio, a panegyric to Hitler and Mussolini; duly monitored
abroad it was assumed to have been officially sanctioned.

While the Archbishop of Toledo ordered a Te Deum to be sung in
all Churches of his archdiocese, to thank God that Spain had been spared
from the war, Falangists found a priest to say a *public* Requiem Mass for
Hitler.* On 15th June the Falange tried to have a second public requiem
for Hitler and Mussolini. The Mass was stopped—whether by Franco's
or the Church's orders or both is not clear. The thwarted Falangists
rioted. There were arrests. Communists were blamed, but few were
deceived—except abroad.

On 19th July Franco published the details of a Cabinet re-shuffle.
While he put the turbulent Falangist Jose Giron, who had been instru-
mental in the organisation of the *sindicatos*, yet again as Minister of
Labour, and one of Jose Antonio's henchmen Raimundo Fernandez
Cuesta as Minister of Justice, Jose Luis Arrese, the Secretary-General
of the Falange who had been ordered to de-Nazify the party a year
previously and had not done so, ceased to be a member of the Cabinet.
Press censorship was at long last taken out of the hands of the Falange.
The choice as Minister of Air of General Gonzalez Galarza, a man
closely associated with Alfonso XIII, seemed to strengthen the Monarchist element in the government, and to be in line with Franco's
reinstitution earlier in the year of the "Council of the Realm", a body
which would enquire of a Pretender to the throne, if need arose,
whether he was fit to ascend the throne, thus reviving a tradition which
had not been observed for centuries.

The resuscitation of the Council with these powers was in fact a slap
in the face for the Pretender Don Juan, looked upon by the Alfonists
as the King of Spain since the death of his father in Rome on 5th
February 1941. In March Don Juan had issued a call from exile for
Franco's resignation and the restoration of the monarchy there and
then. For the monarchy, he said, could "alone provide an effective
guarantee for religion, order and liberty": this the Franco régime
could never do for it was "too closely modelled on the totalitarian

---

* A priest may say a private mass for the repose of the soul of any person
whatsoever: but not a public one for anyone who, if baptised (as Mussolini and
Hitler had been) dies seemingly outside the Church and unrepentant.

system of the Axis powers and contrary to the Spanish character and tradition". In support the Duke of Alba had resigned his Ambassadorship in London but most of Franco's monarchist generals considered Don Juan's call ill-timed.

The important change in Franco's Cabinet was in the appointment of Alberto Martin Artajo as Foreign Minister. Martin Artajo was a Doctor of Laws whose father had been prominent in Catholic Action and Social Studies. He himself had been President of the International Catholic University graduate body *Pax Romana* and later a leader writer on *El Debate*, the Christian-Democrat daily. Here was a man whom no one, except a Communist, could call Fascist.

In the long term Martin Artajo would accomplish for Spain more than all his predecessors. In the short term the appointment had come too late to stop the United Nations offensive against Franco. It had begun in June. The San Francisco Conference had adopted a resolution, proposed by the crypto-communist Mexican delegate Quintanilla, that Spain should be excluded from membership of the nascent organisation. On 2nd August at Potsdam Stalin, Truman and Churchill had agreed to support applications for U.N. membership from all neutrals except Spain. Stalin had earlier demanded of Britain and the U.S. that they should break off all relations with Franco and work actively for his overthrow, or, as he put it, "help the democratic forces in Spain". Churchill would explain later that he agreed to the milder decision "in the hope of inducing Soviet Russia to give [U.N.O.] friendly and generous aid and support".[35]

The Committee of Liberation in Mexico now proceeded to summon a meeting of the Popular Front members of the Republican *Cortes*. The *Cortes* elected Martinez Barrio "President of Spain". Dr. Negrin's connections with the Communist Party in the latter days of the Republic were too well known to expect that he would be acceptable to non-Communist governments. He resigned in favour of Martinez Barrio who then called on Jose Giral to form a new "Government". Giral carefully excluded Communists: except Alvarez del Vayo who then still had the reputation of not being one. Mexico recognised Martinez Barrio and accorded him the honours of a Head of State.

To this "Government-in-Exile" the exclusion of Spain from the U.N. was not enough. Following the ignominious failure of the "invasion", the only hope they had that their name might be shortened was the intervention of foreign powers on their behalf. The three powers in a position to intervene were Britain, the U.S. and France.

In lobbying U.S. Congress and British Labour M.P.s and members
of the French Constituent Assembly some advocated armed intervention: others economic sanctions. In the U.S.A. and Britain they worked
on the old emotions and ignorance of the many who equated the
Spanish words *liberal* and *socialista* with Liberal and Labour. In France
that would have been impossible and it was unnecessary. In the Constituent Assembly the Communists were the largest single group, the
Socialists the second largest: together they had a clear majority.

On 14th September the Spanish police captured two prominent
members of the Spanish Communist Party, Santiago Alvarez and
Sebastian Zapirain. They had crossed the Pyrenees a short time previously. The moment that their capture was confirmed at Toulouse,
the story was put out that they had been executed. On 24th September
Sir Victor Mallet, under instructions from Ernest Bevin (Attlee had
succeeded Churchill during the Potsdam Conference) expressed
Britain's "dismay at their execution". Martin Artajo truthfully replied
that neither man had been executed or even brought to trial. Thereafter
the British Government became more circumspect. Not so the French.
In December they invited Britain and the U.S. to discuss Spain in
Paris. Next, the Foreign Affairs committee and then, on 17th January
1946 the whole of the Constituent Assembly demanded a break with
Franco. Franco took no notice. On 20th February Madrid announced
the execution of ten ex-Maquisards found guilty of common murder
and banditry. The *Confederation Général du Travail*, as well as the
Assembly, now demanded active reprisals. On 26th February the
French Government announced that it would close the frontier on the
28th. Franco's reply was to close it on the 27th. France then declared
her intention to take the "Spanish issue" to the Security Council.
Spain, said the French Government, constituted a danger to world
peace. Washington and London persuaded France into a joint three-
power communiqué, issued on 4th March, stating that as long as
Franco ruled in Spain full and cordial relations with Spain would not
be possible, and that they hoped that the Spanish people would work
out their own destiny without the horrors of civil strife. France, however, persisted in her determination to take the matter to the Security
Council. The U.S.S.R. supported her fully: Britain and the U.S.
considered that France was about to establish a dangerous precedent.

The U.N. was about to be used to intervene in the domestic affairs
of a sovereign state. Furthermore, in the opinion of London and
Washington the effect within Spain was likely to be the opposite to

that desired. Any United Nations action would put the whole of Spain solidly behind Franco. At this juncture, nonetheless, the U.S. Department of State issued the selected fifteen documents to "prove" Franco as the accomplice of Hitler and Mussolini.* France and the U.S.S.R. pushed ahead. The debate in the Security Council opened on 17th April.

It was, like so many of the Security Council debates of the time, long drawn out, dreary and veto-ridden. One speech however must stand the wear of time as a memorial to the credulity of human beings. Oscar Lange, Stalin's nominee as Polish Foreign Minister, had Franco massing a quarter of a million men to invade France, Spanish factories producing the latest aircraft, heavy artillery and tanks—two to six daily from one factory alone—and heavy water being made in Toledo, infering by this and other references to uranium that Spaniards, with the help of German scientists, were manufacturing atom bombs. The Security Council adjourned while a sub-Committee examined the evidence. Giral presented them with a 77-page memorandum in which he wrote of vast industrialisation under Nazi direction and of a Spanish Army of 840,721 men at the ready. After nineteen Sessions the Committee concluded that though Franco's activities did not constitute an immediate threat to peace, the facts were proved and he was a "potential menace". That was the signal for Poland, the U.S.S.R., France and Mexico to demand the imposition of full economic sanctions on Spain, but the seven other members of the Council would not follow them.

"The Case of Spain" dominated the discussions of the U.N. General Assembly from November into December. On 9th December the Soviet bloc, France and Mexico pressed for at least a full break of diplomatic relations. Put to the vote a motion to that effect was a draw at 20–20. The U.S. drafted a resolution expressing the hope that Franco would retire of his own free will. That, too, resulted in a draw —22 to 22. Finally, on 12th December, by 34 votes against 6 and 13 abstentions, the United Nations agreed to exclude Spain from all the U.N. Agencies and recommended all members "to withdraw their ambassadors and ministers plenipotentiary".†

* Spain protested against "the unjust and unseemingly publication of incomplete evidence". She pointed out that thirteen of the fifteen documents were pre-Pearl Harbour and that therefore Britain alone had the right to demand an explanation (Spanish Foreign Ministry Communiqué—18th March 1946).

† The only 'Great Power' affected was Britain, Hayes' successor as U.S. Ambassador, Norman Armour, had resigned in the November of 1945 and had not been replaced.

Franco received the news on the morning of the 13th in the Pardo, the Bourbon hunting lodge on the outskirts of Madrid which had been his official residence and home since 1939. He carried on as if nothing had happened. He spent the whole afternoon painting—a hobby he had taken up during the Civil War.[36] Had he been excommunicated by the Pope he might well have been afraid, for he was at the head of a Catholic people.* His excommunication by a secular organisation of nation-states had no moral value whatever in the estimation of Spaniards. The United Nations might think that they had struck him a mortal blow. He had known for four days already that they had given him new life.

On 9th December, as the U.N. moved to vote on this and that resolution, a body of ex-servicemen had walked to the old Royal Palace where Franco was at work. That far it was an organised demonstration of loyalty to Franco: but on their way they were joined by an ever-increasing crowd. When Franco came out to address them from the balcony, he was met by the roar of his name and cries of *Viva España* from at least a third of a million people.† Here was an unprecedented acclamation by the people. There were rich and poor, young and old, famous men and the mass of the unknown. Franco spoke to them of "the twelve nations of Europe which yesterday were independent and today are in servitude". He recalled the terror of the Communist rule of Madrid. Spain would be free: and he, at their head, would not surrender the freedom for which they had fought: Spain would not be deprived of her victory. The world would come to look to Spain again.

On the following day there were similar demonstrations in other cities of Spain. Queipo de Llano came out of his embittered retirement and estrangement from Franco in Seville, and, with all his oratorical power of the early days of the Civil War, urged Spaniards to place their trust in Franco, and if necessary defend Spain as their ancestors had defended Numantia.

The United Nations had united Spain behind Franco.

* The excommunication of Peron in 1955 was the most powerful single factor in his overthrow from the Presidency of Argentina, a country substantially less Catholic than Spain. The rebellious people and Army flew the Papal flag side by side with the Argentine; and their leader General Lonardi chose as the battle cry *Christus Vincit.*

† Estimates have varied as between 100,000 and 600,000. I have examined photographs and newsreel of the event. I would be prepared to accept that there were even 400,000. 300 or 400,000—the total is quite astounding for a city which then had a total population of a little over a million and a half.

NOTES

1. Doussinague, p. 207.

2. Hoare, pp. 175, 270; Hayes, pp. 58-9.

3. Cf. Churchill in House of Commons, 24th May 1944; and op. cit. Vol. IV, p. 488; Doussinague, pp. 68-70; Hayes, p. 87.

4. House of Commons idem.

5. Churchill op. cit. Vol. V, pp. 474 and 475.

6. House of Commons idem.

7. Cf. Eristov, No. 46. Even field guns, let alone heavier pieces of up to 15 cm. which Franco had in number, could have done considerable damage.

8. Hayes, pp. 87-8; Doussinague, 81-6.

9. Hayes, pp. 89-92; cf. Doussinague, 92, 95-7.

10. The partial mobilisation was decreed on 12th November. Doussinague, pp. 102 *ff.*, 106; Hayes, pp. 77, 93, 126-8, 135, 266-7, 269; Juan de la Cosa, pp. 138-41.

11. Hayes, pp. 100, 103-4, 298. *Das Reich* on 11th June 1943 accused Franco of allowing 40,000 Frenchmen to escape through Spain, adding the comment that it was more than twice as many as the strength of his Blue Division.

12. Eristov, pp. 133-5, Moltke emphasising Franco's criticisms of the Allies. See note 14 below.

13. Hoare, pp. 190-5.

14. Doussinague, p. 229, and confirmed by Military Staff Records. Doussinague, pp. 139-79, for a full account of the negotiations with the neutrals, and pp. 183 *ff.* for subsequent moves. Doussinague gives an interesting account, pp. 127-37, of yet another plot to oust Franco directed by Von Moltke. For German troop concentrations, ibid., pp. 131-2, Churchill to Lord Ismay quoted above. Cf. Hoare, p. 218.

15. For German plans cf. Führer conferences 1943, pp. 19, 21, 38-9; p. 47 for Hitler's objection to Doenitz's further suggestion that flying bombs should be launched from France on Gibraltar. Further references: Nuremberg trials, Vol. XIII, pp. 348-9 and 403-4; Hoare, pp. 169-70. Notwithstanding these German preparations, from December onwards Spain sought hard to buy German weapons. *V.* Doussinague, pp. 206 *ff.*

16. Eristov, pp. 143-52; cf. Doussinague, p. 215.

17. Cf. Hayes, 130-7.

18. Hayes, pp. 156-62.

19. See note 14. The withdrawal, discussed in the Spring, was decided upon at a Cabinet meeting held on 29th July. Casualties suffered in Russia by the Blue Division totalled 12,736; deaths alone, 6,286.

20. Hoare, pp. 220-2. For the Spanish views of this interview *v.* Doussinague, pp. 228-32; and José María Areilza, *Embajadores sobre España*, Madrid, 1947, pp. 57-9, the last a propaganda work.

21. Ibid., p. 222.

22. Hayes, p. 166. Hayes recalls that Hoare "was not only a diplomatist in Spain but a politician in England".

23. Cf. Hayes, pp. 175-9. Hayes' letter to Jordana of 21st October 1943 (Doussinague, pp. 246-7) must be called one of the most naïve expositions of Soviet policy ever to be set down on paper. To expect Spain to publish Soviet war communiqués was really asking too much. The views were not Hayes' but those of the U.S. Government.

24. Cf. Hayes, pp. 105-11, 134-5, for Hayes-Hoare disagreements.

25. Mark W. Clark, *Calculated Risk* (New York, 1950), p. 162; Eristov, nos. 49, 50, 45 and 46.

26. Juan de la Cosa, pp. 148-9, quotes two "documents". They are an amusing example of a singularly naïve forgery: no modern Englishman, even in the Foreign Office, would ever write: "There has come to our knowledge and to that of H.M. Government the magnificent report transmitted by Mr. Harry Hopkins which the Chief of American Secret Information has presented under the eminent and respectable signature of the General Officer Mr. Strong." Of the Laurel incident Doussinague gives the most coherent and best documented account, pp. 286-9.

27. On the Wolfram Affair, Hayes, pp. 181-238; Hoare, pp. 257-64.

28. Hayes, pp. 221-3.

29. Texts available in Hoare, pp. 300-6.

30. Op. cit., pp. 221-31.

31. Hayes, pp. 256-9, gives an account of his own meeting with the *maquisards* in the south of France and their operations in Spain. Eduardo Comin Colomer, *La Republica en el Exilio* (Madrid, 1957), accepts the exiled Republicans figure of 10,000 Spaniards (p. 384).

32. Spanish Army Archives, Hojas de Servicio, monitoring reports of the so-called Radio España Independiente. I have found no satisfactory evidence that more than 1,500 crossed the Pyrenees. If more did so, then their defeat is all the more extraordinary.

33. It should be noted that the *Fuero* preceded the U.N. Declaration of Human Rights with which it has more similarities than differences.

34. *Informaciones* is still published.

35. Churchill, op. cit., Vol. VI, p. 566, and speech in House of Commons, 10th December 1948.

36. Franco-Salgado.

14

FROM ISOLATION TO
VICTORY 1946-53

The Ambassadors of Britain, the Netherlands, Italy and Turkey duly left Madrid; Argentina appointed a new Ambassador. President Peron had seen in Franco a kindred spirit: a military man, authoritarian, nationalist, and a would-be reformer of the social structure. His own plans for Argentina coincided with Franco's for Spain: industrialisation as a means of ending "colonial economic dependence"; Peron had for the United States and Wall Street the same intense hatred that Franco had for the U.S.S.R. and Communism: Argentina had a century-old claim on Britain's Falkland Islands, and Spain had a two-century one on Gibraltar.

In October 1946 Peron had made good Spain's harvest deficiencies with 400,000 tons of wheat and 120,000 tons of maize on credit at a low interest rate. Peron, though himself mainly of Italian descent with a trace of Scots, ruled over tens of thousands of Galician immigrants who, whether they approved of Franco or no, were not prepared to see their relatives starve while they themselves lived in plenty.

With the end of the war, several thousand *Gallegos* had gone back to Spain to visit their families. His "generous impulse" had therefore not been entirely disinterested. His wife Eva Duarte now herself decided to tour Europe. Britain's refusal to receive her in the manner which she considered her due, and Franco's reception of the lady in courtesy, splendour and ceremony—unequalled in any of the other countries of Europe which she visited—led directly to negotiations for a trade agreement with Spain, concluded in April 1948, prejudicial to Britain's interests.

Peron consolidated previous credits to Spain and extended them to £110 million, to enable her to buy yet more grain and some meat. Franco undertook to build for Argentina modern cargo-passenger liners and railway rolling stock, Britain's perquisites up till then. He was also to give Argentina a share in Spanish shipyards and to make Cadiz a free port for Argentina's exports to Europe. In the years from 1950 onwards relations between Franco and Peron would cool, principally because Eva Peron came to consider herself as once having been slighted by the Spanish Ambassador in Buenos Aires (and she was never a person to forget a real or imagined slight however insignificant), and partly because Peron's economic policy ran him into serious economic difficulties of his own; and pressed to pay his own debts he turned on his own debtors. However, without the help given Spain by Argentina in the period 1947-9, the people of Spain would have undergone economic distress even greater than that suffered between 1940 and 1942.

The distress was not of Franco's making. Though 1946 turned out a better year for grain harvests than the five which had preceded it, 1947 was a poor one, and subsequent years progressively worse. The rain just did not fall in Spain. Spain was caught in an economic whirlpool. To make tolerable the food shortages Franco had to use foreign currency with which normally he bought fertilisers. The lack of fertilisers further diminished the yield. The exclusion of Spain from Marshall Aid was thus an appalling blow. When asked at the beginning of 1949 what he felt about it, Franco replied with understandable bitterness: "If there are eight hungry men on a desert island, and a ship arrives with food for seven of them, you can imagine the feelings of the eighth. We in Spain happen to be the eighth man."[1] Black marketeering flourished as elsewhere in Europe where there was a serious food shortage and a lack of competent administrators. Short of putting in prison a sizeable number of the population, there was little which Franco could do: the sudden dismissal in June 1946, that is before the shortages had become really serious, of the General Francisco, Prince of Bourbon, Duke of Seville and G.O.C. the VIIth Military Region, whom popular rumour had as heavily implicated in black marketeering in olive oil, had had little effect. Equally slight had been the popular reaction to the announcement in September that there were over 9,600 men in prison for black market offences.[2]

The drought had another consequence. It severely restricted Spanish industry. Back in September 1941 Franco had founded under his friend Suances the Instituto Nacional de Industria, or National Development Corporation with powers to acquire minority and majority holdings in private firms whose production was judged inadequate in the interests of the national economy, and to embark on new wholly-owned enterprises. In the course of the years since its foundation, it had built new shipyards, opened new mines and established the national airline *Iberia*. It had started off successfully the Spanish cellulose industry. It had also become engaged in a project to extract oil from shale which was to prove as unprofitable, though not as ruinous, as the British ground-nut scheme. Like all such governmental agencies elsewhere in Europe, it aroused strong opposition from industrialists and entrepreneurs. It was accused of deliberately squeezing the small firm out of business; and, being in charge of the rationing of all raw materials, it was suspected of directing an unfair proportion of what was available to its own enterprises. There is no doubt, on the other hand, that the complex departmental procedures which developed did permit officials to contravene with impunity the rationing regulations. There was a black market in imported raw materials no less active than in food. Even where there was no corruption, the clearance of all the documents demanded the private industrialist by the state organisation took time and severely tested the equanimity of the applicants. From a more general public I.N.I. was severely criticised for its construction of grandiose dams and hydro-electric power stations, and its plans to build many more. These had Franco's whole-hearted support. He had rightly been advised that before any large-scale industrialisation could take place, the country's electric power potential would have to be increased many times. In a land of mountains and only poor quality coal, there was little choice on the method. The dams would also make possible schemes for land irrigation on a scale never before attempted in Spain. The old problem of the landless might be solved not only by the politically explosive (and according to some agronomists—wasteful) division of the large estates, but also by bringing new land into cultivation. No one, however, could have predicted the droughts from the statistics available, or that by 1950 the reservoirs would be no more than one-tenth full on average. The production of electric power so far from increasing as had been planned, fell to a long unprecedented low. Industrial Catalonia was particularly affected, and its foreign currency earning textile mills, were almost idle. Franco, however, insisted that the workers should not be dismissed, and that their wages should be maintained by their employers. His *Sindicatos* saw to it that such orders were carried out. The wages inevitably had ever-less purchasing power. The cost of living rose sharply. Franco tried to dampen its full effect by a complicated system of family allowances which, however well thought

out on paper, again did not take into consideration the incompetence of
administrators at the lower levels, and the strength of the temptation
behind the handling of money by civil servants who had themselves
serious economic difficulties.

Fortunately for Spain, Britain and the Scandinavian countries continued to trade with Spain. France had discovered that there was no
adequate substitute for Spanish cork, and rather than have her wine
trade ruined, she forgot her moral objections to her neighbour's mode
of government, and in February 1948 reopened the Pyrenean frontier.
With that Spain began to exploit the possibilities of tourism as a means
of acquiring the much needed foreign currencies that might pay for the
capital goods and the raw materials of industry. Tourists were given
favourable exchange rates.

At first a trickle, the tourist traffic became a steady stream by 1950.
The careful examination of documents and of luggage at the frontiers
by white-gloved customs guards and the ubiquity of beggars, and of
ill-clothed, bare-footed children and adults with haggard faces had also
been characteristic of the years 1931-6; but the majority of the visitors
now crossing the Pyrenees were people seeing Spain for the first time.
Such a careful examination on entry, and such misery, was new to
them. The Frenchman was familiar with the Napoleonic requirements
of registration at the hotel: not so the Englishman to whom the questions then demanded of him—the name of his father and his mother
and whether he was married or single for example—were unwarrantable intrusions into his privacy. On registering at a hotel he would be
asked to surrender his passport. He could not understand why. Again
on certain train journeys plain-clothes policemen would demand it of
him. Fresh from a country where only in wartime was the sight common of an army officer or even rankers in uniform, Spain seemed full
of army men, and of armed policemen in uniforms of various shades
of grey. All this confirmed the visitors' suspicion that Spain was a police
state under a military dictatorship. The face of the dictator in uniform
was everywhere. Every public office, most bars, cafés, had a picture of
the Caudillo enshrined on a wall. His picture appeared daily in every
newspaper. Newsreels in cinemas were full of his presence here, there
and everywhere. The radio gave full details of what he had done that
day. His every action was hailed as of a man of genius. To those not
accustomed to the sight of the image of the Head of State quite so
frequently, it all seemed Fascist, and damnable. Then as the visitor
walked through the streets past shops which had rather more clothes,

cheaper and more varied, than were then to be seen in the shops in Britain, but which seemed to be patronised little other than by tourists, he might be overtaken by a group of the Falange Youth Movement which would recall to him what he had seen on film of the Hitler *Jugend* or the Mussolini *Ballisti*; and as almost invariably the group would have a young chaplain at their head or tail, he could come away from Spain with a certainty that the country was in the grip of a clerico-fascist-face-of-the-poor-grinding conspiracy.

Yet there were other sights to be seen. Spain was a hive of building activity—not so much of housing, but of grandiose monuments: an Air Ministry big enough to house the whole of the NATO air staff, and workers' university buildings which filled the eye with splendour but made the observer wonder whether their purpose or the economy of building had been considered by their architect. Only an economist could realise that with industries which depended on electric power near idle, and few of the necessary raw materials coming into the country to produce goods in factories, the only occupation for tens of thousands of unskilled workers was building. Only a politician could appreciate that one large imposing workers' university was worth any number of small practical village schools or technical schools as a means of impressing both foreign visitor and local inhabitant; for the village school would be seen only by the villagers, whereas the imposing university would become the pride of the whole city and be featured in the magazines of Spain and many other nations.

If the visitor knew Spanish, there was a chance that his vision of Spain as a clerico-fascist-police-military-dictatorship might be modified. He could not be blind to the fact that the Press was rigidly censored; there appeared to be no crime in Spain and no mistake ever by any, even minor, officials. However, if he browsed through booksellers what he could see on sale did not make sense in terms of censorship. There was then an extraordinary variety, quantity and quality of work on every aspect of Spanish history, literature and the arts, new publications by old-established firms, by new private concerns or by Franco's own foundations.* *Persona ingratissima* as he was, and under surveillance amounting to persecution, Professor Gimenez Fernandez, the Republic's ablest Minister of Agriculture, had yet been allowed to publish a monumental work between 1940 and 1942 wholly opposed to the new

---

* The Higher Council for Scientific Research (Consejo Superior de Investigaciones Científicas); the National Spanish Book Institute (Instituto Nacional del Libro Español); the Consejo de Hispanidad.

State's thinking on many sacrosanct points.[3] In translation the works of Marx were not difficult to buy and those of Laski were on public display. There was no "Party line"—because there was no Party in a totalitarian sense.

There were plenty of novels too and book upon book of verse. The censorship of novels, plays and films was a slow process. The only real taboos were obscenity and direct criticism of the State, its institutions or its officers. Other than on those two points, the censors' behaviour was incomprehensible to publishers and producers. Sequences seemingly impeccable would be deleted, yet others expected to be stopped would be passed.*

The visitor could discover also that for all the constant checking of identity documents by the omnipresent grey uniforms and inadequately disguised plain-clothes policemen, people were prepared to criticise the régime and curse all its works and pomps in private conversations, in cafés, and more surprisingly in the wine bars patronised more by the Secret Police than by tourists. There were men who were afraid of the police: those who had held office of any kind in the U.G.T., C.N.T. or other proscribed Republican organisations, but not the rank and file. No action was taken against a critic unless he shouted out his insults or put his views to paper.

The economic plight of the people of Spain at that time indeed did not present a pleasing picture to the visitor. Back in Britain, France or the United States, exiled Republicans heaped all responsibility for it on Franco; and so did Spaniards in Spain who called themselves "the underground". Behind all the propaganda for and against Franco, the

---

* The State's Board of Censors was supposed to examine each work according to the following criteria:

(i) Does it question the Principles of the *Movimiento*, the *Fuero* or the Labour Charter?

(ii) Does it counsel rebellion against the established order?

(iii) Does it criticise any living person in authority in Spain?

(iv) Is it likely to provoke a breach of the peace either by portraying behaviour outrageous to public opinion or by advocating unsocial behaviour?

(v) Does it present as morally good what the Church has ruled morally evil?

(iv) Does it propound any dogma as salutary which is contrary to what the Church teaches?

The Board did not have to give reasons for rejecting a work. I know of two cases where a novel, having been barred by the official censor, was then sent by the publisher to his friend, the diocesan censor for books on religious subjects. The censor read them and thought that they were morally edifying. He then wrote to the State censors asking them whether they knew better than the bishop's censor. The novels were then passed.

drought remained a fact. It was also a fact that though Spain had not been a belligerent, she had been prevented by the European war from re-establishing her trade to 1935 levels and from acquiring the machine tools necessary to her industries. Again it was a fact that in spite of the deaths attributable to the Civil War, the population of Spain had risen from 23·5 million in 1930 to 25·8 million in 1940 and 28 million in 1950:[4] that is to say, Franco's régime had approximately 20 per cent more mouths to feed than the Republic. Spain was noticeably poorer than in pre-war days; but there was blacker bread in France than in Spain, and in the south of Italy there was as heart-rending misery as in the south of the Iberian Peninsula.

By 1950 Spain was one with Western Europe in that any bona fide applicant from Western Europe or the Americas could get a visa for Spain; and once there, the traveller was free alike to see for himself the police that strode the streets, and to talk with whom he chose—the novelists and dramatists frustrated by the vagaries of the State censors, the workers forbidden to go on strike, the men of all classes not allowed to form associations to any purpose except the strictly religious, and if he knew how to set about it, the plotters seeking the restoration of the monarchy or the re-establishment of the Republic, and even to those still hankering for the dictatorship of the proletariat. There was no one to stop him taking photographs of bare-foot children: there were no forbidden zones but one:*[5] civil guards might stop his car to ask him to establish his identity, but there were no roads closed to him (except by landslides or lack of repair).

In the Spain of 1950 there was want and hunger; in twelve nations of Europe there was greater want and hunger. The overall industrial output per head of the population was not quite up to the 1935 level, but Spain was getting the full benefit of what she produced. In Poland, Hungary and elsewhere behind the Iron Curtain, Soviet Russia had taken away whole factories. Coal miners in Spain were poorly paid in terms of purchasing power; but not as poorly as in the coal mines of Poland working for Soviet masters. The fine products of the Catalan textile mills might be beyond the purses of the majority of Spaniards, but the shops were reasonably full of goods: in the Iron Curtain countries there was neither the money nor the goods. In Spain, by the end of 1950, the total prison population was down to under 20,000.[6]

* The Valley of the Fallen where the basilica-mausoleum was still under construction by political prisoners serving out sentences. I exclude of course naval and military installations.

Not even Albania, with under one-tenth the number of the inhabitants of Spain, had as few. In Spain, as in the Communist countries, the trade unions were State-controlled, and strikes were illegal; but individuals who absented themselves were not punished in Spain. A man could leave his work and seek a job elsewhere without Party or police permission.* Students at universities had perforce to join the Sindicato de Estudiantes Universitario (S.E.U.), or University Students' Trade Union; but a total ignorance of the teachings of Jose Antonio was likely to be a recommendation for, rather than a bar, to graduation.† It always helped at all levels of society to have a "pull", but it did not have to be political. As under the monarchy, it was again useful to have a recommendation, especially from a parish priest; such recommendations were not difficult to get, and they were a fairly reliable reference. For Catholics (nominally 95 per cent of the population) there was almost complete freedom of religion—the limitations did not concern the private individual—but neglect of one's religion did not have dire consequences, and there were atheists in high places. The Church even had a weekly *Ecclesia* not subject to censorship, and that paper printed not only papal pronouncements which cut across government policy, but it even took to direct criticism of the government's neglect of the very poor of Andalusia. Only the 30,000 Protestants had serious disabilities: they had freedom of worship, but not of religion.‡

* There was an attempt to restrict the immigration of southerners into Catalonia which already had a labour surplus. The control was highly inefficient. Indeed, the workers of Bilbao had already proved that legally or no, they could go on strike: 20,000 of them had done so after the Civil Governor had tried to dismiss some for not going to work on Labour Day 1947. About a dozen men were tried for causing a disturbance and were given prison sentences subsequently cancelled by amnesties.

† Prominence in the S.E.U. might yield the wardenship of a university residence but not a lectureship.

‡ They were not allowed to propagate their beliefs outside their families. Their chapels were forbidden even to put a nameplate. Protestants had to provide documentary evidence that they were so by baptism as well as by upbringing before they were allowed to marry outside a Catholic church. The Vatican had eventually to bring strong pressure to bear both on Spanish bishops and the Spanish authorities before a more liberal attitude was taken in the 1960s. The whole question of Protestantism in Spain is a complex one, with serious faults on the part of Catholic churchmen, the laity, the State, and Protestant churchmen and laity alike. Cardinal Segura acquired the reputation of being violently anti-Protestant. That was an over-simplification. He distinguished between the English Protestants whom he defined as "very correct, sincere in their beliefs, however mistaken, and often model Christians whom we would do well to emulate in their virtues", and the Spanish Protestants in his diocese whom I discovered to be extreme evangelicals with ideas on the Babylonian Beast which would have warmed the cockles of English-speaking fundamentalist Protestants.[7] In the 1950s I read literature printed

The Catholic hierarchy had its differences with the Head of State, and the Head of State insisted on having a hand in their nomination, but none of the bishops was tortured in gaol, as Beran in Czechoslovakia, Stepinac in Yugoslavia or countless others in the Communist countries of Europe. Bishop Herrera in Malaga might rile publicly against the State's neglect of housing in his city, and himself set about the construction of a whole new suburb, and Cardinal Segura might thunder against the Falange and Franco's "totalitarian state": but neither were silenced.

For all he might wander in 1948 or later in Spain, no traveller could discover the whereabouts of the Army of 800,000 men equipped with the latest weapons of destruction about which the Prime Minister-in-exile Giral had given evidence to the United Nations with such convincing detail. The Army seemed rather to be in the streets of Madrid, Seville, Valencia and all the old garrison cities and towns, as it had been before the war; and its equipment was at best of pre-1939 design, largely worn out and not always clean. The conscripts were worse clothed than the French: their officers, though well-dressed, were known to eke out their salaries by taking spare-time work as private teachers, salesmen and account clerks.[8] An explosion at the naval base in Cadiz in 1947 was blown up by Soviet and exile propagandists into a story that an atomic device had exploded prematurely. Miraculously there appeared to be no deaths or injuries from radiation.

In the House of Commons on 10th December 1948, Churchill had summed up well the situation, though he had never himself been to Spain.

> I say there is certainly far more liberty in Spain under General Franco than in any of the countries behind the Iron Curtain. I do not wish to live in

---

by the Seville Protestants which Anglicans found as offensive as Catholics. It sparked off violence. Two Protestant Chapels were burnt down by youths—some of whom I discovered had not been near a church of any denomination for a decade. The "Bibles in Spain" troubles, too, during Lord Templewood's embassy and subsequently also showed a lack of understanding and of tolerance on all sides. There were at the time available in Spain translations of the complete bible, made and printed in Spain on sale at approximately 60 per cent of the price of English bibles in England. The objections from Catholics to the Bible Society's edition were twofold: first that it called apocryphal certain books which Catholics considered inspired, second that in a number of verses the reading differs from the traditional Catholic one. The State's objection was at bottom a matter of pride: "Spain is not a country of backward natives to be sent these books. After all, there were Spanish translations of the bible before Wycliff" (senior self-confessed atheist government official in conversation with author 1953).

either set of countries, and I expect I shall get into trouble in both cases, but, at any rate, we must look at these facts. The great mistake is to allow legitimate objections to Franco and his form of government to be a barrier between the Spanish people and the Western Powers with whom they have many natural ties, especially with Great Britain, with whom they have the unforgettable association of the War of Independence against Napoleon. There is the folly which, so far from leading to the downfall of Franco, has in fact consolidated his position at every stage. I was sure it would be so. They are a proud people and rather than be spurned and dictated to by the outside world, they have given allegiance to him, which he had never won before, since the Spanish war ended.[9]

While Franco had this unity behind him, he put through a measure which he hoped would consolidate his position.

On 20th February 1946[10] he had declared outright that he was a monarchist. 450 monarchists, including General Kindelan, had thereupon petitioned him to restore the King. That was too fast for Franco. The restoration would come, if at all, in his own time and in his own way. He cut the national Council of the Movimiento to fifty. Next he overhauled the Cortes which he had instituted four years earlier. The Cortes thereafter would have approximately 140 representatives of the Sindicatos, elected by those bodies; 100 representatives of local governments, elected by these: and twenty representatives of Professional Colleges and Learned Societies, also elected by their members. The fifty Movimiento councillors would also be members, and so also fifty city mayors (caudillo appointments), the Rectors of the twelve untiversities (whose appointments were confirmed by the Ministry of Education), the Cabinet and fifty notabilities chosen by the Caudillo from among famous churchmen, soldiers, men of learning, grandees and other noblemen. On paper therefore the Cortes was representative of all classes and occupations in Spain, and over half its members were there by election. Franco would always claim that it was a democratic institution, albeit as Head of State he had the last word in all legislation. It was in truth rather less the rubber stamp than it appeared to be to the people of Spain themselves, let alone to those abroad. The amount of liberty which its members had to discuss what was put before them and amend it, with impunity, varied from year to year.

In the following year Franco had the Cortes choose a special committee to consider a new Law of Succession which he had drafted. They touched it up, amended it in detail, and sent it back to the Head of State. As it was highly controversial, Franco decided to make use of the Law of Referendum which he had had the Cortes approve in 1945. On the last day of March he broadcast to the people of Spain. Capitalism, he said, was "antiquated and unjust", while Marxism was "barbarous and cruel". His new Spain would be human. Its basis would be the doctrines of the Church on social justice. He then announced that on 6th July the people of Spain would have the opportunity to say the simple "Ay" or "Nay" to the following not very pithy proposition: first, that Spain was a Kingdom; second, that the Headship of the State was vested in the "Caudillo of Spain and of the Crusade and Generalissimo of the Armed Forces, Don Francisco Franco Bahamonde"; third, that in the event of his death or incapacitation, his office would be taken over by a Council of Regency, to be constituted by the President of the Cortes, the senior prelate among the members of the Cortes, and the senior serving officer in the Armed Services; fourth, fifth and sixth, that the Head of State would be assisted by the Council of the Realm which would have to be consulted by the Caudillo in all major decisions including his return to the Cortes of any Bill drafted by them, or in his naming of any successor to himself as King or Regent; seventh, that on his death or incapacitation the Council of Regency would assume office in his name and either proceed to swear in the nominee and proclaim him King or Regent; or eighth, if no one had been named, proceed in secret conclave with the Cabinet to choose from among those of royal blood a King or Regent. This King or Regent would have to be male, Spanish, at least thirty years old, a Catholic, capable of fulfilling his office and prepared to swear to uphold the Basic Laws of the Nation and principles of the Movement. The Basic Laws were the *Fuero*, the Labour Charter, the Act of Establishment of the Cortes, the Act of Succession under Referendum, the Referendum Law, and any other Law so classified in the future. The crown having been restored to a King, subsequent succession would be by primogeniture, excluding females who nonetheless would be able to transmit the right of succession.

Don Juan called it a fraud, and the Duke of Alba and the Carlist Count of Rodezno agreed, but the Primate advised the people to vote. 17·2 million were entitled to do so under a rapidly approved Law which was identical with that of the Republic except in that it excluded anyone with a criminal prison record. 15·2 million actually did so. 1·1 returned "Nay", or left the ballot paper blank. 14·1 said "Ay", that is 82 per cent of the electorate and 92 per cent of those who voted.

Thus, on 6th July 1947, Spain became a Kingdom without a King. Franco now revived all the old titles of nobility officially, and gave himself the right to make new nobles.* Rumblings among the monarchists continued. In April 1948 General Kindelan was under arrest for two months after criticising the situation: the Duchess of Valencia was not spared as a woman and given a short sentence as well. Then in August, Don Juan went aboard Franco's yacht, the *Azor*, and in November his son Juan Carlos arrived in Spain to live and be educated there. Here obviously was Franco's choice for successor; but the lad was only nine years old. The Act of Succession made thirty the minimum age for a king: Franco was fifty-six. Of the famous generals who had dreamt of a restoration in their lifetime, Jordana was dead, Kindelan was sixty-nine, and Aranda seventy. Their expectancy of life was short. Varela, one of the younger, Franco's senior by only one year, was to die in 1951, mourned by Franco perhaps more visibly than anyone else since the death at his side of his adjutant in his young days in Morocco. It surprised observers who had seen him outwardly impassive in private bereavement—to the death in a flying accident of his harum-scarum brother Ramon in 1938, to that of his father at the age of eighty-eight in 1944, a pitiful figure in his old age, back once more in the Calle de María, El Ferrol. At his death Franco's elder brother, Nicolas, as head of the family, had provided for his faithful housekeeper and her daughter.

It was, apparently, on his only child, his daughter Carmencita, that Franco had lavished his affection. In 1950, she was twenty-two. The parents of the twenty-seven-year-old doctor of medicine Cristobal Martinez Ortega Bordiu y Bascarán had formally asked General and Mrs. Franco for the hand of Carmencita for their son.

The wedding took place on 10th April, in the Chapel of El Pardo. The Bishop of Madrid-Alcala officiated, and the Archbishop of Toledo, the now Cardinal Pla y Deniel, was present. The bride wore a high-necked white dress with a twelve-foot train. Eight hundred guests attended the wedding breakfast. It was an occasion which in its splendour befitted the marriage of the daughter of the head of a European state, without being unduly lavish or extravagant.

Franco could entertain visitors unstintingly and with colourful pomp and ceremony. In 1949 he had welcomed a more important personage than Eva Peron—King Abdullah of Jordania, who had been delighted with the attention and courtesy shown him by the Spanish Govern-

* A "right" which he had used exceedingly sparingly.

ment and the people. In 1950 Eva turned against the Generalissimo, but it mattered little. The food situation in Spain was easier. The King of Jordan's visit gave Franco a new status in the Arab world. The Regent of Iraq, the son of the Sultan of Morocco, and Egyptian Ministers came to visit Franco. Franco had the Muslims taken to Toledo, Seville, Cordoba and Granada. He glorified Spain's Arab past. He talked of Spain as the bridge between Islam and Christianity. The Arabs for their part were delighted to find a European Head of State who looked upon them as equals, and who knew and understood something of their language and culture. To a limited extent Spain was able to provide them with the manufactured goods which they required, at prices below those of other European countries; and Spain could buy raw materials from them—cotton from Egypt for example, using sterling balances. Above all, however, these Arab friends represented for Spain so many votes in the United Nations.

Since the United Nations had instructed its members to withdraw their Ambassadors, first Argentina and then Paraguay, Peru, Brazil and Colombia in succession had defied the recommendation. Already in 1947 the best that the Soviet bloc could do at the United Nations had been to persuade it to express "concern" only at the continuation of the Franco régime. In the following year the "Spanish problem" had faded into insignificance in the face of the Soviet offensive against Berlin and the West. In May 1949, the Latin American states tried to get the United Nations to withdraw its resolution. Poland and the U.S.S.R. turned the occasion into an attack on the United States and Britain, accusing them of "aiding the Franco régime". The vote for the withdrawal of the original resolution was twenty-six votes for to sixteen against, with sixteen abstentions including the United States and Britain. As a two-thirds majority was required, the Latin American motion was defeated.

What hurt Franco personally on his occasion was that Israel, which had just been admitted into the United Nations, voted against the resolution. The Israeli representative made it clear that his country did so not because the Spanish régime was undemocratic, but because it had been the ally of the Nazis. While the Spanish Government had had no direct hand in the extermination of six million Jews, it had been the active ally of those responsible.

Franco had not expected this, for he thought that Israel at least had some knowledge of one of the more remarkable facets of his close association with Hitler.

Among the arguments used by Franco in persuading Primo de Rivera in October 1923 and July 1924 that it was Spain's duty to retain Spanish Morocco was the residence there for many centuries of "many thousands of Spaniards"—an exaggeration unless he included as Spaniards the Sephardim.* In his account of the evacuation of Xauen, Franco described with unusual sensitivity the plight of the Jews as well as of the Moroccans loyal to Spain.[11] Whether as a direct consequence of this or no (with the arbitrary and unpredictable Andalusian General little can be said for certain) Primo de Rivera decreed on 20th December 1924 that any Sephardi anywhere in the world who so wished it could opt for a fully legalised Spanish nationality.† He gave them until 31st December 1930 to do so. In fact, few did. Primo de Rivera had made the fulfilment of the Spanish military service a necessary requirement. The 1931 Republic promised in its Constitution a new law to give Spanish nationality to the Sephardim, but it never came even to be drafted. A request for a Jewish cemetery in Madrid aroused the wrath of the left-wing which was then secularising all the Catholic burial grounds. The Consulate in Bucharest, however, was instructed to continue as in the days of Primo de Rivera issuing certificates valid for six months to any Sephardi threatened with expulsion or confiscation of goods by the then anti-Jewish Rumanian Government; and there were exchanges of notes with Greece and Egypt[12] renewing the powers of Spain as the protector of locally resident Sephardim.

The Spanish Press during the Republic was even less pre-occupied with the fate of the Jews under Hitler than that of Britain, France or the U.S. To the Spanish Left, Judaism was just another religion only marginally less repugnant than Catholicism. To the Right it was irrelevant to the Spanish scene. There were hardly any Jews in Spain. A few Falangists under Nazi influence tried to arouse anti-Jewish

* Sefarad is the Hebrew for Iberia. The Sephardim are the descendants of the Jews expelled from Spain in 1492. There are sizeable communities of them in most of the countries of Western Europe: the British number 30,000; the French 350,000. In Spain itself there are about 7,000; in what was Spanish Morocco 12,000; and 5-6,000 elsewhere along the north-east coast of Africa to Alexandria; in Spanish America around 250,000. At the outbreak of the war there were some 85,000 in Turkey, 30,000 in Bulgaria, 10,000 in Bosnia (Yugoslavia) and 10,000 in Greece. Many of the Sephardim speak a rather beautiful fifteenth-century Spanish (called Ladino). In Salonica and New York they publish magazines in this language but written in the Hebrew script.

† Under the Montreux Convention of 1837, those in the old Ottoman Empire had the legally rather nebulous status of being "under Spanish protection". The Spanish Consulates kept lists.

feeling, and as we have seen, there were churchmen who identified Jewry with Freemasonry, but then and later, as Serrano would admit to Ciano,[13] Rosenberg's "grotesque theories" (*extravagancias*) were only of interest to "a dozen or so freaks". Franco would come to have references in his speeches to Jews as synonymous with the Masons and Liberals he hated. The Spanish wartime Press had no references to Hitler's persecution of the Jews: but then it had none either to his persecution of the Catholic Church. Nevertheless behind all this, Franco was far from impassive to their fate. He protected the Jews wherever Hitler had power to the limit of his ability. He could not save them as a race, but he could and did save individuals in so far as he could extend to them the legal fiction that the Sephardim were still Spaniards although their ancestors had left Spain four-and-a-half centuries previously.

The whole story is one of constant and complicated diplomatic activity in many cities. On 17th September 1940, for example, the Spanish Consulate in Paris reported that the Sephardim were being treated like others of their race. Franco gave instructions that they were to be registered as Spaniards to make possible their defence as such against the Germans and the French. In November, that is soon after the Hendaye meeting, he gave similar instructions to the Spanish Embassy in Vichy. Sephardic Jews thereafter did not have to wear the prescribed clothing nor did they have their goods confiscated. When in March 1942 cases were reported of Sephardim being molested, Franco had Serrano Suñer order the Spanish Ambassador to take the matter up with the Vichy government, recalling a Protection Agreement of 1862. The Jews concerned were released. Frontier guards on the Pyrenees were instructed to follow the spirit rather than the letter of their instructions. Refugees were allowed to enter without papers, and whereas escaped British prisoners-of-war were treated as illegal immigrants, and as such put into prisons until they were rescued by the British Embassy, Jewish refugees were usually sent to a camp, where conditions were far from ideal but the best that Spain could offer at the time. With Hayes' arrival, a U.S. joint Jewish, Quaker and Catholic relief organisation was established to help them.[14]

Similar action was taken on the Sephardim's behalf by the Embassies and Consulates in Hungary, Bulgaria, Rumania and Greece.[15] The Germans agreed in March 1943 to leave the Salonika community in peace. Nevertheless at the beginning of 1944 the delegate in Lisbon of the World Jewish Congress reported to Nicolas Franco, then the

Spanish Ambassador in Portugal, that there were 400 Sephardim in the
Haidani concentration camp in Greece awaiting deportation. Nicolas
telephoned his brother. Franco had his Ambassador in Berlin take up
the matter. The deportation was stopped. Some had in fact already been
taken to Belsen, and the Spanish Ambassador in Berlin was instructed
to importune the German Foreign Office to obtain their release.[15]
After many excuses—that it was impossible to find out which of the
Jews were Spanish and which not, that they were scattered in various
parts of the country and in different camps—259 Jews released from
Belsen crossed over into Spain by Port Bou on 10th February 1944,
and a further 983 on the 13th. For good measure the Spanish Government got back for them eventually the 44,000 dollars, 55,000 Swiss
francs, 24 million drachmae and the gold and jewellery which the
German police had taken off them in Athens.

How many Jews in all were saved by Franco's legal fiction that they
were Spaniards, does not appear to have been calculated; but the
Sephardic communities of Greece and Bosnia survived the war; and
the first ship to sail from the Western Mediterranean into Haifa after
the war was the Spanish ship *Plus Ultra* with 400 adults and 150 orphans
who had embarked in Barcelona.

By 1949, there were in Barcelona two Jewish synagogues as against
one before the Civil War, and on 2nd January of that year a new
synagogue had been opened in Madrid to replace the one which had
been sacked by Communists during the Civil War.[16] By then also, the
publications of the Institute of Hebraic Studies, part of Franco's Consejo
Superior de Investigaciones Científicas, opened at the very time of the
Hendaye meeting, were beginning to attract international attention.*
On 20th August 1941, Franco had officially confirmed on the 14,000
Jews in Spanish Morocco their right to local self-government and
allotted them a subsidy to enable the Rabbinic Courts to function.

On 31st October 1950, Israel again voted against the revoking of the
U.N. recommendation, but this time only nine other countries did so
—the Soviet bloc, Yugoslavia, Guatemala, Uruguay and Mexico:
twelve abstained including Britain and France: but thirty-seven including the U.S. voted in favour. Spain was now free to join the
United Nations agencies and Britain and the U.S. would be sending
their Ambassadors the following March.

The "providences" on which Franco had been waiting had happened.
Russia, not satiated with her territorial gains in the West had turned

* Today Jewish and Catholic scholars work there side by side.

eastwards: the Korean War was on. The United States was not too certain about the value of NATO. Franco had struck a chord in the minds of American popular opinion when on 31st January, in an interview for the Hearst Press, he had expressed his doubts about NATO and spoken of his willingness to consider an agreement with the United States alone.[17] Back in 1948 the U.S. War Department had spoken of the need to associate Spain with Western defence. U.S. Senators after touring Spain had become convinced that she was more likely to be a bulwark against Communism than France or Italy. Truman, having rejected Congress recommendations for economic aid to Spain in previous years, had agreed to a modest $62½ million allocation in 1950: and now, on 1st March 1951, Stanton Griffis, the new U.S. Ambassador, was arriving to prepare the ground for negotiations which the U.S. hoped would lead to the establishment of air and naval bases in Spain, in exchange for which the U.S. would be prepared to let Franco have the dollars in quantity which Spain needed for her recovery and development.

Admiral Sherman had conversations with Franco on 16th July. There was an outcry from Britain and France. Spain delivered notes to the new British and French Ambassadors protesting against attempted interference in bilateral negotiations between sovereign states. Franco celebrated his new position in international affairs by a minor change in his Cabinet. He relegated his friend Juan Antonio Suances to the post of Director of I.N.I. and split the Ministry left vacant into two— one of Industry which he gave to an ex-military attaché in Washington and the other of Commerce, in which he put a banker who was reputed to be very pro-American. Admiral Sherman died on 21st July, but a U.S. technical and military mission duly arrived in August. Congress earmarked $100 million of aid to Spain for use if and when the negotiations prospered.

Franco was not to be hurried. He needed the dollars but, as he pointed out,[18] it was he who was being asked to close the gap in the Western defences. He would do so on his own terms and in his own time. Another "providence" was occurring which would put him in a strong negotiating position.

In the previous March he had had to face the first major popular demonstration against the State of Spain. When fares were raised on Barcelona's trams, a quarter of a million persons remonstrated. Three were killed, and twenty-one injured, including the mayor. Order was not restored until 3,000 police (of the Policía Armada, the successors of the Republican Asaltos), were drafted into the city, and the Bishop appealed for order; and in April, Franco had on his hands the first serious strike of his reign. A quarter of a million Basques walked out demanding a 50 per cent wage increase. The clergy gave the strikers moral support and *Ecclesia* ruled the workers fully justified in their action as a means of redressing their grievances. Not so Franco. Strikes might be justified, he said, when the law admitted class warfare, but not where tribunals existed to judge conflicts between workers and employees. He accused Communists, foreign powers and, above all, Masons of fermenting disorder.[19] He weathered the strike. Then it began to rain. With the rains there was a bumper harvest. Food rationing was abolished. By the end of the year his reservoirs were 66 per cent full. By mid-May 1952, the water level was up to 85 per cent. Food prices declined. That year Spain's agricultural and industrial production reached record levels. There would be other poor harvests in years to come, but never like those of the 1940s. Industrial production on the other hand, in 1952 nearly double that of 1931, would continue to rise.

With the approaches being made to him by the Americans, Franco could afford another luxury. He could pursue a "tough line" towards the two countries of the West which had been unfriendly towards him —Britain and France—Spain's traditional enemies.

The first person suggested by Franco as his Ambassador in London on the resumption of normal diplomatic relations had been Fernando Castiella. The British Government refused to accept a man who had written and published a book in which he had put forward Spain's claims to Gibraltar in a most undiplomatic manner.[20] Now in 1950 Britain had given Gibraltar legislative and executive councils as a first step towards self-government in the colony. Spain had tried to open talks with Britain on the matter. The Spanish arguments were, in brief, first that Britain had captured Gibraltar on behalf of a claimant to the Spanish throne, but once in possession of it, had treacherously proceeded to make it a British colony; second, that Spain had not surrendered sovereignty over the Rock at the Treaty of Utrecht, but only the installations on it; third, that even if it were held, that Spain, under duress let it be noted, had surrendered sovereignty, Britain was bound under the same treaty to give Spain a first option over it if ever its possession were to be transferred. Britain refused to consider the matter, maintaining that Gibraltar was hers to do with as she pleased.

For the arrival of Sir Samuel Hoare in 1940, the Falange had organised a mass demonstration. Subsequently the Embassy had come under mob attack. In 1951, one of the first tasks of the new Ambassador, Sir John Balfour, was to make a formal protest against an attack the year before on the offices of British European Airways. *Arriba* and several other papers which had never lost their anti-British attitude whipped up Spanish nationalism over Gibraltar. All newspapers were constrained to take and keep up the demand for the return of Gibraltar. There would be commercial treaties, and British tourists would be welcome, but the Gibraltar theme would become an almost permanent feature of the Spanish Press, even of that sector of it which was otherwise pro-British. Franco, for his part, lost no oportunity whenever interviewed[21] to make his position known. Gibraltar was Spanish by right, and so long as it continued to be in British hands, it would cast a shadow on Hispano-British relations. He would be prepared to lease Gibraltar to Britain as a base, but no more.

For the moment Franco could do nothing more than reiterate Spain's claims, but the day would come when he would be in a position to do more than that.

In Franco's development of his pro-Arab policy, France no less than Britain could see a potential danger. 1952 was the peak year of that friendship. Between 4th and 28th April, Martin Artajo, accompanied by the now General El Mizzian, visited the Lebanon, Syria, Jordan, Iraq Saudi Arabia and Egypt. With them went the Marquis and Marchioness of Villaverde, that is Franco's daughter Carmencita and her husband. In a broadcast before their departure, Franco spoke of his gratitude to the Arab states "in defence of Spain and of justice", and paralleled the resurgence of the Arab states to that of Spain. Azzim Pasha, the Secretary-General of the Arab League, spoke of Spain in terms very different from those used by the League with reference to France. Spain, he said, had succeeded in making Spanish Morocco "a bridge between the two people". Not without some misgivings on the part of Spanish prelates, Spain signed treaties of friendship and cultural pacts with the Arab states.

Franco, however, was about to win the major victories of his life.

Since the temporary agreement over the naming of bishops, Franco had wrested other concessions from the Papacy. The most important had been an agreement signed on 16th July 1946 whereby the Vatican had conceded to the Head of the Spanish State the power to choose (subject to a bishop's veto) all Cathedral Deans and half the Chapters and to exercise over the appointment of parish priests a veto "on general political grounds". In exchange the Head of the State had bound himself to consult the Holy See over any legislation on such matters as marriage and education.[22] On 5th August 1950, the Vatican had agreed that the Senior Chaplain to the Forces should be an archbishop, and while Franco had conceded that no person in orders should be called upon to serve under arms, the archbishop had been given the power to demand of bishops priests to serve as chaplains to the forces for a period equal to that of the compulsory military service. None of this however added up to a concordat, which Franco seemingly had come to look upon almost as a sacramental seal of his legitimacy as the Head of the Spanish State. He invoked the name of God in his speeches. He talked of the Catholicity of Spain. He allowed the Church to exercise its mission to a degree unknown for two centuries. Incomprehensibly—to the Spanish establishment—the Vatican held out.* From mid-1952, however, any appreciation of the future was bound to conclude that the U.S.-Spanish negotiations would end with an agreement which would make Franco's position in Spain unshakeable. In the circumstances, the Vatican had to expedite a *modus vivendi*. In the Summer of 1953, it was common knowledge within official circles that the agreements were ready but for minor details. On 27th August 1953, the Vatican capitulated. Franco got his Concordat.

Franco recognised the Catholic Church as the Church of Spain. He promised not to impede in the future direct communication between the Vatican and the bishops, or between the bishops and their clergy or the people (that meant that in future Franco would not prohibit the publication of Papal encyclicals or pastoral letters, or arrest a bishop as he had done in the past). Spain would allow religious organisations to acquire property—as in Britain or the United States. Church feasts would be national feasts. The State, while still keeping the property confiscated in 1851, would negotiate with the clergy tax-free salaries more in keeping with contemporary monetary values. Church building and non-productive property would also be free of rates and taxes. The police would not be allowed to enter church property without higher ecclesiastical authority. The State would not demand of any priest any work not in accordance with canon law. It would

---

* Not incomprehensibly from a universal Catholic point of view. The mind of the Church would come out quite clearly in the years to come, both in Papal encyclicals and at the Vatican Council that no Head of State, however Catholic, has the right to dictate however indirectly who should be or who should not be bishop or parish priest.

allow priests to be tried by ecclesiastical courts for ecclesiastical offences, and never by a civil or criminal court without informing the accused's ecclesiastical superior. The guilty would not be sent to the same prison as non-priests. In courts, the State would recognise the Seal of Confession. The marriage of Catholics in a church would be considered binding in civil law without a further ceremony. The State would also accept an ecclesiastical court's decision on judicial separation or the nullity of a marriage. The teaching of religion would be allowed in schools, though any parent would be free to withdraw his child from such lessons. The Church would have the power to object to the teaching of religion by a particular master. It would also be free to establish its own schools. There would be freedom of association and assembly for religious purposes. The Church for its part would pray for the Head of State (as in other countries), but Franco's *Patronato*, the temporary agreements; over the appointment of bishops and power of veto over lesser posts, became part and parcel of the new Concordat.*

One month after the Concordat, on 26th September, Martin Artajo signed on Franco's behalf, and the then U.S. Ambassador James Dunn on behalf of President Eisenhower, three agreements. Franco granted the U.S. the right to develop and make use of four air bases, one near Madrid, two near Seville and one by Zaragoza, and one naval base, Rota in Cadiz Bay; and he sanctioned the construction of six fuel and ammunition depots. However, their use by the Americans would be limited to ten years, unless the agreements were renewed: Franco reserved the right to call upon the Americans to withdraw at six months' notice. Most important of all, the bases would at all times remain under Spanish command, and the Spanish flag would continue to fly over them.

The Americans for their part promised to spend $191 million in the development of the bases, and in the provision of new equipment to the Spanish forces, and to make available a further $85 million for the

---

* The agreement was condemned by left-wing Spanish exiles as a surrender to Rome, and it was so seen by a number of British and American commentators. In fact the freedom of religion and facilities for its furtherance guaranteed by it to all but a very small number of Spaniards, was no greater on balance than that enjoyed by Christians generally in the U.S. or Britain, whose Catholic minorities, are free to acquire property, to have their own schools (in Britain subsidised by the State) read Papal pronouncements in full (thus the *New York Herald Tribune* would print verbatim *Pacem in Terris* of which the Spanish dailies suppressed sections), and free to form their own societies even ones not strictly of religious character. In both these countries the Pope is at complete liberty to name whom he will as a bishop, and the bishops to choose for themselves their parish priests.

development of Spanish industries or for the purchase of any necessary food stuffs.

Franco's detractors within and outside Spain spoke of his creation of "five new Gibraltars". They did him less than justice. He had directed towards Spain a not unsubstantial sum of money* which would have other money chasing it. He had given nothing away.

On the evening of 26th September, Franco to his friends said: "At long last I have won the Spanish war".[23]

* Not all of the $226 million of course; for the Americans would be bringing over much of the equipment for the bases, and the arms to be provided for the Spanish Army would in no way contribute towards the national economy.

NOTES

1. *Daily Telegraph*, 31st January 1949.

2. Full details were regularly given in the *Boletin Oficial del Estado*. The anti-black market legislation was fierce, much more so than in Britain, but the people lacked the docility or social sense of the British.

3. Manuel Gimenez Fernandez was Professor of Canon Law at Seville University. In his *Instituciones Jurídicas en la Iglesia Católica* (Madrid, Vol. I, 1940; Vol. II, 1942) he showed clearly the abyss between the Spanish State's church policy and Catholic doctrine. The work had the *nihil obstat* of José María Bueno Monreal, Cardinal Segura's eventual successor as Archbishop. He signed Volume II as finished on "6th July 1941, Feast of St. Thomas More", a subtlety not lost on his students. Among many other books alien to the "party-line" there was the racy Professor Elías de Tejada's *Las Españas* (Madrid, 1948) which emphasised the separateness of the cultures of Spain. On I.N.I., cf. *The Economist*, 27th August 1949. But cf. Franco, *Discursos 1951-54*, pp. 46-7, for a defence.

4. On publication of the 1940 figures Jesus Villar Salinas in *Repercusiones demográficas de la última guerra civil española* (Madrid, 1942) was bold enough to estimate that but for the Civil War there would have been 1·1 million more persons than there were. Jackson, op. cit. (pp. 526 *ff*.) used this figure in his general discussion of the number of deaths attributable to the Civil War and its aftermath. However, if the 1960, 1950 and 1940 figures are taken through the same processes in reverse, then there ought also to have been close on a million more in 1930 than there were.

5. In 1951 I walked past the sentries of the fortress in Pamplona. I wanted to settle a doubt about the Emperor Charles V's fortifications. Since it was going to be a matter of a few moments, I could not be bothered to ask for official permission to enter War Department property. A few minutes after my

entering, a sergeant saluted smartly and politely asked me my business. I explained. He asked me to wait. A few moments later he returned with the message: "The Captain presents his compliments and wishes to know if he can be of assistance." "Do please thank him, but tell him I have seen all I wanted to see." The Army would have been within its rights to hold me as a trespasser, or worse. Personally I have never met with anything but extreme courtesy from Spanish officials from the most junior to the most senior, however ill- or well-dressed I went. My only difficulty has been in persuading some of them that I was not a Spaniard.

6. Ministry of Justice figures covering *all* prisoners and not merely the political. *Spain and the Rule of Law*, p. 65, gives the following figures for the prison population of earlier years:

31st December 1939	250,719
31st December 1940	213,373
31st December 1941	139,990
31st December 1944	28,077

However, the official figures for the pre-Civil War years are rather higher than "a minimum of 6,000 and a maximum of 12,500 (in 1934)": *e.g.* on 15th February 1936 the figure was stated in the Cortes to have been 34,526.

7. The total number of Protestants in Spain is 30,000. The attacks on their places of worship (the full list is given in the 1961 report published by the World Council of Churches) are of course indefensible. At the same time the facts cannot be over-emphasised that there were faults on both sides and that the official attitude was not necessarily based on religious motives. I had long conversations on this matter with both Lord Templewood and Cardinal Segura.

8. And to my personal knowledge even as taxi drivers.

9. *Hansard*, 10th December 1948.

10. *A.B..C, ya.*, 21st February 1946.

11. *Xauen la Triste* in *Revista de Tropas Coloniales*—cf. *supra* Ch. 5.

12. *España y los Judíos*: a transcript of documents from the Spanish Foreign Ministry archives. (Oficina de Información Diplomática, Madrid, 1949) and information supplied by the Office of the Haham, London.

13. Serrano, p. 198; *Diary*, p. 483.

14. Hayes, pp. 121-6; cf. 112-21. Hoare, pp. 227 and 237, was less concerned over the fate of the Jews.

15. *España y los Judíos*, pp. 20 *ff*.

16. The old synagogue was in the Calle del Principe: the new ironically in the Calle del Cardenal Cisneros. Cisneros is better known in England as Cardinal Ximenes, who was closely connected with the Isabellan decree of 1492. The

Sacred Scrolls of the old were saved from destruction and hidden in the cellars of a convent in Murcia.

17. Statements to. Karl von Wiegand published in Hearst Press, 13th February 1951; p. 35 of *Discursos 1951-54*.

18. Cf. statements to *Washington Post*, 7th September 1952. *Discursos*, p. 222; cf. p. 278.

19. Speech, 12th May 1951, *Discursos*, p. 57. See also speech to U.N.D.A., pp. 50-1, for attribution to foreign instigators: "the B.B.C. . . . alleged to be semi-governmental, but in fact since long ago in the hands of Freemasonry" —words which must have astounded his international audience of broadcasters who knew the B.B.C. better. On the Labour Tribunals, cf. *Spain and the Law*, p. 33.

20. *Reinvindicaciones de España* by Jose Maria de Areilza and Fernando Maria Castiella (Madrid, 1941): Areilza and Castiella argued Spain's claims not only to Gibraltar but also to Morocco, Algeria and French Indo-Cnina. For a discussion of the legal aspects of Utrecht, *v*. article in *Round Table* for June 1965, pp. 244-51.

21. *Discursos 1951-54*, pp. 67-9, 91-2, 107-8, 134, 360-4.

22. Admittedly the veto on parish priest appointments was to be exercised "only in exceptional circumstances". The one "forward looking" agreement was that re-establishing the Spanish Rota empowered to judge locally nullity suits; though leaving those concerned with the right to appeal to the Roman Rota. For the full text of all agreements, *v*. *Concordato entre la Santa Sede y España* (Ministerio de Asuntos Exteriores, Madrid, 1953).

23. Franco-Salgado.

15

SPAIN 1966

On 4th December 1966 Franco entered his seventy-fifth year. The beginning of the Civil War was thirty years behind him, the end twenty-seven. Twelve days earlier Franco escorted by his mounted ceremonial guard, had been driven in his Rolls-Royce to the Cortes. He had come to put before them a new Organic Law. The old General was planning ahead to the closing years of his life, his death and, if possible, beyond. The Cortes approved it immediately. Ten days later it was put before the country in referendum. The people endorsed it.

The Law was in effect a new constitution. It introduced changes at all the most important levels of government. At the highest it separated the office of Head of State from that of Head of Government. Every five years the long-extant Council of the Realm would put three names before the Head of State. From this trio the Head of State would select the Head of Government. The Council of the Realm (the Law reaffirmed that Spain was a Kingdom) was to be reconstituted. There would be no more nomination to it by the Head of State. Seven of the seventeen members would be *ex officio* as holders of offices such as the Presidency of the Cortes and of the Supreme Tribunal: the other ten would be elected to it by the Cortes from among themselves.

The composition of the Cortes was also to be changed. As before, a few of its members would be *ex officio*, and others representative of the workers, the employers, the professions, learned bodies and local and provincial governments, elected by their peers for a four-year term; but in future there would be a hundred members, two per province, directly elected by the heads of families and their wives, and the Head of State would have the power to nominate no more than twenty-five "distinguished men". Thus the principle of direct election was being reintroduced into Spanish politics: but not of Parties. Franco would have none of them:

Let Spaniards remember that each nation is a prey to its particular furies, and that they are different in each case. Spain's furies are the anarchical spirit, negative criticism, lack of solidarity between men, extremism, mutual enmity. Any political system which nurtures in its bosom the fostering of these defects, the setting loose of these familiar Spanish furies, will sooner or later—much more probably sooner than later—wreak havoc on all material progress and all improvements of our citizens' lives.

The role of the Cortes was also changed. Heretofore its task had been "to prepare and elaborate" laws. In future it would "elaborate and pass" new legislation.

The new Law also modified the *Fuero* and the Labour Charter. The ban in the former on non-Catholic religious ceremonies or manifestations in public was removed, bringing the *Fuero* into line with Vatican Council rulings on religious liberty. In the Charter the State was no longer to be national-sindicalist even in theory. In the future the Sindicatos would not be "instruments serving the State in the execution of its economic policy", but trade, craft and professional unions whose purpose would be to protect and further the interests of their members. Their officials would be freely elected, and not "militant members of the Falange". It seemed therefore that a trade union organisation was envisaged which would be free from State, of Party control. This was a fundamental change which had the approval neither of the Falange, which was thus to lose its hold over the workers, nor the clandestine Socialist U.G.T. whose leaders clung to the Marxist concept of trade unionism as the nursery of revolutionary zeal.

Monarchists, Christian Democrats, Socialists within Spain and Communists from abroad, called upon the people to boycott the referendum on the new Constitution, or to vote against it. Over 90 per cent of the people went to the polls, and over 95 per cent of those who did were said to have voted "Yes".

There were various factors behind the results. The Government had very cleverly mounted a full scale propaganda campaign which did not seek to explain the new Law nor even to extol its virtues: rather it turned the referendum into a vote of confidence and thanks to Franco, and Franco could not have chosen a more propitious moment for a vote of confidence in himself. Spain was enjoying a degree of prosperity unequalled in history. Again, the changes in the Labour Charter in particular had behind them fifteen years of history.

The statistical evidence of national prosperity was overwhelming. In 1935, the population of Spain had been 24 million, by 1965 it had reached 32: that is to say, for every three Spaniards resident in their own country before the Civil War, there were four in 1965; but those 32 million had incomparably more wealth as a body than the 24 million had had. Spain was producing twice as much coal, five times as much cement, six times as much steel, and eight times as much electricity as before the Civil War. Franco's government was building nearly ten times as many dwellings for letting at reduced rents as any of the Popular Front governments: and they were dwellings equipped to take the refrigerators, washing machines and television sets already owned by four out of every ten families. Where workers had walked to work before the Civil War, they now went at least on motor cycles. The cities were full of cars. From scratch in 1950, the output of private cars had topped 200,000 by 1966, and the demand was exceeding supply by the equivalent of a whole year's output. Per capita income at over U.S. $650 was firmly beyond the $500 imaginary frontier which economists generally placed between the rich and the poor countries. Productivity was increasing at a rate well above the 6 per cent which a Four-Year Development Plan for the years 1964-7 had envisaged.

The Basque Provinces and Catalonia were no longer the only industrialised areas of Spain. At Aviles near Oviedo a new steel plant was in operation. Corunna, Vigo, Seville, Valladolid and Zaragoza were rapidly developing into modern industrial cities. An industrial revolution was in progress throughout the country, with none of the miseries of the nineteenth century. Blast furnaces and rolling mills were of semi-automatic operation. Gardens and sports fields were considered of essence in the layouts of factories, and light and air in the design of workshops. Critics of the régime complained that Franco had diverted men's interests away from politics into football. There was perhaps some truth in this, in that the State had fostered clubs in the beginning, but the support now given them was the result of a new leisure. Not that the leisure was as plentiful as in Northern Europe. A dark side to this prosperity was that during the years of scarcity Spaniards at all levels, from management to unskilled worker, had become accustomed to working eight hours a day at one enterprise and a further four or more at another. In consequence the industrial accident rate was unduly high. Yet there were hundreds of thousands of workers with new skills taught them in the new government tech-

nical universities and schools, and under joint government and private
company schemes.

There were at long last in the country enough schools for all children
up to the age of fourteen. The school leaving age had been raised from
twelve for the beginning of the 1966 academic year. A small proportion of the children went to fee-paying schools, many to non-fee-
paying Church schools, but most to state schools. Franco had avoided
the mistakes both of the Liberal and Conservative governments of his
youth and of the left-wing governments of the Second Republic.
Unlike the latter, he had not closed down the Church schools: unlike
the former he had not left it to impoverished religious societies to cope
with a problem beyond their financial resources. From spending a
mere 1·6 per cent of her gross national product on education, Spain
had moved in line with the more educationally-minded countries of
Europe, and the corresponding figure for 1966 was 3·3. Her budgetary
allocation for education compared not unfavourably with that of the
more advanced countries of Europe. Allocations to the Ministeries of
Labour, Industry and Agriculture included sums destined for educational purposes. To remove excuses for absenteeism, school meals had
become general, and transport was being provided in rural areas. The
Ministries of Education, Labour and the Armed Services were co-
operating to retrieve from illiteracy those who had been children in
the less affluent years. Military service was now other than two years
of elementary arms drill and fatigues. For many it was a training school
for a trade. In all there were in the country 5·75 million full-time
students, of whom 99,000 were attending universities or equivalent
schools of study. For the resistance of the older, intellectual élite had
been destroyed. The economy of education had been studied under a
scheme sponsored by the Organisation for Economic Co-operation and
Development, and in consequence the whole educational system was
undergoing a complete revolution. New primary, secondary and
technical schools and universities were being built more with an eye
to "getting the best value for money" in "investment in education"
than to their outward grandiose appearance, a paramount consideration
in the 1940s and '50s. The curricula were being revised, new teaching
methods introduced, and intelligent youngsters encouraged to take up
teaching as a full-time profession in which salaries were increased in
some cases by as much as 100 per cent. Plans had been made for as far
ahead as 1975 when the State would allocate 65,900 million pesetas
(at 1961 values when only 10,520 million had been spent) to provide

for a student body of 7¼ millions. There would then be nearly 200,000 engaged on higher studies, more than half on scientific subjects. Even by 1966, the old adage "everyone in Spain may be assumed to be a lawyer until proved otherwise", was no longer true. Graduates in economics, and social and political studies, had come into their own in industry and commerce and in the Civil Service. The National Director of Primary education was an economist as well as an educationist. The Cabinet had economists of international reputation.

There were two noticeable differences between the men in Ministeries in the mid-1960s and those who had been there fifteen or more years earlier. While proud of the nation's achievements in education, labour, housing, industry and commerce they were not complacent. They had the knowledge of professionals as to what had to be done, of the inbalances between one region of the country and another, and between one and another group. Without prompting they would point out that there were still too many unskilled compared to the skilled, and too few technologists in the middle ranges compared with those at the top; and that there were still some problem areas in the south and pockets of misery even in flourishing cities. They would take the interested questioner to them no less willingly than to the "show places". At most levels, they had the will to do their utmost to correct those inbalances. Again, the new men in the Ministries had minds open to experiments and developments anywhere in the world. They travelled. They exchanged ideas. They were not bound by any particular political ideology. They were pragmatists. As Franco said: "We have changed."[2]

The traveller could see for himself marked changes in the rural areas. He could now go thousands of miles on roads, better than repute, without once being stopped by police. Civil Guards still patrolled the roads, but as much out of a tradition dating back a century and a half as in search of bandits or saboteurs. Neither bridges nor tunnels were being guarded, as they had been, even in 1959.

Now a visitor returning for the first time in four or five years could note, even more than the yearly visitor, that in the countryside the changes were no less astonishing than in the cities. Bare mountain sides had become forests. Re-afforestation was being effected at a rate of nearly a quarter of a million acres a year. As against the pre-Civil War figure of under one million acres of irrigated land there were now close on five million. The principal show place was near Badajoz in the "extremely harsh" province of Extremadura. On 125,000 acres, once arid land, men who in their youth had been driven by the desperation of hunger into anarchism, were living at peace with the world, and comfortably off their produce—fruit, vegetables and cotton, with a market in Seville where one of Europe's largest textile plants was in operation. Badajoz, however, was just one, and not the most remarkable, of several new land settlement areas.

The slow progress of agriculture was nevertheless the economic planner-in-chief, Professor Laureano Lopez-Rodo's, chief worry. Franco had promoted him in 1965 to Cabinet rank. Workers were leaving the countryside for industry, as he had planned, but those staying were not changing their methods of husbandry sufficiently quickly to yield the full 4·5 per cent annual increase which he had considered desirable and attainable. In the circumstances the setting up of agricultural institutes and the sending out of "travelling salesmen" of new methods were being given top priority.

As land reform was the one Spanish need which Franco had apparently hardly touched, the Secretary General of the Communist Party, Santiago Carrillo, made much of it in what he wrote and said in exile.[3] Statistically it did appear that there were still too many large estates, the Duke of Medinaceli owning nearly a quarter of a million acres. Franco had in fact broken up a few of the large estates since 1940, forcing out the particularly inefficient and absentee landlord. In time, however, the large land owners had come to have some economists on their side, who argued that the large holding was not necessarily a serious problem: that given the growing shortage of labour on the fields, the large landlords were already being forced to modernise, and that they could afford to do so more easily than the smallholders: and again that with the labour shortage, the landlords were also being forced to pay agricultural labourers higher wages, thereby reducing the magnitude of the social problem. Franco's agronomist Minister of Agriculture half agreed, half disagreed, conceding that from an economic point of view the over-splitting up of land into holdings of less than 2½ acres was equally serious. It was on their concentration into economically more viable lots that he was spending most of his energies in 1966.

The inveterate opponent of Franco shut his eyes before the factories and the new irrigated and re-afforestated lands, and attributed the economic well-being of the country exclusively to U.S. aid, the growth of Spain into the favourite holiday resort of European tourists, and to the remittances of Spanish workers in Germany, Switzerland and

France. In truth, the total number of Spaniards working temporarily abroad was 675,000, a figure inferior when related to population to that of Irishmen, Greeks or Turks and absolutely to that of Italians. The tourist industry was undoubtedly a money-spinner, the 14·25 millions of 1965 spending $1,157 million: but in fact, the major increases in tourist traffic and spending had occurred after and not before the economic revolution had begun. U.S. aid had been important, not so much in quantity (it was inferior to that received by Britain, Italy or Greece) but in turning the attention of Spain beyond her shores and Pyrenees to ways and means of economic progress.

The immediate effect of Franco's agreements with the U.S. and the Vatican had been to increase rather than diminish his internal problems. Army officers generally approved of the former with its promise of new equipment, though some did wonder how they would be able to compete socially with the far more highly paid Americans. The hierarchy was divided over the Concordat. Some emphasised that it would allow them liberties hitherto not entirely guaranteed by the law: others stressed the evils of State control now to be perpetuated. True Falangists were opposed to both. What had happened to Jose Antonio's principle of a Church–State separation? Was the U.S. not the thief of Cuba and the Philippines! The Cortes had to ratify both agreements, and they duly did so. Significantly Franco took only twenty minutes to present the U.S. trio whereas he spoke for fifty minutes in justification of the Concordat.* *Arriba* had to publish the speeches in full. Nevertheless the Church and the general public were more concerned with the American agreements. Franco had invited into the country men whose religion was heretical, whose manners were barbarous and whose morals were non-existent. More familiar then with the dollar-packed early than with the less spendthrift later American tourist, they worried over the rise in prices that more of such people might cause. Almost the only group who looked forward to their arrival were the shopkeepers who in time were to become the most anti-American, when their expectations were defrauded by the Post Exchanges at the bases.

Against this background of murmurs, the *FET y de las JONS* met in Congress at the end of October 1953, and approved Franco's foreign policies with the resolution: "Spain associates herself in a definite and

---

* A curious speech, in which he considered at length the Catholic view that where there is no conflict there is no need for a Concordat, yet talked round the question why then should Spain have one.[4]

contractual manner with the defence of Europe and, above all, the defence of Western Christianity".

Other resolutions of that Congress showed how the Movimiento did not fit neatly into foreign concepts of left- or right-wing, or of Party. Private enterprise would not be suppressed and wholesale nationalisation would not take place, but financial pressure groups, cartels, trusts and monopolies would be destroyed. A better distribution of the national income through an increase in production was demanded from the government, and so were heavy cuts in food prices, higher wages tied to a cost of living index, incentive bonuses, the redistribution of the land and more and better housing. In retrospect this Congress can indeed be seen as marking the end of Falange supremacy within the Movimiento though the Falange would fight back and recover some lost ground before losing it finally. For all this was more Catholic than Falange social doctrine. In the early days the railways had been nationalised. At a later period the American-owned telephone company, the British-owned Rio Tinto mines, the French, the Germans who had fought so hard for concessions which had yielded them comparatively little, had all been bought out. It now seemed certain that there would be no further nationalisation—as sacrosanct a dogma to Falangists as Clause IV to the British Labour Party. American economic advisers were advocating the opening of Spain to foreign investment, and dissatisfied with the speed at which the bases were being made ready, less government protection for workers and less ministerial control of supplying industries.

Franco's new outward look in 1953 did not extend to Britain except this far: he allowed several thousand Spaniards to go to Britain for the Coronation of Queen Elizabeth II to which she had invited Don Juan as her cousin. The ease with which they obtained the exit permits which were then necessary was interpreted by Falangists as yet another insult to their ideology. However, the Press were instructed to keep up the demand for Gibraltar and not to praise Britain.* Franco made it clear that his alliance with the United States was not an alliance with the

---

* *Arriba* interpreted the orders as permission to intensify their years-old campaign. A double-decker bus overturned in Glasgow in a serious accident. The picture published had a caption implying the untrustworthiness and dangerous quality of the products of the British motor industry. A photograph of gamekeepers protecting a wood in Hampshire from would-be "scroungers" of Christmas trees appeared with a caption warning the Spanish reader of the evil effects of copying British customs. The tragic loss of thirty-six lives in the Comet crash was used as proof of British decadence and insignificance.

friends of the United States.[5] When the Queen's visit to Gibraltar was announced later in 1953, all the Press joined Franco in a protest against her visit to the disputed territory. There was no question that he had the greatest respect for the English monarchy, and for the person of the Queen whose grandfather's funeral he had attended: but Gibraltar, in his view, was a part of Spain.

Falange or no, Franco continued with his preparations for the *eventual* restoration of the monarchy. He wrote to Don Juan asking him to come to talk to him in Spain. Don Juan duly met him the following December. It was the first time for eighteen years that the man whom the Alfonists called John III had crossed the frontiers of his kingdom. His son, Juan Carlos, had completed his secondary studies. Don Juan and Franco agreed on his future: the young Prince would go first to the Zaragoza Military Academy, next to the Airforce and Naval Academies and then to Madrid University, where he would study political science and economics—a total of six years of study. Nothing more was settled at the meeting, but the Falangists were worried. Franco sought to set their minds at rest by reminding them, through *Arriba*, that what had been decided was no more than a prudent measure to enable the Law of Succession, approved by the Referendum of 1947, to be fulfilled in due course. But the *camisas viejas* would have none of monarchy. They used the best weapon to hand, the S.E.U., or Students' University Union, to which all university students had to belong by law but in which only Falangists were active. They were put, in February 1955, on the distribution of leaflets accusing the first six Bourbon monarchs of a long list of crimes, and Alfonso XIII of more of them than all his ancestors. Franco summoned the Editor of *Arriba* and gave him a second "interview".[6] Camouflaging his intentions by saying that he wished to give the lie to foreign commentators, he reminded the readers of the Falangist *Arriba* that more than half the nation knew no more about monarchy than what they had been told. In the first interview he had assured the Falangists that the restoration of the monarchy would not mean the return of a multi-party state: in this second one, he again spoke of the Spanish brand of parliament-arianism as a thoroughly rotten system of government. However, he went on, Alfonso XIII had been its victim. Of the King to whom he had sworn allegiance on being commissioned and whose Gentleman-of-the-Bedchamber he had been, Franco spoke with feeling and praise—and the following day, accompanied by all his Ministers, the Heads of the Armed Services, the Council of the Realm, representatives of the Spanish Cortes and the Diplomatic Corps in strength, he attended a Solemn Requiem in the Escorial for the repose of the soul of Alfonso XIII, and of all the kings and queens of Spain from the time of the Emperor Charles V who lie buried there. Don Juan Carlos began his studies at Franco's old Academy the following July.

Throughout 1955 Franco seemed to lean towards the liberation of the régime and towards the monarchy. The Church campaigned for higher wages, and the Government granted an increase, though one not as high as the Church had demanded. Franco maintained, with politicians and economists of other countries, that the only way out of a wages–prices spiral was by an increase in productivity. Spanish economists as well as industrialists, however, began to murmur that there could be no higher productivity where the State had become the owner of so many industrial enterprises through I.N.I., or so constantly told private companies what they could do or what they should not do. The State relaxed its controls very slightly. *Ecclesia*, the one paper able to do so from its privileged position of not being censored, campaigned against the press laws. The Bishop of Malaga, Angel Herrera, took up the battle in a long correspondence with Serrano Suñer's old press chief, Arias Salgado, now Minister of Tourism and Information. The correspondence was published. In 1953, the first novel dealing with the Civil War in a realistic way had been allowed publication. In the following year a number of books in the languages of Galicia and Catalonia had been permitted and Chairs of Catalan and Galician studies established in Madrid University. In 1955 a Chair of Basque was founded in Salamanca to the surprise of the Basques and the horror of the ultra-chauvinistic Falangists.

The Falange now moved towards violence. On 20th November Franco was insulted to his face by a Falange youth member. The director of the organisation, who had held the post for fifteen years, was called upon to resign. In his New Year message Franco made a call to parents to control their children, and not to listen to "the libertinage of the air and printed word flying from abroad". He appealed to all Spaniards to concentrate on the ideas which united them rather than on points of no importance which caused disunity.[7]

The Falange, and in particular those in the S.E.U., did not heed Franco's words. They continued their anti-monarchist agitation. Now all university students were not Falangists: there were monarchists, traditionalists, liberals, Christian Democrats, Catalan Nationalists and even socialists. There were others who were simply anti-S.E.U., who wished that they had a union to represent them before the university authorities and not one which represented the Falange to the university students. In the February the Falangists organised what was to have been a demonstration against the Bourbons. It became a battle between them and the rest. Riots reached major proportions. A Falangist carrying a gun fired it and killed one of his fellows. Momentarily it looked as if the situation was getting out of hand. Franco suspended two Articles of his *Fuero*: the Articles guaranteeing freedom of movement and freedom from arrest for more than seventy-two hours without being charged. Classes at Madrid University were suspended. The Dean of the Faculty of Law was dismissed. So was the Rector, Dr. Lain Entralgo. He had suggested in public that the students had a case in their demand for a free union.

Franco now acted in the same way as on the occasion of the Falange–Army debacle of 1941. He dismissed on the one hand the liberal and European-minded Minister of Education, Ruiz Jimenez, and on the other the *camisa vieja* Minister without Portfolio and Secretary-General of the Falange, Fernandez Cuesta. Franco, however, now had a potentially more serious problem than students could provoke.

At the end of the war he had withdrawn from Tangier in the face of pressure from Britain, France, the U.S. and Russia,[8] later to return as a member of a new international committee. The Moroccans in Tangiers seemed to welcome the return of the Spaniards. His pro-Arab policy included the frequent insistence that Morocco was a protectorate and not a colony, let alone an oversea province of France or any other power. With this he avoided the troubles of the French in their part of Morocco and the Spanish came to be known as the "happy zone". When the French deposed the Sultan, Mohamed bin Yusuf, Franco refused to recognise his replacement Mohamed bin Arefa, calling him a "quisling". Garcia Valiño, then High Commissioner in Spanish Morocco, allowed Mohamed's supporters to use Radio Tetuan and to take refuge in the Spanish zone. Franco had granted it partial self-government in 1952. The Arabs praised him as their friend. He received a delegation of the Sultan's chief men and assured them that Spain would honour her international obligations, unlike France whose conduct he condemned. The Spanish Press gave as full publicity as the British left-wing press to stories of French police and Foreign Legion violence. When in October 1955 the Riffs attacked the French, the French resident-general in Morocco accused Spain of allowing them to form up within Spanish Morocco, and of letting it be used as a channel for their supplies. Franco expressed sympathy with the Moroccans' "natural desire for independence", and called the French formula of "independence within interdependence" repulsive and contradictory. Furthermore, he said, to impose on Morocco French ideas of democracy would be to expose "a simple people" to Communism. It was Spain's intention to guide Morocco towards independence, but as the Morrocans and not as the French wanted.[9]

The sudden French decision to give Morocco independence under Mohamed V on 2nd March 1956 left Franco somewhat unprepared. Skirmishes began to occur within what had been till then the "happy zone". Franco now acted with the rapidity of which he was capable on occasion. He invited the Sultan to come to Madrid to formalise the end of the Spanish Protectorate.

The Sultan arrived on 4th April. Franco met him at the airport, and Franco's colourful mounted Moroccan Guards escorted the two Heads of State as they drove through the city. The formal negotiations began two days later with a brief speech by Franco. Spain, he said, had undertaken the Protectorate forty-four years previously to restore the Sultan's authority. After thirty years of peace, she was glad to hand the zone over to the Sultan as the Head of the new independent State of Morocco.[10] After an all-night session, the agreement was signed. Spain pledged herself "to help His Imperial Majesty the Sultan, and by common agreement come to his aid in matters of foreign affairs and defence". The rights and liberties of Spanish subjects in Morocco were to be respected.

Franco's real worry was how the Spaniards would take the agreement. There were still the enclaves of Melilla, Ceuta, the island of Alhucemas, and the territories of Ifni and Spanish Sahara, a few islands· and a tiny portion of the West African coast left of the Spanish empire, but nothing more and no prospects that there would ever again be anything more. Several hundred Spanish officers and some thousands of men would presumably now be redundant. Whether the Army were reduced in size or no, service in Africa had carried allowances denied service in the Peninsula. Foreign commentators doubted that the Army would accept the inevitable with good grace. In fact they did. There were some grumbles, but no more than among British Indian Army officers at the dissolution of the Indian Empire. Here, however, was the end to any practical meaning in the Falange's "Will to Empire". The independence of Morocco, therefore, was yet another blow to Jose Antonio's doctrines. However, Franco had had the providential good fortune that the Army had looked upon concurrent student riots with extreme disfavour, and that a group of officers had made it known that they would act against any further attempt by the Falange to disturb public order. The Press and radio were made to follow strictly orders to present the granting of independence to Spanish Morocco as a stroke of genius on the part of the Caudillo. The opposition could not make its voice heard, and the cities of Spain were spared the street deaths which the independence of French North Africa cost France.

Franco himself revealed the discords of the time in a speech to 25,000 Falangists in Seville on 1st May 1956.[11] He spoke of foreign enemies and Masons seeking to divide the Falange and the Army, and of encouraging grumbling in the Army, and of fermenting speculation as to who would succeed him as Head of the State. He challenged anyone to pinpoint any governmental deviation from the Movimiento's twenty-six points (which he did not mention were not quite identical with Jose Antonio's). He assured them that while the Falange could exist without a monarch, a monarch could not survive without the Falange: however, in deference to the peoples of the north and Navarre and their traditions, and they had fought bravely in the crusade, Spain was and would be a monarchy. Mention of the north brought him to speak of "our social justice".

The government had decreed in April a 20 per cent increase in wages. Workers in Pamplona had thereupon gone on strike: the increase was not enough, and in this opinion at least fourteen priests who were later arrested supported them. A nationwide enquiry by Catholic Action had proved over a year previously that at best the Government's fixed basic wages were 50 per cent below what a man needed to maintain himself and his family "in dignity". When police were drafted to break the strike, the workers concentrated on the main square of Pamplona. The police advanced. As they neared the strikers, these took out their rosaries and began to pray. The police had no experience of such resistance, and dared go no further although urged by the Civil Governor. The strikes thereafter spread eastwards into Catalonia and westwards into the Basque provinces.

Franco now admitted that there were social injustices. He was trying to redress these as quickly as he could. What was the answer? Inflation? It would be a catastrophe.[12]

The strikers went back to work, but the Church now took up their case, and issued in the October a pastoral letter signed by every archbishop and bishop denouncing working conditions and the Government's wages policy. At a Cabinet meeting the Minister of Commerce admitted that there was a widespread lack of confidence in the Government's economic policy. In the following months, Franco conceded wage increases of between 30 and 50 per cent.

Franco now decided to give the Falange yet one more chance to lead Spain into unity behind him. Luis Arrese, back in the post of Secretary-General of the Falange in succession to Fernandez Cuesta, was commissioned to prepare a new set of "fundamental laws"—that is a new constitution. The final draft he presented to the Cabinet was for a wholly totalitarian party-state, strictly disciplined though permitting "self-criticism", with a National Council vested with powers identical with those of the Soviet Central Committee and with the Cortes turned into a Supreme Soviet in all but name. The discussion of these laws in the Cabinet continued over several sessions which were said to have been extremely stormy (Franco always allowed his Ministers full liberty of speech at meetings). Copies of them were circulated among those who would recognise their implications[13] and the Church re-acted with some vehemence. Simultaneously trouble broke out again among students and among the workers. The wage increases which they had been granted had been nullified by rises in the price of food.

In the circumstances Franco again changed his Cabinet. He relegated the arch-Falangist Arrese to the post of Minister of Housing. He dismissed Giron. From the University of Barcelona he brought out the Professor of Economics, Pedro Gual Villalbi, and made him a Minister without Portfolio telling him to co-ordinate economic policy. He took an ex-Army officer, Mariano Navarro Rubio, out of one of the banks as whose director he had proved his financial acumen, and made him Minister of Finance; and out of the Madrid University Faculty of Economics and Political Science he cajoled a Professor of Economic History, Alberto Ullastres Calvo, and make him his Minister of Commerce.

None of these three had a party background. Ullastres and Navarro Rubio were known to be, and Gual Villalbi suspected of being, members of a religious society, *Opus Dei*, men pledged by a solemn vow to the dedication to God of all their professional talents.[14]

Franco had had technocrats in his Cabinet before, but never men so beyond the reach of bribery, or popular rumours of corruption, or deviation from duty. They were to lay the foundations for the prosperous Spain of the mid-1960s. They would do so in the face of stiff opposition from the Falangists, for their proposals were to be diametrically contrary to all the nationalism and much of the socialism of economic policy to date.

The first step was for the Bank of Spain to say openly that the State was over-spending, and mis-spending money, and that if Spain was to become more productive, there would have to be an "open door" to foreign capital. At the end of the year they published the fact that Spain's foreign reserves were down to $96·8 million. All this prepared the way for a budget the following year which was revolutionary in that it affected the pockets of the wealthy proportionately more than the rest. The importation of luxury goods was practically stopped. Navarro Rubio and Ullastres uncovered also the illegal holdings of wealthy Spaniards in foreign banks; and Franco backed their action against the culprits, some of whom might have hoped that ties of friendship (or possibly blood) might have spared them. They took Spain into the International Monetary Fund, and into the Organisation for European Economic Co-operation; and they invited advice from these international bodies.

O.E.E.C. published its survey in April 1959. It confirmed the need for radical changes in economic policy. The government was trying to do too much: its planning was haphazard: its industrialisation was dependent on raw materials purchasable only abroad: it was neglecting agriculture and this was leading to a diminishing productivity and creating the need to import essential foodstuffs. Spain's own important citrus fruit harvest could not be marketed abroad competitively.

The reserves dropped to a mere $14 million that July, In the face of this evidence, Franco agreed to the devaluation of the peseta from 42 to 60 to the dollar, and in its support the I.M.F., O.E.E.C. and U.S.A. granted credits of $418 million. His economist Ministers had prepared also, with international advice, a drastic stabilisation plan which would create serious temporary unemployment, but which, they assured him, would in the long run put Spain in a position to create tens of thousands of new jobs. He approved of it, and of the introduction of unemployment benefit to soften the blow. He agreed also to a "stick-and-carrot" policy to encourage private industry to modernise its plant. The plan worked. A year later Spain had a balance of payments of $463 million. Planners and Caudillo had been lucky in that the 1959 harvest had been good, unlike that of 1958, and that the Church had called for support of the plan while seeking greater benefits for the unemployed. West Germany too had agreed to admit Spanish labour.

With this plan, inflation was kept strictly under control, and exports maintained at a high level. In 1961 limited convertibility of the peseta was introduced, loans were serviced and some repaid, yet by December, Spanish foreign exchange reserves had risen to the unprecedented figure of $850 million. Greater efficiency in factories led to higher production. Spain, said Señor Ullastres, was now solvent, but unlikely to remain so. Expansion was now necessary by at least 4 per cent per year to reduce the high figure of unemployment. Spain could achieve 4 per cent if private industrialists were to invest their money in expansion. Franco agreed to allow foreign firms to establish subsidiaries, keeping as much as 50 per cent of the shares. The following April, on the advice of his economists, he approved the formation of the commission under Professor Lopez-Rodo which would plan really systematically and on soundly established statistics, for the first time in Spanish history, the future balanced development of the country. A team of 900 specialists in various fields worked out how Spain could achieve as much as a 6 per cent rate of growth between 1964 and 1967, a figure which was to be exceeded in the event; but while the commission did its work, Franco backed to the hilt his Minister of Finance's preparatory legislation. Over half the decrees whereby the State had controlled industry were discarded. Expanding enterprises would no longer have their every proposition scrutinised by the government, but there was to be no price fixing, market sharing or restriction. Foreign companies were now to be allowed to have even more than 50 per cent holdings in most industries. There was a reform of the antiquated Spanish banking system.

As the date approached for the introduction of the Four Year Plan, which Franco accepted with alacrity, his friend Suances resigned from I.N.I. I.N.I. would in future have fully to justify itself to the Ministry of Finance. It would be allowed to embark on new enterprises only with the express permission of the government, and it would have to compete with private enterprise.

So ended the era of Falange economic nationalism, which may or may not have been justifiable in the 1940s, but which by the early 1950s was holding up Spain's development and indeed taking it to bankruptcy.

Between 1961 and 1966, the per capita income rose by 30 per cent, in real terms, a rate unparalleled in any other country at that time. In May 1966 the number of unemployed was down to 160,000, or under 1·5 per cent of a working population of 12·3 million. It had

become possible to say that freedom from want was being enjoyed by
nearly all Spaniards for the first time in their history.

What of other freedoms?

No man had any cause to fear the police unless he broke the law.
Criminal statistics were low. Juvenile delinquency was exceptional.
The fear that the Americans in Spain would corrupt the nation had
proved unfounded. However, numerous activities considered legitimate in non-Communist countries continued to figure on Spanish
statutes as crimes. It was illegal for men to assemble for any political
purpose, or for any purpose which might be construed as political,
without express permission.[15] It was criminal to attempt to form a
political society or to distribute political propaganda. The publication
at home or abroad of any criticism of the Head of the State, the Army,
Government, officials or State institutions, could render a Spaniard
liable to fines or imprisonment.

Whoever hoped that the agreements with the United States in 1953,
the admission of Spain into the United Nations in 1955, or the economic
liberalisation of the régime which began with the Cabinet changes of
1957 would lead to the repeal of such restrictions of human liberty, was
disappointed. Every year there were arrests and trials of persons who
had broken these laws. Let it be said that those held for longer than
seventy-two hours and brought to trial were a minute proportion of
those who in fact did not respect these laws. The total number in the
ten years to 1963 for these offences and for the more serious ones of
provoking demonstrations and strikes probably did not exceed one
thousand. Wealth, parentage and political history were of no consequence. They included the brother of the Bishop of Malaga, Antonio
Herrera, Serrano Suñer's Director of Propaganda, Dionisio Ridruejo,
the wealthy Basque industrialist Joaquin Satrustegui, and a young
diplomat Julio Ceron.[16] Gil Robles, who had returned to Spain in the
early '50s, was in great demand as defending counsel.

There was a thin trickle, going up to three in 1962, of men tried and
condemned to death for crimes committed during the Civil War. In
almost every case the sentence was commuted. Workers who plotted
to assassinate Franco in 1961 were given prison sentences which came to
an end on the declaration of an amnesty to celebrate the election of
Paul VI to the Papacy. These trials aroused little interest abroad.
However, on 8th November 1962, the police arrested in Barcelona
Julian Grimau, a member of the Central Committee of the Spanish
Communist Party since 1954. Grimau, during the Civil War, had risen

to the rank of commander of one of the notorious *Chekas*,[17] and since
1957 had been back in Spain as a Communist agitator. The first news
of his arrest was given by Radio Moscow on the 11th which thereafter,
with other Communist radios, kept up an almost daily barrage of
propaganda on his behalf as "a hero of the Civil War", and "a member
of the Central Committee". On 18th April, in open court, Grimau
admitted his Communist connections, but denied the written allegations of eye-witnesses and relatives of dead men that he had been responsible for the torturing of prisoners and their assassination during
the Civil War. He was condemned to death. He had presented a sorry
sight in court. According to the Spanish police, he had jumped out of
a first floor window while being interrogated on the day of his arrest.
However, as the police of Barcelona had the reputation of brutality
while interrogating students (*Ecclesia* had published reports of torture
of political detainees in 1960), the world was predisposed to consider
the police explanation of Grimau's visible severe injuries as unlikely to
be true. Franco was sent appeals for clemency from many parts of the
world—among them one from France with the signature of two
cardinals. It was touch and go whether the sentence would be commuted, when Khrushchev appealed personally on his behalf to Franco.
This decided the issue. Franco confirmed the sentence.[18]

Nearly every year from 1953, there were strikes. Till about 1960
they were primarily for better wages or living conditions. Franco kept
to his theory that in the Sindicatos workers had the perfect machinery
for the redress of all grievances. Now from 1958 onwards, there began
to appear in the Basque industrial zone and elsewhere, workers'
organisations totally independent of the Falange or the State. They
were the Workers' Brotherhoods of Catholic Action (Hermandades
Obreras de Acción Católica), which, under the aegis of the Concordat's
guarantee of freedom "for associations of Catholic action ... to
exercise their apostolate", began to disseminate the Catholic view of
workers' rights to strike and to form their own state-free trade unions.
The H.O.A.C. held a meeting in a Bilbao theatre on 1st May 1960, the
proscribed international labour day, with the authority of their bishop,
who attended the meeting. The two main speakers were arrested and
fined. The bishop, in a letter in which he confessed to applauding the
speakers and himself speaking as well, protested at the sentences and at
the presence of the police at a church meeting. On 30th May, 339
Basque priests put their signature to a closely reasoned document
pointing to the abyss between the Spanish State and Catholic doctrines

on the State, social order and the rights and freedoms of the individual. They quoted the Bishop of the Canaries[19] to reinforce their view that the Sindicato was "neither a trade union nor Christian". On 21st September Franco published a new law consolidating existing prohibitions and adding to them. Strikes "inspired by political motives", or which led to "serious disturbances of the public order", were to be considered acts of military rebellion (for which the maximum penalty could be death): so also "spreading false or tendentious information with the aim of disturbing internal public order ... or damaging the prestige of the state, its institutions, government, army or other authorities", and "planning or taking part in meetings, conferences or demonstrations with the above-mentioned ends in view".

Behind the scenes there developed now a struggle between the Falange leaders and the H.O.A.C. As workers, of course, H.O.A.C. members had to be Sindicato members as well. The Cardinal Primate accused the Secretary General of the Falange of "totalitarian methods" in preventing "the apostolic work of the H.O.A.C." in a letter which became public in January 1961. Matters came to a head the following year. A claim for higher wages put in by coal miners in Mieres★ had remained clogged for months in the clumsy slow-moving machinery of the Sindicato when on 6th April the workers' decided on strike action. From Asturias the strikes spread to the Basque provinces and Catalonia. By the beginning of May there were between 100,000 and 150,000 defying the law against industrial action. The Government saw Communist instigation in the movement, and certainly Soviet broadcasters urged the Spanish workers to turn it into revolution; but the strikers had nationwide support, particularly from the H.O.A.C. which issued leaflets urging the strikers to stand firm in their demands for better wages and for the recognition by the government of their right to strike. *Ecclesia* insisted editorially that the right to strike was "a natural and Christian right". H.O.A.C. and *Ecclesia* now had the moral authority of John XXIII's encyclical *Mater et Magistra*. H.O.A.C. proclaimed the necessity for a truly active share for the workers in the undertaking in which they were engaged, its profits and even in its property. Workers, they said, had a right to free association. The government granted a 75 per cent increase in wages. About 300 persons were arrested, all but a handful of whom were quickly released. The most heavily penalised were two leaders of Catholic action on whose behalf the Cardinal Primate had long discussions with Franco. They

★ In Asturias, the epicentre of the 1934 uprising.

were inconclusive. To relieve the tension, the Cardinal eventually wrote a letter in which he gave the assurance that the Church would remain true to the principle of non-intervention in the affairs of state. However, maintaining his personal approval of the H.O.A.C. action, he asked:

> Is it not applying the secular criteria of the partisans of state control* to maintain that it is not the work of the apostolate to "a doctrine contained in the encyclical Mater et Magistra just because it clashes with state legislation? Would it not be more logical rather to reform what ought to be reformed in order to bring it into harmony with this encyclical, in a state which calls itself Catholic and Social and whose leader has declared in many speeches that it follows the social doctrine of the Church?"[20]

The letter was addressed significantly not to Franco but to the Foreign Minister. The inference was clear. Any further action on the part of the State would be a matter of Vatican-Spanish and not Church-State relations.

Into 1964, the Sindicatos did their best, by showing keenness in acquiring better wages for the workers, to arrest the growing demand for independent trade unions. Workers returning from France, Switzerland and Western Germany to take up the jobs now available in Spain, as the momentum of the economic revolution increased, brought with them ideas on the organisation of workers more akin to those of the H.O.A.C. and of Socialists than to those of the official Sindicatos. In the last week of the year the Brotherhoods in their official bulletin openly advocated the establishment of a true democracy in Spain. They postulated the formation of a minimum of two parties in a true freely elected parliament. Simultaneously the non-elected Cortes was discussing a new law of association. It was, in many details, expressly directed at the H.O.A.C. *Ecclesia* considered it "a legal instrument for future violation . . . of a basic human right, freedom of association". Notwithstanding the strong Church opposition and the resignation from the Cortes of the ex-Minister of Education Ruiz Jimenez, the law was promulgated in 1965. Thereafter the Brotherhoods operated less overtly. A new body, the *Alianza Sindical Obrera*, was formed with the aim of uniting workmen of all shades of political opinion and religious belief. The opposition to the passage of the law however did wrest a concession from the régime. In June the

* An obvious reference to the Communist states.

International Labour Office was informed that in future a distinction would be drawn in Spain between strikes caused by economic or social grievances and those with a political motive. The former would no longer be judged or punished as military rebellion.

The year 1965 was singularly free from "economic strikes"; but in March a thousand Asturian miners stormed the police headquarters at Mieres and wrecked the building as they shouted "Liberty, Liberty". The police wisely did not fire. Only one worker was reported arrested. The Government attributed this as all other demonstrations to "Communist conspirators" but confessed that bureaucratic inefficiency had delayed the payment of benefits to victims of silicosis. The attribution of Communist direction of much more serious and prolonged university student demonstrations on the other hand was quickly dropped. Sympathisers with the students included too many figures known for their anti-Marxism. The spark that set them off was a ban in February on a series of expository lectures at Madrid University on the Encyclical *Pacem in Terris*. Professors joined the demonstrators, and four of them were arrested and fined for taking part in "an illegal assembly". At subsequent demonstrations, the cry was taken up "We want free Syndicates". It came to be replaced by the slogan "We are fighting for a democratic union in a democratic state". Truncheons and fire hoses dispersed a body of 5,000 in the heart of modern Madrid. The older generation to whom the name Mieres had overtones of revolution, recalled also the demonstrations of lesser magnitude which had heralded the fall of the monarchy. However, history did not repeat itself; but then, Franco had not repeated history in that he had refused to use troops either against the workers or the students, as his predecessors in government had done.

Franco was moving, or being forced away, from his concept of military discipline as the beginning and end of government. In 1963 he had established a Civil Tribunal of Public Order to take over from courts martial the trial of those accused of causing disturbances; and now, in 1966, eleven years after Bishop, now Cardinal Herrera had battled with Arias Salgado on whether the censorship of the Press was in accordance or no with the dignity of man, Arias' successor as Minister of Tourism and Information, Fraga Irribarne, produced a new Press law, which removed most of the controls on the printed word.[21] The possibility that there might be other changes could be sensed. In March 1965, *Arriba* surprised its readers with a series of articles advocating the creation of an Opposition. In the following year it could well be asked not merely as before what was the Falange, but also where was it? Boy scouts, once a proscribed association, went about Madrid: the Falange youth as such was a rare sight. But for a few elderly *camisas viejas*, a few middle-aged men still anxious to prove to the enquirer that Jose Antonio had been right, some Sindicato officials fearful lest free trade unions should deprive them of their remunerative posts, the Falange had gone back to its 1936 position as a rowdy element in the universities and outside them, holding meetings in theatres and then demonstrations against the Government. The 1966 generation carried banners with the legend: *Falange Si, Movimiento No* as they marched with their arms extended in the Fascist salute abolished by the Government twenty-one years earlier. Only they, the Communists and a few elderly exiles wanted a re-creation of the chaos of thirty years and more past. The rest of the *Movimiento* had moved. Questioned whether he still thought Communism a danger to Spain, Franco answered: "Circumstances and times have changed. We have changed. Governments cannot, or rather must not, stand still."[22]

In the 1957 Cabinet changes, Martin Artajo had been replaced by Fernando Castiella. Franco, it could be said in retrospect, had begun planning for the next battle, like a good general who must be one step ahead. Martin Artajo had done his job with the Concordat and the U.S. and Arab agreements. The next battle would be that with Britain for Gibraltar "a ripe plum ready to fall".[23] For a while foreign policy was deviated. Moroccan irregulars, who had previously been harassing the French, spread over into the Spanish colonies of Ifni, Seguia-el-Hamra and Rio de Oro. There was a major engagement on 3rd January 1958. Spain and France then joined forces as they had against Abdel Krim: and by the end of February had driven the irregulars away. Morocco accepted from Spain a portion of the territory of Ifni, leaving Spain with seven hundred square miles and 50,000 inhabitants in what he then called the overseas Province of Ifni, and 105,000 square miles with 60,000 inhabitants in what was renamed the overseas Province of Spanish Sahara. Spain considered the agreement final: not so Morocco which continued to claim both territories as hers—or Mauretania which also claimed Spanish Sahara.*

* Fernando Po and Rio Muni off and on the coast of Africa likewise became overseas provinces in 1960. They were given autonomy in 1963. Their future in 1966 was most uncertain, some Africans arguing for their independence as a unit; others for their absorbtion by Nigeria and Cameroun.

In 1959 Castiella paid a quick private visit to London to deflect Eisenhower to Spain. Eisenhower changed his plans, and spent two days in Madrid where huge crowds cheered him. He talked with Franco, according to the communiqué "in an atmosphere of cordiality and understanding" giving him "a review of his European trip including the Western Summit conference". Franco had no need to be in NATO, and continued to stress that he had no wish to be so. In the following year, Castiella came officially to London, to sign a cultural agreement. No one recalled the fact that he had once been refused admittance as Spanish Ambassador. Lord Home returned the visit the following year. Other British Ministers took their holidays in Spain.* Trade between Britain and Spain improved. Minor differences were smoothed. There were some Anglo-Spanish naval exercises in the Mediterranean. The sun seemed to be shining on Anglo-Spanish relations: but the shadow of Gibraltar was always there. It figured prominently in the conversations between Castiella, Selwyn Lloyd and Lord Home.[24]

1962 and 1963 were busy years of re-negotiation of the U.S. bases agreement—Franco obtaining better financial benefits than before after some hard bargaining. De Gaulle, too, then had a period during which he seemed to be courting General Franco into his "grand design for Europe". Franco put out feelers to join E.C.E. as an associate member thereby rousing the hackles of the Falange no less than those of such democrats as Gil Robles, Satrustegui and Salvador de Madariaga who with another seventy Spaniards attended the Congress of the European Movement in Munich to express the hope that Spain would not be admitted into E.C.E. before the State undertook to respect the common human liberties.† The Falangists in their new extremist paper *Es Así* published a forthright attack on Franco's policy of Europeanisation as a betrayal of the cause for which Falangists had fought a war.

With the re-negotiation of the U.S. agreements well under way, and terms more favourable to Spain foreseeable, Franco was in a position to start the battle for Gibraltar. His choice of battlefield was the United Nations. His Arab and Latin American friends had seen to the inclusion of Gibraltar as one of the territories whose "decolonisation" would be pressed for by the United Nations Special Committee of twenty-four.

---

* In Africa there had in the meantime been a minor flare-up, but the appointment of General El Mizzian as Inspector-General of the Moroccan armed forces led to a quick settlement.

† On their return to Spain Gil Robles, Satrustegui and others were arrested. They were given the choice of exile or residence in one of the Canary Islands in contravention of Article 14 of the *Fuero* which was suspended.

The Committee first discussed it in any length in September 1963. No member agreed with the United Kingdom that Gibraltar was not within the Committee's terms of reference. Some members, as for example Tunisia and Venezuela, argued with Spain that Gibraltar was Spanish: others, like Iraq and Cambodia on the other hand, wanted Spain and Britain bilaterally to come to an agreement about its future. It was left at that for twelve months when once again, the Committee, at Spain's request, listened to argument from Britain and Spain, and this time also from representatives of the people of Gibraltar and those of the town of San Roque who claimed to be the direct descendants of the inhabitants of the Rock ousted by Britain in 1704. Once again the members of the Committee differed among themselves as to what should be the right solution, Australia alone seeing eye to eye with Britain. On 16th October, the Committee came to the following conclusion: that there existed "a disagreement, even a dispute, between the United Kingdom and Spain over the status and situation of the territory of Gibraltar", and it invited the two countries "to undertake negotiations without delay" in order to find, in accordance with the principles of the Charter of the United Nations, a negotiated solution taking duly into account the opinions expressed by the members of the Committee ... and bearing in mind the interests of the population of the territory". The British representative made it clear that the United Kingdom was prepared to negotiate with Spain on any point except her sovereignty.

Now on 16th October, the Labour Party had won the British Elections. In the June the defeated Sir Alec Douglas Home had been attacked by the now victorious Harold Wilson for permitting negotiations for the construction of frigates of British design for Spain. In the debate Labour M.P.s had shown emotions and used the same language as thirty years previously. On 17th October, the Spanish customs guards at La Linea, across the narrow neck of land separating the fortress of Gibraltar from the mainland, began to enforce customs procedures more according to the book and less courteously. Spain maintained that she was doing no more than was necessary to prevent smuggling through Gibraltar, a matter of which she had complained to Sir Alec and Selwyn Lloyd, and on several occasions before. No one, however, was deceived that Spain's intention was to show how difficult she could make life in Gibraltar. The restrictions increased with the months. Negotiations did not begin until May 1966.

In all these moves and negotiations, Castiella was Franco's operational commander, but he had the whole-hearted support of Franco: and not

merely of Franco but of the overwhelming mass of Spaniards. Franco
in claiming Gibraltar repeatedly, yet saying at the same time that it was
not worth a war, had merely re-echoed Salvador de Madariaga's
words written during the Republic:

> Gibraltar is a permanent offence which we in part deserve for our lack of
> good government: but it does not hinder the normal development of our
> nation and it is not a sufficient cause for us to sacrifice other more valuable
> interests in order to anticipate . . . a fact *which must come about as the restora-
> tion of our nationality evolves towards its logical conclusion*. It seems absurd at
> first sight that our interests should be linked up with those of the only nation
> towards whom we have motives of real resentment. . . .[25]

And before Madariaga a long row of writers back to 1704.

Britain failed to understand the depth of Spanish feeling and sought
to explain the agitation over Gibraltar as proof of Franco's internal
political and economic difficulties: but the truth was that Spain could
now for the first time since Trafalgar challenge Britain's possession of
Gibraltar without damage to her economy: on the contrary, on balance,
benefiting from it.[26] Franco did have political difficulties—from the
Falange as we have seen, no less than from the Church, the democrats
and the Marxists; but his 1961–6 troubles were less serious than those
of say 1945–50 when he had left the matter dormant. He and Spain for
their part failed to recognise the emotions that the word Gibraltar could
still arouse in Britain, or that in this case Britain really did care about
the wishes of the inhabitants. As Franco had said, the Rock would
always cast a shadow over Anglo-Spanish relations, obfuscating the
minds of both contenders from a solution based on freedom and truth,
and just to the three parties in the dispute.[29]

In 1940 and 1941 Franco had refused Gibraltar as a gift from Hitler.
He had no regrets, no doubts in 1966 that his decision had been right,[28]
but a man in his old age tends to remember details of events long past.
The U.S. had befriended him: President de Gaulle had no cause against
him: but in reading what some British M.P.s had to say about him
in the House of Commons every time that Spain was mentioned, he
may well have pondered over Hitler's words as the Führer implored
and beseeched him to let German troops through to the Straits: "Never,
Caudillo, will you be forgiven [your] victory."[29]

Forgiven or no, his victory was complete enough. Spain was now
much more than a source of raw materials and dumping ground of
other more prosperous nations' finished product. In this sense she was

libre—free. Eisenhower's visit had shown her inveterate enemies that she was now *grande*, great enough to be shown deference by one of the only two powerful nations of the world. With the dispersion of industry, Spain was also becoming more homogeneous, but to be *Una*, she still needed that little piece of land, Gibraltar.

Britain's offer to submit the dispute to The Hague put Franco in a dilemma. He was certain that no court of law could give an answer unfavourable to Spain: but for him to agree to the British offer would be to have conceded to the snatching away of the greatest of his victories; for he could not expect to live the years that The Hague (judging by past experience) would take in coming to that favourable decision. The "ripe plum" had to fall into *his* hands, and not those of a successor, that he should be judged by history to have made Spain one.*

The future of Gibraltar was still unresolved at the end of 1966, but Franco could feel well pleased with the results of the referendum. Opponents might seek to explain away the results: but even if 95 per cent were not with him, what evidence was there to contradict his claim that the majority of the nation wanted him to remain as Head of State? He had outlived nearly all his enemies of 1936, and even most of his friends. In 1962 he had promoted Agustin Muñoz Grandes his equal as Captain-General, and made him deputy Prime Minister. Muñoz, a Major at Alhoceima, a Colonel at the outbreak of the war, was ageing more rapidly than he. There remained his cousin, Franco-Salgado, and Admiral Carrero Blanco whom some considered an *eminence grise* since he had survived several government changes as a Cabinet Minister. His old friends had his ear. He would listen to them. He would, for that matter, always hear what his subordinates had to say; but the final decision remained his: as at all times since 1st October 1936, so on 22nd November 1966—when, in introducing his new constitution to the Cortes, he had made his longest speech of all—a speech of triumph lasting close on an hour. Having made his announcement, Franco returned to the house that had been his home for twenty-five years. There, for all the Goya tapestries of the public rooms and the servants, he had always lived the austere life of an hidalgo, rising at a very early hour, hearing Mass (his long battle with the Church, his

---

* There was another reason as well: the support Spain had had in the United Nations from the Arab countries could not be guaranteed indefinitely: a *quid pro quo* would be the surrender of Spanish sovereignty over Ifni and Sahara, if not Ceuta and Melilla.

insistence on the *patronato* and on certain honours due to a bishop but not to a layman do not appear to have troubled his private conscience) taking as simple a breakfast as any labourer—a cup of coffee and a piece of bread; and then, on a normal day, devoting himself to six continuous hours of work, even in his advanced age, without a break for refreshment. At lunch, if there were guests, he would take one glass of wine with them. He never smoked. Lunch over, he might rest, reading a book or painting; he would then return to his desk. Here again his life was like that of his subjects: where they had two jobs, for thirty years he had had three and still retained two. He would have a late dinner— very late by English or French standards—a few hours sleep, and another day would begin again.

Throughout his life Franco retained over himself the iron discipline of his early youth. The only untidy thing about him was his desk with a pile of "pending" files and business. Though capable on occasion of quick decision and rapid action, in minor matters as in major he preferred always "to wait upon providences". He was always, too, a listener rather than a talker: "God has given us two ears but only one mouth". The exhortations to his troops in his youth had always been short. The most constant opening of his speeches as Caudillo was the phrase "Just a few words"; and he fulfilled his promise. He had a fairly high-pitched voice. He rarely declaimed. His longest speeches were those to the Cortes and his "End of the Year" broadcast messages, none longer than 50 minutes.[30]

On Sundays and holidays Franco's delight was to go out with a gun. El Pardo is a hunting lodge—or rather a shooting box—albeit as palatial as befitted the Bourbons. The land around is rich in game. On Christmas Eve 1961 his gun exploded and his left hand was severely injured. He made light of the accident. If his old African stomach wound ever pained him, no one except his private physician knew. When in his seventies it was rumoured that he had Parkinson's disease and heart trouble: if he had, he never cancelled an appointment, and, he could withstand several hours at a stretch of visitors whom he would receive upright: he could carry on a conversation for an indefinite length of time without pause or any visible flagging of energy. That energy was at its height during his annual holidays. He would retire for a few weeks to a house near Corunna by the coast, going out to sea in his small yacht, the *Azor*, his one luxury, deep-sea fishing; and in his enthusiasm he might stay out several days at sea. Every year, too, he would undertake rapid tours of the provinces of Spain.[31]

Popular belief credited his younger brother Ramon with the habits of a libertine, and his elder brother with making use of his position profitably to invest the monies he had inherited. Of Francisco Franco's private life there was never a scruple of scandal. His asceticism had been notorious even in his Legion days. To most men Franco was always an enigma. He seemed aloof from his fellow men: he gave the impression that he held them in disdain. Yet he inspired deep loyalty no less than deep hatred. There were men who said of him that he never laughed even if he always smiled. That was not so. He was fully at home, relaxed and ready to laugh with men of his profession, even foreigners. He claimed that no person had ever had any influence over his life or thought: "Only youth. Yes, youth has influenced me. As a young man I had under my command young men who joined the Army because of intolerable social conditions at home, and young men doing their military service. There were always fresh batches. Then I had under my command the cadets, and would hear their hopes and aspirations —and these did influence me."[32] That he influenced his nation is incontrovertible. Whether it was for good or ill, the God and History by which he always said he would be judged can alone determine.

NOTES

1. Speech to the Cortes, 22nd November 1966: text as in *New York Times*. Full text of speech in Spanish and of new Organic Law and with Basic Laws in *Leyes Fundamentales con las Modificaciones Previstas en el Proyecto de Ley Orgánica del Estado y Mensaje del Jefe del Estado a las Cortes Espanolas* (Madrid 1966).

2. Franco to author in June, 1966. Statistics: Bank of London and South America Quarterly Review, Vol. IV no. 1, Vol. V no. 2, Vol. VI no. 4; Bank of London and South America Fortnightly Review Vols. 30 and 31 (1965 and 1966) *passim*. O.E.C.D. reports on Spain from 1956 onwards. For a useful summary of the economic situation as in October 1956, *v. Spain* (Overseas Economic Surveys—H.M.S.O. 1957). On education: O.E.C.D. *The Mediterranean Regional Project: Spain* (Paris, 1965) and subsequent reports. Other sources: interviews with Directors of Ministerial Departments and rank and file members in various parts of the country 1965–66.

3. Santiago Carrillo: *Despues de Franco Que?* (Paris, 1965) and speeches from Radio Moscow and Radio España Independiente, 1964–66.

4. *Discursos*, 1951–4, pp. 376–84 and 388–409; *cf*. pp. 429–42.

5. *Discursos*, 1951–4, pp. 422, 532.

6. *Discursos*, 1955–9, pp. 7–11 and 12–23.

7. Ibid., pp. 121–40.

8. Cf. *The War and the Neutrals*, pp. 313–16 for the withdrawal.

9. *Discursos*, 1955–9, pp. 115–20. Statements to Director of *E.F.E.* ((Official Spanish Newsagency).

10. Ibid., pp. 149–52.

11. Ibid., pp. 181–90.

12. Pamplona and other details from participants and eye-witnesses interrogated in June–July 1956. Franco speech *Discursos*, pp. 201–38, to Movimiento National Council, cf. pp. 194, 196.

13. I gave the late Dr. Walter Kolarz a copy which had come my way. His reaction after reading it was immediate: "Fascinating: it bears a remarkable resemblance to the Czech constitution. . . . Just change the names of the organisms—Cortes to Supreme Soviet, Consejo Nacional to Central Committee, and add a few stock phrases from Communist jargon."

14. Members of *Opus Dei* also take vows of personal poverty, chastity and obedience in spiritual matters to their spiritual superiors. They make a point of not advertising their membership, though they may not deny it if asked. While a man wishing to live a Christian life more fully than his neighbour without wanting to make it known is understandable, such reticence has led to a partial misunderstanding of what *Opus Dei* is. There are English members. They run an international student hostel in London. The entry of two if not three into Franco's Cabinet at the same time had commentators speaking of *Opus Dei* as a political party. Since they were all economists to talk of a school of economists would have been equally warrantable. In fact they have no unified views on politics, nor on economics.

15. Nevertheless in 1959 the B.B.C. organised "Town Forums" (unscripted discussions on political and economic questions put by an audience to a team of Spanish-speaking Englishmen and Spaniards) with no difficulty in Madrid and Bilbao, and with only minor inconveniences in Barcelona. Permission had to be sought separately from the Ministry of Foreign Affairs, the Ministry of Information, the Department of Internal Security, and in Bilbao and Barcelona from the local provincial delegations of the Ministry of Information. The producer remembers that the only persons who opined that permission would not be granted were British residents in Spain and Spanish exiles.

16. Julio Ceron's case is given in some detail in *Spain and the Law*.

17. Cf. *Crime or Punishment? Unpublished Documents about Julian Grimau Garcia* (Madrid, 1963). The facts were not generally in question. What genuinely shocked the non-Communist world was that he should be tried and executed for crimes committed so many years previously: but the Spanish Government was not at the time the only one with such a long memory.

18. The Cabinet is said to have been equally divided when the matter was put to the vote to them.

19. The Basque priest member of the Republican Cortes, Antonio Pildaín. The Pope had just appointed him Bishop of the Canaries when the Civil War broke out. He was consecrated on 14th February 1937. For text of Basque priests' protest, *v. Spain and the Law*—Appendix 8. Franco's speech to social workers on 18th July 1960 may be seen in his reply. *Discursos*, 1960–3, pp. 71–9: cf. pp. 114–23 End of Year Message; cf. also Cortes speeches 3rd June 1961, pp. 207–53. Franco would come to claim that he had anticipated *Mater et Magistra* by twenty years: an allegation not accepted by those who studied the encyclical. Cf. *Discursos*, 1960–3, pp. 438 and 602.

20. Quoted ibid., p. 46.

21. Copies of newspapers had to be deposited with the Ministry of Information half an hour before they were put on sale in the streets: books, etc., one day ahead per 50 pages.

22. Franco to author June 1966: a theme he took also in his speech of 22nd November.

23. A favourite phrase of Franco's.

24. Cf. *Spanish Red Book on Gibraltar* (Madrid, 1965). On Gibraltar generally, cf. *Spanish Red Book*, White Papers: *Gibraltar—Recent Differences with Spain* (H.M.S.O., April 1965) and *Gibraltar—Talks with Spain: May–October 1966* (H.M.S.O., November 1966).

25. *Spain*, Ch. XXII, pp. 361–2.

26. Cf. *The Rock of Contention:* The Round Table, June 1965, p. 244.

27. Cf. ibid for a solution which up to June 1966 would have satisfied Spanish pride, British interests and the rights of the inhabitants of Gibraltar.

28. Franco–Salgado.

29. D.G.F.P., Vol. XII p. 38.

30. Usually much less. His speech on 22nd November 1966 was in fact one of the longest on record: another long one was that to the Cortes on 3rd June 1961.

31. Franco had great bladder control, to the severe discomfort of his Cabinet ministers.

32. Franco to author June 1966.

SOURCES

I *UNPUBLISHED DOCUMENTS AND BOOKS WITH
RESTRICTED CIRCULATION*

General Franco's personal papers, operational orders and other documents in his Military Household.

General Franco's *Hoja de Servicio* (see note 1 to Ch. 3) and those of his contemporaries.

Documents in the Municipal and Church Registers of El Ferrol and Oviedo.

The Franco Family Papers, compiled by the late Carlos Franco-Salgado of El Ferrol.

MS. Life of General Franco by his cousin and constant companion, General Francisco Franco-Salgado. (The basis for the eulogistic *Centinela de Occidente* by Luis de Galinsoga. Barcelona 1956.)

Colección de Reglamentos de la Armada 1885 and other nineteenth- and twentieth-century naval documents.

Documents relating to the War in Africa and the Civil War in the Archives of the Servicio Histórico Militar, Madrid.

Manuals of Military Training, Tactics and Strategy from 1889 to 1945, in particular the series of training manuals by Jose Villalba y Requelme, Franco's C.O. at the Military Academy, Toledo and in Africa in 1909.

General Franco's own *Reglamento para el empleo táctico de las grandes unidades* (1938) and *ABC de la Batalla Defensiva* (1944).

Historia de las Campañas de Marruecos (Servicio Historico), 2 vols.

Geografía de Marruecos, Protectorado y Posesiones de España en Africa (Servicio Historico), 3 vols.

Military journals of various arms: *Ejército, Revista de Historia Militar* (especially no. 17, 1964); *Revista de Tropas Coloniales* (Edited by General Franco).

The *Anuarios* of the Spanish Army.

General Francisco Franco: *Raza* (Limited edition, Madrid, 1942).

Documents in the Ministries of Justice and Foreign Affairs, Madrid.

Diario de Sesiones de las Cortes Españolas.

Die Wehrmacht. Special number May 1939. *Wir Kampften in Spanien.*

II *PUBLISHED DOCUMENTS*

Concordato entre la Santa Sede y España: Oficina de Información Diplomática, 1953.

Crime or Punishment? Unpublished documents about Julian Grimau García (Madrid, 1963).

Documentos relacionados con la información instruida por el senor general de división, don Juan Picasso sobre las responsabilidades de la actuación española (Annual) en julio de 1921 (Madrid, 1923).

Documents on German Foreign Policy. Series D: Vols. II–XIII (H.M.S.O., 1950–64).

Documents sécrèts du Ministère des Affaires Etrangères d'Allemagne, trans. Eristov (Paris, 1947 and 1955).

España y los Judíos. Oficina de Información Diplomática (Madrid, 1949).

International Commission of Jurists: *Spain and the Rule of Law* (Geneva, 1962), Bulletins No. 7 of 1957, No. 8 of Dec. 1958, No. 9 of Aug. 1959.

International Military Tribunal: Nuremberg (Nuremberg, 1947–9), especially Vols. IX, XIII and XXV.

La Guerra de Liberación Nacional: Papers read at the tenth Study Course of the "General Palafox" Department of Military Studies, University of Zaragoza, 1961.

Les événements survenus en France 1933–1945. Rapport Fait au nom de la Commission de l'Assemblée Nationale. Vol. III (Paris, 1946).

Leyes Fundamentales con las modificaciones previstas en el proyecto de Ley Orgánica del estado etc. (Madrid, 1966), and the corpus of legislation 1940–66 published in the *Indice progresivo de legislación,* ed. Aranzadi.

Réplica a la publicación hecha por el Departamento de Estados los Estados Unidos de America de documentos relativos a España: Ministerio de Asuntos Exteriores, Madrid (March, 1946).

Spanish Red Book on Gibraltar (Madrid, 1965).

The Communist International 1919–43, Selected documents, Vol. III (O.U.P., 1965).

The Führer Conferences on Naval Affairs (Board of Admiralty, 1947).

The Spanish Government and the Axis Powers, Washington, Department of State (March, 1946).

White Papers: Gibraltar, Recent Differences with Spain (H.M.S.O., April 1965); *Gibraltar—Talks with Spain—May–October 1966* (H.M.S.O., November 1966).

III *INTERVIEWS AND INTERROGATIONS* in Spain, France, Britain, Mexico and South America (see Foreword)

Personal notes, despatches, etc., made during frequent visits to Spain, 1950–66.

IV *NEWSPAPERS AND OTHER PERIODICALS 1899–1966,* in particular the following:

A.B.C.	Arriba	Claridad
El Debate	El Liberal	Mundo Obrero
El Socialista	El Sol	La Vanguardia
Informaciones	Ya	CENIT (Toulouse)
Ecclesia	Euzko Deya (Paris)	El Socialista (Toulouse)

Boletín Oficial del Estado

Bulletin of Spanish Studies (Ed. Professor Allison Peers, 1936–44)

The Times, The Guardian, The Economist, Hansard, The New York Times and New York Herald Tribune

Le Monde, Le Figaro

Quarterly and fortnightly Reviews, Bank of London and South America

O.E.C.D. and I.B.R.D. reports.

V PUBLISHED BIOGRAPHIES OF GENERAL FRANCO

To date (1967) fifteen biographies of General Franco have been published in Spanish. All but one are favourable and many encomiastic. *Franco* by J. Arrarás Iribarren (San Sebastian, 1937 and eleven subsequent reprints), *Francisco Franco* by F. de Valdesoto (Madrid, 1945), *Francisco Franco* (*Historia de un español*) by F. Salva Miguel and J. A. Vicente Izquierdo (Barcelona, 1959), and Galinsoga's *Centinela* (see I. above) are the best known, but of limited value to the historian. "Luis Ramirez" in his *Francisco Franco* (*Historia de un mesianismo*) (Paris, 1965) seeks to make the reader believe the General to be a psychopath. He mixes fact too readily with what can only be surmise: an interesting exercise in pseudo-psychology.

Claude Martin's *Franco: Soldat et Chef d'Etat* (Paris, 1959) translated and brought up to 1964 as *Franco, Soldado y Estadista* (Madrid, 1965) is a serious work. His admiration is backed by careful documentation: but it is not a complete biography.

VI OTHER PUBLISHED WORKS

The following is not a complete list of the books consulted, but one limited to those specifically referred to in the notes or which the author considers might be of value to students of Franco's life and times.

(B = Barcelona; B.A. = Buenos Aires; M. = Madrid; N.Y. = New York.)

Aberrigoyen, Inaki de: *Sept mois et sept jours dans l'Espagne de Franco* (Paris, 1938).

Aguirre, J. A.: *De Guernica a Nueva York pasando por Berlin* (B.A., 1942).

Alcala Zamora, Niceto: *Régimen Político de convivencia en España* (B.A., 1945); *Un viaje azaroso desde Francia a la Argentina* (B.A., 1942).

Alcazar de Velasco, Angel: *Serrano Suñer en la Falange* (B., 1941).

Alvarez del Vayo, Julio: *Les batailles de la liberté* (Paris, 1963).

Ansaldo, Juan Antonio: *¿Para qué? De Alfonso XIII a Juan III* (B.A., 1951).

Aparicio, Juan: *Ramiro Ledesma, Fundador de la JONS* (M., 1942).

Areilza, Jose Maria de: *Embajadores sobre España* (M., 1947).

Areilza, Jose Maria de and Castiella, Fernando Maria: *Reivindicaciones de España* (M., 1941).

Arraras Iribarren, Joaquin: *Historia de la Segunda República Española*. Abridged into one volume (M., 1965) (accurate on sources—pro-nationalist in intent).

Aunos, E.: *Calvo Sotelo y la Política de su Tiempo* (M., 1941).

Azaña y Dias, M.: *La Velada en Benicarló* (B.A., 1939); *Memorias Intimas*, ed. Arrarás (M., 1939); *Mi Rebelión en Barcelona* (Bilbao, 1935); *Una política* (M., 1932).

Aznar, Manuel: *Historia Militar de la Guerra de España* (M., 1958–63, 3rd edition) (Pro-nationalist).

Balbontín, Jose Antonio: *La España de mi experiencia* (Mexico, 1952).

Bahamonde y Sanchez de Castro, Antonio: *Un año con Queipo de Llano* (Mexico, 1938).

Beltrán Güell, Felipe: *Preparación y desarrollo del alzamiento nacional* (Santarén, 1937).

Berenguer Fuste, Dámaso: *Campañas en el Riff y Yebala 1921–1922. Notas y documentos de mi diario de operaciones* (M., 1923); *Campañas en el Riff y Yebala 1919–1921*, 2 vols. (Reprint M., 1948); *De la Dictadura a la República* (M., 1935).

Bergamo, Duca di: *Legionari di Roma in terra iberica (1936 XIV–1939 XVII)* (Rome, 1940).

Blasquez, J. M.: *I Helped to Build an Army* (Secker and Warburg, 1939).

Bolín, Luis: *Spain. The Vital Years* (Cassell, 1967).

Bolloten, Burnett: *The Grand Camouflage* (Hollis and Carter, 1961).

Borkenau, Franz: *The Spanish Cockpit* (Faber and Faber, 1937).

Bowers, Claude G.: *My Mission to Spain: Watching the Rehearsal for World War II* (N.Y., 1954).

Brenan, Gerald: *The Spanish Labyrinth* (Cambridge U.P., 1943).

Brussa, J.: *Revolución de Julio en Barcelona* (B., 1910).

Burgos y Mazo, Manuel de: *Páginas Históricas de 1917* (M., 1918); *El verano de 1919 en Gobernación* (M., 1921).

Cacho Zabalza, Antonio: *La Unión Militar Española* (Alicante, 1940).

Cambo, Francisco: *Las Dictaduras* (M., 1929).

Canals, Salvador: *Los Sucesos de España de 1909*, 2 vols. (M., 1910).

Cantalupo, Roberto: *Fu la Spagna; Ambasciata presso Franco, Febbraio–Aprile 1937* (Milan, 1948).

Carr, Raymond: *Spain 1808–1939* (Oxford History of Modern Europe) (Clarendon, 1966). An excellent and considerable advance on previous histories of Spain written in English. Very good bibliography.

Cartas Cruzadas entre el Sr. D. Manuel Hedilla Larrey y el Sr. D. Ramón Serrano Suñer (M., 1948).

Castiella, Jose Maria: *see* Areilza.

Cattell, David: *Communism and the Spanish Civil War* (Berkeley, 1955); *Soviet Diplomacy and the Spanish Civil War* (Berkeley, 1957).

Churchill, Winston: *The Second World War, Vols. I, II, III, IV, V, VI* (Cassell).

Ciano, Count: *Ciano's Diary, 1939–1943* (Heinemann, 1949); *Ciano's Diary, 1937–1938* (Methuen, 1952); *L'Europa verso la Catastrofe* (Milan, 1948).

Colodny, Robert G.: *The Struggle for Madrid* (N.Y., 1958).

Clark, Gen. Mark W.: *Calculated Risk* (N.Y., 1950).

Colvin, Ian: *Chief of Intelligence* (Gollancz, 1951).

Comin Colomer, Eduardo: *La República en el exilio* (M., 1957); *Historia del Partido Comunista de España*, 2 vols. (1965). Massive research vitiated by the author's obsessive theory that Freemasonry and Communism are linked.

Cosa, Juan de la: *España ante el mundo* (M., 1950). Issued by the Spanish Ministry of Information in English under the title "Spain and the World".

Cot, Pierre: *The Triumph of Treason* (N.Y., 1944).

Crespo, Eduardo: *Alfereces Provisionales* (M., 1964).

Cruzada Española: Historia de la: gen. editor J. Arrarás, 36 books in 8 vols. (M., 1943–4).

Diaz, Guillermo: *Como llegó Falange al poder: Análisis de un proceso contrarrevolucionario* (B.A., 1940).

Doussinague, Jose Maria: *España tenía razón* (M., 1950).

Feis, Herbert: *The Spanish Story* (N.Y., 1948).

Fernandez Almagro, Melchor: *Historia de la segunda República Española* (M., 1940); *Historia del Reinado de Alfonso XIII* (M., 1933).

Flores Morales, Angel: *Africa a través del Pensamiento. Español* (M., 1949).

Franco, Francisco: *Marruecos: Diario de una Bandera* (M., 1922); *Palabras* (Burgos, 1936); *Dos discursos Históricos* (Cádiz, 1937); *Franco ha dicho* (3 volúmenes) (M., 1948); *Palabras del Caudillo* (M., 1943); *Discursos y mensajes del Jefe del Estado: 1951–1954* (M., 1955); *1955–1959* (M., 1960); *1960–1963* (M., 1964). *See also* Section I above.

Franco, Comandante (Ramón): *Madrid bajo las bombas* (M., 1931).

Galland, Adolf: *Die Ersten und die Letzten* (Darmstadt, 1953).

Gamir, Ulibarri, General: *De mis memorias* (Paris, 1939).

Goded, Manuel (General): *Marruecos: Las etapas de la pacificación* (M., 1932).

Goma, Cardinal Isidro: *Pastorales de la Guerra de España* (M., 1955).

Graco, Marsa: *La sublevación de Jaca; Relato de un testigo* (M., 1931).

Grossi, Manuel: *La Insurrección de Asturias* (Valencia, 1936).

Hayes, Carlton J. H.: *Wartime Mission in Spain* (Macmillan, 1945).

Hernandez, Villaescusa M.: *La Semana Trágica en Barcelona* (B., 1910).

Hidalgo, Diego: *¿Por qué fuí lanzado del Ministerio de Guerra?* (M., 1934).

Hoare, Samuel (Viscount Templewood): *Ambassador on Special Mission* (Collins, 1946).

Hodgson, Sir Robert: *Spain Resurgent* (Hutchinson, 1953).

Ibarruri, Dolores: *El único camino* (Paris, 1962); (with others) *Historia del Partido Comunista en España* (Paris, 1960).

Iribarren, Jose Maria: *El General Mola* (M., 1945).

Iturralde, Juan de: *El Catolicismo y la Cruzada de Franco*, 3 vols. (Toulouse, 1955, 1960, 1965).

Jackson, G.: *The Spanish Republic and the Civil War, 1931–1939* (Princeton U.P., 1965). (Excellent bibliography.)

Jato, David: *La rebelión de los estudiantes (Apuntes para una historia del alegre SEU)* (M., 1953).

Kemp, Peter: *Mine were of trouble* (Cassell, 1957).

Kindelan y Duany, Gen. Alfredo: *Mis Cuadernos de Guerra* (M., 1945).

Largo Caballero, Francisco: *Mis recuerdos* (Mexico, 1954).

Ledesma Ramos, Ramiro: *Discurso a las juventudes de España* (M., 1939) *Los escritos filosóficos de Ramiro Ledesma* (M., 1941) *¿Fascimo en España?* (Sus orígenes, su desarrollo, sus hombres) (M., 1935).

Lerroux, Alejandro: *La Pequeña Historia* (B.A., 1945).

Liddell Hart, B. H.: *The Other Side of the Hill* (Germany's Generals, their rise and fall, with their own account of military events, 1939–45) (Cassell, 1948); *Memoirs*, 2 vols. (Cassell, 1965).

Lizarra (Andres Maria de Irujo): *Los vascos y la República Española* (B.A., 1944).

Lizarza Iribarren, Antonio: *Memorias de la Conspiración* (Pamplona, 1953).

McNeill-Moss, G.: *The Epic of the Alcazar* (Rich and Cowan, 1937).

Maestre, Pedro: *Divulgación del Problema de Marruecos* (Granada, 1923).

(Col.) Marquez y J. M. Capo: *Las Juntas Militares de Defensa* (B., 1923).

Martin Artajo, Alberto: *El primer lustro de los convenios hispano-norteamericanos* (M., 1958).

Martinez Bande, J. M.: *Intervención comunista en la Guerra de España* (M., 1965).

Martinez Barrio, Diego: *Orígenes del Frente Popular Español* (B.A., 1943).

Montero Moreno, Antonio: *Historia de la persecución religiosa en España, 1936–1939* (M., 1961).

Maura, Gamazo Gabriel: *Bosquejo histórico de la Dictadura*, 2 vols. (M., 1930); *Historia crítica del Reinado de Alfonso XIII en su minoridad* (M., 1925); *La Cuestión de Marruecos* (M., 1905); *Recuerdos de mi vida* (M., 1934).

Maurín, Joaquin: *Los Hombres de la Dictadura* (M., 1930); *La Revolución Española. De la Monarquía absoluta a la Revolución Socialista* (M., 1932); *Hacia la Segunda Revolución* (M., 1935).

Medlicott, W. N.: *Survey of International Affairs: The War and the Neutrals* (O.U.P., 1956); *The Economic Blockade*, Vol. I (H.M.S.O., 1952).

Mendizabal, Alfredo: *Aux Origines d'une Tragédie* (Paris, 1937).

Mola y Vidal, Gen. Emilio: *Obras Completas* (Valladolid, 1940).

Montero Y Arostegui, Jose: *Historia y descripción de la ciudad y departamento naval de El Ferrol* (M., 1859).

Morgan, Gen. Sir F.: *Overture to Overlord* (Hodder and Stoughton, 1950).

Moscardó, José: *Diario del Alcazar* (M., 1943); *Diario de Operaciones* (Toledo, 1936).

Moulin de Labarthete, H. de: *Les Temps des Illusions* (Geneva, 1946).

Ortega y Gasset, Jose: *Annual* (M., 1923); *La verdad sobre la Dictadura* (M., 1925); *Rectificación de la República* (M., 1931); *España Invertebrada* (M., 1922).

A. Orts-Ramos y F. Caravaca: *Francisco Ferrer* (B., 1932).

Otero, Blas de: *Que trata de España* (Paris, 1964).

Payne, Stanley G.: *Falange—A History of Spanish Fascism* (Oxford University Press, 1962).

Peers, E. Allison: *Spain in Eclipse* (Methuen, 1943).

Peirats, J.: *Los anarquistas en la crisis política española* (B.A., 1964); *La CNT en la revolución española*. Three volumes (Toulouse, 1951–3).

Peman, Jose Maria: *Un Soldado en la Historia: Vida del Capitan-General Varela* (Cádiz, 1954).

Prieto, Indalecio: *Cómo y por qué salí del Ministerio de Defensa Nacional* (Paris, 1939); *Yo y Moscú* (Mexico, 1955); *El Testamento de Primo de Rivera* (Toulouse); *Cartas a un Escultor* (B.A., 1961).

Primo de Rivera, Jose Antonio: *Obras completas* (M., 1954); *Textos inéditos y epistolario de . . .* (M., 1956).

Queipo de Llano (General): *El Movimiento Revindicativo de Cuatro Vientos* (M., 1931).

Quilez, José y R. Torres Endrina: *La Sublevación de Jaca; Dos dias de inquietud Nacional* (M. 1931).

Ramos Oliveira, Antonio: *Historia de España* (3 vols.) (Mexico, 1952). (Antinationalist.)

Rojo, Vicente (General): *España Heróica* (B.A., 1942); *Alerta a los pueblos* (B.A., 1939).

Romanones Count of: *El Ejército y la Política* (M., 1920); *Y Sucedió así* (M., 1947); *Notas de Una Vida* (M., 1934); *Las responsabilidades del antiguo régimen* (M., 1924).

Ruiz de Alda, Julio: *Obras Completas* (B., 1939).

Ruiz de Alda, Julio and Ramon Franco: *De Palos al Plata* (M., 1927).

Madariaga, Salvador de: *Spain* (Cape, 1942) Latest edition; *España* (Editorial Suramericana, March 1964). (Outstandingly the most dispassionate commentary on Spanish history written by a Spaniard.)

Sangroniz, J. A. de: *Marruecos* (M., 1921).

Seco Serrano, Carlos: *Historia de España* Vol. 6 (B., 1962) (pro-nationalist).

Sender, Ramon: *Viaje a la Aldea del Crimen* (M., 1933).

Serrano Suñer, Ramon: *Entre Hendaya y Gibraltar* (M., 1947).

Schmidt, Paul: *Statist auf diplomatischer Bühne* (Bonn, 1949) (Hitler's Interpreter. Heinemann, 1951).

Southworth, Hebert: *El mito de la Cruzada de Franco* (Paris, 1963).

Soviet Encyclopaedia, Vol. 29 of 1926 edit. Spanish Communist Party.

Steer, G. L.: *The Tree of Gernika* (Hodder and Stoughton, 1938).

Tamames, Ramon: *La lucha contra los monopolios* (M., 1961).

Thomas, Hugh: *The Spanish Civil War* (Penguin, 1965); *The Story of Sandhurst* (Hutchinson, 1961).

Ed. by Toynbee, Arnold and Veronica M.: *The War and the Neutrals*; *Survey of International Affairs 1939–1946* (Oxford University Press, 1956).

Valdes Rubio, Juan: *Acción de España en Marruecos* (M., 1914).

Vicens Vives, Jaime: *Aproximación a la historia de España* (B., 1952); *Els Catalans en el segle XIX* (B., 1958); *Historia social y económica de España y América*, Vol. IV (B., 1959).

Zugazagoitia, Julian: *Historia de la guerra de España 1936–39* (B.A., 1940) (Anti-nationalist).

INDEX

A

Abaran, 120-1

Abdel Krim, 121-6, 128, 130, 132, 134-5, 137-8, 140, 151, 440

Agrarian Reform: under Republic, 183, 185, 198, 209; under Franco, 397, 423-4

Aguirre, José Antonio, 299n., 303-4

Aid to Axis in World War II, Franco's, 342-3n., 357-9, 369, 372, 373, 374-8, 391

Aid to Western Powers, Franco's, 369, 373-4, 375

Alba, Duke of, 355, 357, 368, 376, 389, 405

Alcalá Zamora, Niceto, 161, 163, 165, 175, 177, 182, 183, 186, 200, 203, 209, 213, 222-3, 228

Alfambra, Battle of, 286-7

Alfau, General, 90, 101, 102

Alfonso XIII, 71, 81, 91, 97, 112, 131-5, 145, 146, 152-5, 159-61, 163-8, 173, 174, 262, 298, 352, 388, 427, 428

Algeciras, 95, 113, 138, 233, 234, 367, 368

Al Hoceima (Alhucemas), 120, 121, 133-40, 145, 151, 296, 444

(Al) Kzar-el-Kebir (Alcazarquivir), 82, 83, 88, 90, 92, 93, 118, 119

Allied and German Plans to invade Spain, World War II, 345-6, 349, 350, 355, 357-8, 365 n.72, 367-9, 371-2, 374, 377, 393 n.15

Alonso Vega, General Camilo, 81, 115, 155, 290

Alvarez del Vayo, Julio, 240n., 389

Anarchists, 32, 37, 38, 55-6, 71, 74-7, 83, 91, 102-5, 122, 132, 146, 148, 171, 178, 179, 181, 182-6, 189-92, 209, 215, 216, 220, 229, 241-2, 243, 251, 252, 253, 262, 276, 278, 298, 300, 302n., 305, 324, 356, 381, 384

"Andrade, Jaime de", 27, 28, 31-2

Anglo-Spanish Relations, 11, 15, 16, 17, 21, 53, 55, 99, 100, 201, 244-5, 283, 284, 287, 296, 303, 340, 341, 343, 353-5, 357-9, 372-9, 386, 389-91, 395-6, 398, 409-13, 426, 429, 440, 441

Ansaldo, Juan Antonio, 204, 205, 217, 236, 238-9 and n., 245

An-Wal (Annual), Battle of, 120, 122, 128, 129, 130, 131, 134, 135, 139, 155, 173

Arab States, Franco's relations with, 406-7, 413, 429-30, 440, 441 and n., 442

Aranda Mata, General Antonio, 287n., 289, 315, 317, 340

Argentine-Spanish Relations, 395-6, 407

Arias Salgado, 372, 428, 439

Army and Politics, 48-50, 101-2, 104-6, 131, 145-9, 159, 160-6, 174, 197, 214-23, 240-4, 256-7, 309, 314, 324; split into pro-insurgent and pro-Government, 240-1; World War II Sympathies, 335, 342 and n., 352, 354, 356, 384; post World War, 430-1

Army, weapons, training, promotions, etc., 62-6, 68-70, 74, 84, 91, 97-8, 110-15, 117, 122, 126, 128, 142 nn. 17 and 19, 200-1, 415; inter-arm rivalries, 149-151; pre 1936 distribution, 151; suppression of Royal Artillery, 152-3, 159; reorganizations: by Primo de Rivera, 155, 159; by Azaña, 167, 170-3; by Gil Robles and Franco, 200-2

Arrese, José Luis, 356, 388, 432

Arruit, Mount, 88, 123, 124, 127, 130

Artillery, Revolt of Spanish Royal, 152-3, 159

Asensio Cabanillas, General Carlos, 247, 249, 260 n.30, 356

Asensio Torrado, General José, 355

Asturias, Revolt of (1934), 170, 188-92, 218, 228, 437, 439. Civil War, 237, 263, 276, 282

Attlee, Lord, 338, 390

Axdir (Ajdir-des-Beni-Urriakel), 121, 134-5, 140

Azaña y Díaz, Manuel, 161, 170-3, 174, 176-182, 186, 187, 200, 202, 207-9, 213, 214, 228n., 298

B

Baamonde, Ladislao (Franco's maternal grandfather), 18, 29, 31, 77

Baamonde y Pardo de Andrade de Franco, María del Pilar Teresa (Franco's mother), 18, 28, 30-2, 61, 66, 67, 77, 128, 130, 154, 187

Badajoz, 179, 247, 424

Bahamonde, see Franco and Puente

Balearics, 187, 201, 202, 220, 237, 254, 271, 284, 287, 338, 377

Balfour, Sir John, 413

*